THE LION AND THE EAGLE

Anglo-German Naval Confrontation In the Imperial Era

1815 – 1919

THE LION AND THE EAGLE
Anglo-German Naval Confrontation
In the Imperial Era

1815 – 1919

David Gregory

Copyright © 2012

All rights reserved. No part of this publication may be reproduced, stored in a retrieval system or transmitted in any form or by any means electronic, mechanical, audio, visual or otherwise, without prior permission of the copyright owner. Nor can it be circulated in any form of binding or cover other than that in which it is published and without similar conditions including this condition being imposed on the subsequent purchaser.

ISBN: 978-0-9572864-0-5

Published by David Gregory in conjunction with Writersworld, this book is produced entirely in the UK, is available to order from most book shops in the United Kingdom, and is also globally available via UK-based Internet book retailers.

Copy edited by Ian Large

Cover design by Jag Lall

www.writersworld.co.uk

WRITERSWORLD
2 Bear Close Flats
Bear Close
Woodstock
Oxfordshire
OX20 1JX
United Kingdom

The text pages of this book are produced via an independent certification process that ensures the trees from which the paper is produced come from well managed sources that exclude the risk of using illegally logged timber while leaving options to use post-consumer recycled paper as well.

To the memory of

Blanche Louise Bingham

who had faith

VOLUME ONE

THE PROTAGONISTS

1815–1914

'Among the Great Powers, England necessarily requires a strong ally on the continent. She would not find one which corresponds better to all her interests than a united Germany that can never make claim to the command of the sea.'

Helmuth von Moltke

CONTENTS

Introduction		*9*
One	The Royal Navy in the Nineteenth Century	*20*
Two	The Birth of the German Navy	*45*
Three	A Fleet against England	*73*
Four	The Naval Race Begins	*102*
Five	Fisher	*120*
Six	The End of Splendid Isolation	*138*
Seven	The Dreadnought Revolution	*159*
Eight	Schism in the Royal Navy	*192*
Nine	The Divisions Intensify	*222*
Ten	The *Daily Telegraph* Interview	*241*
Eleven	Negotiations and Crisis	*254*
Twelve	Britannia Takes to the Shore	*279*
Thirteen	Churchill at the Admiralty	*294*
Fourteen	Olive Branches and Nettles	*337*
Fifteen	Twilight of the Empires 1912-1914	*370*
Sixteen	A Single Shot	*405*
Seventeen	Epilogue to a Long Peace	*439*
Appendix I	Transcript of Wilhelm II's *Daily Telegraph* Interview 1908	*445*
Appendix II	The British and German Fleets August 1914	*447*
Notes to Volume One		*454*
Selected Bibliography		*468*
Index		*483*

LIST OF PLATES

Otto Edouard Leopold von Bismarck-Schonhausen	*57*
Wilhelm in Imperial Pose	*58*
HMS *Empress of India*	*79*
SMS *Kaiser Friedrich III*	*80*
The Kaiser in the uniform of a British Admiral	*87*
Grand Admiral Alfred Von Tirpitz	*88*
'Jacky' Fisher as Captain, c.1883	*129*
Reginald Brett, Lord Esher	*130*
King Edward VII: 'The Great Encircler'	*149*
Théophile Delcassé	*150*
HMS *King Edward VII*	*161*
SMS *Pommern*	*162*
HMS *Dreadnought*	*171*
SMS *Rheinland*	*172*
Admiral Sir Percy Moreton Scott	*179*
Reginald McKenna	*180*
HMS *Invincible*	*187*
SMS *Von Der Tann*	*188*
Admiral Lord Charles Beresford	*205*
Admiral of the Fleet Sir John Fisher	*206*
Bernhard Von Bülow	*249*
SMS *Panther*	*273*
Alfred von Kiderlen-Waechter	*274*
Winston Churchill as First Lord of the Admiralty	*299*
Admiral of the Fleet Sir Arthur Knyvet Wilson	*300*
HMS *Lion*	*309*
SMS *Seydlitz*	*310*
Admiral Sir Francis Bridgeman	*319*
Theobald Von Bethmann-Hollweg	*351*
Sir Edward Grey	*352*
King George V and the Tsar	*387*
Prinz Heinrich	*388*
Archduke Franz Ferdinand with his wife and children	*407*
Gavrilo Princip	*408*
HMS *Iron Duke*	*425*
SMS *Friedrich Der Grosse*	*426*
British battleships fire a ceremonial salute at Kiel	*431*
Gavrilo Princip is arrested	*432*
The High Seas Fleet at Kiel	*441*
The Grand Fleet at Sea	*442*

INTRODUCTION

On the First of November 1914, in the inclement waters of the South East Pacific, off a remote Chilean port named Coronel, there occurred an event unique in the annals of Britain's naval history. A British squadron, on paper not greatly inferior to its adversary, was comprehensively defeated, losing all its major units, and without being able to inflict any significant damage on the opposing force.

In the distant past, there had been very infrequent examples of sea battles resulting in a tactical or strategic setback to British interests. There were no precedents for a defeat so one sided, and so devoid of compensation for the loss of life and materiel as that which was imposed at the Battle of Coronel.

The debacle was a serious blow to British prestige at the outset of the First World War, and was remarkable in the fact that the victorious squadron did not belong to one of the established maritime powers, but to a newly-formed navy possessing neither the tradition nor the experience of battle.

The German nation, as a unified entity, had come into being only after the war with France in 1871. A generation before the First World War, the German Navy scarcely existed as more than a motley collection of coast defence ships and obsolete ironclads. In 1914, only 16 years had elapsed since the beginning of the prodigious effort that had resulted in the building of a High Seas Fleet second only to that of Britain. The rate of expansion had been staggering, but, at the outbreak of war, it was an untried and untested factor, and, resting heavily on its psyche was the colossal deadweight of British maritime supremacy and a tradition of victory that stretched far back into history. Yet, in its first major action, warships of the infant force inflicted a stinging reverse on the most powerful navy the world had ever seen.

How did this come about? And why, despite crippling expenditure that came close to bankrupting an immensely prosperous country; despite robustly constructed and well designed ships; despite highly trained and motivated crews; despite superior technical equipment, gallant commanders, and the utmost fortitude in action, does the engagement off Coronel represent the only unqualified success achieved, in two world wars, by a German squadron over a similarly constituted opponent?

To address these questions is also to lead on to the far more crucial matter of whether the mighty fleet created by the Kaiser's ambitions and produced by Tirpitz's Navy Laws from 1898 onwards, brought any benefits to Germany commensurate to the vast expenditure of resources that its development required. Arguably, in terms of its effect on the First Great War and the fate of the Hohenzollern Empire, the High Seas Fleet ultimately failed in every role – political, strategic, and operational – for which it had been constructed and tasked, and was, in any case, wrongly equipped in terms of materiel to serve its designed purpose. It can be strongly maintained that its very existence was a, if not *the*, primary cause of Germany's defeat in the First World War.

Politically, had the fleet not been created as a deliberate challenge to the supremacy of the Royal Navy, it is unlikely that the British Empire would have been an active participant on the side of Germany's enemies in 1914. That, in itself, would have completely altered the balance of power in Europe, and elsewhere, to Germany's great advantage. Whilst the construction of the High Seas Fleet did not automatically mean that Britain and Germany would eventually go to war with each other, it ensured that, if a general war broke out on the European continent, Britain and Germany would be on opposing sides in the subsequent conflict.

Strategically, from a purely military point of view, had even half of the enormous sums of money; the quantities of munitions and weapons; and the demands on manpower, been diverted to the army – which represented Germany's real military strength – there would still have been sufficient to provide for a surface fleet large enough to carry out all the duties for which it was actually tasked during the course of the war. Had the army been in possession of these extra resources in the August and September of 1914, the Battle of the Marne would very probably have had a very different conclusion, or never been fought at all, and the First World War might well have been over by Christmas – in Germany's favour. The later battles of Ypres, Loos and Verdun; of the Somme, Passchendaele, Picardy and the Aisne, which bled white the cream of the youth of Western Europe, might never have been fought, and the history of the world in the 20th century would have taken a very different turn.

Operationally, the political alienation of Great Britain also placed Germany's naval forces at a huge disadvantage. From the maritime perspective, the geographic situation of the two powers uniquely favoured the British. Germany's only outlet to the oceans of the world lay through the waters of the North Sea, and Britain, from the Straits of Dover to the northern outposts of the Orkney and Shetland Islands, lay like a giant breakwater enclosing that sea area and restricting access and egress to a few clearly defined routes that were relatively easy to monitor and police. The difficulty of overcoming this problem was never solved, and therein lay the conundrum for German strategic planners over two gigantic conflicts. In the Second World War, the conquest of Norway and military possession of the French Atlantic coast gave German naval forces unfettered access to the world's oceans, but, bar the submarine service, without the forces necessary to take full advantage of the situation. In the First World War, a very powerful force existed, but was denied access to bases from which it could deploy to outflank Britain's geographic position.

If this geographic imperative imposed severe restrictions on the use of the German Navy, neither was there, at the highest level of command, the *will* to succeed in breaking the mould. The operational potential of the German Navy was completely stymied by the refusal of the Kaiser and his advisors to risk the High Seas Fleet in action with the British Grand Fleet even when, in the first few months of the war, it very closely approached the numerical strength of its opponent. For a short period, in the autumn and winter of 1914, the British had a dangerously low margin of superiority in terms of battleships and were decidedly inferior both in quality and quantity as regards battlecruisers. No historian has ever disputed that the loss of maritime supremacy following the defeat of the Grand Fleet would have resulted in the loss of the war, regardless of any stalemate on land. There was, at that time, a brief window of opportunity for the German Navy to reach for glory. It was denied the opportunity by its governing authority, and the situation would never again be so favourable. The error of failing to strike in advantageous circumstances was compounded by the later policy of emasculating the surface fleet in favour of unrestricted submarine warfare on trade. Without the latter development, it is unlikely that the United States would have abandoned its highly profitable neutrality for active engagement on the side of Germany's foes.

Materially, apart from the excellent battlecruiser designs, the German naval planners compounded their other errors by building the wrong sort of capital ship. They churned out a series of sturdy, short range battleships that were, admittedly, very difficult to sink but concentrated on defensive qualities to the detriment of all else. Britain had obtained undisputed command of the seas in 1805, at Trafalgar, and that command could only be threatened by ships designed and used primarily for offence. In essence, Germany built an enormous battle fleet that met all the criteria of an immovable object, when her strategic situation and tactical imperatives actually demanded an irresistible force. It is very difficult to challenge the maritime supremacy of an opponent by using ships whose greatest virtue lies in their ability to absorb punishment. Apart from any other factor, it does not display the requisite offensive intent and this inevitably spills over into the tactical arena.[1] The British, in fact, erred in the opposite direction

---

[1] Herein lay an anomaly that persisted throughout the history of Anglo-German naval conflict. The British, in defence of their maritime supremacy, invariably took the operational and tactical offensive, whereas the Germans, who needed to overcome the Royal Navy to gain their nation's ends, were usually very cautious in their operational planning and always defensively orientated in their battle tactics.

and the strategic needs of the two navies, challenger and challenged, would have been better served had some of the designs and qualities of their capital ships been transposed.

If there are germs of truth in all of these various contentions, how was it that the flourishing and vibrant German Empire, on the brink of global economic predominance, could construct a fleet that was so utterly inimitable to its best interests, and which would virtually ensure its eventual ruin? – and why, having made this momentous decision, did it then deploy the magnificently inappropriate weapon it had forged with such operational timidity as to reduce it to progressive demoralisation, mutinous impotence, and ultimately, by its own hand, consign it to the seabed in a British fleet anchorage?

The theme of the work having been set, this first volume sets the scene and introduces the contestants to the arena in which they were to play their part.

The history of the German effort to become a major naval power, and to then, deliberately, dispute the command of the seas with the long-standing supremacy of Britain, is a remarkable tale. It is, though, littered with a comprehensive list of political blunders, missed tactical opportunities, and a singular lack of any strategic insight. These failings were directly attributable to the ruling elite of the country, and to the oppressive restrictions they imposed upon the use of the fleet and on the initiative of its naval commanders.

Despite the notable achievement of creating an effective navy in a remarkably short space of time, the inability to properly direct and utilise such a formidable weapon was to be a characteristic of German military policy in both the great wars. This was the seed that germinated into the writing of this book. If there was one particular drop of rain that served to germinate the seed, it was that which fell on the uninviting waters of the North Sea in early 1915.

I had always felt that the accepted historical assessment of the Dogger Bank action in the January of that year was too trite. The general verdict was that the engagement had been a British success, but only a partial one. The opportunity for a much greater victory had, it was argued, been squandered through command misunderstandings and imprecise communications.

Without at all disagreeing with the facts surrounding the action, it did seem, however, that, if all had gone as the British admiral intended, the result might well have been a catastrophe for his forces, rather than the 'partial' and disappointing victory that was achieved.

Following on from this premise, there were other actions that attracted attention. During the Second World War, there were also missed opportunities for German naval forces in both the Battle of the River Plate, and the *Bismarck* sortie, that had not been fully addressed. In these two cases, the writer is slightly uncomfortable to find himself partially in agreement with Adolf Hitler's judgement of those events – despite the latter's inability to ever appreciate the importance of sea power. If these were the main bones of contention, there were many other, less celebrated, and detailed, incidents in both wars that were variations on the same theme.

In the event, the study of a small piece of history led to a much larger project. Initially, I was only dealing with the British side of events over a limited period. This rapidly diversified and started to stretch back into earlier times. As the Kaiser and Tirpitz came into the picture, so also did Bismarck and many of the characters in the German political and naval establishments. With them came their British and other European contemporaries. The overall histories of both nations in the Victorian era inevitably intruded into the account. Eventually it seemed logical to commence the story at the end of the Napoleonic wars. From there, what started as a short re-assessment of an indecisive action, in which a single vessel was lost, became a fully-fledged book.

I had intended this account to cover the whole period of Anglo-German naval affairs from its beginning through to its end in 1945. This has proved impossible through a combination of reasons and this volume is the first of three that will carry the story through to the natural break point of 1919. A subsequent, two volume, work will deal with the periods 1919-39 and 1939-45. Both these works naturally divide into two sections – the first section describing the 'Protagonists' and covering the circumstances leading up to hostilities; the second recounting the actions of the 'Antagonists' and their consequences. As mitigation for this dereliction of intent in spreading the work over a larger canvas than had been planned (apart from the fact that it would have resulted in an unmanageably large tome), I offer the case of a man who, more than any other, must be regarded as my muse.

The earth into which the 'seed' was sown, and which produced this work, was discovered many years ago, in the 1960s, when I was a young naval officer in the Trucial Oman. By some chance, an English bookshop had been set up in what was then the small coastal settlement of Abu Dhabi. There I obtained, at small cost, the five volumes of Arthur J. Marder's definitive study of the Royal Navy in the years leading up to, and during, the First World War (*From the Dreadnought to Scapa Flow: The Royal Navy in the Fisher era*).

Professor Marder, in the introduction to his monumental work, stated that he had originally intended to write his book in one volume, but that its completion, despite all the advantages of his academic position, contacts, and research assistants, eventually took five volumes and over twenty years of his life. The end product, to anyone with an interest in the subject, certainly justified the effort. The quality of the writing, the depth of the research, the evocation of the time, together with the descriptions of the characters that populated the age, caught the imagination. It also stirred an ambition – not to emulate Marder, which would have been not only impossible, but also presumptuous – to write on the same subject. Strangely enough, part of the impulsion came from what I saw as anomalies in the perceived wisdom of his account and, also, of those of the other respected historians of that period.

Although one of the major purposes of this book is to examine both the reasons for the creation of a German fleet, and to assess its performance in battle, it is also, by necessity, and predominately, a history of the British Navy at that time. It concentrates on the activities of the surface fleets of both nations rather than on the submarine campaigns against trade, which constituted a totally different branch of warfare beyond the remit of this study. In this account, except in the cases of where and when the demands of countering the U-boat threat on trade impinged upon the capabilities of the main surface fleets and squadrons, the first 'Battle of the Atlantic' is left to other chroniclers. That is not to say that submarine warfare against trade did not seriously affect the operations of the surface fleet. On the contrary, the post-Jutland leeching of its best manpower from battleships to submarines effectively destroyed the efficiency and morale of the High Seas Fleet. To a lesser extent, the personnel tied up in anti-submarine duties imposed severe restrictions on the use of the Grand Fleet in the later stages of the war. For all that, the campaign against trade, once the surface raiders were eliminated, is outside the scope of this work.

In justifying this approach, it is relevant to cite two examples that occurred in the course of the next great conflict.

During the Second World War, the second 'Battle of the Atlantic' and the mass heavy bombing offensive of the RAF and USAF against German cities and industries, existed as separate, independent, strategic entities. In the case of the former, the result was absolutely critical to the outcome of the war. Had the Battle of the Atlantic been lost in either war, Britain would have been starved into defeat, regardless of the strength of her fleet, or of those of Germany, Japan and Italy. Militarily, had German submarines made transit of the Atlantic unacceptably perilous, America would have been powerless to intervene in either war. There would have been no Pershing's Army, and no D-Day. The effectiveness of the latter, air, offensive is less easily assessed or justified, and remains contentious to this day. Essentially, they were campaigns and policies that stood on their own without reference to the other, more local, battles being fought (although all of these had their own submarine and air components) on land and sea.

That is not to say that they had *no* effect on other strategies and tactical matters. They were part of the strategic whole in carrying out a world war, and the considerable manpower and materiel required to launch or combat these offensives inevitably meant a significant diversion of resources from other branches of the services – often to the serious detriment of tactical considerations. Half a million personnel of military age diverted to anti-aircraft defence of cities in Germany (and in Britain) was equivalent to several armies that otherwise could have been deployed to the battle fronts. This factor affected both sides in differing degrees and circumstances, and, on several occasions, played a vital role in determining the course of events. For all that, the bombing of Berlin, Hamburg or the Ruhr; or the safe passage of a convoy, whatever the long-term results, could not have an immediate bearing on matters in the field or in contested waters.

The economic blockade imposed by British sea power on Germany during the First World War is more difficult to categorise. Whilst it was conducted by secondary units of the British Fleet, its effectiveness depended on the predominance of the Grand Fleet over its German opponent.

By its very nature, and the limitations imposed by ill-advised treaty obligations regarding the transit of goods in neutral hulls, the British blockade could only be slow to take effect. In a short, sharp, and decisive war on the continent that would be decided by the land armies of the contending nations, maritime blockade had little relevance, and the navies of both Britain and Germany would have been of small consequence in the balance of the conflict. If the immediate battle on land was entirely won or lost, the war was over, whatever happened at sea. This was the established historical wisdom. In the case of the First World War, it would have probably been true. One side would have been the victor and the other the defeated. A negotiated peace would have followed, giving great advantages to the successful nations. Sea power would not have had the time to be of any useful effect and Britain's latent capacity to raise formidable armies for slaughter on the continent would never have been tapped.

Supremacy at sea (and later in the air) ensured that island Britain itself could not be invaded, but, as happened in 1940, the rout of its European allies meant that hegemony over the continent of Europe could not be disputed. The victory of Trafalgar in 1805 did not destroy Napoleon. His armies turned away from the coast of the English Channel and promptly proceeded to demolish, at Ulm, Austerlitz and Jena, the combined forces of the other most powerful nations on the continent. Critically though, Napoleon, like Hitler a century and a half later, left an undefeated foe in his rear, and in charge of the seas. The road to Moscow in 1812, and Stalingrad in 1942, was the same, and it started at Boulogne.

Should hostilities turn out to be a protracted affair, sea power was bound to be a critical influence in the weakening of Germany's economic ability to wage war, and in her failure to prevent the reinforcement of her foes. This situation could only ever have been changed by the defeat of the main British Fleet. That this was never seriously attempted, despite a very favourable balance of strength in the first six months of the first Great War, remains the most compelling condemnation of those charged with the direction of German strategic policies at that time.

Historians, rightly, do not have much regard for the 'What If?' approach to their subject, for the very sensible reason that the whole concept is spurious. *If* Hannibal had taken Rome after Cannae; or *if* Harold Godwinson had not had to fight and win the Battle of Stamford Bridge before marching the length of the country to meet William the Conqueror at Hastings, then history would have been different. *If* old Blucher had been two hours later in rescuing Wellington's flank at Waterloo, then the EEC might have existed since 1815, and might still be run by Napoleon's descendants. *If* Hitler had sold his soul to Franco in 1940 in exchange for Gibraltar then the fascists might have triumphed. The subjects for conjecture are almost limitless, and their consequences infinitely debatable. For better or for worse, history can only disregard the 'ifs' however entertaining they might be, and simply relate what actually happened and explain the background to events.

That said, there are a very great number of 'What Ifs?' that crop up in describing Anglo-German naval relations, and in the subsequent conflicts that ensued between the two nations. Some of them cannot be entirely ignored, as they intrude into the subject of this book. In the process they merge into the altogether different territory of the 'Why Didn't They?' category. At this point the question becomes more respectable, and any form of answer requires an examination of the people, politics, and events of the time.

When addressing the question of 'Why?' the German Fleet did not achieve more, it is necessary to go back to the birth of that navy and trace its development in parallel to the changes that were taking place in what was to be its principal opponent. What is without question is that the eventual naval rivalry between the two nations drove an irretrievable wedge between them that became the critical influence in their polarisation into contending political camps.

In dealing with this subject, I have to apologise to the reader for sometimes appearing to divert from the main theme of the book to address issues of wider international significance. My excuse for this is to put in context the events that led Britain and Germany to be on opposing sides. Naval rivalry remained the prime cause of estrangement between the two nations, but allegiances and entanglements with other powers created the structures within which the rivalry intensified, and the convoluted affairs of the European continent produced the necessary conditions for that rivalry to eventually erupt into active confrontation.

Unlike Marder, and many of the other distinguished historians who have followed in his steps, this writer has not had access to official records, bar the published sources. Nor, time having taken its toll, have I been able to interview or correspond with any living survivors of the period covered. This is not, therefore, a work of new research but an attempt to reassess some of the aspects of the subject. The book has been written, over very many years, at sea, alongside, or ashore, and relies entirely for its facts on previously published material, and a lifetime of research and interest in the subject, allied to the opinions of the writer. The material I have drawn on, apart from the Official War Histories, includes the biographies and autobiographies of all the major players on the stage. It also encompasses many of the other officially published histories of events, newspaper records, as well as the individual memoirs of junior personnel.

I have quoted extensively from other, recent, authors, whose accounts and opinions are both well written and succinctly stated. In many cases, I would have happily quoted them much more but for the fact that this book would have become far too long and discursive. If the reader of this study is encouraged to dig deeper and wider into the subject, then it will have succeeded in its object. Richard Hough's books are particularly readable for their command of the events and their detailed description of men and of action; Robert K. Massie, in writing *Dreadnought*, has provided a wonderful history of the era as well as providing good thumbnail sketches of all the significant personalities of the age; Andrew Gordon, in *The Rules of the Game*, gives a comprehensive view of the British naval command and control mentality at that time; John Campbell gives the definitive materiel dissection of the Jutland battle. Of earlier writers, Arthur J. Marder's works are central to any understanding of the period, as are Winston Churchill's subjective but absolutely essential memoirs. For a background on the navalist mentality of the era, the works of Captain Alfred Thayer Mahan crucially affected the views of all the major players of the day. Very many other writers have obviously been essential to this account, but for reasons of conciseness can only be listed in the bibliography.

That this work has reached completion is largely due to the encouragement, assistance, and patience of my family and also, to a few other special people. My parents, Bill and Joan, have unfailingly supported me in this task and incidentally provided the introduction that gave me the first tentative impulsions to write. As a teenager, on one evening in the early sixties, I sat to dinner opposite the last surviving Great War poet, Edmund Blunden. I was a guest of my parents' next door neighbour, the author Douglas Grant, who was then Professor of American Literature at Leeds

University. Blunden had been Grant's tutor and mentor at university. I left that evening in May 1962 with a signed copy of *Undertones to War* and an insert from Douglas that read:

'This is a first edition of the finest war book in English – & the author is one of the finest of poets and men. May his experience never be yours but may you come to equal, his style.'

I have been blessed with the very great good fortune never to have experienced the likes of Blunden's war service, but, alas, I can never aspire to equal the style or quality of his writing. Nevertheless, over many years, this book has emerged as a piece of work that I hope will partially justify their expectations of the callow youth who shared their table that night.

My great thanks are due to Joan Grant, widow of Douglas, who, before her death, carried out the proof reading of the book's first two volumes. I also owe an inestimable debt to two wives, Janet and Maggie, who have had to tolerate, over many years, the anti-social night owl tendencies of a writer husband. Without their patience and support, this work would never have seen the light of day.

My thanks also go to Graham Cook, Ian Large and Jag Lall, the Writersworld team without whom this volume could not have been produced.

When all the efforts of peacemakers and politicians have failed, and the consequences of that failure have translated themselves into war, there is only left the bleak account of subsequent events. The failures of politicians are frequently translated into their loss of office and reputation. Those who are left to deal with the resulting situation on the field of war often pay with their lives. The accounts of subsequent events are necessarily a record of the loss of human life; the destruction of the machines and weapons to which they were tied; and to the fate of the systems to which they loyally plied their military trade – often against their will and inclination. They are also accounts that frequently illustrate some of the finest characteristics of the human race – albeit exercised in one of its basest pursuits. What remains is a record of gallantry and loss; triumph and defeat. Gallantry is happily remembered; loss, not so, even though it may have been gallant.

Triumph is a relative term, as the cost of its achievement can exceed the benefits of its attainment. The Duke of Wellington once said that that the only thing worse than a battle won was a battle lost. A century later, Reinhardt Scheer, the German Naval Commander for much of the First World War, wrote in the preface to his memoirs, that 'The victor has the privilege of writing the story of the war; for one mistrusts the vanquished…but we are victors and vanquished at one and the same time'.

For Britain, in the two world wars, this anomaly was certainly true. The cost of military victory was ultimately economic decline, dissolution of empire, and, most importantly, the permanent loss of a large proportion of its best young talent. The boldest and most adventurous are always in the forefront of events, and are always, therefore, disproportionately represented in the statistics of slaughter.

If this was the legacy of the victor, what of his opponent? Defeat, in the case of Germany in the First World War, was utterly devastating to the entire social, political, and economic structure of the nation, as well as, consequentially, to the entire continent of Europe. Defeat begat humiliation, poverty, anger and Hitler. Hitler begat the total moral and material destruction of his nation, as well as encompassing the ruin of many others.

Within the overall compass of dreadful conflict, there is a record of people; some exceptional and some ordinary; all of them flawed, but some very gifted, and most of them faced with situations beyond their immediate training, imagination, and experience. The confrontation of Britain and Germany at sea is a record of remarkable events, some remarkable characters, and some of the most stirring episodes in the history of both nations. These are stories that deserve to be retold, and re-read by each generation.

The human race is not renowned for its ability to learn from its mistakes, but, at least, the historian can continue to publicise the evidence of past follies. If by so doing, he can help to ensure that the lessons of the past are not lost to those who would wish to use them to help avoid the pitfalls of the future, it will not have been a vain endeavour. For the pomposity of this statement, I freely apologise, but, if this contribution to the literature on the subject should stir the interest of the reader, it will have served its purpose.

CHAPTER ONE

THE ROYAL NAVY IN THE NINETEENTH CENTURY

'Pax Britannica...The very phrase gives a twofold impression; of a long period of tranquillity efficiently and firmly supervised by the Royal Navy, and of an overwhelmingly powerful nation upon which all others were to a varying extent dependent. Neither impression is fully correct, but both contained a sufficient portion of the truth to secure a widespread acceptance of this overall portrait.'

Paul M. Kennedy

'England can never be a Continental power, and, in the attempt she must be ruined. Let her stick to the sovereignty of the seas and she may send her ambassadors to the courts of Europe and demand what she pleases.'

Napoleon Bonaparte, in exile on St. Helena

At the end of the Napoleonic wars, the Royal Navy reigned supreme on the oceans of the world. In operational strength, Britain could deploy, worldwide, a fleet superior to the combined forces of all the remainder of the other seagoing nations. In the previous quarter of a century, every other major maritime power had been confronted and their fleets destroyed, confiscated, or blockaded in their home ports until all effectiveness as operational units had largely vanished. In 1815, a single, national, naval force dominated and policed the oceans of the world.

This dominance was underpinned by a string of bases strategically situated on the choke points of world trade routes, and, on these routes, the British mercantile marine enjoyed a similar degree of supremacy in the sphere of international trade as did the Royal Navy in its control of the sea lanes.

'The final defeat of France's bid for European hegemony left a victorious Britain the world's predominant naval, colonial, maritime, mercantile, industrial and financial power. In none of these respects would her supremacy be challenged until century's end.

'The number of technological firsts that the French navy (never quite reconciled to Trafalgar) attained around mid-century might appear to contradict that statement so far as naval power is concerned, and several of them did indeed affright the British public, but there was really no cause for alarm.' (1)

The era of Pax Britannica had begun, and it spawned, amongst other things, some very long-lasting clichés. All of these highly general truisms rested on one single, simple, premise. The British Empire had come into being, and was sustainable, because of the Royal Navy. This situation had been in the making for decades, if not centuries, but it was the wars of Napoleon that finally set the seal on its completion. N.A.M. Rodger, in his excellent account of the British Navy in this period, quotes a Prussian Field Marshall of the time, Count August von Gneisenau, in crediting (or blaming) Bonaparte for the final accession of Great Britain to the undisputed crown of the seas:

'There is no mortal to whom Great Britain has greater obligations than this blackguard, for it is the events which he has brought about which have raised England's greatness, security and wealth so high. They are lords of the sea, and neither in this dominion nor in world trade have they any rivals left to fear.' (2) [1]

That the navy had rendered the empire possible produced a corollary. Without a dominant navy the new empire was not viable. Without the riches produced by that empire, and control of the world's trade, a navy of sufficient power could not be financed nor maintained. The one could not exist without the other. The key word, though, was *trade*.

After the loss of the American colonies, there was no deliberate attempt to build a new empire. The hackneyed phrase that 'the (*new)* empire was acquired in a fit of absence of mind', although incorrect, is not without pertinence, as most of Britain's future possessions were certainly not acquired, at least not initially, out of any nationalistic desire for sovereignty.

'The British Empire was not a classic Imperial model, seizing land to control people and markets by military power. Instead it relied on capital and commerce to develop a system of informal empire, in which the cost of local administration was borne by nation states which were beneficially owned by British institutions.' (3)

The bitter lesson of the American experience (which was essentially a civil war between the English-speaking peoples, decided by French intervention), gave colonialism a bad name in British governing circles. Subsequently, the creation of colonies for their own sake was the last thing on the mind of British politicians. What remained vital to Britain was *control* of the sources of trade, and of its safe dissemination throughout the world. To this end, a British presence, both commercial and military, was required in overseas regions. This commitment was sometimes purely commercial, and sometimes purely military – as a means of controlling and

---

[1] There is a certain irony in that two ships named after the same Field Marshall von Gneisenau were to be at the forefront of Germany's efforts to challenge Britain's maritime supremacy in both the great wars of the twentieth century.

protecting the routes on which trade, whether import or export, had to be carried. The British presence was mostly a balanced combination of the two – the balance varying as to the requirements of the time and the specific region. For either to be successful, there also had to be a British administrative authority.

In an era when sail was the only means of seaborne propulsion, the trade arteries were strictly governed by the seasonal winds and currents that dictated the timing and routing of ocean-going mercantile traffic. Of the many areas that were eventually to be coloured pink on the map of the world, some can be seen to be the source of vital or profitable commodities; the rest are sited athwart the routes by which they can be conveyed. If the empire was conceived 'in a fit of absence of mind', there was nothing accidental about its extent and distribution. In the fullness of time, British authority in those areas became formalised and they metamorphosed into crown possessions, if only to prevent other, competitor, nations from intruding. As such they eventually hatched into the protectorates, colonies and dominions of the new empire. Removing such facilities from potential rivals also played a significant role in the process.

Command of the sea also allowed Britain's limited military forces to have much greater effect than would have been represented by the sheer statistics of their numbers. Wellington's successful campaign in the Iberian peninsular was heavily reliant on British control of the sea and of the consequent ability to transport, support, and reinforce his army from a succession of ports. Had, at any point in the campaign, Britain lost command of the sea, Wellington's army would probably have been doomed.

Robert K. Massie has some fun with the clichés whilst emphasising the fact that they were based on reality:

'The Victorian Age, The Pax Britannica, Splendid Isolation, The Empire on Which the Sun Never Sets, existed because Britannia Ruled the Waves. Essentially she ruled unchallenged. Her former antagonists, the Spanish and the Dutch had no navies to speak of; Russia and the United States were deeply engaged in consolidating control over their own continental land masses; the German Empire did not exist. Despite its shattering defeat by Nelson, the French Navy remained throughout the century the world's second largest. But France, after Bonaparte faced decades of political instability and institutional change...Only briefly, at the height of The Second Empire, did France build ships which caused alarm in England. Even then, Great Britain's naval supremacy remained unshaken.' (4)

In an age when intercontinental trade and communications entirely depended on sea transport, undisputed authority on the oceans also gave Britain an effective veto on the ability of any other nation to conduct economic or military affairs beyond their respective shores. In the New World of the Americas, the Monroe Doctrine could have existed only as brave words and a laudable principle without the co-operation, intentional or otherwise, of the British Navy and its political masters.[2] Many general benefits accrued from this situation whereby Britain assumed the role of the world's policeman. Amongst the most obvious and enduring effects were the gradual abolition of the slave trade and suppression of international piracy. Politically, the navy also had a profound global effect. As the American colonies had broken away from Britain in the previous century, so did the possessions of Spain and Portugal choose to replace a distant and unsympathetic authority with self-rule. This did not come easily, and much vigorous and bloody campaigning was involved before the various nations of South America emerged from the debris of the old empires, and settled down to fighting each other. During this transition period the progress to independence of many states on the South American continent owed a huge amount to the active or tacit support of the British Government, and the naval shield, which could, if required, prevent interference from the old colonial powers on the Eastern Atlantic seaboard. The celebrated American naval historian, Captain A.T. Mahan, writing in 1911 remarks that:

'Why do English innate political conceptions of popular representative government, of the balance of law and liberty, prevail in North America from the Arctic circle to the Gulf of Mexico, from the Atlantic to the Pacific? Because the command of the sea in the decisive era belonged to Great Britain.' (5)

Mahan goes on to apply this conclusion to the rest of the world – or at least the large segments of the globe that were then subject to the influence of sea power. The independence struggles of South America provided prime examples for his argument. There was also a considerable influx of support for these libertarian movements from former British Navy and Army personnel. The conclusion of the Napoleonic wars had made redundant a large number of trained military personnel who had no desire to return to penury in Britain. Many chose to take their chance abroad as mercenaries. Some went and settled. Others fought and moved on. One of the outstanding British naval officers of the 19th century, Cochrane, took his chance in

---

[2] In 1823, US President James Monroe introduced a new foreign policy, which stated that any attempt by European nations to interfere in the affairs of states in both North and South America would be viewed as an act of aggression against the United States and would automatically trigger American intervention. The policy became known as the 'Monroe Doctrine', and has been a feature of American foreign policy ever since.

There is a certain historical irony that the president of a nation that had recently, and successfully, fought for its independence from Great Britain could make a declaration on the territorial integrity of two continents that could have no credibility, and was utterly unsustainable, without the tacit approval and naval might of the old colonial power.

Greece and Chile, and is still revered in both those countries as being the driving force behind the creation of their navies. In Chile, they still name one of the finest ships in their navy after him. Many of his sailors, whose exploits have not passed into history, would have had English, Scottish, Welsh or Irish names.

An often overlooked by-product of all this activity was the immense effort Britain put into surveying the world's oceans. Throughout the 19th century (and subsequently), the Royal Navy devoted a great deal of its time and resources into surveying previously uncharted waters. Common sense dictated that most of this activity should be concentrated on the main trade routes and choke points, but much was also done, quite independently, by captains of detached units in distant waters. The excellent series of charts that resulted were made freely available to mariners of all nations.

Above all, protection of the sea lanes ensured the rapid and peaceful development of worldwide trade and the economic expansion of those nations capable of taking advantage of the situation. Prime amongst those nations, of course, was Britain herself, but, if the motives were not entirely altruistic, the effects were beneficial to all.

Apart from its existing maritime supremacy, Great Britain enjoyed two other outstanding advantages during the 19th century. As the first nation to harness the effects of the Industrial Revolution, it was far ahead of rival powers in the capacity to react to advances in technology. For a critical period in the evolution of warships from the wooden walls of Trafalgar to the Dreadnought Battleship, Britain possessed the industrial base to out-produce any potential opponent.

It has been often inferred that British naval construction policy in the 1800s was largely negative in character, being based on the principle of opposing any new development that had the potential to disturb a satisfactory status quo. This was not an entirely stupid position. Britain, after all, had a vested interest in preserving the relative effectiveness of its huge existing fleet. Even if changes to the fleet were seen to be inevitable in the long term, there were good financial arguments for ensuring that they were not made until such time as they became essential.

Obviously, anything that threatened to make this vast armada obsolete was hardly likely to be welcomed by the Admiralty (or, particularly, the Treasury). The board thus generally adopted a policy of doing nothing radical unless and until developments elsewhere forced its hand. It was argued that, if a significant advance was made by a foreign power in warship design or embarked weaponry, then, and then only, would it be necessary for Britain to copy, with improvements, innovations originating from abroad – at which point they could be produced in overwhelming numbers.

'To Admiralty officials, it seemed foolish to have the largest navy in the world pioneer developments that would devalue ships in inventory (as decades later critics accused Jacky Fisher of having done with his Dreadnought). The Royal Navy could afford to leave innovation to others, certain of the capacity of British industry to overtake and outperform any rival whenever it was asked.' (6)

This essentially pragmatic approach was certainly justified in many respects, and on many occasions, but a series of conservative (in the reactionary sense of the word) administrations definitely retarded progress in some areas. For all that, British industry and technology, independent of the Admiralty, was also frequently in the forefront of groundbreaking developments as the age of wood and sail painfully gave way to that of steel and steam.

What is beyond dispute is that Britain, whenever the necessity arose, could out-build any group of nations in the world during this period. That fact, for a good many decades, gave the country a significant advantage over the remainder of the existing, or putative, maritime powers.

The other crucial advantage possessed by the United Kingdom was insularity. Uniquely amongst the world's then major powers, Great Britain was blessed by not having a common land frontier with potential enemies. The English Channel, and the adjoining expanses of the North Sea and Atlantic, remained a moat around the kingdom, and only control of the seas could bridge that tantalising stretch of water.

'Freedom from foreign invasion, conferred by sea power, provided the security which alone made long term investment and economic growth possible. In this way if no other, naval supremacy was the indispensable foundation of prosperity. Add to this the preservation of the lives and liberties of the people, and the strictly defensive achievements of sea power would have been central to British history even if it had never made any other contribution.' (7)

All the major powers of continental Europe rested uneasily on one or the others' borders. All of them were potential friends or enemies in unpredictable combinations and circumstances, and all, therefore, had to maintain large and expensive standing armies to guard against the threats posed by their neighbours. Island Britain, alone of the great nations, could afford to dispense with the cost of keeping significant military forces on her own soil. For so long as the Royal Navy retained command of the seas, invasion of Britain remained an impossibility and negated the need for a large army. 'I do not say they cannot come,' stated the old admiral, Earl St.

Vincent, to a worried questioner during one of the periodic invasion scares in the Napoleonic war, 'but they cannot come by sea.' With the sole exception of the Crimean War in the 1850s (an offensive operation in any case), it would not be necessary to deploy British soldiers against modern well-equipped opposition for the remainder of the century. The richest country in the world could therefore afford to devote a much greater proportion of its overall defence budget to naval forces than could its rival nations on the continent.

'Britain invariably spent far more on its navy than did any would-be rivals with the sole exception of France. Between 1860 and 1890 German naval spending never reached a quarter of Britain's. Italy's barely broached 30%, and then only during the last three years of the 1880s. Russia's, so far as is known, never reached 50%. Austria-Hungary's remained consistently below 15% and typically less than 10%, and the United States, whose naval expenditure ballooned to over twice Britain's in 1864-5, spent less than half from 1868 through 1875, and less than a third for the remaining years of the period.' (8)

John Charmley, in his recent reassessment of Britain's foreign policy in that era, emphasises the point:

'In reality, Britain had established her position as a Great Power by staying out of the "scrum" whenever possible. She had grown great by the use of sea power and money, allowing her Continental rivals to exhaust themselves in costly European wars whilst she picked off their colonial possessions. It was true that after 1808 she had finally made a Continental commitment against Napoleon, but that was in Spain, developed by accident, and it could be afforded.' (9)

He might also have added that the success of Wellington's peninsular campaign had been significantly dependent on the mobility and logistic support afforded to him by the Royal Navy's command of the sea. A much earlier source, the respected naval journalist and political commentator Archibald Hurd, writing in 1912, remarks that:

'England is not the unprotected waif and stray among the nations. On the continent the frontiers that have to be defended are land frontiers, and therefore the military strength of such Powers takes the form of soldiers and the population is compelled to submit to the burden of conscription. No one can accurately calculate the actual cost of those Continental armies, because the burden to the nation is not shown in any financial statement. The actual cost is infinitely swollen by the national loss due to the withdrawal of so many men from industrial occupations.' (10)

In a lengthy extension to his reasoning, Hurd also argued that, for a nation in Great Britain's position, the cost of training and equipping a single soldier for the military was double that of providing a sailor for the navy. What is beyond dispute is that those land forces that Britain did maintain, post-1815, could be largely employed in minor colonial wars and the policing of a rapidly expanding empire – neither of which tasks required the numbers, training or sophistication demanded of the European armies.

The only significant threat to British maritime supremacy in the period following the Napoleonic wars came from the parsimony of complacent government.

'The navy which had smashed Napoleon's dreams was allowed to dwindle away, from ninety-eight sail of the line in 1814 to twenty-three in 1838. Each year the Naval estimates were cut in any way possible, either by Parliament or the Board of Admiralty…Efficiency is not easily bred by such means, for the retention of obsolescent ships and weapons for the sake of economy discourages new tactics and inhibits realistic training… [however] Despite this grinding parsimony the Royal Navy kept an overwhelming preponderance over its nearest rivals for many years.' (11)

Whilst the peacetime fleet remained comfortably able to meet its commitments, little was done by successive administrations to address the problems inherent in the almost mediaeval methods of recruiting and training, and the appalling conditions of service for lower deck ratings. It took the shock of the Crimean War and the sudden emergence of a new breed of warships to prompt a reappraisal of the situation. By that time the devastated navies of the European powers (chiefly France) had reappeared, re-equipped, onto the world scene, and comparisons of relative strength were increasingly becoming of concern.

The Crimean War exposed the parlous state of inefficiency into which political neglect had led the naval forces of the nation. The noted naval writer and academic, Admiral Sir Herbert Richmond, remarks with some acerbity that:

'The Fleet which was sent, after prolonged delay, to the Baltic, was inadequately manned with untrained and undisciplined crews. In the words of its Commander in Chief, "it was not fit to go into action".' (12)

His comment is pertinent. The vast majority of Britain's most experienced seamen were serving at sea under the flags of every mercantile nation on the planet as well as under the red ensign. Few were prepared to exchange what was a hard, unforgiving, and underpaid profession for the even worse conditions of service then on offer in Her Majesty's Navy. The manning of Britain's Baltic Fleet in the Russian war provided a graphic illustration of the problem facing the navy. Foreigners, who were complete strangers to British Navy procedures, weapons, and even the English language, had to be recruited to make up the numbers of experienced seamen to man that force.

Fortunately, that particular fleet was not required to do much more, in the face of a general Russian passivity, than to demonstrate a threatening presence in the Baltic and carry out a few bombardments – in which it had some limited successes. However, the lack of readiness and generally indifferent performance of the navy throughout the war was embarrassingly evident to friend and foe alike. It was said of the Baltic Fleet that it was 'expected to do everything and did nothing', whereas the Black Sea Fleet 'was expected to do nothing, and did it'. The assumed supremacy of the British Fleet, based on the prestige of past accomplishments, and what had become almost a force of habit, was brought into question. Supremacy is as much a state of mind imposed on potential opponents than an actual number of ships deployed in any given area.

The experiences of the Crimean War served to concentrate minds in both military and political circles, and a programme of naval regeneration was commenced with some vigour, although much of this vigour was unfortunately squandered on concepts that would soon become outdated.

Initially, a great deal of wasted effort and money would be expended in the construction of a new generation of very large ships of the line, essentially updated versions of the old three-deckers such as *HMS Victory*.

Since 1815, the only major innovation in warship design had been the introduction of rudimentary steam propulsion into some of the larger fleet units. Otherwise, the ships themselves had altered little for nearly three centuries. The new ships of the post-Crimean War period were designed from the outset with an auxiliary steam engine, and the best of the old wooden walls not already converted were taken in hand for the installation of similar machinery.

In the event, there can be few better examples of an expensive exercise in futility. Before many of these vessels were ready to launch, the era of the armoured warship had arrived, and those majestic final representatives of the age of fighting sail were completely obsolete before water first touched their keels. The very few that were actually commissioned into service had a brief career as magnificent anachronisms, ostensibly leading squadrons made up of armoured frigates, any one of which could have destroyed the flagship with little or no serious damage to itself.

The great majority of these new wooden battleships were laid up on launch or immediately consigned to secondary duties – although as a stopgap measure some of the least advanced were cut down and converted on the stocks to carry a bolted-on armour belt and a single gun deck carrying the heaviest weapons then available for shipboard installation. As such, these hybrids served for a short while to bolster the strength of the fleet during the period of transition to an all-steel navy.

Developments across the Channel had necessarily brought about this radical change in naval thinking.

During the Crimean War, both the French and the British had produced a number of small floating batteries with armour protection to their hulls and upperworks. Their design enabled them to approach close enough to shore fortifications for effective bombardment whilst being sturdy enough to withstand the counter fire. The French units achieved some success in this role during the attack on the Kinburn forts, at the mouth of the Dnieper River, and whilst these craft were in no way seagoing vessels, the concept was clearly capable of a wider application.

In 1859, the great French naval architect Dupuy de Lôme adapted the design of his successful wooden frigate *Napoleon* to carry a bolted-on armour belt covering the waterline and gun deck, affording protection against the heaviest seagoing artillery of the day. The result was *La Gloire* and, although it was not immediately obvious, like the *Dreadnought* 47 years later, she made obsolete every existing battleship in the world, being able to deploy the largest calibre of weapons then in service whilst remaining immune to their effects.

The British were reluctant to admit that a revolution in warship design was taking place, still being preoccupied with their vast construction programme of very large ships of the line – and naturally loath to admit that this extremely expensive investment had been made effectively irrelevant to future requirements. However, considerable disquiet was created, and on the basis of 'if the French have got one, we had better have some as well', the Admiralty went one better, and a year later produced the world's first iron hulled armoured battleship. This ship, *HMS Warrior*, was larger, faster, and considerably superior in every respect to *La Gloire*. Her appearance in the Channel Fleet, followed a year later by a sister, the *Black Prince,* greatly reassured those who correctly interpreted the significance of the new development. Their qualities in service swiftly removed any lingering doubts as to the viability of the design.[3]

The mould having been broken, the pace of development accelerated faster than the ability to assess the relative virtues and faults of new designs,

---

[3] Dupuy de Lôme would have preferred to have constructed *La Gloire* and her successors of iron, but was prevented by the inability of the French industrial base to provide the necessary quantities of iron plate in good time – one example of the advantages enjoyed by Great Britain with her much more developed industrial structure. *HMS Warrior* can be seen to this day. Having passed out of service and been hulked, she eventually found a use in 1909 as a fuelling pontoon in Milford Haven. The need for that facility having ended in 1979, she was acquired for preservation and, magnificently restored to her original appearance, can be found on display in Portsmouth Harbour.

weapons, protection and tactics. There were few opportunities to test new concepts in actual conditions of war, and the infrequent actions that did occur were eagerly seized upon to advance or disprove the various theories advocated by a plethora of differing experts. The limited, and mostly unique, nature of these engagements invariably led to far more wrong than right conclusions being drawn from their outcome.

One engagement did, however, point the way to the future. On March 8th 1862, a Union squadron of wooden frigates blockading Hampton Roads was set upon and largely destroyed by a single improvised Confederate ironclad of bizarre appearance, the *CSS Virginia*, better known to history by her original name *Merrimack*. The one-sided action proved once and for all that sailing generation wooden warships were helpless in the presence of an armoured and engine-powered opponent. The following day, the epic encounter of the *Merrimack* with the equally bizarre Union warship *Monitor* illustrated the tactical possibilities of guns mounted in a revolving turret, which enabled the vessel to train her armament without having to manoeuvre the ship.

Another action, this time a full-scale battle between the Austrian and Italian Fleets, off Lissa in 1866 was less instructive, and encouraged a misbegotten preoccupation with the value of the ram as a tactical weapon. Despite its appearance for years to come on the warships of all nations, it was never again used successfully in action after Lissa, although it achieved some spectacular results against warships of the same navy operating in company and proved, statistically, to be far more dangerous to friend than to foe![4]

The period of rapid change that commenced with the construction of *La Gloire* inevitably resulted in materiel considerations overtaking the human ability to properly control or utilise the new technology. Indeed, this remained the case until the lessons of the First World War could be absorbed half a century later – by which time a new revolution in materiel was already underway and the twin threat of submarines and seaborne air

---

[4] Both Britain and Germany lost important ironclads to collisions whilst squadrons were steaming or manoeuvring in company. In the German case it was a particularly heavy blow to what was still a relatively small force. Undoubtedly the most dramatic incident occurred later when the Commander in Chief of the Mediterranean Fleet went down with his flagship, *HMS Victoria*, after being rammed by her consort, *HMS Camperdown*, during a miscalculated manoeuvre of his own devising. A notable survivor of this disaster was Commander John Jellicoe who will reappear in this account as C.-in-C. of the Grand Fleet during the First World War.

power was about to change all perceptions of tactics and strategy. It can be a fairly held argument that every substantive development in ship design and weaponry since the appearance of *La Gloire* has been fully understood and properly utilised only on the eve of its imminent obsolescence and supersession by a new wave of innovative technology.

Warship design had basically undergone little change for several hundred years, and what change *had* occurred was based on longstanding operational and constructional experience. From 1860 onwards, this process was stood on its head. From then on, the users were playing catch up with developments rather than dictating improvements as had previously been the case. The Royal Navy was particularly affected by the new circumstances, whereas new powers such as Germany, not being burdened by the influences of the past, could start with a clean sheet and concentrate exclusively on what lay ahead.

In Britain, the senior officers of that time had been brought up in the uncomplicated era of total reliance on sail and the 32-pounder gun, and with a tactical awareness that involved little more than ensuring that you placed your ship alongside that of the enemy. They struggled to comprehend, and adjust to, the changes that were occurring around them with bewildering rapidity. Bigger guns were countered by thicker armour, which necessitated even larger guns, and so the escalation continued. Different tactical priorities produced variations in type and distribution of armament; the ram kept intruding into the debate, and the torpedo carried by fast light warships emerged as a threat to a battle fleet that was reluctantly discarding sail in favour of a complete dependency on steam. For twenty years the naval world was in a turmoil of conflicting priorities and theories, and the evolution of ship design scoured many a blind alley and produced some spectacularly inefficient vessels.

If the design and capabilities of the battleship had been radically changed by the appearance of ships such as the *Warrior* and her successors, the principles of fighting a battle were largely unaltered from Nelson's day. It was still expected that actions would be fought at close range between ships, or squadrons of ships, deploying the vast majority of their weapons on the broadside. The admiral's job was relatively simple, and that was to manoeuvre his fleet in good order to within decisive range of his opponent, i.e. the range at which they could not miss. Having done that, the individual vessels could be left to get on with the business at hand until one or the other surrendered or was sunk – and this would depend, given equal skill and bravery, on the numbers and power of the guns carried, vis-à-vis those of the enemy. If the admiral courting action had done his part of the job properly, the opposing fleets would be sufficiently close to make aiming the weapons irrelevant and gunnery skill, therefore, simply equated rapidity of fire.

The great successes of the Royal Navy in the sailing era had been largely as a result of the long months spent at sea in all weathers compared to the experience of its opponents who remained blockaded in their ports for prolonged periods. The wear and tear on men and ships was considerable and the losses to storm and wreck were appalling, but the end product was a thoroughly battle worthy fleet manned by superb seamen. Both in seamanship and in the ability to serve his guns in all conditions, the British sailor had a crucial edge over his enemies. When this advantage was available to an admiral with the tactical vision of a Nelson, the results of an engagement were practically a foregone conclusion, no matter the odds or the oft-proven gallantry of the foe. As has frequently been stated, 'men win battles, not ships', but this distinction became temporarily blurred in the era of change that followed the introduction of the steam-propelled ironclad. From 1860 onwards the adage was effectively reversed.

With the most efficient crew in the world, the best 'Ship of the Line' had no more hope of surviving an encounter with the likes of the *Warrior* than did the latter if pitted against a battleship built ten years after her. Tactics and training took a back seat to hardware for that period.

Up until the turn of the century, naval battles were still assumed to be close range affairs. A maximum of two to three thousand yards was considered the likely engagement range and this would then close as the action became better defined. All the major developments in the second half of the century would therefore be dictated by materiel considerations, rather than the optimum means of utilising that materiel. Every navy had to address the same problems and find its own solutions.

With the introduction of armour plate, any guns that were unable to penetrate that protection became superfluous in a fleet action, and so the trend was towards fewer, bigger guns on a given displacement. This was countered by thicker armour, which, in turn, demanded even fewer, heavier guns, and so the process continued for a while. The advances in gun power and protection were so rapid that a ship would be utterly outclassed before it was completed by the succeeding design taking shape on the stocks.[5]

'Perhaps the most tangible indicator that the world's navies had entered a period of rapid change brought about by mechanisation was the 'see-saw' between the offensive power of the big naval gun and the defensive power of armour plate,

---

[5] Thus the *Warrior* completed in 1861 mounted 7-inch guns firing 112lb shells and carried 4.5-inch armour. Two years later a 9-inch gun with 263lb projectiles was in service, and within a further three years, the *Hercules* was laid down with 10-inch, 406lb guns, and 9-inch armour plate. Against her the *Warrior* would have been helpless. Another three years on came *Devastation* with 12-inch, 608lb guns in revolving turrets and a 12-inch armour belt, utterly outclassing *Hercules*.

which began in the early 1860s and continued for two decades...the swath of armour for new ships was increased. The primacy of defence over offence was reasserted, albeit temporarily...In each instance, however, gun founders quickly designed and constructed larger, more powerful ordnance, and the once-impervious swath of armour was impervious no longer.' (13)

As the increased weight of artillery had to be compensated for by a reduction in the number of guns, so the weight of thicker armour could only be borne, without a huge increase in the size of the ship, by a reduction in the area over which it could be carried. This led to the first major change in design and, such was the pace of progress, it occurred within a few years of *Warrior*'s completion. The 'Central Battery Ship' which resulted, concentrated the armour over the vitals of the vessel (machinery spaces, magazines and gun battery), and left the ends unprotected. If the designer had done his sums properly, the ends could be riddled through and through, but sufficient of the overall volume of the ship would be protected to ensure retention of buoyancy unless the armour could be pierced. This concept was further modified as battle tactics altered during the period when the ram was in vogue.

For some years a considerable body of opinion regarded the ram as *the* potentially decisive weapon in an engagement, and the guns merely as a means of protection and distraction whilst the attacking vessel was closing the enemy. In an era when the size and range of guns was increasing by the year, and torpedoes were already being developed, there was a serious and influential section in the naval establishment of every nation that was demanding a return to the tactics of Lepanto![6]

By the very nature of the weapon, ramming tactics demanded an end-on approach to an opponent, and for this purpose a ship with her main armament mounted all on the broadside was at a clear disadvantage when closing upon, or retreating from, the intended target. The central battery concept was accordingly adapted, and embrasures were provided in the hull so that the fore and aftermost guns in the battery could be shifted to train through ports facing ahead and astern. This arrangement was cumbersome and inefficient, if not impossible, in a seaway, and this totally impracticable concept was eventually superseded by the appearance of the seagoing turret ship.

The revolving gun turret had made its debut on the Union warship *Monitor* at Hampton Roads. This vessel was little more than a twin 11-inch gun turret mounted on a low freeboard barge with just sufficient motive power to retain steerage way when manoeuvring. She was by no means a seagoing ship, and, to prove the point, not long after her day of glory, sank in tow off Cape Hatteras in a moderate sea. The platform was obviously

---

[6] The Battle of Lepanto was the last major naval battle in the Mediterranean fought entirely between galleys, taking place on October 7th 1571.

flawed, but the turret itself promised many advantages over broadside fire. It could train independently on either beam as well as through the arcs of fire ahead or astern of the parent warship. A single gun mounted in a turret was therefore the equivalent of 2-3 weapons of the same calibre carried on a broadside warship that required a similar gun placed on either side of the ship, plus a bow or stern chaser, to achieve the same coverage. The broadside ship also had to manoeuvre itself to enable its guns to bear on the target, and, for the periods when it was so occupied, could not bring its armament into action. The turret, on the other hand, could be trained through 270 degrees, and could engage a target without requiring the ship to be turned – or it could continue to bear whilst manoeuvring was in progress.

Not only was the turret a more versatile means of deploying a weapon of given size, it economised on weight and space, and could guarantee a continuous, and therefore more rapid, rate of fire. Its major shortcoming was that, in order to take maximum advantage of its potential, it required no obstructions to its field of fire. As all major seagoing warships of all nations still possessed a full sailing rig at that time, the masts (usually three) and their associated rigging masked much of the area that could be theoretically covered by the turret, and an overenthusiastic gun crew, in the heat of action, might possibly be capable of dismasting their own ship! A secondary consideration was that action damage to the masts might cause debris to foul the operation of the turrets, whereas guns mounted below decks would be immune to this danger. Attempts to combine turrets with sailing qualities were generally unsatisfactory,[7] and eventually the painful and belated decision was made, in the face of fierce resistance from the traditionalists, to abandon sail as an alternative means of propulsion. This process occurred gradually, and it was not until the 1880s that it disappeared altogether in warship design.

In fairness, the traditionalists had some compelling arguments on their side. Sail training was a wonderful aid to producing fine seamen (as late as

---

[7] In 1867, the Royal Navy commissioned *HMS Captain*, which combined twin turrets with a full ship rig stayed by solid supports (an early precursor of the tripod mast) to try and cut down the interference presented by the clutter of traditional rigging. As designed she was inherently top heavy, too much having been attempted on her displacement, and increases in top weight incorporated during her construction made her dangerously unstable. Nevertheless, her initial trials were carried out without incident and she was commissioned into service. Initially her performance was deemed satisfactory, but shortly into her first commission, she was caught in a gale off the Portuguese coast and capsized, sinking with the great majority of her complement, which included her designer, Captain Cowper Coles. Coles was also the designer and chief proponent of the revolving turret as carried on Royal Navy warships, and the loss of this talented innovator not only retarded development in his particular sphere, but unfortunately, for some time, cast a cloud over the whole concept of seagoing turret ships.

the 1930s there was still a strong movement for its re-introduction), and the transition to a total dependence on steam was neither a simple nor inexpensive matter. Extensive stocks of coal would have to be available wherever a navy deployed its ships. This in turn required the acquisition, and in some cases fortification, of suitable bases. A large fleet of colliers had also to be constructed to resupply these coaling stations. All maritime nations were affected by this development, but Britain with its worldwide commitments was obviously the most seriously involved in the process. In home waters and the Mediterranean, adequate facilities existed, but further afield it was some time before suitable bases could be established. Throughout the 1870s, and well into the next two decades, squadrons detached to the Pacific and South American stations, for example, were still largely dependent on their sails for motive power, and ships had still to be constructed to meet that requirement. The writing, though, was clearly on the wall.

With the increasing reliability of machinery and the introduction of twin-screw propulsion, the days of the ship-rigged warship were obviously numbered – at least to those with the foresight to see the inevitable train of development. Nevertheless the process would be painfully slow in contrast to the other changes taking place.

Central battery ships and a few rigged turret ships continued to be built or acquired in the 1870s, and a few remained in service up to the turn of the century. In the meantime, the turret was adopted for a series of coast defence ships (actually so unseaworthy as to be virtually harbour defence ships) and which, not requiring the endurance essential for seagoing vessels, could dispense with the need for sails. This type developed in parallel with the sailing battle fleet until the British took the logical step and drastically enlarged the design to produce *HMS Devastation*, the first seagoing turret ship totally dependent on steam propulsion. On commissioning, she was looked upon with great suspicion, but was to prove entirely successful in service. Ugly she may have seemed to contemporary eyes, with a solitary stump mast for signalling purposes, but this twin-screw ship, massively armoured, and with a twin 12-inch turret fore and aft, can be considered the forerunner of the modern battleship. Opinion in the navy would gradually come to respect the qualities she embodied, although a further 10 years would elapse before sail would finally be abandoned in the design of British battleships.

The *Devastation* and her lineal descendants represented the way forward, but they continued to exhibit some of the faults of the coast defence ships. Most particularly, limitations on their displacement meant that they could only carry the great weight of their turrets and armour by sacrificing freeboard. Thus, whilst being stable, ocean going vessels, they were very low in the water, and, in any weather, the seas swept their decks, making efficient use of the armament difficult and living conditions on board extremely uncomfortable. Later designs, such as the *Admiral* class of ships, despite substituting barbettes for the turrets and having a different scheme of armour, suffered the same disadvantage in terms of seaworthiness. It was said of the type that they looked like half tide rocks in a storm when steaming into wind and sea.

'In a seaway, because of the low freeboard, they would rise and dip in a smother of green seas and foam presenting a magnificent spectacle. They all shipped hundreds of tons of water through the gun barbettes when seas broke over them.' (14)

Nevertheless, the navy regarded the *Admirals* with some affection, and, in their disposition of main and secondary armaments they became the standard for the designs of the next quarter of a century.

When, in 1886, tonnage restrictions were relaxed, it became possible to increase freeboard without detriment to stability and a truly effective battleship resulted.

In that year, one of the great constructors of the era came to the helm of British warship design. The appointment of Sir William White as Director of Naval Construction ended the period of experimentation in the Royal Navy. No longer would building programmes consist of a succession of one-off designs emphasising one feature or another. The first class of major warships constructed under his auspices (the *Royal Sovereigns*) initiated the standardisation of battleship design for the following 20 years. His arrival in office coincided with one of the periodic scares over French building programmes (as always, more impressive in the intention than the execution). The result was the construction of a series of homogenous warship types possessing most of the virtues and few of the vices of their predecessors. The White-designed ships were classics of their age, and were built more rapidly and in greater numbers than any of the other naval powers could hope to emulate. From the materiel point of view, the Royal Navy could see, in numbers and in quality, a steady improvement in its already pre-eminent position. However, the situation was not totally satisfactory. To operate these vessels to their full potential required officers and men capable of utilising their qualities to the best effect. In that respect, the Royal Navy, with some notable exceptions, was lamentably lacking in suitable candidates.

The experiences of the Crimean War and the subsequent transformation in ship design served to affect a minor revolution in the manning and training of the Royal Navy. Whilst conditions on board remained harsh, it was clear that the new ironclad fleet could not be operated efficiently without experienced, long service crews. Impressment or temporary mobilisation of reserves, for instance, could no longer function as a convenient means of recruitment in an emergency, and, if discipline continued to be draconian, the more obvious barbarities of the past began to be phased out or mitigated.

'The Crimean War did one good service to the Navy. By revealing the full extent of the problem of manpower, which had recently been under consideration, it enabled the Admiralty to implement a regular scheme of seaman entry and to consider the question of reserves. The methods of the press gang could be tolerated no longer.' (15)

By modern criteria, pay was still appalling, the lack of leave scandalous, and the rations abysmal, but a minimum standard came into effect that was no longer subject entirely to the whim of individual commanders. The proof of the pudding was in the eating, and there was no lack of personnel willing to serve in the navy at that time. Few were angels, and many were very hard cases, not only amongst the lower deck, but they reached and maintained a level of seamanship and appearance of the very highest quality, and which was the envy of the rest of the world. Within a few years of the Crimean War and the introduction of the ironclad, the Royal Navy had surmounted its brief personnel crisis and was once again in a position of paramountcy. For all its failings, it was a service that had achieved and constantly displayed a standard to which other navies could only aspire.

Nevertheless, the mentality of the navy remained rooted in a glorious past. The technological advances of the late 19th century rapidly outstripped the abilities and inclinations of many officers who, by dint of their seniority, were unavoidably presiding over the process. When the navy eventually received the finest series of battleship classes then in existence, it was ill-prepared to fight the ships. Courage, seamanship, and an innate sense of its own superiority existed aplenty, but the intellectual and technical abilities to properly harness these qualities to a new age of naval warfare were generally absent. In any case, the latter qualities hardly seemed pertinent in a world where the Royal Navy (at least in the minds of many of its senior officers, not to mention most of the government) continued to exercise a serene supremacy over any combination of her perceived enemies.

An overlong period of maritime security had bred complacency in all but a very few young officers and politicians. To be fair to them, they had met the circumstances of the time but they had not yet perceived the demands of the future. There were not many in either manor, government or service, who recognised the need for urgency in meeting the challenge of a new era. Their contemporaries in every other significant nation had thought and acted no differently. However, as younger powers such as Germany, Japan and the United States began to develop a serious naval capacity, they were not so constrained by traditional criteria. A distinguished naval officer of the period, Admiral Lord Charles Beresford, remarks that:

'The fact was that after Trafalgar this country had attained to so supreme a dominance upon all seas, with so high a degree of sea-training acquired in independent commands, that organisation for war was taken for granted. We were living on the Nelson tradition. The change came with the advent of steam, which altered certain essential conditions of sea warfare. The use of steam involved a new organisation. Other nations recognised its necessity. We did not.' (16)

The senior officers of the day had all learned their trade when sail was the predominant, if not the only, means of propulsion. They were consequently a body of men whose seamanship abilities were superlative, and they naturally preferred to concentrate on aspects of their profession with which they felt comfortable. The advent of engines, which stained and rotted their beloved sails and fouled their gleaming paintwork and decks (particularly during the filthy process of coaling ship[8]), was regarded with the utmost antipathy. Exercising the guns created similar problems and was regarded by many officers as an unfortunate necessity to be conducted as rarely, and as briefly as regulations permitted. The appearance of the ship, and the crew's performance in set drills, were of paramount importance. These, and the rigid observance of a vast minutia of routines, dress regulations and protocol, were the criteria on which the efficiency of an officer was judged, and upon which the route to promotion was dependent. To be fair, an officer who proved to be outstanding in these departments was also likely to be equally effective, given the opportunity, in other aspects of his profession. The problem was that these other opportunities were few and far between, and were hopelessly biased towards out-of-date methods. Suggestions by forward-looking young officers as to how to improve the situation were generally not welcomed, if not actively discouraged. It took a brave man to buck the system, especially if he were without influential friends and family. Harking back to Beresford's comment, Robert Massie remarks that:

'One problem was the Nelsonian tradition. Nelson had achieved absolute victory, Nelson was a naval legend. Therefore, Nelson's way was the only way.

---

[8] Coaling ship was the bane of shipboard life in the ironclad era. Colliers would secure alongside the receiving warship, and, for the best part of a day, sometimes longer, the entire crew of the latter would manhandle thousands of sacks of coal on board and down to the nether regions of the vessel. There, the sacks would be broached and the contents shovelled into coal bunkers. It was backbreaking work, and, at the end of the process, the crew would be utterly exhausted. Coal dust would be everywhere in the air, and the entire ship coated in a layer of black filth. A further full day's work by the crew would be required to clean up the mess. If the ship was carrying out a lot of steaming, this process would take place at regular intervals, and the sheer awfulness of the experience in the tropics can well be imagined. In the latter case, coaling would often take several days due to crew exhaustion, during which time the ship would, of course, be non-operational.

Nelson had ordered his captains to lay alongside the enemy; therefore, even though modern guns could reach out to far greater distances, British captains still dreamed of closing to point blank range. No matter that Nelson throughout his career had been a practitioner of boldness and innovation. His words had been graven in stone, his tactics hardened into glorious tradition. To make matters worse, officers who had fought under Nelson were still around. Any junior innovator thinking of proposing change had to deal not simply with hoary tradition, but with the bleak eye of the old Admiral pacing the quarterdeck.' (17)

Oliver Warner elaborates on this theme:

'Nelson indeed became the patron saint of the service, but his qualities were too often disregarded. His especial virtue as a tactician had been that he treated every situation on its merit, acting accordingly, inhibited by no hallowed rules, disregarding tradition when necessary. He placed generous trust in his subordinates, and he allowed them such freedom of action that they not only did their best at all times under his leadership, but as often as not excelled themselves…Nelson had always been the enemy of rigidity of mind.' (18)

However, if the navy of the time appears hopelessly backward and inefficient to modern eyes, its situation needs to be placed in the context of its likely opposition. To balance the account, it is only just to quote Admiral Sir William James, referring to the navy of 1888:

'Succeeding generations of naval officers often expressed surprise at this absorption in evolutions and cleanliness to the exclusion of interest in the armament, which was the reason for the existence of the ship; but the battle-efficiency of the armament in any period can only be judged in relation to that of other navies. The Kaiser had not yet set his heart on building a navy to challenge us and the French Fleet, the only possible opponent, was at the same stage of armament development; if war had broken out, battles would have been fought unscientifically at short range with each gun or battery of small guns controlled independently by an officer in charge, and superior smartness at drill and a superior fighting spirit would have been the deciding factors.' (19)

Writing of a later period (1906), when rapid changes had occurred in technology and attitudes, James continues:

'…some of the gunnery enthusiasts were postulating that the choice lay between gunnery efficiency and "bright-work", because there was not time for both. That, fortunately died a quick death when the ships that were the smartest and cleanest and best at evolutions were always at the top in the gunlayer's test and battle practice, which was quite natural, as success at anything sprang from the same cause – good leadership.' (20)

There was no doubt, though, that the fleet had become complacent, and was not making the best of its potential.

'The Royal Navy at the end of the nineteenth century, though numerically a very imposing force, was in certain respects a drowsy, inefficient, moth eaten organism.' (21)

After a long period of profound peace, and in a seemingly unassailable position, the navy had stagnated with regard to the business of waging war. Talking about the general attitude of naval officers to their profession, a senior officer who had served during that period remarked that:

'I don't think we thought very much about war with a big W. We looked on the Navy more as a World Police Force than as a warlike institution. We considered that our job was to safeguard law and order throughout the world – safeguard civilization, put out fires on shore, and act as guide, philosopher and friend to the merchant ships of all nations.' (22)

This attitude was soon to be overtaken by the circumstances of a new century and a new threat to the equilibrium of Europe a hundred years on from the emergence of Napoleon Bonaparte. The opponent that it was destined to meet in the next great confrontation of nations could start from scratch; The Royal Navy would first have to painfully discard the suffocating deadweight of its own illustrious traditions and history.

Aggravating the situation, from the British point of view, was the fact that a large proportion of the total manpower was employed on vessels, and in tasks, that had no relevance to the main purpose of the navy. The great fleets of the most up-to-date ships that ploughed the waters of the Channel and the Mediterranean were only a part of the whole entity. In these fleets were concentrated the real muscle of the navy and the nucleus of its capability to wage war. In terms of numbers however, they were far outstripped by the vessels deployed worldwide on great and small duties. Detached squadrons covered China, South America, the Pacific, West Africa, the East Indies, the Caribbean and North America, and the Cape of Good Hope. To each of these stations were attached large numbers of minor warships, from gunboats up to cruising vessels, all employed on the endless tasks of policing the coasts, showing the flag, and generally providing assistance, assurance, protection, and, when required, coercion, for the greater good of the empire. These vessels had no place in modern warfare, their retention being only justified by the fact that they were a cheaper option to carry out minor duties than by utilising up-to-date and more expensive warships. In Admiral John Fisher's words, 'they could neither fight nor run away', and remained inviolate only through the lack of any significant opposition and the knowledge that, in any real emergency, units of the main fleet on that station could be sent to take care of the situation.

The continued retention of this collection of odds and ends owed as much to the influence of the Foreign Office and overseas expatriate interests as it did to the considerable body of opinion in naval circles that still favoured their deployment. The presence of a vessel flying the White Ensign (however feeble its actual fighting capabilities) imparted a sense of security and importance to isolated communities, and was much valued for its contribution to social life. However, it represented a tying up of resources that would soon be urgently needed elsewhere.

These minor colonial units were akin to a second navy, a form of Imperial Coastguard that operated as independent limbs without ever coming into contact with the torso. Almost every officer and sailor served in these vessels at one time or another, but whereas the high flyers quickly returned to the mainstream and went on to greater things, the scattered detachments increasingly became a repository for the eccentrics, the dissolute, and the plain unlucky, of which the navy, like any large organisation, had its fair share. Admiral James remarks that:

'In 1888, the Navy was also approaching the end of an 'Eccentric Age' for the officers. Though the Fleet had often been engaged in conjoint operations with the army and in certain wars, such as the Crimean War and the Egyptian War, had brought all its resources to bear in support of the army, it had not been tested in a major maritime war since the fall of Napoleon. For many officers, service in the Navy in the latter part of the nineteenth century had meant a succession of commissions on foreign stations, often in small ships which spent many months up tropical rivers, and had no electric light, fans, or refrigerators. This form of service tended to exaggerate any slight eccentricities of character and to dull imagination. So, in 1888 there were some strange individuals holding senior rank in the navy.' (23)

Foreign commissions on many varied stations did, however, give one important service to the navy that cannot be underrated. They provided the opportunity to see action.

Apart from the bombardment of Alexandria in 1888, the major units of the navy saw no action whatsoever between the Crimean War and the end of the century. The fleet offered an excellent illustration of an almost perfect deterrent, in that the very fact that it existed ensured that it would never need to be used in anger. It was only in far flung regions away from the main theatres – amongst the creeks of West Africa; the river reaches of China and Burma; the islands of the Indies and Pacific; and beyond the cataracts of the Nile – that the personnel of the navy came under fire and had to prove their mettle in the face of hostile and active opposition. The nature of this opposition was many and varied, and the necessary measures to counter the perceived threats required much ingenuity and encouraged displays of individual initiative. Officers possessing these qualities had a unique chance to make their name and advance their career prospects. In pre-wireless days, the opportunities for men on the spot to control or influence events were obviously much greater than when regular communications with higher authority became possible. In such circumstances did the names of Fisher, Wilson, Beresford, Jellicoe, Beatty, Keyes and Craddock come to the attention of the service and the general public. For all that, it cannot be said that advantages accruing from possession of these colonial detachments could, on balance, justify the heavy overall expenditure of human and materiel resources, on secondary tasks, in areas of peripheral importance. The navy of that time was carrying a good deal of excess fat that would need trimming if it were to efficiently meet the challenges of the 20th century.

The flab was not confined to the backwaters of the empire. At home an assortment of survivors from the era of experimentation swung round their moorings in many of the minor British ports, serving as coastguard ships, and forming what was hopefully termed a 'Fleet Reserve'. Once a year for a few weeks they would be gathered together, their crews topped up with reservists who were complete strangers to the vessel, and go through the embarrassment of taking part in annual manoeuvres with the rest of the fleet. Whatever residual qualities were ascribed to these vessels, many of which still mounted muzzle-loading guns, which had been made obsolete a quarter of a century earlier, their actual fighting value was virtually nil. Nevertheless, they continued to absorb personnel and maintenance resources, not to mention a significant percentage of the naval budget, until belatedly consigned to the scrap yards by Fisher's sweeping reforms. A further 'force' of even more geriatric warships constituted the 'Dockyard Reserve'. These museum pieces, although unmaintained and tying up few personnel, cluttered up the moorings of all the major dockyard ports to the detriment of their efficient use by the active fleet.

Despite the above mentioned factors, British maritime supremacy at the end of the Victorian era seemed as securely entrenched as ever. The 1890s had been a decade of great expansion both in the quantity and quality of major warships joining the fleet. The eight battleships of the *Royal Sovereign* class had been followed by nine *Majestic* and six *Canopus* class ships, all vessels superior to their foreign contemporaries. A further eight more powerful vessels were being built or authorised and three smaller battleships had also been constructed for use on the China Station. They were backed up by 11 older vessels dating from the 1880s, all of which would be replaced on at least a one-for-one basis as they were retired from service. A staggering total of 83 cruisers of all classes had been constructed for trade protection and fleet work. The required strength of the fleet had come to be calculated on the basis that it should be at least equal in numbers and quality to the combined totals of the next two strongest naval powers. This was later revised upwards to permit a 10% superiority over a combination of any other two navies. In 1900, the second and third navies of the world were those of France and Russia respectively, and both these forces were in relative decline. Neither in the quality of their ships nor in operational efficiency were they a match for the corresponding British units – even allowing for the strictures mentioned earlier. The problems afflicting the Royal Navy, apart from those caused by excessive regard for tradition, were equally, if not more, apparent in all other navies of that era.

To the nation as a whole, whatever the politics of the individual, the navy was the rock on which the entire edifice of British power depended. Without it, it was clearly understood, there could be no empire. That was it. Period. Stop. It was, perhaps, the one issue on which all Britons agreed. The politicians might argue vehemently as to whether more or less money needed to be expended on the navy, but any party suspected of neglecting British maritime supremacy was in very deep trouble with the electorate. As the trusted warden of a worldwide empire, the navy was inviolable.

'...the pride of the British people focussed on the Royal Navy, which seemed to embody all that was quintessentially English to the man in the street. No matter what qualities or defects the ships possessed, he saw the battlefleet as the true backbone of the country and the empire.' (24)

What was the British Empire though? It was certainly not a permanent unchanging entity. Whilst it may have seemed, at its zenith, a constant factor in the world, it was, like all empires, transient and in a constant process of change. In recent history it may seem to have occupied a large slice of time, but, overall, it was a brief interlude. The Roman Empire, at its peak, survived more centuries than the British Empire lasted generations.

By the time the last colonies were being acquired, the original colonies were developing into independent nations. Canada, Australia and New Zealand were effectively self-governing states by the early 1900s. South Africa soon joined their number. From henceforth, internal matters in these nations steadily passed beyond the control of Westminster. What remained was a *de facto* British controlling influence on foreign and defence policy – on the basis of *primus inter pares*; Britain being by far the most powerful and wealthy component of the combination – but even this was increasingly a matter for consultation and agreement rather than dictation. At the height of its power, and at the moment of its most ostentatious splendour, the empire was steadily, and voluntarily, taking the first steps towards becoming a Commonwealth of Nations. None of these steps, at least not then, to the slightest degree affected the perception that the Royal Navy was the essential glue that held together the entire edifice – however it might be termed or constituted.

In 1897, on the occasion of the Queen's Diamond Jubilee, a review of the fleet took place at Spithead. In all, one hundred and sixty five warships were assembled in five lines extending a total of thirty miles. It was the greatest array of sea power ever witnessed, and was made even more impressive by the fact that it had not involved the withdrawal of any units from Britain's overseas squadrons. The Fleet Review seemed to demonstrate the futility of any other nation attempting to challenge its primacy. From the British point of view, tinged as it was with a degree of complacency, the situation appeared more than satisfactory, but any sense of long-term security was shortly to be rudely disturbed. The strategic balance between the established maritime powers was about to be obliterated by the emergence to east and west of vigorous young nations with burgeoning ambitions. Japan[9] and the United States of America would rapidly become major players on the world stage, and both their navies would soon eclipse those of Britain's traditional rivals. They would not be the only contenders. A few hundred miles across the North Sea, the greatest challenge to the Royal Navy in a century was about to be launched by a new and very formidable opponent.

---

[9] It might seem inappropriate to term the ancient empire of Japan a 'Young Nation', but its emergence as a major power at the beginning of the 20th century constituted the virtual rebirth of a society that had been cocooned in a mediaeval time warp.

CHAPTER TWO

THE BIRTH OF THE GERMAN NAVY

'A new and mighty state had come into being, sustained by an overflowing population, equipped with science and learning, organised for war and crowned with victory.'

Winston S. Churchill

'Without national unity there could be no navy in Germany. Before 1866, as indeed, after 1945, the short coastal strip and the three main river basins were not controlled by one authority, and without such unified control German naval power had, and has, no real basis. Since geography had inescapably joined the German navy and the German nation, the navy naturally became entangled in the struggle for national identity.'

Jonathan Steinberg

The Royal Navy in the 19th century was a *fait accompli*. It existed as an entity in 1900 much as it had done for the previous two hundred years, i.e. in a state of very occasionally challenged, but invariably maintained paramountcy. Change was generally accomplished at leisure, interspersed with short interludes of painful effort when circumstances dictated. For the duration of that era, regardless of the fundamental revolution in ship design and weapon development that was taking place, the purpose, power, and application of the Royal Navy remained largely unaltered. It was an established, known quantity, and accepted as such by friend, foe and neutral alike.

In complete contrast, its future adversary, the German Navy, was in 1815 non-existent and Germany itself no more than a geographical term embracing those states in Northern Central Europe that were linked by a common language and traditions. No apologies are made, therefore, for treating its creation and gestation period, both indissolubly linked to the rise of Germany as a nation, in rather more detail. The gestation period was remarkably short, and it was a sprat that brought forth a shark.

Of the myriad states constituting the remnants of the Holy Roman Empire as late as the eighteenth century, the Kingdom of Prussia was the pre-eminent power, and the only nation in the jigsaw that comprised the

German-speaking north of Europe that could stand alone as a sovereign entity. The achievement of that status had involved a long drawn out and arduous struggle against what had frequently appeared to be overwhelming odds.

Created by the merging of the territories of the old order of the Teutonic Knights with the Electorate of Brandenburg, Prussia possessed neither natural geographic boundaries nor the obvious prosperity of the more fortunately endowed of other north German states. However, a combination of military prowess, single-minded purpose, and effective leadership had ensured that the nation had survived whilst more superficially viable neighbours had declined into impotence. Nevertheless, beset to the east by Russia, to the south by the Austrian Empire, and to the west by France, the existence of Prussia in the cauldron of Central Europe had, at times, hung by a thread. At several critical periods, and for most of the eighteenth century, that thread had linked the country to the increasing economic strength of Great Britain, and the maritime power by which that strength was sustained and expanded.

As a marriage of convenience, the two states might have seemed something of an odd couple; the one an island nation preoccupied with control of the oceans and overseas possessions; the other a nearly landlocked country striving to hold its own against the great military powers of the continent. The secret of the successful union was that neither posed a threat to the other, whereas most other nations, either directly or through their allies, affected the welfare of both. (At the beginning of the relationship there was also the factor of a newly installed Hanoverian dynasty in Britain to be taken into consideration. Prussia and the hereditary German lands of the new British monarchy invariably gave each other support against a common threat.) The time would arrive when the interests of the two powers would eventually come into conflict and they become mortal enemies, indeed, that is the theme of this book, but for two hundred years, Prussia and Britain generally coexisted as allies to their mutual benefit.

The association had concrete advantages to both sides. The British stranglehold on overseas trade constricted the economic and material ability of Prussia's enemies to wage war, whilst enabling Britain to provide the financial support essential to keep Prussian armies equipped and in the field. On the other side of the coin, the existence of a strong Prussia as an ally in the heart of the continent inhibited the French, in particular, from being able to devote their undivided resources to wresting control of the seas from Britain – which, having a much larger population at that time, France could well have achieved but for military preoccupations in Europe. The benefits were disproportionate, but, if Britain greatly prospered, Prussia more than survived. It is significant that the only serious setback in the otherwise remorseless progress of Britain to world leadership, namely the loss of the

American Colonies, should have occurred when the Anglo-Prussian link was temporarily in abeyance – and when France was able to establish a temporary but decisive local maritime supremacy in North American waters.

During the Napoleonic wars, Prussia came of age as a first class power. Comprehensive defeat at the hands of French armies, at Jena and Auerstadt in 1806, had resulted in an enforced subservience to the 'Continental System' whereby Bonaparte attempted to apply a hermetic seal between the trade of Britain and Europe. For six years, Prussia endured this humiliation until the catastrophic retreat from Moscow ripped the heart out of Napoleon's legions. A year later, Prussia was the major contributor to a coalition that crushed a newly raised French army at Leipzig, and when Napoleon returned from Elba for a final cast of the die, it was the army of Field Marshal Gebhard von Blucher that contested the field of Waterloo alongside the troops of Wellington. German textbooks tell of a Prussian victory with some assistance from the British in the same way that English publications reverse the emphasis, and Wellington is as shadowy a figure to German schoolchildren as Blucher is to their British counterparts.

'When a nation writes its autobiography there is no limit to its boasting and vainglory. When I was young, school books taught that the French were wicked and the Germans virtuous; now they teach the opposite. In neither case is there the slightest regard for the truth. German school books, dealing with the battle of Waterloo, represent Wellington as all but defeated when Blucher saved the situation; English books represent Blucher as having made very little difference. The writers of both the German and the English books know that they are not telling the truth.' (1)

Whoever was the victor of Waterloo, and the probability is that neither could have been without the other, it was Blucher's fresher troops who first entered Paris and rang down the final curtain on the great post-revolutionary drive of the French towards hegemony in Europe. For a nation that had been fighting for its very existence, the ultimate success of the army invested that force with enormous prestige, gave it disproportionate influence in the councils of the state, and diverted attention from other factors that had vitally affected the resolution of the conflict – in particular the application and importance of sea power.

'The Wars of liberation were fought between 1813 and 1815 by a Prussian army whose officer corps was totally dominated by the landed gentry (Junker)…Blucher's victory at Waterloo and subsequent occupation of Paris further enhanced Prussia's role as a dominant land power. Nelson's decisive victories at Aboukir and Trafalgar were not generally appreciated or understood in assessing Napoleon's defeat.' (2)

Nor, it should be added, were the effects of the trade blockade Britain imposed on Europe in retaliation for Napoleon's Continental System properly assessed. Great damage was done to the trade and prosperity of both sides, but Britain always had (albeit disturbed) access to the rest of the world through control of the seas. Europe had to survive from its own internal resources, all of which were disproportionately plundered to support Napoleon's armies of occupation and conquest. If Britain suffered, much of the continent starved, or was otherwise deprived of the raw materials from overseas that had been vital to its industry and prosperity.

In the event, 'Europe blinked first'. Russia, specifically, quickly tired of the prohibitive economic cost of adherence to the Continental System and a new Tsar withdrew from its constraints. In doing so, he incurred the wrath of Napoleon and precipitated the latter's huge retaliatory strike on his nation, the catastrophic results of which were to fatally undermine the foundations of Bonaparte's power.

'When, in 1807, the success of French arms and the acquiescence of Russia finally gave France hegemony over Western Europe, it was Napoleon's inability to exert perceptible economic pressure on Britain at sea that led him to attempt to do so on land, sealing European ports to British trade by the imposition of the Continental System. This measure was probably more than any other single factor responsible for bringing about the collapse of the Franco-Russian entente and setting the *Grande Armée* on the fatal road to Moscow.' (3)

Captain Russell Grenfell, writing under the pseudonym 'T124' in his book *Sea Power* emphasises the point:

'By 1811, Europe was seething with suppressed revolt against the odious continental system, and Napoleon found himself driven from one ruthlessness to another, from the annexation of Holland, to the annexation of the Hansa towns, to the increased coercion of Prussia and the Northern States, to keep his system in operation. At last, the most important of the conforming countries raised the standard of mutiny. Russia made it clear that she would no longer operate the continental blockade of Britain effectively. Napoleon was thus faced with the alternative of an ignominious relinquishment of his economic offensive against Britain or of bringing Russia to heel. He marched eastwards towards Russia and disaster. The Russian campaign destroyed his army and led directly to his downfall.' (4)

This 'influence of sea power on this particular phase of history', to paraphrase Mahan, at that time, and subsequently, never assumed great importance in the corridors of a Prussian establishment focussed upon, and dominated by, its army.

This factor (the ignorance as to the effects of maritime supremacy) was to assume great importance half a century later, after the unification of Germany. The army remained deeply conservative, essentially Prussian in character, and firmly committed to a dominant position for Germany within Europe. The navy, when it finally emerged as a credible force, was a child of greater Germany, and represented the aspirations of a much changed nation searching for a world role. However, in the meantime, it had had to fight for its very existence against the basically conservative inclinations of the long entrenched national hierarchy.

Ultimately, the army and the *Junker* would be perceived by a vastly enlarged country, however grateful and proud of their achievements, as standing for a parochial past, and controlled by an inward looking elite. The navy would become the stepping stone to a glorious future worldwide, supported by the rank and file of an empire driven by immense industrial capacity, rapidly expanding manpower, aggressive and successful merchants, and fuelled by increasing nationalistic fervour. This new awareness of Germany's enhanced status, and the desire to project that status overseas, was to be harnessed and exploited by its political leaders, and was later to become embodied in the term '*Weltpolitik*' (literally, 'World Policy').

In 1815, however, the time was not yet ripe for a basically agrarian society, administered by its aristocracy of warrior land barons, to take a world view of its position. The French writer Mirabeau produced an acidic but penetrating comment on the Prussian nation at that period of its history:

'War is Prussia's national industry. Prussia is not a country that has an army; it is an army which has a country.' (5)

Three more generations would have to elapse before the effects of industrialisation, military conquest and the attainment of Great Power status would combine to focus the eyes of the nation onto the horizons beyond her shores and frontiers. A consciousness of the importance of sea power only gradually emerged in the latter years of that period.

The half century that followed the Battle of Waterloo witnessed the conclusion of the struggle for supremacy in central Europe between the Austro-Hungarian Empire and the Prussian dominated states of the north. In the distant past, once a potential prey of Austria, the virile and increasingly industrialised Prussian nation inevitably prevailed over a Habsburg Empire in terminal decline. In 1866, the undisputed leadership of the German-speaking peoples passed to Prussia when her army decisively defeated the Austrians at Königgrätz (Sadowa). Henceforth Austria would become the junior partner in an alliance with Germany, and dependent on the latter to prop up its tottering regime. By that time, the affairs of Germany were effectively in the hands of the most outstanding statesman of the nineteenth century.

Prince Otto Eduard Leopold von Bismarck-Schönhausen brought to the service of the King of Prussia the finest diplomatic talents and political instincts of his generation. Under his auspices, and with a co-operative monarch, the foundations of modern Germany were created in an extraordinarily short space of time, and with stunning effect.

In his twenty-eight years at the centre of German affairs, Bismarck supervised the final transition of Prussia from being a state of consequence in the balance of European power, to becoming the critical weight in any consideration of that balance. His aims, though, were limited to realising the centuries-old dream of a united, powerful and secure German nation. Having accomplished that remarkable feat, he bent all his energies to consolidating and reinforcing that position. Himself a *Junker* and a product of the old system, he became the last and most influential personality in the bringing of Germany to the threshold of the modern era. His creation would eventually wish to take its evolution further and much faster than its progenitor would have liked.

Throughout the momentous events of his long career, Bismarck never departed from the principle of isolating potential opponents from their domestic or international allies before confronting them with decisive action. He was equally careful to ensure that Prussia itself was never likely to be placed in a similar position. The prospect of a war on two fronts – a permanent dread of German politicians given the geographic situation of their nation – was always in the forefront of his calculations. The culmination of his policies arrived with the crushing defeat of France in 1871, and the subsequent incorporation of all the smaller German states into a new German Empire with the King of Prussia, as the monarch of its most important component, as its head of state – and with Bismarck, most crucially, as the Chancellor, and effectively the controller, of his own creation. 1871 marked the pinnacle of Bismarck's career and, from thence onwards, he devoted his authority and abilities towards holding what had been won.

In the quarter of a century that preceded the formation of empire, the fortunes of Prussia had been carried forward on the lances, rifles and artillery of her incomparable army. Naval warfare had played no significant role in events. Then and subsequently, Bismarck, when he concerned himself at all with naval affairs, was inclined to be a negative influence. He regarded plans for a fleet as at best an irrelevance, and at worst an embarrassment to his overall strategy and foreign policy. Post-1871 he laboured for stability in Europe (on his terms), and considered naval complications as a potentially destabilising factor. Nevertheless, it was on the barren soil of the Bismarck era that the first seeds of German sea power were sown, and from which the first shoots appeared.

Until the revolution of 1848, there existed no German naval forces worthy of mention, nor was there even a coherent concept of such a force. Germany itself existed only as an abstract ideal shared by the thinking classes, and a vague sense of communality in an area occupied by independent states embracing a common language and customs, and linked by economic necessity and fleeting political convenience.

In 1848, the situation changed dramatically. Europe was rocked to its core by a tidal wave of democratic activism. Throughout the continent the long established autocratic monarchies were shaken to their foundations by riots and political upheaval. Not least to be affected was the Kingdom of Prussia, and the regime briefly tottered until the army, with some brutality, restored a semblance of order at the cost of creating an elected parliament. The establishment regained its nerve and out of impending chaos was created a structure that would serve to govern the country through a period of profound change. It was a very imperfect compromise, and relied on the monarchy and the fledgling parliament finding common ground whilst serving very different constituencies. It was at this time that the name of Bismarck first began to be heard in political circles. In 1851 he was appointed ambassador to the German Federal Diet in Frankfurt, an establishment that dated back to the old Holy Roman Empire and which brought together representatives of all the German-speaking nations, including Austria who had tended to assume primacy over the organisation. Bismarck spent eight years in Frankfurt honing his diplomatic skills, and incidentally ensuring that Prussia was treated as at least the equal of Austria in its affairs. Following this service, and with a greatly enhanced reputation, he was transferred, first to St. Petersburg, and later to Paris, as the Prussian Ambassador.

By 1860 the Prussian political system was again in a state of crisis, the most critical of a number of irreconcilable differences arising from parliament's attempts to shorten the length of compulsory military service, a measure utterly unacceptable to the King and his War Minister, von Roon. The latter, who had earlier discerned Bismarck's qualities, recommended his appointment as the King's Chief Minister, but Bismarck would not accept unless given complete control of foreign affairs in addition to domestic policies, and at this, the King baulked. Twice more the offer was made and refused on the same grounds, until, in late 1862 with parliament and King still completely deadlocked, and the latter threatening abdication in favour of his son, Bismarck's conditions were accepted. Armed with unprecedented powers, he immediately confronted the parliamentarians and made crystal clear that he intended to rule in the King's name with or without their co-operation. Parliament considered the ultimatum, lost its nerve, rolled over and capitulated with no serious attempt to call Bismarck's bluff. A hand descended on the helm of state that was not to release its grip for nearly three decades. The political system remained heavily dependent on the strength and capabilities of individual personalities within the structure to ensure its survival. As it proved, for the time being, just one such personality would prove sufficient. In the Prussia of 1862, just as later in the much greater complexities that followed the establishment of empire in 1871, it was Bismarck who provided the centre of gravity around which all the disparate elements of state government revolved, and by whom their orbits were determined. He was, however, constrained to operate within the regulations of a constitution that placed him between an elected assembly and his monarch.

From the beginning of this arrangement Bismarck successfully manipulated or bullied the parliament (*Reichstag*) into supporting his policies. The old King, with a few grumbles, usually also fell into line, but what could not be altered was the fact that a parliament existed, and that however limited in its powers by Bismarck, would henceforth sit as a counterbalance to the throne, and would have a say in the affairs of state. The critical weakness of the system was that for it to work at all, it depended upon someone with Bismarck's abilities as Chancellor, and as he was virtually unique, there were obvious problems for the future. Fortunately for Prussia, and Germany as a whole, that future was a long way off in 1862.

The *Reichstag* was liberal in character, being a product of the democratic revolution, and German, as opposed to Prussian, in its outlook. Its members were drawn from the classes who had business, intellectual, religious, and political connections throughout Northern Europe. In many of them the flame of German unity burned high – some from a historical perspective, some from the profitable consequences of cross-border free trade, and some who just dreamed of a secure future for a people who had suffered too long the many wars and tribulations that descend on the weak and divided. Collectively they represented the previously unheard voice of the non-aristocratic majority. Many of these businessmen and intellectuals, who for the first time had a voice in the nation's governance, regarded the Prussian aristocracy as a narrow-minded cabal of militaristic country anachronisms.

It was from the *Reichstag* that the initial impetus for a German navy was generated – as an essential symbol of, and step towards, the ideal of German unity.

> 'Although the national unity for which they yearned, the constitutional institutions which they admired and the political power after which they strove had all been denied them, German liberals continued to hope. They looked to England which was rich, powerful and free, and they wanted to have what English liberals had. They saw the great British fleet as a symbol of the power of a free, constitutional nation-state, while at home they remembered the bayonets of the Prussian infantry and Prussian cavalry storming revolutionary barricades.' (6)

Immediately after the trauma of the revolution the first tentative steps were taken to create a naval force. They were not auspicious. A dispute arose with Denmark over the status of the territories of Schleswig and Holstein. In 1849 this flared into open hostilities. Prussia had joined a loose federation of north German states, and this organisation assembled a dozen assorted armed vessels under the command of a German national who had served in the American mercantile marine. A brief engagement between three of these vessels and a Danish ship took place off Heligoland (then a British possession, and therefore neutral waters). A few warning shots from the gun batteries on the island sufficed to curtail the action. Apart from that single inglorious incident the motley little squadron remained inactive, and the Danish Navy, hardly the most formidable maritime force in Europe, effectively controlled the sea areas off the German coast.

The naval impotence of Prussia thus evidenced dismayed sections of the establishment who harked back to the days of the *Hansa*, when the ports of the north German coast had had a thriving maritime tradition, and when much of the commerce of the region was transported in German hulls. The Napoleonic wars, in particular the enforced adherence to the Continental System and the consequent British blockade, had effectively ruined that trading base. All the infrastructure of the earlier period of prosperity – the shipbuilding facilities; the trained seamen; the overseas trading links; the ships themselves – had largely disappeared, taking with it the raw materials necessary for the creation of a viable navy. Any new establishment would have to start completely from scratch.

In 1853, Prince Adalbert of Prussia persuaded his uncle, King Friedrich Wilhelm IV, to create a Prussian admiralty. Adalbert's enthusiasm for naval matters stemmed from contacts he had made with the Royal Navy and visits to the British fleets in the Mediterranean and English waters. He was determined to create the foundations of a future naval force based on the standards and practices he had witnessed. Not unnaturally, he became the first head of the new organisation. His expectations, though, were much higher than the possibility of their attainment.

'A committee set up under Prince Adalbert of Prussia during the winter of 1848/9 demanded the formation of a navy of twenty ships of the line, twenty large and ten small cruisers, plus the requisite auxiliary vessels. There was no hope of realising such a programme with the means available at the time and the plans for the Imperial Navy suffered the same ignominious fate as the Reich of 1848 itself.' (7)

Adalbert refused to give up, returning to the subject again and again until he finally succeeded in getting an admiralty established. This was just the beginning of his problems. In 1853, just as had been the case five years earlier, hopes and means were two widely separated concepts.

His creation was certainly no bed of roses. He began with absolutely no infrastructure, never mind ships. Even had there been naval bases and warships, there were no officers and men with which to man, train, and administrate the force. Nor did there exist a port giving access to the North

Sea and from thence to the oceans. There were 'no ships, no officers, no seamen, no naval bases, and – on the North Sea- no seacoast'. (8) However, with the limited funds grudgingly granted him he commenced to purchase, or have built abroad (Prussia also had no shipyards), a series of warships which would form the nucleus of a small, balanced fleet. As experienced personnel were difficult to find in an agrarian, army-orientated state he started by employing trained mercenaries culled from other maritime nations or tempted by preferential terms from the German merchant marine. Shortfalls in numbers were made up by men arbitrarily transferred, often without their consent, from the Prussian Army. This process did not commend itself to the Army General Staff and caused understandable friction between the two services.

During his eighteen year tenure of office, despite the many difficulties, Adalbert achieved a remarkable amount. In 1854, with considerable foresight, Prussia purchased from the Grand Duchy of Oldenburg, a small block of land on Jade Bay opening into the Heligoland Bight.[1] On this site over the next decade and a half was to be constructed the great naval base of Wilhelmshaven, Prussia's first outlet to the North Sea. Following the defeat of Denmark in 1865 and subsequent annexation of Schleswig, the excellent deep water haven of Kiel Fjord passed into Prussian hands. This was to develop into the main dockyard port of the navy, and the major operational base in the Baltic Sea. Training and support facilities were established around the bases, and, by the late 1860s, shipyards in Wilhelmshaven, Kiel, Stettin and Danzig were building the warships that had previously to be acquired abroad. A credible naval force had been created from virtually nothing. The fleet, though still small by major power standards, had modern dockyards and bases from which to operate, experienced crews and the ability to train future generations of personnel, and had become largely self-sufficient in the production of its ships and materiel. Prince Adalbert can justly be regarded as the father of the modern German Navy.

Sadly, Adalbert's ambitions for his young force were to be disappointed in his lifetime. In the decade of conquest and expansion that culminated in 1871 with the defeat of France, the navy played no significant role. In its embryo state it occupied the unenviable position of being too weak to contribute to the momentous events of the age whilst at the same time demanding funds for its development, the utility of which was unproven, and which was generally dismissed as being superfluous to the real military requirements of the nation.

---

[1] In recognition of this event, the Grand Dukes of Oldenburg inherited in perpetuity the honorary rank of Grand Admiral in the Prussian, and later the Imperial German, Navy.

During the war with Denmark in 1864/5, an Austrian fleet under Tegethoff secured German maritime interests. A year later, when Prussia turned on and overwhelmed her erstwhile ally, the campaign was fought entirely on land; Tegethoff's crushing victory over the Italian Fleet at Lissa being irrelevant to the outcome. Humiliation was to follow in the Franco-Prussian War. In spite of the catastrophic defeat of its nation as a whole, the French Navy was able to apply an unopposed blockade on the coast of its conqueror, capturing any and all German merchant vessels rash enough to venture to or from their ports. Forbidden from engaging the vastly superior French Fleet, the Prussian ironclads swung disconsolately round their anchors in Wilhelmshaven, smarting at the disgrace of inactivity whilst the glory of battle, the laurels of overwhelming victory, and the adulation of the people went, as always, to the triumphant army.

In the wake of the war, the reputation of the navy, if it could be said to have acquired one, had sunk to a nadir, and there continued a widespread perception that it could serve no useful purpose for Germany. The army regarded the fleet contemptuously as a waste of money that would be better spent on itself. In the circumstances, even some Admiralty officials 'found it difficult to justify a navy'. When Adalbert retired in 1872, it is a measure of the low esteem in which his service was held, in that he was replaced after a brief interval not by a naval officer, but by an army general. It would be sixteen further years before the official head of the navy would again be an officer with seagoing experience.[2]

The creation of the German Empire and effective unification of the nation was announced in the Palace of Versailles in the immediate aftermath of victory over France. The smaller German states retained some autonomous rights, notably nominal control over their own armies within the overall organisation of a Prussian dominated General Staff. The individual states paid for their military units from their own resources and recruited from within their own frontiers. The navy, however, was established as a purely imperial organisation, recruited from throughout Germany, and paid for out of the imperial budget, which was controlled by

---

[2] It is pleasing to recount that in June 1901, his contribution to the navy was recognised when an armoured cruiser of the latest design was launched bearing his name. The other ships of that category bore the names of great German military and political figures, and the *Prinz Adalbert* was to sail in company with the likes of Bismarck, Blucher, Yorck, Scharnhorst and Gneisenau.

an expanded *Reichstag*. The Kaiser was officially the Supreme Commander of both the combined armies and the navy, but whereas the General Staff were careful to ensure that this was largely a ceremonial role as far as the army was concerned, he was able to exercise considerable control over the composition and utilisation of the navy. When a personality such as Wilhelm II became emperor, even had he not already been preoccupied with naval matters, there was an obvious temptation to concentrate on affairs over which he had genuine influence.

The many complexities of the constitution that bound the empire together are beyond the scope of this account except in relation to their effects on the navy. Suffice to say that the checks and balances incorporated into the system by Bismarck enabled him to exercise effective control over the new super state whilst also becoming its greatest servant. The problem was, as has been mentioned with the Prussian constitution of 1848, that the efficiency of the whole edifice hinged on the personality, prestige and authority of the Imperial Chancellor. Once Bismarck had departed the political scene his successors lacked the strength or ability to maintain the coherence of a government tailored to the requirements of a unique man in a unique situation.

In matters imperial, the relation of the Kaiser to his parliament was closer to the American presidential system than to that of a constitutional monarchy. The *Reichstag* did not initiate policy but it controlled the purse strings by which a policy could or could not be funded. The Imperial Chancellor and his subordinate ministers formulated policies *in the name of, and with the approval of* the Kaiser. The Chancellor would then have to present his proposals to the *Reichstag* with a request that the latter arrange for them to be financed. The matter would then be debated, the Chancellor and relevant ministers taking an active part, and the bill would usually go through, give or take an amendment here, a compromise there. This at any rate was the situation when Bismarck held the Chancellorship. Kaiser Wilhelm I, Bismarck's monarch for most of his time in office occasionally grumbled but usually acquiesced to his chief minister's proposals; the *Reichstag* was no match for his talents and influence. Under a strong Chancellor and a co-operative monarch, the system worked well. Once Wilhelm II became Kaiser and Bismarck banished to the political wilderness, exactly the opposite became the case.

With a wilful but unstable emperor, and weak or sycophantic chancellors, the flaws in the system were rapidly exposed. The Kaiser began to dictate policies and expected his Chancellor simply to be the means of getting them funded by the *Reichstag*. If the *Reichstag* baulked at the proposals, the whole process of government stagnated until the necessary compromises were made, by which time the whole structure of Emperor/Chancellor/Parliament was in a condition of mutual alienation. This occurred on an annual basis. Insofar as this situation affected the

Otto Edouard Leopold von Bismarck-Schonhausen
'The Iron Chancellor'

'The All Highest'
Wilhelm in Imperial Pose

development of the navy, it invariably produced confusion, half measures, and a lack of long-term planning that afflicted the force for many years. Eventually the emergence of another powerful personality who could both channel his Emperor's enthusiasms to his own ends whilst being skilful enough to manipulate the *Reichstag* through argument and public opinion, would bring stability and purpose to naval affairs. The results would be an extraordinary expansion of German naval power in a very short space of time, and a concurrent catastrophic deterioration in Germany's long-term strategic situation. But this is getting ahead of the tale.

The German Empire had been cobbled together by a political genius, given a free hand by his head of state, and with the most formidable army the world had yet seen at his disposal for the realisation of his policies. Military theorist, Carl von Clausewitz's assertion that 'War is just the continuation of foreign policy by other means' was made apparent by Bismarck. Diplomacy was underwritten by the German Army, and all continental Europe had to understand and endure that fact.

Whilst Bismarck held the effective reins of state, there was little requirement for a large navy. The unification of Germany had been achieved without the need for any seaborne assistance. Nor could any maritime effort have prevented its fruition. Subsequently Bismarck had little interest in the creation of overseas commitments that might compromise his diplomatic strategy in Europe. Within that strategy, good relations with Great Britain were a significant factor. To the end of his Chancellorship he cherished hopes of securing some form of alliance between the two countries, albeit with minimum concessions from Germany. 'The preservation of Anglo-German goodwill is, after all, the most important thing', he said in 1889, perhaps with a hint of sarcasm, whilst conceding some minor point of contention, just two years before his fall from office.

In the latter years of his power, Bismarck permitted minor colonial adventures as a sop to the growing expansionist lobby in Germany. He regarded them as a useful distraction to the militant nationalists whilst he got on with the business of establishing the newly fledged empire as the predominant military, economic and political force in Europe.

'Under Bismarck, an imperial policy was pursued for three main reasons. The least important was its economic rationale, that is an attempt to maintain economic prosperity. More important was probably its political and diplomatic rationale in that it pacified the ruling elites at home whilst enabling Bismarck to demonstrate to other European powers that Germany was an Imperial force to be reckoned with. Finally...to Bismarck, an Imperial policy was regarded as a social pacifier. Imperialist adventure would, it was hoped, stimulate nationalism and divert pressure from liberal reform.' (9)

The trappings of a non-productive overseas empire held little attraction for the 'Iron Chancellor'. Much more pertinent was the creation of a secure base on which the enormous potential of the adolescent nation could build. Paradoxically, the very success of this policy would eventually lead to Germany becoming so powerful as to make it inevitable that the country would want to force itself onto the world stage. Unfortunately it would also carry out this process with much less temperate hands at the helm of state.

A notable paradox of Bismarck's policy at this time was that, despite his preoccupation with remaining on good terms with Britain at a diplomatic level, he deliberately encouraged anti-British sentiment within Germany for domestic political advantage. Werner Richter remarks that:

> 'He needed a weapon at the election against the bourgeois left and the Social Democrats, both of whom were enemies of colonialism, and he may well have hoped to inflict heavy damage on them if he pilloried them as allies of Britain and so made them a target for anti-British feeling, while himself posing as the champion of anti-British grievances. He said…"The whole colonial business is a swindle, but we need it for the election."' (10)

Although his position seemed impregnable, it was, to an extent, dependent on approval from above and a majority consensus in parliament. The Heir Apparent to the imperial throne and Kingdom of Prussia, Crown Prince Friedrich, was liberal in his political views (which Bismarck was definitely not), and very pro-British. Richter again:

> 'Another powerful motive behind Bismarck's colonial policy may well have been the desire to drive a wedge between Britain and the German Crown Prince, so that when the latter came to the throne, which might be quite soon, it would be impossible for him to adopt a policy which was markedly friendly to Britain. In…September 1884, Bismarck actually confessed to such an intention.' (11)

At the other end of the political spectrum from Crown Prince Friedrich was the increasingly influential and rampantly nationalistic pan-German movement, demanding expansion overseas in terms of colonies and trading concessions, and resenting the fact that Britain had already cornered the choicest sections of the market in those respects. Bismarck's brief and diffident fling with colonialism must be seen in this context.

> 'The colonial policy was a defensive stratagem. It stimulated patriotism and produced votes; it created an enemy whom Germans could blame for the shabbiness of their overseas possessions. Best of all, inflaming anti-British feeling in Germany weakened the Liberals in the Reichstag and undermined the position of the Crown Prince. Friedrich, as Emperor, would scarcely be able to follow a pro-British policy if, because of the colonial confrontation, most of his people hated England.' (12)

This short-term policy was a complete success. Bismarck got his votes on the domestic front whilst maintaining amicable relations with Britain on the great issues of state, but, for the long term, he had fertilised the seeds of envy and hatred that would have a sombre harvest. In 1884, the British ambassador to Berlin wrote that:

'I am in despair at Bismarck's present inclination to increase his popularity before the general election, by taking up an anti-English attitude; he has discovered an unexplored mine of popularity, in starting Colonial policy which public opinion persuades itself to be anti-English, and the slumbering theoretical envy of the Germans that our wealth and our freedom has awakened and taken the form of abuse of everything in the press. My hope is that this anti-English mania may not last longer, but my fear is that it will increase.' (13)

His machinations to discredit the Heir Apparent, as it turned out, were counterproductive, and proved largely unnecessary. They also led, indirectly, to his own downfall.

Crown Prince Friedrich had been a successful army commander in the war against Austria, and was greatly respected. His liberal views, however, were anathema to Bismarck, who foresaw a loosening of his grip on the nation's internal affairs once the compliant old emperor died and was succeeded by his less malleable son. As Wilhelm I was 74 when the empire was created in 1871, it seemed logical that this succession would take place sooner rather than later. In the meantime, Bismarck set himself to subvert the popularity and influence of the Crown Prince. The unashamedly anglophile stance of the latter, who was married to Queen Victoria's eldest, and favourite, daughter (and who was also something of a tactless dominatrix), provided a suitable lever for the manipulation of public opinion. The instigation of anti-British sentiment was an effective means to discredit Friedrich as a political opponent. Simultaneously, the Chancellor began to assiduously cultivate Friedrich's impressionable young son, Wilhelm. His object was to wean him away from the influence of his parents, and mould him as a potential ally for perceived future differences between Chancellor and Kaiser. As a short- term strategy, this approach was an unqualified success.

'William, secure in the bosom of his regiments, the esteem of his wife, and the approbation of the Bismarcks, was almost completely estranged from his parents.' (14)

All seemed to be falling in place for the Chancellor's long-term plans, but, in this instance it was to be a castle built on sand.

'Bismarck was always aware that he could, with little warning, be forced to deal with a new ruler, in the person of the Crown Prince, Frederick William. This was not a prospect he relished. Frederick William was the very model of a model emperor – a handsome bearded man with a soldierly bearing and a reputation for enlightened views. If life were like romantic fiction, he would have ascended to the throne immediately after his military successes at Königgrätz and Gravelotte, when he was at the height of his powers and was a popular hero. But his father lived on for another eighteen years and the long wait for power frustrated the Prince, blunted his energies, and made him prey to alternating fits of irritation and melancholy. His self confidence was eroded by inactivity as well as by his awareness of the superior intellectual capacity of his wife...the Crown Princess had had a deep personal animus against the Chancellor since the 1860s, a feeling that was reciprocated.' (15)

Gordon Craig's last remark is pertinent in that Bismarck took his personal enmities very seriously and rarely failed to pursue a grudge to its conclusion. In the event, he succeeded entirely in both his immediate strategies, but in them lay the seeds of destruction for the greater part of his life's work. He had created a monster that would demolish the carefully constructed web of alliances and relationships by which he had hoped to guarantee the long-term security of his nation. A most sceptical of politicians as to the value of a navy, he unwittingly became one of the founding fathers of a future naval armaments race that would consume the vital energies of his creation – for German Anglophobia, once established as a trivial electoral ploy would fester and grow until cauterised by dreadful events.

There are two huge ironies at this point. The first is that the old emperor lived to such a great age that a terminally ill Crown Prince Friedrich only survived him by three months. All Bismarck's machinations as to the succession were thus largely irrelevant, whilst they placed a heavy burden on a future for which they had not been designed. The second is that, having cultivated Friedrich's son as a political counterbalance to the father, Bismarck had neither the time nor the opportunity to construct a counterbalance to the son. The most successful political career of the nineteenth century would therefore founder on the rocks of one old monarch living too long, and his successor living not long enough.

In covering these events, the narrative's political aspects have overrun the account of the navy's development. The accession of Wilhelm II would stimulate a radical new attitude towards maritime affairs, but the first two decades of the German Empire were to prove a difficult and confusing period for the navy.

After the Franco-Prussian War, an army general, Albrecht von Stosch was appointed to command a unified German naval force.[3] Stosch had no naval experience, nor did he evince any desire towards becoming a sailor as such. A stiff, unbending Prussian of the old school, he sought to inculcate the navy with the tried and trusted drills and regulations of the army. Not all

---

[3] Admiral Alexander von Monts briefly held the post but died before he could make any lasting impression on the service. No naval candidates were advanced to replace him.

of these were entirely suited to shipboard application, but were conducive to the development of a disciplined and efficient nucleus from which could later expand a more formidable seagoing force than any yet seen in Northern Europe. As the general gradually warmed to his new command (he eventually swapped his rank to that of admiral) he began to foresee the part it could play in the future, as German interests spread beyond the confines of Europe.

If the navy had been born under Prince Adalbert, it was under Stosch that it was weaned. A new intake of officers entered a service that, for the first time, was being established for a set purpose, and with a construction programme geared to specific commitments. Stosch determined that the new Imperial Navy would take a higher profile in German affairs than had previously been the case. One of the new generation of officers was to recall that:

'Stosch started from the idea of developing Germany's maritime interests, of strengthening and protecting "Germanism" and German labour throughout the world...this was not done without some friction with the Imperial Chancellor.' (16)

The officer making that statement was then plain Lieutenant Alfred Tirpitz. Not the least of Stosch's influences on his navy was the lifelong mentor/protégée relationship that grew up, not uncritically, between himself and Tirpitz. The latter, after a fairly lukewarm review of Stosch's period in charge (Tirpitz's memoirs are not notable for their charitable references to his contemporaries) commencing with the dismissive comment that, 'he was never a sailor', concludes by saying:

'Stosch took up again the broken thread of the *Hansa*; he was the first to feel his way towards a future for Germany overseas. He did a great deal also to breathe a fighting spirit into the navy. Mistakes were made, but in those days we were not dealing in trifles; a grave earnestness characterised our work.' [Also] '(Stosch) was way ahead of his time in the energy with which he drove our sea power after centuries of neglect...[he] was convinced that we had to have colonies and that we could not exist for long without expansion.' (17)

In the ambitions of Stosch for a greater Germany, spearheaded and protected by a powerful new navy of unprecedented size and efficiency lay the germs of the great naval expansion that would be initiated and presided over by his most avid disciple.

Stosch produced a comprehensive long-term construction plan for the navy. He envisaged a force that could confidently face either the Russian Fleet in the Baltic or the units of the French Fleet allocated to the North Sea. Beyond that commitment would be cruising vessels deployed to project and protect German worldwide interests. Some progress was made in implementing this programme, but it ultimately foundered on the same obstacle that had stranded the plans of his predecessor.

The progress of Stosch in creating a navy that could serve German overseas ambitions, which were increasing as rapidly as German trade, emigration, and economic colonialism expanded, led to differences between himself and Bismarck. The Chancellor remained preoccupied with the balance of power in Europe, and deeply mistrusted any new factors that might lead to complications abroad, particularly those over which he did not have full control. It is also significant that Stosch was a member of the Crown Prince's circle of unofficial advisors – a fact that would not have commended him to Bismarck. In the event, Stosch's programme was either diluted, or to use a modern phrase, 'put on the back burner'. Frustrated in his ambitions for the navy, and clearly outgunned by the Chancellor and army interests, Stosch finally lost patience and resigned. He left behind him a cadre of officers, committed to his concept of a major role for the navy, aware of their materiel inferiority to potential opponents; and absolutely determined to compensate for that deficiency by achieving the highest possible standards with their existing equipment.

The replacement for Stosch was another army general, Leo von Caprivi, who was later to become Chancellor. His name is perpetrated in the 'Caprivi Strip', an old colonial border anomaly and thin tongue of land, which points like a finger from the northern border of Namibia eastwards into the heart of Africa. Caprivi himself would probably not have welcomed the fame of having a piece of the world named after him. He was a straight, old-fashioned military gentleman, of imposing appearance, sound judgement, and no delusions of grandeur or genius. From Bismarck's point of view he was a safe pair of hands, and his strategic thinking was very much in line with that of the Chancellor:

'This man, who was understood by very few people, lived and wove his plans in the state of mind which he often expressed to me as follows; "Next year we shall have a war on two fronts". Every year he expected it the next spring.' (18)

A thoroughly conventional military thinker, his views faithfully reflected the opinion of the vast majority of his peers. War on two fronts meant, of course, the possibility of simultaneous hostilities with France and Russia, and the Caprivi era would therefore result in the diversion of most naval resources away from a blue water fleet, and more towards a coast defence and interdiction role in the Baltic and the Heligoland Bight. This policy was more in line with Bismarckian priorities, but German naval development stagnated, and the long-term plans for construction of a credible second rank battle fleet, as envisaged by Stosch, withered on the vine.

The major event to occur during Caprivi's tenure of office was the commencement of work on dredging a canal to link Kiel, in the Baltic, to the Elbe estuary, flowing into the North Sea. It was a massive project in its era. Great locks capable of handling the largest vessels in existence had to be constructed at Holtenau, at its eastern end, and Brunsbüttel, leading into the Elbe. This waterway (the present day Kiel Canal) enabled the German Fleet to pass from the North Sea ports to the Baltic without having to negotiate the long, exposed route round the Jutland peninsular, and the narrow waters of the Kattegat between Denmark and Sweden. Strategically, it was an absolutely vital conduit for the navy. It effectively meant that, instead of having to possess two small fleets – one for the Baltic and one for the North Sea, Germany could have one very powerful and flexible fleet that could operate in either environment as circumstances dictated. On completion of the canal, additional naval bases would be developed at Brunsbüttel, and at Cuxhaven, further down the far bank of the Elbe.

In terms of materiel, four reasonably effective battleships (the *Sachsen* class, originating from Stosch's programme) had been commissioned into the navy in 1878-80, but they would be the last for 15 years. Under Caprivi and his immediate successors only a central battery ship of obsolescent design and eight coast defence ironclads would be added over that period. Much effort would be put into building up a large force of torpedo boats, in which great hopes then resided of enabling weaker navies to cheaply nullify the battleship strength of the major maritime powers, and even perhaps of making the battleship itself obsolete. This theory, based on the ideas of the '*Jeune École*', and its guru, the French Admiral Aube, was briefly in vogue with many nations at the time, but could not offer anything more than a coast defence/anti-close blockade facility. The torpedo boats of that era had neither the range, armament nor sea-keeping qualities to operate on the high seas.

If the administration and purpose of the navy had reverted to the traditionalists, the personnel were significantly different to those of the army. Whilst the latter remained the preserve of the aristocracy, and each of the German states retained a measure of control over their own forces, the navy belonged to the nation as a whole and was, from the outset, relatively liberal in its political orientation.

'The Navy became a career for young men of middle-class backgrounds who were barred from advancement in the Prussian Army but who were ambitious and well trained...Not only were these men without ancient lineage, but also without the caste prejudice, snobbery and aristocratic behaviour of the Army.'[4] (19)

---

[4] It has to be said that naval officers, once the service came of age, rapidly began to ape the pretensions of their military counterparts.

Whereas in the army, the 'von' was virtually a prerequisite to obtaining any command, many of the key officers critical to the development and operation of the future fleet only achieved that status, courtesy of the Kaiser, after obtaining the highest offices in their service. Tirpitz himself was the son of a lawyer and not ennobled until after he had become State Secretary for the Navy, and had pushed through the *Reichstag* the crucial First Navy Bill in 1898. Of the two great German commanders of the First World War, Reinhard Scheer, the Commander in Chief of the High Seas Fleet at Jutland, was never ennobled, and Hipper, the outstanding leader of the battlecruisers, only subsequently by the King of Bavaria, his parochial monarch. It would have been inconceivable, in the army, for officers holding commands of that responsibility not to have been members of the aristocracy, and difficult for *any* commoner to hold a senior position over aristocratic subordinates.[5]

Within the ranks, there were also clear differences between the army and naval personnel. The army functioned on a traditional regimental system of long-standing and established disciplines. As the officers of the regiment would be supplied from generations of local landowners, so would the rank and file come from the families who worked the estates or provided the services for that regional aristocracy. The bonds of tradition, loyalty and local affiliation engendered by the system made for a cohesion that could, when the moment came, weather the diluting effects of conscription.

Lacking either a great tradition or a sense of regionality in its units, the navy possessed none of these advantages, and functioned on a much less secure base for its discipline and efficiency. It was also dependent, once it embarked on a vast programme of expansion, on a very high proportion of conscripts in its ranks. The majority of its personnel came from the industrialised centres of Germany, and were by nature and background much more likely to have socialist leanings than their equivalents in the army, and less rapport with their officer corps. For the greater part of its existence this factor was not apparent as the service achieved and

---

[5] On paper there should have been enough scions of the aristocracy to have sated the requirements of both army and navy. Germany was awash with them as it still is today. The inheritance of a title in Germany is not restricted to the eldest son, as in Britain, but passes to all the progeny. To this must be added the fact that the German Empire was comprised of scores of kingdoms, principalities, dukedoms and electorates ranging from powerful countries in their own right down to states barely the size of a respectable parish or a minor town – and all with their individual royal families and lesser nobility. There were certainly enough to go round, but the navy was perceived as being socially inferior to the army, as well as lacking the glorious traditions of the latter. The majority of the aristocracy tended, therefore, to gravitate towards the army, whilst the navy attracted a much greater proportion of its officers from the professional classes.

maintained the very highest standards of efficiency, discipline and morale. Its performance in battle was also exemplary and much admired by its principal opponent, but this inherent flaw, a product of having to advance faster than it could consolidate, finally emerged as a critical weakness when prolonged inactivity and adversity undermined the foundations of its structure. Other factors were obviously important in defining the causes of the mutinies that afflicted the fleet towards the end of the First World War (notably the transfer of many of the best young officers and senior rates into the submarine service), but it is difficult to envisage the same situation arising in the German Army – or, for that matter, in the British Navy.

For so long as German eyes concentrated on her position in Europe, maritime affairs were bound to take a back seat in the councils of state. Unfortunately for the advocates of a purely European focus to policy, the commercial and industrial success of the nation developed a momentum of its own, which spread worldwide, and which, eventually, could no longer be ignored by her rulers. From a situation where successful military and political exploits brought commercial benefits in their wake, those commercial interests were increasingly dictating the pace of events as German trade, population and culture flowed overseas. The ambitions of the nation as a whole began to outstrip those of her traditional leaders.

Within a decade of its creation, the German Empire was bursting at the seams with what seemed to be an irrepressible energy. Even the sceptical and autocratic Bismarck was forced by the groundswell of public opinion into joining the race for the few remaining parts of the world not already colonised by other powers. Between 1884 and 1886, South West Africa, Togoland, the Cameroons, part of New Guinea, and what is now Tanzania came under German sovereignty. None of these acquisitions ever contributed a single Deutschmark to the mainstream German economy, rather the opposite, but Germany had imbibed the heady wine of imperialism, and that first taste intoxicated increasingly powerful sections of her society. In particular, it provided a fertile breeding ground for aggressive nationalism on the world stage, and this would increasingly involve contact and conflict with British interests.

When referring to 'nationalism' there is a very great difference in the way this term could be applied to the populations, and the leaders, of Great Britain and Germany. The former had a natural, and justified, pride in the achievements of their nation, and this had spilled over into a certain arrogance towards the rest of the world. When its interests were threatened, or public opinion outraged by events abroad, there were periodic outbursts of 'jingoism' that lasted for as long as the duration of the crisis. By contrast, German nationalism penetrated into the very depth of the soul of the nation. Germany, in the late nineteenth century, was not just a country – it was a people, re-emerging like a phoenix from the ashes to which it had been consigned in the Dark Ages. It harked back to the legends of Siegfried, and these mystical roots held a dark and powerful attraction on the psyche of the nation. There was almost a religious fervour attached to the process of a united Germany emerging from the flames of a heroic past and once more raising the standard of this departed, more glorious, era. When Wilhelm II became emperor, he consciously donned himself with the mantle of the 'new Siegfried', and, whilst many of his subjects may have questioned his qualifications for the role, there is no doubt that he believed in his part and played it as well as his mercurial temperament allowed. Whatever they thought of their new emperor, a large proportion of the German-speaking world shared his dream.

British nationalism was sometimes strident, and often crass, but it was always eventually tempered by pragmatism imposed by government or trade. In Germany, nationalism tramped roughshod over diplomatic practicalities. Whereas Britain was in deadly serious *competition* with the world, Germany was on a *crusade* to re-invent its origins and traditions, and to prevail over all others.

By 1890, the great victories of the drive to empire were a generation in the past, and the conquests of that era had been digested. New stimuli were required to satiate the appetite for expansion, and a national consciousness arose that, if Germany had a seat at the 'top table' of nations, then she required the appropriate accoutrements of that position, namely an overseas empire. As Wilhelm II later declared, Germany also wanted its 'Place in the Sun'. Inevitably this would lead to a requirement for a maritime presence wherever German colonies and trade began to flourish.

Territorially, the expansion of Germany overseas roused few initial qualms in London, although the bludgeoning style of German diplomacy in obtaining concessions from other nations frequently caused offence.[6]

---

[6] Germany came to empire rather as a member of the *nouveau riche* joins an exclusive club – confident and aggressive in the knowledge of power and wealth, but insecure and envious in the company of those who have occupied its best chairs by right and heredity for centuries. The archetypical *nouveau riche* member is noisy, pushy and resentful of the established status quo it is so anxious to join. Germany was all of that, and, to continue the simile, Britain was, without doubt, the club secretary, and prime target of that resentment.

Possession of relatively unproductive areas of the globe, however impressive on the map and satisfying to national sentiment, did not constitute a realistic challenge to the British Empire.

'By every measure other than size, the new German Empire was a disappointment...By 1914, fewer than twenty-five thousand German citizens, including soldiers and naval detachments were to be found in all the German colonies combined. The cost to the homeland was many times the profits. In 1889, Bismarck even tried to persuade the British government to assume sovereignty over South West Africa because of the expense to Berlin.' (20)

In contrast, of the vast British possessions throughout the globe, hardly any had been acquired purely to gratify the national ego. Almost all had a purpose in the overall scheme of things. The huge natural resources of Canada, the West Indies, Southern and Western Africa, the Indian subcontinent, Malayan peninsular and Australasia underpinned the prosperity of an empire that was heavily dependent on its worldwide trade and the sea power that secured those interests. Trade and sea power had a symbiotic relationship. The first enabled the second to be financed; the latter ensured the security of the former. Many of the smaller British colonies existed not because they contributed directly to the glory and prosperity of the nation, but primarily because they provided bases and sustenance for the navy along the lines of communication on which the major components of the empire depended. In that respect, they had been acquired in order to serve a useful purpose, and were a source of strength. In the case of most of the German possessions, they had been colonised purely for reasons of national prestige (and because they were all that were left), and constituted a source of weakness and distraction for the navy, rather than a means for supporting the service. Only in 1897, with the acquisition of Tsingtao, did Germany create an overseas base of any consequence for her navy, and that colony was so far out on a limb as to be untenable in any conflict with a major maritime power.

Where German expansion did provide a legitimate cause for concern was in the increasing penetration of traditional British markets abroad. Competition in lucrative areas of trade posed an altogether more formidable threat than did a randomly assembled collection of largely unwanted real estate. The importance of economic, rather than physical, colonisation to the long-term viability of great nations could be evidenced by the British experience during the nineteenth century. Paul Kennedy notes that:

'...it is a comment on the short-sightedness of merely looking at the areas painted red on the map to remind oneself that almost 70% of British emigration (1812-1914), over 60% of British exports (1800-1900), and over 80% of British capital (1815-1880) went to regions outside the formal empire.' (21)

The great resources of the largest empire in history were, therefore, only a partial contribution to its overall prosperity, and the means of its preservation.

The challenge in trading matters was emphasised by the fact that the German industrial base was growing so rapidly that it was on the threshold of overtaking that of Britain. By the end of the century, German production capacity in those industries vital to a potential war effort, such as steel, machine tools, precision instruments and engineering, had considerably exceeded that of the British Empire, and the gap was growing steadily.

Having started her industrial revolution much later than Britain, Germany's plant facilities were of a more modern era, and, therefore, more efficient – a fact accentuated by the complacency of too many British industrialists, bolstered as they were by a captive imperial market, who failed to update their factories to meet the challenge of a new situation. Paul Kennedy, in his book *The Rise and Fall of the Great Powers*, pinpoints, in this relative decline of competitiveness vis-à-vis Germany (and especially the United States) in the 1880s, the beginning of the end for Britain as a great world power. Certainly, without that relative decline, it would have been impossible for Germany, committed to maintaining huge land forces against France and/or Russia, to contemplate her later naval rivalry with Britain. As it was, the effort was to place an almost intolerable burden on the economy of both nations.

The basis of German prosperity and power had irrevocably shifted from agriculture to industry during the nineteenth century. Whilst the army, on which all had hitherto depended, was still *controlled* by the *Junkers*, its existence as a predominant force in Europe *depended* on the efforts of the industrialists in an era of rapidly advancing technology. The industrialists needed success on the world market to finance their continued development, and, ergo, the basis on which the army relied for its long-term viability. Extra-continental matters were beginning to affect Germany's influence within Europe. The problem for the statesmen was that, whilst the army might guarantee security for Germany in Europe, it was impotent to protect German interests abroad, not having the means to project its legions overseas or defend subsequent lines of communication and supply. That ability could only be achieved by deployment of naval forces in sufficient strength to match the commitments.

As Germany increasingly began to rival Britain in the sphere of international commerce it became clear that expansion could not continue indefinitely without incursions into British interests. When, rather than if, that occurred, the unpalatable fact had to be faced that, should the two countries find themselves at odds, all German colonies and trading interests would be immediately and hopelessly hostage to British maritime supremacy. As Germany prospered, so there grew an ominous resentment that this prosperity was subject to the dictate of the Royal Navy.

There could only be two conceivable solutions to this problem short of a binding alliance, which was not an option to either country at that time. Either Germany would have to accept the status quo and maintain good relations with Britain, or it would have to challenge the latter by building a fleet of sufficient strength to compete on something approaching equal terms, at least locally. The second option would involve enormous financial outlay and divert industrial effort from other priorities. It would also create political complications on both the domestic and international fronts, and alter the delicate balance of power in Europe. Whilst Bismarck remained Chancellor, there was little chance of this option being adopted – the status quo in Europe was, after all, largely of his making, and consolidation of Germany's existing position was his overriding concern. He was probably also aware that, until Germany had had the opportunity to develop her capabilities much further to her advantage vis-à-vis Great Britain that, in a naval race, his nation was unlikely to end up the winner.

There was an absolute difference in the position of the two countries as regards naval affairs. Germany had attained predominance on the continent of Europe by courtesy of her armies whereas Britain had achieved, at an earlier date, a similar situation overseas by virtue of her navy. Neither nation represented a threat to the other for the very obvious reason that neither could challenge the other's strength.[7] They would have been, as a statesman referred to an earlier standoff between Britain and Russia over Turkey, 'like an elephant facing the whale' – both immensely powerful, but incapable of doing any damage to each other. If, however, Germany were to embark on a programme of naval expansion with the implicit intent of rivalling the Royal Navy, then the equilibrium would be destroyed. That policy would strike at the very heart of British security. Nevertheless, this *was* the policy that was ultimately adopted by Germany, and it is extraordinary that the perpetrators of that line of action never seemed to fully realise (or at least never publicly admitted that they realised) the inevitable consequences that would ensue.

Simply stated, Germany *without* a navy could remain the premier European power with extensive overseas interests and colonies; the British Empire *without* a navy would be indefensible, and Britain herself open to invasion by any of the major continental armies, all of which greatly outnumbered her own military forces. Even Switzerland could boast a bigger army than Britain, and a single, subsidiary, German state – Bavaria – possessed in its own right the 5th largest standing army in the world. To influential sections of German opinion, an effective navy was a prerequisite of ensuring continued expansion; to Britain it was a matter of absolute survival as a power of any kind. A challenge to Britain's maritime position threatened the very existence of the empire, and the sovereignty of the

---

[7] During the conflict between Germany and Denmark for control of Schleswig-Holstein, Bismarck was asked what he would do if a British army landed on the coast to assist the Danes. He replied that he would 'send the police to arrest it'. Had a similar question been posed to the British Prime Minister as to the risks of the German Navy assaulting his own coast, he could well have answered that 'the coastguard will escort it into port'.

United Kingdom itself. Should such a challenge materialise it would be certain that Britain would stiffen every sinew and channel whatever resources were necessary into ensuring the maintenance of naval supremacy for as long as the strength of the nation permitted – and, not having the need to maintain great armies, she could afford to devote a much larger proportion of her wealth to that end than could any rival.

It is an interesting conjecture as to the German reaction had Britain commenced to build up a vast army with the avowed intention of achieving parity with German military forces, whilst at the same time maintaining the strongest navy in the world. The message would have been deafening, 'Germany is at risk of invasion!', and every effort would surely have been made to secure the continued superiority of the army. However, given the need, as perceived by many Germans, for their nation to usurp Britain's position in order to further their long-term ambitions, it might, with hindsight, seem inevitable that there would eventually be a naval competition between the two powers. Nevertheless, the obstacles to Germany were formidable, and the efforts required of an unprecedented scale. Adalbert and Stosch, in their most sanguine moments, could never have contemplated the attention, funds, and political significance that were about to be lavished on their infant creation.

The huge expenditure required to build the ships necessary for a first class fleet represented only a portion of the overall effort. To build the ships there had to be more and enlarged shipyards; to achieve this there had to be a trained workforce; to man the vessels there had to be a dramatic increase in personnel, and therefore payroll; to accommodate and maintain the fleet there had to be more and bigger dockyards and bases from which to operate; and there had to be all the training facilities, supply depots, administrative complexes and all the paraphernalia involved in building a vast entity from small beginnings in a short period – all of which would have to be presided over by the relatively meagre numbers of officers manning and continuing to operate the current naval force. Above all, there had to be the political and national *will* to embark on such a venture, with all its unforeseeable consequences. From where was the colossal financial cost to be met? The event waited on the emergence of the personalities necessary for its fulfilment. In 1888, the first major player emerged from the wings to take centre stage.

CHAPTER THREE

A FLEET AGAINST ENGLAND

'The position of Officer of the Watch on the ship of state has fallen to me. The course remains the same. Full steam ahead.'

Kaiser Wilhelm II

'For Germany, the most dangerous enemy at the present time is England. It is also the enemy against which we most urgently require a certain measure of naval force as a political power factor.'

Alfred von Tirpitz, in a secret memorandum to the Kaiser.

'That William II, himself half-English and virtually bilingual, and Tirpitz, who read English novels for recreation and whose children went to English schools, should have destroyed the amiable Anglo-German ties cultivated by the reactionary Prussian Junker Bismarck is one of the great ironies of modern history.'

Jonathon Steinberg

Wilhelm I, King of Prussia and first Emperor of Germany, died in March 1888. His Anglophile son, Friedrich III, came to the throne already dying of throat cancer and incapable of speech. Ninety-nine days after the demise of Bismarck's 'Old Gentleman', Friedrich followed him to the grave, and the latter's son assumed the title of Kaiser, as Wilhelm II.

The new Kaiser was a fascinating and contradictory character. The last ruling member of the Hohenzollern Dynasty, he has been characterised as a vainglorious bombastic warmonger by those who have had the advantage of being able to assess him from the privileged viewpoint always given to victors. As Napoleon Bonaparte once remarked, 'History is a lie which has been agreed upon'. Wilhelm has also been the subject of much calumny from his own nation, and blamed for many, if not most, of the woes that were to subsequently descend on the German people as a result of defeat in the Great War. As a recent biographer concludes:

'It is perhaps right that we condemn Wilhelm, for if the First World War was not his personal undertaking, the finger of blame points over and over again to the failure of the German diplomacy in which he tried so hard to play a positive role.

Wilhelm saw himself as a major actor on the world stage, yet no one would act with him; and despite twenty-five years of attempts to maintain the peace by reworking Europe's system of alliances, he effected very little beyond reinforcing the convictions of those in power elsewhere; that the new Germany was an unwelcome bad element which exercised a malign influence on the old balance of power.' (1)

He was not, though, the total villain of the piece such that later politicians and historians would conveniently choose to excuse the motives and actions of equally culpable leaders and nations. Many other personalities throughout Europe had equal or more responsibility for what was to happen, but, within Germany itself, the disaster of the First World War has been largely laid at his table. He made a very convenient scapegoat for the failings of others, both in the military and the diplomatic staff. In the wake of defeat and revolution in 1918, one and all of his former acolytes, subordinates, and cronies queued up to desert him and heap disparagement on his head. Wilhelm duly 'took the rap' for a generation of diplomatic and military incompetents. That said, they were generally his appointments, and his own personality impinged on their efficiency. He *was* vainglorious; he *was* bombastic; and he was frequently the despair of even his own diplomats due to his wild swings of mood, which produced ill-considered actions and precipitate statements. As such, he certainly bore his share of responsibility for the dreadful events that were to unfold in his lifetime. However, despite his pretensions to be the 'Supreme Warlord', the 'All Highest', and to having a 'divine right' to rule, he never possessed the untrammelled power of a despot, and the chain of events that would lead to the outbreak of war in 1914 were generated by much more complicated considerations than those which could be laid at the door of one man.

What Wilhelm could, and did, do was to focus German ambitions on becoming a world power, and, in time, to becoming *the* world power. Jonathon Steinberg remarks that the Kaiser was:

'...one of those strange figures in history whose personalities have had more effect on the course of affairs than their deeds...On one point his contemporaries were all in agreement. From the beginning, the Kaiser was an important factor in Germany's growth as a sea power...there is no evidence whatever that his contemporaries regarded him as a freak or as a man impossible to deal with. They complained about his idiosyncrasies, his impulsiveness and his lack of good sense, but they saw those traits in the perspective that historians have too often ignored.' (2)

Paradoxically, some of the strengths of Wilhelm's character exacerbated his weaknesses. He had a quick mind and retentive memory, allied to an exuberant and persuasive power of delivery, and he applied these gifts to an impressively eclectic range of subjects.

'He could make rings round most of the people he associated with. He excelled at summing up the results of a long and complicated meeting. He could speak fluently without preparation or notes. His interests ranged far and wide.' (3)

These interests encompassed art, music, history, archaeology, science, the classics and theology, and so long as his forays were limited to these intellectual pursuits he could cause no harm. Unfortunately, given his position, he was also able to apply his impulsive and boisterously expressed views to graver matters of state, with less happy results. Wilhelm never knowingly understated an opinion, and this spilled over into the written word, which frequently became public knowledge and a source of constant embarrassment to himself and despair to his officials. After fifteen years as emperor, the Chancellor, Prince Bülow, could remark of him that:

'The Kaiser still shows the same youthful freshness, the same power of rapidly grasping a problem, the same personal courage and the same confidence in his judgement and capacity. These qualities, valuable though they might be in a monarch, are still unfortunately outweighed by his refusal to concentrate and go into things thoroughly as well as by his almost pathological desire to take immediate decisions on everything without waiting to consult his advisors, and by his lack of any sense of proportion or of genuine political insight.' (4)

Holstein, the long serving, sinister and vindictive Secretary for Foreign Affairs, acidly noted that, 'Initiative without tact is like a flood without dykes'(5), and a recent biographer commented that:

'William's fluency in speaking meant that he approached all questions with an open mouth...he was constitutionally incapable of preventing himself from saying whatever came into his head, providing he imagined it would contribute to the effect which he was trying to make at that moment, whether of benevolent despot, versatile thinker, skilful diplomat or ruthless leader...as a result his career became a series of what one of his subjects described as "oratorical derailments".' (6)

A distinguished contemporary, Herbert Asquith, the Liberal Prime Minister from 1907-16, sums up the British establishment view of the German Emperor in a remarkably pertinent paragraph:

'William II, if he had been born in a private station, had natural endowments which might have carried him far. His danger, even then, would have been a restless versatility both of mind and character, and a lack of power and will to concentrate, which in the long run makes the difference between the amateur and the expert. If he had been forced by wise training, by self discipline, or by the rigour of circumstances, to choose and to adhere to a definite channel of activity, practical or intellectual, and to throw all his powers into its pursuit, he could hardly have failed to play a useful, perhaps a brilliant part on any stage of contemporary life. But fortune, which seemed to be so lavish in its favours, denied him these restraining and constraining influences, and allowed him free play for all the indulgences of wayward ambition and an uncontrolled temperament.' (7)

As a final comment from one of Wilhelm's peers, Churchill, in his book, *Great Contemporaries*, published many years after the Kaiser's abdication, probably gets closest to the essence of the man:

'William II had none of the qualities of the modern dictators, except their airs. He was a picturesque figurehead in the centre of the world's stage, called upon to play a part far beyond the capacity of most people. He had little in common with the great princes who at intervals throughout the centuries have appeared by the accident of birth at the summit of states and empires. His undeniable cleverness and versatility, his personal grace and vivacity, only aggravated the dangers by concealing his inadequacy. He knew how to make the gestures, to utter the words, to strike the attitude in the Imperial style. He could stamp and snort, or nod and smile with much histrionic art; but underneath all this posing and its trappings, was a very ordinary, vain, but on the whole well-meaning man, hoping to pass himself off as a second Frederick the Great.' (8)

That said, had there been only a very small change in military fortunes in the autumn of 1914, or the Spring of 1918, Germany might well have prevailed in the Great War, in which case the historical perception of the Kaiser would have been very different, as would have been the subsequent history of Europe. It would certainly have been written by different historians, from a very different perspective.

As all the foregoing quotes indicate, Wilhelm disliked restraining influences. There was a strong element of the actor in him, and he played the many roles supplied by his mood swings with unflagging zeal, although, alas, more as Donald Wolffitt than Alec Guinness.

Essentially, he was very far from being a fool, though frequently guilty of foolish*ness* in his grandiose pronouncements and posturings. When he applied himself to a particular subject, especially naval matters, he could bring admirable lucidity and energy (in bursts) to bear. He was one of the first and most committed adherents to the teachings of the American naval officer and historian, Captain A.T. Mahan, whose book, *The Influence of Sea Power on History*, and its sequels revolutionised world thinking on the importance of naval power in the late 19th century. He was also a gifted, if sometimes impractical dabbler in warship concept and design. In his advocacy of the fast battleship as the ideal capital ship, Wilhelm was years ahead of his time, but he lacked the intellectual stamina and self-discipline necessary to see a concept to fruition. Being prone to the influence of the flatterers and sycophants essential to his ego, nor could he distinguish between the parasites and those who could genuinely serve his interests, and those of his nation. There was no effective curb for his misplaced exuberance, and no one had the strength of character to guide his abilities into proper channels – that is bar the redoubtable Bismarck (and he lasted as Wilhelm's Chancellor but two years), and a diminutive old lady across the North Sea.

The relationship between Wilhelm and the British royal family is pertinent to any understanding of the man; his behaviour, and his motives; and to the background effect this had on Anglo-German affairs.

The Kaiser was the grandson of Queen Victoria, nephew of the future King Edward VII, and the cousin of the future King George V. His father had married Victoria's eldest, and favourite, daughter, and was, as previously noted, very pro-British. Whilst his parents controlled his upbringing, Wilhelm was encouraged in the same direction, but, once in his late teens, he began to be weaned away from the influence of his family, mainly at the instigation of Bismarck who wished to manipulate him as a political counterbalance to Friedrich. The British connection however was deeply engrained, and never eradicated.

The links between the British and German ruling families were myriad, and it was not unusual to find members of the German aristocracy visiting, or even serving in, the British Fleet (the British First Sea Lord at the outbreak of the Great War was a German prince who had joined the Royal Navy and taken British nationality early in his career). The adolescent Wilhelm had witnessed the full aura of the British Fleet, and it had profoundly influenced his young mind:

'When, as a little boy, I was allowed to visit Portsmouth and Plymouth hand in hand with kind aunts and friendly admirals, I admired the proud English ships in those two superb harbours. There then awoke in me the wish to build ships of my own like those someday, and when I was grown up to possess as fine a navy as the English.' (9)

His continued connections with the Royal Navy gave him a lifelong preoccupation with warships and naval affairs, and also a lasting respect for the service that had provided his early inspiration. One constant strand that weaves its way through the complexities of the Kaiser's personality was his enduring regard (affection might not be too strong a description) for the fleet of his nation's most potentially dangerous adversary. Parallel to this strand ran another, rooted in envy of the power and traditions of Britain's naval forces and jealous of the empire whose security and prosperity rested on its maritime supremacy.

There is more than a hint of schizophrenia in Wilhelm's attitudes towards Britain. He once declared that the proudest moment of his life was being able to see his Admiral's Flag (an honour conferred upon him by his grandmother) being hoisted on a British battleship during a fleet review. As late as 1904, in the midst of constructing a fleet to dispute Britain's control of the oceans, he was still writing to senior British naval officers of his acquaintance, commenting and advising on ship design, technical developments, and policy. His remarks and criticisms were often pertinent, and evinced a continuing interest in the efficiency and well being of the British Fleet! His predominant characteristic, though, was a burning desire to surpass that which he most admired. His ambivalence towards England persisted right up to the eve of the Great War.

'He oscillated between powerful attraction – "I adore England", he said in 1911 to Theodore Roosevelt – and petulant grievance which came close to hate. He wished to be understood and accepted as an English gentleman, and at the same time feared as a Prussian warlord.' (10)

This split personality evidenced itself frequently, often to the embarrassment of his hosts, his own diplomats, and ultimately to himself. Despite repeatedly adopting violently anti-British positions and launching into sabre rattling speeches, many of his own people never ceased to regard his attitude towards the English with suspicion. The British themselves wondered at this curious man – so belligerent and militaristic in his own country one moment, and the next, revelling in adopting their dress, their manners, and their lifestyle in the country pursuits, on yachts at Cowes Week, and visiting his relatives in their own royal family. Poor Wilhelm was never totally accepted. He was too English for a lot of the Germans and too German for the English in general.

However irrational the Kaiser might have been at times, his sincerity was probably not in question. What he said, he genuinely believed, until someone with his ear convinced him he believed otherwise. If he was childishly fond of pomp, splendid uniforms and gloried in the trappings and obsequities of his own imperial magnificence, he was also simple in his affections towards those whose good opinion he desired or valued. Foremost amongst those was Queen Victoria, whom he revered. She, in turn indulged him rather as someone deals with a high spirited, if occasionally exasperating child. During Wilhelm's life, there seems to have been only one person who fully possessed his devotion and admiration, and that was his grandmother. His respect for her appears quite unfeigned, and, in his correspondence, at times he seemed almost desperate for her approval. One of the most poignant moments at the end of her life was the presence of the Kaiser at her deathbed. His concern and consideration for her family, and his modest and helpful demeanour during the period of mourning did him the utmost credit. The English people naturally warmed to him as never before, and, for a brief moment, he basked in the real affection of the British community.

HMS EMPRESS OF INDIA

Displacement: 14,150 tons; Armament: 4-13.5 inch guns, 10-6 inch guns; Light QF
Dimensions: 410 ft. (oa) x 75 ft x 30ft draught
Machinery: Triple Expansion; 2 screws; 11,000 H.P. = 16.5 knots
Belt Armour: 14-18 inches; Endurance; 4,720 miles @ 10 knots

Laid down in 1889, *HMS Empress of India* was one of seven identical battleships of the *Royal Sovereign* class built under the Naval Defence Act of that year. The initiation and passing of this act had been heavily influenced by the powerful advocacy of Lord Charles Beresford, and probably represents the greatest of the many services that he gave to the navy during his long career before the feud with Fisher devalued his reputation. Fisher's less public influence was also a significant factor at the time. What is often forgotten in the ruins of their later relationship is how well they complemented each other in campaigning for the navy's future in earlier years.

The *Royal Sovereign*s were undoubtedly the finest capital ships of their age, and formed the template for battleship design until the *Dreadnought* ushered in a new era sixteen years later. The chief innovation was the abandonment of a low freeboard and an acceptance that a seagoing battleship could not be constructed within the artificial tonnage limits previously imposed.

The chief weakness of the ships, was that, as in the earlier *Admiral* class ships, there was no protection for the gun crews of the main armament. In the next class of ships, the nine *Majestic*s, this was addressed by placing an armoured hood over the barbettes. In the fullness of time, this arrangement became universal and referred to as a turret.

Empress of India was completed in 1893 and served for 18 years before being expended as a target ship. One of her class, the *Revenge*, later renamed *Redoubtable*, survived to serve during the First World War as a bombardment vessel.

SMS KAISER FRIEDRICH III

Displacement: 11,097 tons; Armament: 4-9.4 inch guns, 18-5.9 inch guns; 14-3.4"QF
Dimensions: 411 ft (oa) x 67 ft. x 27ft draught
Machinery: 13,500; 3 screws; 13,500 HP = 17.5 knots
Belt Armour: 6-12 inches; Endurance: 2,250 miles @ 12 knots

Contemporary to HMS *Empress of India* were the five German ships of the *Kaiser Friedrich III* class. They were poorly armoured, and whilst having a theoretical speed advantage could never have exercised this in an ocean seaway. Nor was their endurance impressive. The main armament was the relatively light 9.4-inch gun which could only deliver a shell of less than half the explosive power of the 12-inch and 13.5-inch weapons available to the likely opposition. German theory at the time was to equip their capital ships with the largest calibre of guns capable of sustaining 'quick fire'. This was a relative term, but, in the 1890s, could not be applied to anything larger than the 9.4-inch gun. This weapon could undoubtedly fire more quickly than the heavier guns of an opponent, but was not capable of causing serious damage at longer battle ranges. *Kaiser Friedrich III* was made non-operational in 1915, became a prison ship at Kiel a year later, and was scrapped in 1919.

The two classes of ship are representative of the different requirements of the navies at that time. The British ships were ocean going vessels that could be deployed abroad; the German designs were 'Baltic battleships' that could not be effectively deployed further than the confines of the North Sea. Later German classes showed many improvements, but there was always this basic difference in emphasis in that Britain was building for a world role, and that the Germany navy, even before Tirpitz and his theories came to the fore, was concentrating on local matters.

His relationships with other members of the British royal family were less fulfilling. For 12 years his 'Uncle Bertie', the Prince of Wales, had had to put up with being alternatively patronised and snubbed by his bumptious imperial nephew, many years his junior. Given Wilhelm's general lack of tact, it is unsurprising that the future king, who, despite being a *bon viveur*, had a profound sense of his own dignity, developed a marked dislike for him. It was equally typical of Wilhelm that he was naïvely unable to comprehend the degree of offence that he was capable of giving. A biographer of Edward VII comments that:

'It is hard to blame the King for having disliked the Kaiser. His nephew all too often cut the figure of one who seems, to a later generation, to have been urgently in need of extensive psychiatric help. The sheer arrogance and childlike desire for status and recognition that the Kaiser had would always make him a difficult man to deal with.' (11)

One of the Kaiser's biographers puts a different slant on the relationship:

'The truth was that the two men were wholly incompatible. The Prince of Wales was more pompous in his public life, more unconventional in his private. The Kaiser could be almost alarmingly direct and friendly when he chose to be, but underneath he was a Prussian and a Puritan and his uncle was almost everything he disliked. He was soft and fat and self indulgent and even at 55 had a sharp eye for the ladies…Most galling to Wilhelm, however, was the fact that the Prince, despite his shortcomings, was the darling of Europe…What was curious about the Kaiser's relations with his uncle was the fact that William credited him with far more brains and ability than English people did. The Kaiser saw him as a mischievous, Machiavellian figure, weaving plots against Germany because of his beloved France; and he did not doubt his shrewdness or his grasp of Foreign Affairs. English politicians and courtiers would have been astonished at this appraisal [but it] was far nearer the truth than the patronising pronouncements of Victoria's officials.' (12)

It might be added that the opinion of 'Victoria's officials' absolutely corresponded with her own assessment of her eldest son. This had been the principal cause of his exclusion from all affairs of state – to his frustration and fury – throughout his mother's reign.

When 'Uncle Bertie' did eventually succeed to the throne as King Edward VII there was no permanent thaw in this relationship, despite the goodwill generated at the time of Queen Victoria's death. Edward was, in any case, a committed Francophile, and was to be one of the driving forces towards a British rapprochement with France and the beginnings of the *Entente Cordiale*. His evident success in this endeavour earned him the undying hostility of the Kaiser. Wilhelm, whilst having a much cannier idea than most of his uncle's abilities, nevertheless overestimated his ability to control events.

The British Monarch had nothing like the theoretical executive authority wielded by the German Emperor, a fact Wilhelm, besotted with an absurd concept of 'divine right' to 'personal rule', was never able or willing to comprehend. Legally and constitutionally the Kaiser had access to sweeping powers over the affairs of his nation.

'The powers invested in the Kaiser included control of foreign policy, command of the armed forces and the right to declare war as well as internal martial law. In addition, he had the power to appoint and dismiss Chancellors and to interpret the constitution.' (13)

At best, Edward could offer his opinion and advice to his ministers, and occasionally, if a particular political initiative attracted his support, he could give it a subtle slap on the back and help it on its way. His active and benevolent support towards developing the *entente* with France was the most striking example of his ability to influence events from behind the scenes. He had no power to initiate the process, but he could, and did, help to create an atmosphere in which it would prosper. It was this particular success that so deluded the Kaiser and led him to suppose that all Germany's subsequent diplomatic and strategic woes stemmed from a malignant web of encirclement devised by his uncle. As a supposition, it had the solitary advantage of him not having to consider any responsibility that he and his ministers might have had in bringing about this state of affairs.

'The greatest point of contrast was not so much in the unique personality of the last German emperor but in the fact that, constitutionally, he was a crucial political figure. Wilhelm may have claimed to be above parties, but he was also at the centre of the governmental decision-making process, and all chains of authority terminated in him. He, and not the Reichstag, was the only body which could select and dismiss the Chancellor. Ministers were *his* men, and not senior politicians from the party or parties which had acquired the largest number of seats in the Reichstag; indeed, ministers could not be members of that institution. The entire conduct of foreign policy was in the hands of the Kaiser, and by delegation in those of the Chancellor.' (14)

Wilhelm, whenever he dealt with fellow monarchs, was never able to come to terms with the fact that they did not have the same executive powers that had been granted to him by the German constitution. His attitude to his British uncle was always blighted by the assumption that Edward had far more political power and influence than was actually the case.

If Edward was a thorn in Wilhelm's side, his son, the future King George V, had by contrast, a marked partiality towards Wilhelm. However, by the time he succeeded to the throne in 1910 events had polarised the two nations, and his lack of political acumen had only a peripheral effect. In any case, Edward VII was the last British Monarch of whom it could be observed was a significant influence in the foreign policies of his nation.

When Wilhelm became emperor, the aging Bismarck was still firmly in control of Germany's destiny. His continued presence in office ensured stability of government and a pragmatic application of German foreign policy. In ideal circumstances he would have been the perfect mentor to the headstrong young man who ascended the throne, and to whom he had already devoted much effort in trying to educate along the lines of Bismarckian political philosophy. It rapidly became apparent that this would not be the case.

Wilhelm's desire for personal rule, however irrational in the state of Bismarck's creation led him to adopt a 'hands on' approach from the outset. Once he had exhausted the novelties of dressing up in splendid uniforms (a pleasure he never outgrew), and dashing around Europe freely giving unsolicited, and frequently unwelcome, opinions to his fellow heads of state, he began to focus on the day-to-day affairs of his empire. He was not content to be just a figurehead, and genuinely saw himself as a latter day Siegfried, destined by God to lead Germany to a predominant position in the world order. At the other end on the scale he also, at least at the beginning of his reign, embraced relatively socialist ideas as to improving the lot of the disadvantaged. This latter tendency caused considerable alarm to the basically conservative establishment, but it proved to be of short duration. Instead of grasping the moment and instituting a dialogue, the professional socialists shot themselves in the foot by showing neither interest in, nor the necessary gratitude for, the new emperor's genuine desire to improve German society. This rebuff had a permanent effect. Wilhelm, true to character, took instant offence, promptly abandoned this approach, and returned to the fold of traditional Prussian illiberalism. The establishment breathed a collective sigh of relief.

Although to some extent a constitutional monarch, his position within that constitution was very different from that of, say, the King of England. As already mentioned, in theory the Kaiser had significant executive clout should he choose to exercise his constitutional authority, and Wilhelm dearly cherished those powers. He also insisted on taking seriously offices and titles that had been formerly treated as honorary. This quickly made impossible a working relationship between the old Chancellor and the new Emperor. There ensued a brief power struggle between the two men as to which of them would be the paramount influence in the dictation of government policy. It was to be Bismarck's last great political battle, and one of the very few in which he was worsted. Within 18 months of the new emperor's accession, Wilhelm accepted the resignation of the greatest German of the century (without hesitation, and on a relatively trivial matter), and the architect of the nation that the Kaiser nominally ruled was cast into the political wilderness. (The Punch cartoon of the time depicting 'The Dropping of the Pilot' remains a classic of its genre. Bismarck's wife had a copy framed and hung on the wall!) With him went the common sense and pragmatism that, however brutally applied, had characterised German foreign policy for the previous forty years. A new era of change and uncertainty was at hand.

'William II repudiated the precautions which were the essence of Bismarck's system. He thought that the Hohenzollern monarchy was strong enough to stand in Germany and Germany strong enough to stand in the world, without checks and balances. When Bismarck left office William II announced "The ship's course remains the same. 'Full Steam ahead' is the order" – the first sentence blatantly untrue; the second the profound motto of his reign.' (15)

Wilhelm shared many of Bismarck's aims, but his simplistic approach to diplomacy was ill-suited to the complications of European politics.

'If Wilhelm II's course was not the same as Bismarck's at least his reign was the natural, almost inevitable, result of the Bismarck philosophy and the Bismarck success. Indeed, it is doubtful whether Bismarck himself could have continued to rule by a policy of restraint for he had kindled desires in the hearts of his countrymen which could not be easily extinguished…*the most striking differences between the regimes was that Bismarck's rule was competent and William's was not.*' [Author's italics] (16)

Bismarck had been the soul of pragmatism. He knew how far he could go in the interests of his country, and he never lost sight of how far he *should* go in those interests. Acutely conscious of his country's geographic weakness, despite its military strength, Bismarck had rarely sought territorial gain from the triumphs of Prussia's armies if that should interfere with his long-term diplomatic goals. After the defeat of Austria in 1866, he insisted on no acquisition of the latter's provinces, preferring only that the Habsburg Empire should accept Prussia as the pre-eminent German nation, and, from thence onwards as a natural ally. In the wake of the crushing of France in 1871, it was only against the qualified objections of Bismarck (one of the very few occasions he did not get his own way) that the French province of Lorraine was absorbed into the German Empire. He rightly saw in that action the inevitability of future confrontation and the impossibility of ever being on reasonable diplomatic terms with his nation's most powerful neighbour. (The army Chief of Staff, Helmuth von Moltke, was being no more than realistic when he opined that, 'What we gained by arms in half a year, we must protect by arms for half a century if it is not to be torn from us again'. (17) In the event, he was not to be granted his fifty years.)

'[Bismarck] devoted his whole power and genius to the construction of an elaborate system of alliances designed to secure the continued ascendancy of Germany and the maintenance of her conquests…everything else must be subordinated to that central fact…This arrangement, under which Europe lived rigidly, but peacefully for twenty years was ended with the fall of Bismarck…new forces began to assail the system he had maintained with consummate ability so long.' (18)

Germany's loss was also Europe's misfortune. It is one of those mournful turns of history that he was unable to devise a system of government that could function efficiently without his presence at its hub. What is certain is that he had groomed his son, Herbert, to be his successor, but the old Chancellor's fall from power also encompassed that of his family and close associates.

'There can be no doubt whatever that, prior to 1890, Bismarck had counted on Herbert being the second Imperial Chancellor, as had Herbert himself. "I know of no-one," the father had said in 1889, "who could replace Herbert. I have made him the depository of all my experience – him and nobody else." Actually, for Herbert the end of the Bismarck era represented a more general beginning of the end. He summed the matter up very simply: "This means the break up of the Empire." In a word Bismarck's most intimate associate foresaw the twilight of the Empire while its inhabitants were just beginning to take its unlimited duration for granted.' (19)

In the vacuum that was created after Bismarck's departure, new and unpredictable influences circulated with disconcerting rapidity. Of all those influences, the one that was to erode most certainly his carefully constructed pillars of German security was the decision to become a major naval power, and to deliberately set out to challenge British supremacy on the high seas.

Prior to Wilhelm's accession, the Emperor had taken, by choice, a back seat in affairs, leaving effective control of events in the capable hands of his Chancellor. While the giant presence of Bismarck occupied that position, the system of his making operated largely to his requirements, although he remained nominally responsible both to his Emperor and to the *Reichstag*. Once men of lesser stature had replaced him, the office of Chancellor declined in influence.

'When the great star fell, many Germans had a chilling presentiment that their country had suffered an irreplaceable loss and that it would not soon again be governed with such intelligence and assurance. Time was to prove them correct, although it must be said that the mistakes of Bismarck's successors might have been less disastrous if he had not contributed to the difficulties of their task by leaving them an anachronistic political system in which he had sought – in the case of liberalism with success – to stifle every progressive tendency.' (20)

His successors were increasingly harassed by the problems of matching the grandiose ambitions of the Kaiser to the willingness of the *Reichstag* to provide the finance necessary for their fulfilment. The creation of a navy capable of supporting Germany's rise to world power status soon became a major bone of contention between monarch and parliament.

The Kaiser was an important factor in the frustration of his own policy. Despite the bluster, he was chronically indecisive, and his attitudes changed with disconcerting rapidity. It was said of him that his opinion depended on that of the last person to have his ear.

'The weakness of the responsible officials of the Empire led to a growth in the strength of all those who were irresponsible. The sheer number of individuals who enjoyed the right of direct audience made it absolutely certain that the responsible officials would lose control over the course of events...The Kaiser's tendency to authorise conflicting plans and to act on whatever his most recent confidant had proposed merely made a bad situation worse.' (21)

Given this failing, an early decree of his reign splitting the supreme control of the navy into separate compartments of responsibility was a recipe for chaos.

'The Emperor wanted to divide the power of the Admiralty, in order to be able the better to intervene himself...The executive command and the Admiralty were separated in 1888; in addition, a special naval cabinet was established, and all three authorities were granted direct access to the Sovereign. The field was now open for move and countermove; for three or four different naval policies.' (22)

In the circumstances, it was hardly surprising that confusion reigned over the ways and means to create and project a German naval force that could best serve the interests of state.

For the nine years after Wilhelm II became Kaiser, policy dithered between the building of a respectable battle fleet; an effective coast defence force, or the construction of cruiser squadrons sufficient to support German interests in peacetime and conduct a *'guerre de course'* on the trade routes in times of war. As late as 1897, Eugen Richter, the chief radical gadfly in the *Reichstag*, was to ironically remark that:

'One State Secretary builds lots of cruisers, the other lots of battleships. If these changes in the navy's leadership continue, eventually we shall have a fine fleet of both.' (23)

The Kaiser in the uniform of a British Admiral

Grand Admiral Alfred Von Tirpitz

If Richter thought what had been built up to then was 'lots', he was soon to be disabused. The events of the previous decade had justified some scorn, but Richter and all the other critics of naval expansion were to be confounded by the arrival on the scene of a consummate expert in the manipulation of public, political and professional opinion. In June 1897, Rear Admiral Alfred Tirpitz became State Secretary of the Navy Office. The second major player in the drama had entered the arena.

The Navy Office was one of the three pillars of power created by the Kaiser's disastrous devolution of responsibility in 1889. The State Secretary was responsible, most importantly, for drawing up, with the Kaiser's consent, the construction programme for the fleet, and then obtaining the approval of the *Reichstag* for the funding of the ships. In times of peace, this office was certainly the most important cog in the naval wheel.

Tirpitz's predecessor, Admiral Hollman, although a competent and decent man, possessed neither the ruthless clarity of purpose nor the political instincts to push through a coherent naval policy. After a series of failures to win the parliament over to his plans for more overseas cruisers (and Wilhelm's desire for more warships whatever their purpose), he was finally dismissed. Tirpitz, then serving in command of the Asiatic Squadron, was, by reputation and obvious ability, seen as a natural replacement. He had a very clearly defined idea of the sort of navy that Germany should possess, and also an absolute conviction that this force would be the only logical means of advancing the interests of his country on the world stage. His views had already been placed in lucid written form before the Kaiser prior to his service in the Far East. In contrast to his contemporaries and peers, Tirpitz had the ability to put his theories into effect. He claimed and occupied a position of authority in the maritime affairs of his nation that became, for most of his nineteen years in office, omnipotent. Tirpitz became the 'Bismarck of the Navy'.

For the Kaiser, the advent of Tirpitz to the post of State Secretary was an unqualified boon. For the first time in his reign he had a man in a position of authority who could not only rationalise his ambitions for a great navy, but also translate the vision into reality. (Equally true was that Tirpitz was dependent on the backing of the Emperor to achieve *his* objectives, and he was assiduous in ensuring the latter's support for each succeeding stage of his programme.) Both men shared the same aims for a greater Germany, and both believed that this could only be achieved by building a navy to challenge that of Britain – albeit one that would never be expected (at least from Wilhelm's perspective) to actually fight the Royal Navy. It was intended as a form of brutal political leverage to advance Germany's world interests in the face of possible British opposition, and in the meantime also to make a splendid show of Germany's prestige and power. From the very beginning of their partnership, whatever public gloss might be applied to the subject, Wilhelm II and Tirpitz set out to build 'A Fleet against England'. The success of their endeavours depended on the acquiescence of the *Reichstag* as to providing the funds, and the necessity of disguising the purpose, for as long as possible, from the intended target.

Between them, Tirpitz and the Kaiser mustered sufficient clout to initiate the project. Long before the term 'propaganda' was coined, Tirpitz became a master of the art of manipulating public opinion – and in this he must have learned much from the success of Bismarck's past methods. He instituted a campaign in the press, focussed on the need for a strong German navy as a prerequisite of imperial ambitions. He also recruited an impressive list of senior academics (the 'Fleet Professors'), industrial tycoons and amenable politicians to support his long-term strategy. All these influences were concentrated on a population that was already besotted with the military successes of the recent past, and aggressively in favour of future national advancement. To round off the effect, a suitable bogeyman was already available, in the shape of Great Britain, to set up as a target for resentment and envy at what were purveyed as intolerable restrictions on German expansion. The anti-British sentiments cultivated by Bismarck were now whipped up into barely controlled hatred. All the resulting public pressure encouraged the compliance of sufficient elected parliamentarians to get a majority in the *Reichstag* and to make it possible for the scheme to proceed as planned.

Despite all these factors, a challenge to the long established position of the Royal Navy was a daunting prospect to even the strongest economy and greatest military power in the world. The question was how could it be achieved?

If Tirpitz has a claim to genius, it must rest in the achievements of his first few years as State Secretary of the Navy Office. He rescued from confusion and demoralisation an organisation that had lost all sense of direction, and imposed upon it a set programme and a reason for its existence. He convinced the Kaiser of the virtues of his theories, and then proceeded to do the same with the bulk of Wilhelm's subjects. Finally he won over the *Reichstag* with the prospect that his plans for the navy would give a much better return for the government's money without costing any more than the discredited programmes of his predecessors (in this respect, there is an obvious resemblance to Fisher's later campaign to sell the reform of the Royal Navy to the miserly controllers of the nation's purse strings). These measures, he proposed to embody in law.

There is a wonderful political audacity about Tirpitz at this moment of his career. He not only managed to inveigle a sceptical parliament into approving a programme for a serious battle fleet, but he also enticed it to enshrine the numerical strength of that fleet in *law*. The *Reichstag* wandered into this legislative trap happily convinced that it was *limiting* future numbers of ships and expenditure on associated equipment. In fact, Tirpitz had been given the leeway to commence a building programme that, once underway, would become virtually self-propagating, and would demand a steadily increasing share of overall government resources.

Superficially, the 1898 Navy Bill made excellent sense. It was presented soberly and illustrated how, with a proper long-term programme geared to an easily comprehended strategy, there could be produced a much more effective force than the existing collection of vessels – and at no extra cost. It established a set composition for the fleet and provided for automatic replacement of vessels once they had reached a set retirement age. This enabled construction programmes to be planned well in advance, with all the advantages of being able to effectively forecast requirements for building capacity and manning levels – and guaranteeing continuity of work for the shipyards. It all seemed very sensible and straightforward, and appeared to ensure the maintenance of an adequate European fleet at an affordable price. In April 1898 the *Reichstag* passed the Navy Bill into law. It established the future strength of the German Fleet at 19 battleships, 8 armoured cruisers, 12 large and 30 light cruisers. This force level was to be reached in 1904 and would involve new construction of 7 battleships, 2 large and 7 light cruisers, over the six years – an increase in strength of less than three warships a year and hardly cause for alarm in other maritime nations.

'Such a fleet was regarded as strong enough for limited offensives against France and Russia. It was not a serious threat to Britain's naval position.' (24)

What was not perceived at the time was the fact that Tirpitz had included in the existing strength of the battle fleet every old ironclad and coast defence ship on the navy list. As these useless antiquities reached the newly established age of retirement (if they had not in fact already done so) the Navy Bill provided for their replacement by ships of the same category. The new vessels would clearly be expected to be more effective than their predecessors, but, in the event, the actual disparity in quality was enormous – the most blatant example of which was the eventual replacement of old 4,000-ton coast defence 'battleships' of the *Siegfried* class by 24,000-ton *Dreadnoughts*! Thus the actual strength of the German Navy mounted rapidly, as did the cost of maintaining, supporting and manning the force. Sooner or later, parliament was bound to come to the conclusion that it had been hoodwinked by Tirpitz, and take a closer interest in his machinations. Fortunately for the admiral, newly ennobled by an appreciative Kaiser, events elsewhere in the world came to his succour. Within two years of the First Navy Bill, he was able to almost double its provisions with the overwhelming approval of public opinion and with hardly a murmur of resistance from the *Reichstag*.

Even with the triumph of the Navy Bill, Germany had a mountain to climb if it was to compete with British maritime power on anything approaching level terms. A comparison of strength between the navies of the two nations in 1900 shows a huge disparity of force, and emphasises the magnitude of the task that faced Wilhelm and Tirpitz. At that time, on a ship-to-ship basis, the modern British units were also considerably superior to their German counterparts (see the table of comparative strength at the end of this chapter). If the British advantage in materiel was impressive, the relative ability to project that force was overwhelming.

Throughout the world, at every crucial focus of maritime activity, Britain possessed long-established dockyards and fortified coaling ports to support her fleet. By contrast, Germany, in 1897, was in the process of claiming her first, and only, overseas colony that could serve as a naval base – Tsingtao, in Northern China. In the circumstances, any attempt to match British strength overseas was out of the question. But, argued Tirpitz, this was, in any case, completely unnecessary.

Like the Kaiser, an avid disciple of Mahan, Tirpitz realised that in any struggle for maritime supremacy, the decision would rest with the main fleets of the adversaries. If the main British fleet confronting Germany should be defeated, then Britain could be invaded and the war won at a stroke. All the overseas squadrons and possessions in the world would be irrelevant to the outcome. Any German colonies and units that were inevitably mopped up by the British in the early stages of the conflict would be restored and multiplied as a result of a punitive peace settlement.

This reasoning presupposed one of the three pillars of Tirpitz's overall strategic thinking, namely that Britain's preoccupation with her imperial commitments would always ensure that a considerable proportion of the Royal Navy would be deployed abroad, whereas the entire German battle fleet could be concentrated in the decisive theatre, i.e. the North Sea. Of the other two pillars, the main one, the famous *Risk Theory*, assumed that, once Germany had assembled a sufficiently powerful fleet, even if inferior to the British Navy, it would be enough to deter Britain from contemplating war – the reasoning being that the Royal Navy would suffer such losses in destroying the German Fleet as to render it vulnerable to a hostile third power, and thus *risk* the maritime supremacy on which the empire depended. The final pillar of the strategy was the rather hopeful assumption that possession of a powerful navy would make Germany a more desirable ally in any hypothetical future combination of states.

At first glance, the gospel according to Tirpitz appeared not unsuited to Germany's immediate interests and future aspirations. In 1898, significant numbers of the Royal Navy's better ships *were* based in the Mediterranean or east of Suez. Britain was also still in her 'Splendid Isolation' phase and her two most intransigent rivals (Russia on the

Northwest Frontier of India and France elsewhere on the colonial scene) were coincidentally Germany's great threats on the continent of Europe. To German eyes, it seemed unlikely that Britain would want to risk a trial of strength with a respectable German fleet when the only benefactors of such an event would be their mutual opponents on the world stage – and it seemed inconceivable, at that time, that there could ever be an Anglo-French or Anglo-Russian rapprochement. At worst, British neutrality would seem to be guaranteed in any conflict involving Germany and the other two powers, and, with every passing year, the quantitive gap between the British and German navies could be steadily eroded.

Within a very short space of time, however, these assumptions were to be proved erroneous, and the whole strategy a disastrous miscalculation. The rise of the German Navy, occurring at the same time as the Boer War, which brought almost universal opprobrium on her head, jolted Britain out of political isolation. In order to meet the situation, in 1902 she concluded a startling defensive alliance with Japan, which permitted the battle squadron in Far Eastern waters to be brought home. Three years later the beginning of a previously unthinkable *entente* with France removed the threat to British lines of communication and supply in the Mediterranean, and enabled the naval forces there to be scaled down. In the same year, Russia also ceased to be a threatening maritime factor following her defeat by Japan, during which her fleet virtually ceased to exist.

'From the strategic point of view, as opposed to the economic or socio-political, the fleet construction programme was supposed to give Germany secure coasts and great political leverage. But from the very beginning, this argument suffered from two grave logical flaws. It overestimated Germany's financial strength while at the same time assuming that the British people would be unwilling to pay the costs of maintaining their decided superiority in naval strength. More important, it was singularly unreceptive to the possibility that Britain might seek an alliance with a Power other than Germany and to the fact that, if it did so, and if that Power were a naval power, all of Tirpitz's calculations would prove to be false.' (25)

The premises of the *Risk Theory* were thus in tatters just seven years from its inception. Instead of having to face a section of a divided British fleet, Germany was to be confronted with almost the full power of the world's largest navy. Worse, in order to concentrate her navy, Britain had been forced from a position of isolation into the arms of her old adversary, France – Germany's most obvious and dangerous enemy. The *entente* with France also helped Britain to settle her differences with Russia, France's long-term ally and in any case no longer a naval threat following the debacle with Japan. The *de facto* alliance with France, almost unthinkable a few years previously, meant that Britain need not be too concerned about the risk of incurring losses in destroying the German Fleet (of the other naval powers, Japan was an ally, and war with the USA was unthinkable – and neither of those two nations was remotely in a position to invade Britain). Jonathan Steinburg comments that:

> 'Germany's growth would, perhaps, have provoked the traditional British reluctance to permit the continent to be dominated by a single power in any case, but the decision to build a first class fleet made British rivalry and resistance a certainty. The first German Navy Law of 1898 was the point of no return in the process, although nobody in Britain and scarcely a handful of men in Germany realised it.
>
> The decision to give Germany a first class fleet was not the only reason for introducing the Navy Law of 1898. That decision by itself was neither unreasonable nor unjustified. In the context of the period, it was probably inevitable. All the other powers were building furiously, and British naval supremacy was equally threatened every time a keel was laid by any one of them. But, in one significant respect, the character of the German Navy Law was different. It alone challenged British hegemony directly and it did so by calling for a powerful fleet of battleships to be stationed in the North Sea...The object of the German Battle Fleet was to give Germany a measure of naval power against Great Britain.' (26)

The strategic element of the naval policy pursued by the Kaiser and Tirpitz had failed almost at the outset, yet it was to be continued with vigour and determination until brought to its inevitable conclusion. Each of the three pillars of the policy had been comprehensively demolished before the architects had seen them a quarter erected. Germany did *not* gain even naval equality, never mind predominance in the North Sea. She did *not* gain allies by the possession of a formidable navy; rather she gifted the alliance of Britain to France and Russia, and, in the process, removed any element of *risk* from the *Risk Theory*. Friedrich von Holstein, First Counsellor in the Department of Foreign Affairs, gloomily, but presciently, commented that:

> 'The Fleet increases the number of our enemies, but will never be strong enough to vanquish them.' (27)

Finally, the German policy concentrated British minds on the threat posed by the challenge to her navy, and ensured that Britain would build whatever ships were required to maintain supremacy. This eventuality was never given sufficient credence by either Tirpitz or the Kaiser. Neither of them adequately addressed the question of why, if Germany could make the huge financial effort to create a formidable fleet, Britain – who, after all, was much more dependent on her sea power – would not make a corresponding effort to retain her maritime supremacy.

'Why did her leaders choose Tirpitz's battle fleet? Why was that battle fleet directed mainly against Great Britain? Because Germany had come to want what Britain had and to believe that they could have it. Britain only became the enemy when men like Admiral Tirpitz and Admiral Senden demanded that Germany achieve the same position of power in the world which she had already begun to achieve in Europe. Britain became the enemy when a great many Germans began to see her as the obstacle to German greatness. Finally, Britain became the enemy because Germany's leaders accepted the view that two great trading nations could not co-exist and that German growth must lead to a struggle between them.' (28)

In 1898, the consequences of the direction Germany had chosen were yet to become apparent, but, with the passing into law of the First Navy Bill, the die was cast, and the first step taken on a road that would lead to a ruinous arms race, and mark a significant milestone towards the ultimate catastrophe of the first Great War.

'For all his great abilities, one is tempted to describe Tirpitz as the evil genius of German foreign relations from 1898 onwards. He had already made a powerful contribution to the worsening of Russo-German relations, for the seizure of Kiaochow (Tsingtao) in November 1897, which was inspired by his reports from the Far East, had infuriated the Russians, who regarded this as an intrusion into their sphere of influence and a threat to their projected domination of Northern China.[1] Now his naval plans succeeded in putting an end to any remaining hopes the German Government might have about winning an alliance with Great Britain.

This was unfortunate, because there were still powerful forces in England that were working for a comprehensive Anglo-German agreement.' (29)

German diplomatic incompetence miserably failed to establish what could have been an entirely sustainable working relationship with Britain. At the same time, the other great powers, apart from the deadweight of the mutually dependent Austro-Hungarian Empire, were successively alienated. Churchill's assessment of the period is as good as any. *The World Crisis*, as a history, is subjective at times, but this comment is indisputably spot on:

'It had been easy for Germany to lose touch with Russia, but the alienation of England was a far longer process. So many props and ties had successively to be demolished. British suspicions of Russia in Asia, the historic antagonism to France, memories of Blenheim, of Minden and of Waterloo, the continued disputes with France in Egypt and in the colonial sphere, the intimate business connexions

---

[1] There is a notable irony here in that Admiral Otto von Diederichs, who relieved Tirpitz in command of the East Asiatic squadron in 1897, was the officer who finally achieved the annexation of Tsingtao. His fierce advocacy for the development of Tsingtao as a self-sufficient naval base for the German Navy in the region led to a falling out between him and Tirpitz. The latter, newly installed as State Secretary for the navy, was completely focussed on all available funds being diverted to the building of a North Sea battle fleet. Diederichs prevailed on the matter of Tsingtao, but it ruined his career. Tirpitz, once crossed, was an enemy for life. Diederichs retired in 1902, recognising that he had no professional future whilst Tirpitz remained in power. (30)

between Germany and England, the relationship of the Royal Families – all these constituted a profound association between the British Empire and the leading state in the Triple Alliance. It was no part of British policy to obstruct the new-born Colonial aspirations of Germany, and in more than one instance, as at Samoa, we actively assisted them…Still, even before the fall of Bismarck the Germans did not seem pleasant diplomatic comrades. They appeared always to be seeking to enlist our aid and reminding us that they were our only friend. To emphasize this they went even further. They sought in minor ways to embroil us with France and Russia. Each year the Wilhelmstrasse looked inquiringly to the Court of St. James for some new service or concession which should keep Germany's diplomatic goodwill alive for a further period. Each year they made mischief for us with France and Russia, and pointed the moral of how unpopular Great Britain was, what powerful enemies she had, and how lucky she was to find a friend in Germany…These manifestations, prolonged for nearly twenty years, produced very definite sensations of estrangement in the minds of the rising generation at the British Foreign Office.' (31)

There were many mistakes yet to be made on the diplomatic front before the alienation of Britain would become final (and these the German Government proceeded to make in a relatively short space of time), but 'The 'Fleet against England' had ensured that, in any future hostilities, Britain and the Royal Navy would not be on the side of Germany.

This was not, as yet, a total disaster. Great Britain, even if she could not be made a bosom ally, had a far stronger antipathy towards Russia and France. These two nations, who were the greatest threat to Germany in Europe, had co-incidentally been Britain's irreconcilable long-term opponents on the world stage. It only remained for the combined efforts of the Kaiser, his Imperial Chancellor, the Foreign Secretariat, and, critically, the Secretary of State for the Navy, to ensure that Britain would not only become increasingly unsympathetic towards Germany, but would actively align herself alongside both these two, previously hostile, nations. Such was the legacy of the 'Fleet against England'.

ANNEX to CHAPTER THREE

COMPARISON OF THE BRITISH AND GERMAN NAVIES IN 1900

WARSHIPS BUILT OR BUILDING

Notes on the Statistical Tables

1. The speeds quoted are the designed speeds of the ships when newly commissioned. Actual speeds in service fell off in proportion to the age and usage of the individual vessel – mainly due to wear and tear on the boilers. Frequently, ships of the same class developed widely differing performances as a result of being particularly hard worked or vice versa. In general, however, it is a fair assumption that, as the ship gets older it is progressively less likely to be able to approach its original best speed.

The quoted speeds are also generally those which have been achieved in ideal sea conditions during builders' trials. In some classes, such as the low freeboard turret ships, even when new their speed rapidly decreased in any sort of seaway, and, at such speeds that they *were* able to maintain, they could not effectively use their armament.

2. Details of battleship armour are included for interest's sake, but these bald figures in no way constitute a valid comparison between classes. Whilst one ship might apparently possess thicker armour than another, the complicated distribution of their relative protection cannot be properly indicated without going into very detailed descriptions. To make a huge simplification; a ship carrying a maximum thickness of 15-inch armour plate spread over 5% of its hull, is not necessarily better protected than a similar sized vessel with 12-inch armour covering 20% of its hull. Rather the contrary.

The relative protection of any one similar sized ship versus another can only properly (and even then only very approximately) be measured by the total proportion of the ship's tonnage that is dedicated to armour. This factor would also be subject to the relative quality of the armour plate. Figures for thickness of armour take no account of the *type* of plate carried. Early ships of the iron clad era were precisely that – i.e. vessels clad in iron armour. Developments in armour technology advanced as fast as any other aspect of warship design in the second half of the nineteenth century. Iron was replaced by steel, and the resistance propensities of the latter were steadily enhanced by a number of processes. At the turn of the century, the thickness of armour was steadily decreasing without any loss in protection. In 1900, a 6-inch armour belt of the latest Krupp system was considered equal to one of 9 inches of the preceding Harvey/Nickel type – which itself was superior to 14 inches of the previous steel plate. All this happened in ten years. (For warship designers, the obvious advantage gained from this development was that less total weight had to be dedicated to the armour and the balance of the saving could be utilised to improve other aspects of the ship, such as extra armament, fuel capacity and seaworthiness.)

3. It is plain from the tables that not only were the ships of the 1900 German Navy heavily outnumbered in every major category, they were, individually, also considerably inferior to their British contemporaries in almost every respect. It was only after the advent of the *Dreadnought* era that Germany started producing capital ships that were the equal of, and sometimes superior to, their British equivalents. What is absolutely clear from the attached statistics is the enormous gap that would have to be bridged before Germany could possess a viable 'Fleet against England'.

Comparison of the British and German Navies in 1900

GREAT BRITAIN

Modern First Class Battleships

Class	Year	Tons	Guns	Speed (kts)	Armour (Belt/Deck)	Units
Duncan	1899/03	14,000	4-12"; 12-6" guns	19	3-7"/2.5"	6
Formidable	1898/02	15,000	4-12"; 12-6" guns	18	9"/3"	8
Canopus	1897/00	12,900	4-12"; 12-6"guns	18.25	6"/2"	6
Majestic	1894/97	14,950	4-12"; 12-6"guns	17	9"/4"	9
Royal Sovereign	1890/94	14,150	4-13.5"; 10-6"guns	16.5	14-18"/3"	8
Trafalgar	1886/91	12,590	4-13.5"; 6-6" guns	16.75	14-20"/3"	2
					Total	39

Modern Second Class Battleships/Older Battleships

Class	Year	Tons	Guns	Speed (kts)	Armour (Belt/Deck)	Units
Renown	1893/97	12,350	4-10"; 10-6" guns	18	6-8"/2-3"	1
Centurion	1890/94	10,500	4-10"; 10-4.7"guns	18.5	12"/2"	2
Sans Pareil	1885/91	10,470	2-16.25"; 10-6"guns	17	16-18"/3"	1
Benbow	1882/88	10,600	2-16.25"; 10-6"guns	17.4	8-18"/2.5-3"	1
Admiral Class	1882/89	10,600	4-13.5"; 6-6" guns	17.4	8-18"/2.5-3"	4
Collingwood	1880/87	9,500	4-12"; 6-6" guns	15.5	8-18"/2.5"	1
Colossus	1879/86	9,150	4-12"; 5-6" guns	14	14-18"/3"	2
					Total	12

Obsolete/Modernised Third Class Battleships

Class	Year	Tons	Guns	Speed(kts)	Armour (Belt/Deck)	Units
Ajax	1876/83	8,510	4-12.5"ML; 2-6"guns	13	15-18"/3"	2
Inflexible	1874/81	11,880	4-16"ML; 8-4" guns	14.75	16-24"/3"	1
Devastation	1869/75	9,330	4-10" guns	14.2	8.5-12"/2-3"	2
Dreadnought	1870/79	10,886	4-12.5"ML guns	14	8-14"/2.5-3"	1
Superb	1873/80	9,710	12-10"ML; 10-6" guns	14.5	7-12"/1.5"	1
Alexandra	1873/77	9,490	4-9.2"; 8-10"ML; 6-4.7"	15	6-12"/2"	1
Sultan	1868/71	9,290	8-10"ML; 4-9"ML; 4-4.7"	14.5	6-9"/Nil	1
Monarch	1866/69	8,300	4-12"ML; 2-9"ML; 1-7"ML	15.75	4.5-7"/Nil	1
Hercules	1866/68	8,680	8-10"ML; 2-9"ML; 2-6"; 6-4.7"	14.5	6-9"/Nil	1
					Total	11

Coast Defence Ships

Class	Year	Tons	Guns	Speed (kts)	Armour (Belt/Deck)	Units
Conqueror	1879/88	6,200	2-12"; 4-6" guns	14	8-12"/2.5"	2
Rupert	1870/74	5,440	2-9.2"; 2-6" guns	14	9-11"/2-3"	1

There were also nine old monitor type vessels of no military value.   Total   3

GERMANY

Modern First Class Battleships

Class	Year	Tons	Guns	Speed (kts)	Armour (Belt/Deck)	Units
Mecklenburg	1899/02	11,774	4-9.4"; 18-5.9" guns	18	4-9"/2-3"	5
Kaiser	1895/01	10,790	4-9.4"; 14-5.9" guns	18	12"/3"	5
Brandenburg	1890/93	10,013	6-11"; 6-4.1" guns	16	12-15"/2.5"	4
					Total	14

Modern Second Class Battleships/ Older Battleships

Class	Year	Tons	Guns	Speed (kts)	Armour (Belt/Deck)	Units
Sachsen	1874/83	7,400	6-10.2" guns	14	8-10"/2-3"	4
					Total	4

Obsolete/Modernised Third Class Battleships

Class	Year	Tons	Guns	Speed (kts)	Armour (Belt/Deck)	Units
Oldenburg	1883/86	5,652	8-9.4"; 4-5.9" guns	13.5	8-11.75"/Nil	1
Preussen	1869/77	6,821	4-10.2"; 2-7" guns	14	4-9"/Nil	2
Kaiser	1872/75	7,645	8-10.2"; 1-8.2"; 7-5.9"	14.5	5-10"/1.5-2"	2
Konig Wilhelm	1865/69	10,591	18-9.4"; 1-5.9" guns	14.5	6-12"/ 2"	1
					Total	6

Coast Defence Ships

Class	Year	Tons	Guns	Speed (kts)	Armour (Belt/Deck)	Units
Siegfried	1888/94	3,691	3-9.4"; 8-3.4" guns	14.5	7-9.5"/1.25"	6
Odin	1892/96	4,100	3-9.4"; 10-3.4" guns	14.5	7-9"/ 2-2.5"	2
					Total	8

Comparison of the British and German Navies in 1900

GREAT BRITAIN

Armoured Cruisers

Class	Year	Tons	Guns	Speed (kts)	Units
Drake	1899	14,100	2-9.2 inch; 16-6 inch	23	4
Monmouth	1899-01	9,800	14- 6 inch	23	10
Cressy	1898	12,000	2-9.2 inch; 12-6 inch	21	6
Orlando	1884	5,600	2-9.2 inch; 10-6 inch	18	7
Imperieuse	1880	8,500	4-9.2 inch; 10-6 inch	16.75	2
				Total	29

First Class Cruisers

Class	Year	Tons	Guns	Speed (kts)	Units
Powerful	1898	14,200	2-9.2 inch; 16-6 inch	22	2
Andromeda	1895/7	11,000	16 – 6 inch	21	8
Blake	1890	9,150	2-9.2 inch; 10-6 inch	20	2
				Total	12

Second Class Cruisers

Class	Year	Tons	Guns	Speed (kts)	Units
Edgar	1890/2	7,350	2-9.2 inch; 10-6 inch	19	6
Crescent	1892	7,700	1-9.2 inch; 12-6 inch	19	2
Challenger	1900	5,880	11 – 6 inch	21	2
Highflyer	1897	5,600	11 – 6 inch	20	3
Arrogant	1896/9	5,750	10 – 6 inch	19	4
Eclipse	1894/6	5,600	11 – 6 inch	19	9
Leander	1881	4,300	10 – 6 inch	16.5	4
Mersey	1883/5	4,050	2-8inch; 10-6 inch	17	4
				Total	34

Third Class Cruisers

Class	Year	Tons	Guns	Speed (kts)	Units
Astraea	1892	4,360	2-6inch; 8-4.7inch	19	8
Apollo	1890	3,400	2-6inch; 6-4.7inch	18.5	21
Pelorus	1895/8	2,135	8 – 4 inch	19	11
Barham	1889	1,830	6 – 4.7 inch	18	2
Pallas	1888/90	2,575	8 – 4.7 inch	17.5	9
Scout	1885/6	1,580	4 – 4.7 inch	17	2
Archer	1884/7	1,770	6 – 6 inch	17	8
Barracouta	1888	1,580	6 – 4.7 inch	16	4
				Total	65

Destroyers

All Classes   Total   108

Torpedo Boats

All Classes   Total   95

GERMANY

Armoured Cruisers

Class	Year	Tons	Guns	Speed (kts)	Units
Prinz Adalbert	1898/00	10,266	4-8.2 inch; 10-5.9 inch	20	4
Prinz Heinrich	1897	9,806	2-9.4 inch; 10-5.9 inch	20	1
Furst Bismarck	1896	10,690	4-9.4 inch; 12-5.9 inch	18	1
				Total	6

First Class Cruisers

Class	Year	Tons	Guns	Speed (kts)	Units
Vinetta	1896	6,599	2-8.2 inch; 8-5.9 inch	18.5	2
Victoria Louise	1895	6,389	2-8.2 inch; 8-5.9 inch	19.5	3
Kaiserin Augusta	1890	6,218	12-5.9 inch	21	1
				Total	6

Second Class Cruisers

Class	Year	Tons	Guns	Speed (kts)	Units
Gazelle	1898	3,033	10-4.1 inch	21.5	6
Gefion	1892	4,208	10-4.1 inch	19	1
Irene	1886	5,027	4-5.9 inch; 8-4.1 inch	18	2
				Total	9

Third Class Cruisers

Class	Year	Tons	Guns	Speed (kts)	Units
Hela	1893	2,049	4-3.4 inch	20	1
Bussard	1888/93	1,838	8-4.1 inch	15.5	6
Meteor	1888/90	1,055	4-3.4 inch	19	2
Schwalbe	1887/88	1,337	8-4.1 inch	14	2
Wacht	1886/87	1,475	3-4.1 inch	18.5	2
Greif	1885	2,230	2-4.1 inch	19	1
Blitz	1881	1,463	1-5 inch; 4-3.4 inch	16	2
				Total	16

Destroyers

All Classes　　　　　　　　　　　　　　　　　Total　　　　10

Torpedo Boats

All Classes　　　　　　　　　　　　　　　　　Total　　　　106

CHAPTER FOUR

THE NAVAL RACE BEGINS

'There was good reason for the British government to interpret the almost frenzied naval policy of Germany as a threat to herself when the first Navy Bill of 1898 was followed by a second in 1900 of a considerably extended scope, accompanied, as it was, by a virulent and widespread demonstration of hostility throughout the country.'

Admiral Sir Herbert Richmond: *Statesmen and Sea Power*

'Englishmen were not unreasonable in looking for some connexion between the German Naval programme, the anti-English press campaign, and the pan-German movement. The pan-Germans were so extreme in their views and demands that public opinion in England did not take them too seriously. At the same time the pan-Germans were never officially disavowed.'

E.L. Woodward: *Great Britain and the German Navy*

'At the beginning of the twentieth century, Germany possessed all the conditions of sea-power: trade and commerce of world-wide importance...The time was short to make good the delay of years. But we were near to our peaceful goal when a calamitous policy set us at war with the four strongest naval powers of Europe, of whom England alone was doubly our superior.'

Alfred von Tirpitz

The few years either side of the end of the century were to witness a profound change in Britain's relationship with the rest of the world. Gradually she would be constrained by necessity into abandoning her aloofness towards non-imperial affairs, and would have to take an ever more active role in determining the international balance of power. It was not a process that commended itself to many British politicians and diplomats. They had been brought up with a long-engrained, and historically justified, suspicion regarding the motives and ambitions of France and Russia. This was not an attitude that could be discarded lightly or easily (the reverse being equally true). What completely changed the situation was the arrival of Germany on the world scene, and a Germany that was determined to overturn the old status quo. And eventually to dominate.

During this period, German diplomacy, if it could be so dignified by the word, was at best heavy handed, at worst brutal; at all times consistent only in its myopic regard for short-term gain. Perceived interests on the international stage were advanced by implied or open threats to other European powers. These were invariably accompanied (and not always assisted) by intemperate and bellicose speeches from the Kaiser. Concessions were not a feature of this policy.

On the face of it, German confidence in the strength of her position was not unfounded. On the continent, her incomparable army underpinned the military supremacy of the Triple Alliance with Austria and Italy (the latter a recent adherent) over the forces of France and Russia. In any case, as one lingering residue of Bismarck's policy, Russo-German relations were close and amicable on most matters. Great Britain, the only other nation of consequence, seemed to have permanent, and irreconcilable, differences with the two latter states, her traditional adversaries in Europe, and now rivals everywhere in the colonial sphere.

The policy of the British Government of the time, as formulated by the long-serving Prime Minister and Foreign Secretary, Lord Salisbury, was enunciated as being that of 'Splendid Isolation'; that is, the avoidance of diplomatic entanglements with any particular power bloc. This oversimplifies the situation. Salisbury expended an enormous amount of his time and energy in trying to maintain good relations with the continental powers. He had a particularly good relationship with Bismarck.

'...British policy was in the hands of a man Bismarck trusted...Bismarck signalled his approval to everyone. "I value Lord Salisbury's friendship more than twenty swamp colonies in Africa."' (1)

Britain never shackled its future decisively to one or the other of the European blocs. The British people as a whole, without comprehending the immense complications that underlay their nation's foreign policy, took pride in this ability to remain aloof from the squabbles and political compromises that were, perforce, attendant on the less fortunately endowed and situated countries of the mainland. The apocryphal news report that fog in the English Channel had cut the continent off from Britain well describes the attitude of the time. The pre-eminence of the Royal Navy was considered sufficient to ensure the security of an empire that did not intrude into the problematic sphere of the continent. Overseas, only the naval resources of France and Russia required to be taken into consideration. It was a simplistic view, but, for many generations, it was one that had been based on a valid premise.

As the century drew to a close, the continued viability of this policy and attitude became increasingly open to question. Not only was the situation becoming complicated by other major nations, such as the United States and Japan, in addition to Germany, emerging as players on the world stage, but second echelon states that had previously possessed no noteworthy naval forces were developing significant maritime capabilities. Brazil, Argentina and Chile were typical of this process, and their rivalry on the South American continent produced, in miniature, a similar naval race to that in Europe and elsewhere. It would no longer be possible for a small detachment of minor vessels to guarantee British interests in either the Americas or the Far East. To preserve Britain's position, either these forces would need to be greatly reinforced, at prohibitive cost, or some accommodation would need to be made with one or more of the other interested states.

From the early 1880s, in fact, Britain's maritime supremacy had been steadily eroded from a position in which her battleship strength was roughly equal to that of the rest of the world, to the point where these vessels comprised less than 40% of the overall total.

'In other words, in 1883 the number of British battleships almost equalled the total of all the other powers combined (thirty-eight to forty); by 1897 this comfortable ratio had shrivelled away (sixty-two to ninety-six)...In retrospect the historian can perceive that the Diamond Jubilee celebrations of 1897 did not denote the zenith of Britain's power, but constituted rather the defiant swan-song of a nation becoming less and less complacent about the increasing threats to its world wide interests. The real apogee of British might had occurred somewhere in the middle of the century; now it was a time, as many politicians and certain other perceptive persons realized, for strenuous efforts and decisive actions to meet the challenges of the coming century when Britain could no longer rely upon those advantages which Palmerston had taken for granted.' (2)

It was still a relatively comfortable position, as the likelihood of having to confront the whole of the remainder of the world at any one time was implausible in the extreme, but the trend of the statistics was there for all to see. The era of Pax Britannica, at least in its naval sense, was inexorably drawing to a close.

For a while, Berlin was able to milk this situation to some advantage, emphasising Britain's relative weakness in terms of allies to extract territorial and commercial concessions in Africa and the Pacific. The German approach was crude, and usually on the lines of, 'Look, we are your only friend in the world; you cannot afford to offend us'. The carrot of future German goodwill in the face of perpetual French and Russian antagonism abroad, was allied to the stick of the possible withdrawal of this benevolence should Germany not continue to be constantly humoured. As a policy this could only succeed for so long as the goodwill was seen to be genuinely attainable as opposed to an ever-receding hypothetical objective. As it was, this form of diplomatic blackmail, not being a particularly amicable form of behaviour, caused considerable irritation in Britain (even the normally emollient Salisbury was goaded into telling the German ambassador that 'you demand too much for your friendship'). That one side always seemed to be the giver and the other the taker had an obvious corollary in that it led to a growing awareness in Whitehall circles that isolation was becoming less splendid, if not positively inimitable to the best interests of the empire.

'The simplistic remedy of increasing the defence budget until Britain's navy and army were capable of satisfying all the demands which were placed on them was financially impossible; and the coming of the Boer War, with the subsequent exposures of the military unpreparedness and inadequacy of generalship, meant that the navy was once again likely to take a back seat to the army in the estimates. The policy of throwing Britain into one of the European alliance blocs, though it appealed to Joseph Chamberlain, contained grave disadvantages and was opposed by many, including the Prime Minister, Salisbury.' (3)

In the circumstances, and as the effectiveness of the aging Salisbury began to wane, influential voices began to be heard advocating the need for Britain to at least develop closer relationships, if not formal alliances, with those of the powers against whom she was unlikely to be in contention, and with whom some commonality of interest could be discerned. Ironically, the first efforts in that direction were to be directed towards Germany.

Most notable amongst the advocates for a change of direction in British policy was the Secretary of State for the Colonies, Joseph Chamberlain, who occupied a position of power in the government second only to that of the Prime Minister. Salisbury himself had never evinced much enthusiasm in affairs outside Europe, but, as the metaphoric tectonic plates of the expanding overseas empires began to rub against one another, potential upheavals in international relations increasingly were to be found in the colonial sphere. There became a real risk that a major war between the European powers could be ignited by disputes over sovereignty or commercial rights in little known and insignificant tracts of real estate in Africa and Asia. Chamberlain's portfolio covered these regions, and Salisbury had granted him wide latitude to deal with, and be responsible for, all matters concerning those areas. As Salisbury's abilities declined, Chamberlain's forceful personality, great powers of argument, and huge electoral popularity, ensured that he would become a crucial factor in the formulation and application of British foreign policy.

The two men were the antithesis of each other, and their personal relationship was never more than cool. Whilst Salisbury's critics accused him of being too passive or appeasing in the defence of British interests he was, in fact, a most consummate practitioner of the art of 'masterly inactivity' and low-key diplomacy. Chamberlain, by contrast saw every problem as needing an immediate, and high profile, fix. There is no doubt that Salisbury's approach was the more sensible, but he despised the common voter and bitterly regretted the necessity to pander to the 'mob' and the popular press. Chamberlain was the product of a new age, and recognised the need to appeal far more to a demanding media and to the more excitable, fickle, and less cerebral, elements of the electorate. Salisbury was appalled by what he saw as the destruction of what had been rational government by an unpaid but devoted elite, and its capitulation to the fleeting whims and fads of a turbulent and ill-informed majority. Unable either by character or inclination to deal with the change in political circumstances, Salisbury was, by necessity, forced to rely on Chamberlain and his likes to garner popular support for his administration.

'Joe' Chamberlain was what would be considered, in this day and age, an anomaly. He was a Liberal Imperialist. The price for his involvement in the basically Conservative government of Lord Salisbury was the introduction into law of what would now be considered socialist legislation. Under his auspices, the foundations of free education and old age pensions were pushed through a not entirely willing parliament. On the other side of the coin, he was passionate in his belief that the preservation and consolidation of the British Empire was of vital importance to the world. He envisaged an English-speaking union of Britain, her dominions, and, eventually, the United States, that would guarantee peace, prosperity, enlightened administration and civilised behaviour throughout the globe. In 1896, this powerful (he was the single most popular politician in the United Kingdom) and able minister came to the conclusion that isolation was no longer a viable option for Great Britain, and that she would have to seek allies amongst the other world powers.

The light on the road to Damascus, as far as Chamberlain was concerned, was the furore emanating from the Jameson Raid into the Transvaal.[1] In the aftermath of that embarrassing fiasco, Britain was subjected to blanket condemnation internationally, no more virulently so than in Germany. The Kaiser, acting both on the spur of the moment, as was his wont and, unusually, also with the encouragement of his foreign office, sent a telegram to the President of Transvaal, congratulating him on the success of his forces. When this communication subsequently became public knowledge, the heat generated by the 'Kruger Telegram', led to a crisis in Anglo-German relations, and a first slow awakening in Britain as to the depth of feeling against her in Germany.

Initially, Chamberlain had favoured an aggressive reaction to the Kaiser's indiscretion, but, in retrospect, he adopted a more sober attitude and drew a worried conclusion. Britain, when challenged, had no friends.

---

[1] In 1895, with the connivance of Cecil Rhodes, his close friend Dr. Leander Starr Jameson gathered together a small volunteer force in Natal and rode into the Transvaal. The objective was to support a planned insurrection amongst the disenfranchised British workers labouring in the gold and diamond mines of the Witwatersrand. The whole enterprise backfired when the rising failed to take place, and Jameson's little force was soon rounded up by the Transvaal authorities. The fiasco served no purpose whatsoever except to inflame relations with the Boers, and thus significantly contribute to the outbreak of formal hostilities four years later.

No help had been expected from France or Russia, but the Transvaal affair had brought confrontation with a power Britain had reckoned, if not amiable, at least not actively unfriendly – Germany. Speaking in March 1896, Chamberlain told his audience that '...the shadow of war *did* darken the horizon' in recent months. The cause, he said, was the '...isolation of the United Kingdom'. (4) Despite the Kruger Telegram, from this moment on Chamberlain began to campaign for closer ties with Germany. On three occasions, in 1898, 1899 and 1901, he made tentative approaches to the German Government as to forming a mutually beneficial alliance. He was probably the only British politician with the clout to deliver such an agreement. On each occasion, his efforts were rebuffed, principally due to lack of commitment on the part of the German Chancellor, encouraged by Tirpitz, who needed Britain as a bogeyman to justify his great fleet-building programmes.

It was the misfortune of both nations that the Chancellorship of Germany was, at that critical time, in the hands of a singularly shallow and cynical opportunist.

On Bismarck's fall, Caprivi, the erstwhile head of the navy, had reluctantly taken his place until succeeded by Prince Chlodwig zu Hohenlohe, an aged and frail aristocrat from a family as old as the Hohenzollerns themselves. Although a sensible and rational old man, he had neither the energy nor the inclination to deal with the rumbustious Kaiser on one hand or an uncooperative *Reichstag* on the other. Hohenlohe was content to plod his world-weary way between the two until released from his unwelcome task in 1897, at about the same time as Tirpitz took over as State Secretary of the Navy. His replacement, Bernhard von Bülow, was to deal with the British initiatives, and his influence was disastrous. The new Chancellor, for all his many abilities, was not the man to preside over matters of such potential import, despite impressive credentials. Given a generally free hand as State Secretary for Foreign Affairs under Hohenlohe he had effectively been in charge of the conduct of German foreign policy for some time. That he failed to capitalise on this experience as Chancellor can be put down to several flaws in his character. Bülow would have made a wonderful ambassador anywhere but he lacked the depth, vision, and grit to occupy the highest posts of government. He was, however, eminently well-equipped to deal with the Kaiser's love of flattery and praise, and, being more practically clever than his sovereign, could use this gift to manipulate Wilhelm's opinions and decisions. Robert K. Massie sums him up as follows:

'It was said of Bernhard von Bülow that he possessed every quality except greatness. Chancellor of the German Empire for nine years, State Secretary for Foreign Affairs for the three previous years, he was the most elegant cosmopolitan figure produced in Imperial Germany. Bülow was a consummate diplomat, urbane and polished, a man of wide culture who spoke several languages flawlessly and moved effortlessly in international society. As a politician, he dazzled even his political opponents with an endless outpouring of classical quotations, discreet jokes, and polished, charming repartee. He was a patriotic German who loved Paris and preferred Italy to most parts of Germany, especially Berlin...

The façade was splendid. Behind lay the driving forces of Bülow's life: vanity and ambition. The characteristics of his work were laziness and cynicism. He grappled ruthlessly for power, but once it was in his possession, he ignored his duties, despised details, and left his subordinates to find their own way...He practised flattery as a high art, lathering and coating with layers of charm, but as soon as the back was turned, he let his malicious tongue dart forth to lacerate and ridicule the object just flattered...For twelve years, German foreign policy lay in the hands of a man who lacked purpose, scruples, courage, and a vision of his own.

People close to Bülow, watching his slippery passage through life were fascinated and repelled by what they saw. Alfred von Kiderlen Waechter, Political Counsellor at the Foreign Office called Bülow "an eel"; on hearing this, Tirpitz snorted that compared to Bülow "an eel is a leech".' (5)

Bülow's personality suited the Kaiser perfectly. The latter's susceptibility to sycophants made him an easy conquest for the former's well-honed talent for judicious flattery, and Bülow took care to adopt only attitudes and policies that found favour with his sovereign. Professor Gordon Craig amplifies Massie's remarks:

'Bülow managed to retain his sovereign's confidence and affection not only for the three years during which Hohenlohe clung stubbornly to office, but for most of the decade that followed his assumption of the old man's place. It is no exaggeration to say that he worked harder at keeping himself in the Emperor's good graces, upon which he knew that his position was absolutely dependent, than he did at any other aspect of his office, and he did not hesitate to employ the most Byzantine forms of flattery to achieve his purpose.' (6)

His flaws rapidly became apparent to many in the upper circles of the German hierarchy, but his influence with Wilhelm was, for a long while, so powerful as to render him impervious to their concerns.

From the first, Bülow was aware of the Kaiser's preoccupation with the fleet, and so happily supported the machinations of Tirpitz, regardless of the consequences, until almost the end of his tenure of office. This refusal to interfere in naval policy was an abdication of responsibility that was to blight relations with Great Britain throughout his occupation of the Chancellorship.

Of all the miscalculations that littered German policy over this period, the attitude of Bülow, supported by his Foreign Office, towards Britain makes the sorriest reading. Certain that Germany was in the driving seat as far as relations with Britain were concerned, he first encouraged, then subsequently snubbed, Chamberlain's overtures, convinced that the longer he procrastinated, the stronger would become Germany's bargaining position.

In his view that Britain's long-term differences with France and Russia were irreconcilable, he was hardly alone. Few in Britain, at the turn of the century, would have disagreed with him, but his blasé assumption that this state of affairs would always be so, and that he could afford to deal with cynical opportunism towards such a powerful empire, is a crushing indictment of his conduct of office. Within a very few years the disparate triumvirate of the Kaiser, Bülow and Tirpitz would destroy Germany's hard won position of pre-eminence within Europe. By a combination of ignorance, arrogance and incompetence, between them they turned what had seemed to be a position of unassailable strength into one of chronic isolation and weakness. Bismarck must have turned in his grave.

The outbreak of the Boer War, in October 1899, was the prelude to a radical reshaping of the world's political map. If the reverberations from the Jameson raid had brought home to Britain how isolated was her position, the effects were now multiplied tenfold. The European powers were unanimously opposed to Britain, and the reaction in the continental press was an explosion of abuse and venom. In Germany, public opinion was wholeheartedly in support of the Boers, with whom they shared a racial and cultural background. Anti-British sentiment swept the nation and was given the most violent expression in speeches and newspapers. The Kaiser characteristically took a lead in broadcasting these feelings.

For the naval lobby in Germany, the climate of opinion was a heaven-sent opportunity to advance its cause. The inability of Germany to influence overseas events, about which the nation as a whole felt so strongly, placed a spotlight on the impotence of the existing naval forces when faced with the might of the British Fleet.

Ideally, Tirpitz would have wanted the greatest possible time to elapse between him saying 'Go', in 1898, and the general realisation in Britain that a naval arms race had started. However, the course of events now presented an opportunity that might never recur. In January 1900, British warships detained three German merchant vessels suspected of carrying contraband to the Boers. The ships were released after search, but the incident provoked fury in Germany, and Tirpitz, seizing his chance, instantly drafted a new Navy Bill, greatly increasing the future strength of the fleet:

'The seizure of German Imperial packet steamers by the English about the end of the year then introduced an element of national feeling into the pro-Boer enthusiasm of the German public, already regrettably high; this facilitated, however, at the beginning of 1900, the introduction of the supplementary Bill to which the Emperor was persistently and impetuously urging me. Moreover, thanks to the co-operation of the political economists, public opinion was much stronger in our favour than even we had hoped.' (7)

The bill 'swept through the *Reichstag* on a tide of patriotism' (8) and became law in June of 1900.

The new Navy Bill effectively authorised the doubling of the German Navy as compared to its envisaged strength of only two years previously. There could no longer be any disguising the fact that a deliberate challenge to British maritime supremacy was being mounted. The published preface to the second Navy Law left little to be deduced. Tirpitz states in his memoirs that:

'When working out the second Navy Bill, we hesitated for a long time whether or not to bring the idea of the English menace into the preamble. I should have preferred to have left England out of it altogether. But such an unusual demand as was presented here, namely, the doubling of our small naval force, made it scarcely possible to avoid hinting at the real reason for it.' (9)

Amongst other references that clearly indicated Great Britain as the potential opponent, the comment was made that, 'To protect Germany's sea trade and colonies...Germany must have a battle fleet so strong that even for the adversary with the *Greatest Seapower* [my italics], a war against it would involve such dangers as to imperil its own position in the world.' (10) The *Risk Theory* had been spelt out in public, and Tirpitz's, and the Kaiser's, ambitions were now in the open.

With this virtual declaration of intent, there came also the fear that a real peril existed to the fleet before the plans for its expansion could take effect. It was seriously considered that, Britain perceiving the threat to her position, might make a pre-emptive strike on the German Navy whilst she could still do so without detriment to her overall maritime supremacy. This element of danger to both powers was a double-headed axe that effectively created the Great Naval Race.

'Along with the risk to Britain of offensive action, and unacceptable losses at the hands of a powerful German fleet, there was also the risk to Germany that Britain, fearing the growing threat of German sea power, might not wait until the mighty German fleet was completed, but would first strike its own offensive blow. History offered precedent for such behaviour.' (11)

The quote clearly refers to Nelson's action against the Danish fleet in 1801, and to the subsequent action of Lord Gambier in confiscating the remains of that nation's navy in 1807. 'Copenhagening' the German Fleet was a phrase used by the more irresponsible organs of the British press at the time, and due note was taken in Germany of what could only be regarded as a confirmation of their own worst perceptions.

A new key phrase was now coined. Tirpitz termed the period of insecurity, before the German Fleet could be brought to a level where it could no longer be 'Copenhagened' with impunity, as the 'Danger Zone'.

He calculated in 1900 that the Danger Zone would be passed in four or five years, when the ships authorised under the first Naval Law had all been commissioned into service. This assessment could only have been based on the assumption that Britain would not react to German naval expansion during that period – which seems extremely naïve for a man in his position. The second Naval Law had removed any ambiguity from the German programme, and the British reaction was entirely predictable.

'The psychological background which prepared the English to distrust a powerful German fleet was the estrangement growing out of the Kruger telegram, the commercial rivalry whose acuteness began to be felt in 1896, and the violent anti-English tone of many sections of the German press after 1895.' (12)

The sense of a growing threat from Germany had become apparent, and a parallel programme of construction was commenced with the specific objective of maintaining an adequate margin of superiority over the perceived future strength of the German Navy, and perpetuating the 'two powers plus 10%' principle of determining Britain's naval needs. This, though, would demand a painful, and politically inconvenient, increment to the annual British naval estimates.

'The balance of naval power was threatened in another way. It was foreseen that Germany's new programme would automatically lead to corresponding efforts by France and Russia, and thus force upon England an ever increasing naval expenditure.' (13)

After 1900, it gradually became clear to British naval authorities that a major future challenge to the empire's maritime predominance was far more likely to emerge from Germany, with her much more advanced military/industrial establishment, than from her traditional enemies. By 1905 the political *entente* with France and the destruction of the Russian Navy in the Japanese conflict had entirely removed both these nations as a potential opponent.

'The question which then arose was the manner in which the established British naval policy of a Two-Power Standard was to be interpreted. The United States had always been specifically excluded from the calculations, Japan was an ally, there was the entente with France; and, though Italy was a member of the Triple Alliance, the possibility of her acting against England could then be discounted. The Austrian navy was small, though not negligible. So, though for the next few years ministers continued to assert that the Two-Power Standard was being, and would continue to be, maintained, the shipbuilding programme was directed towards meeting the German challenge.' (14)

Henceforth, the spotlight would increasingly focus on the development of the German High Seas Fleet, and successive increments to Tirpitz's original naval bills emphasised the sense of foreboding. The threat

The Naval Race Begins

from this new quarter was taken extremely seriously – more so, in fact, than in the past when the relative efficiency of the French and Russian Fleets, whatever their strength on paper, was not usually well-regarded. There was no such sense of complacency when it came to assessing the capabilities of the German Navy.

'More than passing attention was bestowed upon the naval bill in its own right. The German Navy, even before the expansion programmes of 1898 and 1900, had an enviable reputation. The high quality of its ships and personnel, the efficiency of the organisation, and the excellent mobilisation arrangements were testified to by all English experts.' (15)

Effectively, the alarm bells were ringing in the British Admiralty, with steadily greater volume, as from the Second Navy Bill. With the advent of Fisher, as First Sea Lord, in 1904, this unease was translated into a single-minded crusade to stymie the ambitions of Wilhelm II and Tirpitz to build a 'Fleet against England'. Successive naval programmes were approved to ensure that, not only did they match those of its new adversary, but would increase the disproportion in strength between the two navies. Fisher's reforms to his own navy, and the introduction of the *Dreadnought* battleship as the definition of a nation's naval power completely changed the situation.

By 1909, Tirpitz's Danger Zone had not disappeared; rather it had been, by his own assessment, extended to 1915. There can be few more telling admissions of failure than to allow that, after nine years of immense expenditure and effort, his policies had resulted in his country having lost ground as compared with its self-imposed rival. Despite his undoubted intellectual powers, Tirpitz was incapable of acknowledging the failure of his policies, not even to himself. Nor, as it turned out, was he capable of re-positioning himself politically when his star began to set. His memoirs constitute a record of self-righteousness and justification (not unusual in memoirs) – and of pique at the inability of others to see matters from his point of view. In lesser players on the world stage, his attitudes would have been of peripheral importance. In the unique position of influence that he held, at a critical time, they were crucial to the course of Anglo-German relations; and to the alignment of powers in the great struggle to come.

One last, eleventh hour, opportunity for an Anglo-German alliance occurred in 1901. Twice led on by Bülow and abandoned at the altar, Chamberlain made one final effort to forge an Anglo-German compact. In doing so he was acting against the wishes and instincts (and knowledge) of sections of his own party, many of whom were slowly awakening to the fact of overt German public hostility and a provocative naval expansion programme.

With no absolute guarantee of being able to carry his colleagues with him, but confident in his political base, he once more made overtures to Bülow.

This time, there was an added factor. The strategic groupings of the other great powers were becoming more firmly defined and increasingly polarised against each other. Britain's ability to influence world events, despite her colossal empire, and still pre-eminent sea power, was lessened, if not positively threatened, by the power projection potential of these coalescing blocs.

The abilities and energy of the aging, isolationist Prime Minister, Salisbury, were in sharp decline and it was clear to discerning political observers that the days of 'Splendid Isolation' for Great Britain were numbered. When that time arrived, it was equally clear that there were only two viable options for Britain. Either she would have to align with the Triple Alliance of Germany, Austria, and Italy, or make her peace with France and Russia. Chamberlain believed that the former choice was preferable, but it was clear to German diplomats in London that, if this approach failed again, it was likely that Britain would turn to the latter option – despite the enormous historical and political difficulties that would be consequent to that course of action. The adherence of Britain to either bloc was utterly crucial to the overall balance of power. Germany, already predominant in Europe, would become unassailable with Britain on board. That predominance would vanish if Britain were added to the number of her potential opponents. The German Embassy passed their views repeatedly to Berlin as the third Chamberlain initiative unfolded. Their opinions were largely ignored, and there was, in any case, little chance of its success.

The German Chancellor, with the strong concurrence of Holstein in the Foreign Office could not accept that there was any prospect of Britain settling her differences with either France or Russia, which were, admittedly, grave and of long standing. He was convinced that Britain would be eventually forced by the intractability of these disputes to seek an alliance with Germany come what may, and on the latter's terms. In the meantime he was still infatuated by his vision of obtaining all manner of territorial and political concessions by simply dangling the carrot of a future Anglo-German alliance in front of the British, whilst being fully party to the Kaiser and Tirpitz's plan for a 'navy against England'. It was not fertile ground for the planting of Chamberlain's diplomatic seeds. Nevertheless, negotiations recommenced in the autumn of 1900 and were still in intermittent progress when the health of Queen Victoria began to fail.

The Queen Empress had actually been in terminal decline throughout 1900. The initial setbacks in the Boer War had affected her seriously, and, although the war situation had been turned around by the spring, the strain had taken its toll on the eighty-one year old monarch. She genuinely cared about the soldiers who fought under her colours, and felt their losses deeply. Many of the troops who had signed up for the war had come from Ireland, and Victoria resolved to make clear her appreciation of their sacrifices.

In April she embarked on a month long visit to Ireland, in the face of determined opposition from all her advisors, who feared for her safety, and the effect on her health. Not for the first time, the Queen had a better measure of her subjects than their elected representatives. The Irish, many of whom were implacably opposed to the monarchy as an institution, gave a wonderful reception to the old lady whose single-minded devotion to duty, and sense of responsibility to her people, had dignified and adorned her long reign. It was a case of 'the singer, not the song', and a remarkable tribute to someone who had never consciously courted popularity, and to whom the word 'charisma' would have been utterly distasteful. Although it was not then apparent, she was about to leave the stage for the last time. That she was to depart to an ovation from such an audience would surely have gladdened her heart.

The Queen also had a sense of occasion, and, at the time of her visit, she instituted the now renowned Irish Guards as a regiment of the elite Brigade of Guards. She also decreed that the shamrock should be worn by Irish soldiers of the Crown on St. Patrick's Day. This might not seem a huge matter now, but it was of enormous significance then, as it was an emblem of Ireland as an individual entity.

The visit to Ireland was to be her last major public appearance. If concerns for her safety had been unfounded, those for her health were only too well-justified. Her subsequent decline was rapid, and made more painful by personal circumstances.

Alfred, Duke of Edinburgh, her second son, died of the same cancer that had killed her son-in-law, Kaiser Friedrich, and it was clear that Vicky, her eldest daughter and widow of Friedrich, was also terminally ill with another variant of the terrible disease. These family tragedies were dreadful blows to the Queen's morale when she must have started to become aware that her own health was failing.

Throughout the summer she continued to deteriorate. By the autumn she was visibly wasting away, though still faithfully and punctually carrying out her state responsibilities. A week before Christmas, and by then very obviously ill, she travelled from Windsor Castle to Osborne House, the residence that she and her beloved Albert had built on the Isle of Wight. For a few weeks more she continued to carry out her duties and receive officials and dignitaries of state, but on January 17th 1901 it became apparent that she was close to death.

On the 18th, the German Embassy in London telegraphed Berlin with the news. The Kaiser immediately cancelled all commitments and, on his own initiative, set off for England, cabling ahead that he wanted no ceremony as he was coming as a grandson, not an emperor.

In the events that followed, Wilhelm behaved impeccably, and the best aspects of his personality came to the fore. The wardrobe of glittering uniforms was forgotten along with the vainglorious posturing. Gone were the *braggadocio*, ostentation and aggressive self-esteem that had often characterised his life. He was at all times considerate to the wishes of the family, supportive and caring, remaining in the background when required, and being of whatever service he could as the situation demanded. It was certainly not an act. He came to the old Queen's deathbed exactly as he had promised; 'Grandson not Kaiser', and, in the process, his demeanour enabled him to rediscover the warmth of his family ties and endeared him to the country as a whole.

Victoria, Queen of Great Britain, and of all its dominions and possessions, and Empress of India, died just after six o'clock in the evening of 22nd January, attended and supported by Wilhelm II, King of Prussia and Emperor of Germany. It was a moment that marked a turning point in his life, and also with his relationship with Britain (or England, as Wilhelm would always have it). With his grandmother gone, the Kaiser's most enduring tie to Britain was severed. Nevertheless, in the aftermath of her death, he came as close as he ever managed to gaining the acceptance, in her country, that he so much cherished.

A remarkable thaw in the previously frosty relationship between Wilhelm and his uncle, the new King Edward VII, took place as a result of their contact during the last hours of the Queen. When Edward departed for London for constitutional purposes, he delegated Wilhelm to oversee Osborne in his absence. It was an enormous gesture of trust on his part, and Wilhelm responded accordingly. He cancelled his return to Germany and announced to his government that he would be remaining in Britain until after the funeral of the Queen.

In Berlin, this decision was greeted with the utmost dismay. The Chancellor, and all the state officials, knowing their Emperor's emotional nature, feared, with good reason, that the consequences of his personal involvement might produce complications that could derail their overall strategy towards Britain. Particularly frustrating was the fact that, as this was a private family visit, there could be no excuse for him being accompanied and guided by ministers of state. His government had to remain in Berlin in a state of impotent anxiety as to what diplomatic initiatives Wilhelm might take upon himself in a newfound spirit of Anglophilia. No one in Germany seems to have considered that the personal warmth and closeness generated by Wilhelm's presence in England could well have been to the long-term advantage of their nation. In any case, Wilhelm was adamant. He would stay. This was a seminal moment in his life.

Robert K. Massie's description of the occasion has both sympathy and pertinence:

'On no one – not even on her heir – did this loss have greater impact than on the Kaiser. In spite of all, the emotional link between them had never been broken. He was her eldest grandchild, she was his august, but also warmhearted Grandmama. The happiest days of his youth had been spent in the relatively informal atmosphere of Osborne and Windsor, an atmosphere dominated by the personality of the Queen. As the years went by, he never gave up his feeling of tenderness for his aging grandmother and respect for the Queen-Empress. She scolded him, but she also showed him affection and understanding. She criticized him to her ministers, but she also stood up for him, advising Lord Salisbury and others on how to deal with him. In many ways, she was like him: both were sentimental, subject to strong likes and dislikes, capable of gushiness and sharp anger in writing to subordinates. Because Victoria had had Albert and a series of independent prime ministers, she had learned to discipline her feelings and language, as William never had. As long as she lived, she posed for William a model of how an Imperial sovereign should behave. When she died, that model vanished...And so, at forty-two, the Kaiser was left alone to follow his own path, bereft of the presence, the counsel, and the affection of the one human he admired as well as loved.' (16)

Who is to know what might have been accomplished? In the spring of 1901, the *mood* of the British people had been captivated by the Kaiser. Possibly – very probably – it would not have lasted if the German Fleet expansion had continued, but a window of opportunity briefly opened for a better relationship between the two countries. Wilhelm realised this, and telegraphed his government to that effect, causing much consternation in Berlin.

The window was firmly closed by the subsequent actions of the German Government. On such moments do the fates of nations hang. Two years later, the new King Edward VII would visit France, also against the wishes of his government. In a few weeks of skilful informal diplomacy, he converted the *mood* of the French nation from hatred and confrontation into one of unaccustomed benevolence. *This* window, once opened, was immediately padlocked in position by a British administration that took full advantage of the opportunity conveniently provided by their monarch.

Once returned to Berlin, Wilhelm's fleeting personal rapprochement with England was rapidly eroded by the manipulative influences that immediately closed again around him and stifled, finally, any realistic chance of a thaw in Anglo-German relations. These influences were not confined to a myopic government and public opinion. His wife, the stolid, humourless, and intellectually-limited Empress, detested the English side of his family, and the British as a whole. His new mood stood little chance of surviving the joint onslaught, and, in any case, his ambition to possess a fleet capable of challenging that of Britain was unwavering, and that, on its own, would have rendered any long-term agreement with Britain highly unlikely. Robert K. Massie's conclusions tend to support this view:

'The Kaiser did not wish to fight the Royal Navy and he never dreamed of invading the British Isles. He was building a fleet to proclaim Germany's Imperial grandeur, to make the world listen respectfully to the German Emperor, and, above all, to earn England's approval and reduce German dependence on England's favour on the oceans of the world. Because the British Navy was so much stronger, he regarded British complaints about the size of his fleet as impertinent and offensive.' (17)

Wilhelm, unfortunately, could not see that this attitude could not be viewed in isolation from the much more sinister motives of the pan-German nationalists and their supporters in the *Reichstag*. Whilst he could be content with the existence of a large battle fleet as a symbol of German might and his own glory, there were powerful influences within his realm that had much more aggressive intents for its use once it had attained a critical level of strength.

During the protracted and tortuous build up to the world conflict that would break out in 1914 many more efforts would be initiated to try for some rapprochement between the two countries, but 1901 represented the last realistic opportunity for a formal alliance before the rapidly increasing strength of the German Navy imposed an insuperable barrier to any general agreement. This opportunity was finally killed off by a completely impractical German proposal that Britain should join the Triple Alliance and thus be committed to going to war if Russia should attack Austria. Salisbury, in his last effective contribution to foreign policy, roused himself and squashed any consideration of the offer. Chamberlain had already lost patience with Berlin, and, in autumn, the situation descended into acrimony when, in defending British tactics against the Boers in South Africa he suggested that criticism from abroad was unacceptable from countries guilty of much more 'barbaric' behaviour. He instanced the Franco-Prussian conflict among others, and this caused an uproar in Germany. Bülow replied with a vitriolic speech in the *Reichstag* that left diplomatic relations in tatters.

'Bülow's action was also symptomatic because it once again revealed that, faced with a choice of either offending the domestic Anglophobes or annoying the British, he would always plump for the latter. From this time onwards, the bulk of British politicians and press came to regard Bülow with such dislike and suspicion (sometimes contrasting this with Wilhelm's erratic but evident regard for things English) that his continuance in office alone may be said to have constituted a stumbling–block to improved Anglo-German relations in the future. The Chancellor's firm determination to make a strong speech in the Reichstag against Chamberlain and thereby to secure popularity among the agrarians and Pan-

Germans was regarded with dismay by Metternich in London and by Holstein...who sought in vain to dissuade him from this action. Although Bülow gained his domestic-political aim, his "granite speech" had driven a further nail into the coffin of Anglo-German friendship. It was, one Berlin observer felt, "Bülow's first great mistake."' (18)

Between them, Chamberlain, with his predilection for high profile 'instant fixes', and Bülow, the poor man's Machiavelli, had contrived to place a heavy burden on those politicians who were to inherit their legacy.

The failure of the 1900/01 talks was probably preordained. Any formal links between Britain and the German-dominated Triple Alliance would have been disproportionately advantageous to the latter, and would have ensured that Britain became a tied subordinate to Germany in the European sphere, whilst also losing ground to that nation worldwide. It would have been the absolute negation of what had been, for the previous three centuries, traditional British policy towards the continent.

There is a clear irony here. It was by supporting Prussia (amongst others) as a weaker power that the ambitions of Napoleon and Louis XIV towards a continental hegemony were thwarted, and the independence of both Prussia and Britain preserved. The situation was now reversed.

Lest the above precept be questioned, it is only necessary to look at the overwhelming manpower, manufacturing capability, and military capacity on land and sea that could be deployed by a nation that had actually managed to achieve hegemony in Europe. Against these resources, Britain could not have long survived as an independent entity. Even with the total mobilisation of her population, confronted by these odds, British naval predominance could not have been long maintained, nor the empire, which had been built and sustained by that predominance, held.

In 1901, had Britain thrown in her lot with Germany, the hegemony of the latter in Europe would have been virtually guaranteed, with all that this implied. That it did not occur is largely due to the cynical short-term policies of Bülow, the naval ambitions of Tirpitz and his Kaiser, and the manufactured public hostility to Britain generated by extreme nationalistic propaganda dating back to the Bismarck era. When, eight years afterwards, a new German Chancellor attempted to re-establish a dialogue on the subject, the moment had passed. Britain had by then committed herself, however reluctantly, to other attachments and there was no way back. This result was almost entirely due to the actions and attitudes of German leaders. During this period the prescience of the British Government, bar old Salisbury, was not greatly in evidence as a factor.

'The years 1900-2 witnessed a steady deterioration in the relations of the two peoples and the two governments, thereby preparing the great majority of Englishmen to see an immediate threat in the Kaiser's naval plans. The German press and many speakers violently condemned the "buccaneering adventure" in

South Africa, insulted the British army as "mercenaries", and slandered the Queen in gross caricatures. It was in Germany that the British reverses in South Africa were hailed with the most joy. The attitude of the German government was technically correct during the war, but the persistency with which it took advantage of Britain's preoccupation elsewhere to press its claims was deeply resented in England. There was a growing suspicion of German aims. In short, English opinion was becoming unpleasantly Teutophobe. This drift was intensified after the death of Queen Victoria in January 1901.' (19)

The situation was changing beyond recognition, and the dangers inherent in the growing power of Germany were being belatedly recognised by the British establishment, and were coming to the forefront of public debate. This national consciousness of the menace posed by increasing German power was transmitted to the government via the populace, rather than vice versa. From 1902 onwards, the issue of German naval expansion, and the measures necessary to combat the perceived threat, were to become a permanent feature in British political life. It was embarrassingly proved, in 1909, to a pacifistic Liberal government attempting to fund radical social change, that even those most likely to benefit from their policies would not do so to the exclusion of the naval budget. The German naval challenge would be met whatever the sacrifices required in other aspects of British life. During the critical period of the naval race, it would also be impelled and co-ordinated by a personality whose transformation of the British naval establishment would prove to be as profound as that Alfred von Tirpitz had effected in Germany.

CHAPTER FIVE

FISHER

'When Fisher came to power in the Royal Navy, the service which had held back Napoleon's Grand Army a century earlier and changed the face of Europe at Trafalgar was stiff in the joints, asthmatic and reactionary in the few warlike beliefs it held. The Royal Navy was weary with inaction. By its statistical strength, Britannia still ruled the waves. But the monolithic power of the British Empire and its navy was in jeopardy even as its size and wealth reached its zenith.'

Richard Hough

In Germany, the new Emperor Wilhelm had instituted an interest in naval expansion that had struck a chord with his subjects. Germany, as a whole, was not totally enamoured with Wilhelm, but he was an impressive, occasionally inspiring, speaker in public, and his naval policy allied to the *Weltpolitik* theory was generally popular. However, he frequently walked a highly strung wire between his desire to be a 'supreme warlord' and also the 'Emperor of Peace'. Occasionally, he fell off that wire and on such occasions his government had to provide a diplomatic safety net, to their mutual embarrassment and the consternation of the German populace.

Essentially, Wilhelm wanted all the trappings of military might – the armies, the fleets, all the grandeur of regimental uniforms and traditions; but when it came to using these formations for the purpose that they were designed, he was strangely passive. Wilhelm was not a warmonger, but he was besotted by the means of making war. He adored his fleet – his creation – but when, in the end, it came to the crunch of putting it to test, he emasculated his admirals. He couldn't bear to contemplate the loss of his precious ships. When it came to hostilities, the British, by contrast, always accepted that losses were inevitable, however unpleasant. Omelettes could not be made without eggs being broken. When ships were lost, there was soul searching about the causes, the problems were, if possible, addressed, and cures were eventually adopted. Wilhelm was not a natural maker of omelettes; he loved his basket of eggs too much to sacrifice them for that purpose.

His naval mentor, Alfred von Tirpitz, had no such sensitivities. A thorough professional, with great political talent, he was in the process of building a fleet that was intended to be used, and he built the individual ships as stoutly as possible so as to ensure that their destruction would be no easy matter. Whether this defensive pre-occupation suited Germany's strategic naval purposes is debatable. His office, however, gave him no control over their operational activities. Wilhelm jealously guarded this prerogative, and imposed crippling restrictions on their use by the fleet commanders. When war came, this situation frustrated Tirpitz to distraction, but whilst the new fleet was under construction, the two men had a common cause, and for a brief while at the turn of the century, to use a modern phrase, 'they were calling the shots' in a world that had largely yet to divine their ultimate intent.

So far, in this tale, the major personalities have been on the German side. As the new century began they were about to confront their nemesis. A British naval officer of unbounded energy, clarity of thought, and ruthless determination, was to set himself in their path. The naval reforms instituted by this remarkable, albeit deeply flawed, man were central to the whole subject of Anglo-German relations in the period leading up to the First World War. As such he merits a detailed assessment. In the person of John Arbuthnot (Jacky) Fisher, the grandiose ambitions of Tirpitz and the Kaiser were to run onto a rock of formidable character.

Fisher, as a future First Sea Lord, had to operate within a very different system to that in which Tirpitz had learned to manoeuvre and manipulate.

No one person in British governing circles could equate to the position Wilhelm II held in Germany. The British Monarch acted on the advice of the ministers of government, who were effectively appointed by the popular vote of the electorate. During the reigns of Victoria and Edward VII, however, the views of the Monarch had some influence in specific areas. The latter, particularly, would profoundly affect British foreign policy by his unauthorised, but consummately timed, personal initiatives towards France and Russia. Ultimately, though, if there was a complete difference of opinion, parliament would have its way. The pragmatic application of the arrangement by both sides ensured that, despite the odd crisis, this state of affairs never came to pass.

By contrast, in Germany the ministers of state were appointed by the Emperor, as opposed to the electorate, and they dealt, on his behalf, with the *Reichstag*. Wilhelm could, therefore, dictate policy, advised to a greater or lesser extent by his ministers. If the individual ministers, or state secretaries, such as Tirpitz, could gain a position of influence amongst the gang of sycophants surrounding the Kaiser, it was their policies that would eventually be presented to the *Reichstag*.

In Great Britain, therefore, the ministers of the elected government, with the support of the Monarch, occupied the same position as the single personage of the German Emperor in having to present their policies for the approval of the representatives of the electorate. If one is to define Anglo-German adversaries in this sense, it is a case of Wilhelm and his various mentors versus the entire British constitutional system.

On the practical level of the building and effectiveness of fleets, the contest is very much simpler. Effectively it comes down to the navy that Tirpitz wished to create versus the navy that Fisher would revitalise.

In May 1899, at the behest of the Tsar of Russia, the first Peace Conference was convened at The Hague. Not a great deal was expected from this gathering. Indeed, most of the nations attending were doing so only out of respect for the Tsar's wishes, and to ensure that nothing concrete was decided that could fetter their freedom of action with regard to armaments. In this, they were entirely successful.

It was as much a social as a militarist stance that determined the failure of the conference. From the purely naval side, as Arthur Marder remarks:

'One battleship was worth about twenty normal sized cargo boats so far as labour was concerned. One battleship gave two thousand men full employment for two or three years.

'"Warship building means bread to the working-man." Any sudden change of existing conditions would lead to very serious consequences in the industrial world, and the throwing of large bodies of men out of work would result in unrest and possible revolution. That was the argument of the armament journals and of navalists generally, and was conspicuous at the time of the promulgation of the Tsar's disarmament project in 1898.' (1)

It was also the argument that was later used by Tirpitz, and to a lesser degree by the British Admiralty, to justify a fixed, regular programme of warship construction. Unsurprisingly, it had the full support of major industrial concerns, together with the electoral support of their workforces.

The conference marked the first appearance on the international scene of a man who was, more than any other, responsible for the transformation of the Royal Navy to meet the emerging threat from Germany. He made an instant impression.

In 1899, Vice Admiral Sir John Fisher was already well known within his own service. The progress of his career was now to become of interest to a much wider audience.

Known as Jack to his family, and Jacky throughout the navy (though not generally to his face), John Arbuthnot Fisher was born in 1841, the first of eleven children by a young Englishwoman, married to an army officer in Ceylon. Shortly after his birth, Fisher's father resigned from the army and took up tea planting, which venture failed. He subsequently found employment in the Civil Service, but this was not a well paid job, and, with a rapidly increasing family to be fed, his eldest son was sent back to England to live with the equally straightened parents of his mother. Fisher was six at the time, and never saw his parents again. His father died in a riding accident when Fisher was fifteen, but he had already accidentally bequeathed his son a gift of connection that was to shape his life. Influential contacts were a key element in advancing the careers of the non-aristocracy, and one such contact was instrumental in setting the young Fisher on his life's path.

Before leaving the army, William Fisher had been the aide-de-camp to the Governor of Ceylon, whose wife became godmother to his first son. In England, this lady, by then a widow, took a propriety interest in young Jack. One of her family friends was the last surviving member of Nelson's 'Band of Brothers', the captains who had served under Britain's greatest admiral. The gentleman in question was by then reaching the end of a distinguished career, as Commander-in-Chief at Plymouth, one of the most important shore commands. With the godmother's prompting, Sir William Parker sponsored Fisher as a candidate for the Royal Navy. At the age of thirteen, he was duly sent to *HMS Victory*, Nelson's old flagship, in Portsmouth Harbour, to be examined as to his suitability for the service. According to Fisher, this examination was not unduly demanding:

'I wrote out the Lord's Prayer and the doctor made me jump over a chair naked and I was given a glass of Sherry.' (2)

Fisher never knowingly under exaggerated if he had a tale to tell, and the examination probably was slightly more extensive, even, if not rigorous. He always maintained that he entered the navy '...penniless, friendless and forlorn.' (3) Penniless and forlorn he may have been, but to have been nominated by Nelson's last surviving captain was hardly the worst start to a naval career!

Once in the navy, the young man was to do his august sponsor proud. Fisher proved an outstanding success in every post to which he was appointed. Promoted to midshipman in 1856, he served five years on the China station, and saw bloody action on the rivers of that country. Returning to Britain as an acting lieutenant, he had impeccable references from all his commanding officers, and was clearly a man to watch. His boundless energy, exuberance and obvious ability set him apart, not just from the run of the mill, but from other officers of considerable talent.

In England he passed all his examinations for confirmation as lieutenant with exceptional marks, and then proceeded to *HMS Excellent*, an establishment made up of two old wooden walls moored in Portsmouth Harbour. These housed the facilities to train officers in the latest developments in gunnery, and other technologies that were beginning to emerge, such as torpedoes. Fisher, all his life, was an innovator, and nothing gave him greater pleasure and impetus than being at the cutting edge of new developments. A measure of his standing, after his time on courses at *Excellent*, was that he was immediately appointed to the crucial position of gunnery lieutenant on the brand new ironclad *HMS Warrior*.

This vessel was the first of her type in the service and ushered in the revolution that would eventually displace the old wood and sail navy. Her captain was Sir George Tryon, later the most prominent admiral in the service, and all the officers were hand picked. Fisher, as usual, excelled, not just from his obvious abilities, but from the sheer ebullience of his personality, which made him such a natural and popular leader. That is not to say that he was always easy to work for or with – quite the opposite. He was absolutely intolerant of inefficiency and those who perpetrated it. His requirements of those who worked under him were as demanding as the standards he applied to himself, and woe betide anyone who failed to meet those criteria. The same ruthless methods that distinguished his period in high command were already apparent. That said, he also had boundless charm and a sheer *joie de vivre* that made all the ships he served on (once they were to his satisfaction) both supremely efficient and generally very happy.

After *Warrior*, Fisher went back to *Excellent* for five years, this time as an instructor, during which time he was first involved in torpedo development, which he predictably found fascinating. A break at sea again as second-in-command of an old wooden-hulled armoured battleship on the China station was followed by a further four years at *Excellent* as head of the torpedo section. He was responsible for the separation of this section from the core Gunnery School, and became, at thirty three, the first captain of the Royal Navy's first independent torpedo establishment, *HMS Vernon*.

At the end of 1876, Fisher was back at sea again, as captain of vessels of increasing size and importance until, in 1881, he was offered, over the head of scores of more senior captains, the plum command in the Royal Navy. *HMS Inflexible* was, on paper, the most powerful warship in the fleet. Brand new, she carried the biggest guns ever seen in the Royal Navy, and was protected by the thickest armoured belt ever carried on any warship of any nation (twenty-four inches along the central citadel and waterline). She also incorporated many new innovations, including electric lights, and among the many other 'firsts' she can claim the first death by electrocution on a British warship! She also could claim one 'last', as she was the final British capital ship to be built with a full outfit of sails – which anachronistic encumbrances were later removed.

Whilst in command of *Inflexible*, Fisher took part in the bombardment of Alexandria in 1882, the only fleet action (if it can be dignified as such) of the Royal Navy between the Crimean War and the outbreak of the First World War. Subsequent to the reduction of the Alexandria forts, he took command of the naval forces landed to support continuing operations against the insurgent Egyptian elements, a difficult task successfully performed with all of his characteristic energy. It is not irrelevant to future events to mention that he asked for, and received, Lord Charles Beresford as his chief deputy in this matter.

In the course of this duty, he contracted a virulent brand of fever,[1] which resulted in his subsequent complete incapacitation and very nearly proved fatal. At one time he was not expected to live, but was eventually repatriated to England for a prolonged period of recuperation. It was the end of his command of *Inflexible*. He received a much cherished letter from the ship's company attesting to the affection and pride that he had generated during his time on board. Amongst other well-wishers who wrote to him during his illness, were the Prince and Princess of Wales.

Probably the most important aspect of Fisher's time in command of *Inflexible*, was his introduction into the circles of the Royal Family. As the most modern battleship in the fleet, his ship had been present in the South of France when the Queen had holidayed on the Riviera. There, Fisher had been introduced to the Monarch and his frank ebullience had charmed Victoria. For the rest of her life she held a soft spot for him, and he was frequently a visitor during her sojourns at Osborne, on the Isle of Wight. More importantly, he made a friend of the Prince of Wales, who, when he became King Edward VII, was to be one of his staunchest supporters during Fisher's turbulent years as First Sea Lord.

For nearly a year, Fisher was *hors de combat*, until he was considered fit enough to be sent back to his *alma mater*, *HMS Excellent*. He returned as captain of this cradle of advanced naval gunnery training. There he began to instil a new spirit of urgency into the instruction process. Fourteen years before Tirpitz became Naval Secretary in Germany, and that nation's naval forces began to loom large in British consciousness, Fisher was aware that the Royal Navy had lapsed into a state of complacency and needed to be shaken out of this attitude to meet the technological challenges of a new era. He was appalled by the backward looking tendencies of most senior officers and utterly dissatisfied by what he saw as the navy's unreadiness for war in the coming years.

In the intensely conservative navy of the mid 1880s he was very much a lone voice crying in the wilderness, but he had started to attract a

---

[1] In that era the Mediterranean was notorious for its debilitating fevers. 'Malta Fever', which was a pernicious ailment in the Royal Navy's main fleet base on the station, ruined the health of many promising officers and killed not a few. It was eventually traced to contaminated goats' milk in an age when the pasteurisation process had yet to be introduced. Death or incapacitation to disease was then a far greater threat to the Victorian sailor than was the chance of battle or the perils of the sea.

cadre of younger officers who shared his views. During his tenure of command at *Excellent* two of these officers served under him as instructor lieutenants. One of them, Percy Scott, was a stormy petrel who might never have advanced without Fisher's patronage. He became the gunnery guru of the navy in due course, and revolutionised the accuracy and effectiveness of the fleet's firepower. The other, John Jellicoe, a most efficient and balanced officer, was to be Fisher's choice as the future Fleet Commander. Many years later, when war came, even though he was then out of office, Fisher's influence helped ensure that Jellicoe was in place at the critical moment.

He spent only two years at *Excellent*, but, in that time, initiated a series of reforms that transformed the establishment. He picked up on a suggestion of Percy Scott, and a mud bank in Portsmouth Harbour, formed by the spoil from extension of the dockyard, began to be extended and developed to form a new shore base for the navy's gunnery school, replacing the old wooden hulks moored in the harbour. Whale Island, as it was known, became the hub of naval training for the duration of the gunnery era, only decommissioning as a specialist establishment in the 1980s.

Fisher's spell as captain of *Excellent* enabled him for the first time to bring his reforming zeal into actual effect. He had reached a point in his career where his seniority and position enabled him to effect change rather than to just be its advocate. The post also brought him into contact with important figures in the political and media spheres, who shared his concerns, and who, recognising a rising star, wished to promote his influence.

Foremost amongst them was Reginald Brett, later Viscount Esher, who was to become the *éminence grise* behind the reign of Edward VII, and a remarkable man in his own right. A person who was entirely comfortable with being able to influence events without ever being a public personage, he adopted Fisher from this early stage of the latter's administrative career, and supported him through thick and thin during the years of Fisher's great, and often virulently opposed, reforms of the navy.

Fisher had been introduced to Brett by a journalist of enthusiasm and drive that matched his own. W.T. Stead was a soul mate, and they conspired mischief together for many years with undiluted relish. All of them had a common cause; the strength and readiness of the navy to meet its commitments as the defender of the British Empire. In 1884, prompted by H.O. Arnold-Forster, an academic soon to become a senior politician, the three of them combined to produce a critique of the government's neglect of the navy.

The result was a series of articles, written by Stead, entitled *The Truth about the Navy*, and they engendered a furore in the press and in public opinion. This became the first of a series of 'naval scares' that periodically mobilised national opinion for the next thirty years, and served to coerce the government of the day into naval construction programmes that would otherwise have been delayed, subordinated to other political priorities, or simply not contemplated. The detailed and irrefutable information that fuelled Stead's articles obviously came from highly placed sources in the Royal Navy. One of these, of course, was Fisher and was a highly improper departure for a serving officer, but he never let considerations of propriety stand in the way of what he considered the good of the service. As it happened, despite considerable suspicion, no one managed to tie him to the articles. Nevertheless, it was a high risk strategy for a relatively junior officer with ambitions, but, if the ends justify the means, the Fisher/Brett/Stead triumvirate achieved their object. A naval regeneration programme was duly initiated.

By the time he left *Excellent* at the end of 1886, Fisher had become a political animal, the bludgeon to Brett/Esher's discreet rapier, and the supplier of information to Stead whenever he needed public opinion to support his ends. As his career progressed, this aspect of his personality became ever more pronounced.

'The more consequential Fisher became, the profounder his plots. He arranged for friendly questions to be asked in the House of Commons. He conspired with some of the great men of state, men like Arthur Balfour, Winston Churchill and Reginald Esher, an *éminence grise* of the court who was Fisher's confidant for years…He had the ear of Edward VII and made subtle professional use of it. "He would write me long letters," Ponsonby[2] recalled, "apparently intended only for me as they were so outspoken, but really for King Edward to read." Fisher was never a great diner-out – as Ponsonby said, he preferred the back door – and even in his glory days he generally avoided fashionable London society, but once a quarter he would meet for dinner with a remarkably handy trio of friends; Esher, Lord Knollys, the King's private secretary, and the Marquis de Soveral, Portuguese Minister to the Court of St. James and one of the most influential men in London. Fisher knew his velvet ways around the mole-runs of power.' (4)

These contacts and machinations obviously only happened over time, but they developed in parallel with his advancement to the higher levels of his profession.

Fisher's reforms at *Excellent* were so obviously successful as to result in him being redeployed to the Admiralty in the key post of Director of Naval Ordnance (DNO). The supply of guns to the navy was nothing short of a scandal. The War Office, which meant the army, was still responsible for the provision of all weaponry for the British services. Hopelessly overtaken by the advance of technology, it was still supplying out of date

---

[2] The Ponsonbys were something of a Court fixture. Sir Henry Ponsonby had been Private Secretary to Queen Victoria for many years, and his son, Frederick, was assistant Private Secretary to King Edward VII. Another son was a prominent Liberal MP, and the family had considerable influence in the social elite that occupied the border region between monarchy and parliament.

muzzle-loading guns to the navy long after continental navies were adopting far more efficient breech-loading weapons. This situation, in which the premier service was dependent for its weapons on an even more hidebound and inefficient organisation that granted it low priority, had been mouldering along for years. Fisher fought a long and vitriolic battle in the corridors of power before succeeding in getting the navy control over the production of its own guns. Whilst he achieved many other reforms as DNO, this success was the most significant event during his tenure of the post, and brought him to the notice of Lord Salisbury, the Prime Minister, one of whose relatives had been arguing the opposition case.

However much Fisher enjoyed his time afloat, and however much he achieved in advancing the efficiency of ships and fleets that fell under his command, his *metier* was as an administrator and reformer. To properly achieve his ends of modernising his navy to meet the challenges to come, he had to be at the heart of the organisation, and that meant the Admiralty and Whitehall.

He spent nearly six years as DNO, and shortly afterwards, in 1892, was appointed Third Sea Lord and Controller of the Navy, a post that gave him a large measure of responsibility over the materiel aspects of the navy. His most recent biographer notes that:

'The materiel progress of this decade was one of the most eventful in naval history. There was a rapid advance in all fields, in gunnery and new processes in armour construction, and in the creation of altogether new types of warships, and in the introduction of new forms of propulsion. It was also a decade of great international anxiety...For more than half of this decade, Fisher was responsible for the condition of the Navy, to ensure that it was adequate in numbers and efficient and battle-worthy to meet any old or new enemies. It was for Fisher a time of great accomplishments, achieved through constant controversy, and even rancour, and at the price of a reputation for utter ruthlessness. He made many enemies, and among his old opponents the depths of bitterness against him increased with every rebuff which they suffered.' (5)

Fisher, being Fisher, met all opposition head on. At that time of his life, and at that stage of his career, he almost rejoiced at opposition, and took the greatest pleasure in trouncing it. He had reached the foothills of the mountain he felt he was destined to climb, and he assaulted those slopes with unabashed vigour, brushing aside all those who disputed his chosen route.

His time as Third Sea Lord came shortly after the appointment of Sir William White as Director of Naval Construction, and covered the period of the 'Spencer Programme' (named after the First Lord of the Admiralty at the time), which gave the navy an enormous reinforcement of homogenous classes of battleships and cruisers, all superior to anything being constructed abroad. The ships were first class, but Fisher remained sceptical (to put it mildly) as to whether these vessels, designed to meet a French or Russian threat, were on a proper war footing as regards general training and gunnery

'Jacky' Fisher as Captain, c.1883

Reginald Brett, Lord Esher
'The Eminence Grise'

efficiency. The French Navy, at that time, was going through one of its relatively motivated periods, and was posing a genuine threat. As best he could within the parameters of his office, Fisher fought for an increased awareness of the need for efficient use of the materiel available to the navy. All the time, he was expanding his contacts within the political and commercial establishments that served the navy, the latter including key shipbuilding and armaments firms. The more contacts he made, the more information came his way, and he soaked up this information like a sponge, using it to fuel his crusade for efficiency.

At the end of 1896, his term of office as Third Sea Lord came to an end and he was appointed as Commander-in-Chief of the North America and West Indies station. This was not a particularly important detachment of the Royal Navy, but it very necessarily brought him back into contact with the seagoing fleet, and he was delighted at the prospect.

'It was fifteen years since Fisher had held a seagoing command. Much had happened to him in this time. He had acquired great power, he had fought battles, many of them bitter ones, and he had won most of them. He was a veteran warrior from the wars of administration who had not seen fighting since he was a young man. He believed passionately in his causes, believed in himself, and believed in the public figure which he had acquired. He enjoyed his reputation for unpredictable behaviour, for shocking for the sake of shocking, for hurling his weight about and doing everything at full pressure. But this appointment offered him the opportunity to show that he was a real sailor, too, and not just a land-lubber decision maker.' (6)

Needless to say, Fisher brought to his new command the same enthusiasm and drive that characterised all his work. The social and diplomatic aspects of this command also had a high priority, and Fisher revelled in the opportunities thus provided. He was an exhilarating guest, and a splendid host. One of his favourite stories related to the time he entertained an American squadron in Bermuda. Having wined and dined his guests, he proposed a toast to the visiting admiral and to the United States. The reply was a classic:

'I sent the wine round and the Admiral then got up and made the best speech I ever heard. All he said was: "It was a damned fine old hen that hatched the American Eagle."'[3] (7)

Fisher had the greatest regard for America. Its spirit of get up and go, and belief in its ability to conquer any problem by application and enthusiasm, mirrored his own personality. In return, Americans warmed to

---

[3] Jan Morris titled her book *Fisher's Face*. I think any and all of Fisher's biographers and supporters would have given a great deal for a photograph of his face when that reply to his toast was made.

this intensely vital man, so different from the stiff English stereotypes they had been taught to expect. If any one aspect of his tenure of command of this station stands out, it is that he laid the groundwork for the eventual, highly successful, co-operation between the British and American Navies in the latter stages of the First World War.

In 1899, Fisher had been earmarked for command of the Mediterranean Fleet, one of the two premier seagoing appointments in the navy. Before taking up this position, the first Hague Peace Conference intervened.

A naval representative was required to attend this gathering as part of the British delegation, and Salisbury, remembering Fisher's success in arguing the navy's case for control of its own armaments, decided that he was the man for the post. Accordingly, whilst officially being appointed to the Mediterranean command, he was immediately detached to attend the conference.

Fisher, at the conference, was a revelation. He was the single most outstanding personality of the event. Adorned in a white top hat and tails, he brought to the formal meetings an utterly pragmatic voice as to the impossibility of effecting the well-meant intentions of the conference, which was to impose a certain set of restraints on the means of making war. Informally, to a fairly aghast audience, he demolished the principles of making war nicely. To all and sundry, he proclaimed what he saw to be pertinent. In his own words:

'These Leagues of Nations and Freedom of the Seas and all the other items are all damned nonsense. When war does come, then "Might is Right".' Other pronouncements included: "The Essence of War is Violence"; "Moderation in War is imbecility"; "You hit first, you hit hard, and keep on hitting"; and his old oft repeated favourite, "You have to be Ruthless, Relentless and Remorseless". As a final broadside to a conference supposedly focussed on the preservation of peace, and the gentlemanly conduct of hostilities should the former prove unavoidable, he opined, "Its perfect rot to talk about 'Civilised Warfare!' You might as well talk about a 'Heavenly Hell!'" (8)

Remarkably, he managed to voice these violent opinions in such a way as to give no offence. The most blood-curdling sentiments were delivered calmly, even cheerfully, and with an absence of animosity. He was merely stating what he saw to be self-evident truths, and his views, divested of their typical extravagance, reflected those of many fellow delegates who could not, or dare not, utter similar sentiments. Certainly, though, other nations had been given an insight into the character of a man who was obviously destined to be at the centre of the British naval establishment for some time. It must have given them food for thought!

Fisher in fact, was dead set against war unless it became absolutely unavoidable. He dreaded and saw, long before, and more clearly than most, the horrors latent in the use of modern weaponry. He was absolutely certain, though, that the best deterrent to war was for his country's armed forces to be so strong as to prohibit any other nation from contemplating offensive action. US President Theodore Roosevelt's succinct dictum 'Walk softly and carry a big stick', perfectly summed up his case, although Fisher hardly 'walked softly' in his own pronouncements.

For Fisher, the 'big stick' was obviously the Royal Navy. As he once wrote, 'The supremacy of the Royal Navy is the best security for the peace of the world.' (9) He was absolutely sincere in this view. He was about to occupy the highest positions in the service to which he had devoted his life. He would carry out the tasks he had imposed upon himself with complete dedication. In the process, he would drag the protesting navy he loved, kicking and screaming, into a new era. He would also create animosities that tore the service apart, but he absolutely knew what he was doing, and that what he was doing was absolutely necessary.

For all his perceived arrogance, Fisher possessed at heart a genuine humility. He had a simple and absolute belief in God, and, for any virtues that he possessed, he happily gave all credit to the Almighty. His faith gave him the strength to face the trials, tribulations, obstacles and opponents he met during his turbulent career with a sense of generally being in the right. In most cases he was. That is not to say that he met opposition with equanimity. He bludgeoned it to its knees, beat it over the head, and consigned it utterly to the outer darkness. Fisher's Christianity largely confined itself to the Old Testament, from which he so often quoted, and was even then selective. Turning the other cheek was a totally alien concept. An eye for an eye was more his line; and forgiveness was not regularly on the agenda.

After the Hague Conference, Fisher spent three years as Commander-in-Chief of the Mediterranean Fleet. It was his last seagoing command, and was marked by his usual assault on complacency and inefficiency that added to his already impressive list of enemies. Despite the complaints of dockyard staff and the fleet engineers about wear and tear on machinery, he insisted on all manoeuvres and deployments being carried out at maximum speed. There was no point, he believed, in exercising a peacetime fleet in any manner other than the conditions in which it would have to operate during war. His second-in-command was Lord Charles Beresford, another outstanding and outspoken officer who would ultimately become Fisher's fiercest opponent. For the time, although some seeds of dissension were sown, the two generally worked well together. Beresford later generously stated, amongst other positive remarks, that Fisher had transformed his command 'from a 12 knot Fleet with numerous breakdowns' to 'a 15 knot Fleet without breakdowns.' (10).

Whilst in the Mediterranean, Fisher also waged an occasionally acrimonious campaign against the Admiralty over what he saw as a dangerous shortage of some classes of ships, particularly cruisers and destroyers, allocated to his command. He came very close to outright insubordination at times, and was certainly unreasonable in some of his demands. He was particularly antipathetic towards the First Sea Lord, Lord Walter Kerr, a reasonably competent but colourless officer, who occupied the position coveted by Fisher himself.[4]

Despite his differences with the Admiralty Board, at the end of his tour of duty, Fisher was offered the appointment of Second Sea Lord, Kerr remaining at the head of affairs.

Fisher held the post for less than two years, but it was time enough to initiate one of the most radical reforms to affect the service for over a century. The Second Sea Lord's prime responsibility was for the personnel of the navy, and he had very decided views on that subject. There was a strong streak of the socialist in him, and he deplored the class distinctions that were rife at the time, which affected the recruitment of personnel, promotion within the service, and the status of different departments within the navy.

The executive branch of the navy existed as an elite, and it was from this limited pool of talent that the service had traditionally selected its senior officers. Technical specialists, apart from the gunnery and torpedo spheres, tended to be regarded as artisans – valuable and essential certainly, but still artisans. This attitude extended even to the navigation department. Engineer officers were tolerated in the wardroom only because of their unfortunate indispensability to the running of the ship. Fisher wanted all this scrapped, and *all* officers, of whatever specialisation, to have a common basic training in all the disciplines that affected the service. The opportunities of promotion to senior positions would also be opened to a much wider catchment of personnel. Not surprisingly, the entrenched elite screamed blue murder over these proposals, which eroded their privileged status, and Fisher accumulated yet another addition to the numbers of his sworn opponents. Nevertheless, he sold the bulk of his ideas to the First Lord of the Admiralty, Lord Selbourne, the political head of the navy, who put most of its provisions into effect. The 'Selbourne Scheme', as it became known, henceforth became the basis of officer training in the navy, and exists, in part, to this day.

---

[4] There is a certain irony in this. Eight years later, Fisher found himself on the other side of the fence, when, as First Sea Lord, he had to fend off the attacks of Lord Charles Beresford, complaining of a similar lack of support for the Channel Fleet – then Britain's premier naval command. Beresford was even more of a trial to the Admiralty than had been Fisher. Neither episode constitutes a highlight of their respective careers.

Fisher's relationship with the rest of the naval members of the Admiralty Board was decidedly cool, but the rapport that he achieved with Selbourne was of great importance. The First Lord became convinced that Fisher's undoubted abilities outweighed any considerations of unpopularity within the navy, or worries about his volatile temperament. By the time he ended his stint as Second Sea Lord, and was posted as Commander-in-Chief, Portsmouth, Fisher was made aware that he would replace Lord Walter Kerr when the latter's term of office expired. In coming to this decision, Lord Selbourne disregarded the advice of most of his highest placed advisors, and, in doing so, he rendered the Royal Navy the greatest possible service.

Fisher's appointment to the Portsmouth command represented a theoretical demotion, but, in fact, was designed to give him an acceptable means of 'marking time', until Lord Walter Kerr's occupation of the First Sea Lord's post was due to terminate. In the meantime, Fisher was able to concentrate on formulating his plans for the reformation of the navy.

This is not to say that he neglected his duties as Commander-in-Chief, Portsmouth. The man was congenitally incapable of not applying himself totally to whatever task he was allocated.

During his period of command, the Royal Navy's first submarine unit was established in Portsmouth. Fisher took a keen supervisory interest in this fledgling branch of the service, which was placed under the charge of one of his protégés, Captain Reginald Bacon, an exceptionally clever officer. Long before anyone else in authority latched on to the immense potential of this new weapon, Fisher had recognised its importance in the future conduct of war. In 1904 he predicted the inevitability of unrestricted submarine warfare on trade, this at a time when such an idea was regarded with horror and disbelief by his contemporaries – and had not then even been contemplated by the navy that would be its prime exponent.

The Portsmouth command was generally given the full Fisher treatment, but he *did* also utilise the time to hone his ideas and theories on the future of the Royal Navy to the point, that, when he eventually succeeded to the highest office available to a serving officer, his programme was fully thought out and the means of its implementation clear.

A further duty came his way in late 1903, when he was co-opted onto a committee, chaired by the ubiquitous Esher, which was to effect the reorganisation of the army. The early setbacks in the Boer War had come as a severe shock to the British establishment, and were an acute embarrassment to the nation in general. That particular conflict was eventually satisfactorily resolved, but it was only achieved at great cost, some length, and with disproportionate effort considering the nature of the foe. There was clearly something very wrong with the organisation, training, and leadership of the army.

Shortly after the conclusion of hostilities in South Africa, the Prime Minister was pressed to address this problem. A. J. Balfour dealt with the matter by setting up a Royal Commission to investigate the shortcomings of the military establishment, and to propose measures that would effect a radical improvement on its performance. This was the committee on to which Fisher, together with Sir George Clarke, was co-opted. Esher was always an admirer of Fisher, but, even so, it must have taken some nerve to appoint the admiral to help re-organise the generals![5] To the admiral himself, it was an unexpected summons, but he immediately weighed in with his customary enthusiasm and his unique passion for reform wherever he saw incompetence.

If Fisher's appointment was a surprise to himself, it must have been particularly galling to the army, as his views on that service were decidedly uncharitable. In a letter to his son he observed that:

'One does not wonder at South Africa when one sees every day the utter ineptitude of Military Officers! Half the year they are on leave, and the other half of the year everything is left to the Sergeant-Major and the Non-Commissioned Officers!' (11)

Vintage Fisher.

The recommended reforms were duly adopted, and the army placed on a much more professional footing. In particular its staff organisation was utterly transformed (a rather ironic development given Fisher's later antipathy to a similar structure being established within the navy). The success of the measures taken was shown to good effect when war came eleven years later.

In the autumn of 1904, Lord Walter Kerr stepped down as First Sea Lord, and the way was clear for Fisher to begin the even more sweeping transformation of his own service.

On 21st October 1904, chosen deliberately by Fisher as the anniversary of the Battle of Trafalgar, he walked into the Admiralty

---

[5] The army, as will be seen, obtained full revenge for this humiliation. With a much more organised and efficient staff, established as a result of the reforms advocated by the committee on which Fisher served, the army was able to comprehensively outmanoeuvre the navy in the intellectual and organisational argument as to British strategic priorities post-1912. The result was Britain becoming the very junior partner in a continental land war controlled by the French General Staff, and the navy taking a back seat. This was the preferred option of the British Army heads, but unlikely to have been quite what Fisher was intending as the end product of his labours.

building in Whitehall as the professional head of the navy to which he had dedicated his life. No one was left in any doubt that this was to be a period of radical change. Old conceptions, old practices, old preoccupations, were all to be swept away. Fisher had early perceived the challenge represented to British naval supremacy by the rise of the German Navy, and he meant to meet the threat by the complete reformation of his service; the training, the personnel, and the materiel. He recognised that his perceived opponent was already organised and efficient, but only lacked the ships. Given time and opportunity, he had no doubt that they would try to bridge this gap.

For the ambitions of Wilhelm II and Tirpitz, across the North Sea, the advent of Fisher, as First Sea Lord, was the worst possible news. Any chance of there being a sense of complacency as to the threat the German Navy could pose was now, at least within the British Admiralty, no longer a possibility. A single, uniquely talented man, given a strictly limited time in power, was setting himself, and all who would go with him, to meet and confound the challenge.

CHAPTER SIX

THE END OF SPLENDID ISOLATION

'In retrospect the historian can perceive that the Diamond Jubilee celebrations of 1897 did not denote the zenith of Britain's power, but constituted rather the defiant swan song of a nation becoming less and less complacent about the increasing threats to its world wide interests.'

Paul Kennedy

'The abandonment of isolation was the result of Anglo-Russian quarrels in Asia. The issues were political and economic. Nevertheless, to understand fully the origins of the alliance the naval factor must be borne in mind.'

Arthur J. Marder

'Personally, I have always been an enthusiastic advocate for friendship and alliance with France. They never have and never will interfere with our trade. It's not their line, and, really, we have no clashing of vital interests...but we have not been politic toward them. The Germans are our natural enemies everywhere! We ought to unite with France and Russia!'

Vice Admiral Sir John Fisher, in a letter to J.R. Thursfield, November 1901

By the time Fisher became First Sea Lord, Britain's international situation had undergone a rapid and profound change.

The aging Lord Salisbury, generally (and inaccurately) regarded by history as the high priest of isolationism, had finally left office and been replaced as Prime Minister by his nephew, Arthur Balfour. This transfer of office was actually not as significant as has often been claimed, but it came at a time when many of the long-standing political and strategic certainties that had encompassed the European powers were about to be superseded. It also coincided with the death of Queen Victoria, an event which, emotionally and chronologically, inevitably tended to draw a convenient line under both a century and an era.

British foreign policy did not, in fact, drastically alter as a result of Salisbury's departure. The old premier's criterion of avoiding being tied into cast iron commitments to one or another power bloc was never discarded. Salisbury's policy was, in any case, never 'isolationist' in the

bald sense of the word – certainly not in the sense it has been used to describe American parochialism. Throughout his political life he was well aware that Britain, despite its vast empire and its long-term maritime supremacy, had not the power to influence world (or even European) events in 'isolation'. He therefore sought to pursue what he saw as Britain's vital interests by means of leaning to one bloc or another when required by circumstances. He would not commit to any long-term alliance on the grounds that circumstances could change very rapidly, and render such formal commitments both irrelevant and embarrassing to both parties. Britain, under Salisbury's government, would readily commit herself on the basis of what were the demands of the moment – but not be part of an inflexible format that took no regard of imponderable future developments.

If such a policy can be termed 'isolationist', Salisbury can be either credited or damned as its most high profile protagonist. For all that, throughout his career, he was quite prepared to act in concert with the other powers, and diligently tried to cultivate closer relations with all of the European powers. In modern terms, his administration would be better described as 'non-aligned' in principle rather than out and out isolationist as became the American model. Should international circumstances dictate, a certain degree of 'alignment' might be permitted if of immediate and temporary benefit to the international situation. He loathed and despised the Jingoists who rejoiced in slandering foreigners, and had utter contempt for the popular press that encouraged mindless national chauvinism. An old patrician politician, he served as head of the government not from ambition, nor for financial gain – and certainly not for the fickle pleasures of a transient fame. He belonged to an old family, the Cecils, who had served as courtiers, politicians and diplomats since the days of the Tudors and he regarded his position as an inherited bounden duty; a burden not a pleasure. Avoiding unnecessary and costly wars by means of intelligent diplomacy was very much what he regarded as one of his prime 'duties'. One of the constant themes that runs through Salisbury's simultaneous tenure of both the Prime Minister's and Foreign Secretary's offices is his preoccupation with defusing the long-term hostility between Britain and France. Sadly he would not live to witness the rapid progress from *détente* to *entente* that occurred after he left power.

The Foreign Secretary under Balfour was very much out of the Salisburian mould. The Marquis of Lansdowne, who became the new political head of the Foreign Office, is probably one of the most unknown and underrated occupants of that post in the twentieth century. Prior to his appointment, Lansdowne had served, without any particular distinction, in a variety of appointments. As Foreign Secretary, he was an unqualified success. Initially, he did little more than follow the softly-softly precepts of Salisbury's policy and counter the attempts of the more flamboyant and impatient members of the cabinet to promote ill-considered initiatives.

Joseph Chamberlain, the Colonial Secretary, was a particular thorn in his side as the boundaries between the Foreign Office and the Colonial Office inevitably overlapped, and Chamberlain was, in any case, already intent on pursuing his own agenda of foreign allegiances.

It was, however, the old guard, and not Chamberlain, who were responsible for what was regarded as a first step back from isolationism. This move came from a totally unexpected direction, and was driven by fears of the *de facto* alliance between Russia and France in Europe being carried over into the Orient.

Alarmed by Russian penetration into the Far East, and French expansion in Indo-China and Siam, both of which threatened the extensive British interests in China, Britain, in 1902, concluded a treaty of alliance with Japan.

The signing of the Anglo-Japanese alliance has often been characterised as the moment that Great Britain first abandoned the concept of 'Splendid Isolation', but the circumstances of the event were not quite so straightforward. As John Charmley remarks:

'Some historians have seen the alliance with Japan as a first step out of isolation, others have seen it as reinforcing it. Both interpretations have elements of truth in them once the nature of Salisbury's 'isolationism' is appreciated: its traditional Tory distrust of entangling Continental alliances; its reliance on British naval power; its preference for a defence policy which kept taxation low (particularly in view of the cost of the Boer War); all these were compatible with a Japanese alliance.' (1)

The alliance only applied to the Far East, which meant that, whilst it benefited Britain's position *vis-à-vis* the presence of other European powers in that area, it operated in isolation to the political/strategic manoeuvring within Europe itself. However, it removed a potential strain on Britain's military resources and, by doing so, eased the pressure on the British Government to reach an accommodation with either of the European blocs. In this sense, it was certainly a *reinforcement* of Salisbury style isolation – at least in the Western Hemisphere.

For the Royal Navy, already stretched in the east and becoming increasingly wary of the emerging threat from Germany in the North Sea, the alliance came as something of a relief. Curiously enough, the Germans initially failed to digest the importance of this move.[1]

'The Germans were delighted, for they believed that the new alliance would bring Britain into conflict with Russia. They did not perceive that Britain had taken

---

[1] This is a common thread that runs through the entire series of German Foreign Office reactions to all of Britain's diplomatic initiatives over the next few critical years. The Japanese alliance; the *entente* with France; the rapprochement with Russia – all were briefly welcomed by Germany. Only belatedly did it become clear that each step had progressively eroded Germany's predominant position in Europe.

her first decisive step away from Germany; that her long period of isolation was at an end.' (2)

Although British naval forces in the Far East were considerable, the logistics of maintaining this detachment were a significant drain on resources, and the total number of warships was inferior to the combined strength of the Dual Alliance of France and Russia. Germany and the United States also maintained powerful squadrons in the area, and the Japanese Navy was a rapidly expanding presence of known competence (most of the major units of the Japanese Navy had been constructed in British yards, and were at least the equivalent of their British contemporaries. The training and efficiency of the personnel was also commented favourably upon by British officers seconded, as observers and advisors, to the Japanese Navy). Acting on her own, Britain was no longer in a position to dictate even the course of naval events in the region.

'London felt too weak to oppose the advance of other powers without the assistance of a major ally. Not only were they helpless to preserve Chinese sovereignty from the overland advances of the Russians from Siberia and the French from Indo-China, but the naval balance of power was also alarming. By the end of 1901, Selbourne informed the Cabinet, Britain would have four first class battleships and sixteen cruisers in Chinese waters compared to a combined Franco-Russian strength of seven first class and two second class battleships, plus twenty cruisers: the consequences for Britain's interests in a war with the Dual Alliance were obvious, even to those who favoured a concentration in waters nearer home. For this reason, the Admiralty advocated a naval alliance with Japan.' (3)

The combined Anglo-Japanese forces represented a much superior and more homogenous combination than that of the French and the Russians, and the continued enlargement of the Japanese Navy would further emphasise the difference. For Britain, this prospect would represent a huge improvement in her strategic position east of Singapore.

'Equally alarmed at the prospect of a Franco-Russian domination of the Far East, the Japanese were eager to enter into such an alliance. With its signing on 30 January 1902, the British felt that they could breathe more easily in the Orient. Yet even they underestimated at the time the advantages that were to accrue to them from this decisive step.' (4)

The treaty that was eventually signed was limited in its scope, but was of huge importance to both parties. Its terms required either nation to come to the assistance of the other, in the Far East, should they be confronted in war by more than one opponent. Thus, for Japan, it meant that if hostilities arose with either France or Russia, the other member of the Dual Alliance could not become engaged without Britain also being involved. Just two years later, Japan embarked on a war with Russia reasonably assured that the French would be deterred from providing military assistance to her ally by the provisions of this alliance.

The complete and shattering destruction of the Russian Navy during this war removed it, for many years, as a factor in the international balance of power. Not only had Britain gained a significant naval ally, it deducted that force from the list of possible opponents, and, within three years, this new ally had eliminated one of the fleets of Britain's potential rivals. Only the French and German Navies remained in the lists. It was an extraordinary turn of events, entirely to Britain's benefit. Tirpitz's *Risk Theory* was evaporating rapidly, and was about to become utterly redundant, whilst an even greater change to Britain's situation was at hand.

In 1898, Britain and France had come to the brink of war. The unlikely cause was an abandoned mud brick fort on the upper reaches of the Nile, far in the south of the Sudan.

For many years, confrontation between the two nations in the scramble for African possessions had been on the cards. British imperial development on the continent lay on a north to south axis, the French from west to east. At some point it was virtually inevitable that the two progressions would cross. The actual circumstances that attended the event were bizarre.

The vast territory of Sudan, to this day, in terms of area, the largest country in Africa, was a dependency of Egypt, which itself was effectively a British protectorate. Sudan was then, and still is, more of a geographical term than a description of a settled and united society dwelling together in mutual harmony. It was a fractious and divided entity with a largely Arab Islamic north holding tentative sway over the animalist and recently Christianised tribes of the south. The latter supplied the raw material for a flourishing slave trade controlled by the former. The Anglo-Egyptian authorities took measures to eradicate this practice and this gave rise to huge discontent and an eventual insurgency in the Arab-dominated north. Violent clashes between Islamist groups and the meagre government forces followed. In 1885, following the total massacre of a detachment of troops under the command of a seconded British officer, Egyptian government heads, with the support of Gladstone's administration in London, decided to wash their hands of the area and to withdraw their military garrisons from the Sudan. Effectively, this meant leaving the whole region in the hands of a militant religious movement known as the Dervishes. Under their fanatical leader, the Mahdi, the forces of this Taleban-like organisation rapidly filled the vacuum left by the Egyptian Army.

Unfortunately this event, which might otherwise have attracted little interest, was complicated by the actions of the British officer appointed to oversee the withdrawal, General Charles Gordon. Having come to the conclusion that the whole policy was wrong, Gordon refused to abandon the Sudanese capital of Khartoum. There, with a few local troops, he was duly besieged by overwhelming numbers of the Dervish Army.

Coerced into action by public opinion, as Gordon had hoped, an Anglo-Egyptian army was despatched to his relief. After defeating the forces in their way, this army was very close to Khartoum when it received the news that the city had been stormed, and Gordon killed. The reason for the expedition having been removed, it retired back into Egypt.

The death, and martyrdom, of Gordon passed into imperial legend, and engendered a sense of outrage in Britain, but, for ten years, the territory was left in a condition of semi-anarchy; basically what, in modern terminology, would be categorised as a 'failed state'.

This state of affairs came to an end as a result of several factors. One of these was emotional. Gordon's death still festered in the public consciousness, and there was a strong climate of opinion that this should be avenged. Another was based on an influential campaign by the imperial lobby for the construction of a Cape to Cairo railway, linking Britain's African possessions from the Cape of Good Hope to the Mediterranean. There were powerful strategic and commercial arguments for this project, which, whatever the huge engineering and financial challenges, could only be achieved by the pacification of Sudan. Finally, there was the prospect of France occupying the area in the absence of an Anglo-Egyptian presence. In 1898, the French were actually on the point of doing just this.

Two years previously, a small force of French-officered Senegalese troops, under a Captain Marchand, had set out from Western Africa to cross the continent. The expedition was a true epic of endurance, and a triumph over the worst that terrain, climate, and natural hazards could place in the path of human fortitude.

'They walked for twenty-four months, covering 3,500 miles. No army of Dervishes stood in their way; instead they fought swamps, hippopotami, crocodiles, scorpions, mosquitoes, fleas and fever. Nevertheless, on July 10th 1898, the French expedition arrived at the old fort of Fashoda, built by the Egyptians in 1870 to combat the slave trade.' (5)

At the end of their long ordeal, Marchand's little force occupied the ruins of the old Egyptian facility at Fashoda. There, they hoisted the French flag and claimed sovereignty over the region of the upper Nile. It was an act of the most splendid cheek, and deserved a better resolution than was to be its fate. The British had not been idle in the meantime.

For the other reasons mentioned above the British Government had resolved on the re-conquest of the Sudan. Early knowledge of the despatch of the Marchand expedition gave added impetus to this scheme. An army under Sir Herbert Kitchener, prepared with meticulous attention to detail, had been gathering in Egypt. This was launched forthwith into the Sudan, and, on September 2nd 1898 met, and with little loss, utterly destroyed the main Dervish forces at Omdurman, just across the Nile from Khartoum.[2]

Two days later, Kitchener entered Khartoum and was shortly informed of Marchand's presence up river. There he proceeded with overwhelming force and met the French commander on September 19th. Kitchener explained that he was directed to re-establish Egypt's control of its dominion. Marchand replied that he was there on the orders of his government, and could not haul down the French flag without their permission. National pride was at stake.

For all his forbidding reputation, Kitchener dealt with the situation with great tact and consideration. He spoke excellent French, admired the achievement of Marchand, and immediately struck up a cordial relationship with the Frenchman. Having pointed out the obvious superiority of his force (and it being equally clear to both parties that only the presence of that force in Sudan preserved the French from being massacred by the Dervishes), Kitchener permitted Marchand to continue flying the French flag, and he did not interfere with the independence of the little force, even though it became entirely reliant on the British for its sustenance.

The positions of their respective governments were obviously diametrically opposed, but, whilst the solution to the impasse was handed over to the diplomats, relations between the men on the spot remained extremely good.

Politically, however, the situation was bleak. The British Prime Minister, Salisbury, had warned France, when he first got wind of the Marchand expedition, that an incursion into an area that Britain regarded as being within its sphere of influence was utterly prohibited. The French went ahead anyway, and having got themselves into a completely untenable position through Marchand's efforts, which had rightly made him a national hero, could not withdraw without an unacceptable loss of international face, and outraged public opinion on the home front.

The crisis developed to the point where Britain made it clear that, if the French Government did not renounce its claim to the Upper Nile area, and instruct Marchand's beleaguered unit to accept repatriation by the British forces, the two nations would go to war. Should it come to that, there was only one certain loser.

France's powerful army existed to meet the seeming eternal threat from Germany's even more powerful army. It could not be diverted to

---

[2] Winston Churchill took part in this battle as a young cavalry officer, as did David Beatty as commander of a river gunboat supporting the army advance. The two were destined to be reunited at a much higher level in the course of their careers.

invade Britain even if it were able, which it wasn't. The Royal Navy made any such project suicidal. British maritime supremacy also ensured that virtually all of France's treasured colonial possessions, bar perhaps those on the North African coast of the Mediterranean, would be lost in any such conflict.

With nothing to gain, and a great deal to lose, France was forced to back down and accept the inevitable. It was an appalling humiliation to a nation for whom wounded pride was now a paramount emotion. The loss of Alsace and Lorraine to the Prussians in 1871; and now this! The frustrated fury in France itself was predictable, and the unbridled hatred against Britain whipped up by the French press during the Boer War was a vicious reflection of the whole atmosphere.

The Fashoda incident, nevertheless, marked a turning point in Anglo-French relations.

The crisis could easily have proved much worse, and actually degenerated into war, but for the pragmatic attitude of the man at the head of French Foreign Affairs, Théophile Delcassé. This man, on the brink of a war with his nation's traditional enemy, stepped back and took a long hard look at France's strategic situation. His common sense told him that war with Britain, at that time, was unwinnable. His intellect led him to the conclusion that France's long-term strategic interests could not be served if his country was permanently at odds with both Germany and Britain, even if the two latter nations were not in league with each other. On balance, the French Foreign Secretary decided Britain offered more fertile grounds for rapprochement than did Germany. It was a seminal moment. As far as traditional French policy went, at least for Delcassé, this was the light on the road to Damascus.

Delcassé was largely instrumental in extricating France from the Fashoda crisis. In the process he began to lay the foundations for a better relationship with London. In this he was aided by the fact that Salisbury had had no desire to humiliate France, merely to re-emphasise the status quo in a region that had been assumed to be within Britain's sphere of influence. France may well have felt humiliated by the outcome, but Salisbury had absolutely no desire or reason to revel or dwell on the subject. He had made his point, and the incident was over. It did, though, have repercussions that were entirely beneficial to both nations.

The incident had pointed out the dangers inherent to both countries in colonial border disputes. If these disputes over spheres of influence could be sorted out *before*, rather than after, they occurred, it would remove many a bone of contention that stood in the way of better relationships between the two nations.

Delcassé set to his task, and, without pushing things, by the time the Boer War was no longer in the immediate public consciousness, he had made significant progress. His subtle diplomacy was by then striking a chord on the other side of the Channel, where the expansion of the German Navy, and the strident proclamations emanating from Berlin as to Germany's future world role (*Weltpolitik*) were finally causing alarm. The less than spectacular performance of the army in South Africa had also served to reduce any sense of arrogance from the British quarter.

The process of *détente* was greatly facilitated by the long-serving French Ambassador to the Court of St. James. Paul Cambon was an outstanding diplomat whose part in bringing France and Britain together was as significant as that of Delcassé. If the latter can be thought of as the Field Marshall behind the campaign, Cambon was the general in the field. It was a powerful and persuasive combination.[3]

In 1903 the opportunity arose to take matters further. King Edward VII, an ardent Francophile, was planning a Mediterranean cruise that early summer. Without consulting his government, he decided to visit Paris as a preamble to the cruise. Government ministers were not at all sure as to the wisdom of this move, as public opinion on the continent was still hostile towards Britain in the wake of the Boer War. Nor were they pleased that the King's initiative impinged on the constitutional prerogatives of the government, which was normally responsible for the arrangement of state visits. Having failed to dissuade the King, they did their best to present the visit as a private affair, and to be as low key as possible. The King would have nothing of this, and set foot in France on the 1st May adorned in full regalia and accompanied by all the panoply of his monarchical position.

Initially, his reception was cool, but, by his demeanour, courtesy, and well-chosen words, he turned the four-day visit into a personal triumph. By the time he departed, he had effected a notable turnaround in French attitudes towards Britain. Far from discomforting his government, except in its sense of *amour propre,* he had handed it a diplomatic opportunity that proved to be an absolute boon for British foreign relations. To their credit, his ministers were not slow in taking full advantage of the King's initiative.

Two months later, the French President, accompanied by Delcassé, paid a return visit to Britain. His reception was extravagant, and the King played a major role, personally arranging most of the state occasions. During the visit, Delcassé had a meeting with his British counterpart, Lord Lansdowne. The result of this was that the very able Paul Cambon was authorised to commence discussions with the British Government aimed at resolving contentious areas of dispute in colonial matters.

---

[3] It was to Germany's great detriment that, during the whole period leading up to the First World War, it had, in Hatzveldt, Metternich and Lichnowsky, able generals in the ambassadorial field, but all of them completely hamstrung through lack of a competent higher authority. They advised well; they talked sense, but they were speaking to those in power who simply did not wish to hear inconvenient truths.

The talks covered a myriad of problems, large and small. Most important amongst them was the question of spheres of influence in North Africa. This effectively meant Egypt and Morocco.

Up until 1882, Britain and France had had equal influence in Egypt. It was a Frenchman, Ferdinand de Lesseps, after all, who had constructed the Suez Canal, that essential conduit to the east. The vital importance of that waterway made Egypt an area of the utmost consequence for the two nations with their extensive imperial and commercial commitments in India and the Orient.

When Arabi Pasha tried to overthrow the monarchy in Egypt, France decided not to join Britain in resisting the move. Consequently, it was the British Fleet alone that bombarded the Alexandria forts in 1882, and British forces which brought the subsequent shore operations to a successful conclusion. From then on, Britain assumed an ever-increasing role in Egyptian affairs to the point where the country was virtually reduced to the status of a protectorate. A British Agent, with vice regal powers was appointed to virtually run the country in the 'interests' of the Khedive, and British officers took over many of the senior posts in the army – including that of Sirdar (Supreme Commander).

The French bitterly resented their decline in influence, and constantly worked to undermine the British position, which attempts caused much mutual acrimony.

On the other side of the continent, the troubled and shambolic Sultanate of Morocco lay on the border of France's premier overseas possession, Algeria, into which the general anarchy threatened to spill. To protect and advance her position in the region, France wanted freedom of action in Morocco. This was impossible without approval from Britain, whose commercial interests in the country exceeded those of any other nation. Whilst France and Britain remained at loggerheads, French ambitions were stymied.

At the end of nine months of talks, these issues were resolved. France accepted British primacy in Egypt, and, in return, was granted *carte blanche* to take whatever action she considered necessary in Morocco. At the same time agreement was reached on all the other colonial questions.

No formal treaty was signed (or was ever signed) between the two nations, but the agreement marked the beginning of the *Entente Cordiale* (literally 'Friendly Agreement') that would gradually develop more and more into the nature of an alliance. After settling the overseas issues likely to bring them into conflict, it was only natural that the new relationship would focus on the more weighty matters of the European balance of power. It did not take long for this to occur, and Germany, predictably, would provide the impetus.

Initially, German politicians seemed remarkably unconcerned over the Anglo-French rapprochement, but they very soon recognised that the existing balance of power had shifted markedly to their detriment. The removal of potential sources of friction between Britain and France greatly reduced the threat to British maritime communications and trade previously posed by the fleet of the latter. The Anglo-Japanese alliance had eased British concerns about their naval position in the Far East, now the *entente* was to do the same in the Mediterranean and Atlantic. Coincidentally, better relations with France also reduced the threat from France's formal ally, Russia, whose fleet, in any case, was in the process of being obliterated in the war against Japan, which had commenced in 1904.

It became evident in Berlin that, if the Anglo-French connection continued to strengthen, then Britain would soon be free to confront the emerging German Fleet with the overwhelming power of its entire navy. The *Risk Theory* and the other hypothetical children of Tirpitz's master plan would then be dead in the water before they had even reached adolescence. Action was needed.

The German Government, without really thinking through the matter, belatedly resolved to test the mettle of the *entente* whilst the connection was still tenuous, and, by so doing, to break it. A suitable excuse was needed, and, in 1905, this was provided by Morocco.

Prior to 1905, Germany had shown little interest in Morocco. She was, however, a signatory to a half-forgotten treaty signed twenty-five years previously which gave her, together with France, Britain, Spain and Italy, the right to be consulted before any of the other nations took unilateral action within that benighted realm. In 1905, faced by increasing anarchy and corruption in Morocco, which was adversely affecting both the security of foreign residents and the viability of foreign commerce, the French decided to step in. They demanded that control over the security forces and customs be turned over to French personnel.

In taking this action, France was reassured by the recent agreement with Britain, and the previous lack of interest in Moroccan affairs displayed in Berlin. (Germany had actually been encouraging France in its colonial adventures in order to distract her from the German occupation of her two old provinces of Alsace and Lorraine.) Nevertheless, Delcassé gave advance information of his intentions to the other states involved in the old Treaty of Madrid – except, inexplicably, Germany. Whether or not this oversight was intentional, it was a dreadful error of diplomacy and was to have serious consequences, not least to the French Foreign Minister himself. He had given Germany a weapon with which to belabour him, and Berlin duly grasped it with both hands.

King Edward VII: 'The Great Encircler'

Théophile Delcassé

The Sultan of Morocco turned to the German Government for support against what he correctly saw as the first step in what would be a continuing French takeover of his kingdom – on the same lines as the British erosion of Egyptian sovereignty two decades previously. The German government gleefully accepted the opportunity thus presented, and assured the Sultan that Germany still stood by the terms of the Treaty of Madrid, which guaranteed the independence of his kingdom. It was a direct challenge to France, and particularly to Delcassé. Robert K Massie takes up the story:

'Behind this reply to the Sultan lay a major, carefully planned German diplomatic offensive. At the time of the signing of the Anglo-French agreement assigning Morocco to France, Bülow had accepted it as a means of restoring "tranquillity and order" in the Sultan's Kingdom. First Counsellor Holstein had disagreed, arguing that German commercial interests and German prestige both would be trampled by establishment of a French protectorate, but Bülow as Chancellor had prevailed. In the months that followed, Bülow had come round to Holstein's view…When Bülow had welcomed the Anglo-French agreement he had not recognised its larger significance. With the passage of time the implications of Delcassé's achievement dawned; the French Foreign Minister was not simply attempting to remove points of colonial friction; he was trying to change the balance of power in Europe.' (6)

Bülow now belatedly trained his sights on the *entente* and its principal architect.

He was actually in a very strong position at that time. France's ally, Russia, was debilitated by the war against Japan and would take many years to recover. She could offer no effective military assistance for the foreseeable future. The e*ntente* with Britain was still in its infancy and the latter had, in any case, no army of consequence that could be raised in time to help, even if any joint military arrangements had been in place.

Bülow's objectives were threefold. Firstly, he was determined to destroy Delcassé. Secondly, he set out to humiliate France, and by so doing, to demonstrate thirdly, that the *entente* was of no value to France. This latter objective was designed to gain the acknowledgement of France that she would have to accept German primacy in Europe and learn to live with that fact. In the first two objectives, which were short term, he succeeded entirely. In the third, which was long term, and the crux of the matter, he was completely foiled.

Of the weapons at his disposal for the furtherance of his campaign, Bülow first chose his own emperor. In the spring of 1905, the Kaiser embarked on a cruise that would take him to Spain and Italy. To the itinerary, Bülow helpfully added the destination of Tangier on the north coast of Morocco. There, Wilhelm, on the advice of his Chancellor, would make a highly publicised landing and deliver a fiery speech supporting the integrity of that nation.

The scheme descended into near farce. En route, Wilhelm developed cold feet as to his personal safety, and to the wisdom of the entire plan. It was with some difficulty that he was persuaded to go ashore, and was then visibly discomforted when required to ride in procession on a horse that had not been specifically trained for his use (Wilhelm's withered left arm made horsemanship difficult). What with the preoccupations of staying on this beast, and his nervousness as to risks inherent in a badly controlled crowd that verged on being a mob, the Kaiser was not at his imperious best, and departed as soon as he decently could. Nevertheless he made his prepared speech, and by his presence there served Bülow's purpose. The world's spotlight was turned on to the Moroccan question.

The world, however, was puzzled as to Germany's motives, and Bülow chose, for the time being, to keep his cards close to his chest. In retrospect it is clear that he intended France to become increasingly isolated.

'Gradually, the larger purpose began to reveal itself: the Kaiser's landing, the future of Morocco, were only factors in a German attempt to humiliate France. The collapse of Russia had provided the opportunity; France's moves in Morocco provided the pretext.' (7)

As German pressure mounted for the French to climb down from their proposed unilateral action, Berlin genuinely expected Britain to distance herself from the French position. E.L. Woodward comments that:

'The political situation in England was unstable. Everyone expected the fall of the Conservative government...Holstein had always believed that Great Britain would break any agreement rather than fight in a continental war. He had assumed that, if a crisis arose bringing with it the chance of war, the party responsible for the agreement would go out of office and allow their successors to repudiate promises which had been made.' (8)

It was a triumph of wishful thinking, and, in its insulting assumption of a lack of spine in Britain's political establishment, an interesting insight into the arrogant and ignorant attitudes prevalent in Germany's corridors of power. For years, they had swallowed their own domestic propaganda as to Germany's inevitable rise to world leadership – witness the responses to Chamberlain's initiatives for an Anglo-German understanding. Convinced that German military and industrial might had given them the whip hand in international affairs (at least those involving the European nations) they drafted plans in the bland assumption that German power assured their eventual success. This almost contemptuous dismissal of possible repercussions meant that insufficient attention was paid to the formulation of their own policies. As a result, they were about to become badly unstuck over the Morocco situation, a crisis almost entirely of their own making. E.L. Woodward again:

'Yet the situation was likely to develop in a manner not anticipated by Bülow or Holstein. Holstein's belief in English perfidy was wrong. If Germany wished to show that England was only a "platonic friend", and that English support would not be given to France, then it was clearly to the interest of England to be extremely forthcoming. If the entente was worth making, it was worth keeping.' (9)

The initial German goal was achieved. If France were to continue with her stated intentions in Morocco, it was made apparent that she would have to face the risk of war with Germany. The German General Staff was aggressively in favour of this option. They rightly pointed out that the general military situation in Europe was uniquely favourable to Germany at that moment and that a preventive war against France would remove the latter as a threat for many years. Their views were widely known throughout Europe.

Delcassé nailed his colours to the mast, but all around him support was shrinking away, and the German Government made clear that it was no longer prepared to deal with him.

President Loubet, who had faithfully supported him before and during the crisis, was replaced by an appeaser, Maurice Rouvier, who abandoned him to the wolves. Attacked by all sides of the political spectrum, and encouraged only, it seemed, by his English colleagues (and, notably and vehemently, King Edward), he was forced to resign. Round One had clearly gone to Bülow, but the bundling of Delcassé out of office was a significant factor in the realisation of the latter's long-term ambitions for the *entente*. It drew, if it were needed, close attention to the disproportionate power and influence of Germany on the continent, and hardened the determination of British politicians that France must, in future, be given the support to counter this imbalance.

With Delcassé gone, French resolve rapidly crumbled. In the face of overwhelming German might and with no effective military allies, President Rouvier capitulated. France abandoned her immediate intentions towards Morocco and agreed to submit the whole question to international arbitration. If bowing to overwhelming force can be termed a humiliation, then France had duly been humiliated, and her newly-established links with Britain had brought her no relief. Round Two also to Bülow.

In Germany, there prevailed a great sense of satisfaction as to the way events were progressing (the only dissenting voices came from the generals who lamented a lost opportunity to obliterate the French Army as a viable opponent for the conceivable future). There only remained the question of the international conference on the future of Morocco, which was to be set up as a result of German insistence. This was arranged to convene, in January 1906, in the Spanish port of Algeciras, just across the Strait of Gibraltar from Tangier. The German Government looked to its outcome with confidence that the results would further impress their influence on world affairs.

The Algeciras Conference marked a watershed in the German political consciousness of that era. In its aftermath, it gradually started to dawn on Bülow and Holstein that, not only had their appreciation of Germany's long-term diplomatic position been seriously awry, but their cavalier means of advancing its cause had alienated their country from much of the rest of the world. It was a late awakening, and far too late to reverse the trend of opposition that was coalescing against them.

The conference was Germany's child, coldly conceived and nurtured for a specific purpose. It proved fractious to its parent, and was not best served by the diplomats to which its care was entrusted.

The German delegation was headed by that nation's Ambassador to Spain, and Count von Tattenbach, their former representative in Morocco. The former was categorised with Bülow's typically malicious wit as a man 'with a great future behind him'. (Why did he select him then?) The latter scarcely deserved to be dignified by the term 'diplomat'. An arrogant and domineering bully, he represented the worst possible image of German authoritarianism, and managed to successfully offend most of the other delegates. His diplomacy was carried out with all the grace of an obnoxious thug. These two shining examples of Germany's political establishment convened with the representatives of all Europe's major powers.

The ostensible purpose of the assembly was to sort out the future of Morocco, and, to many of the delegates, this remained the focus of debate. However, the underlying reason for the gathering was to emphasise Germany's humiliation of France, and to drive a wedge between France and Britain.

Prior to the event, the Conservative government in Britain had been swept away in an electoral landslide. The new Liberal administration was at pains to assure the French that it fully intended to honour the agreements entered into by its predecessor, and that it would actively back France during the proceedings at Algeciras. Nevertheless, France approached the conference with misgivings.

From the beginning, the Germans attempted to pressurise the British delegation into persuading the French to making concessions. This, they argued, would bring the conference to a rapid and successful conclusion. This thinly disguised stratagem was designed to lower French confidence as to the degree of British support they could expect. The German advances were politely but firmly rebuffed. In the event, the British stood four square behind the French on every issue, and, in fact, frequently defended their (i.e. France's) position more resolutely than the French delegation did itself!

Several times the French showed signs of wavering in the face of German bludgeoning. Each time the British stood rock solid, and, finally emboldened, the French dug in their heels over what became the critical sticking point of the conference – authority over the Moroccan Police Force, which was effectively the key to control of the country. The details of the debate are irrelevant to this account, but, basically, Germany demanded that this should be placed under international control, whilst granting the French supervisory rights over some local units on the Algerian border. The French would not accept less than effective governance of the force. Deadlock ensued, tempers frayed, and swords were sharpened, not least in Berlin.

Holstein, enraged that the conference was not going as he planned, was openly for war. In Germany, the generals pricked up their ears once more, and waited, panting with anticipation, for the call. Bülow, however, was becoming more cautious. The strength of the British support for France had taken him aback, and he was not inclined to tempt providence in battle. The Kaiser also weighed in. He had started to have doubts about the Moroccan policy even before he had landed to make his speech in Tangier. Now he perceived it as a dreadful error. The swords remained sheathed, and a face-saving compromise was eventually reached.

On the critical issue of supervision of the police force, it was agreed that France and Spain would share the responsibility, but that it would be commanded by a Swiss officer! This, and other less contentious points having been settled, the conference dissolved, three months after it had been convened.

On the face of it, Germany had gained a certain degree of success. The French had been prevented from taking over Morocco, at least for the time being. Briefly, in some quarters, Germany was actually credited with a diplomatic victory.

The reality was very different. Morocco, and the Algeciras Conference, was a means to an end. Germany succeeded in obtaining the means, but utterly failed to produce the end.

'At first, because outright French predominance in Morocco had been postponed, some considered the conference a German victory…In time it became obvious that the Algeciras Conference was a significant defeat for German diplomacy. While France had not won the clear predominance she had sought in Morocco, she had gained something more precious…the active diplomatic support of Great Britain. At Algeciras, Germany achieved the opposite of what she intended. She meant to break the Entente before it took on meaning and strength. Instead, German bullying succeeded in driving France and England closer together…This was as clear in Germany as it was in the rest of Europe.' (10)

Far from severing the fragile links that had been established between Britain and France, Bülow and Holstein's actions had helped forge these into a much stronger chain – and much more rapidly than might otherwise have been the case. How Delcassé must have smiled.

As previously remarked, Algeciras was a watershed. German diplomatic strategy up to that moment had been invariably offensive in nature. Afterwards it became defensive. They went into Algeciras aiming at the isolation of France, and came away with an increasing sense of their own isolation, tied only to the ramshackle liability of Austria and the unreliable opportunism of Italy.

Whatever gloss they tried to place on the treaty in Germany, Bülow and Holstein were held to account by a furious *Reichstag*, which clearly divined the real issues at stake. Heads were called for. Bülow suffered a diplomatic collapse at this point and took to his bed. Whilst he was conveniently incommunicado, Holstein foolishly resigned over a tiff with his nominal superior in the Foreign Affairs Department. This was a regular ploy of Holstein's when crossed, and his resignations were never taken seriously. On this occasion, however, Bülow did not intervene, pleading unconvincingly that his malaise had prevented him from being aware of the matter, and, to Holstein's fury his resignation was accepted.

After thirty years as the *éminence grise* in the corridors of power of the Foreign Ministry, Holstein must have momentarily lost his acumen as an office politician. At a time when there was a howl for scapegoats, he obligingly supplied himself.

Bülow, tucked up in his bed, could content himself with the thought that Holstein's demise would probably take the pressure off himself. In Paris, Delcassé's smile must have broadened even further.

The realisation in London and Paris that their tentative relationship had stood the first test of fire had a galvanising effect. Although it continued to remain, in theory, an informal relationship, it more and more took on the aspect of a binding alliance. Military and, to a lesser extent, naval conversations began to take place between officers of each nation's services with a view to co-ordinating their activities if they found themselves at war against a common enemy. Implicit in these discussions, was the assumption that the common enemy would almost certainly be Germany.

For the naval planners, the new situation revolutionised previous thinking. If Britain's strategic problems had been much changed to her advantage, those of Germany had suddenly been placed in a new stark perspective.

Tirpitz's theories, to any perceptive person, had obviously been overtaken by events. Nevertheless, the provisions of the Navy Laws of 1898 and 1900 had taken effect, and the fleet envisaged in these programmes was taking shape. The question was whether to continue on these lines or abandon the attempt to compete with Britain in the changed circumstances with which Germany now had to deal.

The new British Liberal Government, which had a substantial pacifist component, had been expected (at least in Berlin) to be more emollient towards Germany than had Balfour's administration. However, the new Foreign Secretary, Sir Edward Grey, proved to be even less palatable to Berlin than his predecessors. Grey was a Liberal Imperialist straight out of the Joseph Chamberlain mould, albeit lacking the charisma and vote-catching ability of the latter. Although devoted to the concept of maintaining peace amongst the great powers, Grey had one overriding pre-occupation that coloured all his views. He believed, admittedly with some justification, that elements within Germany were hell bent on world domination. The 'Balance of Power', as Grey saw it, was essential to prevent Germany obtaining hegemony in Europe as a first step to that end. In his subsequent pursuit for peaceful relations between the Great Powers, Grey never gave sufficient credence to the possibility that Germany – far from thinking herself powerful – was increasingly insecure as to her future. It has to be said that, from the utterances of the Kaiser down to his government ministers and ambassadors, Germany did not give an impression of weakness, or of a nation that would countenance compromise and concessions in its foreign policy. The impression given was that of a fierce and confident nation, fired by military ardour and with a burning desire to stamp out her place in the world. But genuine concerns lay behind the aggressive façade.

'The personality of Germany as a nation was almost perfectly represented by the personality of the Kaiser as a man. Germany was threatening and blustering one moment, pained and reproachful the next. Germany was able, tempestuous, and unwise, a country with a chip on its shoulder, longing for prestige and acclamation, prone to dark moods of dejection that turned overnight into menacing arrogance…That was the Kaiser, touchy, envious, boastful and uncertain all at the same time.' (11)

For all his good intentions, Grey generally only perceived the former aspect of Germany's character and situation. It remained a crucial flaw in all his subsequent attempts to influence events on the continent that he failed to understand how Britain's increasing attachment to France and Russia was pushing Germany into a corner. The Kaiser's rants against 'encirclement' were not entirely without justification, but Germany's foreign policy remained as intransigent as ever. The results were predictable.

'As early as 1905, it had been apparent to Lansdowne and Sanderson that whatever else was true of Germany, her international position was deteriorating. The assumptions upon which *Weltpolitik* was based were already proving to be incorrect; the 'inevitable' war between Britain and one or both members of the Franco-Russian alliance had not occurred. Britain had not responded to the dangers of isolation by joining the Triple Alliance; and Tirpitz's fleet had, far from intimidating the British, antagonised them. A few more years of Bülow's diplomacy completed the ruin of the diplomatic position which Wilhelm had inherited from Bismarck.' (12)

On the face of it, all logic pointed to a change in German defence priorities back towards the army, and a diplomatic offensive to recover the ground lost at Algeciras. Against this was the continuing preoccupation of the Kaiser as to obtaining a powerful fleet, whatever its useful purpose; and also the political influence of Tirpitz, then at its height, who would continue to stubbornly adhere to his already exploded theories.

It is interesting to speculate as to what would have been the result of this German dilemma had matters remained as they were, but developments in Britain contrived to give the Kaiser and Tirpitz new grounds for hope, and new arguments to reanimate their ambitions. Ironically these stemmed from reforms that were directly intended to reinforce the British position *vis-à-vis* the German Navy.

The introduction of a radically improved battleship design by Britain, which made all battleships constructed up to that point virtually obsolete, offered Germany the opportunity to rejoin the naval race almost from scratch – and not nearly so far behind as before. The advent of the *Dreadnought* effectively bailed out the Tirpitz programme and his already discredited theories for a few more decisive years. That it did so ensured that the German Army would be starved of funding in order to provide for a second class fleet of battleships that, in the event, would not be permitted to fight.

CHAPTER SEVEN

THE DREADNOUGHT REVOLUTION

'I have got 60 sheets of foolscap written with all the new naval proposals and am pretty well prepared for the fray on October 21st.'

Sir John Fisher: Letter to Lord Esher

'I am ready for the fray. It will be a case of *Athanasius contra Mundum.* Very sorry for Mundum as Athanasius is going to win!'

Sir John Fisher: Letter to Arnold White

Sir John Fisher came to the post of First Sea Lord, on Trafalgar Day 1904, with a clearly defined plan of the reforms he intended to make to his beloved navy. His whole professional life had been a preparation for this moment.

In the end, Athanasius *did* triumph 'contra Mundum', but the happy warrior of 1904 was an embittered, exhausted and vengeful combatant by the time he had achieved the bulk of his aims in 1910.

During his time as Commander-in-Chief in the Mediterranean, he had started to hone his ideas into a coherent whole, and to inculcate like-minded officers with his theories. He also encouraged creative input from any officer, regardless of seniority, and adopted any suggestion or theory that could advance or improve his overall concept. His basic, and absolutely undeviating, tenet was that of 'The fighting efficiency of the Fleet, and its instant readiness for war'. (1) Whatever stood in the way of that end, however hallowed, however useful in secondary purposes, was to be ruthlessly discarded and consigned to the dustbin of history. Many senior, or middle ranking, officers in the navy had no desire to go either so far, or as fast, as he wished, and they too, to the best of his considerable ability, were cast out of responsible positions with their careers blighted.

There was no middle way with Fisher. If you were inefficient, you were out. If you were efficient, but disagreed with his ideas or methods, you were also out. Cecil Rhodes' reported last words, 'So much to do; so little time', epitomised Fisher's attitude. He was utterly focussed on what he saw as his task, which was to bring the Royal Navy, materially and effectively, to a level where it *actually* represented what the nation *supposed* it to be – the inviolate guarantor of its sovereignty.

By the nature of the service to which he had devoted his life and energies, he had a limited time, in a limited number of crucial appointments, to achieve his end. This was to drag the navy, kicking and screaming, into the 20th century – in order to be able to meet the future opponent he had already clearly discerned, and which was already challenging the old order. In the process, anyone or anything that got in his way was swept aside.

When he went from the Mediterranean to become Second Sea Lord, he managed to push through part of the first of his reforms, in the shape of the 'Selbourne Scheme', which radicalised officer training. As Commander-in-Chief, Portsmouth, he prepared the rest.

Before officially accepting the offered position as First Sea Lord, Fisher went to Lord Selbourne, the First Lord of the Admiralty, and placed in front of him a plan for the complete reconstruction of the navy. He was resolved that if Selbourne did not agree to every item of the plan, it could not stand as a whole, and he would not accept the post.

Fisher described his plan as 'Napoleonic in its audacity; Cromwellian in its thoroughness'. He obviously enjoyed this phrase, as he used it frequently, to many correspondents. But, to quote another Fisherism, 'Reiteration is the secret of Conviction', and he rarely departed from this principle. By his account, he went to Selbourne determined to have '...the Scheme! The Whole Scheme! And Nothing but the Scheme!!!!!' (2) Selbourne absorbed the verbal assault, which lasted some time, considered the arguments presented, and promised Fisher his support in bringing all aspects of the proposed reforms to fruition.

Fisher's great reforms fell into five categories. The first was personnel reform, which he had already initiated as Second Sea Lord as outlined in Chapter Five. The second, third and fourth were interlinked and inseparable, hence his insistence on the 'whole scheme'. These were the creation of a nucleus crew system for reserve ships; the wholesale scrapping of obsolete or ineffective warships; and the redistribution of the fleet to meet the challenge from Germany.

The nucleus crew system was the only one of his changes that received universal approval.

'Fisher's nucleus crew system was the high water mark of all the reserve systems which had been tried in the world's fleets. He deemed it "the greatest improvement of modern times".' (3)

Up to that point, the operational vessels of the active fleet represented the entire resources of the navy available for some time after a declaration

HMS KING EDWARD VII (1905)

Displacement: 16,350 tons
Dimensions: 454ft x 78ft x 27ft draught
Armament: 4-12inch guns; 4-9.2inch guns; 10-6inch guns; 14-3inch guns; 14QF.
Machinery: Twin screw; 18,000 H.P = 18.5 knots.
Belt Armour: 4-9 inch; Endurance: 7,000 miles at 10 knots

The eight *King Edwards* were the last class of British Pre-Dreadnought. Of well-balanced appearance, their mixed calibre armament marked a transitory stage towards the all big-gun *Dreadnought*. They served with the Grand Fleet until 1916, where their eccentric steering characteristics led them to be christened the 'wobbly eight'. King Edward herself was lost to a mine in foul weather off Cape Wrath at the beginning of that year. By the time of Jutland the remainder had been reallocated to the Channel Fleet, and all had been relegated to subsidiary duties by the end of the war.

SMS POMMERN (1907)

Displacement: 13,191 tons
Dimensions: 419ft x 72ft x 27ft. draught
Armament: 4-11 inch guns; 14-6.7 inch guns; 20-3.4 inch guns
Machinery: Triple screw; 20,000 H.P. = 18 knots
Belt Armour: 4-9.5 inch; Endurance: 4,800 miles at 12 knots.

The third of five *Deutschland* class vessels, *Pommern* was completed two years after the King Edward, and is markedly inferior to the latter in nearly all respects. Most noteworthy is the fact that, despite being three thousand tons lighter, and developing 2,000 horsepower more, than the British ship, the latter has a marginal speed advantage. It is indicative of the technological advantage still held by Britain at that time. The Germans, by this time, had managed to apply the quick firing principle to the 11-inch mounting which was an excellent weapon, and a vastly superior piece of ordnance to the old 9.4-inch gun. The manually loaded 6.7-inch guns were less successful, being too cumbersome for maintaining a high rate of fire. Pommern was lost, almost instantaneously, and with all hands at Jutland after being torpedoed, but her sisters survived the war in subsidiary capacities, and two actually served in the Second World War – where the one had the distinction of firing the first shots of that conflict, and the other that of being the last German capital ship in existence until her destruction five days after Hitler's suicide.

Probably the most significant aspect of this comparison is that it emphasises the very substantial qualitative, as well as numerical advantage available to the British in battleships of the pre-Dreadnought era. Throughout the naval race that ensued, there was always this large discrepancy of power in second line vessels, which would last until the end of the life span of those ships. For so long as the two nations possessed a relatively small number of dreadnoughts, the older ships tilted the balance of power hugely in Britain's favour; but for every dreadnought constructed, that advantage rapidly reduced. It was clearly seen by both Fisher and Tirpitz that within a few years, the *only* measure of a navy's power would be in the number and quality of *Dreadnought*-era capital ships.

of war. A very large number of vessels, comprising the remainder of the nation's warships were laid up in two categories of reserve, neither of which could be rapidly brought forward to the front line in an emergency.

The first category was the Fleet Reserve, which included all vessels intended to be deployed in an eventual war fleet. Ships in planned refits came under this heading, the remainder being laid up with a skeleton maintenance staff on board. The latter could clearly not be made operational before crews could be provided and trained in the effective use of the embarked machinery and weaponry. As such, they did not represent an immediate reinforcement for the fleet.

The second category was the Dockyard Reserve, consisting of ships undergoing long-term reconstruction, and a pool of more or less obsolete warships, of questionable efficacy. The latter were unmaintained, and could not be made operational, even if a purpose could be found for them, without a major refit. The same strictures with regard to finding crews for the ships of the Fleet Reserve, applied, but even more so in their case. The entire mentality pervading the system dated back to the wooden wall era when decrepit old hulks, long past their useful life, were occasionally fitted out and pressed into service to make up the numbers of a theoretical fleet.

Fisher's solution to the problem involved manning all the potentially useful ships of the reserve fleet with a nucleus crew amounting to two fifths of its operational complement. This nucleus would include all the specialist personnel vital to the running of the vessel and its embarked systems. The remainder of the crew could be made up, at short notice, from training and shore establishments, but the core of the complement, familiar with the ship and their individual departments would be permanently in place. The ships were to be regularly activated, and would join in annual manoeuvres with the active fleet. As such, they could provide an almost immediate reinforcement for the fleet at the outbreak of hostilities.

This system obviously required a much higher level of personnel than had previously been the case in reserve ships. Without greatly increasing the manpower resources of the navy, a financial impossibility at the time, from where were these nucleus crews to be provided? The answer lay in the third of Fisher's reforms, and this aroused fierce controversy.

He resolved to raise the necessary manpower by scrapping every vessel in the navy that he did not consider an effective frontline warship and utilising the crews previously employed on those vessels to make up the required numbers. The programme envisaged the removal from service of scores of vessels covering all classes of warship.

It was a vicious culling of the fleet, calling for the disposal of the entire Dockyard Reserve, plus ten old battleships, all the many old unarmoured cruisers, and a vast array of gunboats, sloops and cruising vessels employed on imperial policing duties. Even though his original proposals, in the face of screams of protest from within the service, were watered down somewhat, over one hundred and fifty ships 'by one courageous stroke of the pen' as Arthur Balfour said, were eventually wiped off the effective list of the navy.

In addition to providing the crews he needed, the scrapping policy removed the considerable burden on the naval budget of maintaining and repairing old warships that Fisher rightly regarded as 'a miser's hoard of useless junk', in the case of the Dockyard Reserve, and anything 'too weak to fight, and too slow to run away', in the case of the rest.

Ridding the navy of this excess baggage cleared the main dockyard ports of their encumbering presence, and enabled them to operate more efficiently as well as allowing economies in the number of dockyard personnel.

This policy of concentrating only on essentials resulted in a leaner, but far more effective force than had previously existed. It was, nevertheless, extremely unpopular with those who still placed a token value on some of the withdrawn units, and their views were echoed in certain sections of the press. Much later, at the beginning of the war, when there was a critical shortage of cruisers, there was a chorus of 'I told you so', but in fact, as events were to prove and Fisher had forecast, these vessels would have been more of a liability than of substantive assistance – he was, though, remiss in not constructing sufficient modern replacements for the obsolete cruisers.

The fourth reform was essentially strategic. The distribution of the British Fleet in 1905 took no account of the change in Britain's international situation following the alliance with Japan and the burgeoning *entente* with France. To maintain large forces in areas where there was no longer an obvious threat to British interests was plainly being profligate with available resources. Fisher already had a clear perception that the real threat to Britain lay across the North Sea, in Germany, and he took steps to meet the new challenge.

From 1905 onwards, the major warships of the navy began to be concentrated in home waters. First came the battleship component of the China squadron; later, the Mediterranean Fleet was steadily scaled down. Arthur J. Marder regards this process as the key reform made by Fisher:

'The redistribution of the Fleet to meet strategic ("and not sentimental") requirements was the crowning stroke of all. The distribution had been determined in the sailing ship era, when sea voyages were long and when squadrons to protect trade had to be distributed widely. There were nine squadrons or fleets in 1904. The advent of steam and cable communications, later the wireless, lessened the need for many isolated foreign squadrons. The entire distribution system was rendered obsolete by the Japanese Alliance (1902), and the French Entente (1904), and by the fact that, since 1901-2, the Admiralty had looked upon the German Navy as *the* potential opponent of the Royal Navy.' (4)

This strategic redistribution resulted in another large dose of calumny being heaped on the head of Fisher. Even his most loyal allies, such as

Esher, doubted the wisdom of denuding the foreign stations. The main concern had little to do with the logic of the action; it was based more on a sense that Britain's international prestige would be devalued if a major naval presence were not maintained worldwide.

The redistribution continued regardless, and, together with the culling of extraneous old vessels on foreign stations, it enabled a reduction, or downgrading, of a number of peripheral dockyards and support facilities abroad. Once again, significant economies were made whilst the fleet was better prepared to confront its most likely opponent. In the process, the number of major commands was reduced from nine to five.

This major shake up in Britain's strategic stance took place over the next four years. Basically it involved a steady westerly movement of the centre of gravity of the naval forces. To touch briefly on the details the old Home Fleet, which had previously been largely comprised of aging or reserve battleships, was renamed the Channel Fleet, and would be comprised of the most modern vessels in the navy. Concentrated in home waters, its quantitive strength was augmented to seventeen by the battleships withdrawn from the China station and by a reduction in the number of battleships allocated to the Mediterranean Fleet.

The old Channel Fleet was renamed the Atlantic Fleet and based on Gibraltar where it could reinforce either the Home or Mediterranean stations as priorities dictated. It comprised eight of the next best battleships, and would periodically exercise jointly with either the Channel or Mediterranean Fleets. The latter, although reduced in strength, still comprised a further eight effective battleships based on Malta. Finally, a new Home Fleet was formed, initially made up of ships in the nucleus reserve, but later to include all the new battleships entering service. This force would be based on Chatham, the only extant dockyard port on the east coast opposite Germany, and the long-term intention was for it to develop into Britain's premier fleet. In the meantime, the Channel Fleet, on its own, was more than capable of dealing with the German Navy as it then was. Reinforced by the Atlantic Fleet, three sailing days away at worst, it would possess a crushing superiority.

Elsewhere, the East Indies, Australian and China squadrons were amalgamated into a single wartime command with its focus on Singapore. Although in peacetime, these units would continue to operate independently, joint exercises would be regularly carried out. For the rest, only the Cape of Good Hope station remained as a major command, and took over responsibility for the whole of the South Atlantic, South America and West Africa. A modern cruiser squadron, based in Britain, and specialising in a training role, regularly cruised the West Indies and North American areas, only a few vessels of lesser importance remaining permanently in these waters.

Whatever the grounds for objection that arose as a result of this global redeployment, there is no doubt that it represented a logical and practical reaction to Britain's changed circumstances, and avoided the squandering of the country's available naval resources in areas of secondary importance.

That he was successful in forcing through the programme was not least due to the fact that, whilst greatly improving the effectiveness of the navy, he also reduced the cost to the taxpayer. During his initial three years as First Sea Lord, the naval estimates actually went down. Later, when Germany raised the ante, big increases were required, but, during the first half of his tenure of office, Fisher became the darling of the political establishment – particularly when the Liberals, committed to expenditure on social reform, came to office. There are echoes here of Tirpitz's success, six years previously, in pushing the First Navy Law through the *Reichstag* on the basis that it would guarantee a more effective navy for no additional cost. Tirpitz, though, had a hidden agenda – for Fisher, it was simply a common sense solution to a problem that urgently needed to be addressed.

The fifth of Fisher's great reforms will be dealt with shortly – and separately, as it affected the navies of the entire world, rather than just that of Britain.

The complete reformation of the navy instituted by Fisher is mostly embodied in the core changes he made to the service. This was the skeleton that was to provide the basis for other radical improvements in detail. Of these latter, mention must be made of the revolution in training and efficiency that was set in motion. Along with the structural changes and strategic redistribution he imposed on the navy, he immediately addressed the pressing issue of how to make better use of the excellent ships at his disposal, and realise the full potential of their crews. From every contact that was made with the German Navy, it was apparent that, whatever it currently lacked in numbers and quality of ships, this deficiency was being made good in a very short space of time. The efficiency of its use, high standard of key personnel, and the thoroughness of its training were uniformly impressive. There was no room for complacency.

Fisher gave full rein to the talents of officers who shared his concerns, and soon ensured that they were pressed into service in crucial positions. Prime amongst them was Percy Scott, an abrasive and difficult personality who was nevertheless a gunnery genius. He had a particularly inventive turn of mind, and ate, slept and drank his subject. He had already achieved startling gunnery improvements in the fleet, where his training methods, aided by devices of his own design, made every vessel he commanded the champion gunnery ship of its station. This status was not gained by small margins; his ships regularly hit the target two or three times more often than the average. The remarkable gunnery performance of ships under Scott's command made the naval establishment sit up and take notice. At the same time, his self-righteous and truculent attitude to his peers alienated many who might otherwise have joined his cause and smoothed the way for the reforms he so clearly saw to be necessary.

'The homilies of Percy Scott did a world of good, but unfortunately he was rather like the Old Testament seers, who rubbed those in authority the wrong way. Officers of high standing did not appreciate being told that for years they had neglected gunnery training, and that they should repent and do better. Percy Scott did not know how to gild the pill; so he met with more opposition than would have fallen to his lot had he been more diplomatic. Nevertheless, the Navy owes him a great debt of gratitude for all he did towards increasing our gunnery efficiency.' (5)

Early on, Fisher had recognised this man's unique ability, despite his unfortunate persona, and arranged for him to occupy the most influential positions in the gunnery hierarchy. 'I don't care if he gambles, drinks and womanises – he hits the target!' (6)

After Scott had served as Captain of *HMS Excellent*, the navy's cradle of gunnery, Fisher instigated the new post of Inspector of Target Practice, to which Scott was promptly appointed.

The overall result of Scott's influence, assisted by his disciples and supported by Fisher, was an astonishing transformation in the gunnery efficiency of the fleet. From a navy, at the turn of the century, that was content with hitting a stationary target, at two to three thousand yards range, with 25% of the ammunition fired; within half a decade, it became a navy that could hit a moving target at six to seven thousand yards range 75% of the time. In terms of the relative ability of the fleet to destroy an opponent, it was a quantum leap. This did not mean that it had gained a huge advantage over its future opponent, but it brought it to a level at which it was at least its equal.

The diplomatic events of 1902–1905 were universally detrimental to Germany, and brought into question the whole policy of naval expansion advocated by the Kaiser and Tirpitz, and given expression in the Navy Laws of 1898 and 1900. The alliances made by Britain, and the redistribution of the Royal Navy, more than neutered this policy; they made it utterly redundant.

Not only was Britain now deploying the bulk of its fleet in Northern European waters, ship for ship their contemporary battleships were far superior to those being constructed in Germany.

The phrase 'stolid' comes to mind when trying to describe the uninspired German designs that were to form the bulk of the new fleet authorised by the first two Navy Laws. Between 1900 and 1904, two classes, of five battleships each, were laid down. They were of 13,200 tons, armed with four 11-inch and fourteen 6.7-inch guns, and protected by similar armour to their foreign counterparts. Their speed was unexceptional. Over the same period, the British, in addition to a number of similar vessels, produced eight ships of the *King Edward VII* class, weighing in at 16,350 tons, and carrying four 12-inch; four 9.2-inch; and ten 6-inch guns. These vessels were better protected and had a speed advantage over the German ships. In addition, two other battleships of slightly higher tonnage, and even better protection, were under construction, carrying four 12-inch and ten 9.2-inch guns. The comparison was greatly to the disadvantage of the German ships.

Strategically on the point of collapse, and materially, hopelessly inferior, the whole German naval policy was in crisis. That it survived at all, never mind flourished, was the result of Fisher's final great reform.

This was precipitated by the remorseless advance of technology and design which made inevitable the advent of a radical new type of battleship. If Fisher had vigorously stirred the cauldron of discontent in his other initiatives, he brought it to the boil by the construction of *HMS Dreadnought*, the fifth, and, if possible, the most contentious of all his reforms.

The origins of the *Dreadnought* did not just lie in Fisher's own fertile imagination. The trends that were already in place were moving inexorably towards adoption of this type of vessel. Fisher, however, was one of the first to perceive the logical consequences of the situation, and that it would be fatal to British naval supremacy if other nations pre-empted Great Britain in riding that trend.

There were three factors that pointed the way towards the *Dreadnought* type. The first was the ability of modern naval artillery to accurately reach out to much greater ranges. The second was the absolute necessity of this, given the improved range and destructive capabilities of torpedoes, which made close range action unacceptably hazardous. The third was that effective long-range fire could best be achieved by a large number of heavy guns of the same calibre, firing salvoes. This made ranging much easier, early hitting more likely and continuous hitting the rule rather than the exception. A further two points were firstly, that the heavier the gun, the greater its range, and secondly, the penetrating power and destructive capability of the shell fired increased dramatically with the size of the gun. A twelve-inch shell, for instance, had twice the explosive effect of a ten-inch shell.

The acceptance that future naval battles would be fought at long range made irrelevant all weapons that were ineffective at that range – i.e. those that could not reach, or, even if they could, were incapable of penetrating the armour of their opponents. The only guns necessary, other than the main armament (and this became a contentious issue), would be those capable of supplying an effective defence against torpedo boats, and this indicated a relatively light, quick-firing weapon, albeit with sufficient punch to wreck the torpedo boats of the time.

Even before these principles became enshrined, battleship designs worldwide had been moving towards this end. It is only necessary to look at the drawing boards of the world's naval powers in 1904 to see the shape of things to come. As instances:

Japan: *Satsuma*
19,372 tons: four 12 inch-guns, twelve 10-inch guns.
Laid down 1905.

USA: *Michigan*
16,000 tons: eight 12-inch guns.
Authorised 1904.

Russia: *Imperator Pavel I*
17,400 tons: four 12-inch guns; fourteen 8-inch guns.
Laid down 1903.

Britain: *Lord Nelson*
16,500 tons: four 12-inch guns; ten 9.2-inch guns.
Laid down 1905.

France: *Danton*
18,318 tons: four 12-inch guns; twelve 9.4-inch guns.
Laid down 1906.

Looking at the above statistics, the one that stands out is that of the American ship. In the event, it was nearly six years before she completed, but the first all big gun battleship was authorised before Fisher pushed through the *Dreadnought*. Had the Americans hastened their progress, the word 'Dreadnought' may never have entered the dictionaries. We would now be talking about 'Michigans' as a synonym for battleships.

The Americans had actually got it right, although, by the time the two *Michigans* eventually appeared, they had been overtaken by developments elsewhere. Mixed calibres of 12-inch and 10/9.4/9.2/8-inch guns confused the matter when ranging, and complicated ammunition supply. The lessons of the Russo-Japanese War, then in progress, confirmed that only the heaviest guns had a decisive effect.

Fisher had been toying with the idea of an all big-gunned ship for some time. He had discussed future battleship design with the very able chief constructor of Malta dockyard, W.H. Gard, whilst he was Commander-in-Chief of the Mediterranean Fleet. In those days his preference was for a combination of the lightest heavy gun and the heaviest medium calibre gun (10 inch and 7.5 inch) to be mounted in large numbers on a single hull. He soon reversed this opinion, and, for the rest of his life, became an advocate of the largest possible guns, carried on hulls capable of the greatest possible speed – characteristics more suited to his temperament!

During his time as Commander-in-Chief, Portsmouth, Fisher had continued to work on the concept of a new generation battleship.

His efforts were given additional impetus by the publication in 1903, in the influential *Jane's Fighting Ships*, of an article by the respected Italian naval architect Vittorio Cuniberti who had been responsible for the introduction of an innovative, fast, light battleship class for the navy of his own nation. He wanted to take this design further and produce a much more heavily-armed version, but financial and political constraints in Italy prevented this. He therefore submitted this design, in *Jane's*, within the context of an article outlining his views on a suitable new battleship for the Royal Navy. It called for a ship capable of carrying twelve 12-inch guns. Added to the developments already taking place abroad, the article intensified debate on the subject of future ship design.

Cuniberti's theories reflected those that were taking shape in Fisher's mind. By the time he became First Sea Lord, he had practically decided on a basic specification, but recognised the need to have a broad base of expert backing for the project. Accordingly, one of his first acts was to form a committee on future battleship design.

The committee was chaired by himself and consisted of Sir Phillip Watts, the new Director of Naval Construction; W.H. Gard; a number of the most highly regarded senior naval officers, technical specialists, and much respected figures from outside the service, including Lord Kelvin; and the head of the important engineering concern, Alexander Gracie. Thus bolstered by an impeccable selection of experts, the conclusions of the committee formed the basis for the *Dreadnought* design.

Once the principle was decided, Fisher moved swiftly. It was clear to him that the new type of battleship would render all previous classes obsolete. Britain's huge preponderance in these vessels would be greatly devalued in the process, to the considerable detriment of her overall naval position. He was subjected to virulent criticism in his own country over the introduction of the *Dreadnought* type for precisely that reason, but had correctly assessed that the development was inevitable and, given that fact, it was vital that, in this case, Britain should get a head start. Time was of the essence, and Fisher's energy and drive produced an astonishing performance.

He insisted from the first that he would build this ship in a year. In an era when the normal building period for a battleship, in efficient yards, averaged two and a half to three years, construction of an entirely new type of ship, incorporating many novel features, in a single year, did not seem possible. Nevertheless it was done. To achieve this feat, Fisher cut every corner, and mobilised every resource at his command. As an instance, the main armament of a battleship often took longer to produce than the ship

HMS DREADNOUGHT (1906)

Displacement: 17,900 tons.
Dimensions: 527ft x 82ft x 27ft draught; Complement: 695-773
Armament: 10-12 inch guns; 27-3 inch guns
Machinery: Quadruple screw; Steam Turbines; 23,000 H.P. = 21 knots
Belt Armour: 4-11 inch; Endurance: 6,620 miles at 10 knots

The ship that started the naval revolution. By extraordinary measures, built in just a year and a day. The most obvious feature was the all big-gun armament, but the use of steam turbines to obtain a speed hitherto unknown for a battleship was an even greater innovation. A notable flaw was the lack of an effective secondary battery to combat the increasing size of torpedo boats/destroyers for which the embarked 3-inch guns were inadequate.

SMS RHEINLAND (1910)

Displacement: 18,873 tons
Dimensions: 479ft x 88ft x 29ft draught; Complement: 1008
Armament: 12-11 inch guns; 12-5.9 inch guns; 16-3.4 inch guns
Machinery: Triple screw; Triple expansion engines; 22,000 H.P. = 19.5 knots
Belt Armour: 4-11.5 inch; Endurance: 6,400 miles at 10 knots

One of the first German dreadnoughts. Completed four and a half years after the British ship, she illustrates the characteristics that would continue to differentiate the early German designs from their British contemporaries. Chief amongst these are the shorter length and greater beam which enabled more effective subdivision of the hull and, thus, much better underwater protection against the threat of mine and torpedo. The retention of a medium-calibre secondary armament, whilst being useless for its designed purpose of engaging the non-armoured sections of battleships at the increased battle ranges of 1909, amply met the provisions of an effective anti-torpedo boat defence. What can not be seen from the basic statistics is the much greater proportion of the overall tonnage devoted to armour protection (35%:25%) as compared with *Dreadnought*.

On the downside, the stubby nature of the design resulted in a poor sea boat, and meant that the official speed and endurance figures were only applicable in coastal waters. The space constraints dictated by the retention of bulky and relatively inefficient triple expansion machinery also meant that an additional turret had to be embarked to give the same broadside fire as the British ship, and largely accounts for the fact that an extra 300 personnel needed to be accommodated, with all the associated food and water requirements.

itself. Fisher simply commandeered the guns on order for the two *Lord Nelson* class ships, then under construction. Consequently, these two battleships joined the navy some time after the completion of *Dreadnought*.

His object was achieved, bar, to his chagrin, one day. *Dreadnought* was laid down on the 30th September 1905, and sailed for trials, under the command of Fisher's protégé, Captain Reginald Bacon, on the 1st October 1906.

HMS Dreadnought represented a watershed in battleship design similar to that produced by the introduction of the French ship *La Gloire*, forty-six years previously. By her existence she made every other battleship in the world a second class vessel. From henceforth all battleships would be placed into two categories, 'Dreadnoughts' or 'pre-Dreadnoughts'.

She was a remarkable ship in many ways. The most obvious visible characteristic was the all big gun armament – ten 12-inch guns in five twin turrets, four of which could fire on either broadside, and three (in theory anyway) directly ahead or astern. As such she could deploy two to three times the firepower of her immediate predecessors for a nominal increase in size of less than one thousand tons.

Inside her hull was an even more radical development. For the first time, a major warship was powered by turbines instead of the long-serving triple expansion machinery. Turbines had been used in the latest transatlantic liners, striving for the prestige of the coveted 'Blue Riband', but had never been previously installed in a major warship. Fitting *Dreadnought* with turbines was a calculated gamble that turned out to be a brilliant success. The system proved to be more reliable, and far more efficient, than the old machinery. Bacon comments that, in previous ships fitted with reciprocating engines:

> 'The engine room was always a glorified snipe marsh: water lay on the floor-plates and was splashed about everywhere; the officers often were clad in oilskins to avoid being wetted to the skin. The water was necessary to keep the bearings cool. Further, the noise was deafening; so much so that telephones were useless and even voice pipes were of doubtful value…In the *Dreadnought*, when steaming at full speed, it was only possible to tell that the engines were working, and not stopped, by looking at certain gauges. The whole engine room was as clean and dry as if the ship was lying at anchor, and not the faintest hum could be heard.' (7)

The engines also required much less maintenance after use than reciprocating machinery and were more economical in space. This latter fact enabled the heavier armament to be borne without a huge increase in dimensions, and, in propelling the ship at 21 knots, two to three knots faster than any of her contemporaries, gave her a crucial tactical advantage over such vessels. It was six years before Germany completed a similarly powered battleship; her initial 'Dreadnought' designs suffering badly from an inefficient armament layout dictated by retention of triple expansion engines.

On her trials, *Dreadnought* came up to, or exceeded, all the expectations placed on her by her advocates. She became the high profile symbol of the Fisher revolution, and was thus assailed by all those who had an axe to grind with the admiral.

The reasons for the construction of the ship have already been discussed, as have some of the objections. In the circumstances of the years after 1906, Fisher would have been as damned for not building her, as he was damned, at that time, for her creation – and by the same critics. In 1906, he was thoroughly damned by an impressively broad spectrum of opinion.

From out of the woodwork came an array of superannuated senior officers, supported and informed by numerous anti-Fisher elements in the service. To many of his critics, he had betrayed the paramount position of his navy, and the security of his country that relied so implicitly on the maintenance of that position. To the ranks of those who genuinely doubted the wisdom of his policy were added the increasing numbers of those to whom the First Sea Lord himself was anathema. Both categories included a bevy of distinguished retired admirals, and also many serving officers whose feathers had been ruffled or careers damaged by abrasive contact with Fisher's intolerant and autocratic style.

The chief argument of his gainsayers was that the Royal Navy possessed an unassailable superiority in what would, from henceforth, be termed 'pre-Dreadnoughts'. By consigning these vessels to obsolescence, Fisher was, at a stroke, dismantling the foundations of British maritime supremacy. After the appearance of *Dreadnought*, any nation wishing to challenge Britain at sea could start from scratch, and it would take years, vast expense, and an enormous industrial effort to reassert the status quo, if indeed that would any longer be an option.

'The most powerful argument used by Fisher's critics was that it was wrong policy for the nation possessing overwhelming power at sea and the greatest shipbuilding capacity to pioneer new types of fighting ships; that traditionally it was Britain's role to allow others to experiment, and then herself improve in quality and surpass in numbers.' (8)

What the critics failed to appreciate was that Fisher had come to the same conclusions himself, and did so well in advance of them. It was not a situation of his choosing. He *knew* the consequences that would ensue from the appearance of the *Dreadnought*, but he also *knew* that the development of a ship such as her was inevitable – if it did not happen in Britain, it would very soon happen elsewhere. If such a vessel had first been constructed abroad, Britain would have had the painful task of catching up with developments. By the action he took, he ensured that Britain had at least a commanding lead in the new circumstances. In advancing this opinion, I draw on the magisterial authority of Professor Marder:

'In deliberately nullifying Britain's advantage at the height of her battleship predominance by commencing the construction of all-big-gun battleships, Fisher ushered in a new era in naval competition by giving the Germans a chance to start nearly from scratch. Was the Dreadnought policy Fisher's greatest blunder, or was it a stroke of genius? The writer feels it was the latter...The dreadnought type was on the horizon in 1904-5, and therefore it was, as Fisher realised, imperative to gain for Britain the advantage of leading the way.' (9)

It is also worth noting that, in 1906, Britain, at least *vis-à-vis* Germany, could no longer rely on the old fallback position of being able to build more and faster once a rival produced an innovative design that required countering. Germany's shipbuilding capabilities were almost on a par with Britain by that time, and her armaments industry was the largest, and most efficient, in the world.

The other main criticism that was thrown at him was that the size and expense of new ships of the *Dreadnought* type involved placing too much potential in a single hull. There was a powerful lobby in favour of restricting the size of individual battleships. Also, fewer large ships could be built within a given budget. They pointed to the danger of having too many eggs in too few baskets, and the disproportionate effect on the fighting strength of a fleet that would result from the loss of a single *Dreadnought*. It was more prudent, they argued, to spread the overall strength of the fleet into a greater number of hulls. A subsidiary contention was that there were insufficient docks of adequate size in the country to accommodate the dimensions of the new ships. Providing these would further strain the defence budget. Prominent amongst the advocates of this line of reasoning were not just professional malcontents, or personal enemies of Fisher, but such respected authorities as Sir William White, the recently retired Director of Naval Construction, and that guru of maritime strategy, US Navy Captain A.T. Mahan. Marder pertinently remarks on the latter that:

'However eminent a naval historian, he had no special competence as an authority on tactics or modern construction.' (10)

White was admittedly a renowned constructor, but, like Mahan, he too had no 'special competence' as to tactics or to the requirements of modern gunnery. When in office, he designed ships to meet the specifications of the navy, and achieved great success in that task, but his role had no place in the definition of those specifications.

Their arguments were comprehensibly countered. As Bacon dryly observed, 'Knowing as we did that the *Dreadnought* was the best type to build, should we knowingly have built the second best ship?' (11) An all big-gun armament dictated the size of the vessel, and the advantages of this arrangement to long-range gunnery efficiency were apparent to all those who had studied the subject. It was, in fact, the main *raison d'être* of the design. If there were any lingering doubts on the matter, they were dispelled when the ship made her first appearance at the 1907 fleet exercises. At gunnery practice she scored nearly twice as many hits over a given period as the next best vessel.

As to the risk of losing a ship of this type, and the disproportionate effect this would have on a fleet, a large battleship could naturally incorporate better defensive qualities than a smaller vessel, and the 'eggs' would be in a much better protected 'basket' than would otherwise be the case.

There was also the tactical argument that a fleet of given strength would be easier to handle in battle, and defend as a unit, if its capabilities were concentrated in a limited number of very powerful ships, rather than diffused amongst a large number of much weaker vessels. With the clear speed advantage enjoyed by the type, a fleet comprised of *Dreadnoughts* could concentrate its attention on the corresponding section of an enemy's line, and, by its overwhelming superiority in firepower, obliterate its immediate opponents before the remainder could provide support. These latter could then be mopped up at leisure.

The assertion that docking facilities were lacking for ships of *Dreadnought* size was easily disposed of by the devastating riposte that, if the country continued to build second class ships, there would be no need for any docks at all – as, after its first meeting with the enemy, the whole lot would be at the bottom of the sea!

There could really be no doubt as to the correctness of the decision to build the *Dreadnought*. In 1906 and 1907, a further six, basically similar, vessels were laid down for the Royal Navy. The extreme measures taken to hasten construction of the prototype could not be applied in their case, but, by 1910, all were in service, and, with their prototype, forming the nucleus of a fleet based on the nearest dockyard port to Germany.

Amongst the world's other naval powers, the appearance of the *Dreadnought* imposed a period of pause to take stock of the situation. Several nations were already planning ships of this type, and, as previously recounted, the USA had actually authorised the construction of two such vessels before *Dreadnought* was laid down. As details of her probable armament leaked out, or were surmised, Tirpitz revised his plans for future construction programmes.

As *Dreadnought* was being completed, the German naval programme for 1906 was published. It included three ships of the *Dreadnought* type. They were laid down the following year, but construction was then suspended for a full twelve months whilst the success, or otherwise, of the

Dreadnought's trials were keenly assessed. In the meantime, work proceeded on the last class of pre-Dreadnoughts authorised under the first two Navy Laws. The *Deutschland* class were hopelessly inferior even to contemporary British pre-Dreadnought designs, and continuation of their construction seems curious. The last of the class had not even been launched when *Dreadnought* began her trials, and the logic of stubbornly proceeding with the building of ships that were patently obsolete before they had even entered the water is inexplicable. Common sense would have had them broken up on the slip, and the materials recovered then utilised for new construction of effective warships.[1] The only possible reason for continuing with these vessels was the desirability of providing continuity of employment in the shipyards. This factor probably swung the balance in favour of completing the ships.

The delay in resuming construction of the first German *Dreadnought* class effectively gave Britain a three year start in building a fleet of these vessels. Nevertheless, Germany was relatively in a much better position than would have been the case had the value of fleets continued to rest on pre-Dreadnought strength and numbers. The new situation did, on the other hand, pose new problems, one of which was unique to Germany.

The Kiel Canal, that indispensable strategic conduit for the German Fleet, could not take a vessel of *Dreadnought*'s dimensions, and there was little doubt that the size of subsequent classes would probably further increase. If Germany were to embark on a construction programme of these ships, it would be necessary to both deepen and widen the canal. This was a huge and expensive project, and could not be completed for many years.

It has been suggested that this complication was in Fisher's mind when he originated the *Dreadnought*, but it actually played no part in the decision, which was based purely on operational considerations. This is not to say that he didn't appreciate the resulting burden that was thus imposed on the resources of his country's only logical opponent – on the contrary, he was positively gleeful. In one of his remarkably accurate predictions, he set the date for the outbreak of the war he regarded as inevitable as the first convenient moment to Germany subsequent to the reopening of the Kiel Canal. This, he forecast, would take place in the autumn of 1914, and on a bank holiday weekend. In the event, the canal reopened in June 1914, and hostilities commenced between Britain and Germany on 4th August – a bank holiday weekend.

The first German dreadnought, the *SMS Nassau* was completed on 1st October 1909, three years to the day of *Dreadnought* proceeding on her

---

[1] The final ship of the *Deutschland* class was the *Schleswig-Holstein*. She was not completed until 1908, but managed to carve herself a niche in history. In the early morning of the 1st September 1939, it was shots from her guns, aimed at Polish positions on the Westerplatte, opposite Danzig, that marked the opening of the Second World War.

trials. The *Nassau* was the forerunner of eight basically similar battleships built for the High Seas Fleet. They were solid ships, more beamy than their British contemporaries and better protected, but suffered from an uneconomical distribution of the main armament. This was forced on German designers by the retention of triple expansion machinery. The installation of turbines on the *Dreadnought* had actually been as big a revolution as her all big-gun armament, and brought with it great advantages of space in the siting of the latter.

Rather than sacrifice protection, German designs always put a premium on survivability to the detriment of gun calibre and speed. The British preferred a different set of priorities, and these contrasting approaches to battleship design remained true throughout the Dreadnought-era. The contrast in designs almost served as a metaphor for the officers who presided over their creation.

Tirpitz and Fisher had many things in common. They were sincere patriots of a similar age and came not from a wealthy or privileged family. They had risen up the ladder of their profession through sheer ability and strength of character. Both were primarily administrators rather than fleet commanders, and both could be devious and calculating in obtaining their ends. They also held a shared belief in the power of the press and the need to manipulate public opinion. Both were inflexible in their views. Together they stood like twin colossi over the development of their respective navies in the critical period between 1900 and the outbreak of war.

There the similarities ended. In personality they were diametrically opposed. Tirpitz was as stubborn as a rock in his inflexibility, Fisher volatile and aggressive. Tirpitz became a consummate diplomat – and needed to be. His role was as much political as professional, and he had to personally fight his corner in the corridors of power and the forum of the *Reichstag*. He learned to turn opposition by argument and application of not invariably subtle pressures. Fisher despised politics and politicians, but could leave that side of things to the civilian First Lord, who had to argue the navy's case in parliament. He certainly did not lack political awareness, and possessed considerable cunning, but his automatic reaction was to confront opposition head on, and crush it utterly.

The ships built under the auspices of the two men reflected this difference in approach. Tirpitz strove for the Immovable Object; Fisher for the Irresistible Force.

Whilst the design for the *Dreadnought* was being finalised, Fisher also turned his attention to the future of the armoured cruiser. No less than the pre-Dreadnought battleship, all vessels of this type, built, building, or planned, would be made obsolete by the increased speed of future fleets

Admiral Sir Percy Moreton Scott
'I don't care if he gambles, drinks and womanises – he hits the target.'

Reginald McKenna
First Lord of the Admiralty 1908 -1911

comprised entirely of *Dreadnoughts* capable of 20 to 21 knots. For fleet scouting purposes, a margin of five knots superiority over the battleships was needed for an armoured cruiser to be effective. The speed was necessary to allow rapid advance ahead of their own fleet, and to be able to keep at a safe distance from that of the enemy, whilst reporting his movements. Existing designs gave only 23 knots, which was now clearly inadequate.

Armoured cruisers also had to be able to force through a reconnaissance in the face of opposition from similar enemy vessels. This could only be achieved by a preponderance of power. Any new armoured cruiser design would not only have to be much faster than her predecessors, but powerful enough to at least hold her own against the latest foreign construction. Of these latter, the Japanese had laid down, in March 1905, the first of four innovative warships. The initial pair were of 13,750 tons and carried the extremely powerful armament of four 12-inch; twelve 6-inch; and twelve 4.7-inch guns. The second batch were a thousand tons heavier and substituted eight 8-inch guns for the 6 inch. Speed was 20.5 knots in the first two; 21.25 knots in the subsequent pair. Seven-inch armour protection was carried on the belt. Apart from being a little shy on speed, they outclassed any armoured cruiser under construction elsewhere in the world. A new British design could be expected to at least be their equal.

Fisher, in fact, had decided on an even more radical improvement, matching in audacity the *Dreadnought* concept. Just as *Dreadnought* had made all other battleships obsolete, the new ship would do the same to existing armoured cruisers. Three of these vessels were authorised at the same time as the *Dreadnought*, and the first, *HMS Invincible,* was laid down six months after the battleship. After a few years of existence, they became known as battlecruisers.

Proud though he was of the *Dreadnought*, the battlecruiser represented Fisher's true ideal of a warship. At 17,250 tons, she was only slightly lighter than the *Dreadnought*, whilst being of greater dimensions. As with the battleship, she carried only the heaviest weapons then in service, eight 12-inch guns, plus a light anti-torpedo boat armament of sixteen 4-inch guns scattered around the superstructure and on the turrets. Fisher insisted on an unprecedented minimum speed of 25 knots, and this was to be obtained by sacrificing what he considered to be superfluous protection. Armour, apart from that on the turrets and barbettes, was therefore limited to a narrow belt of 6-inch plate on the waterline and a thin protective deck. This was no better protection than that carried by most armoured cruisers, and neither as thick nor as extensive (relative to the size of the ship) as on the latest foreign vessels of that type.

The last statistic points to the most contentious aspect of her design, and the one that would later condemn the type to universal scorn. This post-Jutland revulsion was overdone, but, for their size and importance, the battlecruisers – or, to be precise, the *British* version of the battlecruiser – were insufficiently robust. When Germany and Japan eventually responded and produced their own equivalents, they had a better balance of qualities and were, by every standard, excellent ships.

Despite rumblings of doubts over their armour, Fisher was sublimely unconcerned. The battlecruisers were his acme of the perfect warship – a vessel that could outrun anything it could not fight (which only meant a *Dreadnought* battleship, or a combination of ships), and could catch anything it could destroy (which was everything else afloat). When questioned, he constantly re-iterated his dogma that 'Speed *was* Protection'.

He had earlier actually expounded a complementary dogma that 'Armour was Vision', meaning that adequate protection was necessary to enable a ship to approach and report on an enemy fleet without being destroyed in the process. When this came into conflict with his concept of the battlecruiser, it was never again mentioned. This was unfortunate, as both statements were equally true and to combine them was to bring about the creation of an ideal fast battleship.

For the First Sea Lord, however, there became only two criteria that counted; the greatest possible speed combined with the heaviest possible calibre of gun.

'If we have the advantage of speed, *which is the first desideratum in every class of fighting vessel...then, and then only,* we can choose our distance for fighting. If we can choose our distance for fighting, then we can choose our armament for fighting.' (12)

With the speed to select your optimum distance from an enemy, having larger guns enabled the opponent to be engaged from a range at which he could not reply. Given these advantages, as Fisher stated elsewhere:

'...you can fight HOW you like, WHEN you like, and WHERE you like!' (13)

There is no better illustration of one of Fisher's weaknesses than this remark. It entirely assumes that all actions will take place in ideal conditions. There is no consideration here that in the North Sea (which area he had declared to be the likely centre of naval operations in the event of war with Germany) there is *very* rarely good visibility. Quite the opposite. Once the visibility is less than the maximum range of the enemy's guns, all the range advantage of having bigger guns is lost, and all the disadvantages of having inadequate armour is immediately exposed. His remarks above are those of a theoretician and materiel expert, not a practical seagoing admiral.

Fisher always thought along simplistic lines, and his arguments were enticing for so long as the battlecruiser type was used in roles for which it was suitable. When the ships were still in the design stage, Fisher himself had stated their purposes on these lines:

1. To be a fast scouting force, capable of forcing through a reconnaissance against a fleet possessing only inferior old armoured cruisers.

2. To act on the trade routes, having sufficient speed and seaworthiness, and possessing the long range, to hunt down and destroy enemy cruisers and merchant raiders – particularly the fast transatlantic liners that were earmarked for war on commerce.

3. To act as a fast wing of the battle fleet, capable of outflanking the enemy forces, pursuing and mopping up cripples, and destroying the opposing scouting forces.

The *Invincible*s met all these criteria and as such were extremely potent warships. They completely lived up to their design specifications, reaching well over 26 knots on trials, and presenting a formidable profile. With three massive slab-sided funnels and four 12-inch turrets mounted on a long high hull they created an instant impression. For their declared intent they were obviously a powerful new factor in the naval plans of all maritime nations.

Where Fisher went badly wrong was in beginning to equate his darlings to battleships. This occurred soon after their introduction:

'The "Invincibles" are, as a matter of fact, perfectly fit to be in the line of battle with the battle fleet, and *could more correctly be described as battleships which, thanks to their speed, can drive anything afloat off the sea.*' (14)

Had Fisher been alone in this opinion, not much harm would have been caused, but an admiral possessing these ships was obviously tempted to utilise their great offensive powers with his fleet, and their commanders were only too glad to comply.

As Fisher's opinions hardened, he advocated that only battlecruisers should be built in future. Fortunately, he was thwarted in this but eventually, as he became increasingly extreme in old age, he advocated even less armour, ever more speed, and fewer but heavier guns for the battlecruiser type. After he returned to the Admiralty in 1914, he managed to get approval for the construction of three such vessels. Unable to push them through as 'battlecruisers', he had them designated as 'large light cruisers'. A completely unbalanced design, they proved to be embarrassing white elephants in service and were eventually converted to aircraft carriers in the 1920s.

Within a few years of their completion, the *Invincibles* lost much of their *raison d'être*, as Germany began to construct similar vessels but with better defensive properties. For scouting and fleet duties, they were now opposed by at least their equals, and their brief period of predominance was over. Nevertheless, in annihilating von Spee's squadron at the Battle of the Falkland Islands, they triumphantly vindicated at least the second of their designated roles.

In Germany, the appearance of the battlecruiser so soon after the *Dreadnought* added to the sense of crisis. The *Invincibles* had been built in conditions of great secrecy, and Tirpitz was completely deceived as to their actual characteristics. He had been expecting a faster, much improved armoured cruiser, and anticipated something on the lines of *Dreadnought*, but with 9.2 instead of 12-inch guns. It was not an illogical expectation, and, to compete, he had laid down a ship which closely configured to the first German dreadnoughts, but with twelve 8.2-inch guns instead of the 11 inch of the latter. The *Blucher* was an excellent ship, capable of nearly 25 knots and better protected than *Invincible*, but she was outranged and heavily outgunned by the British ship. As an armoured cruiser, she would have been probably the best of the type ever built, but the German Navy rated her as a battlecruiser and always utilised her in that role.

The follow-up ship to the *Blucher* came into service a year later and displayed none of the latter's deficiencies. The *Von der Tann* carried 11-inch guns and matched the *Invincibles* for speed whilst outclassing them in protection. She formed the first in a line of German battlecruiser designs that had as good a balance of qualities as any capital ship of the day.

As with *Dreadnoughts*, Germany was now also involved in a battlecruiser building competition with Great Britain. The same conditions applied. The Royal Navy had a slender lead, but its previous crushing advantage in armoured cruiser numbers was substantially devalued. Tirpitz and the Kaiser had been given fresh hope that a naval challenge might succeed. If they stuck to their guns and Britain faltered, there was a chance of approaching parity in capital ships.

In political terms, the German Navy had the advantage of relative stability. Tirpitz was the effective head of its political wing, and, in all, he served nineteen years in the post. He had direct access to the *Reichstag* whenever the navy's case had to be argued. He also dealt directly with the German Chancellor and the Kaiser. All three key pillars of the German constitution were therefore open to his personal influence.

The Kaiser was a constant factor, and a guaranteed advocate of a strong battle fleet.

For over half of the Tirpitz era, the German Chancellor was Prince Bülow, who, however devious in other respects, recognized the advantages of humouring his royal master in naval matters. It is true that in the last couple of years of his Chancellorship, as his star began to wane, he became not uncritical of the naval programmes and their effect on Germany's overall situation. Generally, though, he fell in with the wishes of Wilhelm and the State Secretary of the Navy.

His successor, in 1909, Theobald von Bethmann-Hollweg, was less pliable. He worried about the increasing isolation of Germany on the international scene, and could see the benefits of naval concessions if they served to improve Germany's diplomatic relations with Britain. In the face of Tirpitz's implacable resistance, and the refusal of the Kaiser to countenance any impingement on his imperial prerogative to have as big a navy as he wanted, he was powerless in this respect without the strong support of the *Reichstag*. This was not his to command.

Whilst the composition of the *Reichstag* might alter from election to election, it was the servant of an electorate driven by nationalistic fervour, and nurtured by the long-term propaganda campaign organised by Tirpitz and his acolytes. The great drive for a navy of world standing had developed a momentum amongst public opinion that would have been difficult to arrest. Only a minority of politicians attempted to reverse the trend.

Whatever good intentions Bethmann may have had were wrecked on this one immovable rock. The consensus of power was always against him. As a result, the Kaiser and Tirpitz had a relatively smooth ride whilst building up a fleet to match their ambitions.

On the other side of the North Sea, the man who had set himself to thwart the implied challenge to British maritime supremacy was in a very different position to his German counterpart.

Unlike Alfred von Tirpitz, he did not have the advantage of being able, or having, to argue his case directly to the political establishment. (In this, Tirpitz might have envied him on occasion!) Nor did he have behind him a monarch with significant executive power. King Edward VII was a staunch friend of Fisher, and a very stalwart supporter of his schemes, but he could only work behind the scenes. He could not supply the real, overt, heavyweight, political backing that the Kaiser could throw behind Tirpitz.

Fisher, therefore, was reliant on his political chief to fight his corner. He had a much shorter period of time at the peak of his profession to achieve his life's work, and there was no stability or continuity in the political figures with whom he had to deal. In just over five years at the head of the Royal Navy, he served with four civilian First Lords of the Admiralty (excluding his later association with Churchill) from two political parties that had a very different approach to defence requirements. The first and last of those First Lords stand out as men of consequence. In between them there were the Earl of Cawdor, and Lord Tweedmouth.

The former was an able man, who would probably have made a success of the job. However, he had only a brief tenure before a change of government led to his replacement. In the circumstances, he had only a limited time to make his mark.

> 'Cawdor came direct from an eventful chairmanship of the Great Western Railway, where he had initiated policies destined to benefit that line for many decades to come. Like Fisher, he was a man who by instinct looked ahead and could see through the wall of time to what was coming up behind it; and though their collaboration only lasted nine months, the fruits were memorable.' (15)

Tweedmouth, his successor in the new Liberal government, although not lacking ability, was a comparative lightweight and a disaster in the post. Unfortunately he was not up to the task of dealing with the violent controversies that would rend the navy in the middle of Fisher's reforms. This was exacerbated by the fact that he was suffering from an undiagnosed brain tumour that shortly began to affect his judgement, and led to his eventual transfer to a less demanding post. The unfortunate man died not long afterwards.

Lord Selbourne was First Lord during Fisher's spell as Second Sea Lord and worked with him closely in bringing in the educational and personnel reforms at that time. If the ideas were mainly Fisher's, the success of the First Lord in getting them accepted led to the process being dubbed 'The Selbourne Scheme'. It was the same man that Fisher approached before he became First Sea Lord, and had to convince, when he laid on the table the rest of his radical proposals. As previously related, Selbourne took the whole plan on board and ensured its acceptance.

If Selbourne provided an essential umbrella for Fisher in the early stages of his reforms, Lord Tweedmouth's successor, Reginald McKenna, unfurled it again when the storms were really at their height over the beleaguered head of his First Sea Lord. McKenna, as the situation dictated, both restrained and encouraged the turbulent genius of his principle naval advisor. By that time, even the titanic energy of Fisher was beginning to flag after four years of constant battling against mounting opposition and increasingly vitriolic personal abuse. McKenna gave him unwavering support and was absolutely steadfast in arguing the navy's case in parliament. Selbourne and McKenna both recognized Fisher's faults and regretted his excesses, but both were convinced that he was basically right, and, whilst they may have winced once or twice, they stood four square behind him. Fisher adored them for it. He knew how difficult he could sometimes make their task.

Of all the burdens he threw onto the shoulders of his later First Lords, the greatest of them was the deep and virulent divisions caused in the Royal

HMS INVINCIBLE (1908)

Displacement: 17,250 tons
Dimensions: 567ft x 79ft x 27ft; Complement: 784
Armament: 8-12 inch guns; 16-4 inch guns
Machinery: Quadruple screw; Steam Turbines; 41,000 H.P. = 25 knots
Belt Armour: 6 inch max; Endurance: 3,000 miles at 25 knots

The first battlecruiser. Initially described as an 'improved armoured cruiser', which term more accurately described the vessel, the three ships of this class were the all big-gun cruiser contemporaries of the *Dreadnought* and her successors. As such, they created an enormous impression when they first appeared, being, as Fisher gloated, powerful enough to destroy anything that could catch them, and fast enough to avoid anything that could destroy them. For a period this was true, but in time, when similar, better armoured, vessels were built abroad, they lost their brief ascendancy and immunity. Without doubt they were powerful ships, but their impressive offensive qualities were always likely to see them used in situations for which their protection was inadequate – as was proved at Jutland.

SMS VON DER TANN (1910)

Displacement: 19,370 tons
Dimensions: 563ft x 87ft x 29ft; Complement: 910
Armament: 8-11 inch guns; 10- 5.9 inch guns; 16-3.4 inch guns
Machinery: Quadruple Screw; Steam Turbines; 42,000 H.P. = 25 knots
Belt Armour: 10 inch max; Endurance: 4,400 miles at 14 knots

The German answer to the *Invincible*s, and a much better balanced ship, being more of a fast, light battleship than an armoured cruiser with battleship guns. In their battlecruiser designs the Germans produced a succession of highly successful vessels that were qualitatively superior to their British contemporaries, and a far more effective type of capital ship than their own, rather stolid battleship classes.

Navy by his reforms and his methods of their implementation. When he retired in 1910, his work had been basically completed. The great reforms were largely in place and being made to work. This was probably true two years previously, but there was still much opposition, and he was determined to scotch the obstructionists, doubters, and haverers before he left office. He wanted no dilution of his measures, and trusted no one but himself to ensure that delays would not take place. The whole argument over his programme had also become very personal.

His work had, more than that of any other man, prepared Britain's premier service for the conflict he saw as inevitable. Unfortunately, his abrasive personality; the controversy over the reforms he had instituted; the ruthless discarding of treasured traditions; the arbitrary disregard of normal sensitivities, did not make for a quiet or dignified withdrawal from the highest professional office available to a serving naval officer. His reforms, and his manner of enforcing them, split the navy down the middle. The violent dissensions and personal feuds that resulted spilled over into the public domain. In a service that had previously regarded itself as almost a closed society, this public washing of dirty linen was extremely distasteful, and further polarised opinion in the navy. For a period of time the unspoken sense of loyalty that united the Royal Navy was riven in twain.

For this, Fisher must shoulder a fair proportion of the blame. Utterly driven by his convictions, and conscious of the need for haste, he devoted no time to converting people to his opinions. Instead, he assaulted all those who did not immediately fall in line. As most of his reforms could stand debate on their merits, this approach was both unfortunate and unnecessary; most officers supported some of his policies and a good proportion supported most. The result was that he incensed his confirmed critics (which would not have bothered him), but he also alienated many officers who might otherwise have been sympathetic to those views, and given valuable backing to their implementation. In his autobiography, Lord Chatfield provides a balanced comment from the viewpoint of an officer who served throughout Fisher's years in high command:

'It was his ruthless character and his scorn of tact that led to violent criticism, and enmities that shook the Service, reducing the value of his great work. Fisher's greatness was not then realised. There were many who hated him, and he hated them. His was not the method of leading smoothly but of driving relentlessly and remorselessly. He prided himself on this policy, and boasted of it and of his scorn of opposition.

'Whether the Navy could ever have emerged from its old ways in time for the Great War without his forceful acts is difficult to estimate, but in my opinion it could not.' (16)

Another good assessment of the man, at this point of his career, comes from Richard Hough, a sympathetic, but not uncritical, biographer:

'His fitness for the tasks that lay ahead was beyond question. He had served at sea in almost every corner of the world, and he knew to a fine degree the qualities that made a good naval officer. He was probably better informed on the Navy's *materiel* needs than any other officer alive. His eyes missed nothing, and were those of a prophet. He understood and had acquired a very low opinion of the intelligence and integrity of the general run of those in power in high places. Yet he had developed a wonderful knack of bending their influence to his needs.' (17)

However, as Hough later continues:

'The weaknesses which were eventually to prove his undoing were present for all to see in 1904 – but only a few recognized the truth of them. Although he was so widely criticised it was mainly for the wrong reasons. Probably only Esher, who knew and understood him better than anyone, could recognize all the dangerous defects: the impatience and the weak boyish tendency to throw in the sponge if he did not get his way, all the way; the violent manner of expression which led him to over-state a case and suppress useful and constructive debate, and incense his opponents and tempt them too, to overstate theirs, close their ears to the merits of Fisher's argument, and antagonise them: his readiness to make enemies; his reluctance to consult *after* his own mind had been made up; and finally and most seriously, his pride in his own excesses of temperament and demeanour. In 1904 the first lines in the self-caricature were already being drawn.' (18)

A much less sympathetic commentator is H.P. Willmott, and, for the sake of balance, his views are worthy of consideration:

'Perhaps only one thing can be said with certainty about this whole issue. The great tragedy was that Fisher was retained as First Sea Lord after 1906, when he had clearly outstayed his welcome, and thereafter contributed nothing of value but was a profoundly disruptive and negative influence. This is admittedly not a view which has attracted much interest, still less support. But it is difficult to identify any single act or policy after 1906 that was of benefit to the Royal Navy and Britain as a result of Fisher's being retained at the Admiralty, and there were many matters – most obviously his conduct of personal vendettas and his emasculation of the newly formed staff which he would never accept should wield powers he was determined to reserve for himself – in which Fisher's influence was baleful, to say the least. That point being noted, one must note its rider: many of the people with whom Fisher did battle after 1906, most obviously Beresford and Custance but others as well were not individuals who should themselves attract much in the way of sympathy. Be that as it may, the basic conclusion would seem to hold good. Perhaps very appropriately in many ways, Fisher's time as First Sea Lord can be likened to the *Dreadnought*: major initial impact but thereafter effect not necessarily as intended.' (19)

This is overstating the case more than somewhat, and a sour and negative assessment of the man. He needed to remain for at least a few years after 1906 to ensure that his great reforms were carried to fruition. Had Fisher left the Admiralty in 1906, there was an obvious chance that

Beresford could have been made his successor, and all the sweeping reforms that had just been instituted left hostage to the whims of the latter. At that time Beresford had yet to totally scupper his chances of assuming the post, and it was well known that the only other realistic candidate, Admiral Sir Arthur Wilson, had no desire to become First Sea Lord.

Even had Fisher's personality and methods been more emollient, the drastic nature of his reforms, and the urgency with which they were applied, were bound to cause friction in the service. Nevertheless, and here Wilmott's remarks are pertinent, within two years of becoming First Sea Lord, all the components of his programme were in place. The basic job had been done. The *Dreadnought* revolution was under way.

'At every point the Germans found themselves checkmated by Fisher. The *Dreadnought* and the 'Dreadnought' cruisers had been introduced with a sufficient start to defy their number being overtaken, and by Fisher's skilful strategy, in spite of incurring the most vehement opposition, the distribution of the Fleet had been gradually altered so that one morning the Germans awake to the fact that 86 per cent of the guns of the Royal Navy were trained in their direction.' (20)

It still remained necessary to defend its progress to completion. For that purpose, as mentioned above, and as Willmott emphasised, Fisher was not an unqualified asset. Opposition was hardening against what was seen as his 'personal rule'. Initially lacking in focus, this opposition soon became organised, and it ushered in a period of service infighting that threatened to severely disrupt the efficiency of the navy. It is perhaps the only aspect of Fisher's period in power that brought any comfort to his German counterpart.

CHAPTER EIGHT

SCHISM IN THE ROYAL NAVY

'Dealing now with the criticisms which we have said were levelled at Fisher and his reforms, it must be observed that these were of several different kinds. There was good honest criticism from genuine doubters, or from those who thought they saw better methods of obtaining the same objects. There was criticism of the "made-to-order" from journalists; and, finally, there was criticism from those who had not the welfare of the Navy at heart, but who made the reforms an excuse for launching a personal vendetta and an opportunity for gratifying petty grievances and pent-up spite.'

Admiral Sir Reginald Bacon

'It was Fisher who hoisted the storm signal and beat all hands to quarters. He forced every department of the Naval Service to review its position and question its own existence. He shook them and beat them and cajoled them out of slumber into intense activity. But the Navy was not a pleasant place while this was going on. The "Band of Brothers" tradition which Nelson handed down was for the time, but only for the time, discarded.'

Winston Churchill

At a time when the Royal Navy should have been greatly benefiting from Fisher's programme it descended into a state of internecine strife. The result of this was an inevitable blow to the efficiency of the service. No matter the quality of the ships, the soundness of their deployment, or the underlying strength of its infrastructure, a service divided within itself cannot perform to its potential. This deplorable situation, in which nearly half of the navy's senior officers were not on speaking terms with the other half, came to pass from 1905 onwards, and only began to disperse when the two main antagonists departed the scene. Even then, it left festering enmities that lasted for many years.

The dispute spread into the public and political spheres, and must have been a source of considerable gratification across the North Sea. As such, it deserves treating in some detail.

The opponents of Fisher's reforms, and Fisher the man, eventually coalesced around the personality of Lord Charles Beresford, one of the next most senior serving naval officers.

Beresford was probably better known to the general public than Fisher himself. 'Charlie B' was an able and high profile officer who had distinguished himself at the bombardment of Alexandria. During the subsequent actions in Egypt, and in the Sudan two years later, he several times proved his mettle under fire and became one of the heroes of the hour. He maintained an equally high profile in civil society, aided by influential contacts amongst the aristocracy, independent means, and a very pushy wife. He was also active in politics.

For all his adult life, Beresford had been an ardent campaigner for a strong Royal Navy. When not actively employed afloat (a not infrequent event in the careers of Victorian naval officers), he represented, over the years, various seats in parliament, and used these positions to argue forcibly against governmental policy whenever he felt the interests of his service were being neglected. At times he was both an active serving officer *and* an MP, a conflict of interests that caused him no loss of sleep. In these circumstances, he frequently trod on very thin ice in his relationship with the Board of Admiralty, still his nominal superiors. His conduct, at times, bordered on outright insubordination. None of this would have overly concerned Beresford. An Anglo-Irish peer, he had inherited the fiery nature of his Irish ancestors, and loved a fight.

Some of the causes and views he adopted were of vital importance to the future of the service, and his trenchant airing of these concerns brought them into the arena of public debate. In that respect, he did significant service to the navy, but it has to be said that the manner of his advocacy often tended to undermine his efforts. The downside to Beresford was personal vanity, a huge ego, quick emotions, and a preoccupation with appearances, which sometimes overcame reason and logic. His obsession with being in the spotlight, coupled with a verbose tendency to overstate his case, exasperated supporters and opponents alike. He was not a deep thinker, and his grasp of detail was sketchy. Probably his most valuable contribution to the navy was his long-term advocacy of creating a proper staff organisation. This was undoubtedly a side product of him personally being heavily dependent, as a flag officer, in having a staff to do most of the thinking and organisation on his behalf. Robert K. Massie's statement that he was 'a man of action rather than a man of vision' (1) is spot on except for the fact that Beresford spent very little of his overall career on active service. Compared to most of his peers, his sea-time had been minimal, and he had had to resort to some marginal jobs to even qualify for promotion. Geoffrey Penn comments on Beresford at the time he was appointed to be Fisher's second-in-command in the Mediterranean:

'But to universal amazement, including, apparently, Beresford...he was appointed Flag Officer, Second-in-Command, Mediterranean Fleet, flying his flag in *Ramillies*. After his limited service as a Lieutenant, early promotion to

Commander by Keppel's favour, he had served in only one ship as second-in-command, before returning to another Royal Yacht. He commanded the tiny *Condor*, in which he made his name and was promoted captain. As fourth Sea Lord, having proved unable to co-operate with other members, he had failed to convince them of the very real merits of his views on staffs. He had served the minimum time in command of *Undaunted* and in the Medway Dockyard Reserve to ensure automatic promotion to rear-admiral. His total service since gaining lieutenant's rank was fourteen and a half years, of which six and a half were in Royal Service or as Flag Lieutenant; his total seagoing service, other than in Royal service[1] was five and a half years; many a lieutenant had longer and better experience at sea.' (2)

He was assiduous, however, in promoting the impression of the bluff, salt-encrusted seaman, campaigning selflessly against institutional and political incompetence. Within the service, this hyperbole was taken with a considerable pinch of salt, but he was generally regarded as a good peacetime Commander of Ships and Fleets, capable of inspiring great confidence and loyalty, and was immensely popular with the rank and file of the navy. He came over well as the aristocrat with the common touch. Beresford was never averse to good publicity, and this popularity spilled over into the public domain. He had an imposing and aggressive presence, alleviated by bluff good humour and a truly Irish 'gift of the gab'. To the man in the street, he was the epitome of a British admiral.

'He was always in the newspapers, the wealthy aristocrat who became a popular hero; the captain and admiral idolized by common seamen; the persistent champion of a bigger navy. To most Britons, he was John Bull the Sailor. Photographs of Lord Charles, standing legs apart on a warship deck, his sleeves striped in gold braid, a small naval cap sitting atop his broad, round face, gave a sense of security; England was safe so long as Lord Charles and the navy were on guard.' (3)

Beresford and Fisher were well acquainted. When Fisher was sent ashore to command the units landed after the bombardment of Alexandria in 1882, Lord Charles was his chosen second-in-command. Fisher was then captain of the great battleship *Inflexible*, whereas Beresford commanded the

---

[1] Beresford was one of many well-connected naval officers who spent a considerable proportion of their careers on the various royal yachts. Contact with the monarchy was accepted as a guarantee of future advancement, provided an officer was a reasonably competent seaman and made no social gaffes. But time spent on these vessels was time lost to the professional disciplines of fleet work and keeping abreast of the rapidly changing developments in technology and tactics within the fighting navy.

little gunboat *Condor*. The latter had gone close inshore and taken on a particularly obnoxious fort whose fire was seriously inconveniencing the fleet. A single hit from one of the fort's guns would probably have destroyed the gunboat, but Beresford typically disregarded all hazards and managed to silence the entire redoubt. For this action, he received a congratulatory signal from the commander-in-chief, and was subsequently given accelerated promotion from commander to captain. His initiative and courage on this occasion first brought him to the notice of the navy and the public, and undoubtedly influenced Fisher in selecting him for the perilous and unorthodox operations ashore following the bombardment. Fisher appointed him as the effective administrator of Alexandria as the city descended into an orgy of looting, murder and arson following the withdrawal of rebel troops. With minimal forces at his disposal, Beresford acted decisively but with considered restraint and stabilised the situation within five days.

'This impetuous man, sometimes so foolish in times of peace, was both wise and moderate when faced with a situation which would have dismayed and defeated most of those who got the better of him on the political stage.' (4)

The two men would next serve together in 1899, when Beresford, as a rear admiral, joined the Mediterranean Fleet as second-in-command. Fisher was the commander-in-chief. It was a potentially fascinating combination. Lord Chatfield was then the gunnery officer on one of the battleships:

'Lord Charles Beresford had hoisted his flag in the *Ramillies* as second-in-command. He was famous already, popular and keen; we all wondered how he would get on with the Commander-in-Chief. "Jacky" and "Charlie B" were aware of the strength of each other's characters and position and Beresford was essentially loyal by nature. All went well for a time; the two men seemed anxious to be friends and pull together.' (5)

The relationship was generally a success but there occurred, during this time, a couple of incidents that many regard as the source of their eventual violent feud, although this interpretation of events has probably been over emphasised.

Shortly after joining the station, Beresford fell foul of his superior. Chatfield recounts the incident:

'Then there was a squall. One forenoon Lord Charles had sent his signalmen ashore to the Corradino for signal exercises. He had not asked permission as he should have done by the station orders, an oversight and not a deliberate intention. The Fleet signal officer informed the Commander-in-Chief.

"Make a signal to the *Ramillies*", he said. "*Ramillies* signalmen to return to their ship immediately. Report in writing why station order No____ has not been obeyed." To make such a signal to his second-in-command was unwise. The Fleet took in the signal and pricked up its ears.' (6)

This totally unnecessary signal shows Fisher at his worst. The diplomatic, and most obvious course, would have been to send a private message to his second-in-command reminding him of the station orders, and emphasising that he expected full adherence to these in future. Beresford, of course, would have been furious at what was a failure on the part of his staff, and the responsible officer would have been mercilessly castigated. This would have become common knowledge in the fleet, and treated with some hilarity in the other ships. A public snub to the second-in-command was altogether another matter. Beresford, to his credit, behaved with admirable restraint. He personally visited the commander-in-chief and accepted the rebuke without complaint.

This hiccup was followed later by an even greater breach of normal service etiquette by the commander-in-chief. The Mediterranean Fleet was proceeding into Grand Harbour, Malta. Fisher's flagship had already secured to her buoys, and the admiral had disembarked ashore to observe the rest of the battleships coming in to moor. Beresford's flagship made a hash of the manoeuvre and delayed the entry of the rest of his squadron. This would have been absolute agony for Beresford, himself a competent ship handler. As an admiral, he had to leave the manoeuvring of the ship to his captain, much though he must have itched to interfere. The embarrassment to him, in the presence of the whole fleet, must have been excruciating. There then came a signal to Lord Charles, copied by all the fleet, from Fisher:

'Your flagship is to proceed to sea and come in again in a seamanlike manner.'

In terms of sheer stupidity, this communication takes some beating. Fisher had carried out a crass public humiliation of his deputy. The whole fleet, however, delighted at seeing someone else being caught out, must have winced at the impropriety of the signal. Chatfield, certainly, was not impressed:

'Everyone present tried to dissuade him from making such a signal to his second-in-command, but to no avail...A signal such as Fisher made is not only public property, not only resented by the second-in-command himself and his captain and staff, but rouses the indignation of many aboard the flagship. It is taken up in the club and in the bar or café, and spreads. The harmony of the fleet is lessened.' (7)

For all his virtues, Fisher was not always a good leader. This was actually an example of unmitigated bad leadership, but Beresford, once again, behaved with unexpected equanimity for one of his temperament. No explosion resulted. Many a milder officer might have taken great umbrage and confronted his superior on the matter. It is pure conjecture, but perhaps

Fisher was testing the mettle of his subordinate, and perhaps Beresford was refusing to rise to the bait. Whether or not these incidents formed the basis for the later hostilities between the two men is entirely unproven.

There is no doubt that Fisher's rebukes must have rankled with Beresford. No one with his vanity, and high standards of performance, could fail to have been affected by these public reproaches. For all that, Lord Charles gritted his teeth and took the blasts like a trooper. The service taught every officer, no matter how exalted, to accept the occasional, and often unreasonable, displeasure of their seniors as a necessary evil. All of them would have experienced it at one time or another.

Beresford behaved at this time with complete correctness. If any opprobrium can be spread over these incidents, it must be cast entirely on the head of Fisher, whose lack of tact was inexcusable. This failing, though, was well known within the navy, and generally allowed for as par for the course.

The accounts that try to base the Fisher/Beresford feud on their time together in the Mediterranean do not take sufficient attention of the remarks made by the two men concerning this period. Both professed, at least in public, a very high regard for the abilities of the other. Robert K. Massie gives the Fisher view of Beresford at that period:

'Fisher, who spoke in strong language, and clearly expected those around him not to take offence, had no grudge against Beresford and was as quick to praise as he was to criticize. "Beresford did uncommonly well", he wrote, after fleet manoeuvres in 1900, "and is much pleased at my praising him, which he thoroughly deserved. He is a first rate officer afloat, no better exists in my opinion."' (8)

Admiral Jameson finishes off the quote:

'In the two years he has been under my command he has never failed to do everything he has been ordered, cheerfully and zealously and *has always done it well.*' (9)

Beresford's thoughts on Fisher were equally complimentary. A remark of his on Fisher's rejuvenation of the Mediterranean Fleet has been touched on in a previous chapter. It is worth visiting the entire quote.

'While Vice-Admiral Sir John Fisher was commander-in-chief of the Mediterranean Fleet, he greatly improved its fighting efficiency. As a result of his representations, the stocks of coal at Malta and Gibraltar were increased, the torpedo flotillas were strengthened, and the new breakwaters at Malta begun. Some of Sir John Fisher's reforms are confidential; but among his achievements which became common knowledge, the following are notable: From a 12 knot Fleet with breakdowns, he made a 15 knot Fleet without breakdowns; introduced long range target practice, and instituted the Challenge Cup for heavy gun shooting; instituted various war practices for officers and men; invited, with excellent results, officers to formulate their opinions on cruising and battle formation; drew up complete instructions for torpedo flotillas; exercised cruisers in towing destroyers and battleships in towing one another, thereby proving the utility of the device for saving coal in an emergency; and generally carried into execution Fleet exercises based, not on tradition but, on the probabilities of war.' (10)

The above is an extract from his memoirs, first published in 1914, by which time the two men had been implacable enemies for a good seven years. In the circumstances, Beresford's comments are uncommonly generous.[2]

Six months after taking up his appointment, he was offered the command of the Australian station, but turned the opportunity down in order to remain as second-in-command in the Mediterranean. There, he thought, he would learn more about fleet handling and up-to-date tactics than by playing God elsewhere. Fisher and he may not have been soul mates, but at that time they appreciated and complemented each other's virtues and tolerated each other's vices. There was certainly a level of friendship and co-operation in their relationship at that time.

In private, Fisher complained about Lord Charles' love of publicity; the exaggeration that devalued his comments; the occasionally intemperate speeches, but there is no doubt that he respected his qualities as a fleet commander. After joint manoeuvres between the Mediterranean and Atlantic Fleets – the latter commanded by Sir Arthur Wilson, the greatest fleet handler of the era – Fisher wrote that, 'If anything, Beresford had the advantage and Wilson admitted it.' (11) He also appreciated that Beresford had the good of the service at heart, and that his forays into the public sphere could be quite productive.

For that reason, Fisher was not always averse to Beresford's hogging of the limelight. They were basically working towards the same end, and the latter's high profile served to deflect some of the heat away from Fisher's overall policies. Thus we have Fisher, with deliberate indiscretion, writing to Beresford in February 1902 providing ammunition for a speech the latter was about to deliver in parliament.

*'Private. No one to see this letter except your own self!!!...*You will naturally feel that all I am writing to you thus freely is of the most secret character, but I am sure I can rely on your discretion not to haul me into the matter, but I am anxious you should hit the right nails on the head and not waste your strength and magnificent opportunity on beating the air.' (12)

Beresford, in fact, disappointed on this occasion, magnificently beating the air, and Fisher showed his frustration in a letter to his old First Lord, Earl Spencer:

---

[2] It should, however, be borne in mind that both Fisher and Beresford, in their written correspondence between themselves and with third parties, took some care to be generally complimentary. Verbally, and off the record, this was not always the case.

'There is a good deal in what Beresford urges, but he exaggerates so much that his good ideas become deformities...and his want of taste and his uncontrolled desire for notoriety alienates his brother officers. He promised me faithfully *(for we have been great friends)*, [author's italics] that he would be circumspect and judicious...he has been neither.' (13)

The phrases 'desire for notoriety' and 'alienating his brother officers' are somewhat rich coming from Fisher, as he gloried in his own notoriety and alienated brother officers *ad infinitum*. The two quotes serve perhaps to illustrate the ambivalent nature of their relationship.

Similar letters to the one Fisher sent to Lord Charles regularly went to others of influence, both naval and civilian, for Fisher himself was as assiduous as Beresford in cultivating public opinion for his own ends. Whereas Lord Charles did so openly, in the full glare of the spotlight, Fisher generally worked indirectly through selected sympathetic journalists and by private correspondence with people such as Esher who had great influence behind the political scenes. In the case of the journalists, he took care not to be 'fingered' as the source of their information, however much this was rightly suspected by those in the know.

Both men were intensely patriotic and had a passionate commitment to the effectiveness and welfare of the navy. The vital difference between them was that, for Fisher, this was the absolute be all and end all of his entire professional life; for Beresford, it was also a significant means to personal advancement. (14) As very differing personalities, from very different backgrounds, they were never going to be close friends, but their relationship generally remained affable and mutually supportive until Fisher became First Sea Lord. From then onwards the deterioration was rapid and irreversible.

The Fisher/Beresford feud has all the elements of a modern tragedy. Shakespeare could have done the subject justice. The subject is of two remarkable men, one more remarkable than the other, and the inability of the other to accept this fact. The lesser one sets out to destroy the greater one, and, in all but succeeding, ruins them both as well as his own reputation.

The decisive moment came at the end of 1905, when Fisher was promoted to Admiral of the Fleet. This promotion was not an automatic affair. It rested as a gift of state to a senior officer who had performed particularly outstanding services to the nation. All appointees had to have the approval of the Monarch who, himself, held the rank. It was a very exclusive club in that its numbers were strictly prescribed, and within that very limited quota were included honorary recipients such as the Kaiser and the Tsar. Nor was it a purely cosmetic appointment. All senior officers were normally required to retire on reaching the age of sixty-five, but anyone attaining the rank of Admiral of the Fleet had their period of service on the active list extended by a further five years.

Fisher had been due to retire in 1906, and Beresford might reasonably have supposed to have been on a very truncated shortlist to succeed him as First Sea Lord. Only Sir Arthur Wilson could be thought of as a possible alternative and that most self-effacing of officers had no desire for the post. Beresford, however, positively lusted after the status and trappings of the appointment. Fisher's promotion, allowing him to continue in office until 1911 – an opportunity he immediately grasped – effectively slammed the door on Lord Charles' ambitions. Denied the prize he desired, he became steadily more antagonistic towards Fisher and his works.

The process had already begun whilst he was commander-in-chief in the Mediterranean, a post he assumed earlier in 1905. He held the appointment at a time when the strength of that fleet was being reduced in line with the general redistribution of Britain's naval forces. It is a measure of the vanity of the man that Beresford chose to regard this process as a slight, directed at him personally, rather than as the natural consequence of high policy decisions. His criticisms of the Admiralty measures, and the manner of their accomplishment, became ever more frequent, strident and tactless, and were delivered to all and sundry, in or out of the service. This constant ridiculing of the Admiralty fell on many willing ears, and there commenced a gradual polarisation of the navy between those who supported the views of either Fisher or Beresford. As time passed, more and more officers joined one or the other faction, their positions hardened, and fewer were left uninvolved.

Fisher, at this point, was hardly in the best position to take the moral high ground. During his own tenure of the Mediterranean command he had been a constant thorn in the side of the Admiralty, and had been thoroughly unreasonable, to the point of insubordination, in his demands and complaints. For a time, he himself thought his behaviour had probably stymied his chances of further employment, never mind those of becoming First Sea Lord. What saved him, apart from his obvious efficiency, was the realisation, by a few highly placed men, that he was the only man available who had the drive, the ideas, and the ruthless ability, to transform the navy into a service that could face the challenges of a new era. Fisher survived and duly became First Sea Lord, but the potential problems with Beresford remained to be resolved.

Matters came to a head when Sir Arthur Wilson hauled down his flag as Commander-in-Chief of the Channel Fleet. It was, at that time, the most important seagoing command in the navy, but its status was also in the process of change as part of the overall redistribution of Britain's fleets.

As the new *Dreadnoughts* came into service, they were allocated, not to the Channel Fleet, but to a new Home Fleet based on Chatham. This was the nearest dockyard port to Germany. Thus the Home Fleet, previously consisting of older battleships, and the vessels manned by nucleus crews, was eventually to be transformed into the premier naval force of the nation. Ultimately, it was intended that the two fleets would merge, forming a single, unified command that could be deployed against the threat of the German High Seas Fleet. It was hoped that the gradual nature of this process would be less provocative to Germany than the immediate deployment of all the best existing vessels to a position where they would be obviously aimed at the German Navy.

For the time being, command of the Channel Fleet remained the most prestigious seagoing appointment for a senior naval officer. He would also be the overall commander-in-chief of all Britain's naval forces in wartime. On Wilson's retirement, there was really only one logical successor and that was Beresford. There were no other outstanding candidates of his seniority, and the best new talent had yet to obtain sufficient experience.

Despite severe misgivings, Fisher accepted that Beresford's appointment to the Channel Fleet was inevitable. His first concern was that the gradual shift of emphasis from the Channel Fleet to the Home Fleet would cause friction. He was well aware that problems might arise with the touchy personality of Beresford as this strategy unfolded. He was also in no doubt that Beresford had started to intrigue against him. The latter's comments and attitude during his tenure of command in the Mediterranean had been as tactlessly available to Fisher's supporters as to his own acolytes. Consequently, Beresford was invited to the Admiralty before he assumed his new command where, in the presence of the First Lord, Fisher briefed him on all aspects of policy, particularly those affecting the strategic redistribution of the navy.

It was explained to Beresford that the relative degrading of the Channel Fleet did not affect his position as senior officer afloat. In wartime, and for all manoeuvres and exercises, both the Home and Atlantic Fleets would come under his overall command. However, unless and until those circumstances existed, the other fleets were independent commands directly responsible to the Admiralty. Beresford indicated his understanding and acceptance of the Admiralty's policy. Notes were taken of all the matters discussed during the meeting and, accord having been reached, these were initialled by the First Lord, Fisher, and Beresford. The prospects for future dissention seemed to have been eliminated.

These hopes were very soon dispelled. From the moment Beresford hoisted his flag relations between him and the Admiralty lurched from one crisis to the next. He took a dead set against all Fisher's reforms, even those he had previously supported. His particular venom was reserved for the Home Fleet, and not a month had elapsed before he was writing directly to

Tweedmouth, then the First Lord, describing that force as 'a fraud on the public and a danger to the empire'. Not content with this he repeated the charge to wider audiences, including functionaries of the King.

Fisher, of course, was incandescent. It was an intolerable situation, and could only really be resolved by ordering Beresford to shut up and accept the authority of the Admiralty, or resign. Failing that he would be relieved of his command. To Fisher's disgust, Tweedmouth did not have the spine for such a confrontation, and a new bone of contention soon surfaced.

Beresford started to complain about the absence of detailed 'War Plans' for his command. In fact the Admiralty only ever issued general 'War Orders' to its commanders-in-chief. It was the responsibility of the latter to draft detailed plans to meet the conditions of the War Orders, and submit them for Admiralty approval. Beresford would have been well aware of this, having already commanded two other fleets. The Admiralty patiently reminded him of the procedure, whereupon he responded by producing a completely impractical War Plan involving more ships than the navy actually possessed! For that obvious reason, if for no other, this plan was rejected. Beresford then adopted another tack and maintained he could not produce a plan unless he knew exactly how many ships of every type would be available to him at any given moment. He accused the Admiralty of denying him this essential information, and, to ice the cake of discontent, carped about what he considered to be dangerous shortages in the numbers of cruisers and destroyers allocated to his fleet. His communications with the Admiralty were combative in nature and contemptuous in tone.

Gritting its collective teeth, the Admiralty invited Beresford to come and discuss the various problems and clear the air. The conference achieved little of permanent value. Massie comments that:

'Unfortunately for Beresford, a transcript was kept. It shows the Commander-in-Chief uncertain as to what he wanted, unable to explain his views and – in Fisher's presence – cowed and anxious to please.' (15)

The meeting highlighted one of the admiral's abiding weaknesses. Without a staff to support and advise him, he was hopeless in argument and intellectually limited. When pressed by Fisher or Tweedmouth on a specific, he sometimes could not remember what it was he had actually demanded and it became clear that some of those demands were probably just a means of stirring up trouble rather than any deeply held conviction. On the frequent occasions he was unable to justify his position, his responses dissembled into meaningless waffle.

The end product of the exercise was that the Admiralty, leaning over backwards to accommodate Beresford, gave him some of the extra ships he wanted. Lord Charles professed himself satisfied with this concession and that he was now able to produce draft War Plans for his fleet. With fulsome protestations of loyalty and his cordial acceptance of the Admiralty's paramount authority, he returned to his flagship leaving behind an aura of false bonhomie and an ominous sense of future problems to come. These would not be long delayed. Once back on board, the sniping and niggling immediately recommenced. Just how vital Beresford considered the whole business may be judged from the fact that it took nearly a year before his revised War Plans were submitted to the Admiralty. Having exhausted its potential for mischief, he relegated the subject to the lowest level of priority.

It is apparent that, by this time, Beresford had completely lost his integrity. Whereas previously his weaknesses and excesses could be tolerated on the grounds that he had the best interests of both the service and the country at heart, this was clearly no longer the case. His sole consuming interest had become the destabilising of Fisher's position at the head of the Admiralty. Should he succeed, he had not yet lost all hope of supplanting his rival.

The state of alienation between the Admiralty and its senior seagoing commander had inevitably spilled over into the public domain. What had been a serious enough rift within the navy, now started to become a national issue that steadily increased in intensity and venom. The Conservative press fell in behind Beresford, seeing in him a useful weapon with which to belabour the Liberal government. In the unlikely event of a change of government, Beresford thought it possible that Fisher would be forced out of office and that he would be appointed in the latter's place. This, had he but known it, was pie in the sky. The Conservative leader, Arthur Balfour, although on friendly terms with Lord Charles, also had a great regard for Fisher, and was strongly in favour of his reforms – which had, after all, been set in motion during Balfour's late administration. In any case, Beresford, by his ill-considered actions and general behaviour towards the Admiralty, had probably already disqualified himself as a candidate to head that organisation.

A stream of complaints continued to flow from his pen, delivered with barely concealed insolence. He returned to his old theme of denigrating the Home Fleet and the policies on which its existence was based. He also accused the Admiralty (and by 'the Admiralty', he always meant Fisher) of trying to sabotage his organisation by transferring away his most trusted subordinates. This was a preposterous charge, and easily disproved, but Beresford used it to air other supposed grievances. In a covering letter to the board he noted:

'It has come to my notice that a feeling has arisen in the Service that it is prejudicial to an officer's career to be personally connected with me on Service matters. This may not be a fact, but the impression I know exists. It is certainly borne out by the late procedure...

'It most certainly has the appearance of a wish to handicap and hamper me in carrying out the responsibilities connected with by far the most important appointment within the Empire...

'The ordinary etiquette, civilities, and courteous dealings which officers of high and distinguished command have hitherto so markedly received from the Admiralty have been entirely absent in my case.' (16)

Reading these extracts of a communication from a subordinate officer to the highest authority of the navy, it is difficult (if one assumes his protestations to be sincere) not to conclude that a degree of paranoia had started to intrude into his mental processes.

Beresford had always lived well and moved in the highest social circles. He was a charming and attentive host who clearly enjoyed entertaining, and was thus invariably successful in so doing. He exuded a comfortable authoritarian bonhomie, and shamelessly, but effectively, used these opportunities to play his chosen role as the August Admiral, who was also the Salty Sea Dog. His memoirs provide an excellent and thoroughly enjoyable example of what a superb raconteur he must have been and also of his unabashed enthusiasm for getting himself into scrapes. His good humour and unrestrained relish for the part guaranteed an appreciative audience. These undoubted talents were now employed to further the vendetta against Fisher.

In his frequent spells ashore from the Channel Fleet, Lord Charles entertained lavishly at his Grosvenor address in London, attracting as many influential personages as could be tempted to his well-stocked table. In this, he was greatly encouraged and supported, if not aided, by his wife. Lady Charles Beresford's social ambitions were feral, and those for her husband, if anything, exceeded his own, without being mitigated by any discernable virtue. Whilst Beresford assiduously cultivated his guests towards his point of view, his wife harangued them on the iniquities of his treatment by the Admiralty. Groups of disaffected senior naval officers also began to congregate at his address to plot Fisher's downfall. By now he had started to refer openly to Fisher as 'our dangerous lunatic', or sneeringly as 'the gentleman from Ceylon'. It was effectively a state of open revolt against the constitutionally established administration of the nation's premier means of defence.

In the circumstances, it seems incredible that Beresford was permitted to remain in his command, but Tweedmouth lacked the moral fibre to grasp the nettle and have him dismissed. If he was primarily at fault, the Prime Minister and the rest of the Cabinet provided him with no effective support or encouragement. They were unduly fearful of Beresford's capacity for political mischief if he was kicked out of the navy. The trouble was that the longer they delayed having to face the problem, the more pressing the problem became. Fisher was in despair and was barely able to hide his contempt:

'They are all "blue-funkers" about Beresford and overrate his power of mischief and his influence.' (17)

'Charlie B'
Admiral Lord Charles Beresford

First Sea Lord
Admiral of the Fleet Sir John Fisher

One particular aspect of this sorry saga stands out, and that is of the uncharacteristic restraint displayed at that time by Fisher (at least in public – in private the mere mention of Beresford's name resulted in an eruption). Given his volatile temperament, it might have been expected that an explosion would have emanated from Whitehall. There were, inevitably, occasions when his tongue got the better of him, and he spontaneously combusted before the combined fire brigade of the King, Esher, his staff, and his friends could direct their hoses upon him. The King gave him a stern lecture to the effect that Fisher's occasional intemperance of speech was a source of embarrassment to his own constitutional position, given that it was an open secret that he, the King, was so partisan in his favour. This reminder would have concentrated Fisher's mind wonderfully, and, in general, he refused to be provoked into a public overreaction. His actual feelings did not need to be enunciated, as they would have been apparent to anyone with any knowledge of the situation.

The Admiralty's reply to Beresford's outrageous and impertinent insinuations quoted above was simply a request for him to furnish specific evidence to support his accusations (which, of course, he couldn't, and didn't). Referring to his last paragraph, a tone of irritated exasperation, rather than Fisheran fury, emerges:

'(the Admiralty)...would observe that it becomes increasingly difficult for them in their correspondence with you to avoid overstepping the usual limits of official reserve, while you continue to employ language which has no parallel within their experience as coming from a subordinate and addressed to the Board of Admiralty.' (18)

These words are those of the Admiralty Board as a whole. They are not those that bear the stamp of Fisher's pen, although he would have had to approve the content of the communication. The tone is much more that of Tweedmouth, goaded into tetchiness, and prodded into unwonted censure.

It was not only Beresford's personal relations with the Admiralty that were disintegrating; problems within his own fleet further aggravated the situation. One incident became particularly notorious.

Amongst the senior officers in the Channel Fleet was Sir Percy Scott, who was Rear Admiral in charge of the Armoured Cruiser Squadron. As mentioned previously, Scott's metier, and personal preoccupation, was gunnery. His contribution over the years to the dramatically improved gunnery performance of the Royal Navy had been immense, and Beresford had been one of the senior officers who had unreservedly welcomed his reforms. Scott, however, was in the 'Fishpond', as the phrase went, and, by 1907, anyone associated with Fisher was anathema to Beresford. Massie even suggests that 'Lord Charles saw the assignment [Scott's] as another of Fisher's attempts to place a spy in the nest.' (19) Relations between the two admirals, therefore, were not likely to be warm.

In November, there was a spectacular rift. Scott, with his squadron, was in Portland awaiting the arrival of the commander-in-chief with the rest of the fleet. He occupied the time by sending each cruiser in turn out to sea to carry out gunnery exercises. Beresford, steaming south from Scotland, sent a general signal to his fleet with the information that the Kaiser would be arriving to review the fleet one week hence. All ships were directed to stop whatever they were doing and to concentrate on preparing for the inspection. There was nothing wrong with this order. If the government suddenly require this service of a fleet, then the fleet is necessarily the government's servant. Beresford had no choice in the matter. However, *HMS Roxburgh* of Scott's squadron was at sea carrying out her gunnery and enquired of the rear admiral as to whether she could first complete the exercise. Scott regretted the necessity but, obedient to his instructions, ordered her straight in. The wording of his signal was undiplomatic, but diplomacy had never been Scott's forte: 'Paintwork appears to be more in demand than gunnery so you had better come in in time to make yourself pretty by the $8^{th.}$' It was a ship to ship communication, not a general signal and never meant for a wider audience, but its tone was ill-advised. Such messages tend to leak beyond their intended bounds, and this one was no exception. Within a few days of his arrival at Portland, Lord Charles was appraised of the signal and immediately flew into a towering rage. (20) Scott was ordered to the flagship where he was subjected to a furious tirade on the quarterdeck. This humiliation was carried out in the presence of other officers, and anyone else who happened to be within earshot. He was given no opportunity to apologise, nor even speak. Before Scott had even returned to his flagship, Beresford had made a general signal to the fleet, quoting Sir Percy's original signal to *Roxburgh* and stating that 'this signal, made by the Rear Admiral commanding the First Cruiser Squadron, is contemptuous in tone and insubordinate in character.' (No one can dispute Beresford's qualifications to make this judgement as most of his letters to the Admiralty were similarly adorned!) He directed that the relevant pages in the signal logs of *Roxburgh* and *Good Hope* (Scott's flagship) be removed, and, without further ado, wrote to the Admiralty demanding that Scott be relieved of his command. The Admiralty demurred. The board concurred with the commander-in-chief's rebuke to his subordinate and added their own official 'grave disapprobation' of Scott's conduct, but it did not agree that the severity of Beresford's proposed punishment was appropriate to the nature of the crime (if it *did* agree with that principle, then Beresford himself should have been fired many times over by that time). Lord Charles reacted by virtually banishing Scott's squadron, which was a crucial ingredient of his organisation, from the regular activities of the fleet. Nor would he have any further personal contact with a man who was one of his key subordinates. He continued to fulminate against Scott, and spread accusations outside the service that the latter had been planted on him as

Fisher's mole within the fleet. That, he reasoned, was why the Admiralty had refused his demand to have Scott fired.

It was a ridiculous situation. Scott had carelessly sent a rather stupid signal; Beresford had grossly overreacted. Now there could be no satisfactory solution. No one was in any doubt as to the underlying reasons for a drama being turned into a crisis. If Scott were dismissed it would be seen by one set of partisans as the result of a personal vendetta by Beresford; if he were permitted to remain in his post, the other set would claim that the Admiralty was deliberately undermining the authority of the commander-in-chief.

The whole pantomime now became a general *cause célèbre*. The press got hold of the details and all the navy's dirty linen was being aired in public. It was utterly discreditable to everyone concerned, and all those who held the navy dear were appalled by the developments. Beresford's pompous self-righteousness actually lost him some sympathy among the uncommitted but there arose a general feeling of 'a plague on both their houses'. The principal agency for the defence of the nation's sovereignty, and the security of her empire, was being hazarded by a personal feud that was demeaning the navy.

The Royal Navy had a long and proud tradition of being the 'Silent Service'. It did not glorify or glamorise itself, but, if others wished to do so, it was quite willing to provide the exploits, and welcomed any opportunity to further its reputation. Its problems and scandals, it liked to keep 'in house', so the public nature of the Fisher/Beresford feud was seen by many officers as a disgrace to the service.

If the numbers now wanting both Beresford and Fisher out are added to Beresford's numerous supporters, the First Sea Lord was sorely beset.

If he had been in any doubt before as to the extent of the crisis, Fisher now had none. He was fighting for his professional life and for the reforms that had been the culmination of his career. Beresford had charmed much of society to his side and was winning the public relations battle outside the navy, never mind the fact that most of the press and public were ignorant of the real issues at stake. Within the navy, Lord Charles was supported by a clandestine majority of the most senior officers, plus, openly, by many retired admirals who still had great reputations and influence in and out of the service. The bulk of Fisher's support lay with progressive younger officers who represented the future of the navy, but who had not yet attained heavyweight status. His own minister had no taste for the fray, nor did the Cabinet show any inclination to get embroiled, if that might involve offending Beresford's powerful friends. This (irrational, as it turned out) fear of the political damage Beresford could cause resulted in an unqualified dereliction of responsibility by the government in failing to properly support its appointed officers.

There was a genuine danger in that Fisher was, by nature, an inveterate resigner. Whenever he was thwarted or opposed, never mind how trivial the matter or how minor the detail in an otherwise major conception, his first inclination was to tender his resignation. This is the childish trait mentioned in the earlier quote by Richard Hough. Undoubtedly, his very strong impulse must have been to do the same in the circumstances with which he was now faced. An 'Either Beresford goes, or I go' ultimatum would have been entirely in character. That he did not use this option is down to two factors, one proven and the other a racing certainty.

To deal with the second first; if he had resigned at that point, Fisher would have left the reforms that had been his life's work, and which were still in a formative stage, to the mercy of his successor. Should that successor be Beresford, who had rejected all the reforms as the basis of a campaign against him, they were probably doomed to be mangled beyond recognition. If Fisher wanted his child to survive, he could not become an absentee parent.

The other factor was that a few wise, and very important, individuals rallied to his cause. Esher, that grey eminence in the corridors of power, never ceased to encourage him when he was down. He gave good counsel when it was requested, and tactfully applied restraint when Fisher threatened to kick over the traces. Quietly, he used his considerable influence behind the scenes to maintain support for the beleaguered First Sea Lord. Most importantly though, King Edward VII remained a staunch ally. Although constrained by his constitutional position from any overt comment or gesture that might indicate bias towards an individual or a policy, he nevertheless wielded immense influence, the last British Monarch to do so. As has already been evidenced with the birth of the *entente* with France, he was prepared to use that clout, if necessary stretching his constitutional bonds to the limit of their elasticity.

A quarter of a century earlier, the first meeting of the then Captain Fisher, of *HMS Inflexible,* with his future King and Queen, had laid the foundations of a relationship that was to be of profound significance. When Fisher rose to high command, his contacts with King Edward VII became frequent, and the two men developed a high regard for each other. Regard progressed to a genuine friendship, respectful from Fisher's side, benevolent from Edward's. Early on in his time at the Admiralty, Fisher had written to Esher worrying that much of what he had been earnestly trying to explain to the King about his proposed reforms didn't seem to be holding his attention. Esher's reply is worth quoting at length as it throws a light on all three characters:

'My Dear Admiral,

...What you say about your long talks with the King leaves me full of certainty that you have made lasting and final impressions. H.M. has two receptive plates in his mind. One retains lasting impressions. I have tested this over and over again. The other, only most fleeting ones. On the former are stamped his impression of *people* and their relative value. On the latter, of *things*, and these are apt to fade or be removed by later ones. But, and this is the essential point, if you can stamp your image on number one – which you have long since done – you can rely always on carrying your point, by an appeal to 'authority' – as the Catholics would say. The King will not go into details, for his life is too full for that, but he will always say to himself, "Jack Fisher's view is so and so, and he is sure to be right". I don't think you need trouble about H.M., for he will always back you.' (21)

The King always *did* back Fisher, and Fisher worshipped him for it. As a result, Edward was probably the only person in his life that Fisher obeyed without question or hesitation. Several times, when completely exhausted by the constant assaults on his position, the character assassination aimed at him in the press, and the struggle to keep his reforms intact, Fisher seriously contemplated standing down. On each occasion, a word from the King, reminding him of his duty, was sufficient for him to once again don his armour and return to face the foe.

Although Beresford had impressive support from certain quarters of the press, he did not possess a monopoly in this sphere. Many of the outstanding, and most responsible, journalists of the day, men such as W.T. Stead, J.L. Garvin, Arnold White and J.R. Thurston, tenaciously fought the First Sea Lord's corner.

Nor was he friendless within the navy. Beresford may have attracted a following amongst senior serving and retired officers, but the best of the younger generation – the powers of the future – were generally pro-Fisher. There were those who might not have agreed with his methods, but most supported his goals and saw Beresford's agitation for what it was – a campaign of self-aggrandisement.

All these positive influences helped to keep the aging volcano active, but the strain was taking its toll. For all the arrogant, impregnable public persona that Fisher maintained, in private the barbs and arrows penetrated, and they wounded him deeply. The unrelenting hostile pressure he had to face eroded his reserves of optimism and stamina. To a friend, he stated that when he wrote his memoirs, he would entitle them *Hell, by one who has been there* – this from the man who four years earlier had cheerfully announced: 'It will be a case of *Athanasius contra Mundum*. Very sorry for Mundum because Athanasius is going to win.' Well Athanasius did win through in the end, but the happy warrior of 1904 was a scarred and embittered gladiator by the time the battle was done.

One thoroughly beneficial change took place in June 1908, when the wretched Tweedmouth was transferred to a less responsible post. The circumstances surrounding his departure from the Admiralty were slightly bizarre.

In response to a strident article in the anti-Fisher navalist press calling for the First Sea Lord's dismissal – this being only one of many shrill examples – there appeared a letter in *The Times*. It was from Lord Esher, who characteristically chose the letters column of a respectable newspaper, rather than a more obvious forum, to voice his opinion. After defending the record of Fisher, Esher concluded with the words that, 'There is not a man in Germany from the Emperor downwards who would not welcome the fall of Sir John Fisher'. This was powerful stuff from someone who was known to wield considerable influence on the establishment, but detested the limelight. If Esher's letter was surprising, the reaction it produced was even more startling. The Kaiser always read *The Times*.

Wilhelm absorbed the letter from Esher, who he knew was close to the King of England, and reflected his views, and reacted instinctively. Without consultation with his government, he immediately wrote a personal letter to Lord Tweedmouth complaining that Esher's letter was 'an unmitigated piece of balderdash'. He copied this letter to his uncle, who was not impressed. King Edward sent him an icy response. The King was no more happy with Esher or Fisher for having placed him in this situation.

> 'Needless to say, all this was deeply embarrassing to the King, who wanted nothing more than a quiet life where the Kaiser was concerned. Perhaps the worst side-effect of Esher's indiscretion was that Tweedmouth, a man caricatured as a fool but in fact suffering from the brain tumour that would kill him the following year, wrote back to the Kaiser and revealed in detail to him the building plans of the Royal Navy.' (22)

Fisher attempted to deflect the blame from Esher by pointing out that the latter had only been trying to defend him, Fisher, and therefore the policies that the King endorsed. Edward gave Esher a brief period in the cooler and then normal relations were resumed.

The Kaiser's letter to Tweedmouth was a typical Wilhelmine spur of the moment initiative. Born of genuine good intent, it created diplomatic mayhem. This was not helped by the fact that the First Lord of the Admiralty was dying of a brain tumour, although neither Tweedmouth, nor his colleagues, were then aware of this fact. The unfortunate man had committed a grave disservice to the government by his unauthorised transmission of Britain's forthcoming naval estimates to the Kaiser before they had even been submitted to his own parliament. He compounded this error by telling all and sundry of the Kaiser's letter to him, even producing it at social occasions and reading extracts to the other guests. Belatedly, the Prime Minister realised he had to rid the Cabinet of this embarrassment and shuffled him off into a sinecure. Tweedmouth was replaced at the Admiralty by Reginald McKenna.

The new First Lord was a huge improvement. He was, at age 45, a relatively young and vigorous man, with a concise lawyer's mind and a determined nature. He had little prior knowledge as to the workings of the Admiralty, but was a quick learner and a good judge of character. Fisher was initially concerned that McKenna might have been plucked from the ranks of the 'Economisers' in the Liberal Party, and was worried that the naval estimates were under threat. He was soon disabused of this fear. He and McKenna hit it off almost immediately. They developed a strong mutual respect and became firm friends. The Admiralty Board was immeasurably strengthened by the change.

The first major issue that they had to tackle was the Beresford problem. The latter was soon writing directly to the new First Lord criticising all aspects of Admiralty policy. He should have been left in little doubt that McKenna was a tougher nut than Tweedmouth. Replying to one of Beresford's communications, the new First Lord concludes by remarking:

'In conclusion, I will take the opportunity of laying stress upon the imperative necessity for the cordial co-operation of the Commander-in-Chief of the Channel Fleet in the plans of the Admiralty; and I am sure you will understand the reluctance with which I mention this topic, which is, however, forced on me by my knowledge of the unhappy personal position *in which you have placed yourself* [author's italics] in relation to the First Sea Lord. It is essential for both the success of the Admiralty administration and the efficiency of the Fleet that the most cordial personal relations should exist between the Commander-in-Chief of the Channel Fleet and the whole of the Board.' (23)

Bacon comments on this, that:

'Lord Charles, after receiving this letter, should have realised that the new First Lord was not a man who could be trifled with in the same manner that had been so successful with his predecessor; but he and his advisers had passed the limits of reason. He gambled on the capitulation of the Cabinet under the threat of a national campaign' (24)

In the meantime, Beresford stepped up his efforts to undermine Fisher in the press and within influential society circles. McKenna rapidly came to the same conclusion as his First Sea Lord and wanted Beresford dismissed, but, once again, the Cabinet, fearing political repercussions, baulked at this fence. Herbert Asquith had recently become Prime Minister on the death of Sir Henry Campbell-Bannerman, and showed no more resolution in facing the incipient mutiny than had his predecessor. He was soon to commit an even graver act of unwarranted appeasement.

In the event, Fisher and McKenna soon found a way to solve the immediate problem. It had always been the Admiralty's intention to eventually merge the Channel and Home Fleets as part of the overall strategic re-disposition of the navy. At the end of 1908, this measure was officially promulgated. As a consequence, it was also decided that the command of the Channel Fleet would be reduced to a two year appointment, instead of the usual three. Beresford's term in command would therefore end in March 1909. He was still two years shy of official retirement age, but there was, pointedly, no suggestion that he should receive further employment.

This decision was a purely service matter and thus did not involve consulting the Cabinet. Having failed to support the Admiralty in its earlier attempt to remove Beresford, Asquith and his colleagues were now faced with precisely the situation they had previously so cravenly avoided – at the cost of having the intolerable state of affairs in the navy drag on for a further nine months.

Lord Charles Beresford hauled down his flag for the last time on the 24th March 1909. He was given a rousing send off by the fleet, and an equally enthusiastic reception on his arrival in London. He had lost none of his popularity with the rank and file of the navy nor with the man in the street, and these scenes vividly demonstrated his potential to influence public opinion. Although still on the Active List he immediately launched into a full scale offensive against the Admiralty. His energy was certainly as undiminished as was his desire to avenge his self-perceived martyrdom at the hands of Fisher.

Less than a week after leaving the fleet he had met with both Balfour, the Leader of the Opposition, and then with Asquith. He returned to his twin themes of the unreadiness of the fleet for war, and the incompetence of the Admiralty. He embellished his arguments in a subsequent letter to the Prime Minister, and threatened to lead a nationwide campaign against the government unless it addressed his concerns. This was exactly what the Cabinet had feared when it had previously 'funked' the issue of disciplining the admiral. It now responded with a similar lack of spine.

At this time, neither the government, nor the Admiralty, was in good odour with the electorate. As will be described later, there had just been a major uproar over the naval estimates for 1909, in which the government (with some justification) and the Admiralty (quite unfairly) had been accused of neglecting the defence of the realm. There were other contentious issues brewing which, although having nothing to do with the navy, made the government anxious to avoid any extra controversies. The result was that Asquith capitulated to Beresford's pressure and agreed to his demand that there should be an official inquiry into the recent conduct of the Admiralty.

The mere acceptance of this unprecedented procedure was an implicit condemnation of the Admiralty as it indicated that there was a case to be answered. Fisher was understandably distraught.

> 'He looked on an enquiry as an insult to the navy, the Admiralty, and himself. Even calling the First Lord and the First Sea Lord to account on the basis of the charges of a subordinate had no precedence in the history of the navy; for the government to participate in these charges even to the extent of calling an enquiry smacked of deeper humiliation.' (25)

Fisher again threatened to resign over the matter, but was dissuaded (without much difficulty) by the argument that such an action would be an admission that the charges had substance. The King settled the matter, not this time with a quiet word, but a *command* for Fisher to remain at his post.

The enquiry was flawed in its composition and unsatisfactory in its conclusions. Asquith attempted to spread the responsibility by co-opting as members Sir Edward Grey, the Foreign Secretary; Richard Haldane, head of the War Office; and Lord Morley, a member of the Cabinet with pacifist inclinations. None of them, Asquith included, possessed any qualifications to pass judgement on naval issues.

The Prime Minister was aware of this deficiency and had proposed to include Admiral of the Fleet Sir Arthur Wilson on the panel, an eminently sensible measure. However, he immediately backed down when Beresford objected, on the grounds that Wilson was biased towards Fisher. This was a craven abdication of authority by Asquith, as Wilson was an officer who had scrupulously avoided taking sides in the feud, and whose whole career had been a monument to a selfless dedication to the service. His expertise would have been invaluable to the enquiry, and Beresford feared above all an expert unpartisan dissection of his various allegations. He was on stronger ground in objecting to Esher, who was also touted for the panel, as the latter was a known supporter of Fisher. Nevertheless, Esher would have brought to the enquiry a formidable intellect and a fine appreciation of what was really at stake in its deliberations. Needless to say, Beresford's protestations were sufficient to prevent his inclusion, and the chief accuser of the Admiralty was thus permitted to dictate the composition of the jury that would pronounce judgement on his erstwhile superiors.

The enquiry commenced at the end of April 1909 and comprised a series of meetings that went on for the next two and a half months. Lord Charles was accompanied to these meetings by Admiral Sir Reginald Custance, a clever officer, but a vindictive and unattractive personality, who had supplied much of the intellectual ammunition for Beresford to fire during his campaign. He was the brains behind Beresford's brawn, and had thoroughly briefed his champion on the presentation of his case. McKenna represented the Admiralty, and took the full responsibility for defending its position. He had vowed his First Sea Lord to silence, recognising the serious damage that could be caused by an outburst from that direction. Fisher was at all times present, but only contributed peremptorily when questioned on a specific subject, or when he was invited to explain at greater length the reasoning behind the long-term strategy that had formed Admiralty policy during his period of office. The effect of this restraint on Fisher may well be imagined, and the enduring memories of those who were present testify to the expression of virulent loathing that pervaded his features whenever Beresford rose to speak. It was apparent that, whatever gloss was placed on the enquiry, that this was essentially a clash of the aging titans.

Beresford, being the instigator of the process, commenced by stating his case against the Admiralty. His initial arguments were clearly, concisely and reasonably presented, and impressed the panel. He returned to his long-held position that the Admiralty had failed in its duty to the nation by its neglect of the fleet, and by a faulty disposition of available forces. In consequence, he maintained that the navy was unready for war, and that a major catastrophe would ensue should this situation be permitted to continue. He based this charge on three main premises. Firstly, that, as the wartime commander-in-chief, he had not been given full-time operational control of the Home Fleet, in addition to the Channel Fleet; secondly, to what he saw as a dangerous shortage of cruisers and destroyers; and thirdly to the lack of a comprehensive War Plan.

McKenna patiently and comprehensively demolished these arguments, most of which had been dealt with in detail in previous correspondence between Beresford and the Admiralty. Fisher, who could be accused of bias, and Wilson, who could not, were called upon to clarify certain issues. The result was a complete refutation of these charges. Beresford's key complaint (as far as he was concerned) about the disadvantages of not having control of both the Channel and the Home Fleets was easily met by pointing out that both these fleets had now merged under a single commander-in-chief, which satisfied all his conditions. In any case, this had always been the Admiralty's long-term intention, the reasons for which had been explained to him when he first assumed command of the Channel Fleet – and to which intention he had readily acquiesced. The document recording the meeting, and his acquiescence to its conclusions – initialled by himself, Fisher, and the First Lord – was clear evidence of his awareness as to Admiralty policy, and to his acceptance of its provisions.

Once Beresford was forced to depart from his well-prepared brief, in itself largely the product of Custance and other discontented souls, he again displayed a complete incompetence to argue his case in detail.

'...when he spoke, he rambled; applying logic, he contradicted; offering illustration, he was irrelevant.' (26)

Once he ceased to be the accuser and had to defend his views, his credibility disintegrated. From the Admiralty's point of view, the enquiry seemed to be going very much in its favour, but Fisher, chained to the sidelines, accurately assessed the probable outcome. He early on realised that Asquith was determined to fudge the issue and come up with some sort of acceptable solution that, hopefully, would make the problem, with all its political hazards, go away. Whenever Beresford was pinned down on specifics, or cornered in argument (a situation that became more frequent as the enquiry continued), the Prime Minister would contrive to change the subject or interject in such a way as to relieve the pressure on the man. In so diverting the legitimate interrogation of Lord Charles, and over fearful of the social power wielded by him, Asquith prostituted the integrity of his administration. He was, however, thrown a lifeline.

In one, and only one, aspect of his campaign did Beresford have a genuine gripe. It did not initially form a major part of his campaign against Fisher – the main bones of contention were the ones described above – but it was the single issue on which Beresford was completely right, and Fisher completely wrong. One of the greater services that Lord Charles had rendered the Royal Navy was in pressing successfully for the establishment of a properly constituted intelligence organisation. He saw this as an essential constituent in a larger staff organisation that could co-ordinate plans and advise senior officers on specific issues. The Intelligence Section of the Admiralty had been established many years previously, on the lines recommended by Beresford, and had developed into a vital component of the organisation.

He now advocated the creation of a naval staff similar to that which had been established for the army, and which was already proving its worth. His advocacy for this was not surprising as Beresford had always been heavily reliant on his personal staff to do his thinking for him, and to address the details inherent in any course of action. Ironically, the Army General Staff had its origins in the committee on which Fisher had served, with Esher and Sir George Clarke, whilst he was Commander-in-Chief, Portsmouth. It was a strange aberration on Fisher's part that the eminently sensible proposals he had helped to initiate at that time should not also have been carried into the naval sphere.

There were, admittedly, considerable differences between the two services in the manner by which they prepared for, and subsequently waged, war. What was applicable for one was not necessarily relevant to the other, but the increasing complexities and scale of modern warfare indicated the need for a proper staff organisation. In his defence, Fisher could point to the fact that he had created a war college at Greenwich specifically intended for the study of these matters. Selected officers attended this 'War Course', which provided a valuable opportunity to develop a wider understanding of strategy and tactics, but it had no executive function. A proper naval staff would necessarily be at the heart of the Admiralty and would have accountable responsibility for forward planning and the detailed application of overall policies dictated by the board. This proposal found favour with the committee.

It is difficult not to conclude that Fisher's refusal to consider this action was largely based on the nature of its source. If Beresford had reached the point where he would automatically oppose anything emanating from Fisher, the corollary was also true.

In August, the enquiry completed its deliberations and produced its findings. Apart from agreeing with Beresford on the subject of a naval staff organisation, it rejected all his other charges as being without substance, and fully endorsed the policies of the Admiralty Board. It failed, however, to either condemn outright Beresford's insubordination, or to make a clear statement of support for Fisher. Once again, the real issue behind the enquiry was ducked and, in its general conclusions, the panel made an observation that was deeply damaging to the First Lord. The arrangements for war, it remarked:

'...were in practice seriously hampered through the absence of cordial relations between the Board of Admiralty and the Commander-in-Chief of the Channel Fleet. The Board of Admiralty do not appear to have taken Lord Charles Beresford sufficiently into their confidence as to the reasons for dispositions to which he took exception; and Lord Charles Beresford, on the other hand, appears to have failed to appreciate and carry out the instructions of the Board, and to recognise their paramount authority.' (27)

There followed a final numbing paragraph of clearly calculated, mealy mouthed, blandness:

'The Committee have been impressed with the difference in opinion among officers of high rank and professional attainments regarding important principles of naval tactics and strategy, and they look forward with much confidence to the further development of a Naval War Staff, from which the naval members of the Board and flag officers and their staffs at sea may be expected to derive common benefit.' (28)

It was not nearly the forthright unambiguous statement of support for the First Sea Lord that Fisher required, although every professional naval officer could see the gist of the matter.

Bacon, whilst not an unbiased commentator, puts the committee's remarks in perspective:

'In other words, the Committee found...that Lord Charles's allegations were unfounded; and...that his conduct towards the Board was wanting in discipline. Either of these two findings necessitated, from the point of view of discipline, that he should be placed on the retired list. But no such action was taken. The Prime Minister feared to take a strong line against so seemingly popular an Admiral.

It was from a naval and disciplinary point of view, no part of the duty of the Admiralty to inform an Admiral afloat of their future intentions, intentions that might never materialise, and which in no way affected his present command. The insertion of this statement in the report of the Committee could only have been due to a desire to give Lord Charles some shadow of a grievance against the Admiralty as a set-off to his proved indisciplined behaviour.' (29)

The outcome of the enquiry was a bitter blow to Fisher. He had wanted, and expected, a complete, unambiguous, vindication of his policies and the conduct of the Admiralty. His supporters, notably the King, pointed out that the bulk of the committee's findings had been in his favour, but Fisher knew that its failure to come down unequivocally on his side had fatally weakened his position. Bacon again:

'Thus after nearly five years of unparalleled labour for the country, Fisher found himself deserted by the Prime Minister and Cabinet; who, without one word of commendation for the great work he had accomplished, left him with his authority as First Sea Lord undermined in the Navy, and the quarry of the jackals of the Press.' (30)

It was, in all truth, time for him to stand down. His great work had largely been done, but only at the cost of splitting the service into irreconcilable warring factions. It needed a less divisive personality to carry his reforms forward and to begin the process of healing the wounds that had been inflicted. Fisher himself came to recognise this, and he was anxious that Admiral of the Fleet Sir Arthur Wilson should succeed him as First Sea Lord. Wilson was the only officer of sufficient seniority that he trusted not to betray his legacy, and who had the standing and strength of character to keep Beresford at bay. Fisher was terrified at the prospect of Lord Charles somehow managing to get himself promoted to Admiral of the Fleet – and thus extending his period of active service by five years. This would have made him a potential candidate for First Sea Lord.[3] Alternatively he might have succeeded in getting one of his acolytes, such as Hedworth Meux or Custance, into the appointment. Fisher was uncomfortably aware that Wilson had only two years left on the active list, and it was therefore imperative that his chosen successor be installed as soon as possible. With McKenna's agreement, it was announced that the admiral would retire on reaching his sixty-ninth birthday on January 25th 1910.

---

[3] This was not an idle fear. The Prince of Wales, whilst having to be officially neutral, was friendly with Beresford and tended to his side. After inheriting the throne in 1910, but not with it his father's judgement of character, he proposed Beresford's promotion to the rank. Asquith was not averse to the appointment, but the horrified McKenna, acutely aware of the impossibility of any working relationship with Lord Charles, firmly stamped on the idea.

As will be seen, this was not to be the end of Fisher's contribution to the Royal Navy. Although out of power, he continued to wield considerable influence on Admiralty policy, particularly after Churchill became First Lord, and would briefly but spectacularly, return to his old office at a time of crisis in the early stages of the coming war. In the meantime he declared that he would busy himself in his garden. On hearing this, an old colleague commented, 'All I've got to say is that those roses will damned well have to grow!'

Fisher had departed but the great reforms he had instituted were securely in place. He had made mistakes, and his personality and methods had resulted in much ill-feeling within the service. However, as Churchill wrote, 'There is no doubt that Fisher was right in nine-tenths of what he fought for'. Geoffrey Penn gives an eloquent tribute to the old admiral:

'A tornado of energy, enthusiasm and persuasive power, a man of originality, vision and courage, a sworn foe of all outworn traditions and customs, the greatest of naval administrators since St. Vincent, "Jacky" Fisher was what the lethargic Navy had been in dire need of. His five year tenure of the post of First Sea Lord was the most memorable and the most profitable in the modern history of the Royal Navy.' (31)

As for his great foe, Beresford continued, in parliament and in speeches round the country, to criticise the Admiralty and fulminate against Fisher's legacy. In 1912 he produced a book entitled *The Betrayal*, an epic of self-justification and outraged indignation at all those who had failed to recognise his genius. His feared ability to embarrass the government was soon seen to have been much exaggerated, and he rapidly declined into a rather pathetic peripheral figure whose interventions in parliament became more and more ineffectual.

In retrospect, it was a sad and unfortunate set of circumstances that led to a high profile naval officer and a great character being generally remembered as an embittered champion of those who strove to prevent progress. Both Fisher and Beresford, in their later lives, did little to enhance their reputations, but Fisher's clear achievements ensure his place in naval history as one of the outstanding men of his time. Beresford was hi-jacked by many people who wished to use his position and influence to aid the grinding of their personal axes. They played on his vanity, and his obvious disappointment at being denied the highest position in the Royal Navy – by the presence of Fisher, forever in his way. Beresford possessed many admirable qualities and it was tragic that these were subverted by the twin emotions of envy and jealousy towards Fisher that combined to fatally warp his judgement.

It was, for the navy, extremely fortunate during that period of upheaval, that Lord Charles never occupied the First Sea Lord's chair. Just like Sir Arthur Wilson, as utterly different a character as can be imagined, he would not have been a success behind a desk. He was a natural rebel not a political animal, nor for that matter, an outstanding fleet commander – despite his pretensions to both descriptions. Neither was he particularly gifted in matters of high strategy or detailed planning. Wilson eventually had the post forced upon him, and accepted it, with severe misgivings, through a sense of duty. Charlie B would have grabbed it with both hands – and been equally out of his depth. Percy Scott, an admittedly unsympathetic commentator, does, however, succinctly sum up the man, his career, and his peripheral influence:

'In the Navy we knew he was not a sailor, but thought he was a politician; in the House of Commons, they knew he was not a politician but thought he was a sailor.' (32)

Beresford deserves to be remembered, not for the squalid machinations against Fisher, but for his younger crusading years campaigning for the good of the navy he revered, and also as the outstanding old school 'pomp and circumstance' admiral and natural leader of men he had been.

For all his faults and vanities, 'Charlie B', in his pomp, had been quite special. Perhaps, he should be given, as a loquacious Irishman, the benefit of the last word. At the end of his memoirs (subtitled *Written by Himself*!) Lord Charles gives his own valediction:

'It was a satisfaction to me when I came on shore, and it is a satisfaction to me now, to think that I pulled my pound in the Navy.

'Doubtless, like other men of action, I have made mistakes, but I may justly claim that I have always held one purpose with a single mind; to do my best for the good of the Service and for the welfare of the officers and men of the Royal Navy; and in following that purpose, I have tried to disregard consequences which might affect my own fortunes, and which, in fact, have often proved injurious to them. And to the purpose which I have followed since I was a boy, I shall devote the rest of my life.' (33)

As Fisher had planned, Sir Arthur Wilson was called out of retirement to take his place. He was not a desk man and the trappings of high office held no appeal, but in one respect he was eminently suitable. There was not a man in the Royal Navy who did not utterly trust his integrity and fairness. No taint of partiality attached to him. The navy urgently required someone who could repair the damage to its unity, and Wilson was the only eligible senior officer who had the prestige to fill the position.

The Royal Navy needed to put its house in order. Events in Europe were lurching from one crisis to another, and the threat of war kept emerging from the wings. The Balkans were in turmoil, and the Morocco problem would once again spark a confrontation of the powers.

CHAPTER NINE

THE DIVISIONS INTENSIFY

'In the latter part of the nineteenth century and the early twentieth century war was not regarded in the western world with dread and as a confession that civilization had failed. The pacifists were beginning to emerge and there was much public discussion of the horrors and injustice of war. But this was not the prevalent feeling. A hundred years without a major war had made many people inclined to forget the horrors of war. Moreover, to the pre-1914 generation war was the law of the civilized world as much as of the uncivilized. Clashes between nations were certain to take place.'

Arthur J Marder

The few remaining years that separated the Algeciras Conference from the outbreak of the First World War are littered with well-meaning initiatives, mostly from the British side, attempting to resolve differences between Britain and Germany. All these initiatives concentrated on the one crucial issue that concerned Britain – the question of her naval supremacy. It was the only issue that prohibited good relations between the countries, at least in the short term. That an acceptable arrangement was not reached was not due to a lack of effort, but more to an ignorance of the eventual consequences. Barbara Tuchman argues that there was also a basic lack of understanding, on Germany's part, as to what was reality:

'Germany might have had an English entente for herself had not her leaders, suspecting English motives, rebuffed the overtures of the Colonial Secretary, Joseph Chamberlain, in 1899 and again in 1901. Neither the shadowy Holstein, who conducted Germany's foreign affairs from behind the scenes, nor the elegant and erudite Chancellor, Prince Bülow, nor the Kaiser himself was quite sure what they suspected England of but they were sure it was something perfidious. The Kaiser always wanted an agreement with England if he could get one without seeming to want it…none of them believed England would ever come to terms with France and all warnings of that event Holstein dismissed as "naïve".' (1)

The quote at the head of the chapter accurately reflects the attitudes of the time. The actions of governments and the failure of diplomats in the few years remaining before the outbreak of the Great War need to be seen in this context. Wars had traditionally been carried out by professional soldiers and sailors, and did not directly affect the remainder of the population except in an economic sense. Areas of one country or another were periodically conquered and occupied for a time; occasionally they would change hands permanently, but the physical act of fighting was generally confined to those employed voluntarily for that purpose. The appalling nature of the war to come was then unknown. Had it been foreseen that it would extend its tentacles to whole populations; that mass conscription would be necessary to feed its ghastly maw; and that long-established empires would disintegrate as a result, a far greater urgency might have attended the efforts of politicians – and far greater caution displayed by the militarists.

In the situation that existed after the consolidation of the Anglo-French *entente*, it was still not necessarily inevitable that Britain and Germany should become automatic enemies. That situation only arose if Germany directly challenged British supremacy at sea.

No one in Britain disputed Germany's right to possess a navy commensurate with its world status and colonial commitments. What worried Britain was that this navy was being built, not for that purpose, but as a direct challenge to itself. However often Germany might declare that its fleet was for the protection of its worldwide interests, the fact that none of its battleships possessed the range to pass far beyond the Shetland Islands without running out of coal on the return leg home, rather gave the lie to this postulation. It was perfectly and blindingly obvious to any responsible person that the German Fleet was designed solely and specifically for action in the North Sea. In that area, there was only one possible opponent.

Any British government would have been criminally incompetent had it not taken measures to guard against the threat. From the preface to the Second Navy Law onwards, all indications from Germany pointed to this challenge as being the purpose of the various naval programmes. There is no doubt that this is exactly what the bulk of the German population had also been educated to expect. Britain's natural reaction to this unconcealed threat was not, for some extraordinary lack of reason, assimilated by the German nation.

At no point was the German public ever given a viewpoint into the international ramifications resulting from the policies of their leaders and propagandists. All they saw was an international attempt, orchestrated by Great Britain, to proscribe their natural right to expand, and with it their sea power as the logical vehicle for that expansion. The implicit challenge to the Royal Navy was completely ignored, as was whether the new German Navy actually served the real interests of the nation.

'One may say that the German people as a whole believed that they should possess a strong navy. The figures showing the growth of the German Naval League tell their own story. The matter was not one of right, but of expediency. No one, outside Germany, ever questioned the right of Germany to build as many ships as they cared to build. The problem that the Germans had to answer was a different problem. The building of the German navy would affect the attitude of other naval powers towards Germany. Would the reaction of these naval powers, and particularly the reaction of Great Britain, defeat the purpose of the German navy? Was the navy of any real advantage to German security or a practical instrument for the advancement of German aims? This question must be answered in the historical setting of the world of the early twentieth century. One must take for granted the belief in National Sovereignty and in the nation state as an independent, politically self-sufficing unit…(and) the view that a disarmed nation would be at the mercy of other powers who would at once take advantage of their superior force. This belief was held by the majority of reasonable men in every European country…It is difficult to avoid the conclusion…that the German people did not give very serious thought to the question whether a navy really added to their security.' (2)

There existed, largely thanks to Tirpitz's efforts, a vocal and influential lobby within the empire which built upon the reasonable aspirations of the nation to foster their own, more extreme, agenda.

'An important school of thought in Germany went beyond this view, and interpreted the "general purposes of German greatness" in a wider and more aggressive sense. They believed that their country was destined to world domination – not world conquest, but world domination. It is easy to show that this school of thought, with its extravagant and bellicose plans of expansion, was not supported by the majority of peaceful citizens in Germany. *It is less easy to say that the Pan-Germans and the militarists did not play a disproportionate part in the determination of German policy.*' [Author's italics] (3)

The influence of the ultra nationalistic pan-German lobby, allied to the efforts of the Navy League, and orchestrated by Tirpitz in concert with his other wide-ranging propaganda initiatives, was essential to the success of his plans. The manipulation of public opinion and Anglophobia served the purposes of Tirpitz's grand design admirably, but, like Bismarck a generation earlier, he created a groundswell of emotion and antagonism that, in his case, completely hamstrung the diplomatic interests of his country. The essential difference between the two men was that Bismarck was a truly great statesman who possessed a comprehensive overview of the issues vital to the development and security of his nation, whereas Tirpitz was simply a single issue politician.

Bismarck, in his pomp, had the ability to reverse trends of his own making, should other priorities so dictate; the results of Tirpitz's machinations created an irreversible momentum that was beyond his ability to guide, even had he so wished (there is no evidence that he ever did so wish). He possessed neither the flexibility of thought, nor the sweeping power to properly control the consequences of his creation. Neither did the responsible politicians attempt to rein him in until it was much too late. Jonathon Steinburg comments that:

'In the case of the Navy Laws…The amendments to the Flottengesetz of 1898 were always conscious political decisions. There was nothing automatic or mechanical about them. Obviously the use of fixed naval laws gave the arms race a certain rigidity and posed very real problems for the diplomacy of the empire, but technology as such cannot explain either the treadmill quality of the arms race, nor the bitter determination to carry on with it.' (4)

He might well have added '...and when the logic behind the original policy could increasingly be seen to be flawed, and the results to be the opposite of those intended'.

What is also pertinent is that the question of why a law which was regularly amended or supplemented to *increase* the strength of the fleet, could never be similarly adjusted to *decrease* that programme, was ignored by German politicians, to the exasperation of their British counterparts. They were quite prepared to reduce their own building programmes if Germany would do likewise. If the original 1898 law was supposedly graven in stone, the ease with which it was superseded in 1900, 1902, 1905, 1908 and 1912 gave the lie to the preposterous German claim that each of these legal amendments had tied the hands of government in its ability to alter the pace and scale of the arms race. The means were clearly available to reverse the trend had the political will existed, and had public opinion been subjected to a balanced coverage of the subject, rather than having been bombarded for a decade by one-sided, misleading, and very efficiently co-ordinated propaganda. As E.L. Woodward remarks, why did:

'German society so willingly accept the objectives of the Tirpitz programme and refused to abandon them even when the central paradox of the risk theory began to produce the wrong results. Even if technology had a life of its own or Tirpitz had been a pure technocrat or nothing but a militarist, that society had the power to alter his plans. There was a Reichstag which could have protested. It was elected by universal suffrage and was by comparison with the other parliaments of the day unquestionably one of the more representative. It voted on major pieces of Tirpitz's programme no less than five times between 1898 and 1914, and each time gave him virtually everything he wanted. There was a vigorous Press and an influential academic community. There was a civilian administration and there were numerous parliaments in each of the constituent states of the empire. A concerted resistance to the naval building programme from any of these groups would have forced Tirpitz very quickly to modify his demands. There was no such resistance until the threat of war lay across the land, and even then the resistance was merely directed at the government which had bungled its diplomatic task rather than at the naval administration *which had made that task so hard.*' [Authors italics] (5)

The fact of the matter was that the German electorate had been extremely well manipulated to demand a navy of the first rank as a prerequisite to the continuing expansion and prosperity of the nation. Extreme nationalistic sentiment had been cultivated to that end and focussed on Great Britain, being the most successful imperial power, as the most suitable target for the politics of envy. It was a critical influence in the advancement of the Emperor's grandiose dreams, and Tirpitz's ambitions for a 'Navy against England'.

Once created, such influences and prejudices develop a momentum of their own. It was this, as much as a reluctance to tamper with the law, that really hamstrung the efforts of German diplomats (many of whom genuinely wished to defuse the situation) in their attempts to fight their war on two fronts – in Germany, to apply some measure of control over the activities and pronouncements of a headstrong Kaiser and a powerful naval lobby; abroad, to protect German interests and to pursue German aims within the bounds of accepted international practice.

In the circumstances, the task of moderates within the German political establishment was never going to be easy, and the difficulties that they faced, in the increasingly confrontational European situation after 1900, would probably have confounded the best and most experienced proponents of the diplomatic arts if placed in a similar position. These skills were, in any case, unavailable or ignored.

The German Foreign Ministry did not in fact contain, by international standards, either the 'best' or the 'most experienced' personnel during this period. If example be needed, the efforts of Count Tattenbach at the Algeciras Conference should be sufficient to make the point. It did, however, not lack in men of basic good intentions and common sense. The governing structure of Imperial Germany, under Wilhelm II, prevented the proper application of those talents they possessed.[1]

Germany's diplomatic isolation was compounded in 1906 by a thaw in relations between Great Britain and Russia. This took a similar form to the original Anglo-French compact, and comprised a series of agreements

---

[1] An example can be easily found in the career of Count Wolff-Metternich, the German ambassador to London between 1902 and 1912. Metternich was an outstanding ambassador by any nation's criteria. He managed to cultivate a close, albeit formal, relationship, based on mutual trust, with the British Foreign Secretary, himself one of the most impressive diplomats of the era, which should have been of the utmost value to Germany. This able man's despatches to Berlin, during his tenure of the post, represent an oasis of reason, objectivity and clarity as to the probable effects of German policy on British opinion, and the likely reactions. His reports never attempted to gloss over the problems that would arise in Anglo-German relations as a result of the ongoing German naval programme. His accurate assessments of the British position, without regard as to whether his opinions fitted in with views fashionable at court, were invariably ignored, dismissed or eventually derided by the Kaiser, and led to his removal from the ambassadorship in 1912 – effectively for having spoken the truths that his emperor did not wish to hear – abandoned by his own ministry; a poor reward for a decade of outstanding services to his nation.

on the various colonial issues likely to cause confrontation. These covered territorial and commercial disputes in Persia, Afghanistan, Tibet and the Far East. At first, it was more *détente* than *entente*, but nevertheless represented a remarkable turn round in relations. Only a year previously Britain and Russia had been on the very brink of war.

The Russian Baltic Fleet, at the beginning of its doomed voyage half way round the world to annihilation at Tsushima, had passed through the North Sea. There it encountered, at night, a fleet of British fishing vessels and opened fire on these vessels. One was sunk and several damaged with some loss of life. In the confusion, individual Russian ships even engaged each other, and, but for a lack of competence, might have reduced their fleet to more manageable proportions. The extraordinary reason given for this criminal stupidity was that the fishing craft had been mistaken for Japanese destroyers! This would have presumed a range and endurance for vessels of that size not even available today.

The understandable outrage caused amongst the British public led to demands for an instant declaration of war. The Baltic Fleet was, for a few days, one telegram away from slaughter. Only an immediate apology from the Tsar and entreaties from his ambassador in London stayed the hand of the British Government as the Russian Fleet continued on its way. It remained under surveillance until its shambolic progression took it clear of European waters.

The incident highlights the utter incompetence of the Russian Navy at that time. Britain and Japan were allies, and this inexcusable action offered ample justification for Britain to join in the conflict – in which case, it would have saved Admiral Rozhestvensky's ships a long and arduous journey to a watery grave in the Far East. His ships would have been at the bottom of the sea well before he was past Gibraltar and the crews spared many privations and future agonies.

That prospect had been a distinct possibility. Lord Charles Beresford's Channel Fleet was ordered to close and shadow the Russian ships, which by then had reached Vigo, in North West Spain. When he left port after coaling, Rozhestvensky was soon in the presence of eight efficient British battleships, which remained at short notice to intercept and engage him. In the meantime, the ships moved southwards whilst waiting for the situation to unfold.

Any engagement between the fleets would have been a foregone conclusion. However numerous the Russians, they were no match for Beresford's battleships in either quality or efficiency. The British commander-in-chief, well aware of his actual superiority, quixotically proposed to attack the Russians with only half his fleet – to make a fairer fight of it! 'It appeared to me that this would be only chivalrous under the circumstances.' (6) As previously related, this generosity of spirit was neither shared nor appreciated by the Admiralty. Nelson himself would have been appalled by the suggestion. 'Only numbers can annihilate' was a principle both Nelson and Fisher would have shared. A hard-fought action involving massive casualties was a situation they would strive to avoid if overwhelming might could produce a cheaper and more complete victory with minimal loss of life. It would be less glorious perhaps, but more compassionate as regards the participants on both sides. Glory, for the press and the public, who happily do not have to share the experience, is a term that generally goes hand in hand with the deaths of those to whom they are not related.

In the end, the issue was settled by referring it to the International Court at The Hague. The subsequent judgement, awarding financial compensation to Great Britain, was gladly accepted by Russia, greatly relieved at having narrowly avoided a catastrophic addition to her already desperate woes. Russia would have grovelled if pushed, but sensible diplomacy avoided that necessity and Britain certainly acquired a moral bargaining counter for the future. It also served to oil the wheels of the *Entente Cordiale*.

That the matter did not degenerate into open hostilities probably hinged on the fact that both countries now had close ties with France. In Russia's case, this was an alliance of long standing and was of vital importance to both sides. For Britain, to have gone to war with Russia at this point, would have put a serious strain on the new *entente* with France. The probability is that Anglo-Russian hostilities at that time would have wrecked the embryonic alliance. There is no doubt that this fact had a restraining influence on the British Government's reaction to the crisis.

The fiasco in the North Sea represented the absolute nadir of Anglo-Russian relations in that era, yet the overall trend was already moving in the opposite direction. There are very close similarities between Britain's rapprochement with France and that which would now take place with Russia.

The North Sea incident was the Anglo-Russian Fashoda. The part of Théophile Delcassé was now taken by Sir Edward Grey, except that the latter was operating from a position of strength rather than of weakness (Russia was beset by problems – internally from revolutionary dissent; externally by the disastrous war with Japan). The role of Paul Cambon, in London, was now played by Sir Arthur Nicholson, the British ambassador in St. Petersburg. On the other side, Izvolsky, the Russian Foreign Minister, assumed the mantle of Lord Lansdowne. Once again, the pivotal interventions of King Edward VII oiled the wheels of the process.

Prior to 1906, the Monarch had already made a contribution to affairs. Two years earlier, on a private visit to Copenhagen, he had met the Russian ambassador. During informal conversation, the King brought up the subject of Anglo-Russian relations, and how beneficial to both countries would be a resolution of their differences on the lines of the *entente* with France. The ambassador's demeanour and diplomatic responses favourably impressed him, and he later wrote to his cousin, the Tsar, expressing his appreciation of the man's qualities. The ambassador was Izvolsky, and the King's remarks cannot but have advanced his career prospects. Be that as it may, when, two years later, the position of Russian Foreign Minister became vacant, he was appointed to the post. Within a month he had begun tentative negotiations with Britain.

A rapprochement between the two countries posed greater difficulties than those presented by the *entente*. In contrast to France, Russia's relations with Germany at that time were generally good. Many in the deeply conservative Russian establishment advocated even closer ties, and certainly would have preferred to favour Germany over Britain with its newly elected Liberal government. Izvolsky had to tread very carefully to avoid alienating this faction, or for that matter, Germany itself. The problem was compounded by the fact that there was little enthusiasm for the Russian regime from within the governing party of Great Britain. Most Liberals deplored what they saw as the repressive autocratic tyranny of the Tsar and his ministers. The British Foreign Secretary had to tread equally carefully to keep his party with him.

In the event, Grey and Nicholson adopted the same 'softly softly' approach that Delcassé had used with the British Government. Talks went on for over a year. No attempt was made to press the Russians, but, with a suggestion here and a proposal there, matters gradually progressed until a general agreement was achieved.

At the end of August 1907, the Anglo-Russian Convention was signed and sealed. It removed all the outstanding colonial and commercial irritants that stood in the way of improved relations between the nations.

King Edward VII once again emerged from the wings. Behind the scenes, he had been prodding the politicians for some time to show more initiative in cultivating better relations with Russia. This had posed obvious difficulties for a Liberal government, many of whose members regarded the Tsar as little more than a blood soiled despot. Even Conservatives were antipathetic.

> 'English imperialists regarded Russia as the ancient foe of the Crimea and more recently as the menace looming over India, while to the Liberals and Labour, Russia was the land of the knout, the pogrom and the massacred revolutionaries of 1905 and the Czar, according to Mr. Ramsey McDonald, 'a common murderer'. The distaste was reciprocated. Russia detested England's alliance with Japan and resented her the power that frustrated Russia's historic yearning for Constantinople and the Straits. Nicholas II once combined two favourite prejudices in the simple statement, "An Englishman is a *zhid* (Jew)"...But old antagonisms were not as strong as new pressures.' (7)

Edward took it upon himself to change the mood, accepting the fact that this initiative would be controversial and unpopular in many circles. In

1908, to the great annoyance of many Liberal MPs, he travelled to Russia in the Royal Yacht to meet the Tsar and his ministers. He was given a splendid reception although, due to security fears, he never set foot ashore. Once again, to some irritation in his government, he overstepped the strict bounds of his constitutional authority. Without consultation, he created the Tsar an Admiral of the Fleet in the Royal Navy, and received a similar honour from his delighted host. Once again, the King displayed a better sense of occasion than his ministers. His visit cemented the new atmosphere of goodwill generated by the Anglo-Russian Convention.

In another striking similarity to the events surrounding the Anglo-French *entente*, the German reaction was initially one of unconcern. Prior to the signing of the convention, Izvolsky had anxiously travelled to Berlin in order to sound out the views of Bülow. The Chancellor voiced no objections to the process, and even welcomed it as a means to defuse international tensions. For such a devious operator as Bülow, this was strangely naïve, especially with the *entente* and the events of Algeciras so fresh in his memory. Had Bismarck still been alive and in power, the alarm bells would have been instant and clamorous, and there is little doubt that his formidable talents and energy would have been arraigned against both initiatives from the moment of their inception.

If the inherent dangers to Germany's international position had yet to dawn on Bülow, they became apparent within a year. In a grim foretaste of 1914, the actions of Austria in the Balkans drew Germany into confrontation with Russia.

The Balkan situation was chaotic, then as now, and far too complicated to describe in detail. The Ottoman Empire had been in a state of imminent disintegration for as long as anyone could remember. It only remained intact due to the fears of the major European powers that one or the other might acquire a disproportionate share of the carcass should it finally and entirely collapse. In 1878, after a ruinous war with Russia, its status and boundaries had been defined and guaranteed by the major powers at the Congress of Berlin. The new nations of Romania, Bulgaria and Serbia were created from old Turkish territories, and Greece enlarged. Turkey, however, still retained large tracts of the Balkan peninsular, spreading through present day Macedonia and Albania to the Adriatic. Different ethnic groups and religions spilled over the various borders, and the whole area seethed with discontent stoked by ancient hatreds. The situation satisfied virtually no one, but, for thirty years, the ramshackle arrangement somehow held together.

One of the more curious anomalies thrown up by the Congress of Berlin concerned the twin provinces of Bosnia and Herzegovina, which lay between the new state of Serbia and the Austrian Empire. These provinces remained nominally under Turkish sovereignty, but were administered by Austria. Their strange status was now to cause a major crisis.

In 1908, sickened by the impotence, corruption and inefficiency of the Sultan's government, a group of young nationalist politicians and army officers staged a successful *coup d'état* in Constantinople. Although the deposed Sultan was replaced by his brother, the latter was reduced to the role of a ceremonial figurehead. The real power in the country now rested in the hands of these 'Young Turks', who were resolved to arrest the decline of their nation.

In Austria, this development was viewed with alarm. It was thought that the new government might try to reassert Turkish control of Bosnia and Herzegovina. To forestall this possibility, Austria determined to annex the two provinces outright. This action was bound to outrage Serbia, who had her own designs on the territories. If the façade of Turkish sovereignty was to be abandoned, then Serbia considered she had the better claim to succeed that authority. The predominately Muslim Bosnians and the Catholic Croats of Herzegovina were fellow Slavs, and both provinces contained a substantial minority of Orthodox Serbs. As subsequent events, right up to the present, have brutally shown, there was no lack of animosity between these groups, but a shared hatred of Austrian rule gave at least a temporary unity of purpose.

Militarily, Serbia was no match for the resources of the Austrian Empire but she possessed a much more powerful ally. Traditionally, Russia, as the only Slav major power, had always vigorously defended the interests and security of her distant kinsmen. Without Russian approval, Austrian opportunist activity in the Balkans was a dangerous adventure.

At this point, Izvolsky, still basking in the success of the Anglo-Russian agreement, makes a reappearance. With his reputation at its zenith, he promptly proceeded to commit political suicide.

In 1871, the strait of the Dardanelles, separating Europe from Asia Minor, and being the only outlet from the Black Sea, had been closed by treaty to the warships of all nations. Ever since, having this vital waterway (over ninety percent of Russian maritime commerce passed through the straits) reopened to its navy had been a constant theme of Russian strategic policy. During his negotiations with the British, Izvolsky believed he had obtained their tacit approval for this to take place. He now approached the Austrian Foreign Minister, Count von Aehrenthal, with a proposal for a *quid pro quo* deal. Russia would not interfere with Austria's annexation of Bosnia and Herzegovina, if the latter would accept the reopening of the straits. As both actions would be in breach of international treaties, it was agreed that their announcement would be made simultaneously. This, it was thought, would neutralise the perceived opposition from the other powers. If Germany felt obliged to back her ally, Austria, she could hardly make a song and dance over the Russian action, and the same applied to France *vis-à-vis* Russia and Austria. In suggesting this rather sleazy bargain, which was very necessarily not made public, Izvolsky deliberately abandoned Russia's traditional policy of support for the Serbs. It was an audacious move, but in the process, he left himself as a hostage to fortune.

The Divisions Intensify

'Izvolsky had placed himself in a precarious position. He was preparing to betray the Balkan Slavs, to whom Russia had deep historical and psychological commitments. He was preparing to defy the Great Powers, possibly including his Entente allies. And, desiring exclusive credit for this coup, he had informed neither the Tsar nor Prime Minister Stolypin. Unfortunately for Izvolsky, before he was ready to betray the Balkan Slavs, Aehrenthal betrayed him.' (8)

By his extraordinary failure to consult either his royal master or his prime minister, Izvolsky left himself out on a limb. Almost immediately it was chopped away. Within days, Aehrenthal, concerned about the rapid changes in Turkey, decided he had to act unilaterally and announced the Austrian annexation of Bosnia and Herzegovina. In this declaration there was no mention of the Dardanelles question – nor could there have been, as this was still Izvolsky's and Aehrenthal's private arrangement.

Stunned by this development, Izvolsky vainly struggled to retrieve the situation. He attempted to put pressure on Aehrenthal to honour his side of the bargain, but was helpless in the face of the latter's bland threat to make public his incriminating correspondence with the Russian prior to the agreement. The matter was, in any case, soon out in the open and, if Austria's action in violation of the treaty created outrage throughout Europe, Russia's part in the intrigue was hardly to her credit. There was now absolutely no chance of the other European powers agreeing to a change in the status of the Dardanelles. Tempers ran high and a first rate crisis ensued that seemed likely to escalate into open hostilities. Serbia, incensed by the Austrian *fait accomplis* and equally with Izvolsky for his betrayal of their interests, mobilised its army. Austria threatened to attack Serbia if the latter refused to accept the change in sovereignty, and began to mass troops on her borders. The Russians responded with their own concentrations on their common frontier in Galicia. It was practically a dress rehearsal for the events of July 1914. Grey remarks in his memoirs that:

'It is impossible to recount these events of 1908-9 without being struck by an ominous parallel with the crisis of 1914. In 1908, as in 1914, Austria acted without full consultation with her ally – so the world was told by von Bülow in the first, and by von Bethmann-Hollweg in the latter crisis. In 1908, as in 1914, Germany, whilst deprecating the headstrong character of Austria's action, thought it necessary to support her Ally. In 1908, as in 1914, Russia felt herself challenged to support Serbia. There the parallel ends. In 1909, Russia preferred humiliation; in 1914 she faced war.' (9)

The anger of the other powers seemed as much focussed on their delinquent allies as on their potential enemies. France virtually disowned Izvolsky's actions, and the Kaiser, who, with his government, had been kept in ignorance of the Austrian intentions, was furious at being placed in the position of having to support 'a piece of brigandage'. He was also embarrassed by the fact that his country had been making great efforts to cultivate a closer relationship with Turkey and having to countenance the arbitrary usurpation of that nation's nominal authority over the two provinces was not calculated to advance this process.

Nevertheless, Germany had to prop up its ally. Russia, however, weakened by the war with Japan was still more than a match for Austria, and the addition of the Serbian Army to the equation further increased this superiority. For three months the situation simmered dangerously until Germany brought it to the full boil. Tired of the impasse, Bülow issued an ultimatum to Russia. If Russia failed to acknowledge Austrian sovereignty over Bosnia and Herzegovina and continued to support Serbia, Germany would give Austria a blank cheque to take any action she saw fit against the Serbs. An immediate response was required, and no compromise solutions would be tolerated. The implication was brutally clear: if Russia attempted to intervene, it meant war with Germany.

Faced with this unequivocal threat, Russia capitulated and recognised the illegal annexation of the Balkan territories. Abandoned by the only ally capable of offering effective assistance, the Serbs were forced to accept the inevitable and fall in line. Their frustration and rage found an outlet in clandestine societies and groups of fanatics dedicated to turning Bosnia and Herzegovina into Austria's poisoned chalice. From within these organisations, many of which had the tacit support of the Serbian authorities, came the spark that, six years later, would ignite the powder keg of Europe.

The rest of the powers were stunned by the rapid turn of events, but, in reality, Russia had no choice other than to acquiesce. Her military forces were debilitated by the recent defeat in the Far East, and were in no state to confront the might of the German Army. It was an utter humiliation, but bred a determination that such a situation could not, and would not, be repeated. Should a similar circumstance arise in future, Russia would be better prepared and would not shrink from the consequences of defiance. The advantage of having powerful allies, and keeping them 'on side', was also apparent.

Once again, recent history was repeating itself, albeit for a different reason. The humiliation of France in 1905 was a deliberate German ploy to drive a wedge between that nation and Great Britain. The ploy backfired. By contrast, the facing down of Russia was the result of Germany being more or less coerced into a confrontation she did not will by the precipitate actions of an irresponsible ally. The result, however, was the same. Germany, once again, was seen to adopt the role of 'Bully Boy' in the playground of Europe. Russia, with whom she had had reasonable relations up to that point, and with whom the Kaiser, in particular, nurtured hopes of a lasting compact, was driven into the arms of the opposition. It had been another Pyrrhic victory. The ties between Britain, France and Russia grew steadily more resilient, and the sense of encirclement, which reached paranoid levels in the Kaiser and certain sections of the press, became ever more pronounced. Grey remarks that:

> 'The Germans worked up the theory of an "encircling policy", and attributed it particularly to King Edward. I did not think that the German Government seriously believed this theory. It seemed incredible that they should not realise that, if Germany had alliances, other countries must have them too. It seemed to me that they surely must see that the Franco-Russian Alliance was the inevitable outcome and counterpart of the Triple Alliance.' (10)

Grey, accomplished diplomat though he was, never properly appreciated the fortress mentality that steadily took over in Germany in the years after the Algeciras Conference. Germany's genuine insecurities were admittedly not reflected in or by the language and policies of her leaders. The tragedy, from Germany's point of view, was that the alienation of yet another major power, namely Russia, made her even more dependent on maintaining the decaying edifice that was the Austro-Hungarian Empire.

The light of history, blessed with hindsight, illuminates no obvious winners from this episode. One clear loser, though, was immediately apparent. Izvolsky, whose career and reputation had experienced a meteoric rise in the preceding few years, now saw those cherished commodities plummet like a stone. Remarkably, although he had completely lost the confidence of the Tsar and his other ministers (never mind the respect of his international colleagues), he was suffered to remain in his post for almost three more years. He was, however, a broken reed, and was eventually put out of his misery by being posted to Paris as Russian Ambassador, where he served out the remnants of his career with mixed results. As demotions go, this was a very well-cushioned fall. Belgrade would have offered a considerably less comfortable landing.

If at any stage of this era Germany deserved sympathy, it was at this point. She had been unwillingly dragged into the Balkan dispute and emerged as one of the villains of the piece. Whilst this contretemps was still in progress, Britain suddenly contracted one of its periodic naval panics. These had previously been brought on by the occasional efforts of the French to challenge British supremacy. Now Germany was the perceived danger. Political, commercial and press interests combined to put pressure on the government to increase the naval budget in order to meet the German challenge. Those who supported this move suspected that the declared German naval programme was being exceeded, that this fact was being deliberately concealed, and that the potential existed for Germany to obtain parity, or even supremacy, in numbers of battleships, within a few years.

Germany, in fact, never departed from the published provisions of her Navy Laws (which were unpalatable enough for British tastes), and the accusations of deception were wholly unwarranted. Nevertheless, German naval expansion was a justifiable cause for alarm, and the British governments of the time were anxious to try and find a way to reduce the level of competition whilst maintaining an adequate margin of supremacy.

Between 1905 and 1914, on several occasions, initiatives were put forward to try and stem the ruinous and accelerating naval competition that continued between the two nations. All were to founder on the inflexibility of Tirpitz and the ambitions of his emperor – who invariably flew into a fury whenever he felt his right to build as many ships as he wanted was being questioned.

For all that, a continuous dialogue was maintained through normal diplomatic channels. Throughout this period, the British Foreign Secretary, Sir Edward Grey, maintained close relations with the German ambassador in London, Count Metternich. Over and over again Grey emphasised to his diplomatic colleague that the only substantive issue that stood athwart better relations between Britain and Germany was the question of the naval construction programmes of both countries. The Liberal government was anxious, desperate even, to reduce naval expenditure in order to divert funds to the social programmes it wished to institute, and which formed a major plank of its appeal to the British electorate.

Grey's constant theme was that any slowing down of German naval construction would enable Britain to make a proportional cut in her effort, to the mutual benefit of both nations. On the other hand, if Germany stuck to her declared programme, Britain could not relax her efforts. Whatever other issues absorbed the British electorate, the maintenance of her naval supremacy, however painful that proved to the Exchequer, was not negotiable. It was the one issue that, however reluctantly, united the supporters of every political grouping. Metternich accurately gauged the British position and, encouraged by Grey, continued to provide realistic reports to Berlin of the climate of opinion in Britain. His was a voice crying in the wilderness (see earlier footnote).

The first crisis in the overall situation did not take long to materialise. As mentioned above, in late 1908, an outcry arose in Britain as a result of a largely manufactured scare over the possibility that Germany had the ability and intention to secretly accelerate her naval construction programme. It was based on information that materials were being stockpiled for the construction of German capital ships that had not been officially ordered. Some of the information was correct, but was wrongly interpreted. It was meat and drink to the navalists.

The action had been taken in Germany to anticipate the construction of ships already approved within the Navy Laws. It was done for the sound economic reasons of ensuring a continuity of cash flow for the building yards, and employment of the workforce. There was no intention to exceed the provisions of the Navy Laws, and a revision of these laws, publicly debated in the *Reichstag*, would have been necessary to change the published construction programme. In any case Tirpitz had only just pushed through the *Reichstag* a new supplementary Navy Law. This had reduced the useful life of German battleships – the age at which they would become due for replacement – from 25 to 20 years. The mechanics of this process meant that German construction could be accelerated, and for the four years 1908-11 she would lay down 3 battleships and 1 battlecruiser annually. Subsequently, the rate of construction would reduce to two capital ships a year. This measure was quite open, and it was highly unlikely that additional covert construction could, or would, be contemplated. There was, in fact, about to be a highly contentious debate in the *Reichstag* as to whether the existing plans for the navy could be funded at all!

Had this fact been explained with any degree of frankness, the resulting furore might have been avoided – to Germany's benefit. The German Government failed to respond quickly to the situation, and waited for Tirpitz to clarify the matter. Tirpitz, however, was stubbornly ambiguous in his response to what were legitimate enquiries. This generated an atmosphere of suspicion. Analysts in Britain started to look at the *potential* ability of Germany to accelerate her rate of shipbuilding. Commercial and political interests promptly jumped onto the bandwagon, and worst possible scenarios were hawked about for their purposes. As it was, the German supplementary law represented, in itself, a sufficient cause for alarm. Britain had actually reduced the number of battleships in the 1906 and 1907 estimates from four to three and, in 1908, this was further cut to just two.

In the circumstances, the scaremongers soon acquired the ear of the public. By some of the gloomiest calculations, Britain's battle fleet of modern dreadnoughts could be overtaken by that of Germany within a few years.

This led to a national uproar, amidst an acrimonious debate on the 1909 naval estimates. The Admiralty, alarmed by the new German construction programme, had asked for funds to build six dreadnoughts and battlecruisers (an unprecedented number). The economists within the Cabinet, led by the Chancellor of the Exchequer, David Lloyd-George, and firmly supported by Winston Churchill, vigorously disputed the necessity for this and demanded that the programme be reduced to four ships. Only then could funds be provided for the social welfare programmes which had been a keystone of the government's appeal to the electorate. The electorate, sadly for the economists' expectations, failed to measure up to their concerns for its wellbeing.

A national campaign was whipped up to ensure Britain's naval security. Instead of six ships, the public was encouraged to demand eight! The rallying cry went round the country of 'We want eight, and we won't wait'. The campaign attracted widespread public support from throughout the political spectrum. Appalled, the economists attempted to regroup, but their efforts were scuppered by developments in the Mediterranean.

Lloyd-George and Churchill had more or less resigned themselves by this time to the original programme of six capital ships. However, in the midst of the debate, came the announcement that Austria was about to lay down four dreadnoughts. Italy immediately followed suit.

These two nations, both formally linked in an alliance with Germany, were scarcely on speaking terms with each other, having many historical and territorial differences. If one developed a new military capacity of any sort, the other was almost bound to follow suit. The overwhelming probability was that their naval capabilities would be cancelled out by mutual hostility (and general inefficiency), but the fact still remained that, on paper, dreadnoughts built by either country represented a potential reinforcement to Germany. In the face of this development, the economists accepted defeat. Churchill wryly comments that:

'In the end a curious and characteristic solution was reached. The Admiralty had demanded six ships: the economists offered four: and we finally compromised on eight.' (11)

In the end, the dreadful predictions of the alarmists never materialised and the scare was seen to be what it actually was – just a scare. However, when Churchill became First Lord of the Admiralty three years later, he was very grateful for the extra ships. His perceptions by then had been much changed by circumstances. With typical magnanimity, he reflected that:

'Although, the Chancellor of the Exchequer and I were right in the narrow sense, we were absolutely wrong in relation to the deep tides of destiny. The greatest credit is due to the First Lord of the Admiralty, Mr. McKenna, for the resolute and courageous manner in which he fought his case and withstood the party on this occasion. Little did I think, as this dispute proceeded, that when the next cabinet crisis about the navy arose our roles would be reversed; and little did he think that the ships for which he contended so stoutly would eventually, when they arrived, be welcomed by open arms by me.' (12)

The British situation was further improved when the governments of Australia and New Zealand both voted funds for the construction of a battlecruiser. This meant that no less than ten vessels of the dreadnought type were laid down in a single year. The New Zealand ship was unconditionally allocated to the Admiralty, whereas the Australian unit came under the orders of the newly formed Royal Australian Navy. The latter, however, always worked within the overall imperial defence policy, and *HMAS Australia* served much of her operational life with the Grand Fleet.

The Divisions Intensify

If the scare over the 1909 naval estimates had been spurious, it had at least concentrated attention on a serious potential threat to Britain's security.

By the end of 1910, before the new programme had come to fruition, Britain had completed seven dreadnoughts and three battlecruisers to Germany's four and two (counting *Blucher*), respectively. In itself, this was an adequate superiority for the British, but if both countries continued to build at the same rate thereafter, it would be entirely inadequate. A British superiority of only four or five capital ships, in future fleets of more than twenty vessels each, would put her control of the seas in grave danger.

The Germans, if they wished to challenge the Royal Navy, could always do so at their moment of choice – that is, whenever they could arrange for all their ships to be available. In the meantime, if they so wished, they could lay up half the entire fleet for refit and repairs until came the moment that all were battle worthy and ready for a specific operation. The British, on the other hand, had to permanently be ready for this critical moment, which entailed being constantly at short notice for sea (and involved greater wear and tear on the ships than would otherwise have been the case). Refits and repairs had to be routinely cycled into this general state of preparedness, which meant that there would always be a proportion of their fleet absent at any given time.

In London, this fact was plainly recognised, and thus the German construction programmes were closely monitored, and changes in the Navy Laws regarded with mounting concern. By this time it was becoming clear to senior British politicians and the naval hierarchy that the old 'two power plus 10%' standard, which had previously determined the strength of the fleet, had been overtaken by events. Although not officially admitted until 1912, this standard was being effectively discarded from 1906 onwards. Thereafter, Britain was building against Germany alone.

The huge construction programme resulting from the 1909 naval estimates eased British worries as to their relative strength *vis-à-vis* the German Fleet, but the whole furore had concentrated minds on the continuing threat from across the North Sea. The government had been made painfully aware that their sweeping plans for social reform could not be financed at the cost of neglecting the navy. This posed a dilemma for the reformers.

However much the majority of the electorate approved of their programmes, there was the problem of how to find the necessary funds to provide for their implementation. If the naval budget continued to burgeon in order to meet the German challenge, insufficient resources were available without recourse to increased taxation – and this would be a very unpopular move. One logical solution was to try and reduce the level of naval competition between the two countries. The resulting economies would help to release funds for more productive purposes. The British Government continued to work towards this end.

There were some grounds for optimism, as Germany was feeling the pinch as well. Additional levies had already had to be made in order to finance the existing fleet expansion programmes, and there were rumblings from the army that it was being starved of resources by expenditure on what it regarded as an irrelevance to Germany's military priorities. The bulk of German public opinion was wholeheartedly in favour of a fine fleet, but was not enthusiastic about the means of paying for this armada if it involved personal sacrifice. The richest landowners were the most vehement opponents of this suggestion and regarded with antipathy the prospect of being taxed to fund what many of them considered to be an irrelevant collection of ceremonial ships.

Bülow, whilst Chancellor, took the line of least resistance and humoured the Kaiser in his desire for a great fleet. His successor was less pliable and broadly supported the view that either naval construction had to be limited, or Germany would have Britain as an enemy. This rational appreciation of the situation was unfortunately not available until 1909. As early as 1902, the then British First Lord of the Admiralty, Selbourne, had identified the potential conflict of interest between the naval and military authorities that would result from the expansion of the German Navy.

> 'The great naval expenditure on which Germany has embarked involves a deliberate diminution of the military strength which Germany might otherwise have attained in relation to France and Russia.' (13)

Four to five years later, this prediction had become an undeniable fact. In France and Russia, this distraction of German resources, to armaments not immediately threatening to them, was a welcome development. To many throughout Europe it seemed that Germany was diluting its real source of power in order to provide the Kaiser with a showpiece fleet. Holstein's glum comment that 'the fleet increases the number of our enemies but will never be strong enough to vanquish them' became ever more pertinent.

These doubts did not afflict the State Secretary of the Navy. Tirpitz, with the full support of the Kaiser, stood firm. He was gambling on the stamina of his own nation's economy to outlast that of Britain in a long-term naval armaments race. Who knows what might have happened in the course of another ten years of peace? Germany was improving her economic position relative to that of Britain at a steady rate, and, unlikely though it was, the British might have tired of the competition. It was from the British Government that all the initiatives originated for a reduction in naval construction. Tirpitz interpreted this as a sign of weakness, and a justification for his intransigence. His policies were, however, subject to a more searching scrutiny when Bülow was replaced as Chancellor. This occurred in July 1909.

Bülow's successor, Theobald von Bethmann-Hollweg, was a much more straightforward character and less tolerant of Tirpitz's influence with the Kaiser. He also made it one of his first priorities to improve relations with Great Britain. In pursuit of this end, he insisted on being personally responsible for all matters affecting Germany's dialogue with the British Government. As the main bone of contention was always naval construction, Bethmann and Tirpitz were immediately locked into a power struggle for the ear of the Emperor and the support of the *Reichstag*. From the point of view of the Kaiser, this was obviously an unwelcome development. It was, however, a situation largely of his own making, and was exacerbated by one of his typically cavalier forays into the arena of foreign affairs.

CHAPTER TEN

THE *DAILY TELEGRAPH* INTERVIEW

'My actions ought to speak for themselves, but you listen not to them but to those who misinterpret and distort them. That is a personal insult which I feel and resent. To be forever misjudged, to have my repeated offers of friendship weighed and scrutinised with jealous mistrustful eyes, taxes my patience severely. I have said time after time that I am a friend of England, and your press – at least, a considerable section of it – bids the people of England refuse my proffered hand and insinuates that the other holds a dagger. How can I convince a nation against its will?'

Kaiser Wilhelm II, as quoted by Colonel Stuart-Wortley

The change of Chancellor was actually influenced by one of the Kaiser's self-inflicted diplomatic crises. Bülow played a characteristically slippery role in this process, and, by doing so, eventually lost the remaining trust that Wilhelm had reposed in him.

In late 1907, Wilhelm paid a state visit to Britain. He was not in the best frame of mind at that time, as one of his closest confidantes, and behind the scenes 'fixer', Prince Philip 'Phili' von Eulenberg, had been implicated in a sensational and much-publicised homosexual scandal. The affair had, by then, reached the courts. This was in an age when homosexuality was not only a criminal offence, but socially tainted anyone associated with those touched by suspicion. As Eulenberg was known to be an intimate friend of the Kaiser, the trial was an excruciating embarrassment to the latter. Far too late, Wilhelm attempted to distance himself from his former favourite. Already perceived, in the eyes of many of his subjects, as lacking judgement in his choice of friends, he now stood accused of compounding this error with the additional charge of disloyalty.

The self styled 'All Highest' and 'Supreme Warlord' was deeply humiliated by his exposure to the often caustic press comment, public censure, and private ridicule that ensued. In the circumstances, the acutely depressed Wilhelm did not feel in the mood to undertake a planned visit to Great Britain, and it was only with some difficulty, and stiff pressure from the British, that he was persuaded to meet his state obligations.

As it happened, the Kaiser's visit was a considerable success, and both governments were well satisfied with the results, which gave a boost to improving mutual relations. The enthusiastic reception given to Wilhelm raised his flagging spirits somewhat, and, at the end of the official leg of the visit, he decided to stay on in a private capacity. His incorrigibly Anglophobe wife had returned to Germany immediately, and, released from her influence, Wilhelm was happy to relax away from the immediate problems awaiting him back in Berlin. The Eulenberg unpleasantness could be cast from the mind for a while.

He hired a small castle on the south coast of England and invited the owner, Colonel Stuart-Wortley, to stay as his guest. There he entertained and mingled with the local gentry. For Wilhelm, it was an opportunity to play one of his favourite roles; that of the English country squire. It was also a much welcomed opportunity to be rid of the stultifying pomp and circumstance of the Prussian Court – paradoxically, a burden he assiduously perpetuated once he returned to his native soil.

Wilhelm never mastered the language of diplomacy. He pronounced as an emperor or he spoke man to man. He was a stranger to most of the stages that intervened between these conditions. In the latter mode he often pontificated, but he was erudite, amusing, and frequently indiscreet. His natural exuberance spilled over into his conversation, and he was prone to making exaggerated statements to emphasise the points he was trying to make. These were not intended to be taken entirely literally. Such statements, if transposed to the written word, tend to lose their immediacy and informality and assume a weight that the argument was not designed to bear. For the finer purposes of diplomacy, such informal discussion never translates into good print.

In private, most public figures regularly have frank conversations, or make comments and statements that they take good care to ensure will remain 'off the record'. The Kaiser made the profound mistake of permitting his private observations to be transmitted verbatim into the public arena. Whilst walking the grounds or sharing the table with his paid host, Wilhelm unburdened himself as to his views on Anglo-German relations. The colonel faithfully recorded all these observations, and, naïvely impressed with the Kaiser's evident good intentions, later wrote to him asking whether he might publish the text of these conversations – as a contribution to a better understanding between the two nations. Wilhelm, back in Germany, readily agreed on his part, but sent the proposed article to Bülow for final approval. Bülow, by his account (which is suspect), did not read it through and merely had it forwarded to the Foreign Ministry for vetting. Having made some minor corrections of fact, the ministry returned the document to Bülow who again maintained that he did not bother to read it before passing it back to the Kaiser with his approval for its publication.

Bülow's protestations of ignorance as to the proposed article's content have a hollow ring. It is almost inconceivable that he would have neglected to at least scan the contents of a proposed article that was based on the observations of his sovereign regarding the crucial subject of Anglo-German relations. He could have been in no doubt that the publication of such an article, from such an exalted source, would receive widespread attention and would thus be a significant contribution to the development, or detriment, of those relations. He was also no stranger to the Kaiser's lapses of judgement and tact in both his verbal and written communications. This, alone, should have demanded that Bülow give full scrutiny to any planned publication reflecting Wilhelm's views of the moment.

However hazy may be the evidence of Bülow's knowledge, or lack of it, as to the matter, he stands condemned on either count – on the one hand for gross incompetence; or on the other, for deceit and disloyalty to his royal master. There is not, and there never will be, any conclusive proof as to the German Chancellor's degree of involvement in this affair (and he was chronically lazy about detail) but, to this writer, the latter scenario seems marginally more likely. Bülow may well have calculated that the inevitable, and embarrassing, repercussions from publication of the article might have a salutary and restraining effect on Wilhelm's enthusiasm for impromptu interference in foreign policy. It is only fair to add that when the whole affair inevitably turned into a diplomatic disaster, Bülow erupted in a highly convincing appearance of rage at both his sovereign and his subordinates. If it was acting, then it was well done.

On October 28th 1908, the *Daily Telegraph* published Colonel Stuart-Wortley's account of his interviews with the German Emperor. Wilhelm's remarks were undoubtedly well intentioned, and had been made privately and aimed purely at a British audience. If left as such, they would not have caused a major furore. By allowing them to be published, he completely overlooked the fact that they were then available to the world in general – a readership for which they were clearly not designed. The account of the interview immediately caused a stir amongst the diplomatic establishments of the rest of the world, and, in Germany itself, provoked an unprecedented torrent of outrage and criticism.

The full text of the interview is attached in Appendix I. In its more contentious remarks, it managed to offend or embarrass most of the other major powers. With regard to Great Britain, Wilhelm helpfully offered the opinion that 'You English are mad, mad, mad as March hares' in rejecting his frequently extended offers of friendship. There then followed an embittered tirade against the anti-German tone of the British press (the considerably greater vitriol towards Britain emanating from his own fourth estate was conveniently ignored). This, he averred, seriously hindered his efforts to improve bilateral relations, particularly as the majority of his subjects 'were not friendly' to the British. As evidence of his goodwill he volunteered the information that, when the early stages of the Boer War were going badly for Britain, he had consulted his Army General Staff as to the best strategy for winning the conflict, and had passed on their conclusions to London via the Queen. He also asserted that he had refused to be drawn into a suggested coalition with France and Russia aimed at supporting the Boers and 'humiliating England to the dust'. More than that, he claimed that he had threatened the French and the Russians with German reprisals should they initiate such a measure, and he maintained that this information was also communicated in a telegram to his grandmother. Turning to the huge increase in the strength of his navy, the Kaiser denied that it represented a specific threat to Britain. He defined its primary purpose as the protection of Germany's overseas colonies and its rapidly expanding global trade. He darkly hinted that, in view of Japan's growing power in the Far East, Britain might one day be grateful for the existence of a strong German fleet.[1]

The *Daily Telegraph* article, ironically, caused the least stir in Britain. Depending on the viewpoint of the reader, it was treated with amusement, scorn, or exasperation, and as further evidence of Wilhelm's unbalanced personality. When questioned as to the existence of Wilhelm's alleged correspondence, the British Government stated that it was unable to trace the relevant documents. Elsewhere, the French and Russians were outraged. Both governments vehemently denied the accusation that they had plotted a continental combination against Britain and had been thwarted by the Kaiser. The Tsar actually stated to the British Ambassador in St. Petersburg that the reverse had been the case. The hooded allusion to possible dangers from future Japanese expansionism caused offence to that nation where it was seen, at best, as a clumsy attempt to drive a wedge into the structure of the Anglo-Japanese alliance.

It was in Wilhelm's own country, however, that the greatest exception was taken to his misconceived initiative. There had always been a great unease at the Kaiser's obvious desire for 'Personal Rule' regardless of his legal status. His conception of the 'Divine Right of the Monarch' was completely at odds with his actual constitutional position, and this now came to a head. From every strata of German society, whether on the right, left, or centre of the political spectrum, there came a furious, blanket condemnation of his actions. The tone and manner of his remarks were seen as inappropriate as coming from the ruler of a great power. The contemptuous reaction abroad to them, and the inferences that they were indicative of a mental instability in their emperor, were deeply humiliating to the German population – more particularly so as many of his own subjects shared this latter suspicion. No one enjoys having their private concerns open to public debate.

---

[1] In this remark, Wilhelm totally ignores the fact that his entire battle fleet had been consciously designed with insufficient range and habitability to embark on extended operations beyond the confines of the North Sea. Its only possible use could be against the British Fleet. Indeed, it was the sacrifice of 'Blue Water' qualities that contributed materially to the better protection displayed by German dreadnoughts as compared to their British counterparts.

It was the content of the interview, however, that generated the greatest anger. It was bad enough that France and Russia had been publicly and needlessly antagonised, and the Japanese gratuitously offended, but it was the revelations about South Africa that really put the cat amongst the pigeons. The Germans felt a strong racial kinship with the Boers, and, throughout the South African war, public opinion had been overwhelmingly and passionately on the side of the latter – and correspondingly hostile towards the British. It had been precisely this strength of feeling, and the associated sense of frustration at German impotence to project its influence overseas, that Tirpitz had tapped in order to secure the passage of the Second Navy Law. Now, their own monarch had publicly asserted that he had, at that time, ignored the will of virtually his entire nation with regard to the Boers, and, furthermore, had actively conspired to effect their defeat! The country seethed with fury. In the eyes of many, the Kaiser was guilty of treason against the state, and there were calls for him to abdicate. The *Reichstag* determined on holding a censure debate.

Coming on top of the continuing Eulenberg scandal, this crisis was too much for Wilhelm. He was literally traumatised by the strength of feeling against him and eventually suffered a form of nervous breakdown. Behind the splendid façade and ferocious posturing crouched a chronically insecure personality. In the deep depression into which he was thrown, Wilhelm completely withdrew from public appearances, and became almost pathetically dependent on Bülow to rescue him from the consequences of his own indiscreet utterances.

In placing his fate in the hands of Bülow, the Kaiser was tempting providence, as he was not the only person whose position was open to attack. Bülow's castle was also under siege, and he had a highly developed sense of self-preservation unconstrained by loyalty or scruple. The wily Chancellor immediately took steps to extricate himself from the situation. He wrote to Wilhelm tendering his resignation. Cleverly, he painted himself in the light of the Kaiser's conscientious servant, nobly taking upon himself responsibility for the failings of the Foreign Ministry. In taking this approach, he was well aware that the Kaiser regarded the Foreign Ministry with some antipathy. Confident that Wilhelm, in his current frame of mind, was incapable of doing without him, he added the proviso that, if his royal master wished him to remain at his post, it could only be on the understanding that he would be given an absolutely free hand to defend them both. Shortly afterwards Bülow visited the Kaiser at the latter's Romintern estate, near the Russian border, whence he had fled from Berlin. He found Wilhelm in a 'very pitiable' state, and easily obtained from him the necessary consent to act as the Chancellor best saw fit.

Bülow quickly moved to consolidate his reprieve. Expanding his role as the noble martyr, he now presented himself to the *Reichstag* as selflessly shouldering the blame for both the Foreign Ministry *and* the Kaiser. This ploy entirely succeeded.

'Bülow successfully avoided the storm, managing to incriminate the Kaiser, exonerate himself, and present the image of a brave and chivalrous Chancellor, willing to absorb all blows, just and unjust, and persevere for the sake of Crown and nation.' (1)

Bülow, in his explanation of the circumstances surrounding the incident, made a compelling, and superficially convincing, speech to the *Reichstag* minimising his involvement in the matter. The *Reichstag* responded enthusiastically to his defence, and, in the process, Wilhelm's position deteriorated even further. The general feeling was that it was intolerable that the Kaiser, by his irresponsible behaviour, and by his unconstitutional efforts to exercise 'personal rule', should have placed such a worthy public servant in an impossible situation. For the time being, Bülow emerged triumphant with what seemed to be an improved reputation and an increased authority. This apparent success was destined, however, to be transitory, and it proved to be Bülow's last hurrah on the political scene. Briefly though, he was able to milk the situation to his advantage.

The Kaiser had deliberately removed himself from Berlin for long periods during the crisis and had furiously occupied himself with hunting parties in far-flung estates. These took place in an atmosphere of almost desperate artificial bonhomie. Bülow encouraged him in this activity despite the fact that the Monarch's absence at such a critical period gave rise to further rumbles of disapproval from the *Reichstag* and the press.

Even in a self-imposed internal exile, ill-fortune continued to dog the Kaiser's steps. In the chosen company of his male sycophants, Wilhelm's idea of 'entertainment' tended towards crass schoolboy humour, practical jokes, and a ritual humiliation of his close entourage. They were used to humouring him, but it all went badly wrong when the Chief of the Military Cabinet, fetchingly attired in a tutu, collapsed and died whilst performing an after dinner ballet sketch in the presence of the 'All Highest'. With some difficulty, the stiffening general was divested of the trappings of the Sugar Plum Fairy and re-united with his uniform and service decorations before his funeral. In itself, the incident could have been regarded, with some black humour, as an untoward embarrassment. Unfortunately, although such matters could be hushed up for a time, word inevitably spread, and this was one incident that could no longer be treated in isolation. It emphasised, to a now completely exasperated establishment, the lack of gravitas that surrounded Wilhelm's inner circles, and it reflected on his ability to uphold the dignity of his position as Head of State. Coming on top of all that had occurred before, he had become an embarrassment to his nation and an annoyance to the bulk of his subjects.

The death, before his eyes, of General Count Hülsen-Haeseler, a childhood friend, marked the absolute nadir of the Kaiser's fortunes.

Overwhelmed by the repeated blows of what he came to see as malign fortune, Wilhelm's remaining reserves of fortitude collapsed. Shortly afterwards, Bülow applied the *coup de grace* to his self-respect.

The Chancellor's late honeymoon with the *Reichstag* was proving to be short lived. Once his silver tongue had ceased to lap over the assembly, questions arose as to why he had not intervened to prevent the publication of the article. On two occasions he had had the opportunity to either censure, or kill outright, the contents of the *Daily Telegraph* interview. The initial enthusiastic approval of Bülow's conduct was beginning to give way to a scepticism as to his motives, and to a healthy suspicion that the parliament had been manipulated to his ends. No organisation that prides itself on its integrity and abilities enjoys the thought that it might have been used for the purposes of an individual who considered himself cleverer than its combined intelligence.

As a sublime political animal, Bülow recognised the dangers of the situation. By the German Constitution he could only be appointed or dismissed by the Kaiser. To function effectively as Chancellor, he needed the support of the majority of the *Reichstag*. To survive, therefore, he needed to have both the agreement of the Kaiser for all policy initiatives, and the approval of the *Reichstag* for their funding and the means of their attainment. He decided to bolster his position by obtaining a public declaration of support from his emperor. Consequently, he drafted a statement for Wilhelm to sign, which gave a blanket endorsement of Bülow's recent performance in the *Reichstag*:

'Uninfluenced by the exaggerations of public criticism, which seem to him unjustified, His Majesty the Emperor regards it as his chief Imperial task to assure the continuity of Imperial policy, while at the same time, maintaining his constitutional responsibilities. His Royal and Imperial Majesty has accordingly approved all declarations by the Imperial Chancellor in the Reichstag, at the same time assuring Prince von Bülow of the continuation of his confidence.' (2)

The Chancellor confronted the Kaiser, who had returned to Berlin, with this document, and, in the latter's depressed state had no trouble in obtaining his signature.

Behind the fig leaf of the first sentence, the statement represented a gesture of humility totally at odds with Wilhelm's normal conception of his role as supreme leader of a great nation. This latest blow to his fragile self-esteem was too much for him to absorb. However readily he had approved the document, he cannot have regarded it as other than an act of self-abasement, and it resulted in him sinking deeper, if that were possible, into the slough of despond. In the aftermath of Bülow's visit, Wilhelm became tearful, took to his bed, and began to speak of abdication. In this state, he was visited by his eldest son. The Crown Prince commented on this moment:

'My father had returned. Prostrated by these exciting and violent events and still more by the lack of understanding he had met with, he lay ill at Potsdam. The incomprehensible had happened: after twenty years, *during which he had imagined himself to be the idol of the majority of his people and had supposed his rule to be exemplary* [author's italics], disapproval of him and of his character had been quite unmistakably pronounced...I was shocked by his appearance...He seemed aged by years; he had lost hope, and felt himself to be deserted by everybody; he was broken by the catastrophe which had snatched the ground from beneath his feet; his self confidence and his trust were shattered.' (3)

Although the impulsion to abdicate soon dissipated, it was weeks before Wilhelm recovered his confidence sufficiently to resume his public appearances. In the meantime, there occurred profound changes in his attitude towards Bülow. The first was an entirely human reaction. In retrospect, he was acutely embarrassed by the memory of his disintegration in the presence of the Chancellor, and the pathetic figure he must have cut. The embarrassment was such that he was no longer comfortable in Bülow's company. Out of this embarrassment grew resentment, and, during the long period of brooding that followed, he became increasingly critical of the Chancellor's performance on his behalf. The Crown Prince, whose powers of judgement have not generally received the acclaim of history, nevertheless states his father's case with admirable clarity:

'In a perfectly loyal way, the Kaiser sent it (the original draft of Stuart-Wortley's article) on to the Imperial Chancellor and asked him for his opinion. The proceedings were consequently all absolutely correct; and nothing improper had occurred, unless the remarks themselves are to be characterised as such; and even then, one must give the Kaiser credit for having made them with the object of improving Anglo-German relations, just as General Stuart-Wortley, with the same intention, conceived the idea of making them known to a wider public.

'The manuscript was returned to the Kaiser with the remark that there was no objection to its being published – only, unfortunately, through negligence and a number of unfortunate coincidences, none of the gentlemen who were responsible for this judgement had actually read the text with any care. And so the mischief began...And yet the man who was called upon by my father's trust...to cover and defend him, that man failed...[The Kaiser]...was rudely torn out of his security and unsuspecting confidence and felt that he was deserted and abandoned by the Chancellor.' (4)

The above remarks do not constitute a plausible defence of the Kaiser's miscalculated initiative, but they do highlight some mitigating circumstances. The key points are probably those of the Kaiser's benevolent *intentions* for improved Anglo-German relations; that his statements had been made to that end; and that they were delivered with due regard to the fact that he was addressing a British audience. Bülow could, and should, have employed these facts to take a little of the heat off Wilhelm in the assembly. That he did not so choose is a clear contradiction of his fervently declared loyalty to his sovereign. It was also an uncharacteristic blunder by

'The Eel'
Bernhard Von Bülow

the Chancellor, in that, whilst offering such mitigating arguments would not have unduly harmed his own defence, the failure to make such obvious points cast suspicion on his own motives and integrity. In the circumstances, he had been far too clever for his own good. Even the most inveterate of Wilhelm's critics, or of Bülow's political opponents, could accept that it was one of the latter's constitutional duties to make the best possible case for the Kaiser. No one would have thought any the less of him had he done so. Indeed, it would have probably enhanced his standing. In the fullness of time, his conspicuous lack of effort in Wilhelm's defence resulted in public opinion starting to swing away from him.

If the Kaiser's failings remained apparent, and his role in the matter unforgiven, some sympathy for his predicament also emerged. He had clearly been badly served by his Chancellor. Unsurprisingly, this view also took a firm hold in the mind of the Emperor. From that moment on, Bülow's days as Chancellor were numbered.

As Wilhelm gradually began to recover his precarious equilibrium, and, with it, his self-confidence, so his relationship with Bülow declined. On the surface, all seemed well for a while. Wilhelm made a show of affection for the Chancellor, and, in their conversations, returned to something approaching his old good humour and ebullience. It was, however, a public charade. In private he was increasingly hostile towards Bülow and spoke of his 'betrayal' by the Chancellor. Some intimation of this attitude must have reached Bülow as he regularly returned to the subject in his audiences with the Kaiser, repeatedly attempting to justify his address to the *Reichstag*. He continued to emphasise that he had done everything in his power to defend the Emperor's position. His efforts were in vain. Wilhelm had decided to rid himself of the Chancellor as soon as he had a convenient excuse. It was not long before a suitable opportunity presented itself. It was provided by the requirement to finance the German naval programme.

By 1909, the dreadnought revolution had resulted in a large increase in the unit costs of individual battleships. The subsequent amendments to the Navy Laws of 1898 and 1900 had also resulted in older ships being due for decommissioning at an earlier date than was originally contemplated. This meant that more ships than originally planned had to be constructed within a given time span if the provisions of the Navy Laws were to be met. Tirpitz, of course, had realised that this would be the case when he drafted the first bill. As previously stated, he was essentially a single issue politician. Once he had gained his end, his involvement ceased. It was left to others to arrange the funding, and deal with the political ramifications that resulted from his programme. Both these factors now came to the fore.

Bülow, up to that point, had managed to raise the funds by uniting a majority of the *Reichstag* behind the banner of *Weltpolitik* – literally 'World Policy' – of which the navy was to be an essential ingredient. By the spring of 1909, however, Tirpitz's demands were far exceeding the available revenue. Germany could no longer fund its naval programme without either making economies elsewhere in its state expenditure or by finding a means to raise extra cash. The first alternative simply did not exist as a practical option. Between them, the army and the navy absorbed an overwhelming proportion of the nation's wealth, but, whereas the army was supported by each individual component of the German Empire, the navy was a purely imperial institution, and the means of its funding involved the necessity for controversial legislation. This needs a short explanation.

When Bismarck cobbled together the German Empire in 1871, it was very much a conditional federation of previously independent states. The constitution that bound them together was deliberately loose and required them to act as a single nation only on certain essential matters such as common foreign and defence policies, and as a unified trade market. There was also to be a common, elected, parliament, the *Reichstag*, which had power of veto over imperial proposals, but which could not initiate proposals of its own. For most other purposes, each state retained many sovereign rights, and continued to levy its own taxes to support the administration and public services of its own population.

This situation extended to the various armies. Each state maintained its own regiments which were financed by its own internal taxation system. The central direction of the combined armies, in time of war, came from the Imperial German General Staff, but individual responsibility for the raising of troops and their field command was retained by the parent states. Some of these states were insignificant and their levies were combined into larger units, but others could raise a full army in their own right. Bavaria, for example, could mobilise an army that, on its own, would rank as one of the ten most powerful military formations in the world – a distinction that was not shared by the British Army of that time! The nearest equivalent, strangely enough, is that of the British Empire, apart from India. By, or shortly after, the beginning of the 20th century, Canada, Australia, New Zealand and South Africa were effectively self-governing nations who recruited and trained their armed forces from their own resources but almost invariably, in practice, placed them at the disposal of an overall defence policy for the empire.

By contrast, the German Navy depended for its existence on funds raised from the empire as a whole. Obtaining these was not an easy or straightforward process. First of all, most of the taxes that brought in serious revenue were already being levied by the individual state governments and used for their own purposes. Secondly, any new imperial tax, levied across the board, was bound to be unpopular with a considerable section of the electorate. The *Weltpolitik* argument could not be milked indefinitely. Thirdly, if the funds were levied from the section of society most able to afford it, it would alienate the most influential political lobby in the land.

There was a fourth alternative, and that was to curtail the naval programme. Given the intransigence of Tirpitz, with the full support of the Kaiser, this option never reached the discussion stage. Bülow was instructed to find a solution to the problem and to get it accepted by the *Reichstag*. Wilhelm made it clear that Bülow's retention of office hung on this matter. An adverse vote in the assembly would require the resignation of the Chancellor.

Bülow, to his credit, did his best, and very nearly succeeded. He tried to put together a package that would spread the load equally throughout German society. No one would be hit so hard as to have a real grievance, but all would be required to contribute. His efforts foundered on the matter of an inheritance tax, which adversely, but only marginally, affected the landowning classes.

> '...thus the navy came home to roost, directly challenging the interests of conservative landowners...they crushed the inheritance tax proposal and passed the burden of taxation on to business and urban interests. The economic consequences of *Weltpolitik* had divided, not united, the different forms of property ownership.' (5)

Their opposition to him was crucial. When it came to the ballot in the assembly, it was desperately close. In the end, out of 382 delegates who registered, Bülow's motion was rejected by 8 votes – four delegates either way. With the rupture of his power base in the *Reichstag*, it was effectively the end of his career.

In accordance with the Kaiser's stipulations, he tendered his resignation as Chancellor. Despite his disquiet as to Wilhelm's attitude towards himself, he was not entirely expecting this pre-arranged deal to be taken seriously, and it was with some chagrin that he found his offer instantly accepted. The turnaround in his fortunes had been dramatic. Only seven months had elapsed since his triumph in the *Reichstag*. It took some time for him to realise that this decision was final, but, on July 14th 1909, it was publicly announced that he was standing down and would be replaced by Theobald von Bethmann-Hollweg.

The net result of the affair was that the Kaiser's authority and influence was undermined. After a while, he recovered his equilibrium to some extent, but the events had a permanent effect. On the face of it, this was no bad thing, but some historians contend that it was a very mixed blessing.

> 'Given the fact that the German constitution was designed to rest on the Kaiser's command – above all in the areas of war and diplomacy – Wilhelm's subsequent loss of confidence left a vacuum which was probably even more dangerous to Germany than his earlier assertions of authority.' (6)

There was now a new Chancellor who was less of a sycophant, and more inclined to challenge the validity of Wilhelm and Tirpitz's naval programmes. Consequently, the latter could no longer rely on having a clear run whenever he chose to upgrade those programmes, and the stage was set for a change in tone and approach to Germany's external relations.

CHAPTER ELEVEN
NEGOTIATIONS AND CRISIS

'Bülow had managed the Reichstag by use of *Weltpolitik*. But when Bethmann-Hollweg became chancellor the financial implications of the navy's expansion ensured that *Weltpolitik* was deeply divisive in its effects. Bethmann therefore foreswore *Weltpolitik*, at least in its more aggressive forms, for a policy of détente. He did so for reasons not of Foreign policy, a field in which he had no previous experience, but of domestic political necessity. Indeed, even had he tried to manipulate the parties by the use of nationalist appeals, he might not have succeeded...An Anglo-German naval agreement was therefore the main means by which Bethmann sought to extract himself from the problems.'

Hew Strachan: The First World War

'Grey's fixed version of the "balance of power" prevented him from appreciating what was becoming only too apparent to the Germans, which was that the changes in it since 1906 had been uniformly unfavourable to Germany.'

John Charmley: Splendid Isolation?

The new Chancellor's inheritance was certainly no bed of roses. Germany's increasing isolation in Europe was beginning to assume critical proportions.

The problems that faced the nation were daunting. At the turn of the century, her position had been one of great strength, but, in a few brief years, her international position had been severely eroded. Running through this period was a constant strand; the rise of Germany as a naval power, which, on paper, increased her military strength; and, on the other hand, the corresponding alienation of Great Britain, which weakened her strategic situation. By the middle of 1909, despite the considerable strategic advantages of a central position and unified internal lines of communication, Germany was faced by an increasingly united front of Russia, France and Great Britain – with the emerging power of Japan as an ally of the latter.

The Kaiser's pre-occupation with the 'encirclement' of his country, even if that had not been intentional, was not simply paranoia. A glance at the map of Europe and the Mediterranean in 1909 illustrates the extent to which the power blocs had coalesced into a central core represented by Germany and the Austrian Empire, and an outer ring comprising the 'Triple

Entente' and the possessions of France and Great Britain in North Africa. It is true that the adherence of Italy to the central powers represented a theoretical breaking of the ring, but this was something of a moot point. The latter nation was a powerful new factor on the international scene, but was an unpredictable quantity and an unreliable ally. Italy had bitter historical differences with Austria, together with territorial claims, and between these two nations there was an atmosphere of mutual hatred and loathing. It was hardly a situation that lent itself to a happy alliance or encouraged co-operation in any form. As a further negative factor, the general feeling in Italy, at that time, was very pro-British.

The crucial moral support of the British Government, and the practical assistance given by the Royal Navy during Garibaldi's campaign to unify Italy, half a century previously, still ranked high in the consciousness of the new nation. Any Italian government would find itself in a dreadful quandary if pushed to join a war coalition against the country that had so materially contributed to its existence. The small print in the alliance gave her a let out, in that her involvement was conditional on the other two nations being *attacked*. If either of the other two nations initiated hostilities, Italy was not committed to their support. Should, therefore, with debatable reason, Germany and Austria-Hungary find themselves engaged in hostilities with an alliance containing Great Britain, Italy's involvement on their side could not be taken for granted – and so it proved in 1914.

Bülow's legacy to Bethmann was, therefore, something of a poisoned chalice. The problems he had to face would have tried the most experienced diplomat, and the new Chancellor was a complete stranger to the tangled web of foreign affairs that had been spun by his predecessors. To briefly recapitulate: The Anglo-Japanese alliance in 1902 had been followed by the Anglo-French *entente*, which was cemented by the first Moroccan crisis and the subsequent Algeciras Conference. The Russo-Japanese War in 1904/5 removed Russia as a naval threat to Britain and facilitated the Anglo-Russian agreement of 1908. This agreement was consolidated by the 1909 crisis in the Balkans, which further alienated Russia from Germany. In both the Morocco and Balkan crises, Germany had achieved what were arguably tactical diplomatic successes, but were, in fact, severe strategic reverses, the political consequences of which were the equivalent of effectively having lost a war.

Of the other major powers, the United States of America was far away to the west across the Atlantic Ocean and, in any case, isolationist by temperament. Even had America wished to involve itself, it would have been impotent to affect matters if not allied to one or the other European powers. To the east, however, there was one very significant nation, whose involvement could immediately, and radically, affect the balance of power – providing it so chose. The Ottoman Empire, on the periphery of Europe had yet to align itself with any particular bloc. Seeking an outlet and ally in the east, a circumstance which would also serve to isolate Russia's southern borders from any French or British assistance that might have been forthcoming through the Mediterranean, Germany commenced a vigorous diplomatic offensive to bring that nation into the fold of the central powers. Berlin's wooing of Istanbul remains the only unqualified success achieved by German diplomats during the period leading up to the First World War.

On the face of it, the rotting edifice that was the remnant of the great empire that had once conquered or terrorised most of Europe, the Middle East, and North Africa was a poor choice for an ally. For several centuries it had been in a state of steady decline as the corruption and incompetence of its rulers eroded the foundations of its prosperity and influence. For most of the previous hundred years it had been propped up by outside powers, not for its own sake, but as a buffer between themselves – and because none of those powers could accept any of the others obtaining control of the Bosphorus and the Dardanelles, which gave access from the Mediterranean to the Black Sea, and from Europe into Asia Minor and the Middle East.

At the beginning of the 20th century, the Turkish Empire was moribund. By land and by sea it was surrounded by predators, restrained only by mutual suspicion. Should any of them make a fatal strike there would be, in their wake, vultures aplenty queuing up to feast upon the carcass. Chief amongst the scavengers would be the newly independent nations of the Balkans. Serbia, Bulgaria, Greece and Rumania, all of whom had been under the Ottoman heel for half a millennium, cast greedy and vengeful eyes on the considerable remaining Turkish possessions in Europe, and all of them wanted a disproportionate slice of the kill.

For all that, the Ottoman Empire was not a power that could be disregarded. In population, situation, and in martial tradition it remained a significant player on the world scene. Its potential, though, was severely undermined by the fact that the nation was irredeemably bankrupt.

The Sultan and his administration, even had they been marginally competent, simply could not afford to arm or pay the forces that were necessary to maintain control over the empire's extended territories. Neither were there any facilities to manufacture the essentials for the nation's requirements, even had funds been available. The Industrial Revolution had arrived and passed without touching Turkey, and everything and anything that was required to enable the country to progress to the modern era had to be purchased from abroad. This, obviously, came at a price, and the price was exorbitant.

Whatever the wealth generated by the empire, which was considerable, the great majority of it vanished into the pockets of privileged landowners, distant governors, and, of course, the Sultan and his courtiers.

There was insufficient left after these depredations to pay for the various projects commissioned by the government, however pressing their need. Consequently, loans, at ruinous rates, had to be raised to meet the costs of developing the country. This prospect did not seem to unduly alarm the Sultan and his advisors who continued to commission projects until the entire nation was in a state of what is now known as 'negative equity'. The various Ottoman rulers during the 19th century had effectively mortgaged their country for many times its worth until even the entire income of the empire was incapable of servicing just the interest payments. The price of this insolvency was not just financial. It also severely affected the freedom of action of the Turkish Government. The country was in hock to a number of creditor nations, and, the bigger the overall debt accumulated with these nations, the greater the influence the latter had over Turkish policy and actions.

For nearly a century, Great Britain had been the principal buttress of the Ottoman Empire. This was not an altruistic position, only what was seen to be an unfortunate strategic priority. Successive British governments had deplored the necessity of having to prop up such a regime but there had simply seemed to be no alternative option. By her geographical situation, Turkey was the only power of consequence capable of preventing Russia from advancing her borders to the Mediterranean. This possibility was a constant dread of nineteenth century British politicians and military leaders, and was regarded as a far greater evil than the antidote – however exasperating, and often fruitless, were the attempts to mould the Turks into an effective barrier to Russian expansionist ambitions.

It is true that, during the Greek struggle for independence from Turkish rule in the post-Napoleonic era, Britain was a source of active and moral assistance to the insurgents, and that their eventual success was greeted with elation in an upper class society that harked back to the classical roots of their education.[1] Otherwise, however, the British establishment generally strove to sustain the Ottoman Empire as a viable entity. Even during the administrations of Gladstone, who loathed the Turks, and despite frequent evidence of their appalling atrocities against the

---

[1] The fact that the latter day Greeks had absolutely nothing in common with Archimedes; the idealised warrior gods of the *Iliad*; the Athenian philosophers; or the great poets and dramatists of the Classic Age was generally overlooked. As it was, a large section of the independence movement was comprised of bands of bloodthirsty brigands, motivated by greed, vengeance, and the prospect of local predominance. They were capable of appalling atrocities at least the equal of anything perpetrated by the Turks – and had no hesitation in extending these to any of their own countrymen who threatened their authority, profits, or any of their other interests. Today's folk heroes in the Balkans are frequently the mass murderers and torturers of the past.

populations of their turbulent provinces, British public opinion was always ultimately swayed by the need to confront the perceived threat from Russia. This was invariably manifested by the threatened or actual intervention of the British Mediterranean Fleet whenever Russia seemed on the brink of overwhelming Turkish forces and advancing to Constantinople and the Bosphorus.

At the beginning of the twentieth century, however, British attitudes were starting to change. The Russian threat became less of a pre-occupation, particularly following the displays of military and naval ineptitude that characterised Russia's conduct in the war with Japan. The awesome potential of Russia's huge population, area, and resources was still acknowledged, but the war had shown that these admitted advantages were stultified by the institutional incompetence of an arrogant, ignorant, and oppressive regime that supplied, from its scions, all the senior commanders of the armed forces. Within the military administration, inefficiency and corruption was endemic, and, particularly within the ranks of the navy, morale was low, respect for the officers almost non-existent, and indiscipline rife. In less than two years of conflict in the Far East, Japan, to the astonishment of the entire world, utterly demolished the credibility of Russia's military machine, in the process eliminating its navy as a factor on the international scene.

By 1906, the British Government had become sickened and frustrated by the continuing unwillingness of the Sultan's administration to curb the corruption within its ranks, and to seriously address the growing problems throughout the fractious provinces of its empire. The Turkish connection also no longer seemed as vital to British interests as it had in the past. Russia was a bogeyman who no longer frightened the children. However, as a positive move, a British naval mission was established in Constantinople to try and resuscitate the Turkish Navy, which had fallen into a state of advanced decomposition. Otherwise, Britain took a considered step back from her previous position in relation to the ailing empire, and, as relations with Russia gradually warmed, inevitably those with Turkey gradually cooled.

As Britain stepped back, so Germany stepped in. No region of influence is ever left long in a vacuum. The secret of good policy and diplomacy, in that situation, is to ensure that, if you have to leave a vacuum, it should be filled by a benevolent replacement. The British governments of the time signally failed in this respect, and Berlin took full advantage of the situation.

As its Ambassador to Constantinople, Germany sent one of its few diplomatic heavyweights. Baron Marschall von Bieberstein had previously been the Secretary of State for Foreign Affairs and was a robust, uncompromising representative of his government's policy. His brief was to wean, bribe, bully, or do whatever else was necessary, in order that

Germany should supplant any other nation as Turkey's most favoured benefactor and potential ally. Marschall was to achieve considerable success in this role, and he was certainly a good, experienced diplomat to have in place at a time when the country to which he was accredited was about to be convulsed by extraordinary events.

The Ottoman Empire itself was entering a period of transformation, triggered by defeat and adversity, into the first stage of metamorphosis from which would eventually emerge the modern, secular, Turkish state. These matters, though, are outside the parameters of this chapter.

The major powers were obviously the defining influences in the European balance but they were not the only states of consequence.

There were a number of second line European states whose addition to the balance of power, one way or the other, would have been significant. Some of these nations, such as Belgium, Holland, Denmark, Spain and Portugal, still presided over large overseas empires. All possessed reasonably well-equipped and trained armed forces on a moderate scale. Taken in isolation, their forces were not significant, but one or the other could be a most valuable, and perhaps critical, addition to the overall strength of an alliance. However, none of these nations, very wisely, had evinced any desire to tie themselves to one side of a confrontational power struggle. In any future conflict, all of them, with the addition of Sweden, would most probably remain neutral unless, and until, their sovereignty was violated by one side or another. For some of them, a long general war between the Triple Entente and the Triple Alliance would be nothing but good news, providing that they, themselves, could arrange to be uninvolved. There were mouth-watering profits to be made from the misfortune of others.

There only remains to mention the turbulent nations of the Balkans. All of them possessed large numbers of armed personnel, some official, some not. Of these countries, Serbia was the sworn implacable enemy of the Austro-German axis. The others, Bulgaria, Rumania and Greece, were beset with divided loyalties. All had monarchs of recent Germanic ancestry whose sympathies lay in that direction, but this was counterbalanced by a large section of their political establishments, which leaned towards France, Britain, and/or Russia. In the event of war between the major power blocs, their attitude was likely to be determined on the opportunist basis of which side appeared to be the probable winner. The only certainty was that of their mutual hatred for each other – which would intensify during the events of the next few years.

This then was the unfolding general situation that confronted the new Imperial German Chancellor as he assumed office. He was an accomplished bureaucrat who had steadily risen through the ranks of his profession, and had most recently occupied the position of Imperial Secretary of the Interior (the equivalent of the British Home Secretary) and Vice Chancellor. A tall, bony man, he had an imposing presence, which tended to disguise the fact that he was studious by nature, and schoolmasterly, rather than inspiring, in his pronouncements. He was generally well respected, regarded as a safe pair of hands and a good choice to replace Bülow – and was, in fact, the latter's recommendation for the post. He was hampered, though, by a lack of experience in foreign affairs, never having served in an ambassadorial capacity abroad and having had no dealings with the other players, German or otherwise, who strolled that particular stage. He recognised this shortcoming, and was also sceptical of his ability to control the Kaiser. Personally, unlike Bülow, he had no driving ambition to be Chancellor, and had none of the talent for flattering the Emperor that had distinguished and prolonged the career of his predecessor. He accepted the job out of a sense of duty, not for self-glorification or for the social status attached to the position.

In one way this diffidence made Bethmann a much more suitable occupant of the post than did Bülow. Having no burning desire for this advancement (and, in fact, regarding it as something of a poisoned chalice), he was far less likely to betray his convictions in order to retain the Kaiser's favour. This became apparent when he immediately turned his attention to arresting the deterioration of his country's strategic situation.

So long as Germany occupied the old French provinces of Alsace and Lorraine, and remained tied to the support of Austria-Hungary, there was little prospect of removing either France or Russia, respectively, as potential opponents. With regard to Great Britain, however, the situation was not totally beyond redemption.

Although the agreements the latter had made with France and Russia were unlikely to be renounced, they were not yet graven in stone. Indeed, the British Government had taken great care to stop short of committing itself to a formal alliance with either nation. Whilst it might be said that Britain had a moral duty to assist France should the latter be attacked by Germany (which action would inevitably also bring in Russia), there was no such obligation in the case of France being the aggressor – no matter what the provocation or circumstances. The British Liberal Party, which then possessed a massive majority in parliament, contained a large pacifist element and would not have tolerated any treaty binding Britain to such a commitment. It was also the case that only a single issue – the question of German naval expansion – stood in the way of improved Anglo-German relations. From the day he took office, Bethmann-Hollweg determined to address this problem, and made it the cornerstone of his foreign policy.

He was aided in his ambitions by the fact that, following the crisis over Bosnia and Herzegovina, the cauldron of the Balkans had subsided into quiescence for a while, and the general European situation entered a period of relative calm. This lasted for the first two years of his Chancellorship.

To compensate for his own lack of qualifications in the field of foreign policy, Bethmann arranged for the appointment of an experienced diplomat to the post of Secretary of State for Foreign Affairs. Alfred von Kiderlen-Waechter was a very different personality to the Chancellor. He was the archetype of a certain kind of German: self confident, loud and aggressive; a hard drinker with a heavy-handed sense of humour. For all that, he had genuine diplomatic ability, usually sound judgement, and he got things done. He was a Count Tattenbach with brains and a more amiable presence. Importantly, his thinking was in harmony with Bethmann's views on the vital issue of how to improve relations with Britain.

Less than a month after taking up his position, Bethmann found himself at odds with his sovereign. The circumstances were typical of the haphazard way policy had tended to be initiated in Wilhelmine Germany. In a meeting with the Kaiser, Albert Ballin, the influential head of the Hamburg-America Line (then the world's largest merchant shipping concern) put forward the suggestion that Tirpitz and Fisher be brought together to discuss contentious bilateral naval issues. Ballin's suggestion was doubtless well meant, but Bethmann, who was present, overheard his remarks and was furious. He immediately intervened, and with some heat, made clear that he, and he alone, was responsible to the Kaiser for originating all policy initiatives directed towards Great Britain, and that included discussions on naval matters. There could be no question of parallel private schemes being sponsored on impulse without the prior approval of the government.

This was the Chancellor's first experience of the manner in which formation of policy often originated from those who happened to have Wilhelm's ear at any given time. The Kaiser himself was taken aback by the strength of Bethmann's reaction, but was in no position, so soon after the *Daily Telegraph* affair, to take matters further. Having so recently dispensed with the services of Bülow, he could hardly risk the uproar that would certainly result if Bethmann resigned.

As for poor Ballin, he must have wondered what had hit him. He clearly had no wish to cross the Chancellor, but, after the twelve long years of Bülow's administration, had simply not taken into account the change of personalities. His approach to the Kaiser would have caused scarcely a ripple in the *laissez-faire* atmosphere of the previous era. Bülow was too indolent, and too anxious to avoid irksome confrontations with the Kaiser, to have made such a scene. Recognising that he was unlikely to win any arguments on that subject, and would only become unpopular in the process, he had largely washed his hands of naval matters. He left Wilhelm and Tirpitz to play with their floating toys whilst he got on with the more important business of just being Chancellor.

The new Chancellor took a more combative approach. Having had an early insight into one of the problems of working with the Kaiser, Bethmann took immediate action to try and stamp his authority on the government. He sent a directive to all branches of the administration, making it clear that he was personally assuming responsibility for all aspects of Anglo-German relations, most particularly those concerning naval matters.

When this edict landed on the desk of the State Secretary for the Navy, its effect may well be imagined. Tirpitz had no intention of relinquishing one iota of his control over the naval construction programme without a fight. Nor would he ever consent to any amendment of the existing Navy Laws. Although nominally subordinate to the Chancellor, he had, for the previous twelve years, operated virtually as a law unto himself. He knew he had the Kaiser on his side; that they shared the same agenda; and that he had direct access to his sovereign, who had a casting vote, or an effective veto on the matter. This had been the case ever since his triumph in forcing the First Navy Bill through the *Reichstag*. Bülow had recognised that the Navy Minister's position was impregnable, and, until the last few months of his Chancellorship, had never attempted to challenge the status quo. Only as his star quickly waned did he begin to publicly question the efficacy of the Risk Theory and advocate a degree of flexibility in the rate of battleship construction – if this might help to bring about a diplomatic rapprochement with Britain.

In Bülow's case, this conversion came much too late to matter. For Bethmann-Hollweg, it was, from the first, a principle that would be the centrepiece of his policy until the outbreak of war rendered all such considerations irrelevant. The stage was set for a drawn out contest of attrition between Bethmann and Tirpitz that would extend beyond their active careers and into the battleground of their memoirs. In the process, they developed a marked dislike of each other, which feeling was only thinly veiled by the niceties of diplomatic language.

It was for the Chancellor to take the initiative. He had already proposed to the British Government that negotiations should take place with a view to reducing the level of mutual naval competition. For two months he set his mind to establishing what concessions he could offer, and what would be an appropriate *quid pro quo* from the British.

It was soon apparent to him that the basic provisions of the German Navy Laws could not be altered. He simply did not have the necessary support, in or out of parliament, to have any chance of altering the planned composition of the battle fleet. The only room for manoeuvre that he possessed was in the rate of construction required to achieve this ordained force. A reduction in the rate of German construction would result in the same number of battleships being built, but obviously the process could be spread over a longer period. The extent of any agreed delay in construction would be a useful bargaining chip in any negotiations. This concession would enable the British to correspondingly reduce their building programme, whilst still being able to preserve whatever they regarded as a necessary margin of superiority. The size of that margin would be up to the British government of the day.

A proposal on these lines offered great benefits to both nations. The British Government was exasperated beyond measure at having to react to the German naval programmes when it urgently desired to deploy its wealth elsewhere. In Germany itself, Bülow's career had officially foundered on his inability to obtain sufficient resources from the *Reichstag* to fund the new battle fleet. Money was beginning to be a problem on both sides of the North Sea. The huge, and increasing, unit cost of a modern dreadnought was only the tip of the financial iceberg. As the numbers of battleships increased, so were more cruisers required to scout for the enlarged fleet, and many more destroyers needed to provide an adequate screen. As the speed of the newest battleships also increased, so, rapidly and proportionately, did the older and slower escorts become obsolete. More and bigger berths and docks were necessary to base and maintain the vessels, and the annual running costs in such categories as fuel, ammunition, wages, food and clothing mounted proportionately.

Clearly, Germany would actually lose little by making such a concession. The relative strength of the fleet *vis-à-vis* that of Great Britain would remain the same. The strain on the budgets of each country would proportionately lessen. Looked at logically, it was hardly a concession at all and more in the nature of a gesture. For that gesture, Germany stood fair to gain, in her diplomatic relations, a far more significant reward.

Having established what he thought he could possibly offer to attract British interest, the Chancellor then considered what should be his *quid pro quo*. He set his sights very high indeed. He aimed at nothing less than a declaration of British neutrality should Germany become involved in a major war.

Had Bethmann achieved this ambition, it would have ranked as one of the greatest diplomatic coups of the age. Obtaining British neutrality would have been worth the sacrifice of the entire German Fleet; built, building, or planned. Nothing that fleet could have accomplished in battle, even by the most unlikely and sweeping victory could have surpassed this achievement. Removing Britain from the list of potential enemies meant that it would be unnecessary to challenge her navy. The money and manpower resources that were currently being poured into a fleet, which would almost certainly remain inferior to that of Great Britain could be utilised for other pressing needs – such as reinforcing the army to the point that it could absolutely ensure future German continental hegemony. Once that object had been attained, and Britain thus deprived of potential allies, the long-term results would have been almost inevitable. The resources available to Germany in a pacified Europe of client states would have guaranteed her eventual ability to overwhelm Britain. This had been Napoleon's aim a hundred years previously, and, had the Russian campaign of 1812 been a triumph instead of a disaster, who is to say that he might not have succeeded?

It is inconceivable that Bethmann saw himself as a latter-day Bonaparte or even fully realised the long-term implications of his policy, should it have succeeded. By contrast, the British Foreign Secretary, Sir Edward Grey, immediately discerned the inevitable consequences of such a one-sided deal. He earnestly desired better relations with Germany, but this theoretical goal could not be achieved at the expense of existing, tangible, agreements with France and Russia. However, having settled on his agenda for negotiations, Bethmann stuck faithfully to its basic provisions – a reduction in the intensity of naval competition in return for Britain's declared neutrality should Germany become involved in a continental war. The remarkable thing is that he later came close to obtaining an agreement that went some way towards meeting his conditions. In October 1909, he indicated to the British Ambassador in Berlin that he was ready to open negotiations with London and outlined his proposals.

The response to Bethmann's approach was initially lukewarm. Whilst welcoming the opportunity for dialogue, the British Government baulked at accepting, as a basis for any agreement, anything less than a reduction in the planned strength of the German battle fleet. Bethmann explained that this would be impossible for him to achieve. A year later, the British abandoned their insistence on this condition, but the other facet of the proposal proved intractable.

The *entente* with France had become established as a cornerstone of British foreign policy. The Cabinet was united in its opposition to any action that would endanger this relationship. A formal treaty of neutrality such as Bethmann envisaged would clearly have rendered the *entente* meaningless, and all the British Government would contemplate was a declaration that Britain harboured no hostile intentions towards Germany and was committed to the maintenance of a mutually friendly relationship. This was manifestly inadequate for Bethmann's purposes.

An associated sticking point was the chronology of the process. The Imperial Chancellor insisted that a deceleration of the German naval programme could only be instituted following the conclusion of a political agreement. Grey was adamant that the reverse had to be the case. Politically, neither was in a position to make concessions without first being able to show a concrete achievement from the process. Neither nation trusted the other sufficiently to make the initial move.

Nevertheless, the mere fact that talks were continuing was a positive sign, and, in one respect, there was a gleam of encouragement. Grey had made the suggestion that both countries should exchange advance information on each other's naval programme for the subsequent year. This would remove the danger of a misunderstanding such as that which had caused the recent naval scare in Britain. The German Government, although initially unenthusiastic, eventually agreed in principle to this proposal. Details had not been worked out before the proceedings were rudely interrupted.

For over a year and a half the talks had proceeded sporadically without being able to break the impasse over the essential bones of contention. Further progress then had to be shelved as a new crisis erupted to disturb the brief period of international calm. Events in Morocco once again triggered a confrontation between the European powers.

Six years had elapsed since the first Moroccan crisis had brought Europe to the brink of war. The Algeciras Conference had applied a temporary salve, but the country continued in a state of semi-anarchy, and the major issues concerning the long-term future of the Sultanate remained to be resolved.

The provisions of the accord reached at Algeciras cast a diplomatic veil over the fact that France had been granted what amounted to a supervisory role in the affairs of Morocco. In the intervening years, the French had not been noticeably subtle in exploiting this advantage and consolidating their position. This process had not gone unnoticed in Berlin, and had led to strained relations between the two countries on more than one occasion.

As time passed, and the carefully phrased announcements were digested, it had become apparent to the German public that, politically and strategically, Germany had suffered a bloody nose at Algeciras. This fact rankled with a nation that had become accustomed to arrogantly dictating terms to the rest of Europe. Events in Morocco thus occupied a higher profile in the German consciousness than might otherwise have been the case.

In 1909 there had been a financially ruinous civil war in the country, at the end of which the Sultan was overthrown by one of his brothers. In the process, damage was caused to foreign properties and businesses, and compensation for this was demanded. The sums involved far exceeded the resources of Morocco's Exchequer, which by then were virtually nil, and new taxes had to be levied to meet the shortfall. This measure caused widespread discontent, in the wake of which yet another of the royal brothers fermented a rebellion. By March 1911, with the country again in a state of civil war, and huge resentment mounting over the foreign presence and financial demands, France decided that the situation was sufficiently dangerous to justify armed intervention. There can be little doubt that, whatever the merits of this decision, the French had recognised an opportunity to consolidate their position of dominance in the country.

Invoking a clause in the Algeciras agreement which gave any of the signatory powers the right to intervene should their expatriate population be at risk, France duly gave notification to the others that she was mounting a military expedition to the inland city of Fez, where the dangers of the situation were deemed acute. In Germany, this development was immediately discerned as threatening her prestige and commercial influence in the region.

As the crisis unfolded, Bethmann was on leave and Kiderlen-Waechter was left to deal with the situation. He responded by warning the French Government against taking its proposed action. He considered, probably rightly, that this expedition was intended to be the prelude to a complete French takeover of Morocco. He doubted the veracity of French assurances that, as soon as the situation had been stabilised, the troops would be withdrawn. In this, he was proved correct.

Undeterred, the French chose to ignore Kiderlen's warning and went ahead with their plans. For three months there was an ominous superficial calm as the underlying situation gradually began to deteriorate. Once established in Fez, the military expedition soon began to assume the appearance of a permanent presence. The German Foreign Minister's reaction to this perceived provocation was predictable. In any action he chose to take, he had the full support of national public opinion, and of German business interests who had covetous eyes on the potentially rich, but as yet undeveloped, mineral resources of southern Morocco. He was also placed in a favourable bargaining position by the French Government's precipitate action. It was as clear to France's allies as to her potential opponents that the Fez adventure had become a smokescreen for a *de facto* French annexation of the populous north of the country. This, of course, went far beyond the bounds of the Algeciras pact. Germany (or any other of the signatory powers for that matter) had every right to complain about this process, and had good grounds to demand compensation for the relative loss of influence and business opportunities that would inevitably result from French control of the Sultanate. This latter situation would not be acceptable to Germany without substantial commercial or territorial concessions elsewhere in Morocco or further afield. Hard diplomatic bargaining would probably have achieved this end in any case (and, in fact, negotiations were already under way), but Kiderlen eventually decided on a more aggressive approach. (Although Bethmann was back in harness, he was content to leave the immediate conduct of matters in the hands of his Foreign Minister whilst himself maintaining a watching brief.)

Following the line taken by the French in justifying the Fez expedition, Kiderlen cited a request for protection from 'endangered' German citizens and interests in the south of Morocco. On this pretext he obtained the consent of the Kaiser (reluctantly, and only after some argument) to order a German warship to the small port of Agadir, the only tenable harbour along the barren coast of the region. Although the consequences of this action brought about a major international crisis, some of its aspects had the elements of high farce.

The only German warship in the immediate vicinity was the *SMS Panther*, which was returning to Germany after a prolonged commission in African waters. Despite its imposing name, the vessel was little more than a colonial gunboat that entirely matched Fisher's definition of a ship that could 'neither fight, nor run away'. As a vehicle for the projection of national power, it was a most unlikely candidate, but *Panther*'s chance availability thrust the little vessel into the glare of the world spotlight. On July 1st 1911, she came to anchor in Agadir roads, there to wait upon events. If the vessel's actual fighting qualities were practically non-existent, her deployment was nonetheless highly significant. Her arrival at Agadir represented a German military presence in the country and as such was a direct challenge to the French. The main difficulty that now presented itself to the German Foreign Ministry was in providing adequate justification for what was an overtly provocative move. This proved to be something of a problem.

There was also the question of whether Britain would support the French initiative in the face of German objections. There was certainly a degree of irritation in London that the situation had come to pass. Grey, the British Foreign Secretary, remarked that:

'As long as it was possible, I deprecated any action by either Power, but things got worse in Morocco and eventually France sent a force to Fez and Spain landed troops in her zone. Then suddenly the Germans sent a ship, the *Panther*, to Agadir. Agadir was a port not open to commerce; it was said to be suitable for a naval base. The German action at once created a crisis, and for weeks the issue of peace or war hung in the balance. We were bound by the Anglo-French agreement of 1904 to give France diplomatic support. This engagement we fulfilled in letter and spirit, while doing all we could to steer for peace not war.' (1)

The clear inference is that Grey and his Cabinet colleagues were not best pleased at being placed in this position by the precipitate action of their new-found allies.

The French, in mounting their expedition to Fez, could at least point to the fact that the area was genuinely in turmoil and that there was a considerable expatriate community whose lives and property were under threat. Germany could hardly claim the same in Southern Morocco, which was thinly populated and had yet to develop any foreign commercial infrastructure. It was true that several German concerns had designs on the mineral resources of the region, but these had yet to take any substantive form. Nevertheless, in casting about for an excuse to justify his action, Kiderlen chose to ignore this inconvenient fact. He approached the companies who *intended* to establish themselves in the area, and, with little difficulty, persuaded them to request military protection for their as yet non-existent property and personnel. To give substance to this ridiculous appeal, one of the firms directed an employee from elsewhere in Morocco to proceed to Agadir, there to beg rescue from the supposed hordes of marauding, bloodthirsty rebels. Unfortunately for the credibility of this plan, the gunboat reached Agadir well in advance of the distressed expatriate's arrival to formally request assistance. It was three days before the man eventually appeared on Agadir beach, by which time a second, and more substantial, German warship, the light cruiser *Berlin*, had also anchored in the roads. He was duly 'rescued' by a sea boat and evacuated to the sanctuary of the naval ships.[2]

This cynical ploy was an insult to the intelligence of the other powers who were very well acquainted with the actual state of affairs. Kiderlen recognised this, and was fully aware that they knew that *he* knew! Nevertheless, he remained supremely confident in the strength of his position.

The German challenge was blatant, and there only remained to be considered what would be an appropriate response.

The French had, for some time, been in discussions with Kiderlen. They were adamant that there could be no question of partitioning Morocco, but, in return for German acceptance of French predominance in that country, were offering the prospect of colonial concessions elsewhere in Africa. These negotiations were thrown into utter disarray by 'the *Panther*'s leap' (!). Within a few days, the German Government further intensified the

---

[2] I cannot resist quoting Massie's description of this incident: 'When Wilberg arrived at Agadir on the afternoon of July 4th, the *Panther* had been at anchor for three days. Wilberg saw the warship, but was too exhausted to make contact. The next morning when he awoke he saw that a second larger German ship had entered the bay and anchored during the night. Immediately, Wilberg tried to let his countrymen know he was present. At first he had no luck; the men on the *Berlin* took the man on the beach running up and down waving his arms and shouting faint cries, for an excited native, perhaps with something to sell. The Admiralty had given strict orders that men were not to be landed without further instructions. Wilberg, seeing the men on the ships staring at him without apparent interest, became dispirited and stood motionless, looking back at the two grey ships lying silent in the bright sunshine. His posture identified him: suddenly an officer on the *Panther* was struck by the lonely figure on the beach standing with his hands on his hips. Africans did not employ this stance. A boat was launched, and soon Wilberg, the 'Endangered German', was taken under the protection of the Imperial Navy.' (2)

crisis by publicly stating its intention to establish a permanent presence in Southern Morocco. This declaration was received with acclaim by the German population – in particular, by the nationalist pressure groups and the associated media. It was also a significant mistake in that it is never a good idea to announce the result of events long before they have been concluded. Tirpitz, in his memoirs, draws the same conclusion:

> 'A flag is easily tied to a staff, but it often costs a great deal to haul it down again with honour.' (3)

Kiderlen's overweening confidence had, in fact, led him into committing a serious error of judgement. By the premature disclosure of his agenda, he had painted his government into a corner. As the nation responded with patriotic fervour he had left himself no room for diplomatic manoeuvre. A negotiated compromise with the French that did not give Germany all that she demanded would be seen in Germany as tantamount to a humiliating climb down and involve an unacceptable loss of face. He had committed the cardinal political sin of bringing high policy into the public market place. Once there, it was hostage to emotions beyond his control. To compound the error, he had discounted as irrelevant the possible response of France's friends and allies. This mistake, born of misplaced arrogance, was to prove fatal to his designs.

> The despatch of the *Panther* to Agadir was a very brusque way of opening negotiations with the French: the Germans followed it up by a disregard of us that led to a dramatic incident.' (4)

The French reaction to the precipitate German action was one of shock. The situation, although admittedly delicate, had been in the process of resolution through normal diplomatic exchanges. The abrupt change in the German posture came completely out of the blue, and its timing was doubly unfortunate as the French Government was in a state of flux. A freak accident at an air show in May had killed the War Minister and maimed the Prime Minister so seriously as to force his retirement. Coming at such a critical moment in Franco-German relations, the loss of two key players in this untoward event severely affected the French Government's ability to co-ordinate its response to Kiderlen's offensive. There is little doubt that this factor played a part in the German Foreign Minister's calculations, and the timing of his initiatives.[3]

---

[3] The importance of this factor should not be overstressed. The French political system was highly volatile – far more so than any other nation of consequence. Senior ministers arrived and departed (and were frequently re-appointed) with bewildering rapidity, even in the normal course of events. Of all the extant political structures, the French version was most practiced in carrying on a general policy despite the constant change of key figures. Nevertheless, the tragic accident to the two politicians could not have occurred at a more inopportune moment.

Whatever the dislocation in the French Government, it was apparent that a first rate crisis was in the making. Germany was once again displaying the 'bully boy' tendencies of its personality, and France, once again, was to be its victim.

To a detached observer, nearly a century removed from these events, it must seem extraordinary that a dispute could arise, between two powerful nations at the heart of what was then regarded as civilisation, over relatively unimportant tracts of African territory. France was obviously stamping its authority on the northern regions of Morocco, which comprised 90% of the country's population and commerce, and Germany wished to grab the rest. However immoral the procedure, a mutually acceptable agreement should not have been beyond the abilities of French and German diplomats without recourse to the threat of war. Instead, the confrontation was permitted to develop to the point where national prestige was at stake. As the positions on both sides hardened, the strength of public opinion in both Germany and France left the politicians with little scope for compromise.

As the tension increased so the militarists in Germany inevitably began to agitate. The Army General Staff was quite prepared to go to war over this issue – or any other for that matter – and there emerged a real danger that the situation could escalate into open hostilities. At this critical stage of proceedings, the British Government also became involved.

Shortly after the arrival of *Panther* at Agadir, Sir Edward Grey had made a formal request to the German Ambassador in London for a statement of Germany's position and intentions on the Moroccan question. No response was forthcoming. This was an inexcusable lapse on the part of the German Foreign Ministry, suggesting, as it did, a deliberate intention to ignore legitimate British concerns. As the days passed, and the tension increased between France and Germany, so the continued silence from Berlin began to arouse anger and suspicion in London. Of all the nations, Britain had, by far, still the largest commercial investment in Morocco and, whilst she had granted France political pre-eminence in the area, her interests could hardly be ignored in any consideration of that country's future status.

The German challenge raised concerns of more than a commercial nature. As with the previous Moroccan crisis, it was also seen as a test of the Anglo-French *entente*, and illustrated both the dangers and weaknesses that came as part and parcel of that *de facto*, but informal, alliance.

The initial French action had been taken without consulting the British Government, and this was a source of some irritation to the latter. The French had clearly not expected the startling German response, but the fact remained that, by her unilateral action, she had stimulated a major confrontation – and, by so doing, had involved Britain in an unwonted crisis. The importance of the *entente* meant that Britain could not avoid becoming embroiled in an affair that was not of her making or of her liking.

It was to be the first of many such commitments covering half a century that are notable only for the absence of any significant gratitude or even acknowledgement from the benefactor. Rather the opposite.

The fact was that the *entente* was not a formal treaty, and it meant that France had no binding obligation to act in concert with the British Government. Had this not been the case, the situation in Morocco might have been very different. The French action would have been taken in the context of an Anglo-French alliance, and, as such, would probably have been accepted, after some grumbling, as a *fait accomplis* by the rest of the world, including Germany. It is extremely unlikely that the little gunboat *Panther* would ever have set eyes on the beaches of Agadir had it been clear from the outset that France and Great Britain could not be considered separately.

Britain's involvement in the crisis was not entirely altruistic. Politically and publicly, German interest in Morocco was perceived to be unwelcome. On strategic grounds, informed British opinion was greatly concerned at the possibility of Germany gaining a foothold on the North African coast. These fears were shared by many in the government. The principal cause for alarm stemmed from the prospect of Germany being able to develop a fortified naval base in the area (at Agadir, for instance), which would lie athwart the trade routes and lines of communication linking Britain with the Cape of Good Hope and South America.

These fears were, in fact, largely unfounded. The difficulties of establishing, maintaining, and defending such a base were so daunting as to make the concept utterly impractical for Germany, even in the highly unlikely circumstance of the necessary funds being available. In the event of hostilities it would have immediately been blockaded by the British Navy and open to land assault by the French forces in the north of the country. The most telling reaction, or lack of one, was from the British Admiralty. Sir Arthur Wilson, the First Sea Lord, was utterly unperturbed by this prospect. If anything, the Royal Navy would have warmly welcomed such a development. From the point of view of Wilson, and many other senior officers, the creation of an isolated German base, with its lines of communication and re-supply horribly vulnerable to both the British and French Fleets, offered mouth-watering opportunities to bring the High Seas Fleet to action.

An exposed naval station on the Atlantic coast of Morocco, such as the alarmists feared, offered only a hostage that might tempt the main German Fleet into battle. Only by forcing its way past the British ships and out of the North Sea could the High Seas Fleet have relieved the distant outpost. Even if it succeeded in this aim, once there, the subsequent logistics of supporting the fleet would have proved insurmountable. These facts were, however, disregarded by a large section of the population for whom any German presence anywhere was regarded as a danger to the empire.

Matters came to a head on the 21st July. The British Cabinet came to the conclusion that it could not wait indefinitely for a statement of Germany's intentions. The continuing failure of Berlin to make any form of response to their request for information was nothing short of an insult to Britain. Subsequently, Grey had a meeting with Metternich and made clear his government's irritation over the matter. Rumours were abounding of unacceptable territorial demands being made on the French and he stressed the need for urgent clarification of the situation. This placed the German Ambassador in an embarrassing position, as he had received no brief on the subject from his Foreign Ministry and was no more aware than Grey as to Kiderlen's motives and aims. He was therefore unable to give the British Foreign Secretary any pertinent reply to his pressing demand for information. However, that same day, a speech was made that brought the whole affair into the open. It came from an unexpected source, and was all the more effective as a result.

David Lloyd-George, the Chancellor of the Exchequer, belonged to the pacifist wing of the British Government, and had previously been notably pro-German in his attitude and utterances. His opposition to inflated naval estimates has already been noted. It was this influential politician who, after long consideration, came to the conclusion that, in the face of Germany's refusal to disclose the extent of her ambitions in Morocco, the British position on the matter must be stated in such a way as to ensure there could be no misunderstandings as to her stance. He foresaw that, unless this stance was made absolutely clear, there was a danger of Berlin miscalculating Britain's strength of resolve and, by so doing, to inadvertently precipitate a war. He was due to make a speech on the domestic economy to a gathering of bankers, and, quite independently, decided to insert a passage that obliquely, but unmistakably, referred to the international situation. Having made this decision, and having cleared his text with Asquith and the Cabinet earlier in the day, he delivered the scheduled speech that evening. Grey remarks that:

'I thought what he proposed to say was quite justified, and would be salutary, and I cordially agreed. I considered there was nothing in the words that Germany could fairly resent.' (5)

The speech could hardly be described as overtly inflammatory. Most of its content dwelt on the sober aspects of managing the economy, but, in emphasising that all the calculations of the Exchequer were based on an assumption of the continuance of peace, he led in to his prepared statement on Britain's international position. Very deliberately, he concluded that:

'I would make great sacrifices to preserve peace. I conceive that nothing would justify a disturbance of international good will except questions of the gravest national moment. But if a situation were to be forced upon us in which

SMS PANTHER
An unlikely candidate for the projection of national power.

Alfred von Kiderlen-Waechter
Secretary of State for Foreign Affairs 1910-1912

peace could only be preserved by the surrender of the great and beneficent position Britain has won by centuries of heroism and achievement, *by allowing Britain to be treated, where her interests were vitally concerned, as if she were of no account in the Cabinet of nations*, [authors italics] then I say emphatically that peace at that price would be a humiliation intolerable for a great country like ours to endure.' (6)

On the face of it, these remarks were not provocative, but, in the subtle language of diplomacy, the italicised section could only be seen as a reference to Germany's disregard for British sensibilities in the ignoring of her request for a statement of intentions. The message was certainly not lost in Germany itself. The speech caused an outburst of indignation at supposed British interference in what was regarded as a purely Franco-German affair. It was quite wrongly assumed that the British Government had deliberately used Lloyd-George, as the most pro-German member of the Cabinet, to give added emphasis to a thinly veiled warning.

Whatever the resultant furore, the speech produced exactly the effect that Lloyd-George had intended. Kiderlen was forced to accept that, in any action he proposed to take, he would not be dealing with France in isolation and that to threaten war with the latter in the pursuit of his ends was now a much more hazardous option. Conversely, the French were greatly encouraged in their resolve to stand firm against the German demands. For a few days the situation was critical and the angry rhetoric from Berlin produced a genuine war scare in Britain. However, the cooler heads prevailed. From that moment on, the German Government began to modify its position and the level of tension declined, to a huge sigh of relief from the rest of Europe.

Initially Kiderlen had demanded either a slice of Morocco, or in compensation for the establishment of a French protectorate over the country, the cessation of the entire French colony of the Congo to Germany. German public opinion had been primed to the point where anything short of this would have been unacceptable. Nevertheless, after several months of negotiation, the unacceptable had to be countenanced. When agreement was finally reached, France was confirmed in her Protectorate of Morocco, and, as a fig leaf to Berlin, relinquished a minor portion of her territory in the Congo for incorporation in the neighbouring German colony of the Cameroons.

It was impossible to gloss over the fact that Germany had suffered another humiliating diplomatic reverse over Morocco. Tirpitz regarded the debacle as:

'...the first serious diplomatic defeat since Bismarck had taken over the political leadership of the nation, and it hit us all the harder because the clay image of our position in the world at that time did not rest so much upon power as upon prestige.' (7)

Tirpitz, if he believed the words he wrote, clearly had not appreciated the importance of the earlier Moroccan crisis. It was the Algeciras Conference in 1906 that had cemented the Anglo-French *entente*. Agadir merely confirmed it in its solidarity. It is also difficult to take him seriously when he refers to a 'clay image' of German power given the situation that his country possessed the most effective army in the world – a fact that had been demonstrated throughout Europe for the previous third of a century, and which was a source of great pride to his nation. To be charitable, Tirpitz may only have been referring to the inability of Germany to deploy its peerless army outside the confines of Europe. Sir Edward Grey had it about right:

'The end was almost a fiasco for Germany; out of this mountain of a German made crisis had come a mouse of colonial territory in tropical Africa. France was left with her prestige intact and free of the Morocco thumb screws.' (8)

In the wake of the debacle, the fury of the German population focused on the figure of Kiderlen-Waechter, as the architect of the failed policy. His career was effectively in ruins. He had always been a heavy drinker, and this habit now progressed to the point where its effects were increasingly evident. It was probably a major contributory factor when, little over a year after the conclusion of the Agadir Crisis, he collapsed and died, ostensibly from heart failure.

Morocco was proving a graveyard for foreign ministers. Delcassé had been forced from office, and Holstein's position fatally undermined, as a result of the first crisis over that unfortunate state. Now Kiderlen's career had foundered on the same rock. If we add the eclipse of Izvolsky following his bungled initiative in the Balkans, the direction of foreign policy in the tangled affairs of Europe was becoming a graveyard for the ambitions of both aspiring politicians and well-intentioned diplomats.

As the dust settled after the Agadir Crisis, it became possible for Britain and Germany to contemplate the resumption of talks on the limitation of naval construction, and the associated political factors. If anything, the recent events had brought an added urgency to the table. It was clear to powerful interests in both countries that any agreement which contributed to an overall reduction in tension and lessened the prospect of confrontation was an objective to be ardently pursued.

When negotiations resumed, the British approach was affected by radical changes in some of the key personalities at the head of naval affairs. If Britain's involvement in the Morocco question had been limited to a supportive role for France, the proximity of war had led to a major reappraisal of strategy – in particular with regard to the conflicting priorities adopted by the high commands of the army and navy. The revelation that the two branches of the British armed forces were pursuing totally different strategies and neither wished, nor were required, to communicate with each other, came as something of a shock to the government. The matter clearly needed to be addressed, and a commonality of purpose established. This could only be achieved by one side or the other yielding primacy to the other. Their respective positions were too far apart for a compromise.

The navy had a deep antipathy, based on good historic precedent, for joint operations with the army. Excepting Wellington's campaign in the Iberian peninsular, most operations involving co-operation between the services had been notable only for disagreements between the respective commanders. The results had been delay, frustration, and confusion, leading to failure of the operation. A satirical verse penned during the Napoleonic Wars, and after a spectacularly botched combined operation, perfectly summed up the position as seen by a sceptical naval establishment:[4]

'The Earl of Chatham with sabre drawn, was waiting for Sir Richard Strachan,
Sir Richard, eager to get at 'em, was waiting for the Earl of Chatham.'

For those who believed that the Royal Navy was the absolute guarantee of the nation's independence and the security of its empire, it seemed inconceivable that the service would have to play second fiddle to the army. The army, it was held, in the oft-quoted phrase, was a 'projectile to be fired by the navy' where and when the situation warranted. It was a long-accepted premise that the relatively small British military forces could tie down much greater numbers of the enemy simply because they could be landed anywhere on the coast of Europe as a result of naval supremacy. The enemy, therefore, had to guard all his seaward flanks against this possibility, thus depleting his main armies without a single British soldier having to set foot on the continent. The validity of this concept was based on the conditions of the early nineteenth century, but had, to a large extent, been eroded by the development of railways and other internal communications that permitted the rapid, and mass, redeployment of men, artillery, and munitions throughout a land area.

In the past, troops could be transported by sea from A to B faster than they could march that distance, and, allowing for seasickness, they would normally arrive at 'B' in better condition. The development of a European rail network completely negated this advantage. Armies, henceforth, would

---

[4] For non-British readers, the name 'Strachan' is generally pronounced 'Strawn'.

increasingly rely on rail transport to enable mobilisation, redeployment and support of their troops. As regards a country's ability to react to an amphibious assault on its coast, or one of its ports, the railways ensured that reinforcements and supplies could be delivered to the point of contact faster and with more security than could those of the invading force.

For all the alterations in the conditions of making war, the most radical change in British strategic thinking resulted from the *entente* with France. From the moment that this came into being, there arose, within the British military establishment, a core of very able officers who considered that a Franco-German war was probably inevitable in the long term, and that Britain would have to support France if the latter was not to be overwhelmed. These officers largely dominated army thinking by 1911 and were of the opinion that the best and only effective contribution that Britain could make to the *entente* would be to immediately send as much of the British Army as possible to serve alongside the French, and to be subject to the general French plan of campaign. Subsequently, British forces on the continent would be steadily enhanced until the war was, hopefully, won. The duration of hostilities, before this happy result was achieved, was not expected (by either side at that time) to be more than a few months. The British Navy's role in all this was to ensure the safe transport of the troops to France and to secure the subsequent supply lines to the Channel ports.

This strategy was complete anathema to the naval officers at the head of their service. To them, it involved Britain abandoning all the advantages and independence given to her by geography, inclination, competence, and tradition in order to fall in with a French plan of action that was entirely self-centred. It was hardly likely that the Admiralty Board would welcome the opportunity for the world's greatest navy to be reduced to a transport and security service for an army that was roughly half as strong as the Swiss armed forces. The admirals and the generals simply did not communicate, the result being that neither had made any plans to fall in with the other's strategy. When this fact became apparent to the government during the Agadir Crisis, there was a very understandable sense of outrage at what was an utterly preposterous (and dangerous) state of affairs. It was clear that some heads had to be banged together and a sensible common policy defined. This process was certain to be extremely contentious, and it was inevitable that some of the heads that were banged together would also subsequently roll. The severed heads, of course, would be those on the side that had lost the argument.

The resulting upheaval brought to the forefront of affairs the man who was to become the most famous Englishman of the 20th century.

CHAPTER TWELVE

BRITANNIA TAKES TO THE SHORE

'Wisely or unwisely, the Germans had attempted to separate Great Britain from France. The failure of this attempt could not but affect Anglo-German relations. Germans would feel more sharply the need for a strong fleet; Englishmen would consider the use to which Germany might put this fleet.'

E.L. Woodward: *Great Britain and the German Navy*

'The new Director of Military Operations was free of all harassing doubts or hesitations. His ideas on what should be done were fixed and definite. He believed that the largest possible British Army should go across in the shortest possible time after the outbreak of war to join up with the French Field Army. To further these aims he bent all his energies, from the first day of entering a Post which placed him in a unique position to prosecute them.'

T124 (Capt. Russell Grenfell): *Sea Power*

1910, the year before Agadir impressed itself on the world's consciousness, witnessed 'Jacky' Fisher's departure from the office of First Sea Lord. Within a few months of the admiral's retirement, the figure who had provided his staunchest support during the years of his great naval reforms had also left the scene.

King Edward VII had not been in good health for some time. His refusal to temper his addiction to cigars and good food undoubtedly hastened the decline. Weakened by persistent bronchial infections, by the late spring of 1910 his condition had become grave. The end came on the 6th May. He suffered a series of heart attacks during the day, lapsed into unconsciousness, and expired just before midnight. In a gesture of extraordinary generosity, the Queen invited her husband's long-term mistress and companion, Mrs. Alice Keppel, to visit him before he died. It was the end of an era in more ways than one.

The King's death was a serious blow to the nation. During his relatively short reign, his influence on the country's affairs had been far more profound than could be accounted for by his constitutional position.

'He had in a very high degree the gift, proper and valuable in a Sovereign, for ceremonial. No one knew so well as he how ceremony should be arranged, ordered, and carried through in the manner most effective and impressive. By his own person, and by the part he took in it, he added dignity to it...There was however, something more that gave a spirit and aspect to it all, and this was due to his individual personality. Warm human kindness was of the very substance of the man...He had a capacity for enjoying life, which is always attractive, but is particularly so when it is combined with a positive and strong desire that everyone else should enjoy life too. These, it may be thought, are not very uncommon qualities, but King Edward had a peculiar power of making them felt. There was, in fact real sympathy and community of feeling between himself and his people. It was the same wherever he went. I was told it was perceptible even in the short time of his visit to Berlin, though there was no political entente to predispose to popularity.' (1)

In Berlin, so it was in Paris and in Russia. Despite a profligate youth, and without ever losing his appetite for life, he matured into a wise and usually benevolent monarch whose advice and guidance to his ministers – although not always to their liking – was mostly of great benefit to the state. Behind the amiable exterior, however, was a very steely core, and he was not a man to cross. Abroad, he was held in general esteem, and on his visits, invariably warmed the ground in advance of political initiatives. He became known as the 'Uncle of Europe', not only because of his family connections to most of the crowned heads of the continent, but also for his avuncular appearance and manner. Only in Germany was his death greeted with ill-disguised jubilation. His nephew had no doubts about the existence of a 'steely core'.

The Kaiser had always had a pronounced inferiority complex with regard to his *actual* uncle. This bordered on paranoia, and their relationship was rarely other than frosty. The accidental foibles of royal succession placed Wilhelm, as an immature young man, on the throne of Germany a generation before the much older British heir apparent attained the same status. In the intervening years, the future King Edward VII was subjected to various snubs and patronising behaviour from his nephew that deeply offended a man who had a pronounced sense of dignity and proper manners. Briefly, such as at the time of Queen Victoria's death, the underlying animosity was put aside as the best aspects of the Kaiser's personality came to the fore and 'Bertie's' natural magnanimity responded in kind. In general, though, the new British Monarch was deeply distrustful of the style, ambitions, and aggressive tone of Imperial Germany – and he was particularly wary, from intimate experience, of Wilhelm's unpredictable and impulsive personality.

For all the failings of his nation's traditional enemy, he accurately discerned that France was a better bet as an ally. He was a Francophile in any case, but clearly saw that meeting German conditions for an alliance would result in Britain becoming the second class partner in such an arrangement. Accordingly, he used what influence he had to break down Anglo-French antipathy. History, I think, rightly judges this as a defensive reaction to the German drive for predominance on the world stage – a drive that was being vehemently, and categorically, supported, and inflamed, by a large and influential proportion of the German press, and, consequently, by the bulk of German public opinion.

The British Government and electorate were as aware as the Monarch of the threat presented by an utterly dominant Germany, but Wilhelm chose to personalise this conflict of interest. Having considerable executive powers himself, he never came to terms with the fact that other heads of state, excepting the Tsar, were not in the same position. His lack of grasp of the realities of world politics (or, for that matter, the practical limitations of his own position) led him to regard his uncle as the arch-villain in the thwarting of his ambitions for a greater German Empire

In every diplomatic setback suffered by his nation, Wilhelm detected the hand of Edward VII, ceaselessly manoeuvring to isolate Germany from potential allies and to form combinations aimed at restricting Germany's growth – the 'Great Encircler', Wilhelm called him. For all that, the Kaiser put on a good show at Edward's state funeral where he was received with considerable enthusiasm by the huge crowds. The rank and file of the British nation was still prepared to embrace and welcome Queen Victoria's grandson when he came in peace and mourning.

His relationship with the new King George V was much more amicable than with the latter's father. Wilhelm had no sense of inferiority *vis-à-vis* the new British Monarch, who was of the same age, and also a much less formidable player on the political scene. This was not an unqualified asset in Anglo-German relations. The new King was a steady, solid man who possessed a good measure of common sense, uncluttered by any great intellect. He hadn't a tenth of Wilhelm's intelligence, flair, and wide-ranging interests, but he was stable and reliable. George lacked the political *nous* and flair of his father, and, at times, his naïvety in foreign affairs caused concern amongst sections of the establishment. He was also a very poor judge of character in his dealings, as a *monarch*, with the officers of his erstwhile service. The King was 'old navy' before his time, and preferred the company of the dandies and the pomp of the Beresford version of the navy rather than the focussed and efficiency-driven atmosphere of Fisher and Scott's vision for the service. This was a problem.

Any monarch is surrounded by numerous military aides who carry out duties large and small according to their rank. The Monarch obviously has a say in these appointments, and he will want around him the people with whom he feels comfortable. In the case of George V, the majority of his naval aides were of the Beresfordian persuasion, and they consequently served to reinforce his natural prejudices.

For the newly retired First Sea Lord, lately created Lord Fisher of Kilverstone, the death of his Monarch, 'the best friend I ever had', was an immense personal blow. It also filled him with a great fear for the future. The new King, George V, had spent much of his adult life in the Royal

Navy and had risen, to some extent on merit, to the rank of captain – which probably represented the ceiling of his professional capabilities. He had had no particular training for the role into which he was now thrust and entirely lacked his father's experience and skill in foreign affairs. In itself, this was of no abiding concern to Fisher. What really worried him was the fact that George had one foot in the Beresford camp, and he dreaded the possibility that Lord Charles might somehow use the new situation to inveigle himself back into a position of power – even, perhaps, as First Sea Lord. It was partially to forestall this possibility that Fisher had brought forward his own retirement. This was to ensure that his chosen successor, Admiral of the Fleet Sir Arthur Wilson, had sufficient time to establish himself in the post. Wilson only had two years to go on the active list, but this was long enough to effectively block any chance of Beresford, who was of similar age, staging a comeback.

Sir Arthur Wilson had actually been in retirement until he was persuaded to assume Fisher's mantle. This he did with extreme reluctance. An austere, self-contained and rather distant personality (although he could be charming company), he had no aptitude for office politics and had no illusions to the contrary. His great contributions to the service had been made at sea rather than behind a desk, but, in one vital sense, he was an eminently suitable choice. As well as commanding universal respect, he was recognised throughout the Royal Navy as being utterly impartial. In a service that had been torn asunder by the internecine strife between the Fisher and Beresford factions, he was a guarantee that such partisan behaviour would no longer be tolerated.

Wilson was a living legend in the Royal Navy. He was a magnificent seaman and almost certainly the best fleet commander of his era. He was also very technically minded by the standards of the time and had made significant contributions to the development of torpedoes. As a commander of men he was a very hard taskmaster and disciplinarian; a character of firm beliefs, stubbornly held; and was motivated, to the exclusion of all else, by a formidable work ethic and an absolute devotion to duty – standards he rigorously imposed on all those who served under him. Not for nothing was he known in the Navy as 'Old 'ard 'eart', a nickname that was used with a degree of reluctant affection. The modern phrase, 'What you see is what you get', is entirely applicable to Wilson. There was no hidden side to him, and everything that was seen was impressive.

'The utmost effort of which a man was capable was the expected norm. Praise was superfluous, and rarely given. His signal to a cruiser, returning to port "sunk" by the umpires after performing particularly well on manoeuvres, "I am sorry to lose you", was so notably effusive as to be memorable…In spite of his dictatorial ways he was without conceit, though he believed that age, experience and application had endowed him beyond his fellows. Personal merit did not come into it.' (2)

His ascetic self-discipline extended into the limited recreational time he permitted himself or his subordinates, and he kept himself in hard physical shape.

'His short, sturdy, upright body was as hard as nails, seemingly impervious to fatigue, heat or cold...Even off duty he lived to a rigid code. To clear his head and harden his body he would land for long tramps ashore with a gun and an old dog or with some perspiring companions...He would cover the miles at high speed, usually in silence. The places he liked best were wild and desolate...He was never observed to enter a theatre or other place of amusement...Indeed he seemed to have no taste for the relaxations of ordinary men...though a kind and generous host he rarely smoked and bothered little what he ate or drank. He liked to entertain his officers at dinner, encouraging them to talk particularly on service matters. Alert and interested he would listen to their views, showing by his brief remarks that they had the whole of his attention.' (3)

It will come as no surprise to learn that he remained, fortunately, a lifelong bachelor. Any Wilson household would probably have resembled the early regime of the musical Captain von Trapp – before the latter was converted to more frivolous ways!

Utterly devoid of any sense of self-importance, he shunned the limelight and had no time for the baubles and titles that adorned the careers of his successful contemporaries. (He refused the offer of a peerage – what was it for? Wilson's attitude was that he had only done his duty to the best of his ability. In his eyes, this made him no more deserving than anyone of lesser rank and responsibility who had done the same.) Winston Churchill, who first effectively sacked Wilson, and later re-employed him, had this to say:

'He was, without any exception, the most selfless man I have ever met or even read of. He wanted nothing and he feared nothing – absolutely nothing...everything was duty. It was not merely that nothing else mattered. There was nothing else. One did one's duty as well as one possibly could, be it great or small, and naturally one deserved no reward. This had been the spirit in which he had lived his long life afloat, and which by his example he had spread far and wide through the ranks of the navy. It made him seem very unsympathetic on many occasions, both to officers and men...All the same...[he] was greatly loved in the Fleet. Men would do hard and unpleasant work even when they doubted its necessity, because he had ordered it and it was "his way".' (4)

There was one award he did possess that paid testament to his physical courage. Like several of the naval officers who came to prominence at the turn of the century, Wilson had served on detachment with the army in Sudan. At the Battle of El Teb, in 1883, the British square was penetrated by a Dervish army. Wilson was pivotal in sealing the breach and, saving the day, fighting with his sword until it broke at the hilt, after which he used it as a knuckleduster. For his actions on that occasion he was awarded the Victoria Cross, and was turned by the press into a national hero. Perhaps the best illustration of Arthur Wilson's personality is given in the few written references he ever made to the event. In a letter to a friend, he gave a bald account of the action, playing down his own role as incidental, and as being the automatic reaction of anyone confronted with such a situation.

'In some men this might have been false modesty, but Wilson was writing nothing less than the absolute truth. Physically and morally he was all his life quite without fear. He simply did what he conceived to be his duty. It never occurred to him to do otherwise.' (5)

On returning to Britain, after his exploits in Sudan, there is a terse entry in his diary – 'Docked Ship. Received the VC.'

For all his outstanding qualities, Wilson, apart from significantly helping to restore unity in the service, was not a success as First Sea Lord. Behind a desk, he was a fish out of water. To quote William James again:

'Wilson was a great commander rather than a great administrator. His habit of working alone, of issuing orders rather than laying down policy, his almost pathological reserve which prevented him from discussing matters with his subordinates and his consequent failure to decentralise, were grave handicaps.' (6)

Wilson was also out of his depth in dealing with politicians, a key aspect of the First Sea Lord's responsibilities. He had no great love for the breed, a view he shared with Fisher, but whereas Fisher could plot and connive with the best of them, such activities were hateful to his successor. Fisher could also be compelling in argument, unlike Wilson, who was stilted and unconvincing in debate, and an autocrat of few words rather than a persuasive diplomat. He was well aware of his failings in this respect, and that awareness had been the prime cause of his reluctance to take the post in the first place – only the unfailing appeal to his sense of duty having the necessary effect. This ultimately turned on an order from the Monarch. Richard Hough, in his biography of Fisher, quotes the latter as saying:

'The King sent for Wilson to Sandringham and the King told me himself the curious nature of the interview. Sir Arthur Wilson reluctantly consented but he said to the King, "Only once, Sir, have I asked a favour of anybody since I entered the Navy and that was of Sir John Fisher, who, when he was about to lay down the appointment of Controller of the Navy, Fisher had already arranged for his successor but he cancelled the arrangement and secured the appointment of me. I assure you, Sir, that I was absolutely the worst Controller the Navy has ever had and if I am to succeed Fisher again I may probably become the worst Sea Lord in the annals of the Navy."' (7)

These are Fisher's informal words, and, as is usual in his case, were almost certainly an embellishment on the actual words spoken. However, it is probably a fair summary of the gist of what Wilson said to his King. For all his protestations, Wilson was manipulated by Fisher and constrained by his Monarch to accept a post for which he knew himself to be unsuited.

None of this should detract from his absolutely deserved reputation as one of the greatest naval officers of his age. Nelson, that most revered of all British naval heroes, would probably, for very different reasons of character, have been a disaster as a Lord of the Admiralty. Wilson, actually, was extremely incisive in memoranda, and was capable of utterly demolishing any half-baked initiatives or ill-thought through ideas. He was not, however, flexible enough to accommodate the new line of thinking as to the establishment of a proper naval staff, or to realise that this could complement the position of the First Sea Lord rather then usurp his authority.

At the height of the Agadir Crisis, the British Government was faced with the problem that, in the event of being drawn into a Franco-German war, there existed no overall strategy for the involvement of Britain's armed forces. The *entente* had been kept deliberately informal by the British but there *had* been conversations between representatives of both army high commands, which had assumed the character of a joint plan of action. On the British side, this had been pursued by a group of very able and dedicated enthusiasts whose activities were largely unknown, not only to most of the Cabinet, but also all of the public, and, incidentally, the Board of Admiralty. It immediately became apparent that there was a complete lack of co-ordination between the army and the navy as to the means and measures necessary to support France should a conflict with Germany arise. Although the immediate danger of war had receded in the month following David Lloyd-George's crucial speech, this situation clearly had to be addressed. To resolve the problem, the Prime Minister ordered a meeting of the Committee of Imperial Defence, which duly convened on the 23rd August. Asquith himself chaired the meeting, the other Cabinet members being Sir Edward Grey, McKenna, Lloyd-George, Churchill and Lord Haldane, the War Office Minister. The two services were represented by the Chief of the Imperial General Staff and the Director of Military Operations, on behalf of the army, and by Sir Arthur Wilson, as the professional head of the navy.

The War Office, which represented the army, had been given advance notice of the event – indeed, it had lobbied for it. The Admiralty had not. There was, inevitably, a discrepancy in the preparation and briefing between the two arms of Britain's military forces.

The format of the meeting was that the committee would be addressed in turn by the representatives of each service during which they would outline their respective war plans. The proceedings would be initiated by the army presentation, delivered by Sir Henry Wilson, the Director of Military Operations.

Henry Wilson was a man of formidable intellect and personality who was lucid in expression and persuasive in argument. He could leaven the most turgid discussion with a dash of humour. To these qualities was added a natural gift for detailed organisation. He was consequently a most impressive advocate of the army's strategy. If he had a failing, it was that he was Francophile to a fault and believed the French High Command to be the fount of all military wisdom. This blind spot coloured all his professional thinking and utterly blighted what was otherwise a brilliant mind. His presentation to the committee was a masterpiece of logic based on the absolute assumption that the bulk of the British regular army would immediately proceed to France on the outbreak of war and take its place within the overall organisation of the French forces. All the discussions with the French General Staff that had taken place since the forming of the *entente* had been based on this premise, and the resulting plans had been prepared with meticulous, and almost Teutonic, attention to detail. The committee was given an operational plan that could be translated into immediate effect from the moment that Britain became involved in a general war, right down to the minute to minute schedule for troop trains on both sides of the channel. The forethought and organisation that had gone into this concept was a tribute to good staff work and rightly created a most favourable impression within the select audience. The army obviously had its act together. It was then the Royal Navy's turn to give its views as to the future conduct of hostilities.

Whilst the professional and political heads of the army were only too willing to offer a presentation for which they were well prepared, the navy was a reluctant participant in the process. Sir Henry Wilson had revelled in the opportunity to push his case and had spent weeks preparing his case; Sir Arthur Wilson had to be ordered to attend and his presentation was ill-prepared and largely off the cuff. The navy had been effectively hi-jacked into this meeting, and the First Sea Lord was, accordingly, not as impressive as his army opponents. As in all meetings of this kind, those who are aware in advance of the agenda generally have the advantage in pressing their argument. As good soldiers, the army had taken control of the high ground before battle commenced. In the circumstances, A.K. Wilson would have been at a severe disadvantage even had he been a master of dialectics. That he was not.

As already mentioned, the First Sea Lord was not a good speaker in council, but, within his limitations, he argued powerfully that the deployment of the entire British Army to be an adjunct of the French would be a serious error. When questioned, he grudgingly affirmed that the Royal Navy could guarantee the safe transport of the army to France should that be required, but that this should not take place before the expected destruction of the German Navy in a fleet action. He believed, in any case, that the best possible use of Britain's limited military forces should be in amphibious assaults in the Baltic; on islands in the Heligoland Bight; or on the flank of a German advance into France and Belgium. Using the mobility granted by sea power, the mere threat of Britain's small army being deployed in a number of potential locations would tie down a disproportionate number of the perceived enemy – far more than would be required to meet it on a one to one basis when acting as an additional French army corps. This argument was entirely in line with Britain's traditional policy whereby war strategy was based and projected from a position of strength – i.e. a dominant navy, rather than from the weaker posture of being very much the subordinate in a massive continental land campaign.

However compelling this strategic reasoning, and not having had any notice of having to put forward these concepts – and further lacking any staff appreciation of the ways and means of accomplishing them, the First Sea Lord's presentation fell far short of the comprehensive argument provided by Sir Henry Wilson for the War Office's case.

A.K. Wilson was also utterly antipathetic about disclosing any of the Royal Navy's war intentions in an open forum. On the subject of War Plans, he was obsessively secretive. As with Fisher before him, he believed that the overall conduct of naval operations should be directed by the First Sea Lord, and that the detailed plans to deal with this strategy should be confined to his head alone. The more people given access to any plan diluted the secrecy, and therefore the effectiveness, of such a plan. In particular, he had an utter contempt of the War Office, and believed that any information imparted to it would find its way into the press within a few days. In any case, he argued, the actual circumstances of any new war were likely to be unique, which rendered detailed advance planning irrelevant. If the army was inflexible in its structure, the navy was capable of thinking on its feet. The matter would have to be dealt with, as it unfolded, by the Board of Admiralty of which he was the head. That was the responsibility of the post. Politicians could decide if, where, when, and with whom Britain went to war; after that, the conduct of operations rested with the professionals, using what materiel the government had thought fit to provide for the purpose.

Sir Arthur Wilson's address to the Committee of Imperial Defence was uncompromising, but something of an oratorical mess. It consisted of a series of general pronouncements based on the assumption that the only practical employment for the army was in it being used independently for campaigns or strikes behind the enemy lines rather than as a minor component of an allied army facing the main force of the enemy. The absolute crux of the matter, as far as he was concerned, was in following the traditional British policy of gaining uncontested dominance of the sea first, and deciding where to best use the army afterwards. As a policy, this had both the virtue of simplicity, and that of concentrating on the nation's real strength. Unfortunately, it ignored the political realities and commitments that were now attendant on the *entente* with France and, to a lesser extent, Russia.

The meeting descended into acrimony, with the much better prepared army officers tearing into Sir Arthur Wilson on matters of detail he could not answer. They absolutely rejected, as military experts, the chances of success of random descents on enemy territory, given the new factors of extensive internal rail and road communications that could deploy troops far more quickly than they could be shipped, or supported, to oppose them. They cited the impressive coast defensive measures already installed along the German coast. On balance, without a prepared defence, Sir Arthur Wilson did not adequately counter these arguments. McKenna, as First Lord, weighed in, as he always did, in support of his beleaguered colleague. He made the point that a German attack on France would, in all likelihood, rapidly overwhelm the French Army. Sending a small British Expeditionary Force to the latter's assistance would doom it to share the same fate. It would be insufficient to have any significant effect on the outcome, but its loss would deprive Britain of the core of its military capability. This, as will be seen later, was also the opinion of the German General Staff. McKenna's comments were pertinent, but he was not a critical influence in what was basically a confrontation of professional opinion.

The meeting broke up without a decision one way or another as to whether the army or navy strategy should be adopted – although the War Office presentation had clearly been the more effective. What utterly impressed itself on all the politicians present was the appalling fact that the two services were completely on different tracks as far as their war policy was based, and that there was no communication or cooperation between them as to aims and means. The navy was clearly seen to be the villain of the piece.

The overwhelming consensus of the politicians present at the meeting was that this situation could not continue, and that either the army would have to fall in line with the navy's view of things, or vice versa. Haldane, the War Minister (political head of the army), stated he would resign from the government unless there was a change in the Admiralty and the institution of a proper staff such as he had established with the army. His pressure was probably unnecessary, as Sir Henry Wilson's presentation had carried the day in the minds of most of those attendant on the meeting of 23rd August.

It is doubtful if even the generals realised the full implications of what had occurred at that fateful meeting. In fact, its results had turned on its head the strategy that had dominated British thinking for centuries. In a single working day, the basis of British foreign and military policy was shifted from a maritime to a continental emphasis.

Sir Arthur Knyvett Wilson was one of the outstanding naval officers of his time, but, without him, or almost anyone else, really comprehending it, he had lost the greatest battle of his life in one single meeting around a table occupied by a few politicians and army officers more glib, prepared, and practised in argument, than himself.

Following on from the slick army presentation, Wilson's inability to state his case clearly was a disaster for the navy, and also for an entire generation of the male population of Britain. It is impossible to overstate the importance of the First Sea Lord's failure to adequately fight his corner. This is the exact starting point on the road that was to lead to Ypres, Loos, the Somme, and Passchendaele. It is the point where Britain changed from a 'Blue Water' to a 'Land Based' strategy.

There were very powerful arguments that could, and should, have been made against the unqualified commitment of Britain's entire military resources to serve as an adjunct to the French Army, and to thus operate within a strategy dictated by the plans of the French High Command. It was inevitable, given the huge initial disparity in numbers between the French and British military forces, and the fact that the planned campaign would take place on French soil, that the British would have to settle for a subordinate role. This course of action also involved a reversal of traditional British policy as to its strategic involvement.

For most of Britain's existence as a world power, it had been accepted by its rulers and populace that the naval forces of the country were a guarantee against invasion from the vastly superior armies of the nations of continental Europe. The Royal Navy had also projected and secured British power, trade, and influence throughout the world beyond Europe, and eliminated competition in those areas. Stemming from this, almost incidentally, grew the empire that reached its apogee in the latter years of Queen Victoria's reign. These benefits, coupled to the fact that Britain managed to get a head start in the Industrial Revolution, had produced wealth and influence to the point that the country had become the world's first super power; except in one respect – it could not field a regular army commensurate to that of any of the other major powers.

Maritime supremacy had negated the need for an island nation to waste its resources on huge armies. All it had needed was an imperial police force. Should it need to coerce other nations, it could effectively blockade a nation from importing or exporting any materials by sea. In an age where the great bulk of all trade was carried in ships, this was a potent threat. It was reinforced by the fact that every overseas colony of the other European nations was hostage to the Royal Navy, and the troops that could be conveyed under its protection.

Briefly, and occasionally, Britain had become seriously involved in large-scale military operations on the continent. Those involvements, most notably the campaigns of Marlborough and Wellington, included many of the most glorious episodes in British military history, but they represented special situations, and were exceptions to the general rule that had guided long-term national policy.[1] However, from time to time, the question kept arising as to whether Britain should shift its strategic emphasis to a continental rather than a maritime policy. With the forming of the *entente*, and a general perception of the threat from Germany, this once more became a subject for fierce debate.

The *entente* had certainly changed Britain's thinking as to the potential threats to her shores. With France now a *de facto* ally, the centuries-old danger from that direction had suddenly vanished, and been replaced by a new and seemingly even more formidable foe in the shape of an all powerful Germany. In itself, this did not represent any radical shift in Britain's traditional policy. This had always been to oppose the predominant power on the continent by means of assisting those nations that could prevent the one obtaining hegemony over the many – and by so doing form a bloc so powerful that it could, and must, create an overwhelming combination against Britain.

For two centuries, highlighted by the reigns of Louis XIV and Napoleon Bonaparte, France had been the primary threat. In the altered conditions from 1871 onwards, it was plain that Germany, not France, had become the predominant European power, and had not yet nearly begun to satiate its appetite for further expansion. In the circumstances, the *entente*, however startling it was to many citizens of two nations with such a long history of enmity, was neither surprising nor illogical. It was actually *inevitable*, in that, as the French yielded supremacy in Europe to Germany, Britain, by all her historical precedents, would be bound to support the weaker nation.

Militarily, the new situation *did* require a completely new set of thinking. A considerable body of opinion tended to the view that Britain required much larger military forces as a defence against invasion, and also to be able to participate as a significant factor in any future European confrontation.

In the forefront of this argument was the most senior officer in the British military hierarchy. Field Marshall Lord Roberts, V.C., the venerable hero of Britain's eventual success in the Boer War, severed his formal

---

[1] Wellington's triumphant Peninsular campaigns were entirely dependent on the fact that he could be supplied and reinforced from the sea, courtesy of naval supremacy. This is not to denigrate the achievements of his army, rather it is to emphasise what can be achieved by land and naval forces operating in harmony for their mutual benefit. Before and since, this was rarely the case until such operations were perfected during the Second World War.

connections with the army to head a campaign for compulsory conscription – and thus the establishment of a standing army capable of playing a major role in any future continental war. His action had the tacit support of many in the military hierarchy, particularly the Francophiles who were beginning to occupy most of the key positions. The campaign for an army of sufficient strength to affect the balance of power on land in Europe began to gather momentum. It was naturally fiercely opposed by the navalists.

In Britain, such a change in the balance of traditional strategy involved controversies equal and opposite to those raging in Germany as to the relationship between the roles of the army and the navy. In each case, the traditional defenders of the realm were threatened by the diversion of vital resources to a competitor.

In Germany, there was almost a frantic concern on the part of the Army General Staff, that the Kaiser's pre-occupation with creating a huge navy would impinge on its ability to face the established armies of France, and the rapidly re-arming forces of Russia. Despite the humiliating debacle suffered at the hands of the Japanese, and the incipient threat of revolution in that nation, some strategists had calculated that, by 1917, Russia would be capable of facing Germany on her own unless there were significant increases in Germany's land forces. This could not be achieved whilst vast sums continued to be allocated to building up a fleet of battleships, which even the admirals admitted would never be able to meet its designated opponent on equal terms. For each battleship rolling down the slipway, the Army High Command saw the loss of an army corps in the field.

In Britain, the situation was not as clear cut. There was a general sense of 'ditherance' in government policy. Having adopted in principle the continental strategy advocated by the War Office, no major increases were made in the army whilst the huge costs of maintaining an adequate naval superiority over the ever-expanding German Navy continued to be met. When war finally came, Britain would find itself committed to a policy of sending its army to the aid of the French without having established a big enough army to radically affect the balance of power. That the British Expeditionary Force in 1914 would have a pivotal role in the Battle of the Marne was a matter of chance, place, and circumstances rather than calculation.

The change of strategic emphasis in the respective roles of the army and the navy was obviously not welcomed by the latter. It went against every precept of the maritime strategy that had generally served the country so well for the previous three centuries. If the change of policy was unpopular with those naval officers privy to the information, the subsequent change of its responsible minister was an additional blow that caused great apprehension.

It was plain that the soldiers had won the battle of the 23rd August. It was equally plain that the Admiralty, as it was then constituted, would not accept the result as final.

After reflection, the Prime Minister decided that there must be a change at the Admiralty. Unwilling to grasp the nettle of forcing the dismissal of Sir Arthur Wilson, he resolved on replacing McKenna, who continued to remain steadfastly loyal to his professional advisors. In his place, the Prime Minister intended to appoint a minister who would impose the government's will on the admirals. This was the easier option for Asquith, who was a natural compromiser and flinched from confrontation. McKenna's transfer to head another ministry could be presented as a promotion within a government reshuffle, whereas the sacking of the First Sea Lord could not be seen as anything other than just that – and would be bound to stir up unwelcome controversy, particularly when the officer concerned was such a revered figure as Sir Arthur Wilson.

Once this decision had been made, there only remained the question of who would succeed McKenna. It boiled down to a choice between two men – Lord Haldane, the War Minister, who was keen to carry through his reforms of the army staff into the naval sphere; and Winston Churchill, the Home Secretary. A few years earlier, as a junior minister, the latter had belittled the post of First Lord of the Admiralty as 'a poor ambition' to a colleague offered the position. He was now avid in his pursuit of that same appointment, even though it would mean a theoretical demotion. As Home Secretary, he ranked fourth in the Cabinet pecking order, only the Chancellor of the Exchequer, the Foreign Secretary, and the Prime Minister himself having precedence. Churchill, however, clearly saw that, in the conditions of time and place, the Admiralty then offered the highest possible profile for a politician. He was also, and ever remained, a man on whom warfare, and the means of its prosecution, exercised a compelling fascination.

Asquith would probably have preferred Haldane, who was an old political crony, had all things been equal. However, two things mitigated against the War Minister. He had recently been raised to the peerage, and this meant that he could not present, in person, the naval estimates to the House of Commons each year, or take part in the extended debate that followed. Given the fact that these estimates were now so large as to be one of the most contentious issues of the day; and given also that they were now inextricably connected to foreign relations with Germany, it was felt that the minister responsible had to be able to argue his case in the Commons. Asquith had rather painted himself into a corner in that respect. On replacing Sir Henry Campbell-Bannerman, in 1908, he had more or less made this requirement one of the conditions of his acceptance of the office of Prime Minister.

'The King accepted a radical constitutional departure from his new Prime Minister. He told Admiral Fisher...that Asquith had convinced him that, in future, it was essential that the ministers in charge of big spending departments should sit in the Commons.' (8)

The other consideration that told against Haldane was that he had been one of the sternest critics of Admiralty policy and its organisation. Whilst he may well have been a good choice to 'cleanse the stables', the hostility his appointment would have created within the navy would not have made the anticipated changes any easier to consummate. Another consideration was that there would certainly have been problems with McKenna, who would have been unlikely to take, lying down, the humiliation of being superseded by the man against whom he had been so recently arraigned.

Asquith had both men join him for a private weekend in the country. After some discussion, it was decided that it would be Churchill who would go to the Admiralty. This was to occur at the earliest possible moment and would involve a straight job swap with McKenna.

When he learned of this decision, McKenna was none too happy about his promotion. He had been, by most reckoning, an extremely effective First Lord who had gained the trust and respect of the service. The navy, and particularly Fisher, had gradually warmed to this rather dry lawyer who had fought their corner so stubbornly. McKenna himself had become increasingly attached to his department, and it was only with great reluctance that he relinquished his post to Churchill.

Within the navy, the abrupt supercession of its political head was rightly seen as portending a period of change. The Cabinet reshuffle that resulted in the removal of the trusted McKenna as First Lord of the Admiralty, and his replacement by Winston Churchill, was regarded with the utmost antipathy and foreboding. Churchill had been the most vociferous supporter of Lloyd-George when the latter had attempted to cull the naval estimates during the 'scare' in 1908. He was seen to have been imposed upon them as an economiser and a reformer, neither of which roles generated any enthusiasm within the service. He was, though, to prove something of a surprise.

Churchill did indeed institute reforms. It was, after all, the reason he had been drafted into the post, but he also became as doughty a defender of the navy as ever had McKenna or any of his predecessors. The successive naval estimates, during Churchill's period at the Admiralty, each marked new record levels of expenditure, and were the cause of a political estrangement between him and his long-time ally at the Exchequer, David Lloyd-George. Although each retained a great respect for the other's abilities, from henceforth they were fighting from opposite corners within the Cabinet. For Churchill, who was not over-endowed with political friends, this development left him considerably isolated within the upper levels of government. He was not deterred by the challenge.

CHAPTER THIRTEEN

CHURCHILL AT THE ADMIRALTY

'Although my education had been mainly military, I had followed closely every detail of the naval controversies of the previous five years in the Cabinet, in Parliament, and latterly in the Committee of Imperial Defence; and I had certain main ideas of what I was going to do and what, indeed, I was sent to the Admiralty to do. I intended to prepare for an attack by Germany as if it might come next day.'

Winston Churchill

'It would be stupid to pretend that everything was right with the Navy in August 1914. There were many weaknesses, but there were also great strengths, and the improvement since 1911 had been immense. Churchill had grasped the torch of progress lit by Lord Fisher and had carried it bravely forward.'

Vice Admiral Sir Peter Gretton

Winston Churchill has been the subject of so many biographies and assessments that it would be quite pointless to rehash the details of his life and character in this volume. However, for the purposes of this story, it is relevant to take a look at the man as he was in 1911.

As one of, if not *the* most famous and revered statesmen of the 20th century, it is perhaps difficult, nowadays, to appreciate just how little respected or liked was Churchill at this stage of his career. His exceptional abilities were grudgingly recognised, but, as a politician and a person, he was widely regarded as untrustworthy, disloyal, and solely motivated by a consuming desire for self-advancement. To that latter end his propensity for courting favourable publicity was offensive to many traditional politicians. Worse, he had been a Conservative MP up to the time of the split in that party over the issue of free trade. Churchill went further than most and crossed the house to join the opposition Liberals. This had effectively made him an utter pariah as far as the Conservatives were concerned, and, whilst the Liberals had welcomed his defection as a political coup, they regarded him personally with no particular warmth. Leaving one party to join another has always been regarded as a treasonable offence in politics, and no one loves, or trusts, a traitor – not even his new colleagues. Nor, throughout his life, and despite his wonderful powers of advocacy, was he always correct in his judgement of personality and events – although it has to be said that he usually got the really big issues right.

Another factor was his age. Churchill was only 36 when he inherited the post of First Lord. Characteristics that are acceptable in older age are frequently resented when displayed in youth. What is seen as wisdom in an elder statesman is regarded as presumption and arrogance in a person of lesser years. Churchill never attempted to sugar the pill. He knew he was special, and, whilst he made every effort to carry the party along with his policies, he made little attempt to court popularity amongst its MPs. Consequently, he had no substantial power base within parliament except amongst the more radical members of the Liberal Party. Although the latter had no particular love of him as an individual, his fight to cut the 1909 Naval Estimates was a recent memory, and the influential pacifist wing of the party consequently saw him as an opponent of bloated military expenditure. On that assumption, his appointment to the Admiralty was welcomed. They were to be sorely disillusioned by his actual performance in office. The erstwhile economiser soon proved to be 'gamekeeper turned poacher', and the naval estimates during his term of office increased to an unprecedented level. The radicals then rapidly rejoined the majority of senior politicians in regarding him as a bumptious, unprincipled opportunist.

It has to be admitted that Churchill changed horses more than most during his long career. When, in the 1920s, he became Chancellor of the Exchequer, the 'poacher' instantly reverted to the most assiduous 'head game keeper'. The navy had to fight for its very life to squeeze minimal funds from its erstwhile First Lord. As Chancellor, Churchill could point out, with some justification, that it was his bounden responsibility to fight, to the very best of his ability, the corner of whichever government ministry had been entrusted to his care. It was the job of other ministers and the opposition to oppose him as and if they thought fit. Nevertheless, this lack of a consistent political stance was a primary cause of his alienation from most of his contemporaries.

It was only much later in his career that Churchill was seen to put principle before advancement, and, when that time came, it was generally reckoned, and welcomed by many, as an act of political suicide. His unswerving opposition to the policy of appeasing the Fascist dictators; his absolute antipathy towards the granting of Home Rule to India; and his doomed but doggedly loyal support for King Edward VIII – all attitudes that were directly opposed to the government policy of the time – seemed to ensure that he would be consigned indefinitely to the political periphery, eventually, presumably, to fade from the scene as do all politicians who have not quite scaled the highest peak. All this, though, was a long way in the future.

What was relevant, in 1911, was that Churchill was generally detested. The fact that he was so obviously cleverer and more energetic than most other politicians simply compounded their irritation. Churchill, therefore, had few influential backers in parliament. That he rose so far, so quickly, was entirely due to his own ability, single-minded determination, and soaring ambition.

Arthur Marder comments on Churchill at this point in his career:

'He was far more brilliant than McKenna, but without McKenna's solid qualities. All the traits that were to win him global renown in World War II were clearly discernable before World War I: self-confidence, vivacity, inexhaustible vitality and power of work, courage, eloquence, temperament, and a great brain. He had wonderful argumentative powers in the Commons or when putting a case before the C.I.D. [The Committee of Imperial Defence] or Cabinet. He was aggressive and truculent in his official capacity, showing a disregard for the opinions and sensibilities of his opponents; but he was full of charm and tolerance and amiability in social intercourse.' (1)

Paradoxically, some of his virtues were also part of one of his most dangerous weaknesses. His self-belief and determination, allied to an immensely creative mind and formidable powers of argument, led him into decisions and initiatives without giving adequate consideration to very valid objections. Time and time again, Churchill would have an inspiration on a subject or a course of action, and, carried forth on a flood of creative enthusiasm, only those arguments that helped his case would subsequently be absorbed. The rest would be discarded as obstructive or irrelevant. His fertile brain churned out a stream of ideas – some utterly impractical: a few brilliant – and all these had to be immediately addressed by his staff. It also has to be admitted that, given Churchill's enjoyment of stimulating company, plus his 'night owl' tendencies, some of these ideas originated at a time of day when, to quote a delightful euphemism applied to him, he 'had dined well'!

It was extremely difficult for those overworked and long-suffering subordinates to arrange for the wheat to be sorted from the chaff. It also stifled any initiative from the supposedly competent officers who made up his staff. They were kept far too busy, either advancing his practical initiatives (or trying to thwart those that were obviously impractical), to have any time left to advance theories of their own. People who should have been making a vital contribution to thinking and policy were reduced to ciphers. Fisher used to group them under a heading of 'Winston's facile dupes'.

This was a conspicuous waste of talent where and when it existed (which was not necessarily everywhere or always). The fact was that the workload placed on Churchill's subordinates often prevented them from properly doing their appointed job – even if, on a specific issue, their opinions, backed up by a lifetime of specialist experience, were of particular value. It is a valid criticism of Churchill, throughout his political life, that he would not countenance any views that did not fit in with his personal appreciation of a policy or situation. Any criticisms or dissension, no matter how relevant or well backed up with inconvenient, but incontrovertible facts, would be entirely ignored. If Churchill were thwarted once he would pause for a moment to regroup and consider the opposition. After reflection, and with renewed counter-arguments and fervour, he would return to the subject over and over again. More often than not, by his extraordinary powers of persuasion, persistence, and sheer stamina he would gradually wear down the most adamant opposition. Experienced politicians and admirals would find themselves supporting (or at least not obstructing) policies and actions to which, for very pertinent reasons, they were fundamentally opposed. This side of Churchill never changed – it was as much in evidence in 1939 as it was in 1911 – and would have been disastrous during the Second World War had he not possessed a very strong Chief of Staff, in Alanbrooke, to curb his worst excesses.

Within the navy, Churchill's arrival as its civilian head was greeted with considerable apprehension. The very reason that the radicals had initially approved of his appointment, i.e. he was expected to cut the naval estimates, was a matter of great concern to the admirals. Although this fear was soon seen to have been unfounded, the first impressions he created were not favourable. His conduct, and interpretation of the rights and responsibilities, of the First Lord's office may have been within the letter of his remit, but they totally went against the spirit in which all his predecessors had applied them.

Traditionally, the First Lord of the Admiralty, whilst having overall responsibility for the strategy and performance of the navy, and possessing the power of veto, largely confined himself to matters affecting policy and the general administration of the service. He was the representative of the navy in the Cabinet and had an obvious great interest in operational matters, but did not usually interfere with the dispositions and orders to the fleet as promulgated by the naval officers on the Board of Admiralty. Nor did he dabble in the technical aspects of ship construction and weaponry. These were generally acknowledged to be within the domain of the responsible naval experts. It was on their advice that the First Lord formulated a strategy pursuant to the policies of the government of the day. This advice was rarely disputed or contradicted. Matters of detail were left to the professionals.

The practical application at sea of the overall strategy was also the exclusive preserve of the delegated naval commanders–in-chief on the various stations. This had been the way the system had worked, generally to everyone's satisfaction, for as long as any serving officer could remember. The government supplied overall war policy and objectives; the Admiralty planned the campaign strategy; and the commanders at sea won the tactical victories. This was the way it had always been done; this was the way that had always succeeded. Ships and the conditions of warfare had obviously changed drastically in the preceding few decades, but the means of managing the process had not. Service opinion was firmly in favour of preserving this status quo.

Churchill, however, had other ideas. He describes his initial perception of his new duties thus:

'How then is a civilian Minister appointed for political or parliamentary reasons and devoid of authoritative expert knowledge, to acquit himself of his duty?...I interpreted my duty in the following way: I accepted full responsibility for bringing about successful results, and in that spirit I exercised a *close general supervision over everything that was done or proposed*. Further, **I claimed and exercised an unlimited power of suggestion and initiative over the whole field**...Moreover, it happened in a large number of cases that seeing what ought to be done *and confident of the of the agreement of the First Sea Lord*, **I myself drafted the telegrams and decisions in accordance with our policy**, and the Chief of Staff took them personally to the First Sea Lord **for his concurrence before dispatch**.' [Author's italics and emphasis] (2)

He immediately made clear, on taking office, that these were not idle words. More than any First Lord of the Admiralty, before or since, he immersed himself totally into the structure of his department and all its branches. With all the immense energy at his disposal he threw himself into an exhaustive programme of visits to shore establishments and the ships of the fleet. Everywhere he went, he questioned and probed. There was nothing he did not want to know, and no information that was not absorbed into the filing cabinet of his memory. He took full advantage of the Admiralty yacht that was placed at his disposal, and used it to such an extent (six months out of his first eighteen in office) on his tours of inspection that, by the beginning of the war, he had spent more time afloat in that period than many serving officers! It was an impressive and unprecedented performance.

That this was also a mixed blessing was inevitable given his character. For all his efforts to learn about his new department, his knowledge could only be partial, selective, and unconnected to practical experience. This fact did not, however, encourage any self-restraint on his part when it came to offering opinions or pronouncing decisions. Churchill was, and remained, an inveterate meddler and interferer. He was never a subscriber to the adage that 'a little knowledge can be a dangerous thing' – at least not in his specific case. The remarks of Dudley de Chair, who succeeded Beatty as Secretary to the First Lord, give a good idea of the difficulties faced by the professional heads of the navy:

Winston Churchill as First Lord of the Admiralty

'Old 'Ard 'Art'
Admiral of the Fleet Sir Arthur Knyvet Wilson, Bart; V.C., GCB, OM, GCVO

'Winston certainly made us realise that he was clever and hard-working, but he was also impulsive, headstrong, and even at times obstinate. As a result of this, I, as Naval Secretary, found it difficult to keep the balance even, especially as he thought he knew more about the naval personnel than any of us in the Admiralty, who had been all our lives in the Service. We thought he considered himself more like Napoleon and Marlborough than any living man, and he appeared to have an immense amount of courage and initiative…Many were the times that I tried to dissuade him from appointing some one to a post whom I knew perfectly well would not be a success, and on one occasion he replied that, as he had instituted the Labour Exchange, he could tell from a five minutes' talk whether a man was suitable or not for a post.' (3)

Some of his impromptu forays into service matters caused huge offence and were the source of continual friction with the naval officers on the Admiralty Board who had to deal with the repercussions. At one time or another, every one of the four Sea Lords on the Board was on the point of quitting over Churchill's transgressions of accepted protocol, or intrusions into their specific areas of responsibility. On one occasion, all of them were within measurable distance of a joint resignation that would have caused the most appalling political furore. This one particular incident is worthy of quote as it encapsulates the difficulties that the navy had in accommodating the personality of the new First Lord, and also Churchill's own incomprehension as to the damage his often ill-considered words and actions had on the stability and morale of the service.

In November 1913, Churchill had been on one of his circuits in the Admiralty yacht, and had put into Sheerness, there to inspect the facilities and to visit *HMS Hermes*, an old protected cruiser converted into a seaplane tender. As such, she was the parent ship of the embryo Royal Naval Air Service (RNAS), and her captain (Gerald Vivian) was much involved in the development of the branch and of its facilities.

Vivian had recently had to make a decision on the usage of some land on the Medway that had been allocated to the RNAS. His decision had not met with the approval of one of his junior officers on *Hermes* who took the opportunity of the First Lord's visit to buttonhole Churchill and express disagreement with the policy of his own commanding officer. This act of extraordinary insubordination was compounded when Churchill (instead of telling the officer to put his objections on paper and send them, through his captain, to higher authority) chose to support his case. Marder, quoting from letters written at the time, takes up the story:

'…one of the young Lieutenants held other views very strongly. These he very improperly expressed to the First Lord, who, impressed, sent for Vivian and told him the Lieutenant's proposals were to be carried out. Afterwards the young officer had lost his head in discussing the matter with Vivian. He informed him that (as reported by the Captain) "if he did not get what he wanted he would write to the First Lord and that he (the First Lord) had told him so". Then the row began.' (4)

Captain Vivian was, not unnaturally, incensed that some upstart under his command had arranged to by-pass his authority and supposedly have a direct line to the civilian head of the navy. In high dudgeon, he duly donned his sword and medals and went to see his commander-in-chief to whom he made a vehement protest.

Admiral Sir Richard Poore was the C.-in-C. the Nore, and he was equally incandescent about this breach of discipline and naval protocol that had, apparently, been approved by the First Lord. He immediately took up the matter with the Second Sea Lord (at that time Jellicoe), who had overall responsibility for naval discipline.

'Churchill, who somehow got wind of the correspondence that had been initiated, asked Jellicoe to send him immediately any dispatch on the subject received from the C.-in-C. But Jellicoe, when Poore's letter reached him found it couched in such strong terms that he returned it for some amendment. Enclosed was a private letter from Jellicoe with comments.' (5)

What happened next was scarcely credible in the context of the time.

'When, a few hours later, Churchill learned what had happened, "he went dancing mad" and telegraphed the General Post Office, asking that the letter should be found and returned *to him*! He got it back from the G.P.O. and, of course read it, although he claimed not to have read Jellicoe's private letter. Churchill announced that he intended to telegraph Admiral Poore, ordering him to haul down his flag. Jellicoe threatened to resign from the Board if Churchill went ahead, and to make his reasons public. The Third and Fourth Sea Lords...were ready to resign with Jellicoe. Battenberg, the First Sea Lord, was talked out of joining his colleagues by the First Lord. At one point in the crisis it seems that all four Sea Lords had signed their resignations and that Poore was about to follow suit.' (6)

Dudley de Chair, who was then Naval Secretary to the First Lord, gives his own version of events:

'...one of the Private Secretaries came into my room, and told me that the First Lord was very angry with the Commander-in-Chief at the Nore for some letter he had written, that he intended to make the said C-in-C haul his flag down, and that he was going to order this to be done at once, without any reference to the Sea Lords...they had been trying to prevent the First Lord from doing such a thing, but he was quite unmanageable, and they asked me if I would see him. Consequently I walked into his room...and found him in a very excited state. I said, "Good morning, First Lord, you seem disturbed this morning." He turned on me and said, "Disturbed! I have been insulted by the C-in-C at the Nore, and I am dictating a telegram to him to haul down his flag at sunset, and give up his command... I read what had been written, and saw at once that the First Lord was about to do an unjust and ill-considered action, and I told him so. I also told him that he should put the matter before the whole Board, and if he had been insulted the matter would be put right. To this he replied, "Do you think I am going to humiliate myself before the Sea Lords? Either his flag comes down or I go. I refuse to discuss the matter further." (7)

De Chair went back to his office and considered his position. He felt compelled to resign in protest. However:

'Before doing so, I felt it my duty to warn the Sea Lords, and see if they could prevent the First Lord doing such a mad thing. Prince Louis was away, so I went to see Admiral Jellicoe. He said, "Don't resign. If the First Lord persists in this action we will all resign, and you can come with us, and it will make it all the stronger. I will endeavour to see the First Sea Lord now." When Prince Louis heard he came back to the Admiralty, and…it was decided that (he) should see Churchill and persuade him to put the whole matter before the Board. Churchill eventually agreed, and it transpired that the entire Board were against his action, until the facts of the case from the C-in-C's point of view could be heard.' (8)

After this meeting, the sense of crisis gradually receded. The Sea Lords approached Poore privately and, after some difficulty, persuaded him to withdraw his letter and express regret for any of its contents that might have caused offence. 'Under vast pressure' (9), he agreed not to resign.

The lieutenant whose actions had precipitated events was reprimanded for his importunity. He was also induced to make an official apology for his conduct to both his captain and to the First Lord.

There the matter rested. Poore retained his command for the full term of the appointment, and the board resumed its normal affairs. However, the fact that this particular incident took place some two years into his tenure of office indicates that Churchill had not been mellowed by his exposure to the service he represented.

For all his formidable talents, the incident over Sir Richard Poore shows Churchill, at this stage of his career, very deficient in man management. He simply did not have time for such niceties at a moment when there existed the immediate challenge of preparing the navy for war. Whilst he persistently made himself an annoyance, he was nevertheless reasonably diplomatic in dealings with his peers and those people higher up on the career ladder than himself (who, nevertheless, also found him a considerable trial). To those under him, he was a hard taskmaster, and often unpardonably rude to those who, by their subordinate position, could not answer back. He was an extraordinarily multi-faceted character who possessed great generosity of spirit and warmth allied with a genuine humility, but it is pointless to deny the fact that another of those facets was that of a terrible bully. The former aspects of his personality were unfortunately not much in evidence when he took over the Admiralty – whereas examples of the latter were only too apparent, and became common knowledge within the service.

His most unforgivable sin, as far as the navy was concerned, was his complete lack of respect for its traditions, its competence, and its commitment. There was also his scarcely disguised lack of regard, bordering on contempt, for many senior officers who held important positions – the Poore affair being a perfect example. Even for those not exposed to the lash, it was a serious concern that respect for the constituted authority, essential to a disciplined service, was being undermined. It ill-behoved a 36-year old *arriviste* to start dictating terms and policies to professional officers who had dedicated their entire lives to the study of the subject, as if they were children. This was, nevertheless, the route that Churchill chose to follow. Those who failed to fall into line were ruthlessly discarded. First to go was the most senior, and the most respected, serving officer on the active list of the country's armed forces.

The relationship between the new First Lord and his chief naval advisor was never likely to be a viable long-term success. Churchill had been specifically appointed as the 'new broom', to 'cleanse the stables'. The strategies and attitudes of the Board of Admiralty, in particular those of the First Sea Lord, were clearly at variance with government policy as to the future deployment of Britain's military forces. Quite apart from Sir Arthur Wilson's complete antipathy towards large military campaigns on the continent as an adjunct to French interests, his absolute opposition to the concept of a naval staff organisation meant that he and his new civilian chief would be instantly at loggerheads. One of the specific reasons for Churchill replacing McKenna was in order to force this measure through. It was clear to all in the navy that changes were in the offing. It only remained to be seen how soon and how sweeping would be these changes.

Churchill quickly brought matters to a head. He made clear that he intended to create a naval staff, somewhat on the lines of that adopted earlier by the War Office for the army. He invited Wilson's comments. These, when they came, were predictably uncompromising and utterly opposed to such an organisation. The First Sea Lord would not bend to the political wind. In Wilson's opinion, such an establishment might be appropriate to the army, but was irrelevant to the very different needs and conditions pertaining to the navy. Some of his arguments had merit, but effectively the decision had already been made, and Churchill only solicited his views in order to make absolutely clear the impossibility of any progress whilst Wilson remained on the board.

Having established that the positions of the First Lord and the First Sea Lord were completely incompatible, Churchill wrote to Asquith and obtained his agreement to Wilson's supercession. 'Old 'ard 'eart' was in any case due to retire within a few months, but Churchill was unwilling for the stalemate to drag on longer than necessary. In his letter to the Prime

Minister, the First Lord made clear that the existing situation could not be permitted to continue, but he also provided a convenient (and not totally irrelevant) excuse for bringing forward a change of First Sea Lord:

'The enclosed memorandum from Sir A. Wilson is decisive in its opposition, not only to any particular scheme, but against the whole principle of a War Staff for the Navy...it would not be difficult to continue the argument. But I feel this might easily degenerate into personal controversy, and would, in any case, be quite unavailing. I like Sir A. Wilson personally, and should be very sorry to run the risk of embittering relations which are now pleasant. I therefore propose to take no public action during his tenure.

[But]...If Wilson retires in the ordinary course in March, [the letter was written on 5th Nov] I shall be left without a First Sea Lord in the middle of the passage of the Estimates, and his successor will not be able to take any real responsibility for them. It is necessary, therefore, that the change should be made in January at the latest.' (10)

In an interview with Wilson, he informed him of this decision to advance his retirement. Wilson accepted the situation without demur – he was almost certainly aware that there existed no alternative – and the meeting was probably more of a strain for Churchill than it was for the admiral:

'Sir Arthur Wilson and I parted on friendly, civil, but at the same time cool terms. He showed not the least resentment at the short curtailment of his tenure. He was as good humoured and as distant as ever. Only once did he show the slightest sign of vehemence. That was when I told him that the Prime Minister was willing to submit his name to the King for a peerage. He disengaged himself from this with much vigour...I could not help thinking uncomfortably of the famous Tenniel cartoon "Dropping the Pilot", where the inexperienced and impulsive German Emperor is depicted carelessly watching the venerable figure of Bismarck descending the ladder.' (11)

Churchill's account of the interview is obvious tinged in his favour, and there are others who have suggested that it was not such a bland encounter, and that Sir Arthur's 'vehemence' stemmed from the clumsiness in which the offer of a peerage was made to appear as a bribe for him to go quietly. Should that version of events be given any credence, it would indicate an extreme lack of judgement on Churchill's part as to the character of the admiral. It would also fly in the face of all evidence as to Churchill's very obvious respect for Wilson as a man – a view often expressed in the former's memoirs. Whatever were the true facts of the matter, the abrupt departure of the revered First Sea Lord, so close to his natural retirement, outraged most of the service.

However tactlessly handled, the decision was undoubtedly correct in the circumstances. If changes were to be made, it was better that they be made sooner rather than later, and there were no advantages to be gained by putting off the process for four months.

There were, at that time, few outstanding candidates who possessed the seniority and experience to replace Wilson. After some consideration, the choice fell upon Admiral Sir Francis Bridgeman, the Second Sea Lord and recently Commander of the Home Fleet. Churchill had ascertained that their views coincided in most essentials, and, whilst Bridgeman was not a particularly forceful character in committee, he was a very competent and sensible officer who was well-respected in the fleet. He had, in fact, been previously considered for the post at the time of Fisher's retirement. Then, he had been discarded as a candidate on the suspicion that he might be out of his depth in dealing with politicians, and in his ability to aggressively argue the navy's case in council – although he would surely have been no worse than Sir Arthur Wilson in that respect! For Churchill, these perceived failings were of little matter in any case, as he fully intended to monopolise that particular side of things. Bridgeman's supposed malleability, compared to Wilson, was also of no concern to the First Lord. Rather, he would have regarded this as a positive bonus. Further, and most importantly, he was already receiving all the professional guidance, inspiration and exhortation he needed from another quarter.

For the whole of Churchill's period at the Admiralty prior to the outbreak of war, there was an unofficial First Sea Lord in the background who had far more influence than the actual occupant of that position. Unbeknownst to all but a very few, but suspected by a good few more, Churchill and Fisher were in constant communication from the moment the former took up his new responsibilities.

The two men had met for the first time in 1907 whilst both were visiting the King in Biarritz. The old admiral and the young politician struck it off immediately. Both had boundless enthusiasm, were highly opinionated, and were brimming with projects and visions that were expounded with passion and colour. King Edward was amused to observe them constantly in deep and animated discussion and dubbed them 'the Chatterers'. At this meeting, it was Fisher who dominated the conversation. He was then in his pomp, with all his great reforms beginning to reach fruition and the *Dreadnought* newly commissioned. He regaled Churchill with the reasons behind his policies; berated the scoundrels who tried to obstruct him; and predicted future developments with what, in most cases, was uncanny accuracy.

Churchill was captivated by this extraordinary man, and, for once in his life, shut up and listened as the ideas and opinions flooded from his companion. He was fascinated by Fisher's vivid descriptions of the challenges that he, personally, and the navy, as an entity, was preparing to meet. This was, essentially the long-term security of the empire, and the peace of the world. The commitment, vibrancy, and enthusiasm of the admiral struck an immediate chord. From having known next to nothing about the Royal Navy, apart from the generally perceived wisdom that it was a good thing, preserved peace, and secured the empire, Churchill was given a crash course on every aspect of its strengths and weaknesses. He was bombarded with information, and he soaked it up with relish. The two men continued to correspond subsequent to this meeting (both were prolific writers), and even the furore of the scare over the 1909 Naval Estimates, which found them adopting diametrically opposed positions, failed to shake the foundations of their relationship.

When Fisher retired, he took himself out of the country for lengthy periods and deliberately vanished from the spotlight of naval and political affairs. That is not to say that he did not continue to influence policy. He had the greatest regard for McKenna, who had been his trusty shield against the barbs and arrows directed against him in the last years of his administration. The respect was mutual. Complete opposites in temperament and personality, they gelled as a team. The two men remained on close terms subsequent to Fisher's retirement, although more on a personal than professional level.

For a person of Fisher's temperament, McKenna's supercession by Churchill presented something of a problem. However much he wanted to immediately assault his fellow 'Chatterer' with his plans for the future of the navy, he did not wish to offend or embarrass McKenna. His loyalty to the latter was never in question. Caught between the civilised, but rather prickly transfer of office between two politicians, both of whom he respected, Fisher tried to take himself out of the equation. In any case, far from cultivating recalcitrant roses in England, he had gone into a form of deliberate quiescence in Switzerland. Nevertheless, as soon as he realised that the Churchill/McKenna swap was a *fait accompli*, and in advance of the official announcement, he was immediately in touch with Churchill with recommendations as to which officers should be placed in the key positions for the development and the command of the service. For Fisher, the interests of the navy were paramount and transcended all other considerations. Churchill wasted no time in grabbing this opportunity, and, even before he had taken over the reins at the Admiralty, arranged an informal meeting – at which McKenna was also present – to discuss the most pressing naval concerns. From then on, they remained in regular and frequent communication. The period between 1912 and the outbreak of war in August 1914 can properly be termed the first phase of the Churchill/Fisher administration.

For so long as their relationship remained unofficial and informal it worked wonderfully well. Fisher spewed forth the lava of his knowledge and genius, and Churchill absorbed it all like a sponge. Everything of value was channelled into his administration of the navy, whilst the occasional impracticalities and personal aberrations were, in most cases, tactfully sidelined.

In many respects, it was almost a perfect arrangement. Fisher's best ideas could be translated into reality without any of the violent opposition that would inevitably have ensued had his name been associated with any particular project. Churchill could filter out the extreme personal prejudices that so obstructed and potentially devalued Fisher's initiatives. There was also the bonus that, being so pre-occupied with the constant stream of advice and exhortations that emanated from the old admiral, Churchill's attention was diverted away from possibly misguided initiatives of his own. This, obviously, was not always, or entirely, the case, but it certainly was a factor at this stage of their relationship. What is beyond dispute is that their collaboration in the two years preceding the outbreak of war was of profound benefit to the navy and the nation, and crucially affected its readiness and ability to meet the impending challenge.

Inevitably, given the strength of egos engaged, there were bound to be disagreements – hence the comment above that it was 'almost' a perfect arrangement. Old age was not mellowing Fisher; rather it was confirming him in his more extreme opinions and attitudes. When Churchill, without consulting him, approved the appointment of three admirals, all of whom were old Beresford supporters, to influential positions, Fisher instantly broke off all relations with the First Lord, accusing him of an unforgivable 'betrayal of the navy'. There followed a prolonged sulk, which was only terminated a month later when he was enticed from Switzerland to join the Admiralty yacht *Enchantress*, which was then visiting Naples en route to Malta. The Prime Minister, Asquith, was embarked, as was Lord Kitchener, then the Sirdar of Egypt. Also present were senior members of the Admiralty Board and, of course, Churchill, to whom the yacht had become his preferred means of transport in his visits to the fleet. In the midst of this exalted company, and after a fairly frigid beginning, the two men buried the hatchet and were soon once again gleefully discussing plans for the navy and for the confusion of its enemies.

This incident highlighted the difficulties that were increasingly apparent in any dealings with Fisher. If his wishes were thwarted in any way, no matter how trivial, there would be a major rupture. It was symptomatic of the problems that would arise when he once again became an *official* member of the Admiralty. Tantrums, sulks and prejudices can be catered for outside the corridors of power. Allowances can be made for age, temper, and eccentricity. Within the constrictions of those disciplined corridors, there is not the same freedom of action or expression. This, though, was in the future.

As a footnote to this tiff, it must be said that, of Churchill's three nominees for the positions that had so incensed Fisher, two were perfectly adequate. The third would come back to haunt him. Sir Archibald Berkeley Milne, a reasonably competent officer of little initiative, but a dandy and a court favourite, was appointed as Commander-in-Chief, Mediterranean Fleet. This post, the responsibilities for which Milne was not qualified, either by

HMS LION (1912)

Displacement: 26,350 tons
Dimensions: 700ft x 88ft x 28ft; Complement: 997
Armament: 8-13.5 inch guns; 16-4 inch guns;
Machinery: Quadruple Screw; Steam Turbines; 70,000 H.P. = 27 knots
Belt Armour: 9 inch max

The long-time flagship of the British battlecruiser forces, she was involved in all the major North Sea engagements, and was heavily damaged at both the Dogger Bank and Jutland. It was from her bridge that Admiral Beatty, having witnessed the blowing up of two of his other battlecruisers, made his famous comment, 'There seems to be something wrong with our bloody ships today'. Like all the British battlecruisers, she was an immensely impressive looking vessel whose offensive capabilities exceeded her ability to absorb punishment.

SMS SEYDLITZ (1913)

Displacement: 24,988 tons
Dimensions: 658ft x 94ft x 31ft; Complement: 1,108
Armament: 10-11 inch guns; 12-5.9 inch guns; 12-3.4 inch guns
Machinery: Quadruple Screw; Steam Turbines; 67,000 H.P. = 26.5 knots
Belt Armour: 11.75 inch max

The most heavily engaged of all the German battlecruisers during the war. As Hipper's flagship at the Dogger Bank action, she nearly blew up when a shell wiped out both her after turrets together with their entire crews of over 150 men. She was only saved by an act of individual heroism that enabled her after magazines to be flooded before the flames reached them. At Jutland she was reduced to a wreck by over 20 heavy shells plus a destroyer torpedo and would certainly have foundered had she not been close to home and in sheltered waters.

It was the horrific experience of *Seydlitz* at Dogger Bank that taught the Germans about the risk of flash fires in the ammunition chain. *Seydlitz* survived, the lessons were learned, and measures taken to deal with the problem. It was not until Jutland that the British were made fully aware of the danger, and, in their case, it involved the loss of three battlecruisers with nearly all hands. *Lion* herself would have shared their fate but for an individual action similar to that which had saved *Seydlitz* in the earlier engagement.

temperament or by any particular competence, he still occupied at the outbreak of war. Milne was not a dreadful officer, simply a dreadful choice for the most senior seagoing post in the navy excepting the Grand Fleet. On the other side of the coin, Churchill had readily acceded to Fisher's advice as to the future command of the Grand Fleet – the most important seagoing appointment in the navy, and pivotal to the prosecution of the war with Germany that Fisher was convinced would occur in late 1914. Fisher was exultant when it was decided that his protégé, Sir John Jellicoe, would be groomed for the role. Jellicoe, a most competent and conscientious officer, and a meticulous organiser, was earmarked for the appointment as Second-in-Command of the Home Fleet, which effectively meant that he was the heir apparent to the prime command of the British Navy.

Churchill also made another very significant appointment. At the beginning of his administration, a young rear admiral called David Beatty had requested an interview. Beatty had been unemployed for some time as a result of having turned down the position of Second-in-Command, Atlantic Fleet when he was first posted to flag rank. Refusal of such offers was almost unheard of, and did not commend itself to the establishment. Beatty had subsequently been 'beached' to presumably await compulsory retirement. This was not a cause to disturb many of his contemporaries who considered him too flashy by far and one who had risen too high and too fast. He had, in fact, been made the youngest admiral in the service since before the Napoleonic Wars – this as a result of accelerated promotion for exceptional leadership and gallantry, first in the Sudan and then in China during the Boxer rebellion. He had also married into money, had matinee idol good looks, and had a high profile in society. Inevitably, all this attracted a fair share of envy and resentment. At his interview with Churchill, the First Lord reportedly said to him that he 'looked rather young to be an admiral'. Beatty replied that Churchill 'looked rather young to be a First Lord'. (12)

Whatever the truth of this, Churchill immediately took Beatty on as his Naval Secretary, a post that had great background influence within the Admiralty, and was particularly concerned with the appointment and deployment of senior officers. Beatty so impressed Churchill that, when the plum appointment of commanding the battlecruiser force of the Grand Fleet was made vacant, the First Lord ensured that he was given the post – over the head of many more senior and more obvious candidates.[1] Thus Jellicoe and Beatty, the two great British fleet commanders of the First World War were in place when hostilities put the Royal Navy to the test of maintaining the command of the seas.

---

[1] The post of Naval Secretary to the First Lord had a traditional, and considerable, 'perk'. Having had an influential say on the appointments and postings of senior officers, the naval secretary was normally given considerable scope to choose his own next job when his tour of duty in the Admiralty was over. Whether Beatty used this unofficial privilege to advance his cause is unknown. What is more likely is that Churchill considered him ideal for the post, and Beatty avidly grasped the opportunity.

In these appointments, the First Sea Lord should have had a considerable say, but, in fact, he was scarcely consulted. The decisions were made whilst Sir Francis Bridgeman was pre-occupied in taking over from Sir Arthur Wilson, but it is indicative of the subordinate position that Churchill wished to impose on whoever was the incumbent First Sea Lord. This immediately became a problem, as Bridgeman, contrary to expectations, had absolutely no intention of seeing the prerogatives of his office usurped without a fight.

Sir Francis, although he was in general agreement with Churchill's overall programme, proved to be an obdurate protector of the First Sea Lord's position in the Admiralty hierarchy. Historians have generally dismissed him as a 'mediocre' officer who was out of his depth with politicians. In the sense that he lacked charisma, and had a very unsatisfactory year as Churchill's chosen First Sea Lord, that judgement is probably correct. For all that, Bridgeman was certainly nobody's fool. Nor was he prepared to submit to Churchill's constant niggling presence in matters that were more properly in the sphere of the Sea Lords. Arthur Marder has it about right in his comment that:

'Bridgeman did possess sound judgement and he might have made a moderately successful First Sea Lord had he served under anyone but Churchill. The two simply did not get along, the root trouble being Bridgeman's resentment against the First Lord's interference in everything.' (13)

The result was that there was an impasse. Their ideas as to the relative responsibilities of their offices did not coincide, and their personalities simply did not gel. The more Churchill intervened, the more Bridgeman obstructed. The more Churchill pushed, the deeper Bridgeman dug in his heels.

Within a year, it was clear that the situation had become impossible, and Churchill resolved to rid himself of yet another First Sea Lord. Bridgeman had suffered some health problems, and had inadvisably made some remarks as to the strains imposed upon him by his office. Churchill, on hearing of this, leapt on these hostages to fortune and used them to bulldoze Bridgeman into retirement. This campaign was not carried out with any degree of subtlety. Within the navy it caused considerable offence and was an undoubted setback to the process of his acceptance by the service – which had been making some headway. Politically, it was to cause him considerable discomfort.

The outrage amongst many senior officers as to Bridgeman's summary treatment, coming so soon after the similar dismissal of Sir Arthur Wilson, spilt over into the political arena and there was a subsequent storm in parliament. Churchill was called to account in the House of Commons and given a severe grilling as to his actions and motives. Several of his many enemies used the occasion to attack other aspects of his style of administration, particularly his tendency to interfere in professional matters.

It was perfectly obvious to everyone with any knowledge of the situation that Churchill, to use a recent phrase, was being 'economical with the truth' in his reasons for compelling Bridgeman to retire. For all that, Churchill got his way and survived the inevitable backlash, albeit not without further besmirching his reputation. Bridgeman was replaced by the Second Sea Lord, His Serene Highness Prince Louis of Battenberg (of whom more later), and this arrangement certainly worked to more harmonious effect. Battenberg was a very able officer, but (possibly with the recent fates of Wilson and Bridgeman in mind) did not obstruct Churchill, and was happy to take something of a back seat in their professional relationship.

A final comment on Bridgeman would only be fair. He was a small stroke of the brush on the canvas of events, but, if he was not outstanding and something of a grey personality compared to the likes of Fisher and Wilson, his contribution to the navy should not be overlooked. All the major decisions of 1912 could not have been translated into effect without his support. He may not have been the driving force behind the policy, and his working relationship with Churchill, as previously mentioned, was a disaster, but his active opposition would have seriously impeded, if not damned, the process. It was fortunate, in the circumstances that he was in agreement with much of what Churchill hoped to achieve. If Bridgeman can be termed a failure as First Sea Lord, it was mainly because, by training and inclination, he was unable to reconcile himself to Churchill's methods – particularly to the arrogant usurpation of what had been previously accepted to be the First Sea Lord's prerogatives of initiative. Many of the justifiably praised achievements of Churchill's regime at the Admiralty cannot be disassociated from Bridgeman's contribution to the process.

In all reality, none of Churchill's First Sea Lords ever had a chance of being a success in that role. Fisher was the only naval expert that Churchill treated with any reverence. So long as the old admiral remained his mentor, all the initiatives for the navy came from that direction. The Sea Lords, at this time, were merely functionaries in the translation of these ideas into practical realisation. If this arrangement was not exactly correct, the results produced were startlingly effective.

What was really impressive about this informal collaboration was the rapidity with which crucial decisions were made and then translated immediately into practical effect. It was a characteristic of everything both Churchill and Fisher did as individuals that decisions and actions took place quickly. When both were focussed on the same object, things happened very quickly indeed. By the spring of 1912, at which time Churchill had been in office for a mere six months, some of the most important developments affecting the future shape of the navy had been initiated and the measures to implement the process were already in train.

The first priority that confronted Churchill was to establish a Naval Staff. This was, after all, the prime reason that he had been installed in place of McKenna, and why Sir Arthur Wilson had been ousted as First Sea Lord. The establishment of a staff organisation duly took place, but, considering the contentious circumstances of its creation, the measure caused surprisingly little stir – mainly, probably, because Bridgeman was already a confirmed supporter of the process. The initial effects of this development on the running of the navy were actually rather insubstantial. Churchill himself acknowledged that it would take a generation of training before real benefits were reaped from the system. In the meantime, the staff came into existence as another level of the Admiralty strata, acting in an advisory capacity and capable of exerting considerable influence, but possessing limited executive authority.

As will be seen, when faced with the demands of war, the infant system proved inadequate for the purposes of its creation. Only after three years of conflict, in 1917, was the matter resolved to any degree of satisfaction, when the First Sea Lord himself became also the Chief of the Naval Staff – which immediately gave the organisation the executive clout it had previously lacked. This matter was one in which Fisher had no influence – indeed, the whole concept was anathema to him. In all the other matters that Churchill so readily addressed, his input was crucial, and his involvement pivotal to most of the major decisions made as to the materiel and structure of the Royal Navy. This was immediately apparent when the designs and armament of new battleships for the navy came to be considered.

When the German Navy had increased the size of its battleship guns from the well tried 11-inch guns to a new 12-inch weapon, the British had already anticipated the situation. Under Fisher's auspices there had been introduced into service for the latest British designs, a highly successful 13.5-inch gun. This more than adequately preserved the British advantage in weight of shell. If only Germany needed to be taken into consideration, there the matter might have rested for a while, but developments elsewhere in the world caused the Admiralty to re-assess the situation.

The expansion of the German Navy was the immediate pressing concern, but Britain, as a world empire totally dependent on naval supremacy, had also to consider long-term requirements outside the narrow confines of the North Sea. Both the Japanese and the Americans were adopting 14-inch guns for their new classes of capital ship, and it was felt that Britain could not fall behind in this respect. Churchill was particularly concerned about the situation, and felt that 'we should go one better'. On appraising Fisher of the problem he found the admiral, not surprisingly, vehemently in favour of developing the larger gun. This decided the matter. Consequently, the design and production of an experimental 15-inch gun was commenced.

There were problems involved here, as the guns to arm battleships frequently took longer to produce than the ships themselves and the new class of British dreadnoughts authorised in the naval estimates was already in an advanced stage of planning. If it was desired to mount this weapon on the new ships, it would be in the knowledge that there would be no time for the normal testing and proving procedures for the gun to take place. It was something, therefore, of a leap in the dark. However, fortified by the confidence of the manufacturers – and of the Third Sea Lord, who had particular responsibility in this area, the leap was taken. It was a gamble that turned out to be the most extraordinary success. The British 15-inch gun proved to be probably the best and most reliable capital ship weapon ever produced.

The adoption of the bigger gun was not simply a huge advance in capability. It also opened up the prospect for a radical advancement in battleship design. In terms of weight of shell the 15-inch weapon fired a projectile of 1,920 pounds as compared to the 1,400 pounds of the latest version of the British 13.5-inch, or foreign 14-inch gun. There were also other benefits, including the technical fact that the larger the shell, the greater would be the accuracy at long range, and that the new gun could outrange anything in existence. By simple mathematics alone, eight of the larger guns, in four twin turrets, had a hitting power and potential accuracy superior to the ten in five of the smaller ones.

From this fact came a singular conclusion. The new ships could discard the amidships turret of the ten-gun design and utilise the saved weight and space to provide an enormously increased propulsion plant. This opened up the prospect of being able to produce a battleship that possessed a speed bordering on that of the early battlecruisers, and far superior to that of any contemporary design. The horsepower, in fact, was tripled to 75,000 and it was hoped that this increase would produce 25 knots in the new ships. The result would be a squadron of battleships that could act as a fast wing of the fleet and it opened up exciting tactical possibilities for any commander possessing such ships. Once again Fisher's influence was an important factor in the decision. A combination of speed and the heaviest guns was his ideal of a capital ship.

The third innovation in the design was probably the most radical and far reaching of all. It was decided that the vessels should be powered entirely by oil fuel. Arthur Marder regarded it as 'the most vital decision Churchill made'. Previously, all major British warships had been predominately coal-fired ships. Oil, though, had considerable advantages over coal. It was much more efficient and economical as a fuel and obviated the necessity for large numbers of stokers to feed the boilers. This considerably reduced the manpower required to complement the ship. Fewer personnel meant that more weight, supplies, and space could be devoted to other priorities in the design of a particular ship. An oil-fired system also meant that maximum speed could be maintained indefinitely, rather than being dependent on the stamina of hard pressed stokers. Given proper facilities it was also much easier to embark than coal.[2]

Oil could be embarked much more rapidly than coal by simply connecting up a number of hoses from the receiving ship to a tanker or a fuel jetty, and it could be done without the human stress or the plague of the all-pervading coal dust. If efficiency were the only criterion, then the choice of fuel would seem to have been obvious. However, there were two compelling arguments, one from a purely British point of view, the other from constructional considerations that tended to militate against this change.

Coal, in abundance, could be supplied from the mines in the valleys of South Wales. In terms of quality, it was the finest steaming coal in the world, and came from an absolutely secure source. Oil, if it were to be decided upon, would have to be imported from unstable nations outside the empire, and its availability would be subject to a long and potentially hazardous period of transit over many thousands of sea miles. There was also the secondary consideration that the coal bunkers of a ship contributed to the overall protection of its design. Oil fuel was normally carried in tanks within the double bottom, whereas coal was stowed in compartments on either side of the ship on or about the waterline area. As such it provided an extra layer of protective insulation to the vitals of a warship. If the change in fuel was to be adopted, ship design would also have to be adapted to reflect this factor. This latter consideration could eventually be dealt with by the naval architects in the department of the Director of Naval Construction. The problem of obtaining a guaranteed source, and secure supply, of oil was a different matter altogether.

If the mechanics of design and construction involved in changing from coal to oil were not too demanding, the geo-political ramifications were a very real concern that needed a great deal of thought and

---

[2] Looking back on all the memoirs of that era, one consistent emotion emerges, and that is of utter detestation towards the process of coaling ship. From the highest to the lowest, there was a common loathing attached to this unfortunate but unavoidable procedure. It was filthy debilitating work and took the ship itself out of action for a day at a time, whilst exhausting, if not incapacitating, its crew. Cleaning the ship, and their own bodies, afterwards took the crew almost as long as the actual coaling evolution. When compared to this recurring nightmare, the prospect of something better, easier and cleaner must have sounded a chord in the heart of every person in the navy.

organisation. To address the matter, Churchill appointed a committee which had a sweeping remit to examine all aspects of the question. Its recommendations, if adopted, would have a significant impact on the shaping of policy – not just naval policy, but also foreign policy. The importance placed on these deliberations enabled Churchill to entice Fisher out of retirement to become chairman of the committee. He did not need much tempting. It was a subject close to his heart. All his famed, and undiminished, drive and enthusiasm was brought to bear on the task.

However it was described, this was not a forum constituted to discuss whether or not oil should be adopted as the future fuel for all major British warships. That essential decision had already been made at the highest level. The prime purpose of the committee was to investigate the ways and means of realising this end. By the summer of 1913, Fisher's committee had delivered the bulk of its conclusions and Churchill was able to announce in parliament that, henceforth, oil would be the prime source of propulsive fuel for all classes of warship in the Royal Navy.

Apart from the obvious effect that this development would have on future generations of warships, perhaps the most significant consequence that emanated from Fisher's recommendations was the decision of the government to purchase a controlling interest in the Anglo-Persian Oil Company. Excepting the vast oil concerns within the United States, this organisation was then the most important developer of oil resources in the rest of the world, and, just as Welsh coal had been, the quality of the oil extracted from that region was ideal for shipboard use. From that moment on, the umbilical cord of the British Fleet would reach to Basra and Bushire rather than to South Wales and the Tyne/Tees region. From the purely logistical point of view, it was a huge decision to make. For all that, the political ramifications were even more significant. Henceforth, Britain would also become inevitably and inextricably involved in the political affairs of the Persian Gulf, in particular, and the Middle East in general.

Previous to this point, the only practical interests Britain had had in this area were with regard to the suppression of piracy and the slave trade. There had also been an underlying geo-political imperative for at least a token British presence in order to deter Russian ambitions in the area (the hypothetical threat of Russia obtaining use of a warm water port on the flank of British lines of communication to India was taken very seriously by the Foreign Office). From 1914 onwards, the fractious and murderous affairs of the nations and tribes of the Arabian peninsular and the peripheral Gulf states would become a matter of profound importance to every succeeding British Government. Over ninety years have passed since then and *plus ça change,* but this is a digression. The material consequences to the Royal Navy of the change to oil fuel and the introduction of faster battleships filtered down to every other class of warship.

When the *Dreadnought* had arrived on the scene in 1906, with a speed of 21 knots, she made obsolete not only her lesser-armed predecessors, but also the entire force utilised to scout for, and screen, a battle fleet. Cruisers needed a good 5-knot superiority over the battleships to carry out their prescribed purpose. Destroyers required a margin of speed over the cruisers for the same reason. The classes of ship built subsequent to *Dreadnought* reflect exactly this tactical requirement – 25/26-knot cruisers and 30-knot destroyers.

The introduction of battlecruisers into the equation had posted a problem. These huge and impressive vessels were intended, in one of their primary roles, to screen and scout for the battle fleet. The earliest, and slowest, examples of their type were capable of well over 25 knots. Subsequent classes became ever faster. However, they had become so large, so expensive and so important an asset as to themselves acquire the status of capital ships. Hence they required their own high-speed screen. Nothing had been done to provide this facility, and, in any sort of a seaway, a battlecruiser squadron of 1911 would have had to apply the brakes in order to allow its supposed screen of the most modern cruisers and destroyers to catch up. This problem had not been properly addressed. The introduction of a new design of ship, in the shape of the fast battleships that became known as the *Queen Elizabeth* class, brought matters to a head.

New classes of cruisers and destroyers were authorised to reflect the future requirements of the navy. Churchill became particularly and enthusiastically involved in the production of a new type of small cruiser, designed primarily for fleet work. The ships that resulted proved to be remarkably successful. After a first batch of eight *Arethusa* class light cruisers, a further twenty-eight vessels, of progressively increased capability, were produced. All the later ships were given names beginning with the letter 'C', and, not surprisingly, it is as the 'C'-class that the whole generic type came to be known. From the second year of the Great War to the mid 1930s, they formed the backbone of the British Fleet cruiser force and it was a measure of their utility that thirteen survived to participate with distinction in the Second World War. (The intensity of their continued employment was reflected in the fact, and manner, that six were lost in that conflict – one to air attack in the fjords during the ill-fated Norway campaign; four to bombs and torpedoes in the cauldron of the Mediterranean; the last, *HMS Curacao*, tragically run down by the *RMS Queen Mary* whilst escorting the great liner on a transatlantic trooping run.) When, in 1939, after his years in the political wilderness, Churchill returned as First Lord, he must have seen these ships, the fruits of his labours a quarter of a century previously, as old friends.[3]

---

[3] A representative of this class exists to this day. Decommissioned in 1924 to become a R.N.V.R. drill ship, *HMS Caroline*, still sound in body and instantly recognisable for what she was, continues to serve this role in Belfast. As such, she is the last remaining survivor of the Battle of Jutland.

Admiral Sir Francis Bridgeman
A fine sailor, with the full confidence of the service afloat.

Parallel to the development of the new cruiser type, an extensive construction programme of larger and faster destroyers was instituted. Capable of 34-35 knots, they maintained the margin of speed superiority for their type required by the corresponding increase in the speeds of the larger units of the fleet. Nearly a hundred of these vessels were eventually produced and they formed the core of the Grand Fleet's flotilla force for most of the Great War.

If developments in the composition of the battle fleet were the most obvious manifestations of Churchill's period at the Admiralty, they were not, by any means, the whole of the story. Every department felt the weight of his influence and significant attention was paid to the development of materiel both above and below the sea.

The growing potential of the submarine as a weapon of war was very apparent to the First Lord. Were he in any doubt of this, Fisher was constantly reminding him of the fact and berating him for not accelerating the production of these craft for the Royal Navy. Churchill, in fact (and in common with almost every other naval expert or politician of the day) saw submarines simply as being a great future influence on naval operations. He (and they) was not, however, able to foresee what Fisher had discerned years earlier – that the submarine was destined to become the commerce raider *par excellence.* Fisher's prediction had been universally condemned as unrealistic on three counts. Submarines were, firstly, very vulnerable on the surface. Secondly, they did not possess the crew numbers or the sea boats to board, examine, and take possession of merchant vessels. Lastly, they had no space to accommodate prisoners. Fisher disputed none of these facts, but, alone amongst his peers, he took the argument a logical stage forward from the thinking of a previous era. The very limitations of a submarine, he argued, made it certain that in most cases it would have to sink, rather than capture its prey. For reasons of self-preservation, this would have to be done without warning and any survivors would have to fend for themselves. Considerable loss of civilian life was, in the circumstances, inevitable. He further argued that, if a warring nation had no prospect of disputing the command of the seas on the surface, then it would have to resort to these methods.

These views were regarded with horror and disbelief at the time. It may seem naïve nowadays, when we have sadly become, to some extent, inured to the many atrocities that have subsequently been committed in the prosecution of wars, but it was a genuine reflection of the attitudes of that age that such behaviour was considered unthinkable. It was sincerely held that no civilised nation would ever contemplate such barbaric measures. Nevertheless, Fisher's prediction almost exactly described the state of affairs once Germany first declared unrestricted submarine warfare in 1915. As history has shown it became a (if not *the*) critical factor in the resolution of both the great wars of the twentieth century.

For the British Navy, submarines only had significance as weapons of defence or offence against the military forces of an opponent. They had no application with regard to trade. During hostilities, enemy commerce would be swept from the seas by the surface fleet in the time-honoured manner. Submarines did, however, possess qualities that were ideally suited to the prosecution of war against continental nations such as Germany. Offensively, they could impose a close blockade on the military ports of an opponent; defensively, they could provide a potent deterrent to surface raids on British ports. It was in providing for these tasks that Fisher continuously implored Churchill to speed up the construction of submarines. Had he been able, Churchill would probably have complied, but he was hamstrung by the necessity to use most of his authorised finance in providing for battleships and battlecruisers to meet the German construction programmes. In this respect, Britain, although to a less drastic extent, was having to follow the same path as Germany.

Tirpitz had staked all on a viable, short-range, battle fleet. Into that flowed the great bulk of available funds. In quantity and quality, all other classes of vessels were subordinated to this prime requirement and compromises had to be made in their designs and capabilities. This was particularly evident in the cruisers constructed for the High Seas Fleet. Designed as 'all rounders' to be capable of operating with the battle squadrons and also to act on the trade routes, they fell between two stools. Whilst being splendid ships they could never be exceptionally good in either role. It is also a notable irony that, Tirpitz, for most of his career, had a very poor opinion of the potential offered by submarines, and begrudged any funds allocated to their development – which might otherwise be more usefully employed in advancing his battleship programme. It was only in the second year of war, when his star was on the wane, and his battleships rotting round their anchors in Wilhelmshaven, that he eventually saw the light on the Damascus road, and became the complete convert to unrestricted submarine warfare.

By 1912, the British naval estimates had become so high, and so politically contentious, that similar constraints to those imposed on Tirpitz were necessary to preserve the core of the overall programme. However much Churchill might have wanted to raise funds for accelerated development of the submarine service, this was, in the financial climate of the time, simply unaffordable.

The same conditions applied to naval aviation. In 1911, the navy possessed just two aeroplanes, and its single airship, rather pessimistically, but presciently, named the *Mayfly,* had been wrecked on the ground without ever making a flight. Nevertheless, the enormous potential of both airships and aircraft to affect the conditions of naval warfare was beginning to be realised. In most naval circles, this potential seemed to be confined to the surveillance and reconnaissance advantages that accrued from the possession of flying machines. Only a few, far-seeing, officers (Fisher, unsurprisingly, was one) fully discerned the long-term possibilities of air power – namely the fact that, as aircraft inevitably and rapidly developed in capability, they could be deployed both in a strike and defence capacity. As such they stood to revolutionise naval warfare rather than being just a useful adjunct to its prosecution by traditional means.

In 1912, this insight into the future was granted only to a few visionaries and, within the establishment, the use of airships and/or seaborne aircraft was primarily focussed on their ability to extend the vision of the battle fleet. This was not limited purely to reconnaissance duties as it was recognised that, if suitable communication links could be provided, aircraft could also 'spot' for the fleet – i.e. they could observe the fall of shot on an opponent and, therefore, aid gunnery accuracy in conditions of poor visibility. This applied not just to fleet actions, for the facility obviously could be also utilised for the purposes of shore bombardment.

For the British naval establishment it was clear that some form of air capability needed to be developed. The problem was that it was not simply a matter of deciding on the relative virtues of airships and seaplanes to fulfil individual tasks and then produce numbers of both to fit into specific staff requirements. Budget constraints dictated that funds could not be made available for both lines of development and there could be no 'Rolls-Royce' solution on the 'and/or' basis. The 'and' was financially impossible, and it had to be a choice between one 'or' the other. With the benefit of many years of hindsight, the decision seems easy, but, in the particular conditions of the time, it was actually far from being straightforward.

The concept of the aircraft carrier, able to act as a mobile floating airfield, was still some years short of realisation. In the meantime, the level of development that had been reached by the air*ship* and the sea*plane* had progressed to the point that both had established themselves as concepts capable of practical military application.

The airship, as conceived and developed by Count Zeppelin in Friedrichshaven, was very much as its name suggested, a small vessel and its crew transported into the air – the means of elevation being a huge balloon filled with a gas lighter than air. Within the envelope provided by the balloon could be carried stores, water and the fuel to supply whatever engines were fitted to propel the craft. These latter, together with control surfaces and the 'gondola', containing the crew and equipment, were suspended on the undersides of the colossal gasbag that kept it in the air. By its very nature, it was a huge and cumbersome structure that was extremely difficult to control on the ground during the process of getting it ready for flight or recovery. This could only be done within strict weather parameters. Once in the air, however, it truly merited the description of 'airship'. It was much faster than a warship, had long endurance, an acceptable level of accommodation for the crew, and the space to fit whatever equipment and personnel were required for specific tasks. The pilots could concentrate on handling the craft whilst navigators, communicators, and spotters carried on, undisturbed and undistracted, with their duties. Wireless contact with surface warships could be maintained at ranges far exceeding that possible on a ship to ship basis. In perfect visibility conditions, one of them could, in theory, see and report everything that moved on the surface of the sea within a seventy-mile radius. Once airborne, and on station, their endurance enabled them to provide this coverage for an extended patrol period, and sufficient staff were carried to enable a watch system to be maintained for the duration of the operation.

If the launch and recovery of an airship posed problems, the same was also true of the early seaplanes. They had to be lowered into the sea by means of a crane on the parent ship and then hoisted back on board at the end of the flight. Obviously, for such frail machines, this procedure could only be attempted when sea conditions were ideal, and this limitation was equally relevant to the act of take off and landing. In 1912, the first experiments were being made in launching aircraft from makeshift platforms installed on the foredeck of warships. The results were promising but these had yet to be translated into practical operational application.

Early aircraft were also very limited in their range and endurance, and were much inferior to airships in this respect. They also had the serious disadvantage of having but a single pilot to carry out all the duties that were, in an airship, spread amongst a large crew. Thus, in addition to physically flying the aircraft, the pilot also had to be his own navigator, wireless operator and spotter. Obviously, he could not carry out these tasks with the same degree of efficiency that could be maintained (and for much longer) by the specialist staff carried on the airship. On the other hand, aircraft, in addition to being far cheaper per unit, were faster and much more manoeuvrable than airships and there was a vast scope for future development of the type. By contrast, there was not the same potential for improvements in airship design. The concept was capable of further sophistication but there could be no quantum leaps in performance comparable to those that eventually took place in aircraft design.

A lengthy, and lively, controversy arose concerning the relative virtues of the two types. The two schools of advocates came to be classified as 'Heavier than Air' and 'Lighter than Air' men. This debate had been going on for some time before Churchill arrived at the Admiralty. He immediately entered the fray.

'In keeping with his character, he did not confine himself to exhortation from behind a desk. He took to the air as often as possible, and endeared himself to his instructors by his zeal and unexpected humility as a pupil.

'But the instructors were "frightened stiff of having a smashed First Lord on our hands", and he was passed on from one to another because no one was prepared to take the responsibility of sending him up solo. Although he did many hours of dual instruction and flew over 140 times, he was unable to take his certificate before family pressure forced him to give up this dangerous pursuit.' (14)

Although he later tried to distance himself from this view, Churchill was initially on the side of the 'Lighter than Air' (i.e. airship) men. By that time, however, the argument had almost been decided in favour of the aircraft. The disaster to the *Mayfly*, caused by structural weaknesses in her design rather than any fault in the concept, had resulted in a board of enquiry, the conclusions of which came down heavily against further development of the type. This view had the formidable support of Sir Arthur Wilson, who was then still the First Sea Lord. The question seemed to have been settled on the 25th January 1912 when, during a meeting at the Admiralty, the decision was made to discontinue airship production and concentrate on the development of aircraft.

There the matter might have rested had anyone other than Churchill been First Lord. Reinforced by eyewitness reports from, among others, Sir John Jellicoe, on the success of the German Zeppelin programme, Churchill managed to have the argument resuscitated a few months later. It rumbled on into 1913, and, eventually, the original decision was rescinded and the Admiralty given the authority to resume a very limited programme of airship construction. By that time, however, Britain was hopelessly behind Germany in airship development and none of these craft were available to the Admiralty when war broke out in 1914. In stark contrast, by then, the German Navy had at its disposal a highly efficient fleet of Zeppelins, able to provide advanced reconnaissance and direction at ranges far exceeding those available to the British. That this facility was not used to greater effect is due to the infrequency and temerity of their employment rather than to any lack of capability.

The main result of this whole saga was that British resources were concentrated on advancing the development of aircraft. Whilst, by mid 1914, this had not resulted in a facility comparable to that provided by the German Zeppelins, there was a rapidly dawning realisation of the immense and varied potential offered by future advances in aircraft technology. With this realisation came a sense of urgency in finding better ways and means of operating aircraft from seagoing platforms.

As mentioned earlier, the first experimental steps had been taken to investigate the possibility of launching seaplanes from a specially constructed ramp on the foredeck of a ship. These trials, on the pre-Dreadnought *HMS London*, had proved successful, and, in theory, provided a much better solution to the problems of launching the machine. The outbreak of war gave added impetus to this line of development, and, during Churchill's time as First Lord, a number of fast, cross-channel ferries were commandeered by the Admiralty for conversion into seaplane carriers. They incorporated the launching ramp together with a hangar for seaplanes on the foredeck. On the aft section of the ships was a second hangar and a lifting crane. Thus, although seaplanes could be launched directly from the vessels, recovery still depended on them landing in the sea and then being hoisted inboard. It was, though, a considerable improvement on previous practice, and the option existed, provided the seaplane had sufficient endurance, for it to divert to the coast if sea conditions made landing dangerous. Otherwise, as before, the machine would be forced to ditch next to a convenient warship. So long as seaplanes, rather than conventional aeroplanes, were operated, it was impossible to surmount this difficulty. While a seaplane could be launched from a trolley, its floats prevented it from landing anywhere other than in the water.

The complete answer was, of course, to be found in the aircraft carrier, and the first proposal on these lines was made as early as January 1913. Interestingly enough, this came, not from the visionaries such as Fisher or Churchill, but from the august pen of Sir Arthur Wilson. Although by then retired from the navy, he remained a member of the Committee for Imperial Defence (CID), and, in a paper arguing against airships, he suggested an old cruiser be converted so that normal aircraft, as opposed to seaplanes, could both take off and land on the vessel. His proposal was not for an aircraft carrier as it would now be recognised – i.e. with a continuous flight deck – but one with the existing type of launching ramp forward, and an additional landing deck aft – this latter area to be provided by removing the mainmast and after superstructure, and hinging the after funnel. Cranes would transfer aircraft from aft to forward around the remaining superstructure and funnels. It is almost certain that this idea would have been unworkable as an almost identical configuration was tried, in 1918, on the converted light battlecruiser *Furious*, a very much larger vessel than that suggested by Wilson. It proved a failure as the air turbulence created by the residual superstructure made the process of landing extremely hazardous. Nevertheless, in Wilson's proposal can be discerned the genesis of the modern aircraft carrier.

All in all, Churchill's arrival at the Admiralty coincided with a great upsurge of interest in naval aviation coupled with rapid advances in technology. His wholehearted involvement in these developments gave further impetus to the process, and, when Battenberg relieved Bridgeman, in 1913, he had an equally enthusiastic ally in the new First Sea Lord. The results were dramatic. By the outbreak of war, nearly a hundred seaplanes and conventional aircraft, manned by well-trained pilots, were operated by the newly formed Royal Naval Air Service. Subsequent development continued unabated.

'The Royal Naval Air Service, when it was absorbed into the Royal Air Force in 1918 was the largest and most efficient air force in the world. By his active encouragement and forthright methods Churchill cut red tape, dispelled mistrust and helped to produce miracles. He must be credited with a considerable share in a remarkable achievement.' (15)

It is one of the tragedies of British military history that, from this position of acknowledged world leadership, the formation of the RAF resulted in naval aviation becoming the poor relation in Britain's overall air strategy. The result was a period of stagnation between the wars, during which the RAF concentrated limited resources on its own priorities, and seaborne air power became very much the poor relation both in numbers and in quality of aircraft. By the time the Royal Navy belatedly regained control of its own air arm, in 1938, it had completely lost its predominance in maritime air power and had fallen well behind the navies of the United States and Japan, both qualitatively and quantitatively. The Second World War commenced long before this situation could be redressed, and there was then a bitter price to pay in lost ships, aircraft, and far too many lives, before the situation could be redressed – largely through the loan of American built and designed aircraft.

The improvements in materiel during Churchill's tenure at the Admiralty received most of the publicity. Less spectacular, but of great importance, were the personnel reforms that were also instituted at that time.

When Fisher, as Second Sea Lord, pushed through the 'Selbourne Scheme', which dealt with the training and career structure of naval officers, it was only the first stage of what he intended to be a much more sweeping programme that would affect the entire service. For one reason or another, chiefly lack of time, this had not materialised by the time he left office. With Churchill installed as First Lord, the subject received a new airing. Even had he not had Fisher to encourage him, Churchill would undoubtedly have fought for change in the conditions of service for the lower deck. He was always very concerned for the welfare of what was termed the 'working man', and this involvement went much deeper than just the cynical self-interest of a professional politician protecting his constituency vote. Both Churchill and Fisher had a strong socialist streak in their make up.

In 1911, discontent on the lower deck was becoming a real problem. In almost every aspect of his life, the naval rating was significantly disadvantaged compared to his civilian counterpart. Following the army reforms instituted by Haldane, his conditions of service had even fallen behind those of the soldiery.

Naval pay had not been substantively increased for sixty years and, although inflation in those days was low, each year that passed found the naval rating relatively worse off. This unpalatable fact was impressed upon him every time he went home on long leave and had to confront an increased cost of living. It was exacerbated by contact with civilian workers whose interests were being promoted by the rapidly increasing power and influence of trades unions. Even on duty, no sailor was immune from this influence, as, every time his ship was docked for refit or repair, he was given first-hand evidence of a new militant mood amongst the workforce of the nation. Shipyard and dockyard workers were in the forefront of the trades union movement. Strikes, and obstructive work practices, adopted to enforce long-overdue improvements in their conditions of employment, were not only being carried out on the quay where the ship was berthed, but by groups of dockyard workers making modifications within the ship itself. The results were curious but instructive.

Instead of allying themselves with the trades unionists, most sailors generally regarded the dockyard workers, and their practices, with contempt. The term 'Dockyard Matey' was, and remains, an indication of the sailor's disgust at the venality and laziness of what they considered to be an overpaid, idle, inept and fractious branch of mankind that made a careless filth of every ship on which they worked. The problem was that these turbulent people were achieving improvements in their quality of life, whereas the loyal, disciplined, servicemen were not. Virtue and restraint were receiving no reward, whereas irresponsible militancy clearly was.

A serviceman had no recourse to a trade union in order to improve his lot in life and he was entirely dependent on the Board of Admiralty or the War Office to recognise and properly serve his interests. It was a source of growing resentment to naval ratings that these interests were being consistently ignored. It was not just pay that was the problem. The standards of accommodation, and the conditions of leave, recreational facilities, discipline and career advancement had received no attention for many years. The War Office had managed to do something for the soldiers; the Admiralty had done nothing for the sailors.

Although the various types of ships in which naval personnel served had progressively increased in size and sophistication, this was not reflected by any improvement in accommodation – rather, it had deteriorated. Increasingly, the living quarters on warships were being squeezed into whatever spaces were left after the paramount considerations of armour, armament, increased sub-division, and machinery had been incorporated in the design. They were, consequently, cramped, claustrophobic, and poorly ventilated. For off-watch sailors, relief from these conditions afforded by access to the upper deck was also no longer as attractive as it had been in the past. Most of the fleet had been concentrated in home waters to meet the German challenge, and the weather conditions around the British Isles for much of the year were less conducive to open-air recreation than was the case in, say, the Mediterranean, or on other foreign stations.

With regard to leave, and access to his family, the sailor was a poor relation compared to his army counterpart. An off duty soldier could walk out of his barracks into the surrounding town every evening. If he was married, it was likely that his family would be domiciled in that town. This state of affairs also applied to seamen when their ship was docked in its home port, but, for long periods, the squadrons in which he served were deployed elsewhere, either on seagoing duties and exercises, or at anchor at remote bases around the coast of the British Isles. The sheer numbers of vessels now concentrated in home waters meant that there was insufficient space in the established dockyard ports to accommodate them all. New dockyard facilities had been planned and approved, most notably at Rosyth, but development was proceeding at a snail's pace. Once again, funds could not be spared to accelerate the process without affecting the battleship programme. The effect of this shortcoming was that many sailors had only a very limited opportunity for shore leave. An Admiralty memorandum submitted by Churchill in late 1912 summed up the problem thus:

'The life of the bluejacket and stoker in our finest ships of war is one of pitiable discomfort, which cannot, while the present competition in armaments continues and the present types of warship construction prevail, be effectually alleviated…As a rule, half the fleet have to lie at Portland or Harwich, and the men have to travel to their homes at their own expense. As regards short leave, when the ships in the course of cruising visit frequented ports, there are nearly always great difficulties in getting the men to and from the shore…and when a man does get on shore in a strange port in Home Waters, there is hardly anything for him to do except loaf around and spend his money…For long periods at a time the ships are at sea or off unfrequented places carrying out gunnery practices or manoeuvres, and then the sailors, when their work is done, have nothing to do in their leisure but potter about the crowded decks under constant supervision.

'If these conditions be compared with life in the Army in time of peace, the contrast is very great. A soldier has a comfortable barrack room and recreation room and ground; he can smoke, read or play billiards in comfort while off duty. In the ordinary routine he has practically all his afternoons free. He can make his home near his place of duty with certainty that he will not be ordered away to the other end of the kingdom at a moments notice. Service ashore is looked upon as the greatest luxury in a sailor's life: it is the ordinary experience and routine of the soldier.' (16)

Despite better conditions of service, the soldier was also paid more than the sailor. Army pay had been significantly increased during and after the Boer War. As the memorandum continued:

'No corresponding increase was, however, made in the pay of the Navy, and in consequence their position in relation to the soldier has been substantially impaired...This deterioration of the sailors relative position has synchronised with the increased severity and discomfort of the naval service afloat and the rise in the cost of living ashore.

'In consequence...there is a deep and widespread sense of injustice and discontent throughout all ranks and ratings of the Navy.' (17)

Whilst pay, leave and living conditions were probably the biggest bones of contention, the adherence of the navy to an old-fashioned, draconian, and often illogical, concept of discipline also caused much anger.

There was also the fact that, in an era of ever increasing complexity in the technology of naval warfare, the chances of promotion for a much more educated workforce had not significantly improved from those of Victorian times. Once a rating, by dint of ability, experience and character, had reached the level of Chief Petty Officer, there were very limited opportunities for further advancement. Admittedly, a 'Chief' who had attained warrant rank could eventually achieve a commission, which gave him the professional (although certainly not, then, the social) status of a junior officer. This stage, though, was not reached until late in the man's career, and, at best, the highest he could expect to ascend up the ladder was to reach the rank of lieutenant. For many senior ratings, the change, from being at the top of the lower deck tree to the permanent bottom of the officer pond, held few attractions.

Aggravating the whole situation was the fact that sailors were recruited into the service when they had only just reached the age of thirteen. At that point in their life, they were required to sign on for fifteen years employment. This was an iniquitous system by which immature boys, sometimes encouraged by their parents, were inveigled into a binding contract at an age when they were incapable of understanding the consequences of their commitment. Exposed to the conditions of service mentioned above, it is hardly surprising that a great many chose to leave the navy, for the greener fields of civilian life, at the first available opportunity. Consequently, the navy underwent a haemorrhaging of personnel in their late twenties – just at the point when a combination of youth, training and experience meant that these ratings were reaching the period of their greatest potential. In the rapidly expanding fleet of the last pre-war years, this annual loss of trained personnel was an intolerable drain on a service that actually needed to increase its manpower.

Churchill attacked the problem with his customary energy. In all but the matter of pay, he was able to address the situation within the existing structure of the navy, although some areas were obviously more difficult to tackle than others. It was, for instance, out of the question to alter the living conditions on ships already completed or in building. It was, however, possible to ensure that greater attention was given to this matter when the designs of new classes of ships came to be considered.

A real improvement was made in the career prospects for ratings. Increased opportunities for promotion to officer rank were provided, and these were not limited to the most senior warrant officers, as had been the case in the past. A radical (for the time) scheme was introduced to select promising young senior ratings for officer training – what would nowadays be termed 'fast tracking'. The successful candidates from this scheme were young enough to join the career ladder only a few years behind the direct entry officer intake, and, apart from ability, from then on there were no barriers of access to the highest ranks in the service. As touched upon above, this programme was not just an altruistic measure to improve lower deck prospects. As the navy continued to expand, there was a critical shortfall in the numbers of junior officers available to fill all the seagoing billets. It was absolutely necessary that a new source of recruitment be tapped, and it was of unqualified benefit to the navy that these positions were opened to a pool of talented young men with already proven seamanship and specialist abilities.

The matter of service discipline was also given much thought. Certain practices that were a leftover from early Victorian times were abolished, and the powers of the universally hated Ship's Police were severely curtailed. Seamen were given much readier access to the process of appeal against unjust sentences and punishment, and summary discipline, carried out on the whim of an individual captain or commander, was placed within strict legal boundaries. A very firm code of discipline remained, but it was constrained by a sense of humanity, and those who abused the power of their rank could expect to be brought to account.

One of the main disadvantages of the traditional system was that the day to day running of a ship, in all its manifestations, was the responsibility of a single man. This was not the captain of the ship, it was his second-in-command. The commander dealt with every single detailed aspect of the ship's routine. The captain drove and fought the ship, and had a huge influence on the personality of the vessel, but it was the commander who did the drudgery. Efficiency in drills; cleanliness; the standard of food; smartness in dress; the appearance of the ship; the health and general well-being of the crew; all received his personal attention. Discipline was also his problem, and the commander had to carry out all the duties of a local magistrate with regard to the crimes, failings, and indiscretions of the crew. Too much authority, and too much work, was concentrated in the hands of a single man, however efficient that officer might be. The commander simply did not have the time to properly consider the general welfare of the crew.

A very welcome change was brought to this situation by the institutionalising of the divisional system. The various specialist officers on board had always obviously had a proprietary interest in the welfare of crew members serving in their department. This interest was now formalised, and the divisional officers became responsible for many personnel matters, such as leave, recreation and minor offences, that had previously to be referred to the commander. The latter retained overall responsibility, and still had to deal with serious disciplinary and welfare problems, but his workload was sensibly eased and the sailors received more detailed attention from their respective heads of department than had previously been the case. The divisional system thus instituted remains largely unchanged to this day.

Despite the improvements mentioned above, the biggest bone of contention faced by Churchill was that of pay, and, in this matter, the Admiralty could not operate in isolation. Any increase in salaries had to be paid for out of the annual naval estimates, and these were subject to the approval of the Chancellor of the Exchequer, David Lloyd-George. Churchill's one time ally in the fight against bloated naval programmes had not changed his spots, and, as the cost of competition with Germany inexorably rose year after year, each successive set of estimates was subjected to minute scrutiny in every detail as the Chancellor sought to trim expenditure. In the end, Churchill was forced to accept a reduction in his pay proposals in order to preserve other essential priorities. A modest increase in sailors' pay was achieved, but Churchill was bitterly disappointed that he was unable to do more.

All the measures taken, however welcome, did not remove the general causes of discontent, but they were clear evidence that the problems had started to be addressed. The fact that the Admiralty was making a real effort to improve the lot of the sailor had an effect on morale out of all proportion to the actual results. For the first time in very many years, the interests of the lower deck were seen to be receiving long overdue attention, and this was genuinely appreciated. Grievances remained, but the general attitude of sailors towards the Admiralty became markedly warmer.

There is one vital remaining feature of Churchill's time at the peacetime Admiralty that needs to be mentioned, and that is the change in strategic policy that took place during his tenure of office.

For centuries, British maritime policy had been to impose a close blockade on the enemy's coast and naval bases from the moment hostilities commenced. The policy was aptly summed up in the adage that 'Britain's first line of defence is the shoreline of the enemy'. In the altered conditions of the 20th century, this had become an option fraught with hazards. Torpedo boats, submarines and mines posed an increasing threat to any fleet attempting to operate on the doorstep of a hostile power. The probability of continuous attrition to the fleet by these means, coupled with the difficulty of maintaining ships on station now that fuel had replaced sail as the motive power of the fleet, led to an inevitable conclusion. After much soul-searching, the decision was made that close blockade was no longer feasible, but, specifically, in the case of Germany as an opponent, a policy of 'distant blockade' would serve just as effectively.

The unique geographical position of Britain in relation to Germany made this option possible. By establishing a hermetic seal on the outlets from the North Sea, Germany would be cut off from all overseas trade just as completely as if the British Fleet was operating in her territorial waters. With the English Channel blocked by mines, submarines and destroyers backed up by a fleet of the older battleships, the southern approaches to the North Sea could be denied to the enemy. The Scotland/Norway gap would be covered by the main fleet based on Scapa Flow, and effectively preventing any German naval activity or trade on the oceans of the world. The Kaiser's grandiloquently termed 'High Seas Fleet' would be confined to the Baltic and to sorties into the North Sea unless it could break through the British cordon – and this is what the Royal Navy fervently hoped it would try to do. Eventually, it was thought, the effects of the blockade would force the German Fleet to come out and offer battle – and having done so, it was confidently expected that it would be destroyed.

This radical change in British strategy was, sensibly, not broadcast at the time, and it was very successfully kept from the Germans. As will be seen, the German admirals confidently expected an immediate descent on their shores by the Royal Navy as soon as war was declared. They positively welcomed this prospect, as their whole strategy was based on weakening the Grand Fleet by attrition until a rough parity in numbers had been achieved. Only when that point had been reached, would a full-scale trial of strength be attempted. Clearly, if the British Fleet was chancing its arm in local German waters, then the opportunities for attrition were greatly enhanced. It is curious that they did not credit the British Admiralty with the ability to come to the same conclusion.

The many achievements of Churchill's administration have been detailed, but there were also some significant failures. These stemmed from the same source as had partially frustrated his efforts to improve pay.

Constraints on the budget meant that the planned development of naval bases was seriously retarded. All the existing dockyards had been constructed in an age when the navies of France, Spain and Holland had constituted the major threat to Britain's security. Consequently, the main naval bases were on the south and west coasts of Britain, and in the English Channel. With Germany now the threat, a fleet base on the east coast was seen as essential to cover the North Sea, and, in 1904, approval had been given for a naval dockyard and fortified anchorage to be established at Rosyth, in the Firth of Forth. Due to lack of funding, construction had proceeded slowly, and Rosyth was still incomplete when war broke out. In the meantime, it was decided that the main fleet base in any war against Germany would be the vast and remote sheltered expanse of Scapa Flow in the Orkney Islands. A further fleet anchorage and base was established in the Cromarty Firth, roughly halfway between Rosyth and the Orkneys. However, neither Scapa nor Cromarty had docking facilities, and the latter could not accommodate the whole fleet. As to the other options, the Tyne had dockyards, but was a constricted river with no space to anchor a fleet, and the Humber had space in plenty, but all of it too shallow for capital ships. These two harbours, together with Blyth, Sunderland and Hartlepool provided useful bases for light warships, and could accommodate the odd old battleship as a guard ship, but were completely inadequate to the requirements of handling a large modern fleet.

Aggravating the problem was the fact that the fixed defences of all these bases was not the responsibility of the Admiralty, but of the War Office – and, given similar pressures on its budget, the army put a low priority on defending naval facilities. Consequently, none of the bases were adequately protected in 1914, although the Admiralty managed from its own resources (by removing guns and searchlights from old ships and manning them with reservists) to make Cromarty reasonably secure. The situation was far from satisfactory, and, when the extent of the submarine threat began to be realised in the early months of the war, the Grand Fleet was forced to evacuate Scapa until suitable defences were provided. For several months the fleet wandered about at sea or retired to anchorages in Northern Ireland and the west coast of Scotland. The strain on men and machinery was considerable, and the temper of senior officers sorely tried.

A further aspect of the navy's readiness for war that suffered for want of funds was the provision of adequate fuel reserves for the fleet. Coal stocks were not a problem, but, having made the momentous decision to rely on oil for all future major types of warship, the infrastructure to provide for this was badly neglected. There was a pressing need to construct massive storage facilities for oil and to purchase quantities of the fuel sufficient to support the fleet for an extended period. The oil committee chaired by Fisher had recommended that reserves capable of supporting the normal operations of the fleet for four years should be accumulated and stored, but such a provision was a complete impossibility in the prevailing economic conditions, and this figure was savagely pruned. It was only after a threat of resignation by Jellicoe, then the Second Sea Lord, that agreement was reached for four and a half *months'* worth of stocks to be provided. The result was that inadequate reserves of oil existed when war was declared, and, as more and more oil-fired ships joined the fleet, the situation progressively worsened. Although war loosened the purse strings, supply did not keep up with demand, and, by 1917, the chickens had come home to roost. The vast numbers of escorts required at sea on the, by then, paramount task of combating the submarine menace meant that the Grand Fleet had to curtail its sea time – and effectiveness – through lack of fuel. Arthur Marder comments that:

'During several months of 1917 the shortage of oil fuel was most critical, due to successful submarine attacks on so many British oil carrying vessels. Oil was down to a three weeks' supply as a whole, and to six days' supply at some of the fuelling bases...The pre-war politicians were responsible for that state of affairs.' (18)

In some technical areas there were also failings, notably in the quality of heavy shells supplied to the fleet. This did not become apparent until after the Battle of Jutland, in 1916, but the lack of quality control in production, and the absence of any proper measures for proving the effectiveness of the shells, was a telling indictment of the responsible Admiralty department. Jellicoe, when in charge of this branch, had been preparing a comprehensive testing programme to this end, but he was promoted out of the job before this reached fruition. His successor, through incompetence, idleness, or both, failed to progress the plan – with disastrous consequences for the navy. This matter pre-dated Churchill's arrival at the Admiralty, and was, in any case, a specialist concern on which he was not qualified to pass judgement (not that this proviso deterred him in some other areas!). He was not alone in his ignorance of the problem. It was shared by virtually the entire navy at that time.

If imperfections existed within his administrative sphere, the balance of judgement on Churchill's peacetime Admiralty has to be very markedly to his credit. Profound improvements had and were being made to every aspect of the Royal Navy. The sense of purpose he instilled was also impressive, and actions followed decisions with no tolerance of delay.

By the spring of 1912, when he rose to address parliament, Churchill had been in office for a mere six months, but most of the critically important decisions affecting the future shape of the navy had been made, and the measures to implement them were already in train.

Churchill's presentation of the first naval estimates of his administration was, by the reckoning of most contemporaries, an impressive performance. He had something of a tightrope to walk in that he was caught between the political demands of much of his own party versus the practical requirements of the navy, for whom he was now the chief spokesman.

In an attempt to placate the pacifists in the governing Liberal Party he was obliged to regret the necessity for increased expenditure. He then proceeded to make unanswerable arguments for that absolute necessity. As one of the erstwhile 'economists', his arguments bore particular force. A politician with a history of 'Big Navy' connections could not have had nearly the same effect.

In the course of his speech, Churchill startled many members of parliament by openly admitting that the government had abandoned the old 'two powers plus 10%' calculation that had previously determined the strength of the Royal Navy. For the moment, Britain was building against Germany alone, and a 60% percent superiority in capital ship numbers was to be maintained over that nation. This had actually been official policy for several years, but it was the first time that it had been announced in public.

Of all the previous First Lords, none had ever had the clarity of expression, never mind the inclination, to so clearly state the policy of the Admiralty in relation to the challenges it had to meet. Nor had there ever been so refreshing an openness in the manner with which he elucidated the problems facing his department, and the proposed measures by which these problems were to be effectively addressed.

Within the navy, it also gave his critics pause for thought. This was obviously not just an opportunist politician that had been foisted upon them. He had demonstrated in parliament that he was also an advocate who, in a very short time, had clearly mastered his brief. The content and the manner of his speech in presenting the estimates spoke of someone who was fully committed to the service that he represented.

As time went by, the navy began, grudgingly, to appreciate the positive qualities of the First Lord. The senior officers still grumbled about his tendencies to 'personal rule', but the progress being achieved was undeniable and there was no doubt that he was an excellent champion of the service's interests in parliament. Despite the regular gaffes and irritating breaches of service etiquette, it was plain that he was wholeheartedly on their side so long as they could prove that they were right.

History has rightly concluded that, from 1911 until the outbreak of war in August 1914, Churchill was probably one of the most outstanding occupants of his office in the annals of the Royal Navy. His performance as a wartime First Lord is a much more contentious issue, but, as Kitchener said to him at the dark moment of Churchill's dismissal from the Admiralty, 'There is one thing at least they cannot take away from you. When the War came you had the Fleet ready.' (19)

CHAPTER FOURTEEN
OLIVE BRANCHES AND NETTLES

'At the beginning of 1912 there was the strongest disposition in the British Cabinet, which was, I believe, sincerely reciprocated by Herr Von Bethmann, to settle outstanding differences between the two Countries.'

Herbert Asquith

'My naval concession was absolutely uncompensated...England was only concerned with making us give one-sided concessions without receiving anything in return.'

Alfred von Tirpitz

'Why should we attack Germany for building ships when we could ourselves build more ships quicker and cheaper? Why incur the guilt cost and hazard of war when a complete remedy was obvious and easy?'

Winston Churchill

By 1912, there was an acute awareness throughout Europe that intolerable tensions between the great powers were being fuelled by the general increase in arms and the lack of any purposeful dialogue between contending nations. Nowhere was this more pronounced than in the case of Anglo-German relations. For all that, the last two years before the outbreak of war witnessed a considerable improvement in the atmosphere between London and Berlin. Whatever the ultimately insuperable difficulties over the ongoing German naval programme, relations between the two countries in the summer of 1914 were probably more amicable than at any time in the previous twenty years. For a brief while there did seem to be genuine grounds for optimism as to the ability of both nations to co-exist on a peaceful basis, even though they might be the most ferocious of commercial rivals. Olive branches and nettles were both there to be grasped. All that was lacking was firm hands on both sides that could accommodate both plants.

If the aftermath of the Agadir Crisis had resulted in upheaval at the British Admiralty, in German naval circles subsequent events conformed to a familiar pattern. Whenever Germany had experienced diplomatic or strategic setbacks, these had been used to press the argument for a more powerful fleet. It was contended that only by strengthening its naval forces could Germany avoid the sort of humiliation caused by the climb down over Morocco. This argument was highly simplistic and could have been refuted on several levels.

Essentially, Germany's problems had arisen as a result of over-aggressive policies towards other nations, supported by incompetent diplomacy. The strength of the German Navy was irrelevant to this process and would remain so unless it could be raised to the point of possessing maritime supremacy – at which point Germany would have been in a position to do anything she liked whenever and wherever she wanted. It was recognised, even by Tirpitz and the Emperor, that this was not possible until Germany had achieved the dominant economic status required to fund both the strongest army and the strongest navy in the world. This was never a serious prospect. Even had Britain's naval power collapsed or been overtaken in the long term, the vast economy of the United States, should it be properly applied, would have prevented any German global hegemony.

Nevertheless, the basic tactics were never altered. The impotence of the imperial navy during the Boer War had given Tirpitz the opportunity to double the provisions of the original Navy Law. Similarly, the diplomatic reverse suffered at the Algeciras Conference in 1906 enabled him to further increase the programme. Tirpitz's propaganda machine had no difficulty in milking nationalist sentiment to ensure popular support for these measures. True to form, he utilised the Agadir fiasco to draft yet another amendment to the Navy Law. This became known as the 'Novelle', and, whilst its provisions were likely to remain unknown prior to it being laid before the *Reichstag*, word soon reached London that something was afoot – and, whatever that something was, it was unlikely, from the point of view of the British Government, to be a welcome development. Once again, however, it concentrated minds on the desirability of obtaining a diplomatic solution to the naval arms race, and, to that end, resume the contacts which had inevitably been suspended during the Agadir Crisis.

The initial impetus to renew Anglo-German negotiations came from an unexpected source. We have already come across Albert Ballin, the German shipping magnate. It was he whose approach to the Kaiser in 1908, concerning the possibility of opening conversations with the British Government about naval matters, had so incensed von Bethmann-Hollweg in the early days of the latter's Chancellorship. Four years on, and four years wiser, Bethmann was much more receptive when Ballin resurrected his initiative. Ballin's original approach had come about as a result of an introduction to the eminent Anglo-German banker, Sir Ernest Cassel. The two men had struck up a close relationship, and, in their discussions, discovered a common interest in reducing the tension between their respective countries. They remained in frequent touch subsequently, and, after the Agadir affair had blown over, considered it worthwhile to make a further effort to bring the two sides together in an attempt to defuse the situation.

Ballin was head of the Hamburg America Line, which had grown to become the largest shipping concern in the world, eclipsing even Cunard and White Star. A highly astute businessman, he had taken great care to cultivate the goodwill of the Kaiser, and encourage his interest in the projection of German power by means of maritime power. In many respects, Ballin was genuinely in tune with Wilhelm's ambitions, and, in the commercial sphere, he had already achieved what Tirpitz never managed to approach in military terms – dominance of critical areas and markets. To further his relationship with the Emperor, Ballin often placed the most prestigious of his vessels at Wilhelm's disposal whenever the situation warranted. It was on one of his ships that Wilhelm made his ill-fated visit to Tangier in 1905. Permanent, private, suites were installed for the Emperor on all the latest liners launched for the company. In due course, Ballin became one of Wilhelm's closest confidantes, although, being a Jew in a society that had a strong anti-Semitic element, he remained clear of the innermost circle of sycophants. Given the general nature and personality of the latter, it is unlikely that this would much have disturbed him.

Cassel was also Jewish and had been born a German. His family had emigrated to England where he had become naturalised. In due course he had founded one of the most powerful banking empires in the world, which, in turn, led him into the upper echelons of British society. There he met the future King Edward VII, and they became firm friends. Over the years, Cassel virtually became the King's personal banker. Although Edward died in 1910, Cassel retained enormous clout within the British business community and within the 'establishment'.

Both men were extremely patriotic. Ballin was in no sense 'pro-British', whilst Cassel's commitment to his adopted country was beyond question. Nevertheless, they recognised the dangers inherent in the ruinous naval competition that was taking place. Cut-throat competition between commercial rivals was an accepted fact of life in the world of business, but the prospect of an arms race ending in military hostilities would be disastrous to the business of both nations. The two men took an entirely pragmatic view of the situation. The nature of any future war was, as then, unknown, but there was a vague, deep-seated premonition that neither country stood to prosper from such an event. Ballin, certainly, had realised that any war that set Germany against Britain would result in every ship of his line being either captured, interned, or laid up to rot until hostilities ceased.

The attitudes of these two men accurately reflected the prevailing opinion of the time – at least within the business community. It was thought that the common economic links that tied the major nations together had made war between them an obsolete concept. As an early argument for the benefits of globalisation, it was to prove premature.

When Ballin put feelers out on the prospect of governmental contacts, using himself and Cassel as intermediaries, he found Bethmann in a much more compliant frame of mind than he had evidenced in 1908. This mirrored the prevalent attitude in London, where all were aware that any further expansion of the German Navy would have to be tracked by proportionate increases in the British naval budget. To avoid this unpleasant necessity, Britain was prepared to offer concessions elsewhere. The new First Lord of the Admiralty was particularly keen to divert German efforts towards the direction of imperial ambitions:

'We knew that a formidable new Navy Law was in preparation and would shortly be declared. If Germany had made up her mind to antagonize Great Britain, we must take up the challenge; but it might be possible by friendly, sincere and intimate conversation to avert this perilous development. We were no enemies to German colonial expansion, and we would even have taken active steps to further her wishes in this respect. Surely something could be done to break the chain of blind causation. If aiding Germany in the colonial sphere was a means of procuring a stable situation, it was a price we were well prepared to pay.' (1)

Ironically, there are unmistakable echoes here of Bismarck's policy towards France, post 1871. German diplomacy actively encouraged the French to concentrate on colonial expansion in the vain hope that it would distract the Gallic mind from the loss of the provinces of Alsace and Lorraine. The depth and vehemence of French public opinion meant that there was never any chance of that particular policy succeeding. Churchill's hopes, in the face of German national feeling, were equally impracticable, and his intentions equally unattainable.

Returning to Ballin's initiative, he was able to arrange an audience with the Kaiser at which it was agreed that Cassel would come to Germany with proposals for a meeting between a senior minister of the British Government and the German establishment. Initially, both Ballin and Cassel were thinking on the basis of Churchill sitting down at a table with Tirpitz to thrash out points of difference (what a wonderful prospect that would have been!), but this, for various reasons, proved impossible. In the event, though, Cassel's visit produced the desired result, and both sides approved the principle of governmental contact, to be arranged on an informal basis.

The meeting had taken place in a very positive atmosphere, and, importantly, Cassel was able to return to London with the basic outline of the new German Navy Law. This information was supplied by Bethmann, with the Kaiser's approval (and to the chagrin of Tirpitz), and certainly indicated a desire to be open on the subject. Cassel immediately transmitted this information to the Admiralty, where it was perused with growing alarm.

Essentially, Tirpitz was manoeuvring within the bounds of the laws that he, himself, had created. He was, therefore, in a unique position to know how to stretch the elasticity of those bounds to their fullest extent. One particular opportunity presented itself in the actual ages of the battleships in the fleet.

The lifespan of an armoured ship had originally been established at twenty-five years. The rapid advance of technology had rendered this timescale obsolete. Tirpitz, therefore, had little difficulty in arguing that the effective life of a warship should be officially reduced to twenty years. This principle was adopted, without question, by the German parliament.

The result of this change in the age categorisation of warships was that many of the older, and, by then, effectively worthless, ships in the German Navy ceased to be considered as operational. They could, therefore, be scrapped or reduced to auxiliary duties. In the absence of these old ships, modern battleships, of the greatest power, could be constructed as replacements without exceeding the stated numerical limit of the fleet.

To meet this requirement, there had to be an acceleration in construction above and beyond the standard two capital ships each year that had been the originally planned rate of construction from about 1913 onwards. Initially, Tirpitz wanted three dreadnoughts to be constructed annually until the agreed fleet strength was achieved, but he later modified this demand to the extent that the third ship would only be laid down every other year. Overall, the new programme envisaged the creation by 1920 of a main battle fleet comprising three squadrons of eight modern battleships (as opposed to the two squadrons previously planned), plus a flagship. At the same time, older armoured cruisers would be replaced by battlecruisers, bringing the numbers of the latter up to eight and giving a total of 33 capital ships in commission. The mathematics of this programme meant that, from 1912, Germany would be constructing battleships per annum at a rate of 3-2-3-2-3. A battlecruiser would also have to be constructed every other year, which effectively gave Tirpitz his three capital ships per annum.

The British had already accepted a new criterion for its navy as having at least a 60% superiority in battleships over those that could be deployed by Germany. Only dreadnought battleships were now considered to be frontline units. It had also been agreed, that, for every extra German battleship built above the original programme, Britain would build 'two keels to one'. Any increase in the previous German programme, therefore, required Britain to lay down double the number of the extra German capital ships. These decisions had yet to be made public knowledge, and there was some concern as to their presentation to the country. Obviously, meeting the criteria meant an increase in the British naval estimates, which, in turn, would be deeply unpopular in a parliament intent on diverting money towards social problems. When Cassel approached the government with his, and Ballin's, suggestions for an informal contact, at ministerial level, between the two nations, the British Cabinet did not take long to grasp the opportunity. The decision was made almost immediately, and the only question that remained was that of who should be the emissary.

After some thought, Asquith nominated Lord Haldane, the War Office Minister, to undertake the mission on behalf of his administration.

Haldane was, in fact, a first class choice. Born into a strict Scottish Baptist family, he had broken free and carried out his studies at the universities of Göttingen and Cologne. Consequently he spoke German fluently and had developed a great admiration for German culture and traditions. In his spare time he read Goethe, and, when he went on holidays, they were spent in Germany. Given these connections, there was no great speculation in the press when, on 8th February 1912, Haldane was sent to Germany, ostensibly to study the processes of German technological education. Had any other minister been sent, the press would have scented that a meeting of great significance was about to take place. Neither government wished the discussions to become public knowledge.

When Cassel first went to Germany to break the ice, he had been thoroughly briefed by the Cabinet as to the agenda of any subsequent meetings. His immediate priority was to establish that the question of how to reduce naval construction and associated expenditure was to be the first item on that agenda. As a *quid pro quo*, he was authorised to offer the prospect of Britain's active support for further German colonial expansion as well as a mutual non-aggression agreement. It was also to be made plain that any slowing down of the German naval programme would lead to a similar, and proportional, relaxation of British construction, that could only be of financial advantage to both nations. It was agreed that the discussions would be informal and non-binding, but that they might lead to greater things. It was on this basis – hope of a more amicable relationship, and perhaps some concrete proposals on how to reduce the naval competition – that Haldane then set off for Berlin.

In the end, the Haldane Mission was a failure. It foundered, in detail, on the rock of Tirpitz's intransigence as it concerned the naval situation, and, in general, because Britain could never give Germany diplomatically what the latter required without abandoning the *entente* with France. Nevertheless, the obvious goodwill generated in the talks had a beneficial effect on the relationships between the two nations. Tirpitz excepted, all the major players on both sides developed a greater understanding of the problems each other faced in dealing with their respective ambitions and electorates. The remarkably open and frank discussions that took place were a model of how constructive diplomacy could be conducted. It was also (and how this must have grieved the establishment *apparatchiks* on both sides of the North Sea) very off the cuff.

When Haldane arrived in Berlin, the British Ambassador briefed him as to his programme of hastily-arranged appointments. Otherwise, he was completely unprepared for the format of his visit. The manner of his mission was highly irregular in the normal run of diplomatic activity, and, as neither government had wished it to be unduly publicised, had to be carried out on an *ad hoc* basis.

First of all, Haldane met Bethmann at the British Embassy. There had been an official lunch at which the attendance of both men would not have aroused comment. Afterwards, they repaired to a room and spoke alone. Two well-meaning men sat down and discussed the causes of difference between their two nations – differences and a situation that they both deplored. Haldane, from the outset, stated that he had no authority to make formal commitments. He was there to discuss the basis on which future agreements might be made. Bethmann, in his own mind, put a greater emphasis on the results of their talks. He still held to his impossible dream that, if he could meet British requirements as to the naval competition, there was a chance of obtaining a declaration of British neutrality should Germany become embroiled in a conflict with either France or Russia – or both. This was well beyond Haldane's remit from his government, but he made clear that, if Germany were to be attacked, unprovoked, by any nation, Britain would not join the attackers whoever they might be – although this obviously was not quite the same thing as an outright statement of neutrality in any circumstances.

Whatever agreements with other nations that had been made by the British Government, these were of a defensive nature. There was absolutely no question of Britain ever being involved in an offensive combination against Germany *unless* Germany gratuitously provoked the confrontation. Haldane indicated that Britain was prepared to make a formal declaration to that effect. That, however, was never going to be enough for the Germans. Bethmann made the point that Germany might be forced to make a pre-emptive strike before potential aggressors against his nation were in a dominant position. Germany might appear strong, but her geographic situation was dreadful, having to face both east and west with no natural borders. Historically, the country had been ravaged on many occasions, by both the French and the Russians, and there was a deep sense of insecurity in that the nation was being encircled by a hostile coalition.

Haldane went as far as he could to assure Bethmann that Britain would never enter an aggressive combination against Germany. He spoke for all his Cabinet colleagues in saying that an attack on Germany would never be supported by his government. He made clear that whatever agreements Britain had with France and Russia were exactly, and only, what had been publicly stated. There were no secret agendas and no hard and fast commitment to an anti-German alliance. On the other hand, he could not, and would not, say that, in the event of an unwarranted attack by Germany on France or Russia, that Britain would remain neutral. Sticking to his brief, Haldane returned to the subject of the naval competition and made clear that any thaw in diplomatic relations would be largely dependent on the ability to curb the nautical arms race. Bethmann fought his corner on the basis that any alterations to the Navy Law could only take place after a formal and satisfactory diplomatic agreement had been achieved.

The two points of view on the crucial issues were diametrically opposed, but the willingness of both to see each other's side of the argument, and to try and find a way round the problem produced an excellent atmosphere for the continuation of talks. There were also secondary matters on which it was much easier to confer. Haldane, for his part, came to the meeting with a package of possible colonial concessions that were greatly beneficial to Germany's overseas ambitions. These, it has to be said, were to be largely achieved by the transfer to Germany of Portuguese and Belgian territory in Africa, neither of which nations had been consulted on the matter! Britain, though, would materially influence and assist German aspirations and negotiations towards that end. The end product would have been such as to create a single German territorial bloc extending from its existing colony of South West Africa (Namibia), through Angola and the Congo, and into German East Africa (present day Tanzania). Thus, Germany would possess a band of territory that crossed the African continent from the South Atlantic to the Indian Ocean. There was the undoubted carrot of being able to possess an overseas territory of such size and resources, that it might become a productive and strategic entity, instead of a useless drain on the Imperial German budget – as was the case with most of Germany's overseas territories.

However impractical this rather cynical scheme may have been, there is no doubt that the mere suggestion of it would have been music to the ears of the Kaiser and the pan-German imperialists. Tirpitz commented, and it is difficult to disagree with him on this specific, that:

'The extravagance of this offer of colonial possessions which did not belong to the English and were not at their disposal was calculated to suit the Emperor's temperament. It made a painful impression on me because the method was too crude and the design too obvious.' (2)

All this pie in the sky depended, though, on the settlement of the two major issues under discussion. Haldane and Bethmann had broken the ice, but, in practical terms, they were still a long way from establishing a common position. Both were overly optimistic as to the long-term prospects of the talks.

It had been a remarkably frank and forthright discussion between two men who had clearly developed an immediate respect and liking for each other. When the meeting was over, both Haldane and Bethmann felt that they were on the brink of a real breakthrough in Anglo-German relations. Bethmann went to the Kaiser in a mood of considerable optimism and found the latter in a most receptive frame of mind.

Wilhelm was in one of his best 'world statesman' moods, and determined to do his utmost to maintain and advance the good feeling that had been established between his Chancellor and Haldane. When he set his mind to it he could be the most charming and attentive of hosts, and these characteristics were in full play the following day when Haldane was invited to lunch with him and his family. Bethmann and Tirpitz were the other guests.

After a convivial meal and some champagne, the Kaiser took Haldane and Tirpitz aside, and the three of them sat down at a table to discuss naval matters. It was a remarkable meeting – the effective creator of the German Navy and the British War Minister stating their completely incompatible positions whilst the Emperor of Germany acted as a benevolent referee and tried to bring them together!

For a long while there was no progress, but, eventually, with Wilhelm's encouragement, Tirpitz reluctantly conceded the possibility of a very small reduction in the rate of battleship construction. He actually stated that 'he sacrificed the ship', meaning a battleship, but this is patent nonsense. The concession was hardly of any consequence in the long term – it merely delayed the laying down of a ship. Its construction was not cancelled and the same number of ships would be built as per Tirpitz's plans, albeit the programme would run on for a couple more years than was originally intended. Haldane was not sufficiently *au fait* in naval matters to pick up on the importance of Tirpitz's long-term intention to build and maintain three squadrons of eight dreadnought vessels (plus a flagship) in full commission. This was a huge advance over a fleet of two squadrons that was largely non-operational over the winter months. Had Haldane known of the eventual plans Tirpitz had for the German Fleet (40 dreadnoughts, in five squadrons, plus up to 20 battlecruisers), he would have realised the impossibility of any constructive negotiation with the German Naval Secretary.

Positively, for both sides, the mere fact that there had been any concession at all was evidence of a willingness on the German side to compromise in the cause of better Anglo-German relations. There is little doubt that even this insignificant measure would never have been agreed had the Kaiser not been determined to show a concrete result from the talks. Tirpitz grumbled that, 'A really business-like deal with Haldane was rendered difficult by the presence of the Emperor', (3) but, left to themselves, Tirpitz and Haldane would have remained in deadlock. Whilst their discussion was carried out with all the politeness of diplomatic language, it was clear that they had no common ground and there was none of the warmth and sincerity that had attended the meeting between Bethmann and the British minister. Haldane found Tirpitz something of a cold fish, and the latter was practically paranoid in his suspicion of British motives, whatever their source.

Tirpitz was nothing if not consistent. For him, there were only two possible reasons why a British minister would want to have talks with him.

If the British Government had been forced to the negotiation table, then it meant that his policy was working – the Risk Theory was vindicated; on the other hand, if they hadn't been forced to the table, then it was certain that there was a sinister motive behind the talks that would inevitably be aimed at confounding German interests. He never changed his views. The British would be damned if they did, and damned if they didn't. This quote from his memoirs is his comment on the Haldane mission, and says far more about Tirpitz himself than his intended target:

'Haldane did not proceed on strictly business lines; he tried first of all mock negotiations, ready to sugar our subjugation and to grant us the appearance of a political agreement and the acquisition of colonies if we practically entered into a vassalage in return.' (4)

Even accepting the fact that he was a bitter old man when he wrote those words, they are evidence of a certain professional paranoia and a complete inability to see matters other than from his own standpoint. Germany was the premier military state in the world and hardly met any of the criteria to qualify as a helpless victim to British oppression. The Kaiser, Bethmann, and practically everyone else, then and since, has accepted that Haldane's mission was a genuine attempt to improve Anglo-German relations, and to reduce the crippling burden on the Exchequers of both nations caused by their mutual naval competition.

If the attitude of Tirpitz was a problem, a further hindrance to the eventual purpose of the mission resulted from a speech by Churchill whilst Haldane was still in Berlin. In the course of his oration, the First Lord, in trying to define the differences between the situation of Britain and Germany, made the remark that:

'There is, however, this difference between the British naval power and the naval power of the great and friendly Empire – and I trust it may long remain the great and friendly Empire – of Germany. The British Navy is to us a necessity and, from some points of view, the German Navy is to them *more in the nature of a luxury*. Our naval power involves British existence. It is existence to us; it is expansion to them...Germany was a great Power respected and honoured all over the world before she had a single ship.' (5)

Churchill, in coining the term *luxury*, caused unintended mayhem. The obvious point he was making was that Britain depended on its navy for its very survival whilst the same conditions applied to Germany as per its army. The German Navy, however important to its nation's ambitions, was above and beyond its needs for basic security as a major power. Unfortunately, the sense in which he used the word 'luxury' did not translate well into German, where it was used to describe irrelevant vanity and frippery. Not unnaturally this caused some offence – which was gleefully pounced upon and exploited by the nationalist press. Whilst this development did not affect Haldane's talks with the other principals (he actually thought it contributed positively to a lively debate), it soured the public atmosphere then and afterwards.

On the third, and last, day of his visit, Haldane was once again closeted with Bethmann and the two men went over the content of the talks, and the developments that could arise as a result. Both felt that the concession that had been wrung out of Tirpitz, to spread the capital ship construction programme over a longer period, was a positive contribution to further dialogue – which, it was agreed, would take place in London at an early opportunity. It was also agreed that these further contacts would continue to explore the possibility of closer Anglo-German relations without detriment to existing alliances. The subject of colonial acquisitions, border adjustments and commercial matters – mostly, as previously mentioned, to Germany's benefit – would also be discussed. Amongst these other token sweeteners, Haldane had hinted that the island of Zanzibar, positioned just off the coast of German East Africa, might be restored to Germany (the British Government had accepted sovereignty of this East African potentate, previously a centre of the slave trade, in return for ceding the strategically vital island of Heligoland to Germany).[1]

If the talks had concentrated on a few matters of central concern, they had not been the only subjects on the agenda. There were also wide-ranging discussions on the pressing matters of trade and influence, such as the Baghdad railway. This latter project, German financed and organised, sought to project a German presence through the Turkish Empire to the shores of the Persian Gulf. The British Government regarded this development with the utmost antipathy, suspecting (rightly) a disguised German attempt to penetrate an area previously assumed to be within the British sphere of influence. This, and many other areas in which Britain and Germany differed were brought into the open and the problems addressed. These were, though, secondary issues. All hinged on the settlement of the naval problem, and both Bethmann and Haldane were very well aware of that fact.

---

[1] This had been arranged during the reign of Queen Victoria, who was most displeased – and rightly so – with her government of the time. It was a very poor bargain in the first place and this was made all the more apparent once Britain and Germany became naval rivals. Heligoland controlled the approaches to all Germany's North Sea ports, and, thus, the access of her fleet to open waters. That this (by then heavily fortified and nigh on impregnable) island was in German, and not British hands in 1914 was a critical factor in the subsequent conduct of the naval war. Had the island still been British territory, it may not have been defensible, in the conditions of 1914, but its harbour could certainly have been rendered unusable to an enemy for some time. Instead, the Germans had had many uninterrupted years to heavily fortify the island and to develop its port as a focal point of local defence in the Bight, and as a base to launch sorties of submarines and light forces into the North Sea.

There was one final, and very significant development. Before he departed from Berlin, Haldane was given by the Kaiser the complete draft of the 'Novelle' to take back with him to Whitehall. It was a remarkable and unprecedented gesture, particularly as the bill had yet to be presented to the *Reichstag*, and was a compelling token of Wilhelm's commitment to the process of *détente* with Britain, at least for the moment.

Haldane always maintained, and there is no reason to doubt this, that he never looked at the draft for the 'Novelle' before presenting it to the Cabinet and the Admiralty. It being extremely complex and technical, and not being versed in naval matters, he would, in any case, have been quite unable to draw many conclusions from the document other than those from the obvious details of the battleship programme – and these, it is fair to say, were all that mattered to the vast majority of politicians and the public. He felt that the mission had gone well. Once back in London, he turned the papers over to the Admiralty, where Churchill and the First Sea Lord rapidly sifted through the information. The more they read, the greater became their alarm.

For the eagerly expectant eyes in the Admiralty, the sting was in the small print. The provision that first caught the eye in the proposed legislation, i.e. the increased rate of capital ship construction, was, paradoxically, the one which caused them least concern. They had already been prepared, and provisionally allowed, for that development. Buried in the document were other measures that greatly increased the capabilities and potential of the German Navy as a whole.

The 'Novelle' required a 20 per cent increase in active personnel, an enormous increase in submarine construction, and the provision for a permanently operational force of at least 100 destroyers. The terms 'active' and 'operational' are significant. No navy (or army or air force, for that matter) can operate efficiently with a high proportion of semi-trained conscripts and reservists in its ranks – not instantly at any rate.

The influx of inexperienced and unqualified personnel and the consequent diversion of frontline officers and senior rates into training roles inevitably reduces overall efficiency and dilutes the effectiveness of any service. It is the quality of trained men, rather than numbers or weapons that wins battles and wars. Every lesson of warfare in the last century and a half points to the fact that it cannot be waged successfully with a high proportion of trainees and conscripts, until time and experience has brought them up to an acceptable professional level. To a lesser extent, the same proviso applies to reservists. The latter have the basic skills and discipline, but are not abreast of the latest technology and need a certain amount of retraining if they are not to be exclusively employed in second line duties. The provisions of the 'Novelle' directly addressed this problem.

The increase in permanently employed personnel meant that a much greater proportion of the German Fleet could be kept on a full-time operational footing. Previously, the navy had been lumbered with the problem that faced any rapidly expanding military force – how to recruit and train sufficient people to man the new ships whilst still managing to retain efficiency on the operational units. The only viable solution for the German Navy up to that point had been to lay up much of the fleet over the winter months and utilise the released personnel for training duties. This had the effect of writing off the German Fleet as an effective force for a significant proportion of each year – a fact that went not unappreciated by the British, who took full advantage of this lower level of readiness and utilised the period to carry out essential refits and repairs on their own major units, and to grant leave to their own crews. For limited periods it also allowed elements of the main fleet to get away from home waters, and cruise some traditional areas with a more benign climate. This would now have to stop.

The provisions of the 'Novelle' enabled an enlarged German fleet to remain operational on a year-round basis. In practical terms, it doubled the effectiveness of the Kaiser's navy. In the medium term, i.e. around 1920, Tirpitz was aiming at having three full squadrons of dreadnoughts, plus a flagship – a total of 25 modern battleships – in permanent commission. The number of battlecruisers would rise to at least eight. He expected that this would force the British to maintain 40 dreadnoughts (five battle squadrons) in service, with a similar margin of numerical superiority in terms of battlecruisers.

Although it is irrelevant to the provisions of the 'Novelle', it is of interest that Tirpitz eventually envisaged a German fleet of *five* operational squadrons of modern battleships, plus a flagship, and up to twenty battlecruisers – sixty-one ships, all of which would be dreadnoughts as the older pre-Dreadnoughts were progressively replaced – for which he later happily stated that he would have been prepared to accept a British fleet of eight squadrons – i.e. *sixty-four* dreadnoughts, plus enough battlecruisers to have a similar margin of superiority over his planned twenty. There is evidence of megalomania creeping in here, as these sort of programmes for either nation would have been completely impractical on either political, financial or manning grounds. From which portion of the air Tirpitz was planning to pluck the funds or the men necessary for this programme was never established, as the outbreak of war and the pressing demands of the army for more resources stymied his plans. Nevertheless, just the wind of his intentions caused the utmost consternation in London.

Even if the basic provisions of the 'Novelle' were all that were carried out, the consequences for Britain were serious. Existing plans allowed for a fleet roughly equivalent to that of Germany being permanently deployed in home waters and capable of being reinforced within a few days by the Atlantic Fleet of six battleships based on Gibraltar. A further six battleships of the Mediterranean Fleet were available at Malta, but these were nine days hard steaming away and might not be available in time should an early clash take place. The proposed increases to the German Fleet dictated that Britain would either have to increase its own battleship construction programme, or bring back from abroad its remaining detachments of those vessels – or, more likely, it would have to do both.

Once the full import of the 'Novelle' was digested, it was clear that any negotiations would have to proceed on a revised basis from that of Haldane's approach. It was something of an embarrassment to the British Government that it had informally suggested through Haldane that territorial concessions could be made to Germany in return for a slowing down of the latter's naval programme – the clear assumption, and fervent hope, in this case, being that, as a result of this bribe, Britain would be able to cut back on its own naval expenditure. The reality of the 'Novelle', once its provisions were fully appreciated by the experts, meant that the opposite would be the case. Churchill estimated that, even if the slowing down of the rate of construction, reluctantly conceded by Tirpitz, took place, the British naval budget would have to be bolstered by a further £18 million pounds over six years to maintain the status quo between the respective fleets.

This was not a scenario that would encourage the government to grant Germany any of the territorial acquisitions, as one of the *quid pro quos* that Haldane had suggested as the basis for an agreement between the two nations. The negotiations now recommenced in London, with Haldane and Sir Edward Grey, the British Foreign Minister, in session with Metternich, the German Ambassador. From the beginning of these discussions it was made clear that the full implications of the 'Novelle' had not been apparent to Haldane during his talks in Berlin, and that detailed study of the programme had given rise to questions that had not been previously covered. Until these were resolved, any general agreement on other matters would be impossible.

There is absolutely no doubt that this course of action was excruciatingly painful and embarrassing to the British. The government had been in a state of some elation as a result of the early assessments of Haldane's mission, and of his reports of the very good, and optimistic, atmosphere in which the discussions had taken place. There was a feeling that the obvious goodwill from the German side was a breakthrough in inter-governmental relations, and should be warmly reciprocated. Then came the damper. All sense of this mood had been thrown into disarray once Churchill had advised the Cabinet of the full implications of the new German naval legislation. If detailed perusal of the 'Novelle' document had shaken him, and his department, it was a dreadful blow to the aspirations of

Theobald Von Bethmann-Hollweg
German Chancellor 1909-1917

Sir Edward Grey
British Foreign Secretary 1906-16

his government as a whole. It is fair to assume that, up until that point, the full extent of German naval ambitions had not been entirely appreciated by many in the government. Even so, the realisation of the fact came as a hard blow, and it was distressing to have to throw an extremely wet blanket on the high German expectations aroused by the visit, and to have to disavow some of Haldane's informal propositions.

The situation for the British was not made any easier by the subsequent insistence of the Kaiser and his ministers that Haldane had been making concrete proposals, with the full approval of the British Government, rather than merely taking part in informal discussions. This had clearly never been the case as far as London was concerned, and was an irksome development. The British Government had been particularly careful to stress, from the very beginning, that Haldane was in Berlin to follow up the Ballin/Cassel initiative, and to float ideas, looking for some common ground for future negotiations. Haldane, himself, had made this position apparent from the outset of his mission. He was not intended to be an emissary making commitments that would tie his government in any way. To Asquith and his Cabinet, this had appeared clear, and they thought that they had made it abundantly clear.

'[It] was an honest attempt, not to arrive at a final arrangement, but to examine the ground with the object of finding out whether there was a road by which such an arrangement might be reached. Lord Haldane's function was not that of a plenipotentiary, or even of a negotiator in the full sense; it was rather that of an explorer.' (6)

Haldane also thought that he had established, in Berlin, that his position was that of an intermediary, not a bearer of concrete proposals. Not so, stated the Germans.

Retrospectively, the Kaiser; to a much lesser extent, Bethmann; and particularly Tirpitz – for his own reasons, chose to misinterpret, or ignore, the degree of executive authority that Haldane had brought to the negotiating table. In the case of Wilhelm and his Chancellor, it was probably a simple case of frustrated over-optimism. They took Haldane's tentative suggestions as substantive commitments on behalf of his peers. As a result, when the British Cabinet had to bite the bullet and tell Bethmann that nothing that had passed during Haldane's mission was in any way binding, some umbrage was taken. The Kaiser felt betrayed and insulted, as was his wont; Tirpitz shrugged his shoulders, and effectively said 'I told you so'; whilst Bethmann, who had had great hopes from the discussions, was utterly distraught and offered to resign. The Kaiser refused to release him from his post.

The German Chancellor was nothing if not persistent. Stubborn adherence to a line of thought was both one of his qualities, and one of his failings. In the latter case, if a policy had failed, or was impractical, he would continue to flog the dead horse. His intentions were admirable, but he did not possess the acumen to know when one approach should be abandoned and another line of negotiation adopted. In the process, he greatly weakened his own position *vis-à-vis* Tirpitz, which was a disaster for the governments of both nations. From then on, Bethmann was associated with a policy that everyone in the German political establishment knew he disagreed with. His credibility was, perforce, seriously undermined, and, despite his best efforts, he became increasingly an isolated voice in the corridors of power. For all that, he was still the Kaiser's appointed Chancellor and he still entertained ideas of being able to improve Anglo-German relations.

In the event, he determined that the positive aspects of Haldane's visit should not be thrown away, and so embarked on a course that directly challenged the strategy according to Tirpitz. In this well-intentioned initiative, he did not have the active support of the Kaiser, but neither did Wilhelm discourage any attempt to improve Anglo-German relations. Bethmann, through the channel of ambassador Metternich, held out to the British Government the prospect that the 'Novelle' might not be presented to the *Reichstag* for approval if Britain agreed a treaty of neutrality with Germany. Tirpitz, of course, was furious at this possible threat to his plans for the fleet. The two men were now in a state of permanent alienation as to the future course of Germany's foreign and military policy. In the event, Tirpitz fretted without reason. The Chancellor's requirements were beyond the capacity of satisfaction by any British government.

Bethmann, in trying to resurrect the negotiations, displayed all his great qualities of dogged determination. Despite the clear impracticality of the concept, he was still pursuing his dream of a pact with Great Britain that would ensure the latter's neutrality in the event of Germany going to war with any of her continental rivals – effectively France and Russia. This, of course was absolutely impossible. Asquith later made the point that:

'...the formula of neutrality which we were asked to accept was of such character that if there had been no *entente* at all Great Britain would have been bound to refuse it.' (7)

The sheer effort of will that had been required for Britain to disregard the enmities of centuries, and come to a working agreement with both those latter nations, had made it inconceivable that any of the political arrangements subsequently arrived at could be discarded at will. Nevertheless, serious and continuous talks took place in London for a further month.

As far as the 'Novelle' or, for that matter, any further increases in the German Navy was concerned, the British Government made it known that for every extra German capital ship built beyond the old programme, Britain would reluctantly lay down two equivalent vessels. This 'two keels to one' policy became accepted as a dogma in British circles. Its message was absolutely clear. The more ships Germany built; the more inferior its fleet would become to that of Britain. If that became the stick of the British approach, they also attempted to provide a carrot by offering to Germany something in the nature of a non-aggression treaty. This became the chief subject of the discussions between Sir Edward Grey and Metternich, but however close the two sides came to agreement, the talks eventually, and inevitably, foundered over a single word – neutrality.

The British Government was prepared to declare that it would never attack Germany, and that, furthermore, that it would never support a French and/or Russian attack on Germany. Effectively, therefore, if either or both of Germany's great continental rivals were to declare war on her, Britain *would* remain neutral. This was insufficient for Berlin. What the German Government required was an agreement that Britain would also remain neutral if a war against France and/or Russia was *forced* upon Germany. This was clearly too far for the British to go as it would have given Berlin virtual *carte blanche* to declare war upon those two nations whenever it liked, subject only to the provision of first having to supply any convenient reason for having been 'forced' into that position. It was all too easy to manufacture a spurious border incident to justify hostilities.[2] Such a treaty would have rendered Britain's existing agreements with France and Russia utterly worthless, and was thus out of the question. There was no further room for manoeuvre in the talks.

Ultimately, the British Government sent, through Metternich, a final draft declaration. Both the ambassador and Grey knew that this would almost certainly not be sufficient for Bethmann, in Berlin, to win his battle against Tirpitz and the powerful naval lobby. It read:

'England will make no unprovoked attack upon Germany and will pursue no aggressive policy towards her. Aggression upon Germany is not the subject and forms no part of any treaty, understanding or combination to which England is now a party, nor will she become a party to anything that has such an object.' (8)

Their fears were justified. Bethmann was in despair when he read the final British offer, and, realising the battle was lost, was ready to resign again. There was an awkward sequel to this. Grey, realising Bethmann's problems, and regarding him as the most reasonable element in the German establishment, tried to bolster his position. The British Foreign Secretary took it upon himself, rather stupidly for such an intelligent man, to inform Metternich that so long as Bethmann remained Chancellor there would be

---

[2] Hitler did just that in 1939 with the Poles. On the eve of war, in 1914, the French, considerably to their disadvantage, withdrew their troops ten kilometres back from well-fortified positions on the frontier precisely to avoid this possibility.

good personal relations between London and Berlin, which could only be beneficial to the peace of Europe. He then virtually egged the ambassador into reporting this remark back to his government. Metternich's wording of the conversation was that Britain regarded the continuance of Bethmann as Chancellor as the best guarantee of peace. The Kaiser, of course got to hear of this, and threw a major tantrum, for which he might be conceded some reason. He rightly concluded that it was most improper for a senior representative of a foreign power to dictate who would be the most appropriate chief minister of another sovereign state. Being Wilhelm, he was probably far more miffed that the influence of his own personage was not given prime importance.[3]

Bethmann, in the event, did not resign despite the fact that his position had been totally undermined. Asquith regarded this decision, or lack of it, as 'a fatal blunder'. The Tirpitz faction had triumphed and the fact that the Chancellor remained in office gave its views the appearance of having been generally accepted.

Any chance of disinterring the talks vanished subsequently in the wake of Churchill's presentation of the 1912/13 British Naval Estimates to parliament. As mentioned in the previous chapter, his speech did not beat around the bush. Marder remarks that:

'Unlike McKenna's speeches on the subject, which were apologetic and sometimes confused, Churchill was almost brutally clear and frank. The sham of the two-power standard was now publicly abandoned. He brushed aside the last remnants of pretence and stated bluntly that they were building against one power, and one power only – Germany.' (9)

Churchill openly declared what had been the official policy for some time, i.e. that the strength of the British Navy was now being calculated on the basis of it retaining a 60% superiority over that of Germany in terms of Dreadnought-era capital ships. The great preponderance of British pre-Dreadnought battleships would no longer take any part in comparisons of relative strength. In addition, he categorically stated, with the full agreement of the Cabinet, that this percentile figure only applied to the existing German naval programme. Should additions be made to the latter – clearly a veiled reference to the, as yet, unpublished 'Novelle' – Britain would build two ships for every extra keel laid down by Germany. Furthermore, any additional capital ships financed by the British Dominions were not going to be taken into consideration when calculating the extent of future building programmes. It was an uncompromising message, and spelt out the fact that

---

[3] He might also have forgotten his own representations to his grandmother, derogatory to her then Prime Minister, Lord Salisbury – for which he had received a very frosty response.

an increased German building programme could only result in the High Seas Fleet being in a position of greater inferiority than would be the case if the provisions of the 'Novelle' were not introduced. Adding a final shot to this broadside, Churchill stated that the 60% margin of superiority would only continue to apply whilst Britain retained a huge advantage, both in numbers and in quality, of pre-Dreadnought vessels. As these ships vanished from the effective list, the margin would have to be adjusted to reflect the loss of this considerable superiority in second line vessels.

One aspect of Churchill's speech that did not go down well with British public opinion, was the declaration that the Mediterranean Fleet would be scaled down in order to concentrate all the most modern ships in home waters. Given the logic of the overall argument that Germany was now the prime, if not the only, threat to British maritime interests, it was a difficult decision to contest. However, it was a blow to the sense of imperial pride that a long-established, and pre-eminent, naval presence in an area of strategic consequence was having to be denuded to meet the requirements of the new situation. To the traditionalists, this intention was akin to the Romans having to 'call the legions home' when the heartland of that great empire, the Italian peninsular and Rome itself, was under threat of invasion by the barbarian hordes. It had been a defining moment in history, and not one with which they were comfortable or wished to see repeated.

In retrospect, the simile is not inapt, and it was certainly seen by a perplexed public, reared on the glories of imperial expansion, as a retreat from empire at the very moment that, to all but the most farseeing, it seemed to be at its zenith. However it appeared to the average Briton, to the rulers of Germany this action sent another very unpalatable message. The threat to Britain represented by the German Fleet had been absolutely recognised, and nothing whatsoever – no matter how painful to British opinion and interests elsewhere – was going to distract the British Government from taking the necessary measures to meet that threat with overwhelming power. Tirpitz, in his memoirs, chose to interpret this development as a justification for the High Seas Fleet. He referred to the German Fleet as a 'Trump Card' that had been placed at the disposal of his diplomats:

'...one must remember that in consequence of the concentration of the English forces *which we had caused* [authors italics] in the North Sea, the English control of the Mediterranean and Far-Eastern waters had practically ceased.' (10)

This seems a somewhat risible and desperate attempt to present the subsequent situation in a favourable light. Forcing a potential enemy to concentrate superior strength against you does not come across as a stroke of strategic or tactical genius! Even more serious was the fact that this supposed triumph had forced Britain to adopt a course which resulted in her having to make alliances with other powers potentially hostile to Germany – entanglements that the British Government would, by preference, have otherwise avoided. A British commentator, Sir Frederick Pollock, accurately sums up the inheritance of Tirpitz and the pan-German nationalists:

'The Germans will go down to history as people who foresaw everything except what actually happened, and calculated everything except its cost to themselves.' (11)

By reducing its fleet in the Mediterranean, maritime protection of Britain's interests in the area became, perforce, dependent on the French maintaining the bulk of their fleet in that sea. There was no formal agreement to that end, but, in the event, the French Navy withdrew all its modern heavy units from the Atlantic and English Channel coasts, and redeployed them to Toulon and Algeria.

Intentional or not, this placed a definite burden of moral responsibility on the British Government should France happen to be assaulted on her western coasts – which, arguably had been deliberately denuded of protection to cover for the British in the Mediterranean. That this informal, and unacknowledged, state of affairs was uncomfortable for the British is without doubt, and it was firmly intended that, once the naval building programme permitted, the re-establishment of a strong British battle squadron in the Mediterranean would take place. That, however, could not be achieved, at the best estimate, until at least 1915. In the meantime, a force of three or four battlecruisers, an armoured cruiser squadron, and other vessels, was to be based on Malta to preserve a significant and versatile 'presence'. However unpleasant this decision must have been for the British, it was, despite Tirpitz's assertion, a disaster for Germany. Churchill's views on the subject emphasise the political discomfiture caused to the British by this state of affairs. Britain was being pressured into a much closer commitment to France than she would otherwise (Sir Henry Wilson, and the Army General Staff apart) have desired:

'The only "trump card" which Germany secured by this policy was the driving of Britain and France closer and closer together. From the moment that the Fleets of France and Britain were disposed in this new way our common naval interests became very important. And the moral claims which France could make upon Great Britain if attacked by Germany, whatever we had stipulated to the contrary, were enormously extended. Indeed, my anxiety was aroused to try and prevent this necessary recall of our ships from tying us up too tightly with France and depriving us of that liberty of choice on which our power to stop a war might well depend.' (12)

He expressed his concerns in a lucid and well-reasoned letter to the Foreign Secretary:

'The point I am anxious to safeguard is our freedom of choice if the occasion arises, and consequent power to influence French policy beforehand. That freedom will be sensibly impaired if the French can say that they have denuded their Atlantic seaboard and concentrated in the Mediterranean on the faith of naval arrangements made with us. This will not be true. If we did not exist, the French could not make better dispositions than at present. They are not strong enough to face Germany alone, still less to maintain themselves in two theatres. They therefore rightly concentrate their navy in the Mediterranean where it can be safe and superior and can assure their African communications. Neither is it true that we are relying on France to maintain our position in the Mediterranean…*If France did not exist, we should make no other disposition of our forces.* [authors italics]…Every one must feel who knows the facts that we have the obligations of an alliance without its advantages, and above all without its precise definitions.' (13)

Britain had been forced into a position she did not wish to occupy, and that position was absolutely detrimental to German strategic interests.

The results of the decision to run down the Mediterranean Fleet (albeit only until such time as numbers of ships permitted its re-establishment) in order to concentrate the bulk of the navy in home waters, should have sent a powerful message to the naval lobby in Germany. That, and all the other weighty matters Churchill addressed whilst presenting the estimates, should have been absolutely apparent to the German establishment.

On the face of it, in view of the First Lord's speech, only a fool in Germany would want to go ahead with the 'Novelle' for the sake of a few more battleships. This, however, was not the main point. As already mentioned, the sting of the 'Novelle' was in its tail. It was the increases in personnel and subsidiary classes of vessels that provided the main cause for worry, and why Tirpitz was so anxious for its acceptance. These other factors would enable a large proportion of the German Fleet to be fully operational, and supported, on a year-round basis. It represented a huge enhancement of the fleet's capabilities – far more than could be achieved by just adding extra dreadnoughts to its existing strength. These other matters, though, could not be mentioned at the time of Churchill's speech. As he explains:

'It would of course have been a breach of faith with the German Emperor to let any suggestion pass my lips that we already knew what the text of the Navy Law was. I was therefore obliged to make my first speech on naval matters on a purely hypothetical basis.' (14)

Whatever Churchill was unable to say, the coded message to Germany, given in his address to parliament, was crystal clear. The threat to British interests presented by the German Fleet would be met. The challenge would be repulsed. Britain would be adamantine in the preservation of its naval supremacy.

Despite the trenchant content of Churchill's speech, there was also extended an olive branch towards Germany, of which more later. Essentially, though, his address to parliament had the effect of cutting through the diplomatic verbiage that had previously surrounded the subject of naval rivalry. It categorically stated the realities of the situation, and of the measures that were being taken to deal with the immediate consequences of *being* in that situation.

If his address was well received in the British parliament, it cut little ice in Berlin. The Kaiser termed it 'arrogant' and 'offensive'. In any case, the failure of the diplomats to agree on a formula for a non-aggression treaty had already scuppered Bethmann's dreams of a rapprochement between the two nations. Churchill's words merely served to confirm the long-held prejudices of his opponents. Logic and reason were set aside, and the Chancellor conceded the stage to Tirpitz. Within a fortnight the terms of the 'Novelle' were officially published, and, over the next six weeks, the law was duly presented to, and rubber stamped by, the *Reichstag*.

The first casualty of this process was the German Ambassador in London. For a decade he had accurately reported and assessed the mood of the British people and their leaders. He had consistently emphasised the impossibility of improving Anglo-German relations whilst the question of naval competition remained unresolved, and, just as consistently, this advice had been ignored. He had become tarred with the brush of being 'incurably' Anglophile. Now, in the hallowed tradition of shooting the messenger if he did not bring good tidings, Metternich was relieved of his post. The British Prime Minister of the time gave a good assessment of the German Ambassador, and, by inference, the fact that he would be a loss to the German diplomatic corps and to the cause of better Anglo-German relations:

'Count Metternich was a man of the highest honour, a vigilant and pertinacious custodian of all German interests, and at the same time genuinely anxious to maintain not only peaceful but friendly relations with Great Britain. His disposition was not genial, and he led a retired and almost isolated life in London. He was stiff and reserved in his methods of expression. He was, however, a shrewd and dispassionate observer both of men and events, an expert chronicler of what he saw and heard, with a sturdy and independent judgement. He was not well adapted to serve under such masters as the wayward and opinionated Kaiser and his vacillating though dogmatic chancellor. He had a considerable measure both of insight and foresight, qualities in which they were both lamentably lacking.' (15)

Metternich's replacement was the one time Secretary of State for Foreign Affairs, and, for the previous fifteen years, German Ambassador to the Ottoman Empire, Baron Adolf Marschall von Bieberstein.

Marschall was an imposing personality and an undoubted political heavyweight. His philosophy towards Britain was seen to be more robust than that of Metternich, and much more in tune with that of the Kaiser, and the Tirpitz clique.

'"...no Minister had done more than Marschall to awaken understanding of the political and economic disadvantages of our not having a fleet, before the period of systematic popular instruction which began with the appointment of Admiral Tirpitz to the Admiralty"...In contrast to his predecessor Freiherr v Marschall immediately began to study seriously the concrete numerical and constructional proportions of the two navies one to the other...In connection with this task he came to see me shortly before his departure for London, and in the course of a long conversation we arrived at perfect unanimity with regard to the naval policy to be pursued.' (16)

Unfortunately for both the latter, his appointment was to be of the most fleeting nature. Marschall briefly visited London to inspect his new embassy and then departed on leave to his estate in Germany, where he promptly, and inconveniently, expired. Tirpitz remarks that:

'His early death was a loss of incalculable effect to Germany, *so poor in real statesmen.*' [Authors italics] (17)

Without wishing to seem heartless, there is a delicious irony in this unexpected turn of events – in that the official reason given by Berlin for the supercession of Metternich, a genuinely 'real statesman', was on grounds of health.

A new ambassador had to be found at short notice, and there were few obvious choices. The mantle eventually fell on Prince Karl Max Lichnowsky, a *Junker* from Silesia who had had no diplomatic appointments for the previous ten years. Without in any way impugning the reputation of Lichnowsky, who proved to be a capable and respected ambassador, it is a comment on the dearth of talent within the German diplomatic establishment that there were no other, more qualified, candidates immediately available for this key posting.

Lichnowsky, to the chagrin of the Kaiser, took very few weeks in his new appointment before coming to exactly the same conclusions as had Metternich. His subsequent relations with Berlin proved to be as equally difficult as those of his predecessor. As it was, all his representations were generally undermined by a junior member of his own staff.

Tirpitz had, some years before, installed one of his minions as Naval Attaché in London. This officer, whose pedigree was impeccably pro-navalist and pan-German, was encouraged to send his own appreciations of the diplomatic and naval situation direct to the State Secretary of the Navy, and behind the back of the ambassador, his nominal superior. From Tirpitz, these reports were privately relayed to the Kaiser, behind the back of the German Chancellor. The navalists thus successfully bypassed the official channels of communication. Being more palatable to the taste of the 'All

Highest', the Naval Attaché's appreciations were generally given credence over the balanced and reasoned reports of Lichnowsky or his predecessor. With Bethmann neutralised, the higher direction of German policy towards Britain was in the hands of a mercurial monarch and a single issue naval militarist whose policies were fuelled by the support of a virulent nationalist cadre. Despite the well-intentioned efforts of all those who disagreed, German policy towards Britain and the naval question would henceforth proceed on the well-honed and comfortable basis of ignorance and arrogance, and, as the inevitable consequence of the two, stupidity.

If Churchill had wielded the metaphorical stick towards Germany during his speech on the naval estimates, he also proffered a carrot – this being one entirely of his own cultivation. He posted the suggestion of both nations taking what he termed a 'Naval Holiday'. He describes it thus:

'Take, as an instance of this proposition I am putting forward for general consideration, the year 1913. In that year, as I apprehend, Germany will build three capital ships, and it will be necessary for us to build five in consequence.
'Supposing we were both to take a holiday for that year and introduce a blank page into the book of misunderstanding; supposing that Germany were to build no ships that year, she would save herself between six and seven millions sterling. But that is not all. In ordinary circumstances we should not begin our ships until Germany had started hers. The three ships that she did not build would therefore wipe out no fewer than five British potential super-dreadnoughts. That is more than I expect they could hope to do in a brilliant naval action. As to the indirect results within a single year, they simply cannot be measured.' (18)

This is a wonderful example of a typical Churchillian proposition – eloquently born out of inspiration and optimism, but untrammelled by hard facts or realities. He was saved from the ignominy of being disavowed by his own colleagues by a surprisingly courteous response from the Kaiser that terminated the whole idea. Wilhelm, through the Ballin/Cassell conduit, informed Churchill that, whilst appreciating the sentiment, 'such arrangements were possible only between allies'. The Kaiser, by stamping on the idea from the outset, prevented Churchill from taking what was folly, further. That is not to say that this idea did not continue to ferment within his extremely active mind, and he was never one to readily abandon a concept once it had taken root in the fertile soil of his intellect.

However attractive the idea might have seemed, it was simplistic in the extreme, and took no account of the economic and commercial realities of the time. Over a five or ten year period of peace, it was entirely possible that the economy of a country could be gradually weaned off a diet of ships and armaments, and the workforce transferred into other industries that could be developed as alternative employment. It was ridiculous, though, to suggest that the two contending nations could simply take a year off building ships, channel the money saved into more worthy causes, and then start all over again twelve months hence. Many of the shipbuilding firms of both countries would have been faced with bankruptcy unless they were to lay off a considerable proportion of their workforces for the period of the 'holiday' – in which case, tens of thousands of skilled workers would have been thrown into the unemployment queues, and priceless skills lost elsewhere. Continuity of work was essential to the viability of the armaments industry in both countries.

Churchill never lost his enthusiasm for this impossible scheme, and tried to resurrect it later, but there was never any realistic chance of it receiving serious consideration on either side of the North Sea. At best, the initiative was seen as well-intentioned, if impractical. As such, it deserved commendation for at least being an original attempt to break out of the grip of the arms race. It might even have been the starting point for a wider and more comprehensive debate that could have led on to greater things. However, to the likes of Tirpitz and his ilk, it was just another political smokescreen to cover up Britain's dark intentions to keep Germany forever in 'vassalage'. There was nothing that could have been done or said by Churchill, or any other senior British politician, that would ever have dispelled the suspicions of the people who now dominated German public opinion and government policy.

Dramatic events in Europe now began to overtake the limited sphere of Anglo-German negotiations, but, for the purposes of continuity, it is convenient to follow the progress of that relationship to its conclusion.

If all the great hopes raised by the Haldane Mission had been dissipated by subsequent events, the frank and generally amiable nature of the talks had represented a welcome breakthrough in the ability of London and Berlin to conduct a reasonable and sensible dialogue. In that sense, the process had been thoroughly worthwhile, and it had produced a much more positive atmosphere for any future contacts between the two governments. As Marder comments:

'The Haldane Mission was not, however, without beneficial results. Relations between the two governments became somewhat more cordial. During the negotiations Grey had expressed the hope that even if no agreements were reached, the Mission and the free and open exchange of views that it had brought about might serve as a basis for a more candid and confidential relationship in future. This expectation was partially realised.' (19)

Co-operation in areas of mutual interest and the tone of communications between Britain and Germany distinctly improved in the next two years, and was an important factor when international crises once again began to flare up in the Balkans and elsewhere. There continued to be a dialogue on matters of mutual concern, including the subject of possible colonial acquisitions for Germany.

A particular concern of Britain was also addressed as part of the overall picture. This was the contentious issue of the Baghdad railway, a German-financed and controlled project to link Europe with the Middle East. At that time, before the era of the car or the aeroplane, railways had a massive strategic and economic importance. Before they existed, the world's trade and military activity was either conducted by sea or on foot (whether of the two or four legged variety). Of the two, sea transport was generally faster, more suited to bulk, and the only method of venturing beyond a specific land mass. The railway revolutionised transport, and, with it, the whole concept of the movement of goods and people. Critically, it was also able to rapidly deploy, reinforce, and resupply fully-equipped armies.

In the case of the two great continental powers, Russia and the United States, railways provided the means to pacify and unlock the almost limitless potential of their vast interiors. Elsewhere, in Africa, South America and Asia, other industrialised nations constructed railways to tap the resources of their colonies. Where colonies did not exist, private European companies, heavily sponsored by their respective governments, competed for the contracts to build and run railway systems. To the successful companies (and, as an automatic extension, to their parent country) it gave enormous influence within the host nation. This was extended by granting loans to those nations in order to finance the construction of the project. The bigger the loan, the more indebted each country became to the purveyor of the finance. Economic colonialisation is not just a recent trend.

From the strategic point of view, therefore, the concept of a continuous railway that could link Berlin with Baghdad via Constantinople was a tempting objective for German planners. Germany was making a determined effort, with considerable success, to court the Ottoman Empire as a potential ally and as a market for German products and expertise. It could also act as a conduit to extend German influence to areas previously beyond the bounds of its ambitions. These would encroach on a region that had become absolutely vital to British interests.

As previously related, for most of the previous century (Gladstone's administrations excepted), Britain had attempted to prop up the increasingly ramshackle Ottoman Empire as a buffer against Russian expansion and penetration into the Mediterranean and the Middle East. The task had proved largely thankless due to the corruption and incompetence that pervaded the

Turkish realm. Not for nothing was the Sultan's regime contemptuously referred to as 'the sick man of Europe'. For all that, what passed for a government in Constantinople had generally been very Anglophile for many decades. The British Mediterranean Fleet had long been, after all, the most powerful guarantor of the declining empire's territorial integrity, particularly against the threat from Russia. This attitude began to change following the 'Young Turk' revolution in 1908, and German influence gradually came to supplant that of Great Britain. Although the British still maintained a naval mission in Constantinople charged with the thankless task of trying to improve the efficiency of the Turkish Navy, it was to Germany that the Ottomans turned for assistance with the much more significant matter of reforming the army. German military officers poured into the country and, although officially there only as advisors, effectively took over many of the leading staff and command positions in the Turkish land forces. This was not an inconsequential development.

As mentioned earlier, Britain had made a momentous political decision, with regards to her navy, in turning from home produced coal to oil as the optimum means of fuelling all her future major warships. From the moment that the British Government adopted this new policy, the Persian Gulf region became of prime importance to the operational effectiveness of the Royal Navy. At the time of the decision, it was recognised that it involved the abandonment of a safe and guaranteed source of fuel for one that was far distant and very much less secure. The oilfields that would supply this vital demand lay in South-Western Persia, on what is now the Southern Iraq/Iran border, and this region directly abutted onto the Mesopotamian province of the Ottoman Empire, with its capital in Baghdad. Completion of the Baghdad railway would represent a potent threat to British interests in the area in that it would enable the Turks (and Germany, if allied to the Ottoman Empire) to rapidly deploy and support a much larger force, much more efficiently, than had hitherto been the case. Additionally, although the original plan had envisaged the railway terminating at Baghdad, it was clearly not a difficult matter to extend a spur the remaining few hundred miles to the port of Basra, on the Persian Gulf. This option was soon adopted, although, in the end, the outbreak of war prevented its immediate realisation.

If a railway to Baghdad rang alarm bells in the British establishment, the prospect of its extension to the Gulf ratcheted up the volume of the tocsin. The Persian Gulf was the natural access to the area from the open seas, and the only conduit by which any British forces could be sent, if necessary, to protect the Persian oilfields from outside interference. As such, this small and enclosed offshoot of the oceans was beginning to assume considerable strategic importance. In that context, it was not irrelevant that German commercial interests had already established themselves in the area, intent on developing the mineral resources on several of the islands, and exploiting the other trading opportunities offered by the region.

British naval interest in the Gulf had previously been limited to dealing with the minor irritations of Arab piracy and the slave trade. This had been part and parcel of its routine role as the world's policeman. As a result of these concerns, a small, but permanent, shore presence had been established in the area, and treaties made with certain of the sheikhdoms that surrounded the coast of the region. This presence, unless considerably reinforced, would become tenuous when, rather than if, a Turkish (and German-controlled) rail link was established to Basra.

It was one of the positive results of the atmosphere created by the Haldane Mission that this situation was able to be discussed by the politicians and civil servants of both Britain and Germany in a reasonable manner. A frank exchange of views took place, following which there were extended negotiations. Eventually, an agreement emerged.

Britain's legitimate interests in the area were acknowledged, and her concerns addressed. Germany accepted that the Persian Gulf was a region that came within Britain's sphere of influence, and that any German commercial penetration of the area would be subject to British control and regulations. On the other side of the coin, the Baghdad railway project would go ahead, and Britain would have equal rights with Turkey and Germany to utilise its facilities once it was completed. This was about the best deal the British could have achieved. Realistically, the railway was probably going to be completed whether she liked it or not, and the political concessions extracted in recognition of this were of real value.

If nothing else, the settlement of the Baghdad railway question showed that Britain and Germany could negotiate in a reasonable manner to sort out their outstanding differences. In the couple of years between 1912 and 1914, there were to be other instances in which the two nations co-operated in their mutual interest, and maintained positive contact in all matters of international concern. Basically, in most situations, the two nations were not at all incompatible. The one nagging issue that separated them, and the one which always proved to be completely insuperable, was the question of Germany's challenge to British maritime supremacy.

The 'Novelle' of 1912 proved to be the high water mark of German naval ambitions and expansion. No further additions or adjustments to the German Navy Laws were to take place before the Great War drew a final line under the arms race. In any case, there had commenced a certain swing in opinion within Germany which militated against further expenditure on the navy.

After many years of having to play second fiddle, at least in terms of publicity, to the navy, the pressing requirements of the army began to be re-established in the national consciousness.

After the humiliating defeat by Japan, Russia had set about the regeneration of her armed forces. Although too weak, at the time of the Bosnian crisis in 1908, to face the threat of conflict with Germany, the Russian Empire had been rapidly regaining its strength. With her enormous reservoirs of manpower and natural resources, Russia had always been capable of attaining the status of a superpower. That she had not previously reached this point was mainly due to the incompetence of the ruling class and to the gross inefficiency and corruption that pervaded the bureaucracy. Nevertheless, sufficient progress was being made in resurrecting the military capabilities of the state to be a cause of worry to Berlin. Pessimists in the German establishment calculated that, by 1917, the country would be in a position of military inferiority if confronted by both France and Russia. This produced an alarming conclusion.

Cold logic dictated that this situation could only be averted by means of a pre-emptive war against one, or both, of these nations whilst Germany still possessed the means to guarantee success in the endeavour. This attitude was, of course, prevalent amongst the Army General Staff, and the extension of this logic pointed to a strengthening of the army regardless of any other claims on the nation's resources. In terms of Germany's basic security, the army's interests were paramount and the fleet had, indeed, become a relative 'luxury'.

Even Tirpitz recognised the danger, and the 'Novelle' would most probably have been his last sortie into the pockets of the taxpayers for many years. The German naval construction programme had been established on a secure basis for the foreseeable future, and a period of consolidation was in order. That this, in itself, still caused alarm abroad was evidenced by the continuing efforts of British politicians, Churchill in particular, to curb German naval expansion.

In his speech to parliament, presenting the naval estimates for 1913/14, Churchill returned to his pet scheme for a 'naval holiday'. He must have known by then that this proposal was a non-runner, but, perhaps, resurrected it as a sop to the pacifist element of his party. To no one's surprise, the suggestion was again dismissed by Germany even more cursorily than when it had first been aired. The whole question of Anglo-German naval rivalry did not, however, go away.

There is a footnote to the naval situation which has something of an ironic humour about it.

During Metternich's period of duty as ambassador in London, Tirpitz had installed one of his acolytes as the German Naval Attaché at the embassy. This officer, a Captain Müller, was encouraged to send his reports direct to the Naval Secretary without submitting them for approval to his nominal superior. These reports differed greatly in their assessment of the naval situation from those of the ambassador, and were used as ammunition by Tirpitz to discredit Metternich's opinions with the Kaiser. Whereas the ambassador's reasoned and pertinent communications were usually telling Wilhelm what he wished to ignore, the thoughts of Captain Müller were of a more robust nature, and much more in harmony with the 'All Highest's' perception of affairs. When Metternich was relieved of his position by, first, Marschall, and then Prince Lichnowsky, Müller remained in place, still rendering his despatches to Tirpitz behind the back of the ambassador. The naval attaché had become aware that his reports were being passed on, via Tirpitz, to the Kaiser, and were being given more credence than the official communications from the Embassy. Captain Müller duly became besotted with his apparent ability to influence the decisions of the mighty. Tirpitz's mole duly became a severe irritant to his erstwhile master.

The naval attaché in London was attaining a personal status with the Emperor that threatened to supersede the influence of Tirpitz himself. Müller was not unaware of this and became increasingly sure of himself and more strident in his reports. In the face of these, Tirpitz was forced to make what was, for him, an astonishing admission. To his bumptious former acolyte in London he offered the opinion that 'the bow is overstrung here as much as in England'. As E.L. Woodward remarks, it was:

'...a confession which he had never made before the year 1914.' (20)

Tirpitz would have further astonished his contemporaries by a statement in his memoirs in which he suggested that he had argued for the navy's requirements to be subordinated to those of the army. This extraordinary assertion referred to a time at which he was concentrating all his power and influence on forcing through the provisions of the 'Novelle':

'The army was kept too small in time of peace, and the fatal omission was made of not drawing sufficiently on Germany's defensive powers. At the end of 1911 the Chancellor introduced an Army Bill. This, however, was not big enough, and the 1913 Bill came too late to take full effect during the war. I myself had proposed to the Minister of War...just before Christmas 1911, that together with me he should insist upon the immediate introduction of a Defence Bill, and I expressed my readiness to subordinate my demands to those of the army.' (21)

He continues with a remark of sublime and bland ignorance as to the effect naval expenditure had had on the resources available to strengthen the army:

'The opinion at General Headquarters in the autumn of 1914 was that the war against France would have been won if the two army corps had been there which the General Staff had allowed itself to be done out of in 1911-12, contrary to the demands of the experts.' (22)

The resources that could have supplied the missing two or three army corps that might have made the difference between victory and stalemate in 1914, had already been expended on a fleet of battleships that was not permitted to play any useful part in the crucial turn of events. The money, the men, the armour and the guns that probably would have made the critical difference were tied up in ships tethered to their moorings in Kiel and Wilhelmshaven, or swinging round their anchors in Jade Bay. There they remained, forbidden to make any contribution to the conflict, and, in particular, to even strive to prevent the reinforcement of the army's immediate foe.

Woodward's encapsulation of the Tirpitz period, and the results of the policy to which he had held so firm, is clearly and plainly stated:

'Tirpitz's acknowledgement that any further increase in the German navy would be a "great political blunder" is a curious "last word" in the history of the naval competition between Great Britain and Germany. Fourteen years had gone by since the Navy Law of 1900. The danger-zone was not yet passed. The 'risk' theory had lost any political meaning. Great Britain might hesitate for a score of valid reasons from entering upon a naval war with Germany. These reasons did not include the calculation that even a victorious war with Germany would leave a weak British fleet open to attack from France or Russia, the United States, or Japan. The "alliance" value of the German fleet had been one of the main arguments of the advocates of a strong navy. The effect of the fleet had been to draw Great Britain more closely to France and Russia. The fleet was one of the causes of the isolation of Germany, and yet it was not strong enough in time of war to protect German commerce or the German colonies, or to meet its main rival on the open sea…Finally, although the financial burden of the British navy was heavy on the taxpayers, and although there might be complaints that this burden was unnecessarily severe, the first signs of actual exhaustion came not from Britain but from Germany.' (23)

All these considerations would now become academic. War came suddenly upon the scene and obliterated the long years of effort that well-intentioned diplomats on many sides had devoted to maintaining the semblance of equilibrium in Europe.

For more than two generations, involvement in the turbulent affairs, and bitter rivalries, of the Balkan states had regularly pushed the major powers of Europe to the threshold of hostilities. On each previous occasion, reason and self-interest had intervened in the nick of time, and those nations had stepped back from the brink of catastrophe. The next Balkan crisis was to be prolonged, and it would not have a peaceful conclusion. This time, Europe was to be propelled over the precipice, and it was utterly ignorant as to the extent of the abyss that lay beyond. It would engulf the bones of many millions more than that of Bismarck's 'single Pomeranian Grenadier'.

CHAPTER FIFTEEN

TWILIGHT OF THE EMPIRES 1912-1914

'Two vast combinations, each disposing of enormous military Resources, dwelt together at first side by side, but gradually face to face.'

Winston Churchill: *The World Crisis*

'Those who entrust the destiny of their country to war...incur unforeseeable risks which may be fatal to them and the land they love.'

David Lloyd-George: *War Memoirs*

'What it seems fairly clear that Germany did not want, was war.'

Hew Strachan: *The First World War*

It was inevitable that the affairs of the fractious, unstable and semi-formed states of South-Eastern Europe would continue to torment the stability of the continent. Thirty-five years earlier, Bismarck had predicted that the next great European conflict would have its origins in this region.[1] His forecast proved to be sadly accurate. By 1914, Europe was a vast magazine of previously unimaginable explosive potential. The Balkan peninsular was its tinderbox.

The Balkan wars that broke out between 1912 and 1914 might not seem to be strictly relevant to this account, but they directly affected the relations between the major European powers – and not entirely in a negative sense. Not only did the brutal conflicts in the region pose a threat to the already delicate status quo in Europe, but they also provided an opportunity for the established power blocs to get together in a common cause. For a brief while, the tribulations of the south-east corner of Europe served to bring together the Triple Alliance and the Triple Entente in an effort to co-operate on a matter of genuine and pressing mutual concern. On

---

[1] It was also the region that he famously suggested was not worth the bones of a single Pomeranian Grenadier. It was, directly or indirectly, to claim the bones of more soldiers, of any designation, than Bismarck can possibly have imagined.

the other hand, the road to Armageddon was becoming clogged with uninvited ramblers – many of whom were strangers to the concept of international diplomacy.

The liberation of the Balkan peninsular from Turkish rule had been a stop/start process for over forty years (ninety, if the Greek independence struggle is taken into consideration), and had yet to be resolved. Greece, Rumania, Bulgaria, Serbia, and Montenegro had all come into existence as independent nations by a variety of convoluted routes and stages over that period, but the Turkish presence continued to be a major factor in the region. Albania, Macedonia, Kosovo, and much of modern-day northern Greece remained part of the Ottoman Empire. The weight of Turkish influence still rested heavily on the entire area from the Bosphorus to the Adriatic, although the power of the central government was clearly on the wane. Misha Glennie remarks that:

'The great powers had begun to anticipate the dismemberment of the Ottoman Empire a century before the Great Eastern Crisis. Since the end of the eighteenth century, Paris, London, Vienna and St. Petersburg maintained operational plans to deal with convulsions in the East. Prussia was the one power that showed little interest in the region...France, and especially Britain were prepared to use diplomatic and military methods to keep the sick man alive. Russia and Austria-Hungary were open to the idea of dividing his Ottoman spoils. These plans changed as the sands of international relations shifted unpredictably but rarely took account of the aspirations of the people who actually inhabited the region.' (1)

As the disparate races of the area coalesced into sovereign nations, their 'aspirations' began to intrude on the established ambitions of the major powers, and to further destabilise the already volatile situation in the Balkan peninsular.

The various newly-fledged states had little love for each other but all coveted portions of the remaining Turkish possessions in Europe. Due to the fact that the different races and religions were greatly intermixed and that their individual territorial ambitions overlapped to an alarming extent, it was a devil's brew and a recipe for conflict. The situation was exacerbated by the ancient and virulent hatreds that had festered for hundreds of years between the Balkan races, and which had only been partially constrained by the long centuries of stern, but mainly fair (or at least equally unfair), Ottoman rule.

None of the new nations were yet strong enough to act alone against the still formidable military machine available to the Turkish Government, but, in combination, they possessed more than adequate resources and manpower to prevail – albeit only if they could agree on a co-ordinated plan of action and an equitable division of the subsequent spoils. The first proviso proved to be briefly attainable; the second, impossible.

Nevertheless, by the autumn of 1912, with the aid of Russian brokerage, an alliance of sorts had been secretly concluded between Serbia, Bulgaria, Greece and Montenegro.

The Balkan League, as the alliance was named, had as its object the conquest and division of all the remaining Turkish provinces in Europe. Unfortunately, there was no prior formal agreement, should success attend their efforts, on where to draw the future borders between their countries. That problem would not be addressed until after the resolution of the impending conflict. Given the mutual loathing between the component states of the League, and their greed for territory, the chances of an amicable settlement on the subject of new frontiers was something of a pious hope. There was also a notable absentee from the Balkan League.

Rumania, not having a common frontier with any of the Ottoman possessions, had not been closely involved in the negotiations that led to the alliance. Nevertheless, the government of that nation resented the fact that it had been excluded from the vultures' feast on the perceived corpse. Although one of the most powerful of the Balkan countries, Rumania regarded with some foreboding the potential expansion and strengthening of her neighbours, particularly Bulgaria. For the moment she stayed her hand.

At this late point, Russia began to have well-justified doubts about the wisdom of the enterprise, fearing that it could escalate into a general European war that would set her against Germany and Austria – a confrontation for which she was not yet ready. In the first week of October 1912, when the preparations for war could no longer be disguised, Russia did something of a *volte-face* and joined Austria in a joint warning to the Balkan League that no annexation of Turkish territory should be contemplated, even in the case of a successful military campaign. As an example of muddled thinking, this belated attempt to limit the consequences of a certain catastrophe is a classic. The whole, and sole, point of the imminent conflict, from the Balkan League's point of view, was that of the annexation of territory. The League had no other purpose or reason.

The Austro-Russian warning, in any case, came much too late to influence events that were already under way. Matters were brought to a head from an unlikely source. Whilst Serbia, Greece, and Bulgaria hesitated, the King of tiny Montenegro took positive action and declared war on Turkey.

'This rare unity of Vienna and St. Petersburg failed to impress King Nikita of Montenegro, who had played the game of Balkan diplomacy for more than half a century and could distinguish a genuine threat from a pious hope. Claiming that Turkey was exercising an intolerable tyranny over Montenegro's Albanian neighbours (whose very existence the Montenegrins had done their best to ignore for 500 years), Nikita declared war on the Sultan on October 8th...it was a development of great significance. The Balkan kingdoms were no longer content to remain puppets of the Great Powers. They were assuming an independence and initiative unknown in previous crises.' (2)

It is slightly absurd that one of the smallest, least developed, and most insignificant states in Europe should have provided the catalyst for a ferocious conflict that would permanently alter the political map of the continent. However, the events that were about to unfold bore little resemblance to a 'mouse that roared' script. There were few comic moments to come. The sheer barbarity of the war that was about to erupt constituted one of the most revolting episodes in the history of the twentieth century, and has left scars on all the participants which refuse to heal to this day.

There was, though, a preamble to the imminent war in the Balkans that would be critical to its outcome. The Turkish ability to react to the threat had already been weakened by the necessity to meet an attack from elsewhere.

Italy had been reunified as a state some ten years before the German Empire was established, but, lacking the industrial base and population of the latter, her development had not proceeded at the same breakneck speed. Nevertheless, like post-Bismarckian Germany, Italy also wanted her 'place in the sun' and to join the top table of nations that could boast of imperial possessions. The problem for Italy was that the cake had already been divided and very few crumbs remained on the plate. This, for Italian imperialists, posted something of a dilemma, but a solution was found in the shape of the last remaining possession of the Ottoman Empire on the continent of Africa. Very conveniently, it was also within easy range of Italy itself.

Between French-governed Tunisia and the (all but in name) British protectorate of Egypt, lay the lands of Tripolitania and Cyrenaica – present day Libya. This area, although internally largely self-governing, was still under the official sovereignty of Constantinople. It was policed and protected by substantial regular units of the Turkish Army, and administered by the appointees of the Sultan.

In 1911, in order to appease nationalist sentiment, the Italian Government cynically set out to rob this province from its long-term ruler. The risks involved seemed minimal, and any moral considerations as to the justification of the action (which were non-existent, it being simply an act of territorial greed) were happily disregarded.

The mechanics of the enterprise were hardly daunting. The Turkish ability to re-supply and reinforce the area by land had vanished many years previously when Britain had effectively occupied Egypt. Even had this block not existed, the logistics would have been insuperable in the conditions of the time. Consequently, Turkey could only rely on the efforts of her standing local forces in Tripoli and Cyrenaica to repel any invasion once war broke out. In fact, some reinforcement of the province by sea had been carried out in time to meet the threat but it proved to be a mistaken strategy. The forces sent were insufficient to tip the balance against the invaders, but at the same time they critically depleted the Turkish forces in Europe and Asia Minor where they would shortly be desperately required. Once the Italian Navy established local control of the contested waters, no further reinforcement of the beleaguered province was possible, whereas supplies of manpower and equipment flowed unimpeded from the ports of the aggressor.

The Italian Navy, although, as always, very much more impressive on paper than in terms of operational effectiveness, was still vastly superior to the obsolete and inefficient collection of warships that constituted Turkey's shambolic maritime defence force of the time. Italian warships, therefore, dominated the Eastern Mediterranean for the duration of hostilities. This domination also facilitated the Italian acquisition of the Dodecanese Islands, in particular Rhodes, a development that was of some irritation to Britain. The British Government had no wish to see a member of the Triple Alliance in possession of such strategically situated islands athwart the trade routes converging on the Suez Canal. The Italian occupation of the Dodecanese would have been a major diplomatic concern had not the advent of the First World War, and a reshuffling of allegiances, rendered such considerations irrelevant.

For all Italy's obvious advantages, the acquisition of Libya proved a lot more difficult than her planners had predicted. What was supposed to have been an uncontested invasion turned into a logistical nightmare through lack of efficient preparation and organisation, and the greatly inferior Turkish forces in their African province fought with spirit, and for some time. Even when the official Turkish resistance was inevitably overcome, the invaders were unable to rest on their lightly-bought laurels. The Italians inherited a long-term problem in the intransigence of the indigenous population. The Senussi tribes, who were thinly spread within the inhospitable interior regions of the country, had even less liking for their new rulers than they had had for the representatives of the Sultan. At least, in the latter case, they had a shared religious belief. With the Italians, there was no mutual area of contact, nor any convergence of interest. The result was a long, drawn-out insurgency that lasted intermittently for the entire period of thirty years that Italy claimed governance of the area. At best, effective Italian control of the region only ever extended to the coastal strip and isolated strong points in the interior.

This is a diversion away from the main theme, which is that the war with Italy materially detracted from Turkey's ability to meet the imminent threat from the Balkan League. The forces sent to Tripolitania and Cyrenaica were inadequate to affect the issue in Africa, but ensured a vital depletion of Turkish strength in her European possessions.

A side-effect of this conflict was that it constituted, just as had Austria-Hungary's annexation of Bosnia-Herzegovina four years previously, an unwelcome irritant to Germany's efforts to court influence with the Turks. Yet again, an ally of Germany had attacked the interests of a nation with whom Berlin was attempting to cultivate close relations. The Triple Alliance was utterly failing to establish a co-ordinated foreign policy beyond its stance towards the *Entente* powers.

A week after King Nikita's unilateral declaration of war, the remaining members of the Balkan League overcame their concern at the Austro-Russian warning, and – correctly assessing that the long-term differences between the two great powers meant that they probably never could, or would, act jointly – entered the fray with decisive effect. Serb armies from the west, Greeks from the south, and Bulgarians from the north descended on Kosovo, Macedonia and Thrace, outnumbering the Turkish defenders by two to one. It was a short and vicious war, lasting but seven weeks, and resulted in appalling casualties to all its participants.

The outcome of the war was inevitable. By late November, Turkish forces had been expelled from almost all of Europe. The fortresses of Ianina in the Epirus, Scutari in Albania, and the city of Adrianople (present-day Edirne), still held out, although all were closely invested by, respectively, the Greeks and Bulgarians. Constantinople itself was virtually under siege; the remaining Turkish forces having retreated to the Chatalja lines, the last defensible position outside the city. On the Gallipoli peninsular, a further, isolated, Turkish army stood behind improvised defences on the Bulair neck. In a hopeless situation, the Turks were rescued from complete collapse by the weather. Torrential rain swept the area between Adrianople and Constantinople from mid-November onwards, rendering the roads impassable for military transport. The Bulgarian forces were, themselves, also close to exhaustion. Almost within sight of the city that held an importance in the Christian mind second only to that of Jerusalem, and which controlled one of the great strategic maritime highways of the world, the momentum stalled.

'The thud of shells could be clearly heard in the great city on the Bosphorus and wild rumours of imminent disaster began to circulate. But the Bulgarian offensive had come to a halt. For days it never seemed to stop raining. The retreating Turks had sought to destroy the railway tracks and now the weather completed their task for them, washing the ground from under the sleepers. Water stood in deep pools around the encampments and there were gloomy tales of cholera in some Bulgarian units. It was no better in the Turkish lines...the fighting died away as chilly gusts swept in the first scuds of snow from Anatolia.' (3)

In these dreadful conditions, there was one final, desperate, offensive push by the Bulgarians that failed, at great cost in lives, to break the last-ditch resistance of the Turks defending the outskirts of their capital. The intervention of the weather, at this critical point in the war, probably had a profound effect on the subsequent map of Europe and the relations between its more powerful states. Had decent conditions prevailed for no more than a couple of weeks in late November 1912, Constantinople would probably have fallen to the Bulgarians and the modern-day Turkish state would have had, as its western border, the Asiatic side of the Bosphorus. As it was, Bulgaria fell tantalisingly short of its objective.

'To the Bulgars Constantinople was as remote and unattainable as ever. It was no compensation to discover that, while eight Bulgarian divisions were engaged in Thrace, the Serbs and Greeks were acquiring all the cherished prizes in Macedonia.' (4)

This perceived injustice was to have melancholy consequences, and these would not be long delayed.

On December 3rd, the Turkish Government accepted that the war was lost and concluded an armistice with the Serbs and Bulgarians. The Greeks and Montenegrins continued operations against the isolated strongholds of Ianina and Scutari, and Adrianople remained unconquered. This brief truce, born of mutual exhaustion, only lasted into January of 1913 when a military coup took place in Constantinople. Disgusted by the incompetence of the political authorities, a group of disaffected 'Young Turk' army officers, led by Enver Pasha, assumed control of the government. Their avowed intent was to regenerate the strength of the army and to reverse the humiliations of the recent war.

The first results of the coup were inauspicious, as its immediate effect was the abandonment of the truce between Turkey and the forces of Serbia and Bulgaria. The victorious Serbian Army sent reinforcements to aid the Bulgarians in the siege of Adrianople. On March 26th, the starving, plague-ridden, and exhausted defenders of the city capitulated. Ianina and Scutari also fell after prolonged fighting, and all the remaining pockets of Turkish resistance in Europe, excepting only the defenders of Constantinople and Gallipoli, were eliminated. At this point the major powers, alarmed by the extent of the Turkish collapse and its uncertain consequences intervened, and imposed an armistice. This was not achieved without a certain amount of coercion. King Nikita of Montenegro, as he had been at the beginning of the war, proved to be the least malleable of all the Balkan rulers. It was only when Austrian troops mustered on his northern border and the combined fleets of Britain, France, Italy, Austria and Russia appeared off his coastline that the recalcitrant monarch agreed to submit his cause to international arbitration – a process that was expedited by a substantial transfer of cash to his personal bank account.

A conference in London was convened to settle peace terms and to, rather hopefully, establish stable borders within the newly liberated areas of the region. The conference was attended by the London ambassadors of all the major European powers, closely briefed by their foreign ministers. As an exercise in diplomatic harmony, it was a roaring success. The representatives of the various nations got on famously and could have solved the Balkan question very satisfactorily had it not been for the inconvenient fact that none of them represented the interests and ambitions of the inhabitants of the area.

The conference, did, however, achieve two results; one lasting, the other temporary. The concrete result was the establishment of the sovereign state of Albania, which has survived as such, albeit with great tribulations, to this day. This piece of nation creation incensed Serbia, Greece and Montenegro, all of whom had expected to carve up the area and annex various portions to their existing territory. The appearance of an independent Albania completely stymied these ambitions.

The temporary benefit of the conference was in the much improved relations between the European powers that resulted from the generally amicable and positive conversations that took place within the forum. In addressing the Balkan problem, the governmental representatives of all the chief European nations were able to sit together and put their various points of view. A large measure of agreement attended their deliberations, and, at the end of May 1913, they secured a peace treaty between Turkey and the Balkan League.

The treaty, however, was fatally flawed in that it did not include a definitive agreement as to the permanent borders of Albania, nor to the satisfactory division of Macedonia and Thrace between the recently victorious combatants. These matters were shelved for further consideration by the ambassadors. Unfortunately, their efforts were overtaken by events. A more immediate solution to these problems was required by the nations of the Balkan League, and they soon took matters into their own hands. Having briefly acted in unison against a common enemy, they now turned on themselves.

Bulgaria had borne the brunt of the recent conflict, had committed more troops, and suffered greater losses in the common cause than had any of the other states. To opinion in the country, her gains from the war were not considered commensurate to her contribution, although possession of Adrianople and much of Thrace was, admittedly, a significant addition to the realm. Nevertheless, Serbian forces occupied much of the Macedonian territory that Bulgaria regarded as her rightful spoils, and the jewel of

Turkish Europe, the great multicultural city of Salonika, had fallen into the hands of the Greeks. In the latter case, the Bulgarian Army had only been beaten by a short head in the race to occupy the city, and a small detachment of her troops had actually established a foothold within the boundaries of the metropolis.

Possession of Salonika, as well as Eastern Macedonia, became a critical issue in Bulgaria, and inspired much passion that threatened to destabilise the government. Aware of these pressures, the Greeks and Serbs concluded a secret agreement to act jointly should Bulgaria attempt to challenge the extent of their conquests.

If Bulgaria had not enough problems, at this point the Rumanians decided to enter the equation. Despite playing no part in the First Balkan War, the government of that country demanded that it should be compensated for the gains achieved by the blood of her neighbours. The Rumanian argument, if it can be so dignified, was that Bulgaria's accession of territory in Thrace should be compensated by her agreeing to cede to Rumania some of her lands south of the Danube (the southern Dobruja – incidentally the most fertile land in the region). This was clearly unacceptable to the Bulgarians, and the military, aware that the situation was slipping out of their control, decided on pre-emptive action.

The war was lost, for the Bulgarians, in the space of ten days. Ruination followed. With all its forces engaged with the Serbs and the Greeks, the country was then assaulted by a new enemy on its undefended northern and eastern borders. The Rumanian Army crossed the Danube virtually unopposed and occupied the southern Dobruja. Seizing the unexpected opportunity, reinforced Turkish armies broke out of the Chatalja lines and Gallipoli, and very quickly re-conquered eastern Thrace. On the 23rd July, Adrianople, the one great Bulgarian gain from the First Balkan War, passed again, and finally, into Turkish hands. Seven days later, in an impossible situation, and militarily helpless, the Bulgarians sued for peace. The Second Balkan War was over.

The effects of the two wars were profound and extended far beyond the actual accretion of territory to the Balkan nations and the bundling of Turkish influence out of South-Eastern Europe. The Balkan states had flexed their muscles independently of the influence of the major powers – in many cases, directly contrary to the wishes of those powers – and had, with the notable exception of Bulgaria, greatly profited from the experience. There was a significant change in the mentality of the victorious governments, particularly that of Serbia. Far from being sated by the gains of the recent conflict, the mood of the moment was that of relentless expansion. Flushed with the sense of victory, the baleful eye of Serbian nationalists (although not most members of the government, who recognised that, militarily, Serbia had, for the moment, shot its bolt) now focused on their ethnic brethren in the Austrian provinces of Bosnia and Herzegovina.

Whilst the government of Serbia could not be seen to officially support the policies of its more extreme nationalist groups, it had to cope with the fact that there was much popular sympathy with the latter's aim to create a 'Greater Serbia'. It was also no secret that key figures within the administration had active links with these groups. One such organisation, the 'Black Hand', had, as a clandestine sponsor, the Serbian Defence Minister. It was with the latter's connivance that weapons were issued to an idealistic bunch of incompetents in Bosnia in order to attempt the assassination of the Austrian Crown Prince during the latter's state visit to Sarajevo, the capital of the province. This particular decision, by a subordinate minister of a relatively minor European state, was to result in the most catastrophic conflict, in terms of loss of life that had ever been experienced by the continent. It would also mark the end of the dynasties, which, for centuries, had ruled the most powerful nations in the world. Bismarck's old forebodings were swiftly transferred into reality.

The empires of Europe, in 1914, existed in an uneasy balance with each other. The one thing that they had in common was in the intense desire of the ruling elites to retain control of their realms. Self-preservation surmounted all other considerations. To that end, they bargained together with a view to preserving the sometimes frail status quo. Each, though, had their own agenda, interests, pre-occupations and prejudices. However amiable were the diplomatic relations at any time, these basic differences were bound to be a source of constant disagreement. Within this turmoil of international relationships, Great Britain and Germany could not act independently to sort out their bilateral differences – which, in effect, boiled down to the naval question and little else. In nearly all other matters, the two countries had few bones of contention, and frequently were in active co-operation on the world stage. The main problems, excepting naval matters, were with the actions and policies of their respective allies.

Essentially, the power brokerage of Europe boiled down to the relations between five nations: Russia, Germany, France, Great Britain, and Austria-Hungary. Italy hovered on the fringe of this group, whilst the Ottoman Empire remained a peripheral poor relation at the table. Briefly stated, the positions and policies of these nations were as follows:

Russia was in internal turmoil as the autocratic government of the Tsar wrestled with an increasingly strident revolutionary movement within the country. In 1905, tensions had come to the boil and, despite brutal countermeasures, there were violent demonstrations on the streets and mutiny in the forces. The immediate consequence was a tentative and unwilling move towards democratisation of the society, but this was insufficient in scale, and too slow in its rate of progress, to halt the rising tide of discontent. This was evidenced by continuing public unrest and a spate of assassination attempts against members of the government and aristocracy, some of which were successful. Both a Prime Minister and a Grand Duke fell victim to such attacks. The failures of Russia's foreign policy served only to fuel the pervading sense of malaise.

The disastrous war with Japan had dealt a heavy blow to Russia's military capabilities, not to mention her prestige, but her huge resources of manpower and territory still far exceeded those of any other European nation, and great efforts were made, post 1906, to strengthen and modernise the army, and to rebuild a credible naval force. These efforts were severely hampered by the corruption and inefficiency endemic in the regime, and by the relatively primitive state of her industrial capabilities. However, eight years later, considerable progress had been made and the potential for further improvement was clearly evident to all the other powers, in particular to her most likely future adversaries. Of these, the principal threat to Russia came from Germany, not because of any great divergence in policy between the two nations, but because the latter power was reluctantly committed to the necessity of preserving the integrity of its chief ally – the ramshackle Habsburg Empire.

Externally, there were two main considerations that were a constant in Russian foreign policy. Firstly, there was the traditional support for the fellow Slav populations of Eastern Europe, and for their nationalistic aspirations – albeit with the proviso that Russia's pre-eminence should be recognised, and that her long-term interests in the region were to be of paramount concern. The latter consideration was inextricably linked to Russia's second (but not secondary) priority – control of the Bosphorus and Dardanelles. This had been her abiding ambition/policy for more than half a century, and, if the Ottoman power was ever forced to relinquish its hold on this crucial conduit to the Mediterranean, it would have been unacceptable for any nation, other than Russia itself or a puppet state, to have occupied the hinterland controlling the straits. Had, for instance, Bulgarian forces succeeded in taking Constantinople during the First Balkan War, Russia would have insisted on control of the waterway. Fully a third of her total overseas trade, and nearly four-fifths of her grain requirements, were dependent on seaborne traffic through the straits.

If the theme of Slav unity would have had to have been subordinated to this strategic imperative, it could not have been entirely discarded. The Balkan states existed as a natural barrier between Austria-Hungary and the remains of the Ottoman Empire. The possibility of the Austrians (and also, as an inevitable consequence, Germany) having unimpeded access to the region would have been a strategic nightmare for the government in St.

Petersburg. By necessity, therefore, even if the ethnic link had not existed, Russia had a vested interest in the survival of the newly independent nations. This single fact ensured that her interests clashed irrevocably with those of the Austro-Hungarian Empire, and, by extension, to those of Germany.

If Russia's internal problems were a matter for concern, they paled in contrast to those of her most likely enemy. The ongoing travails of the Habsburg Empire were immediate, continuous, and without long-term solution. For many centuries the predominant power in central Europe, Austria-Hungary was in terminal decline. Crushing defeat, to Prussia in 1866, had resulted in the ceding of leadership in the German-speaking world to her conqueror. Bismarck's diplomacy had resulted in the two nations managing to resume close ties despite the conflict. However, the creation of the German Empire, in the wake of the Franco-German war, five years later, made it clear that Vienna would be the permanent junior partner in any future alliance with Berlin. What resulted was a Faustian bargain in reverse. The manifest power of Germany was applied to maintain the fragile and tottering regime of Austria. In doing so, Germany lost its freedom of action and was tethered, often against its will, to the actions and policies of its weaker partner.

The prime source of Austria's weakness lay in the sheer diversity of its population. The might of an overweening central government and fear of a common foe had held these diverse elements together for centuries. At its height, the tide of Ottoman expansion had swamped much of central Europe and had lapped onto its western fringes. Only the combined resistance of the various races in the region had sufficed to stem the onrush. This supreme effort had required a central controlling focus which eventually coalesced under the umbrella of the Habsburg Empire. As an entity it was always a quarrelsome forum. Apart from odd remnants of the Holy Roman Empire, it contained, within its eventual boundaries, Germans, Magyars, Poles, Rumanians, Serbs, Croats, Slovenes, Czechs, Slovaks and Italians. Once the Ottoman tide started to recede, the glue that held these disparate ethnic groups together began to lose its adhesive qualities. This process became even more pronounced when the kinsmen of many of these races began to establish independent states adjacent to the frontiers of the empire. For a while, though, the ghastly events accompanying the independence struggles of many of these nascent states were a compelling reason to stay, at least temporarily, within the fold of the old authority.

Eventually, however, it was always probable that those nationalistic influences would prevail, and that the ethnic minorities within the empire would seek to amalgamate with their independent brethren. With the gift of hindsight, it is easy to argue that the creation of sovereign ethnic states in the place of Turkish-occupied Europe spelt the inevitable doom of the Habsburg Empire. This it did. But, certainly, it was not perceived as such at the time by the finest political minds of that generation. It was, however, a total preoccupation of less agile brains, particularly those that dwelt in most of the heads of the higher echelons of the Austrian establishment. Even to some of these, it must have been apparent that they were fighting a rearguard action, but they were nevertheless intent on the preservation of their position – and, if needs be, to take offensive measures to that end.

The Habsburg Empire had already commenced the disintegration process in the middle of the nineteenth century. A schism developed between the two dominant races in the realm – the German-speaking Austrians, and the Magyar-speaking Hungarians. This split was papered over by the creation of a 'Dual Monarchy'. Hence emerged the term of the 'Austro-Hungarian Empire'. Basically it was devolution on a grand scale. Whilst retaining a common foreign and defence policy, and with the key imperial offices shared between the nominees of both races, the sprawling empire was effectively divided into two autonomous states. Both allowed allegiance to the personage of the Emperor as its monarch. This political compromise enabled the realm to stagger on for a remarkably long time with an outward show of unity. In fact, it was deeply divided.

The Austrians and the Hungarians had a deep mutual antipathy, and disagreed on almost everything except for the need to keep the structure of the empire intact, and that no other races should be permitted to join the power-sharing arrangement. This unholy alliance of cynical self-interest excluded the possibility of any other of the ethnic citizens of the empire having a say in its (or their) governance. Essentially, it excluded the right of its Slav population, which (after the official acquisition of Bosnia and Herzegovina) amounted to nearly a third of its inhabitants, to have any part in the decision-making processes that affected their regions.

The Hungarians, in particular, resisted any attempt to alter the status quo. Having attained a privileged position, they were not going to dilute their influence by agreeing to the introduction of a third party. On the Austrian side, there were not many dissenters to this point of view. However much their detestation of the Hungarians, very few Austrians wanted a Slav presence in the government. Even if it would dilute the Hungarian presence, it would also reduce their own influence.

One important Austrian was, however, in favour of the idea and his opinion bore some weight as he was the heir apparent to the throne.

Archduke Franz Ferdinand was something of a maverick within the establishment, and his views made him deeply unpopular, not only amongst the Hungarian ruling clique, but also to his uncle, the Emperor, and the Austrian hierarchy. When he eventually succeeded to the throne, as, given the advanced age of the Emperor, seemed likely within a few years, his views were bound to have a strong influence on policy. Whether or not a Slav presence as an equal partner in a tri-monarchy would have staved off the collapse of the empire remains unproven, as the theory was never put to the test. On balance, however, the arguments against the likelihood of success are the more convincing.

Externally, the threats to the stability of the empire were several, and pressing. Italy, a nominal ally, had designs on the Tyrol and on the Istrian peninsular, including the large port city of Trieste. She also harboured designs on several enclaves on the Dalmatian coast. A substantial proportion of the population in these areas was of Italian origin, and nationalist sentiment was an issue on both sides of the border. Franz Conrad von Hötzendorf, the Chief of the Austrian General Staff, had actually advocated a pre-emptive war against Italy to crush the latter's army and thereby quash her territorial ambitions (for this apostasy he was sacked – only to be re-instated in time to press for the same action against Serbia). Similarly, the Rumanians coveted the region of Transylvania for which, in ethnic and geographical terms, they had a plausible claim. The most immediate threat, however, came from Serbia. Emboldened by victory in the Balkan wars, the Serbs were brimming with confidence and aggressive in intent. Far from sitting back to digest at leisure their recent gains from Turkey, the extreme nationalists transferred their attention to the Slav-populated regions in the neighbouring provinces of the Austrian Empire. Of these, Bosnia and Herzegovina presented the most obvious target, as a substantial percentage of the inhabitants were not only Slavs, but also ethnic Serbs.

The official government in Belgrade was relatively moderate and had no desire to antagonise the Austrians. The successes of the Balkan wars had extracted a terrible toll on the Serbian Army and the economy of the nation. This was compounded by a mutiny within its Albanian units in 1913, which led to further extensive bloodshed. The more sober-minded politicians in the Serbian establishment recognised that a period of recovery was in order before further military adventures could be contemplated. Unfortunately for the peace of the region, the rational politicians in Belgrade were not in full control of events within Serbia.

Ever since Austria had made official her *de facto* sovereignty over Bosnia and Herzegovina, in 1908, various semi-independent groups in Serbia had set out to destabilise the province. These efforts were patently obvious to the governments in both Vienna and Belgrade. Indeed, there was clandestine support for the movement from key members of the Serbian regime, and these links could not be totally disguised. The secret society 'Union or Death', better known (or perhaps more notorious) as the 'Black Hand' had infiltrated the highest levels of government and had a very different agenda from the moderates who represented the acceptable face of Serbian politics. The Austrian Government was well aware of this schism, and that the Black Hand,

and other similar movements, were more truly representative of the mood of Serbia than were the careful declarations of her ministers and ambassadors. There was an obvious threat to Austria from the nationalist ambitions of Serbia, and, to the more militant members of the Viennese establishment, there seemed to be only one logical course of action.

If the Austro-Hungarian Empire wished to remain a major power, and avoid dissolution, it had to be seen to be strong and to be able to crush any threat to its territorial integrity. The retention of prestige was essential to maintain the façade. Should it crumble in one area, it would disintegrate everywhere. A serious threat to this façade obviously existed, in the shape of Serbia, and action needed to be taken before the latter state became sufficiently powerful to render such action unduly hazardous. All that was required was a suitable excuse.

The danger of a pre-emptive strike against the Serbs was that it might involve hostilities with Russia. This prospect, for Austria, was an unacceptable peril without German involvement. Even though Russia had been militarily weakened by the disastrous war with Japan, her subsequent recovery had been rapid, and the resources of the Austro-Hungarian Empire were inadequate to countenance a confrontation whilst simultaneously carrying out a war with Serbia. An unprovoked attack on the latter was, therefore, out of the question. What Austria needed was an excuse for such action that would be so cast iron as to ensure Germany's support. In that event, Vienna hoped that the threat of German intervention would stay the hand of the Russian Government, and that the Austrian Army would be left to deal, unimpeded and undistracted, with the Serbian problem. Such an ideal solution required an act of supreme stupidity to be initiated by the Serbs. As it happened, not for the first, nor for the last time, they were not to be found wanting in that respect.

Outmanoeuvred by Bismarck's diplomacy, and outfought by the combined armies of the German states in 1871, France had henceforth to dwell in the shadow of her eastern neighbour. From then onwards, the nation that Napoleon had nearly carried to complete dominance of Europe was constrained to endure a progressive decline in its relative status on the continent. In terms of trained working population and industrial capacity, France steadily lost ground by comparison with the vibrant new German Empire.

In the aftermath of the 1871 catastrophe, France had been forced to cede the sovereignty of two of its most productive provinces, Alsace and Lorraine, to her conquerors. These areas were part of the coal, iron and steel centres of North-East France. That this loss rankled and festered in the French psyche goes without saying, particularly as Germany administered the regions more in the nature of colonies than provinces. But the prospect of their recovery grew ever more remote as the power of the united German nation inexorably increased. However much nationalist French sentiment yearned for the re-capture of her lost provinces, the reality of her position was starkly apparent. Far from contemplating a restoration of these territories, France's main concern was to avoid further erosion of her position in Europe. This, essentially defensive, policy led to the alliance with Russia. Neither nation could individually confront Germany with any chance of success, but, in combination, they stood a chance of maintaining a precarious balance.

The alliance with Russia was a double-edged sword. Whilst it gave France a degree of security against the German threat, it also involved her in complications that would result from an Austro-Russian confrontation. These would inevitably involve Germany as well. As a result of the tie with Russia, France was drawn into the convoluted affairs of the Balkans.

A huge bonus for France was the 1904 *entente* with Great Britain. Not only did it remove a potential source of conflict, it began the process of persuading the most powerful empire in the world to take sides – and, essentially, the side of France.

The *entente* was a massive boost to the overall French position. But, there was no formal, binding, treaty, and, even had there been, Britain could not immediately provide more than a token military presence should France be faced by an all-out assault by the bulk of the German armed forces. Should, however, any conflict be long drawn out, the effect of British sea power was bound to become progressively more telling. The ability to blockade Germany's maritime activity, and to safely convoy the enormous strength that could be drawn from her overseas empire, would potentially be the decisive influence on the matter.

In 1914, France had no offensive territorial ambitions, although, in the wake of a successful war against Germany, she obviously would have laid claim to the return of Alsace and Lorraine. There was no question, however, of her initiating such a conflict. It would have to be forced upon her. In the meantime, the French, in common with all the other European powers, continued to plough a large proportion of their gross national product into the maintenance of the most powerful and well-equipped army that population and industrial capacity could bear. This was something of another double-edged sword. If France reasoned that she needed this force to deter further German aggression, by its very possession, it represented a potent threat to Germany's own position – and, therefore, was as much a danger to French security as it was a guarantee.

The complex, and often contradictory, linkages that dictated relations between the main power blocs meant that the presence of the French Army in the west was a preoccupation of German strategists (with their permanent dread of a war on two fronts) in the event of their country being drawn into hostilities on its eastern frontier, between Austria and Russia. With the Franco-Russian alliance an accepted fact, there was an obvious prospect that, if war was imminent with Russia, Germany would attempt to first destroy the French Army, before the cumbersome machinery of Russian mobilisation could take effect. This, in fact, is exactly the sequence of events that took place in August 1914, and the strategy, that from the German side had been in place for over twenty years. Military imperatives duly superseded the last desperate efforts of the diplomats to avoid a catastrophic war.

Up until 1891, German military strategy had been dominated by the massive presence of Helmuth von Moltke, the army chief-of-staff, and the architect of the successful campaigns against Austria and France that had led to the creation of the empire. When the Franco-Russian alliance was concluded, Moltke had decided that Germany's military resources could not be evenly split in the event of a war with these two nations. His strategy would have been to deploy the bulk of his army against his strongest perceived opponent – which was then the Russians in the east – whilst in the meantime holding a defensive line against the French. Once the Russian offensive ability had been crushed, as was confidently forecast, the main body of the German Army would transfer to the west and deal with the French. In 1891, old Moltke was succeeded by Graf von Schlieffen. The new chief-of-staff did not dispute the basics of Moltke's reasoning, but, in view of changed military circumstances, he reversed the attack priorities. On German mobilisation for war, the vast bulk of her armies would be immediately directed against the French.

Schlieffen's change of policy had been influenced by massive fortifications newly constructed in Russian Poland which made problematic a rapid offensive thrust by the German Army in the east. There was also the fact that the much more advanced road and rail systems, in a much more compact and organised country, would enable France to mobilise her army, at the critical point, faster and more effectively than her ally. It was also supposed that the considerable forces available to the Austro-Hungarian Empire would serve to divert and occupy an equivalent number of Russian units. In consequence, he decided that France was the more suitable target for the initial German assault, and had devised a strategy to ensure a quick, and overwhelming, victory in the west. This would be followed by a mass transfer of the army to the eastern front. Germany's great advantage in any such scheme was her internal lines of communication, and the most efficient and comprehensive transport network in Europe. Every single railway and major trunk road in Germany was designed to meet military as well as civil requirements. No other nation could match her in the ability to rapidly re-deploy whole armies to meet strategic necessities.

The subsequently famous 'Schlieffen Plan' required the vast bulk of the German Army (over 80% of its total strength) to be deployed on her western

'Georgie and Nicki'
King George V and the Tsar

Prinz Heinrich
Younger brother of the Kaiser and Grand Admiral in
the Imperial German Navy.

frontier immediately after mobilisation for war. Only a few army corps would be left to defend Prussia's eastern border against the Russian threat, and, on their right flank, the Austrians were to be trusted to hold their own.

The novelty in Schlieffen's strategy lay in his plan of action against the French Army. Instead of attacking it within the well-protected confines of its own borders, a portion of the German Army would concentrate on a holding operation along this front. Having tied down (or 'fixed' as the military would term it) the main French force on their frontier, the bulk of the German armies would sweep, without warning, in a vast outflanking movement through the weakly defended neutral countries of Belgium, Luxemburg and Holland and descend on northern France. It was intended that the power and speed of this advance would carry it, in a huge right hook, to the east and west of Paris before curling back to take the French armies in their rear. This strategy assumed that the French would be unable to disengage their forces on the frontier without risking a headlong retreat, but, if they stayed put, would be effectively encircled and, inevitably, doomed. It was a plan of staggering scope and audacity, and dependant on the most meticulous precision of its execution. Nevertheless, given the superiority of force that Germany could initially deploy, the prospects of its success were very favourable. The minute calculations of the German Army Staff did not entertain ventures of an impractical nature.

The Schlieffen Plan did, however, introduce a new factor into the larger sphere of international relations. Whilst the military heads were quite unconcerned about marching through neutral nations en route to confronting the enemy of choice, this action posed something of a dilemma to the German Government and its diplomats.

This diversion into German military strategy may seem prolonged and spurious, but it is not without relevance. Schlieffen's strategy pre-supposed the automatic and instant violation of the sovereign integrity of states who had neither the intention, nor the inclination, to be part of any German war against France or vice versa. Luxemburg was an irrelevance and Holland, in the event, and greatly to its financial profit, was not to be involved. The case of Belgium, though, was an entirely different matter.

The metamorphosis of Belgium to the state that exists within its present borders had gone through many stages of domination or occupation by virtually every major nation in Europe bar the Russians. Napoleon's fate had been finally decided on its soil, by the Anglo-Prussian armies at Waterloo. When it eventually emerged, from a centuries' old larva, as the butterfly of an independent nation in the wake of the Napoleonic wars, it was recognised as such by all the major powers on the continent, plus Great Britain.

With such a set of godparents, the treaty that established Belgium's existence as a sovereign state was a powerful document, and, to paraphrase what would become its most important clause, it guaranteed the nation's neutrality. In practical terms, it meant that, if any of the signatory nations of the treaty violated Belgian neutrality (i.e. invaded the country), it would be a *casus belli* for the rest. Although it was Prussia, not the German Empire, that had signed the treaty, it was not disputed that the treaty applied as much to modern Germany as it did to the old kingdom. The responsibilities of Prussia were inherited in much the same manner as the new empire inherited the ruling house of Hohenzollern. Wilhelm's ancestor had signed the document, and he was not one to lightly disregard history or heredity. The mechanics of the Schlieffen Plan, however, absolutely required Germany to abandon her treaty obligations in an immediate and violent manner if war was imminent.

This would not have been a problem to Germany, apart from the ethical factor, if she only had to take into consideration her continental neighbours. In the circumstances, she would have in any case been making war with or against all of them. The great imponderable would be the attitude of Great Britain. Many of the German leaders, including the Kaiser and Bethmann-Hollweg still cherished hopes, as late as August 1914, that Britain would contrive to remain aloof from a continental war. These hopes were not entirely fanciful.

A large number of influential and intelligent people in the British establishment, and in commercial circles, were absolutely against the idea of involvement in any continental conflict. The spirit, even if not the reality, of 'Splendid Isolation' remained strong. There was also a very powerful pacifist element within the ruling Liberal Government, including key members of the Cabinet, that was bitterly opposed to war on almost any terms. German diplomats were well aware of this situation. Nevertheless, the war plans of their Army General Staff posed a weighty problem for the Kaiser and his ministers, and the importance of the issue of Belgian neutrality to Anglo-German relations was not adequately grasped.

The naval rivalry between the two nations most probably meant that they would be on opposite sides in any future European confrontation, never mind their existing commitments to contending alliances. It was not *absolutely* certain, though, that this would translate into active hostilities. What was not properly understood in Berlin was that, despite deep pacifist sentiment in the British governing party, any German violation of Belgian neutrality would turn that probability into the *absolute* certainty of Britain actively joining her foes.

The army had been ready and willing to go to war for many years, on any pretext, whilst Germany was still able to impose her military will on Europe. The generals feared that Germany's dominant position would be steadily eroded if Russia and France continued to improve their military capabilities. The progressive strengthening of the *entente* between these two nations and the previously aloof Great Britain was even more alarming, as it threatened a decisive alteration in the balance of power. The geographical nature of the putative alliance of these three nations gave a powerful, and not unreasonable, impulse to the theory that Germany was indeed being 'encircled'.

It was a strong belief, in army circles, that a preventive war was needed whilst Germany still possessed a decisive superiority over her potential enemies. Substantial support for this view existed throughout the German establishment, but this attitude, whilst generating some sympathy, did not reflect the considered opinions of the political hierarchy. Although obviously concerned by adverse diplomatic developments, the Kaiser and his ministers were not anxious to initiate a major European conflict. The army staff, and Tirpitz, on the naval side, could confine their attentions to the pure mechanics of conducting a successful war; the politicians had to deal with the wider consequences of such action.

Wilhelm II, despite his bluster, occasionally bellicose stances, and ferocious speeches had not the stomach to be a warmonger. Nor were the ministers of his government anxious to provoke general hostilities between all the major powers. By and large, Germany was content with the extent of her domain in Europe, and her pre-occupation was not to expand these borders, but rather to ensure their security. The ambitions of her leaders, embodied in Bülow's old self-serving principle of *Weltpolitik* were concentrated on global, rather than continental expansion. Economic colonialism and power projection abroad had become the political priority, not least because this had been the focus of internal propaganda for many years. It was this road that was seen as the preferred route to Germany's eventual international predominance.

Berlin's intentions in this respect were frequently stymied by her alliance to Vienna. As the power blocs in Europe coalesced, the preservation of the Austro-Hungarian Empire had become absolutely essential to Germany. Within the Triple Alliance, only the most naïve politician regarded Italy as a reliable ally and, consequently, Germany was shackled to the policies and actions of her only dependable associate. This would not have posed a great problem had there been more frank communication between the foreign ministries of both nations. The Austrians, unfortunately, took automatic German support for granted, and as a licence to do as they pleased – without bothering to properly co-ordinate a joint approach to matters of international importance.

Once before, in the crisis of 1908/9, Germany had been dragged into a confrontation with Russia as a result of Austria's precipitate action in unilaterally assuming sovereignty over Bosnia and Herzegovina. The threat of German power had prevailed in that instance, but both the Kaiser and his ministers were infuriated at the irresponsible, and unheralded, action of the Austrians (Wilhelm privately termed it an act of 'brigandage'), and regretted the need for intervention – for which Germany received the calumny of general world opinion. The German bull had been led by the nose by the Austrian ass, and a major European war had only been narrowly averted. It was a lesson that Berlin should have better learned. On the next occasion that the situation arose, the results would be fatal for the dynasties, and national structure, of both nations.

As already mentioned, one consequence of the crisis over Bosnia and Herzegovina was particularly irritating to Germany's government. Throughout the period of Wilhelm II's rule, he had made a concentrated effort to establish amicable relations with the Ottoman Empire. Faced with what they perceived as 'encirclement' by the Triple Entente, the Kaiser and his advisors saw South-Eastern Europe and Turkey as the only feasible area in which to prevent the completion of a hostile ring around the central powers (the potential outlet to the south, via Italy, was sensibly regarded with some scepticism given the unreliability of that nation as an ally). The unilateral action of the Austrian Government in 1908, however reluctantly supported by Germany, dealt a blow to this policy. Subsequently, an assiduous and largely successful effort was made by the Kaiser to re-cultivate good relations and economic links with the Turks. In the midst of world disgust and opprobrium over the Turkish massacre of Armenians, in 1912, Germany alone stood aside from the general condemnation. Whilst this furore was in progress, and Turkey had become an international pariah, Germany continued its wooing of the Ottoman Government. The Turks were duly grateful, and German influence, both economic and military, rapidly flourished. Politically, Germany also obtained the allegiance of key players in the Turkish hierarchy. This was to have far-reaching consequences.

Previously the French and the British had been the major influences on Ottoman affairs. Through long-term diplomatic complacency, inertia, incompetence, and moral hypocrisy, their position had been usurped by Berlin. By the time war broke out, Germany and Turkey were on the brink of concluding a formal alliance that would almost guarantee the eventual participation, on Germany's side, of the still formidable strength of the Ottoman Empire.

For Germany, Turkey and its residual possessions represented a vital outlet for economic and political expansion to the east. However, the Balkan states imposed a barrier on the direct access to the area. Bulgaria and Rumania were amenable to German influence, but, at the heart of the region, the belligerent and recalcitrant nation of Serbia was a continuing source of concern. This was the one point that German and Austrian foreign policy merged in complete harmony, albeit for different reasons. The neutering of Serbia was essential to the ambitions of both empires. This fact alone meant that an Austrian confrontation with Serbia, should the latter be seen to initiate the situation, would not be unwelcome to the German Government. Any justifiable train of events that served to debilitate Serbia would be granted full German support.

The balance of power on the continent of Europe, in 1914, was not weighted overly on one side or the other. Of the 'Big Four', Germany remained the dominant military nation, but her chief ally, Austria-Hungary, was gazing into the abyss of dissolution. Nevertheless, the latter could still field a substantial military force, and had a far from negligible armaments industry. Russia and France together could not expect to prevail against the combined forces of these two nations, and their alliance was essentially defensive. Neither was committed to joining the other in an offensive adventure. As an additional deterrent, Italy was allied to both the central powers, and was treaty bound to come to their aid should they be attacked – but was not so committed should either Austria or Germany initiate hostilities. In the circumstances of the time, unless forced, neither France nor Russia would chance their arm against Germany. Nor were there any plans to so do. Churchill remarks that:

> 'Although the groupings of the great Powers had thus been altered sensible to the disadvantage of Germany there was in this alteration nothing that threatened her with war. The abiding spirit of France had never abandoned the dream of recovering the lost provinces, but the prevailing temper of the French nation was pacific, and all classes remained under the impression of the might of Germany and of the terrible consequences likely to result from war.
>
> 'Moreover, the French were never sure of Russia in a purely Franco-German quarrel. True, there was the Treaty; but the Treaty to become operative required aggression on the part of Germany. What constitutes aggression? At what point in a dispute between two heavily armed parties, does one side or the other become the aggressor? At any rate there was a wide field for discretionary action on the part of Russia.' (5)

In 1914, therefore, Germany herself was in no danger of attack by any foe with the capability of defeating her incomparable army, nor did her government have offensive intentions on her neighbours. Germany's policy on the continent of Europe was belligerently stated but essentially defensive. If, however, hostilities beckoned, her military strategy was absolutely geared to the offensive. If Germany was threatened with war, she was fully prepared to initiate the process, and to do so with overwhelming force.

All of Germany's war plans were meticulously researched by her military planners and covered almost every eventuality in the event of war against a combination of France and Russia. The involvement of Great Britain was not considered to be pivotal to any land battle. In its dismissive attitude as to the capabilities of the British Army, the German General Staff actually encouraged the unopposed transport of the British Expeditionary Force to the continent. This was on the grounds that it would be much easier to destroy it there and then, in the process of mopping up the French, than having to face it later in any attempt to invade Britain. It was a miscalculation that would have a profound effect on the course of the forthcoming struggle.

Despite her concerns with the growing strength of her continental rivals, Germany had no doubts about her military superiority over her potential adversaries even if they could field equal or even superior numbers of troops. In a short land war it was believed that there was not a formation in Europe that could prevail against the power and efficiency of the German Army, backed, as it was, by the most productive armaments industry in the world, and supplied by the most comprehensive and flexible transport system in all of the developed nations. Where the danger existed for Germany was in the possibility of the first blow not being absolutely decisive. A quick result was vital. Should the German Army fail to knock out France in the initial offensive shock, the prolongation of the war would steadily erode Germany's advantages. Should Britain be drawn into the conflict, there would be a steady and formidable reinforcement of the French position. Time, therefore, was of the essence in accomplishing Germany's war aims. There was also, at least in the opinion of the Kaiser and his Chancellor, the possibility that Britain might not choose to become embroiled in any hypothetical European conflict. This wishful thinking was fatally flawed if the German Army maintained the battle strategy of the Schlieffen Plan.

Although Britain would not willingly engage in a continental war, unless she was more or less forced into that eventuality, the effecting of the Schlieffen Plan, and its consequent violation of Belgian neutrality, would place her in a position where such action was practically inevitable. Even if she did not have moral obligations to France, as a result of the *Entente Cordiale*, circumstances would have demanded action or else the complete loss of international credibility and self-respect. Even the very influential pacifist lobby in the British Parliament could not disregard the breach of a solemn treaty to which she was a signature. This fact failed to assume its real importance in the calculations of the German Government. An exasperated Bethmann-Hollweg later referred to the treaty document as a 'scrap of paper'. It was a revealing comment. On such 'scraps' exist the reputation and authority of nations.

In the summer of 1914, however, British pre-occupations did not include the possibility of a major European conflict. Internal divisions seemed to be of a far more pressing nature.

Britain had been in increasing political turmoil over the previous few years. A crisis had arisen over the impossibility of getting the Liberal government's economic budgets accepted by parliament. Time and again, measures that had been approved by the House of Commons, where the elected Liberals had a large majority, were obstructed by the unelected House of Lords – where the Conservative peers had a similar predominance, and a power of veto over government proposals. The result to the political process was a damaging, and increasingly acrimonious, deadlock that defied resolution.

The situation was repeated on the highly contentious issue of Home Rule for Ireland. In the Commons, with its large bloc of Irish Nationalist

MPs, there was substantial support for this measure; in the Lords, there was an equally adamant opposition to its adoption.

Determined to impose the will of the elected parliament on these two critical issues, the government instigated a third crisis by deciding to effect the reform of the House of Lords, severely reducing its powers to block legislation. This bill, of course, had absolutely no chance of being approved by the peers. The phrase 'turkeys voting for Christmas' springs to mind. Consequently, the government took the drastic action of approaching the King with a request to create sufficient new peers of its choosing to overturn the Conservative majority in the House of Lords.

This request, which was actually more in the nature of an ultimatum, was received with horror by George V, to whom it was personally abhorrent. It placed him, at the very beginning of his reign, in the centre of an unwanted constitutional crisis that had the potential to destabilise the monarchy, never mind the whole political system. Nevertheless, he had little choice in the matter without countenancing the most serious schism in the political process since the English Civil War. As a constitutional monarch, the reality of his position was that he would eventually have been forced to either bow to the will of his elected parliament, or to suspend it – and the latter course of action was utterly inconceivable. After much agonising, George reluctantly made it known that he would, if absolutely necessary, accede to the wishes of his government. At this point, realising that the game was up, the Conservative peers (or at least sufficient of them to ensure the passing of government legislation) capitulated to the inevitable. The wholesale creation of new peers would be avoided, but the House of Lords would lose its power to veto legislation – although, by parliamentary means, it would still retain an ability to delay and amend government proposals.

If the government thought it had finally solved its problems, it was soon disabused of this illusion. Confronted with the inevitability of an Irish Home Rule Bill becoming law, the Loyalist politicians of largely Protestant Northern Ireland, supported by many of their English colleagues, rose in fury at the prospect of being subordinated to the Catholic South and domestic rule from Dublin. The possibility of an armed revolt by Loyalists against the provisions of the Home Rule Bill became a serious matter of concern. To guard against this prospect, the government decided to order army units based in Dublin to the north. When these intentions were made known, a significant number of the senior army officers stationed at the Curragh barracks, outside Dublin, openly stated that they would refuse to be deployed against the Loyalists in Ulster. This was virtual mutiny, and, in the meantime, paramilitary forces on both the Nationalist and Loyalist sides were making obvious preparations to contest the issue. Politicians from both wings of the dispute made haste to join the fray. The dreadful prospect arose of a civil war in Ireland that would have profound effects on the entire United Kingdom.

In the circumstances, it is hardly surprising that British attention was focussed on its own problems, rather than those of Europe. In any case, relations between the Great Powers seemed to be going through a period of comparative calm. There was no intimation of the explosion to come. The future British Prime Minister, Harold MacMillan, writes in his memoirs that:

'The First World War, in contrast to the Second, burst like a bombshell upon ordinary people – a real "bolt from the blue". It is true that the large expansion of the German Navy was regarded by many informed observers as a serious portent. But the German retreat at Agadir and the somewhat better relations that followed seemed reassuring. Indeed, in the summer of 1914 there was far more anxiety about a civil war in Ireland than about a world war in Europe…the occasional outbursts of the Kaiser were treated as pardonable indiscretions. Germany, after all, appeared to be governed by men of solid reputation, and a civilized background. Her rulers were not in any way comparable to the ruffians led by Hitler who were to seize power in the next generation.' (6)

MacMillan's views were undoubtedly shared by the majority of the British establishment, although his somewhat mildly expressed reference to the ongoing development of the German Navy would not have reflected the more robust views that were generally prevalent at the time.

The naval question, as earlier chapters of this book have made abundantly clear, was the one, overriding, and insuperable, difference that prevented closer relations between Great Britain and Germany. Even more significant was that it was also the defining issue that enticed Britain into the camp of Germany's potential enemies. However reluctantly and partially Britain discarded her independence of policy and freedom of action, the necessity to concentrate her navy against the potential German threat meant some form of collusion and co-operation with France – and, to a lesser extent, Russia. Her earlier alliance with Japan had not been designed particularly with Germany in mind, but well-served that purpose as circumstances changed.

Unlike the Anglo-Japanese alliance, the *entente* with France never developed into a formal treaty, but its consequent military ramifications imposed an overwhelming moral obligation on Britain. Since the critical meeting of the Committee of Imperial Defence, in August 1911, when Sir Arthur Wilson famously botched the Admiralty's case, there had been only one imperative in British war strategy. The Army General Staff, incurably besotted with the supposed infallibility of the French High Command, had virtually committed all of Britain's meagre land forces to a continental campaign. It was assumed, correctly, that, if there was to be a future war, whatever its extent, France and Germany would be in opposition. The involvement of the British Army, on French soil, in a conflict against Germany, had been, therefore, taken for granted, and plans for this deployment had been drawn up and scheduled with the utmost precision.

There were no plans for a different situation or for consideration of alternative strategies. The navy's role in this grand concept was to carry out its traditional task of controlling the trade routes, transporting the army safely across the English Channel, and protecting Britain from invasion whilst the soldiers were being slaughtered elsewhere. There was also the necessity of imposing a maritime blockade on the coasts and trade of the designated enemy.

To carry out all or any of these duties, the Royal Navy had to be prepared to meet, and defeat, the High Seas Fleet. To guarantee success in all these tasks required a considerable margin of superiority over the German Navy. Given the existing force of the latter, and with the continuing accretion of units to its strength, this necessitated the vast majority of modern British warships to be concentrated in Home Waters – particularly in the area of the North Sea. The sheer scale of German naval expansion over the previous decade meant that available British resources were no longer sufficient to allow of them being spread across the globe. The Anglo-Japanese Alliance (ironically, at the time, a measure against French and Russian ambitions in East Asia) had permitted the re-deployment of the six battleships on the China station back to British waters. The Anglo-French *entente* resulted in a much more significant re-distribution of force.

The British Mediterranean Fleet had been, for over a century, an integral component in the projection and preservation of Britain's many interests in the area. With the opening of the Suez Canal, the Mediterranean also became a vital conduit in the military and commercial communications of the empire. Throughout the post-Napoleonic era, therefore, Britain had maintained a fleet of its most modern and efficient capital ships in the 'Middle Sea', based on the major dockyard port of the superbly situated island of Malta. Well-equipped support facilities, which were being upgraded to full dockyard status, also existed at Gibraltar, from where the narrow entrance to the Mediterranean could be controlled. For almost all of that time, the main perceived opponent of this fleet had been the French Navy. With the advent of the *entente*, however, came a radical change in the strategic situation of both nations. Britain no longer had to worry about the security of its Mediterranean communications, and France could discount a British threat against its Atlantic and Channel coasts. In these new circumstances, it was illogical for the navies of the two countries to continue duplicating their efforts in both areas. Common sense prevailed, and, within a few years, the French had concentrated all their effective battleships in the Mediterranean whilst Britain had severely pruned the strength of its fleet based on Malta. The British ships released from the Mediterranean inevitably went to swell the concentration of naval force against the German threat.

It was never officially acknowledged that this redistribution of forces was as a result of a formal agreement between the two countries, but it could hardly be dismissed as a coincidence. Churchill, however, always maintained that these were independent decisions reached by the respective naval authorities, and made a point of emphasising that the French could not have made a better distribution of their navy even had the *entente* not existed. This was somewhat ingenuous. He based his reasoning on the premise that, since the French Atlantic Fleet was no match for the German Navy, it was better off in the Mediterranean, where its reinforcement of the main fleet would at least ensure French maritime supremacy in that area. There is a certain amount of diplomatic obfuscation here, for, had the *entente* not existed, Britain could never have considered withdrawing her naval forces and permitting a potentially hostile French fleet to fill the void.

In the event, the French denuded their western coasts of significant naval protection, and, whatever the politicians said, then or afterwards, the great majority of the thinking population could, and would, draw its own conclusions. In the event of Germany and France going to war, there clearly existed a moral obligation for British naval forces to protect the French Atlantic coast and Channel ports. In that circumstance, the French would have certainly made the point publicly and loudly. Failure to respond would have left the British Government morally bankrupt in the eyes of the world, and also in the eyes of most of its own population (and eligible electorate).

'...however much the British might deny a legal obligation to protect France, they had assumed a moral one to defend her northern coastline against German attack. Like so many compromises, the agreement was unsatisfactory to both sides. In 1912, however, the question of the withdrawal from the Mediterranean was probably of greater concern in London, simply because of what it implied: the decline of Britain's world position.' (7)

This concern made the proposed abandonment of the Mediterranean deeply unpopular across a broad sweep of British public and professional opinion, and the government was pressured into diluting the full scope of its proposals.

'Following meetings of the Cabinet and C.I.D.[2] this was modified in July to the compromise:

'There must always be provided a reasonable margin of superior strength ready and available in Home Waters. This is our first requirement. Subject to this we ought to maintain, available for Mediterranean purposes and based on a Malta port, a battle fleet equal to a one-power Mediterranean, excluding France.' (8)

The carefully worded informality of the *entente* agreements with France and Russia (and, indeed, even within the separate Franco-Russian convention) could not disguise the reality that these were all *de facto* treaties, albeit hedged with conditions and not graven in stone. For all practical purposes, however, the agreements constituted an effective alliance should any one of them be attacked by another Great Power.

---

[2] The Committee for Imperial Defence.

The glue that held Britain to this combination was her fear of the German naval programme that threatened the maritime supremacy essential to the preservation of her empire, and to her own national security and sovereignty. Without the Kaiser and Tirpitz's 'Fleet against England', there would probably have been no question of Britain tying herself into allegiances with Germany's potential foes. Although feral competitors in trade and influence worldwide, Britain and Germany had no specific differences in their approach to international issues. A great measure of agreement attended their diplomatic conversations, and, if they were commercial rivals, they were also amongst each other's best customers. The business and financial relationships between the two countries were cordial and productive. The one problem was the naval race, and it was a problem that refused to go away. If repetition be the secret of conviction, as Fisher would have it, The 'Fleet Against England', to the despair of the merchants and bankers of both nations alike; to the worst fears of their politicians and diplomats, and to the ultimate utter desolation of their populaces, irrevocably turned Britain against Germany, and forced her into association with the latter's rivals.

The remaining two major powers on the continent, Italy and Turkey, had recently been at war with each other, and, in terms of power, could not be considered the equivalent of the 'big five', although Italy certainly aspired to that status. The former was already a member, with Germany and Austria, of the Triple Alliance, whilst the latter was on the brink of concluding a treaty of friendship with Berlin. However, they faced very different circumstances and had very contrasting ambitions.

The Italian conquest of Tripoli and the Dodecanese Islands, in 1911/12, had whetted her appetite for further expansion. The many ultra-nationalists in the Italian political spectrum harboured dreams for the creation of a new Roman Empire. This ambition was given extra spice by the disaster and humiliation that had attended an earlier attempt to carve out new domains.

In 1899, having annexed the territory of Eritrea, on the western coast of the Red Sea, Italy had embarked on the invasion of the ancient 'empire' of Abyssinia. Despite the possession of up-to-date weaponry, and the supposed advantages of a modern European military system, the expedition came to a grisly end. Confronted by the relatively unsophisticated forces of the Abyssinians, at Adowa, the Italians were utterly routed and hounded back into Eritrea. The memory of this debacle, with its consequent loss of prestige to a nation with grandiose ambitions, rankled for years – and eventually was only, albeit briefly, expiated by Mussolini's conquest of Abyssinia in 1935.

The successful war against Turkey restored Italian prestige to some extent and she possessed, on paper, a considerable army and a powerful, modern navy. Nevertheless, she was not a reliable ally, and the terms of her adherence to the Triple Alliance included an escape clause that released her from the obligation of joining in hostilities should Austria or Germany be the aggressors. The harmony of the alliance was not improved by the fact that Italy and Austria were most unlikely bedfellows. There was, between the two nations, a hearty sense of mutual loathing, and Italy had territorial designs on several regions within the Austro-Hungarian Empire. Added to this was the fact that the Italians were very Anglophile. This feeling dated back to the very real encouragement and covert assistance that had been given by Britain and her navy during the reunification process. Involvement in any war that brought Italy into conflict with Great Britain would have been very unpopular with significant sections of her public opinion.

Italy, then, remained something of an enigma, both to her nominal allies and to her potential adversaries. None of them knew what course of action she would take in the event of a general war. It is fair to comment that neither did most Italian politicians. The general trend of Italian policy was opportunistic, and would be decided on the basis of prevailing circumstances, rather than an adherence to any firmly held principles or commitments.

The disastrous wars against Italy and the Balkan League between 1911 and 1913 had marked a new nadir in the fortunes of the Ottoman Empire, but it remained a far from negligible factor in the balance of power. Although Turkey retained only a tiny foothold in the south-eastern corner of Europe, and had been entirely expelled from the continent of Africa, she still occupied a crucial strategic situation athwart the Bosphorus and the Dardanelles, and her surviving domains covered much of the Middle East. Turkish rule still extended over the lands of modern day Syria, the Lebanon, Iraq, Palestine, Jordan, and the eastern shores of the Red Sea as far as the Yemen. Within these realms rested the holy cities of both Jerusalem and Mecca, and, consequently, as custodian of the centres of faith, the Ottoman Empire claimed the leadership and allegiance of the Muslim world (rather as Saudi Arabia does today, in the case of Mecca). This was, or should have been, a matter of some concern to Great Britain, as the population of the latter's vast empire contained a large Muslim element. In sheer terms of numbers, at that time, the British Empire actually encompassed the largest Islamic community in the world. Fisher, an ardent Turkophile, always emphasised this fact when arguing for the need to maintain close ties to the Ottoman Government. He frequently quoted Sultan Abdul Hamid (the ruler of the Ottoman Empire at the time Fisher had taken the Mediterranean Fleet on a visit to Istanbul) as saying to him that Britain and Turkey were the two great Mohammedan nations.

Strategic situation and faith were not the only measures of the nation's latent strength. The heartland of Turkey also possessed significant manpower resources, and the Anatolian peasantry, from which the bulk of her armies were drawn, were to demonstrate that, when properly trained, equipped and led, they could be formidable fighters.

If the government of Turkey drew one, indisputable, lesson from the catastrophe that had engulfed its empire, it was that, in isolation, the country could not prevail against the nationalist forces that threatened its borders. Belatedly, Turkey recognised that her defeat in the recent wars had been due to the fact that she had no binding alliance with any of the other major powers. As a result, she had been left unsupported to face the attack of the Balkan League. A serious effort was initiated to redress this situation, and approaches were made in turn to Great Britain, France, and even to her traditional enemy, Russia, in order to secure a mutual defence pact. All these approaches, for one reason or another, were rebuffed. Eventually, a faction in the government turned to Germany, despite fears about German ambitions and potential involvement in Turkish affairs.

The dominant figure in the Committee for Union and Progress (the CUP, but better known as the 'Young Turk' movement), which had assumed control of the government after the 1913 coup, was a thirty-three year old army officer of proven bravery, and with something of a Napoleon complex. Enver Pasha had had a meteoric rise through the military and political ranks, and was, in early 1914, appointed Minister of War. His influence far transcended the boundaries of his official portfolio, and he was ardently pro-German.

'His dynamism enabled him to rise rapidly in the councils of the CUP, which attracted many go-ahead young officers, so that he played a leading role in the revolution of 1908-9. His reward for that was the plum post for a progressive officer of military attaché in Berlin. The brief tour of duty there reinforced his conviction that the Germans were the nation of the future and the right people to side with in the event of international conflict.' (9)

Enver, and a few like-minded colleagues, in fact only represented a minority of the CUP leadership. The majority opinion, as the European crisis deepened during the July of 1914, had veered to the view that Turkey had been so exhausted by the ravages of the recent wars that a policy of neutrality was the only sensible course of action – at least until she had had time to recover her strength. The Enver faction was, however, able to circumvent the opposition, and the German presence in the military and political affairs of Turkey became ever more prominent. Its most conspicuous manifestation was in its role of revitalising the army.

From the moment the Young Turks first laid a hand on power, in 1909, an urgent effort was initiated to modernise the nation's infrastructure and, particularly, its armed forces. German assistance was requested and provided, in the case of the army, whilst the British agreed to establish a naval mission with the task of reconstructing the navy. Neither of these programmes involved anything in the nature of a formal alliance, and neither had had sufficient time to take effect by the time of the outbreak of the Balkan wars, and were thus unable to influence the result. Henceforth, however, Great Britain and Germany were jockeying for poll position in a contest to be the prime influence on Turkish affairs. As a contest, it was rather one-sided, as the Germans devoted a far greater political and military effort to the issue.

'...the influence of Germany remained predominant after the Kaiser's visit in 1898; Britain was the only power in a position to displace the Germans, thanks to its naval supremacy and a long history of friendship. The British however...lacked motivation, and, as the threat of a general European war grew, limited their aim in Turkey to achieving a benevolent neutrality in Constantinople. The Germans were playing for much bigger stakes.' (10)

If the task of modernising the army was, as Dan van der Vat remarks, 'most daunting', it was child's play compared to the problems confronting the British Naval Mission. The Turkish Army, although badly organised, poorly trained, and ill-equipped, was an extant force with a large body of fierce and committed men on which to call. The navy was little more than a collection of unmanned, mouldering, obsolete hulks that had, for decades, been rotting at its moorings. Nevertheless, some progress was made, and the navy was able to play a minor, though unsuccessful, part in the wars of 1911-13.

The British commitment was half-hearted and received little encouragement from the Admiralty in London. Battenberg, the First Sea Lord from 1912, questioned the relevance of the Naval Mission, and thought it demeaning that the reputation of the Royal Navy should even be associated with such a shambolic force. There was, however, one positive development in that the Turkish Government was persuaded to order two, state of the art, dreadnoughts to be built in British yards. The vessels were approaching completion in 1914, and crews had been trained by the Mission to take them over once the builder's trials had been concluded. As will be seen, this development turned out to be very much a mixed blessing.

In contrast to the British approach, the Germans, from the beginning of the commitment, devoted their full attention to the cultivation of their relationship with Turkey. Strong diplomatic ties were forged with Enver and his clique, and German military officers flooded into the country, taking over most of the key command, staff, and administrative posts in the Ottoman Army. With them came German methods, and as many armaments as could be spared, subject to the difficulties of their transportation.

The German authorities were determined to weld Turkey to their side, and, by the end of July 1914, by which time war was imminent, they had largely achieved their aim. A clandestine mutual defence treaty was drawn up between Germany and the Enver faction, which was shortly presented as a *fait accomplis* to the Turkish Government. This provoked outrage amongst those Turkish ministers who had been unaware of the machinations going on behind their backs, and many of whom largely disagreed with its provisions. It became the subject of an increasingly acrimonious debate, which was still in full flow when the war broke out in Europe. Until this debate had been settled, the immediate ambitions of Germany (and Enver) to draw the Ottomans into a cast iron alliance remained unfulfilled. In the event, Turkey would initially adopt a position of armed neutrality whilst her governmental infighting continued, but the pro-German faction was better organised than the opposition and had the stronger personalities. It became a question of when, rather than if, Turkey became a full ally of Berlin.

For the previous decade and a half, the complicated entanglements of these seven empires had been steadily evolving. At the same time, all the major powers were feverishly engaged in increasing the sophistication and strength of their arsenals, and the numbers of their trained servicemen. A self-perpetuating, and financially ruinous, arms race had taken over from rational thought, and it defeated all the well-intentioned efforts of the statesmen who attempted to impose restraints on its insatiable growth. For all that, as 1914 entered its summer months, relationships between the dominant European nations were at their most amicable for several years.

'Not even the astutest and most far-seeing statesman foresaw in the early summer of 1914 that the autumn would find the nations of the world interlocked in the most terrible conflict that had ever been witnessed in the history of mankind; and if you came to the ordinary men and women who were engaged in their daily avocations in all countries there was not one of them who suspected the imminence of such a catastrophe.' (11)

Lloyd-George's colleague, Winston Churchill, despite being at the hub of navalist affairs, was no less sanguine. His remarks closely reflect those of Harold MacMillan, quoted earlier:

'The spring and summer of 1914 were marked in Europe by an exceptional tranquillity. Ever since Agadir the policy of Germany towards Great Britain had not only been correct, but considerate. All through the tangle of the Balkan Conferences British and German diplomacy laboured in harmony. The long distrust which had grown up in the Foreign Office, though not removed, was sensibly modified. Some at least of those who were accustomed to utter warnings began to feel the need of revising their judgement. The personalities who expressed the foreign policy of Germany seemed for the first time to be men to whom we could talk and with whom common action was possible.' (12)

Despite this deceptive calm, the tangled web of alliances and interests that connected the various powers almost guaranteed that hostilities between any two of them would draw in the others. Had the full horror of a modern mechanised war been then apparent, and had the shattering national consequences that came in its wake been even dimly perceived, it is certain that more notice would have been taken of those who sought to avert conflict. The tragedy of 1914 is that no one, civilian or military, in any nation, could predict the appalling nature of 20th century warfare, and of its total involvement, and effect upon, entire populations. By the time the lessons of the Somme, Verdun, Passchendaele and the Eastern Front had been absorbed, an entire generation would have been sacrificed to the carnage as a result of the ignorance of their pre-war elders.

Of this collection of European nations, only one would partially profit from the impending conflict, and, even then, only at great cost to her youth. Italy would have to wait until the Second World War before her grandiose ambitions for a new Roman Empire were to be ignominiously scuppered. Of the rest, defeat and revolution meant that four would cease to exist as dynastic entities in the next few years, two of them disintegrating entirely. The supposed victors would suffer such losses in manpower and wealth as to cripple their position in the world hierarchy. Britain, as a constitutional monarchy, and France, as a republican democracy, were exhausted and impoverished by their efforts in the events to come, but at least their structure of government survived the experience, and their overseas empires, for a couple more decades, remained intact.

Of the major powers, the only winners in the course of the coming conflict would be America and Japan – who profited greatly, either economically or territorially, from the agonies of both their enemies and their allies. The great loser was not an individual nation, but the European continent as a whole. In the three to four centuries leading up to the conflagration of 1914, Europe (at least in terms of the western hemisphere, and, latterly, most of the rest) had been the hub of cultural, economic and military power and influence. This situation could not have endured indefinitely – history dictates otherwise – but the First World War was a cataclysm that fatally damaged its predominance and accelerated its relative decline. It truly marked the end of a historical era

The potential for self-destruction had become greater by the year. Europe had developed into a vast powder keg, the explosion of which only waited upon the provision of a single spark. On the 28th June 1914, that spark was duly struck.

CHAPTER SIXTEEN
A SINGLE SHOT

'The world on the verge of its catastrophe was very brilliant. Nations and Empires crowned with Princes and Potentates rose majestically on every side, lapped in the accumulated treasures of the long peace. All were fitted and fastened – it seemed securely – into an immense cantilever. The two mighty European systems faced each other glittering and clanking in their panoply, but with a tranquil gaze…The old world in its sunset was fair to see.'

Winston Churchill

'The first seven months of 1914 saw the British nation living like some prosperous settlement on the glacis of a volcano. Few understood how thin was the crust, and how at any moment it might be rent by chaos and death.'

John Buchan

'It is nothing.'

Last words of Archduke Franz Ferdinand

For many centuries, the city of Sarajevo, capital of the province of Bosnia, had been a comparative haven of tolerance in the turbulent arena of post-renaissance Europe. In its environs dwelt an eclectic mix of nationalities and religions that had generally managed to co-exist in relative harmony. Jewish refugees from persecution in Spain had established a thriving community in the city alongside Catholic Croats, Orthodox Serbs, and indigenous Muslims. Each community had its quarter, with its respective mosques, churches and synagogues. All of them came together in the vibrant central suq where the business and commerce of the city was conducted. Despite sharing the volatility and occasional violence that was endemic in the region, the city could claim in many respects to be a model of successful multiculturalism. Today, as a result of the events of the twentieth century, the name of Sarajevo conjures up a very different image – that of internecine strife, nationalist and religious bigotry, and military atrocities. The frightful acts of genocide that took place in the surrounding province in the 1990s first spawned the modern, mealy-mouthed, euphemism 'ethnic cleansing'. It was not always thus.

For Sarajevo, the years of relative obscurity, peace and reasonable prosperity came to a melancholy close in the latter part of the nineteenth century. In 1878 the major European powers convened at the Congress of Berlin in an attempt to re-define the frontiers and settle the affairs of South-Eastern Europe – and to remove the potential for mutual confrontation between themselves. In the sense that it removed the threat of immediate conflict, the congress achieved its object, but its deliberations and decisions merely delayed a process that was held over for the attention of a later generation. Far from solving a problem, it exacerbated the difficulties that would have to be addressed by the politicians of the future.

The conference took place in the aftermath of a Russo-Turkish war that had thrown the future of the whole Balkan peninsular into turmoil. Despite heroic Turkish resistance, the Russians had eventually prevailed and in the wake of the war the hitherto Ottoman provinces of Rumania, Bulgaria, Montenegro and Serbia had progressed to independence. The Congress of Berlin established their borders and sovereignty although anomalies remained in their relationship to Constantinople. Outside the realms of the new nations remained the residual territories of the Ottoman Empire in Europe. Of these, the provinces of Bosnia and Herzegovina became subject to a curious compromise in terms of their status.

Almost isolated from the rest of the Turkish possessions bar a narrow connecting corridor of land, the two provinces became a prime target for the territorial ambitions of Serbia. This prospect had been very evident to the Austro-Hungarian Government at the time of the Congress of Berlin, and that imperial nation had no desire whatever to see a vibrant new Slav state emerging on its south-eastern borders. Austria, therefore, only agreed to the creation of an independent Serbia on the basis that Bosnia and Herzegovina would be maintained as buffer territories between the two states, and that Vienna had to have absolute control over their administration and security. The result of this insistence was that, whilst Turkey retained nominal sovereignty over the provinces, Austria occupied them with all the powers of a colonial authority. The Turkish flag still flew over the territories, but Austro-Hungarian control was complete and its influence was paramount.

This situation did not rest easily with the Slav nationalist element in Bosnia, who ardently desired the region to be incorporated as part of a greater Serbia or, even better, a unified southern Slav state. It remained a constant source of grievance and discontent. This came to a head when, in 1908, Austria formally annexed the two provinces. There was predictable outrage from both Belgrade and the Bosnian Serbs, but the political priorities of the major powers imposed their imperatives on the situation, and the nationalists on both sides of the border could only rage at their impotence to affect the issue. As Serbia became increasingly powerful, spectacularly so after the Balkan wars, her sense of impotence steadily declined whilst the rage remained a constant factor. There was certainly no

Archduke Franz Ferdinand with his wife and children

Gavrilo Princip

lack of committed young idealists prepared to risk their lives in order to destabilise Austrian rule in Bosnia. Several clandestine groups of these militants came to be formed within Bosnia itself. In the summer of 1914, one such group took the opportunity to play its part in the grand cause. The intention of its members was nothing less than the assassination of the heir to the Austrian throne.

Archduke Franz Ferdinand von Österreich was not the most popular citizen of the realm in which he was designated the heir apparent. He was deeply conservative in his views, loathed Hungarians, and despised the Slavs. He firmly believed in the necessity, and indeed the inevitability, of a preventive war against Serbia if the territorial ambitions of the latter were to be properly curbed. Had the opportunity arisen, he would have advocated the total conquest of Serbia and its subjugation to Austrian rule.

Acceptance of his views was hindered by his unsympathetic personality and demeanour. He possessed a foul temper and had alienated many members of the establishment, including his uncle, the Emperor. The latter permitted him little involvement in the government of the realm and largely limited his role to ceremonial duties. The Archduke had also outraged the rigid social hierarchy of the Habsburg Empire by marrying a Czech commoner, Sophie Chotek, to whom he was utterly devoted. Franz Ferdinand's love for, and loyalty to, his wife evidenced a more human side to his personality than that portrayed by his public image. The Emperor had insisted that the marriage be morganatic, and, whilst Sophie was given the rank of Duchess, she was forced to trail far behind her husband in state processions and gatherings, separated by a throng of higher-ranked aristocracy. This ritual humiliation of his wife did not tend to better relations with his peers, nor did it improve his disposition.

The Crown Prince's few supporters within the Austrian establishment were mainly fellow reactionaries, but even they had many differences as how best to address the manifold problems facing the empire. Prominent amongst these semi-willing, but personally antipathetic, allies was the Chief of the Austro-Hungarian General Staff, Count Franz Conrad von Hötzendorf, whose views made Franz Ferdinand appear a relative moderate. Hötzendorf was positively welded to the creed of preventive war (and, indeed, had previously been dismissed from his post for advocating such action against Italy – only to be re-instated a few months later). Hötzendorf's enthusiasm for offensive action was unfortunately not complemented by any great ability as a military strategist or tactician. What influence he had with the Crown Prince was, therefore, generally malign and unbalanced. Berchtold, the Austrian Foreign Minister, was much more moderate in his views and one of the few politicians who had an amicable personal relationship with Franz Ferdinand. However, he was also an advocate of pre-emptive action against Serbia. If the Crown Prince's own prejudices and inclinations were already well-established, they were absolutely confirmed by his choice of advisors.

Here arose a paradox. Despite his antipathy towards the Slav constituents of the empire, Franz Ferdinand's hatred of the Hungarians took precedence. Accordingly, he adopted the very unpopular view that the dual monarchy should eventually expand to include representatives of the Slav population in its government. His prime motivation for this was not from any humanitarian concern as to the plight of disenfranchised Slavs. Rather, his intention was to dilute Hungarian influence at the centre of government and to remove Hungarian control over the Slav provinces in the Balkans. It was hardly surprising that there was virulent opposition to his views in both Hungary and Austria. Less obviously predictable was the reaction of Slav activists who also took a dead set against the proposal. For the Serb nationalists in particular Slav participation in the government of the Austrian Empire would rob them of justification for a separatist agenda, or at any rate dilute their appeal to the middle ground. Franz Ferdinand, therefore, had powerful enemies on all sides of the political spectrum.

In the summer of 1914, as was usual at that time of year, military manoeuvres were due to be held within the Austro-Hungarian Empire. For that particular year it had been decided that they would be carried out in Bosnia and Herzegovina. The exercises were scheduled to take place during the month of June, after which, in time-honoured fashion, the bulk of the rank and file of the regular army would be released from their duties in order to assist with the harvest in their respective provinces. The old Emperor was by then too frail to attend these events and had delegated the duty to the Crown Prince. As the latter held the largely ceremonial title of 'Inspector General of the Armed Forces' he would have been present in any case. The plan for the exercises was published in March and it included the information that on their conclusion Archduke Franz Ferdinand, as the representative of the Emperor, would make a state visit to Sarajevo. This would take place on the 28th June.

The date of the visit was not particularly well chosen as it coincided with one of the main Serbian festivals, in honour of the patron Saint Vitus. This festival was noted for its displays of nationalist fervour, and Austrian intelligence was well aware of the existence of extremist cells that might be expected to disrupt the occasion. There were, therefore, well-grounded forebodings amongst the Archduke's friends and advisors as to the wisdom of his visit at that time. Their professed concerns produced a stony response.

Franz Ferdinand dismissed their counsels and was almost fatalistic about the possible consequences. He replied to one such cautionary source with the words, 'I am sure your warning is justified, but I do not let myself be kept under a glass cover. Our life is constantly in danger. One has to rely on God.' (1) Franz Ferdinand went further in requesting that no exceptional security arrangements be made for his visit. This may have been an act of bravado that was not intended to be taken seriously, but the subsequent measures for his protection (or, more pertinently, the lack of them) initiated by the governing authorities in Bosnia would seem to indicate that they took him at his word. For all that, nemesis for the Archduke came from a most unlikely source.

As the person who would provide the spark that would ignite a world war, Gavrilo Princip was not the most obvious candidate. He was a Bosnian Serb who had studied at a university in Belgrade. Physically frail and not particularly gifted with great intelligence or common sense, he nevertheless possessed the boundless enthusiasm of a genuine fanatic. He was a fervent Slav (rather than purely Serb) nationalist and believed that the cause of his race could only be advanced by acts of violence and assassination. To that end he had joined an underground group of fellow spirits known as the 'Young Bosnians'. This organisation was no friendlier towards the Serbian government than it was to Vienna. Its members were anarchists and atheists who would have swept away all the existing regimes and united the southern Slav race in some romantically inspired but structurally undefined manner. They were a disorganised bunch of incompetent teenage dreamers, but no one could fault their depth of commitment. They were quite prepared to die for their cause. The group was based in the young student's home city of Sarajevo and had established loose links with the Black Hand society in Serbia.

In 1912, Princip and a friend from Belgrade had joined a huge influx of volunteers who made their way south to enlist in the Serbian forces that were about to assault the Turks in Kosovo and Albania. The pair presented themselves at a recruiting office in the town of Prokuplje close to the front. Misha Glennie recounts the incident:

'Among the students were two teenage Serbs, one from Belgrade, strong and handsome, the other from Bosnia, pale and weak with sunken blue eyes...Here they found Major Vojin Tankosic, a gruff senior officer with responsibility for organising the volunteers, who was also a leading member of the Black Hand. As the two teenagers entered his office, Tankosic was reinterpreting the legend of William Tell by firing his pistol at a cigarette packet resting on the head of one of his soldiers. When introduced to the sunken-eyed student from Bosnia, Tankosic dismissed him with a snort. "You are too small and too weak", he barked, ordering him out of town and threatening to have him beaten up if he did not comply immediately.

'Humiliated and in despair at his rejection, Gavrilo Princip returned first to Belgrade and soon after to Sarajevo. By then he was determined to prove Major Tankosic wrong.' (2)

In 1914, Tankosic had become a senior member of a Serbian Defence Ministry that was heavily infiltrated by members of the Black Hand society.

When news came of the impending visit of Archduke Franz Ferdinand to Sarajevo, a member of the Young Bosnians contacted the Black Hand organisation in Belgrade with a request for weapons and ammunition. The stated intention of the cell was to attempt the assassination of the Austrian Crown Prince. After some discussion, the Black Hand leadership approved this request, without much thought as to the possible consequences, and Tankosic dealt with the matter personally. He arranged for four pistols and six bombs (actually very basic grenades) to be collected by the conspirators – one of whom was the student he had so contemptuously dismissed at the recruiting office in Prokuplje eighteen months previously. He thoughtfully added six cyanide pills to the requisition, these to be taken in the event of the conspirators being captured alive. This action by him was necessarily of a very clandestine nature, being directly against the then prevailing policy of the Serb Government, the leadership of which had no desire to antagonise Austria. Vladimir Dedijer, a Serbian partisan fighter, politician and historian, makes this clear:

'The Serbian government had no reason to provoke a conflict with Austria-Hungary in 1914. After two Balkan wars and the Albanian mutiny (when Albanian units in the Serbian army mutinied) the Serbian army was decimated and had nothing like enough weapons and ammunition for a major conflict. The country needed peace badly. The Serbian government did its best to stop any incident during the arch-duke's visit to Bosnia, as Serbian documents, recently found, prove.' (3)

The effects of the Balkan wars, whilst being territorially beneficial, had also exhausted the Serbian Army, and there were many problems involved in absorbing the newly acquired provinces. Although probably inevitable in the long term, it would be a number of years before Serbia had recovered sufficiently to challenge Austria over Slav nationalist issues. Government officials in both Berlin and Vienna were well aware of this fact. The former German Chancellor, Bernhard von Bülow states in his memoirs that:

'Although the horrible murder was the work of a Serbian society with branches all over the country, many details prove that the Serbian government had neither instigated nor desired it. The Serbs were exhausted by two wars. The most hot headed among them might have paused at the thought of war with Austria-Hungary, so overwhelmingly superior, especially since, in Serbia's rear, were the rancorous Bulgarians and the untrustworthy Rumanians. Thus at least did…our minister in Belgrade sum up the position, as did also the Belgrade correspondents of every important German newspaper.' (4)

Dedijer also provides a quote from a 'special emissary of the Viennese Foreign Ministry', Friedrich von Wiesner, that confirms that the Austro-Hungarian establishment was also very well aware that the Serbian Government was anxious to avoid any provocative incident:

'On July 13th, Wiesner telegraphed: "There is nothing to show the complicity of the Serbian Government in the direction of the assassination or its preparations or in the supplying of weapons. Nor is there anything to lead one even to conjecture such a thing. On the contrary, there is evidence that would appear to show that complicity is out of the question."' (5)

What becomes crystal clear is that both Germany and Austria-Hungary, in their subsequent attempts at laying the blame for the assassination at the door of the Serbian Government, were completely conscious of the fact that they were perpetrating a known lie. Whilst they might have briefly congratulated themselves on the success of this cynical exercise in power diplomacy, the consequences would return to haunt them to the grave of their empires.

It is entirely possible, but unproven, that Black Hand involvement in the assassination attempt was only agreed on the basis that the plan stood little chance of success. It is known that Tankosic and his superior, Dragutin Dimitrijević (better remembered by his pseudonym, Apis), regarded the capabilities of the Young Bosnians with some contempt and probably felt that the operation would be botched. However, any action that encouraged instability in Bosnia and provided nationalist martyrs had obvious attractions to the leadership. The Young Bosnians were pawns in a much greater game than they knew. What is without question is that their weapons were supplied by the Black Hand for that one specific operation.

The Black Hand assessment of the Young Bosnians' potential to cause mischief was not far off the mark. Nevertheless they offered an opportunity to embarrass the Austrians without, it was probably thought, much likelihood of any serious political mayhem being traceable back to Belgrade. Although speculative, it has to be admitted that there was a good basis for this argument. The recent history of the Balkans had been littered with failed assassination attempts by similar groups of uncoordinated idealists and malcontents, and the young fanatics in Sarajevo hardly seemed likely to buck the trend.

'The six conspirators...formed one of the most disorganised and inexperienced squadrons of assassins ever assembled. The most enduring mystery surrounding the assassination is not who did it or why, but how they ever succeeded.' (6)

If Apis and Tankosic gambled on the likely failure of any assassination attempt, they had the odds on their side. On the other hand, the consequences of its success were potentially disastrous to their nation and their cause. As with all unsuccessful gamblers they would have been staking more than was worth the risk.

The River Miljacka runs through the middle of the city of Sarajevo. On its right bank there is a long, broad boulevard known in Habsburg times as the Appel Quay. About half way along this avenue a small side road connects the riverside to another major concourse, then called the Franz Josef Strasse. Nowadays, there is little to distinguish the building on the corner that leads off from the boulevard. A small plaque next to a closed door indicates that there is a museum within. Its theme is unstated. In the June of 1914, the lower floors of the building were taken up by a general store called 'Schiller'. It was a modest venue for an event that would change the world.

The state visit took place as planned, and, in the morning of the 28th of June, Archduke Franz Ferdinand proceeded in a motorcade along a four mile route to attend a ceremony at the town hall. Much of the designated route was along the Appel Quay, which was thronged with spectators. Only a hundred and twenty policemen and a few soldiers guarded the procession, and they were swamped by the crowds. Mingling within the mass of humanity the six conspirators with their pistols and grenades elbowed their way to the roadside. What followed was true to Balkan form and confirmed the opinion of Tankosic and Apis as to the capabilities of the Bosnian activists.

As the motorcade passed along the Appel Quay, five out of the six potential assassins either lost their nerve or could not deploy their weapons in the crush. One, however, managed to throw his grenade. It lobbed onto the rear of the Archduke's car, bounced off, and exploded under the following vehicle, wounding two officers of the Crown Prince's entourage. The procession continued, minus the damaged vehicle, to the town hall.

The incident did not commend itself to the Archduke's notoriously violent temperament. On arrival at the town hall he was incandescent. The attempt on his life was personally obnoxious and an insult to the state of which he was the Emperor's representative. In high dudgeon Franz

Ferdinand changed the arrangements for the return route of the motorcade. It had been planned that the procession would veer off from the Appel Quay, down the little road past Schiller's store, and then progress along the main street of Franz Josef Strasse. The Archduke cancelled this arrangement and ordered that the motorcade would proceed directly back along the Appel Quay so that he could visit the hospital where the wounded officers from the abortive bomb attempt were being treated. As it happened, his concern for the members of his entourage was to prove both fatal to himself and also to the long-term future of his nation.

Franz Ferdinand's car was second in the line of the motorcade as it proceeded back from the town hall and along the Appel Quay. At the corner by Schiller's store, the driver of the lead car, momentarily forgetting the changed route, turned right, as had been the original plan. Realising his mistake, he stopped and prepared to reverse. The driver of Franz Ferdinand's car had automatically followed the lead car into the turn, and he too had to stop. For thirty seconds, the car carrying the Heir Apparent to the Austrian throne was stationary next to the kerb by Schiller's store. Standing there was a disconsolate young anarchist called Gavrilo Princip.

Utterly depressed by the failure of the earlier attempt on Franz Ferdinand's life, Princip had tried to merge into the crowd and ended up by Schiller's store. Suddenly, the open limousine with Archduke Franz Ferdinand in its back seat stopped exactly next to him. For good or ill it was the single chance of a lifetime and the young man did not hesitate.

Princip had never fired a pistol at a human being in his entire life but he was only a few feet from his target and could hardly miss. A policeman was almost on his shoulder, but the crush of the crowd prevented intervention. At point blank range Princip fired his pistol, hitting the Archduke in the neck. He attempted a second shot, aimed at the Governor of Bosnia, General Oskar Potiorek, but, by that time he was being grappled and the bullet found an unintended target. Passing through the door of the car it mortally wounded the Archduke's wife. The dying woman slumped into her husband's lap. At first it was thought that she had just fainted, but she was soon perceived to be dead. Franz Ferdinand, aware of his own mortal wound, attempted to revive his wife. His penultimate words were, 'Sophie, Sophie, don't die. Live for my children'. By the time he uttered these words his beloved Sophie Chotek was gone. It was their wedding anniversary. The Archduke did not long survive his consort. His last words were a constant repetition. Over and over again he kept saying, 'It is nothing', until death intervened. Misha Glennie comments, rather unsympathetically, that:

> 'Although frequently wrong in his lifetime, the Archduke was never quite so wide of the mark as he was in the minutes before his death.' (7)

Immediately after the assassination, and with the certainty of being apprehended, Princip duly took the cyanide provided by the Black Hand. True to the shambolic character of the entire plot, the poison had degenerated to the point that it induced agony but not death. To this misfortune, if it could be so termed, was added a brutal beating at the hands of the Austrian police. Under this pressure, Princip and his fellow conspirators revealed the links between them and the Black Hand leaders at the heart of Serbia's governing elite. Once this information became public there was a general sense of outrage within the ruling cliques of Europe. The assassination was perceived with horror and condemnation by even Austria's most ardent enemies and Serbia's most devoted allies. It became absolutely clear that Austria would have the general support of all the major European powers in demanding recompense from Serbia. In the remaining three years of his short life Princip became aware of the enormity of his act and of its terrible consequences. It haunted him to his grave. Misha Glennie remarks that:

'By killing Franz Ferdinand, the Young Bosnians signed Serbia's death warrant. Gavrilo Princip was also horrified by the outcome of his deed. The Habsburg Empire did collapse, although Princip did not live to see it as his pain-wrenched, fettered body finally expired in Theresianstadt...a year before the event. But according to the psychiatrist...who interviewed him a number of times in 1916, he was stricken with guilt about the retribution unleashed on the Serbs during the First World War. "The news about the Golgotha which his people were experiencing destroyed him utterly.'" (8)

What had taken place was unacceptable to the international community and it was apparent that Serbia would have to pay a heavy price for the misdemeanours of its irresponsible citizens. There only remained to be decided the terms of the inevitable Austrian ultimatum to Belgrade. For nearly a month, matters remained seemingly in limbo. An outward, and very deceptive, calm prevailed in European relations. Behind the scenes, the reality was very different.

Whatever the level of responsibility for subsequent events that can be laid at the door of Kaiser Wilhelm, his initial reactions to the assassination provide the most compelling, and damning, evidence of his influence on the unfolding catastrophe.

True to character, after a brief dither his response was entirely aggressive. He assured the Austrian Government that Germany would stand four square behind Vienna in confronting Serbia. He made it clear that he expected nothing less than a punitive war to take place and actively encouraged the Austrians to make such demands on Belgrade as to render this inevitable. The terms of an ultimatum were to be so severe as to make Serb compliance impossible without utterly compromising the sovereignty of the nation. In this attitude, the Kaiser was supported by his chief minister, Bethmann-Hollweg, and the Army General Staff. In a meeting with the Habsburg Ambassador, Wilhelm pledged his unconditional support for any action that Austria might choose to take against the Serbs.

'It was a historic moment. The Supreme War Lord of the German Empire, permitting the bellicose side of his nature to take command, had given his ally a blank cheque to strike down Serbia. If Russia intervened, he accepted the risk of a German war against Russia. And, based on the war plan of his own General Staff, Germany would also fight France.' (9)

With this guarantee of Germany's unqualified support, (the 'blank cheque' to which Massie and other historians refer), the Austrian demands, when they eventually materialised, were bound to be ferocious. Even so, when, on July 23rd, the Austrian note was finally delivered to Belgrade, its terms stunned the other governments of Europe. The British Foreign Secretary described it as 'unexpectedly severe; harsher in tone and more humiliating in its terms than any communication of which we had recollection addressed by one independent Government to another.' (10)

The ultimatum commenced with the statement that Serbia was responsible for acts of terrorism against the Austro-Hungarian Empire. There followed ten demands on the Serbian Government, which included the closing down of what were perceived as anti-Austrian newspapers; the arrest and prosecution of members of such groups as the Black Hand; removal from office of named politicians and authorities unacceptable to Vienna; and censorship of school history books and other teaching publications to eliminate anti-Austrian propaganda. These measures were to be supervised by Austro-Hungarian officials operating from within Serbia. Belgrade was given 48 hours, on threat of war, to agree to the terms. The document represented an assault on the integrity of a sovereign nation (however deserving of rebuke), and a clear attempt to either provoke war or force subservience on the government of that country.

Throughout the period between the assassination of the Archduke and the delivery of the Austrian note to Serbia, the German establishment behaved with a cynical disregard for honesty and transparency. As has already been related, both the Germans and the Austrians were well aware that the Serbian Government was innocent of any involvement in the assassination. The worst crime that could be laid at its door was that of failing to control an extremist group of its citizens – albeit some of whom held governmental positions. Nevertheless, from the beginning of July, Berlin was pressing Vienna to force the issue to the point of war. There were even concerns in the German capital that the Austro-Hungarians might lose their nerve and accept a diplomatic solution to the crisis. In the meantime, the Kaiser, the Chancellor, the Foreign Minister, and the military chiefs were professing ignorance as to any knowledge of Austrian intentions. When worried ambassadors requested clarification of the position with regard to Serbia, both Berlin and Vienna blandly assured them that there was no serious cause for alarm. After all, Europe had survived many such crises over the previous decades. To support this tissue of lies, an elaborate subterfuge was concocted to deliberately deceive the rest of the world as to the real perils attendant on the situation.

Having decided that nothing would be done to alert the other powers as to anything untoward, the Kaiser duly boarded the royal yacht and proceeded on his regular summer cruise to the Norwegian fjords. The Chancellor and the military heads likewise commenced their usual holidays although all remained in constant contact with Berlin. A similar charade was played out within Austro-Hungarian circles. This ploy was largely successful and no sense of impending crisis disturbed the deliberations of the other European nations as the month of July progressed to its conclusion.

'The European powers were indeed misled by this camouflage. The British and Russian Ambassadors in Berlin took their summer vacations. The Russian Ambassador even left Vienna on July 21, after the Austrians had assured him that they would not make any demands that could lead to international complications [This, two days before the note to Belgrade!]...This only underlines one important observation: the Entente Powers had to wait, in any case, to see what the Central Powers would do after Sarajevo. They could only react to whatever action the Central Powers were to take.' (11)

Vienna applied a final touch to the deception by deliberately timing the delivery of the note to coincide with the departure of the French President, Prime Minister and Foreign Minister from a state visit to Russia. This ensured that the heads of the French Government would be at sea, and effectively incommunicado, when the storm broke.

The success of the subterfuge meant that consequently, when the details of the Austrian note became known, it came as a bolt from the blue and found the governments and military organisations of the other powers unprepared to deal with a situation that was developing too rapidly to be controlled. Diplomats on all sides desperately attempted to achieve a last minute solution to the crisis, but matters, by then, had passed beyond their competence.

It had been recognised by all the major European powers that the Habsburg Empire had a legitimate cause to claim redress from Serbia for the outrage that had been perpetrated in the assassination of the Archduke. Even

Russia, traditionally the stalwart supporter of fellow Slavs, accepted that some punitive repercussions to Serbia were both inevitable, and to some extent justified – and, whatever Russia's commitment to Slav nationalism, the Empire of the Tsar was an aristocratic autocracy that, for obvious reasons, did not encourage the killing of members of their own class. There had been, therefore, general sympathy and support for the Viennese regime, even amongst its natural enemies. All this vanished abruptly in the wake of the Austrian note to Serbia, which was seen exactly for what it was – a blatant and cynical attempt to precipitate an unjustified war that had the potential to destabilise the entire continent. It was quite plain to even the most committed optimist that this was a crisis that would not be averted by a leisurely transition to a diplomatic congress such as had occurred in the past. The mere fact that Vienna had placed a 48-hour deadline on the ultimatum indicated that the Austrians had no interest in the prospect of international arbitration – rather, by the imposition of a totally unrealistic time scale, they had rendered any diplomatic solution impossible.

The sudden transformation of the crisis came as a particular shock to politicians in London. Up until that point the British Government had been entirely preoccupied with its own problems in Ireland, where it seemed as if matters might degenerate into a form of local civil war. The news of the Austro-Hungarian ultimatum to Serbia broke whilst the British Cabinet was meeting to address the Irish situation. Churchill describes the moment when the prospect of a much greater disaster began to dawn on himself and his colleagues:

'The discussion had reached its inconclusive end, and the Cabinet was about to separate, when the quiet grave tones of Sir Edward Grey's voice were heard reading a document which had just been brought to him from the Foreign Office. It was the Austrian note to Serbia. He had been reading or speaking for several minutes before I could disengage my mind from the tedious and bewildering debate which had just closed. We were all very tired, but gradually as the phrases and sentences followed one another, impressions of a wholly different character began to form in my mind. This note was clearly an ultimatum; but it was an ultimatum such as had never been penned in modern times. As the reading proceeded it seemed absolutely impossible that any state in the world could accept it, or that any acceptance, however abject, would satisfy the aggressor. The parishes of Fermanagh and Tyrone faded back into the mists and squalls of Ireland, and a strange light began immediately, but by perceptible graduations, to fall and glow upon the map of Europe.' (12)

In Paris, St. Petersburg, and Rome, as well as the other capitals of Europe, diplomats and politicians were also suddenly preoccupied with the seriousness of impending events. Quite remarkably though, those who genuinely desired peace were thrown an eleventh hour lifeline. It came, quite unexpectedly, from Belgrade.

There were very few politicians in Europe who could have imagined that the Serbian Government would ever accept the terms of the Austro-

Hungarian note. Nevertheless, within the wholly unreasonable 48-hour time limit of the ultimatum, the Serbs effectively agreed to all of the conditions in the document bar one. It was a capitulation and humiliation that very few diplomats could have foreseen. However, the Belgrade Government baulked on the one single issue that Austro-Hungarian officials would oversee and monitor, on Serbian soil, the processes required by the other provisions of Vienna's demands. That would have been one humiliation too far.

For a brief moment it seemed as if catastrophe might be averted. In Berlin, the Kaiser, having hastily curtailed his Norwegian cruise, was beginning to have second thoughts on the consequences of his earlier inclinations and was counselling that the Serbian concessions should be the basis for further negotiations. By then he was not the only person in the German and Austrian establishments attempting to take a step back from the brink. Surely, it was argued, Serbia's humiliating acceptance of 90% of Vienna's demands would be sufficient to avoid a general war. Unfortunately for the wavering politicians, military imperatives were now dictating the course and timing of events. The dogs of war had slipped their leash and were already far beyond the call of their masters.

Unaware that Austria and Germany would force the issue to war regardless of Serbia's concessions, Britain, France and Russia had heaved a collective sigh of relief. Given Belgrade's unforeseen willingness to meet the Austrian conditions it was assumed that a compromise could probably be reached. It must have seemed possible that officials of other nations, including those of Germany, could be given the role of monitoring the provisions of any agreement. This would have settled the one sticking point on the Austrian demand without prejudice to the latter's interests. The pious hope that this prospect was ever on the agenda was quickly dispelled.

The Emperor of Austria-Hungary himself was of the view that the proposed actions of his government could lead to a world war. In this opinion he was supported by many members of the Austrian establishment. Nevertheless, it was the view of the war party, urged on by their German sympathisers, that prevailed. The Serbian capitulation was termed 'unacceptable', and, on the 28th July 1914, the Empire of Austria-Hungary formally declared war on Serbia and effectively signed its own death warrant.

It is an irony of history that the military influences in Austria, having brought upon the continent the dreadful prospect of war, were far from prepared for the event. As was usual, a good proportion of the army had been released after the summer manoeuvres to help in gathering the harvest.

Conrad von Hötzendorf did not anticipate being in the position to commence hostilities before the 12th of August. However, overwhelming pressure was brought to bear by the German General Staff, and this succeeded in determining the matter. On the 29th July, Austrian artillery on the north bank of the Danube, which at that point formed the border between the two nations, began a bombardment of the Serbian capital, which lay just across the river. The First World War, with all its appalling, albeit then uncomprehended, consequences for the population of Europe, had commenced. It only remained to be seen how many of the other European nations would be drawn into the conflict, and to what extent would be their individual involvement.

The first reaction to the Austro-Hungarian declaration had come from Russia, and was predictably hostile. Whilst diplomatically phrased the communication spelt out a clear warning to Vienna. Russia, it was stated, could not be 'indifferent' to the fate of the Serbs. In undiplomatic language it meant that Russia would not stand on the sidelines whilst the (on paper) overwhelming forces of the Habsburg Empire effected the conquest of Serbia and the destruction of her army. In the meantime, Serbia, recognising the inevitability of war, ordered the mobilisation of her army and prepared for the worst.

On the 25th July, Russia decided on a partial mobilisation of her army. The order came into force on the 29th July as the Austrian bombardment of Belgrade commenced. It was initially a precautionary measure against the prospect of the Austro-Serbian confrontation spilling over into a wider conflict and was only targeted at units on the Galician front, where Russian territory bordered on the Austro-Hungarian Empire. The partial nature of the mobilisation was deliberately intended to show no hostile intent towards Germany.

However well-intentioned, this gesture was to prove entirely in vain. Over the previous few days, in a series of telegrams to St. Petersburg, the Kaiser had attempted to bully or alternatively persuade the Tsar into aborting the Russian mobilisation. In this effort he entirely failed. Russian public opinion, even from the avowed opponents of the regime, was completely in favour of deterring the Austro-Hungarians from an assault on Serbia. The Tsar was not in a position to suddenly and arbitrarily reverse the process without alienating the support of virtually every component of his nation. Consequently, when a final German demand was made on the 29th that Russia either suspend its mobilisation or Germany would have to commence her own, the Tsar had no room for manoeuvre and it was already far too late to affect the process.

The only effective means of reversing the procedure without causing utter chaos was to continue the process to its logical conclusion and then subsequently de-mobilise according to the plans laid out for that eventuality. The entire process of mobilisation and de-mobilisation, in all nations, was by its very nature a highly organised and inflexible operation that could not be simply stopped at the snap of a politician's finger – or even at the decree of an absolute ruler. The only hope that remained was that Germany would stay her hand and wait upon events. This hope was immediately scuppered by the German ultimatum to St. Petersburg on the same day that the Russian mobilisation commenced and Austrian shells started to fall upon Belgrade. Systems, rather than personalities, were beginning to dictate the course of the crisis. Robert Massie remarks that:

'Germany now faced the growing likelihood of war with Russia. German policy had been to encourage a localized Balkan war, punish a regicide state, and restore the fortunes of a crumbling ally. Russian intervention had been discounted. The Tsar's army was considered unready and the Kaiser and his advisors had expected Russia to give way, as she had five years earlier in the Bosnian Crisis. The prospect was glittering: localization accomplished; general war avoided; Serbia crushed; Austria reborn; Russia stripped of her status as a Great Power; the balance of power in the Balkans and Europe realigned. Russian mobilisation against Austria demolished this dream.' (13)

If Massie over eggs the cake somewhat in terms of Austro-German aspirations, there is no doubt that the Russian reaction to the crisis was far more robust than the Central Powers had expected. The calculation that diplomatic browbeating, such as had occurred in 1908, would suffice to win the day had clearly proved not only incorrect but downright dangerous. By her ultimatum to Russia, Germany had placed herself in an untenable position. Withdrawal of the ultimatum would have been a humiliating and unacceptable climb down, whilst maintaining its provisions almost certainly ensured war. In the end, Germany lacked the courage to lose face.

At this point it is in order to define the effect that the act of 'mobilisation' had on the freedom of action available to diplomats of concerned states.

In effect, the act of mobilising the armed forces of a nation meant acceptance that a particular situation had passed beyond the capacity of diplomatic solution. It was also a crossing of the Rubicon in the sense that, once it had been initiated, it could not be revoked. This fact was not fully appreciated by many politicians – and certainly not by the Kaiser, whose military education, and role as 'Supreme Warlord', should have encompassed such details.

The complications involved in concentrating, at pre-arranged points, the whole military potential of a nation, including all its reservists, imposed an extraordinary burden on the state. The entire transport system of the nation, whether it be road, rail, horses, mules or men, had to be immediately utilised to meet the requirements of a unique situation. By its very nature, the organisation and disruption involved impinged on the total resources, and the daily routine, of the entire state. The activation of this process was, therefore, a matter of profound consequence, and, once having been commenced, could not be readily halted. At the risk of stating the obvious, this was in an era when communication systems, if they indeed existed, were relatively primitive. Wireless was in its infancy and vital information needed to be coded and decoded at either end of the link to avoid interception by the enemy. Telephone lines were often few and far between. Communications between military units and their headquarters, and between the latter and the government, were therefore frequently a matter of many hours and dependent on telegram or courier for their delivery. It was not a situation that could be easily resolved or changed by a simple phone call. Once commenced, mobilisation could not be arrested any more than a dart could be recalled from its flight to the board.

These factors combined to produce one indisputable conclusion. There had to be an absolutely concrete strategic policy on which the mobilisation process could be based. There had to be a plan that said, at the moment of mobilisation, this is where the troops have to go and this is going to be their purpose. If Germany had its Schlieffen Plan, this imperative also applied to every other nation. Mobilisation, therefore, had to be firmly attached to a pre-conceived strategic concept that had been engrained and accepted by both the military and the government of any particular country.

Once the overall strategy had been decided at the highest levels of government, it was the responsibility of the Army General Staff to ensure the efficient translation of national policy into the effective deployment of its military forces. In practical terms, therefore, once a government had decided on 'mobilisation', the actual conduct of events passed temporarily out of its hands and into those of the generals. This was only partially true in the special case of Britain, whose insular position coupled with maritime supremacy allowed considerable flexibility in the deployment of her small, but very efficient, regular army. However, it was certainly applicable to all of the continental European states. In the particular case of Germany, these considerations had resulted in General Schlieffen's plan, albeit somewhat diluted and modified by his successors.

It is in this context that all the ineffective efforts of the diplomats, politicians and rulers of nations should be judged. From the 23rd July onwards they were reacting to events rather than controlling the situation. The control and initiative to determine the actions of states was by then in the hands of the 'Captains of War'. In the context of the summer and autumn of 1914, it was the long-prepared plans of the military that dictated the subsequent course of history.

In recent years there has been some play on the phrase 'Domino Theory', in which it is assumed that the collapse of one regional state will automatically trigger the ruin of its neighbour, and that the whole process will then continue down the line until all the regional dominoes have fallen. A very similar argument has been directed at the 'mobilisation' process as it applied in the summer of 1914. One mobilisation begat another, which begat another and so on. In the case of Europe, though, it was not a symmetrical process. The dominoes fell in unpredictable directions, but, in the end, they all did fall, whether it be one way or another.

The mobilisation process took its inexorable course. In reply to the Russian action, the Austro-Hungarian Government announced, in the name of the Emperor, that it would commence a full mobilisation of its armed forces on the 30th July. A day later, the Russians responded by making their own mobilisation total as opposed to partial. Germany now entered the arena and an ultimatum was sent from Berlin requiring Russia to abandon its mobilisation or face a declaration of war. The Russian Government was given just twelve hours to comply with this demand. This was the critical moment at which the fragile peace that had encompassed the continent for many decades was finally shattered. St. Petersburg did not deign a reply, and, on the expiry of the time limit, Germany duly declared war on Russia and announced the general mobilisation of its own armed forces. By the very nature of the German war programme this also meant war against France. There only remained the small matter of devising an excuse for a German declaration of war on her western neighbour and unwilling combatant.

The Schlieffen Plan committed the bulk of the German Army to the invasion of France, through neutral Belgium, as an absolute prerequisite of its overall strategy. First, the French Army would be destroyed. Afterwards the German armies would be transported east to demolish the Russians. In this scenario, the French had little choice. Whether they liked it or not, they were part of the German War Plan. However much they might have wished to remain uninvolved, and however much they strived to avoid giving Germany the excuse for hostilities, they would be attacked by the most formidable military machine in the world.

The German Government actually went through the façade of a diplomatic process in its dealings with the French. An ultimatum was issued that, in its terms, made the Austrian note to Serbia seem positively mild. France would have had to commit herself to a position of benevolent neutrality whilst the Austro-German combination disposed of her chief ally. Amongst its other provisions was the demand that France turn over to Germany several of its key frontier fortresses for the duration of hostilities. Acceptance of these terms would have involved the complete emasculation

HMS IRON DUKE (1914)

Displacement: 25,820 tons
Dimensions: 623ft x 90ft x 30ft; Complement: 925 (1,193 as flagship)
Armament: 10-13.5 inch guns; 12-6 inch guns
Machinery: Quadruple screw; Steam Turbines; 29,000 H.P. = 21 knots
Belt Armour: 4-12 inch; Endurance: 7,780 miles at 10 knots

Flagship of the Grand Fleet at the outbreak of war. Essentially a logical follow on from previous classes, but, for the first time since the *Dreadnought*, carrying a medium-calibre secondary armament in an armoured battery. This gave her an additional armoured area above the waterline, and also a more effective defence against attack from light warships. She was a good all round design, but was quickly superseded by the introduction of the *Queen Elizabeth* class vessels in 1915. *Iron Duke* was de-militarised in 1931 according to the terms of the Washington Treaty, and converted into a Gunnery Training Ship. In that capacity, she was damaged by bombing in Scapa Flow in 1939, beached, and served as a depot ship throughout the Second World War. Jellicoe's Jutland flagship was patched up and towed to the scrap yard in 1946.

SMS FRIEDRICH DER GROSSE (1912)

Displacement: 24,724 tons
Dimensions: 566ft x 95ft x 30ft; Complement: 1,088 + Flag personnel
Armament: 10-12 inch guns; 14-5.9 inch guns; 12-3.4 inch guns
Machinery: Triple screw; Steam turbines; 26,000 H.P. = 20 knots
Belt Armour: 6-12 inch; Endurance: 7,900 at 12 knots

Flagship of the High Seas Fleet at the outbreak of the war. A great improvement on previous classes as she was fitted with turbines, which also permitted the reduction of one turret whilst retaining the same theoretical broadside. Like *Iron Duke*, she was a good all round design but soon put in the shade by subsequent developments. Interned at Scapa Flow at the end of the war, Scheer's flagship at Jutland was scuttled in 1919. In April 1937, the hulk was raised and scrapped in Britain.

of France's ability to defend itself or support its treaty obligations to Russia. Churchill remarks with some emotion that:

> 'Not until she was confronted with the direct demand of Germany to break her Treaty and abandon Russia, did France take up the challenge; and even had she acceded to the German demand, she would only, as we now know, have been faced with a further ultimatum to surrender to German military occupation as a guarantee for her neutrality the fortresses of Toul and Verdun. Thus there never was any chance of France being allowed to escape her ordeal. Even cowardice and dishonour would not have saved her. The Germans had resolved that if war came from any cause, they would take and break France forthwith as its first operation. The German military chiefs burned to give the signal, and were sure of the result...She would have begged for mercy in vain. She did not beg.' (14)

If the matter had not been so serious, the German ultimatum would have been risible. It was an insult to the intelligence of the lowest peasant, never mind to that of the international diplomatic community.

However crass the German communication, it had its desired effect. The ultimatum was rejected by the French Government, thus 'justifying' the inevitable declaration of war by Germany that followed on the 2nd August. Even so, the French Government took extraordinary measures to avoid any action that could be construed as provocative. To the fury and despair of its own field commanders, who were in well-prepared positions, the French Army was ordered to withdraw all its advanced units ten kilometres back from the Franco-German frontier – so that there could be no question or danger of a border incident that could be inflated into an excuse for German aggression.

In some respects it was a bizarre situation. Austria-Hungary had initiated war by commencing actual hostilities against Serbia, but was still officially at peace with the rest of Europe – and remained so for some days afterwards. (As will be related, this anomaly was to have significant consequences in the Mediterranean.) In the meantime, Berlin had declared war on both Russia and France despite the fact that neither nation had directed its armed forces against Germany. By this precipitate action Germany also dealt a severe blow to the structure of her own defensive alliance.

The German declarations of war let Italy off the hook as far as her commitments to the Triple Alliance were concerned. The third member of the alliance was only treaty bound to join in hostilities if Germany or Austria were *attacked* by any of the other powers (Serbia was not considered to be covered by that definition). Italy was not required to assist her treaty partners in the event of either of them initiating hostilities – which both had. To no one's great surprise, Italy took the option of declaring herself neutral and waited on events to clarify which side seemed to be the likely victor.

In Rome, the opportunity to utilise the let-out clause was a huge relief to the Italian Government. War against France, Russia and Serbia would have been acceptable (if undesirable) but if, as it seemed likely, Britain were to be drawn into the conflict it would have placed an intolerable strain on the Italian political structure. Anglo-Italian bonds were very strong at that time. British support for Italy, both tacit and practical, during and after the reunification of the nation was still fresh in the memory of the Italians and there remained a deep sense of gratitude and goodwill towards their erstwhile patrons. It would have been almost unthinkable that Italy and Britain be placed in the position of having to declare war on each other.

At this critical moment, Italian neutrality was a huge bonus for France. It released the military planners from the nightmare of having to divert significant forces of an already outnumbered army to meet a second threat on the Franco-Italian border. All the forces that could be mustered were therefore available to concentrate against the impending onslaught from Germany. Unlike her chief opponent, France, at least, did not have to fight a war on two fronts.

At this point, at the end of July, it was clearly inevitable that Germany and the Austro-Hungarian Empire were going to war against France, Russia and Serbia. The involvement of the other European nations was still in question. Unbeknownst to the rest, Germany had already concluded an alliance with the most influential clique in Turkish governing circles that would eventually serve to bring that still powerful nation, with its absolutely vital strategic position, into the fold of the Central Powers. As for the other significant Balkan states (Greece, Rumania and Bulgaria), they were up for grabs as allies, just as was Italy, depending on the diplomacy and military success of one side or the other.

In Western Europe, the matter was rather more clear-cut. There were nations who did not intrude into the immediate area of conflict, several of whom grasped the opportunity to profit greatly from the tribulations of their less fortunate neighbours. For Holland and the Scandinavian countries, the First World War was an economic boon and they milked the situation for all it was worth. The more the graveyards of Picardy and Poland filled, the more their pockets bulged.

For Belgium, and the tiny nation of Luxemburg, the immediate future was much less rosy. As was the case of France, they were going to be invaded whether they liked it or not, and no action on their part could have prevented the violation of their territory. The German war plan explicitly required the use of their lands in order to attack France. The only question that remained was whether the invasion would be resisted. Luxemburg, having no military forces, did not enter the equation, but Belgium, possessing a sizeable second rank army – and with impressive fortifications defending its border cities and the great port of Antwerp – was an entirely different matter. The diplomatic status of Belgium was also of immense consequence, and proved to be pivotal in the involvement of the one remaining great power in Europe.

As has been described in the preceding chapter, the governing Liberal Party of Great Britain had a strong pacifist element. Churchill states, in his chapter on John Morley in *Great Contemporaries*, that 'the majority of the Cabinet was for leaving France and Germany and the other powers great and small to fight it out as they pleased'.(15) Even though all the major figures in the government (with the possible exception of Lloyd-George) held a contrary view, there was considerable uncertainty as to whether the British would be able to honour their moral commitment to the *entente* with France and Russia without splitting the party and causing a parliamentary crisis. To quote Churchill again:

'There was an invincible refusal on the part of the majority to contemplate British intervention by force of arms should the Foreign Secretary's efforts fail and a European war begin. Thus, as the terrific week wore on and the explosion became inevitable, it seemed probable that a rupture of the political organism by which the country had so long been governed was also rapidly approaching.' (16)

In these circumstances the integrity of Belgium's neutral status assumed critical importance. Britain was bound by treaty, as was Germany (although, in the latter case, it had long been an irrelevance), to be a guarantor of this status. Should Germany invade Belgium en route to outflanking the French Army, the British had a concrete *treaty* (as opposed to a moral) obligation to intervene. This diplomatic nicety was the key factor in swaying uncommitted members of the Liberal Party towards the majority opinion of the senior ministers in the Cabinet. Britain's involvement in the forthcoming war was, therefore, largely in German hands. If Germany abandoned the Schlieffen Plan and respected Belgian neutrality, Britain might be kept out of direct hostilities – or, at the very least, would be debilitated by a long and damaging political crisis that would seriously affect and delay her ability to support her allies.

'So unprepared was the national mind to envisage war as a fact, that a declaration that we would stand by France, if made anytime before August 3rd, would have split the Cabinet, would have been repudiated by the House of Commons, and probably would not have been accepted by the majority of the people. Britain had to be educated into a new mood, and it was only the crisis of Belgium which expedited that education.' (17)

On the 4th August, the whole matter became academic.

Two days previously Germany had issued an ultimatum to Belgium which was effectively a demand that the German Army should be permitted unopposed passage across Belgian territory and that the virtual occupation of the country would ensue for the duration of war against France. The Brussels Government was given just 12 hours to comply with this demand. For a brief moment events remained in limbo, and many diplomats expected King Albert and his ministers to bow before the overwhelming might with which they were now confronted. However, within 9 hours, a forthright answer to Berlin was delivered. The ultimatum was abruptly and decisively rejected, and the armed forces of Belgium were instructed to stand to arms and prepare for the inevitable onslaught. Shortly afterwards, in the early hours of the 3rd, King Albert sent a message to the British Monarch requesting that Britain honour its treaty obligations to defend his nation's integrity:

'Remembering the numerous proofs of your Majesty's friendship and that of your predecessor, and the friendly attitude of England in 1870 and the proof of friendship you have just given us again, I make a supreme appeal to the diplomatic intervention of your Majesty's Government to safeguard the integrity of Belgium.' (18)

The ball was now firmly in Britain's court, and events were moving swiftly. It was in these circumstances that the notably non-histrionic British Foreign Secretary uttered the words for which he is best remembered. As evening fell and he watched the street lamps being lit on the pavements outside his office he remarked, 'The lamps are going out all over Europe. We will not see them lit again in our lifetime.' (19) He prophesised better than he knew; over thirty years would elapse before the matter was finally laid to rest in the devastated heart of Berlin.

On the morning of the 4th, in accordance with the long prepared plan of the their Army General Staff, spearhead units of thirty-four German divisions crossed the border into Belgium and commenced the invasion of the country. Everywhere, the incursions were fiercely resisted and German hopes for a trouble-free transit of its armies through Belgium rapidly evaporated. With these hopes also went any lingering prospect of limiting Britain's involvement in the conflict. In an address to the *Reichstag* later in the day, Bethmann-Hollweg left no doubt as to the illegality of the German actions:

'We are now in a state of necessity, and necessity knows no law! …We were compelled to override the *just* protest of the Luxembourg and Belgian Governments. *The wrong – I speak openly – that we are committing* we will endeavour to make good as soon as our military goal has been reached. Anybody who is threatened, as we are threatened, and is fighting for his highest possessions, can have only one thought – how he is to hack his way through.' (20) [Authors italics]

The remarks of the Imperial Chancellor, who was undoubtedly one of the most reasonable influences within his domestic political sphere, rather give the lie to the efforts of Germany's later apologists.

Five days before the shot that brought the world to war.
British battleships fire a ceremonial salute at Kiel.

A Single Shot

Moments after the shot that brought the world to war.
Gavrilo Princip (second from right) is arrested.

Had Belgium acceded to the German ultimatum and become an unresisting conduit for the Schlieffen Plan the political situation in London would have remained extremely delicate. Even at that late stage, the Kaiser and his Chancellor had still harboured hopes that Britain could be kept out of the war. The Belgian decision to contest the German assault ended all speculation. When news of the invasion was received in London, the British Ambassador in Berlin was instructed to inform the German Government that, unless the operation immediately ceased, and all the invading troops were removed from Belgian soil, a state of war would exist between Britain and Germany. This ultimatum would expire at midnight, continental time, on the 4th August (11pm British time). Even amongst the optimists there was, by then, little hope that its conditions would be accepted. In the event, as the hours passed, and the diplomats clung to the last vestiges of hope, there was not even a reply. Events had passed beyond diplomatic control. As the deadline approached, all the responsible ministers and functionaries of the British Government repaired to their respective offices awaiting news of some last minute reprieve that might somehow defuse the situation. They waited in vain.

At the Admiralty, Churchill and the Sea Lords gathered, together with senior French liaison officers, and watched the minutes tick by. Eventually, the last few seconds of peace passed into history.

'It was 11 o'clock at night – 12 by German time – when the ultimatum expired. The windows of the Admiralty were thrown wide open in the warm air night. Under the roof from which Nelson had received his orders were gathered a small group of Admirals and Captains and a cluster of clerks, pencil in hand, waiting. Along the Mall from the direction of the Palace the sound of an immense concourse singing 'God save the King' floated in. On this deep wave there broke the chimes of Big Ben; and, as the first stroke of the hour boomed out, a rustle of movement swept across the room. The war telegram, which meant "Commence hostilities against Germany" was flashed to the ships and establishments under the White Ensign all over the world...the deed was done.' (21)

When Churchill joined the rest of the Cabinet he was able to report that the entire British Fleet was fully mobilised and already at its war stations. That he was able to do so was the result of an entirely fortuitous decision made many months previously.

On the 23rd June, a squadron of four battleships, amongst the most modern in the British battle fleet, carried out a week long visit to the great

German naval base of Kiel. The visit was attended with much pomp and ceremony and was treated as a matter of considerable import by both the hosts and the guests. The Kaiser and Prince Heinrich, as well as Admiral von Ingenohl, the commander of the High Seas Fleet, took a prominent part in the proceedings. As well as the ceremonial aspects of the visit, it was also an opportunity for the officers and men of each navy to mix and weigh each other up. For nearly ten years there had been a concentrated press and propaganda campaign on both sides of the North Sea that had postulated the two navies as future combatants. In the circumstances, there was obviously much curiosity on both sides as to the nature of the ships and the men that they might have to meet in battle. Ships of both navies had regularly met and co-operated with mutual respect, and a good degree of friendship, on foreign stations, but there had been few contacts between the main fleets in European waters. Given the tensions of the time, relations between the senior officers of the two fleets were necessarily civil and correct rather than amiable. A German officer, seconded to the British squadron on liaison duties, summed up the general mood:

'The German officers adopted a cool and reserved attitude, and the English more or less did the same, so that, in spite of formal courtesies, the political tension could be observed. In the subsequent festivities I failed to notice anything similar, especially in the intercourse of the junior officers, who were very soon good friends. At all the balls and dinners the young English officers could be seen getting on famously with the German officers and flirting outrageously with the German ladies.' (22)

Generally speaking, the British naval visit to Kiel went very well. Both Britain and Germany were going through a period where all their political differences on the international stage seemed to be non-confrontational and none of them were incapable of diplomatic solution. The two navies had been plainly built to face each other, but had rather more mutual respect for each other than they had for the fleets of their respective allies – as had been regularly evidenced whenever British and German warships met and co-operated on foreign stations.

Five days into the visit came the news of the assassination of Archduke Franz Ferdinand. No great disruption of the occasion ensued, although the Kaiser had to cancel some scheduled appearances in order to return to Berlin for consultations with his ministers. On the 30th June, as scheduled, the British squadron weighed anchor and proceeded to sea. As the four ships of the *King George V* class battleships with their accompanying three cruisers, departed Kiel, there were the usual exchanges of signals and salutes that adorn such occasions. The battleships would only ever see each other again twice. Once, and briefly, in the evening mists and cordite fog of the Jutland battle one of them might have sighted the other. On the second occasion a demoralised rusting and mutinous remnant of the

High Seas Fleet would be ushered into internment. Not a single officer or man of either fleet would have ever heard the name Gavrilo Princip or realised that his action during the British visit to Kiel had condemned the two fleets to war against each other.

The reason that British naval squadrons were able to pay diplomatic visits to the other European powers at that time was a result of a much earlier decision to cancel the annual naval exercises that normally took place at that time of the year. This was an unprecedented change in its normal routine. Had the latter still pertained, the fleet would have been gearing itself up for a test of mettle in which tactics and reputations were exposed to a very searching inquisition. For the ambitious officers of all ranks in the fleet it was an opportunity to make their mark and impose upon others their views on tactics and materiel. Annual manoeuvres were a very important part of the fleet's year, and regarded as essential to the ongoing efficiency of the navy. The procedure was, however, also very expensive as there was a vast amount of coal consumed and ships were generally steaming at uneconomical speeds for much of the exercise, which could last for weeks. The naval budget had become an embarrassment to the government, and, pressed to make cuts, Churchill was trying to trim operational costs. Consequently, in the spring of 1914, the Admiralty decided, as an economy measure, to substitute for annual manoeuvres a practice mobilisation of the entire fleet.

In the circumstances, no more fortuitous decision could have been made. The mobilisation exercise was scheduled for July and had been publicly announced many months in advance of its initiation. As a result, there could be no sinister motives attached to this process, occurring, as it did, just as the European crisis erupted. By an entirely accidental piece of timing, the British Fleet, including all its reserve units, was in full commission as the drama on the continent was played out to its sombre conclusion.

The mobilisation exercise was carried out to general satisfaction, and, on its completion, the entire fleet mustered in the Solent for a review by the King. The Fleet Review of 1914 provided the greatest concentration of naval power ever seen and in scale dwarfed even that of the Diamond Jubilee review in 1897. After the review it was planned that all the reserve ships would return to their home ports and decommission, whilst the active units of the fleet would disperse to their designated bases. However, this long-prepared process had to be rapidly reconsidered in the face of the deteriorating situation on the continent.

When news of the Austrian rejection of Serbia's response to her ultimatum became known it was clear that there was a very strong likelihood of a major war, although its extent and consequences were still imponderables. At that very moment, the British Fleet was already dispersing to its home ports and the reserve ships were arranging to discharge their temporary crews. It was a Saturday, and Churchill (assuming, as did most politicians, that there was not an imminent danger) had departed for a weekend with his family in East Anglia. The First Sea Lord, Battenberg, had, however, remained in Whitehall, and instantly realised the seriousness of the situation. On his own initiative he issued orders to immediately suspend the demobilisation process. Subsequently he was able to contact Churchill who fully endorsed his action and passed on the information to the Cabinet. In his rapid and decisive reaction to the crisis, Battenberg did as great a service to his country as any other he had provided in a long and distinguished career. For a considerable number of years, Churchill was given the credit for this action, but, whilst he undoubtedly approved of the First Sea Lord's initiative, it was Prince Louis who grasped the nettle on behalf of the country. When later on the admiral was forced out of his post, helped by a scurrilous press campaign that focussed on his German origins, his vital contribution to Britain's readiness for war was never properly recognised.

Demobilisation of the fleet having been cancelled, there remained the business of despatching its units to their war stations. In the case of the most modern capital ships, constituting what would be known as the Grand Fleet, this involved the transit of the English Channel and then the passage off the east coast of Britain to the Orkney Islands and the great natural harbour of Scapa Flow. According to the recent change in British naval policy towards a strategy of 'distant blockade' this deployment would enable the main fleet to close off access to the North Sea between Scotland and Norway. The only other exit to the Atlantic Ocean from the North Sea, through the narrow waters of the English Channel, would be protected by the bulk of the older pre-Dreadnoughts and numerous flotillas of destroyers, torpedo boats and submarines.

On the morning of the 29th July, the main body of the British battle fleet, comprising all of its most modern units, weighed anchor and departed from Portland where it had been concentrated. That night it made transit of the Dover Strait and set course to the north.

'We may now picture this great fleet, with its flotillas and cruisers, steaming slowly out of Portland Harbour, squadron by squadron, scores of gigantic castles of steel wending their way across the misty, shining sea, like giants bowed in anxious thought. We may picture them again as darkness fell, eighteen miles of warships running at high speed and in absolute blackness through the narrow straits, bearing with them into the broad waters of the North the safeguard of considerable affairs.' (23)

Behind it, the Grand Fleet left an equally large collection of older ships that were to constitute the Channel Fleet and which deployed to their various positions based on the dockyard ports of the south coast and the

Thames estuary. Substantial light forces detached to various of the main non-naval ports, and a major concentration of modern units was established at Harwich, covering the Heligoland Bight and the northern approaches to the English Channel.

By the 4th August, all these ponderous movements had been completed, and every ship of the Royal Navy was at its pre-arranged station. Warning telegrams had already been sent to every overseas command that war was imminent. In the wireless rooms and on the bridges of hundreds of ships, in every ocean, there would have been an unnatural tension and sense of excitement as officers and men waited for the signal that all must have suspected was inevitable – 'Commence Hostilities against Germany'.

On the other side of the North Sea, the High Seas Fleet had carried out its normal summer deployment to Norwegian waters. This generally coincided with the Kaiser's yachting excursion to that area. As the political situation in Europe rapidly deteriorated, Wilhelm hurried back to Berlin and the fleet returned to its base ports. There it waited on the turn of events.

For German naval commanders, the outbreak of war posed something of a problem. In terms of its war employment, the navy only had a subsidiary role. It was entirely subordinated to the policy of an Army General Staff, which was naturally concentrating on the great land campaigns that it had placed in motion. The generals, in fact, had little use for the fleet, and had even vetoed its use against the transport of the British Army across the English Channel to France. The Army Staff was sufficiently confident of victory to welcome the relatively small British force onto the continent. They reasoned that what the Kaiser referred to as 'the contemptible little British Army' could be wrapped up in the general destruction of France, and could be easier dealt with there rather than leaving it intact across the channel as a future threat. For the fleet, therefore, the prospect of immediate action and glory was not high unless the British descended on the German coast. Nevertheless, the sense of anticipation and tension in the German ships must have mirrored that of their British counterparts. The light forces that spread out as a screen into the Heligoland Bight from the Elbe and the Ems estuaries, and from behind the coastal islands, were in a state of profound and high alert.

As midnight on August 4th 1914 came to Berlin, and as the chimes of Big Ben tolled out 11 o'clock in London it marked the end of a long period of peace between the two nations. At that moment, as it lay at its moorings in Kiel and Wilhelmshaven, without putting to sea or firing a shot in anger, the High Seas Fleet had lost its first and greatest battle. Constructed at immense cost and absorbing a significant proportion of its nation's military manpower, it had failed in its prime object – which was to deter Britain from joining Germany's enemies. Instead, its development had actively encouraged a reluctant Britain into their arms. Henceforth it would search for a role to mitigate the consequences of that failure. Once again it would prove unsuccessful, and by its very existence be a material factor in Germany failing to win the war on land. For all that, in the drawn-out consequences of its failure, the gallantry and commitment of its officers and men would ensure that the deeds of Germany's sailors, and the ships in which they served, took their proper place in the history of their nation, and would earn them the utmost respect amidst the awful events that were about to unfold.

CHAPTER SEVENTEEN

EPILOGUE TO A LONG PEACE

This volume has addressed the background to events that found the British and German Fleets in opposition to each other at the outbreak of war.

Britain and Germany, for the most part of their existence as nations in the 18th and 19th centuries, had been natural allies. The ties between the two great empires that had emerged from the period were strong, based not only on the emotive dynastic links between their ruling families, but also from a common history of struggle against their mutual enemies. For all that, the outbreak of the First World War found them on opposing sides; both irrevocably committed to support nations with whom they had traditionally and, often jointly, been enemies.

For the two navies, the situation was particularly fraught. Long-term political imperatives since the turn of the century had placed them in an arms race that had set them against each other. All the training and planning on both sides of the North Sea, from about 1904 onwards, had been based on the assumption that Germany would attempt to challenge Britain's maritime supremacy – at least locally in the North Sea. The end product was a naval arms race that utterly hamstrung the best efforts of well-meaning politicians on both sides of the divide to defuse the situation. As the rivalry intensified, Britain was forced more and more to rely on the Japanese alliance, and *entente* with the French, both very unpopular policies to the British electorate, so as to be able to concentrate the bulk of her naval forces against the perceived emerging threat from Germany. Any chance of a rational approach to the problem from the other side of the North Sea was being loudly and vigorously demolished throughout the German media and through the many influential organisations that had been set up to propagate and distribute the gospel according to Tirpitz.

The reliance on other countries to look after Britain's naval interests in the Mediterranean and Far East did not sit well within many establishment circles and certainly not within the navy itself. It was, however, a *fait accompli*, and the navy had to learn to live with the fact. Nonetheless, the rank and file of the service had little empathy with the new scheme of things, and the prospect of having to successfully co-ordinate operations with the navies of France, Russia, and, later, Italy was regarded with some justified scepticism. The Royal Navy, as an institution, did not rate the effectiveness of its potential allies very highly. As regards the High Seas Fleet as a potential opponent, there was no similar sense of implied disparagement. It was expected to be beaten, but no one was in any doubt that it would be a hard-fought process in which materiel superiority would probably be the deciding factor.

On the German side, no one in the senior naval hierarchy thought it possible to take on and beat the Grand Fleet before its perceived numerical superiority could be reduced by attrition. This, though, was thought to be a real possibility. There was a genuine belief that, immediately after the outbreak of hostilities, the British would venture into German coastal waters where individual units could be picked off by torpedo boats, submarines and mines. There was also the possibility that a mistake by British commanders might offer the opportunity for a detached squadron of the main fleet to be engaged by the full German force. This, in fact, very nearly occurred on one occasion.

The naval confrontation that commenced in 1914 was, therefore, almost entirely an Anglo-German matter. Other nations, allied to either side, had forces that, on paper, appeared formidable, but their contribution was negligible in the context of the conduct of the naval war and their presence frequently an embarrassment, distraction, and annoyance to the main protagonists.

Napoleon, when once asked which force he had most feared, is reported to have answered, 'Allies'. In 1914 there existed a similar frame of mind within the Admiralties of the two premier naval nations. Neither had a great deal of faith in the reliability of their allotted allies whilst they retained a high degree of mutual respect for each other's naval capabilities. All the individual contacts between seagoing officers of the two nations, home and abroad, had tended to reinforce this attitude, as did the almost invariably successful co-operation, in foreign waters, between British and German naval detachments engaged in joint operations.

Certainly, neither side underrated the efficiency of the other. What remained uncertain was the relative effectiveness of their materiel given the fact that the conduct of naval warfare would take place under entirely new conditions. These would be dictated by the application of weaponry and techniques for which there were no adequate precedents.

The Russo-Japanese War of 1904/5 had offered some clues as to the complexity of modern naval warfare, but advances in the previous decade, allied to the 'Dreadnought' revolution, had already rendered these lessons largely irrelevant. The pace of development had overtaken the ability to apply its consequences. Exercises and formal annual manoeuvres by all navies had attempted to address what each authority perceived to be the problems of the future, but only the acid test of war could provide the experience that would decide what tactics, materiel, (and leaders) needed to be discarded – and what radical measures needed to be adopted – to meet the demands of a new era.

Both navies were saddled with the equipment they had been given, and constrained in their use by the strategic and political imperatives that had determined their construction. There was also the question as to whether they would actually be relevant to the war.

The High Seas Fleet at Kiel

Epilogue to a Long Peace

The Grand Fleet at Sea

The perceived wisdom of most politicians and army commanders was that the outcome of hostilities would be decided within a few months as a result of the battle on land. If the war were to be over by Christmas, as was generally assumed at the time, a German campaign against the trade routes, or a British naval blockade of Germany would be inconsequential to the outcome. Neither would have had the time to take any long-term effect. This was undoubtedly a major factor in the Kaiser's policy of not taking risks with his fleet at a time when it was best placed to challenge the British Navy. A quick, successful land war, with a powerful fleet still intact, would have given Germany all the trump cards at a subsequent peace conference.

For the Royal Navy, an early showdown with the High Seas Fleet was what it most urgently desired – but it would have been a hazardous enterprise at the time. Its margin of superiority over its opponent was small, and its materiel deficiencies had yet to become apparent. Fortunately, the Grand Fleet (its main body) was not put to the test at the moment of its greatest vulnerability.

Circumstances dictated that the two main fleets would only meet once, at Jutland, in 1916, by which time the war had taken on a much different aspect. By then, deadlock on the Western Front had seriously undermined Germany's strategic situation, and, in terms of relative naval strength, Germany's position had also considerably deteriorated. For all that, the two navies fought a long campaign against each other that was absolutely crucial to the outcome of the conflict. Had, at any stage up to the summer of 1918, the German Fleet prevailed, there is no question that the Allies would have lost the war. On the other hand, had the British Fleet managed to destroy its opponent, hostilities may not have immediately ceased, but the war would certainly have been brought to an earlier conclusion. In either event, some of the catastrophic losses in the obscenity of the trenches would have been avoided, and a generation of Europe's youth granted a few more survivors.

The two navies were actually playing each other for extraordinarily high stakes. The definitive awful battles of the 'Great War' which have etched themselves on the consciousness of the 20th century all took place on land. For all that, it was the Royal Navy's retention of control of the seas that ensured that the formidable might of Germany's military establishment would eventually be defeated. That the High Seas Fleet remained in being ensured that the conflict would be played out to its bitter end. There were, however, many determined efforts by naval officers on both sides to break what amounted to a strategic deadlock, and, as related in the next two volumes, they encompassed some of the most stirring episodes and exploits to adorn the maritime history of the two nations.

APPENDIX I

TRANSCRIPT OF WILHELM II'S *DAILY TELEGRAPH* INTERVIEW 1908

"You English," he said, "are mad, mad, mad as March hares. What has come over you that you are so completely given over to suspicions quite unworthy of a great nation? What more can I do than I have done? I declared with all the emphasis at my command, in my speech at Guildhall, that my heart is set upon peace, and that it is one of my dearest wishes to live on the best of terms with England. Have I ever been false to my word? Falsehood and prevarication are alien to my nature. My actions ought to speak for themselves, but you listen not to them but to those who misinterpret and distort them. That is a personal insult which I feel and resent. To be forever misjudged, to have my repeated offers of friendship weighed and scrutinized with jealous, mistrustful eyes, taxes my patience severely. I have said time after time that I am a friend of England, and your press – at least, a considerable section of it – bids the people of England refuse my proffered hand and insinuates that the other holds a dagger. How can I convince a nation against its will?

"I repeat," continued His Majesty, "that I am a friend of England, but you make things difficult for me. My task is not of the easiest. The prevailing sentiment among large sections of the middle and lower classes of my own people is not friendly to England. I am, therefore so to speak, in a minority in my own land, but it is a minority of the best elements as it is in England with respect to Germany. That is another reason why I resent your refusal to accept my pledged word that I am the friend of England. I strive without ceasing to improve relations, and you retort that I am your archenemy. You make it hard for me. Why is it?"

His Majesty then reverted to the subject uppermost in his mind – his proved friendship for England. "I have referred," he said, "to the speeches in which I have done all that a sovereign can do to proclaim my good-will. But, as actions speak louder than words, let me also refer to my acts. It is commonly believed in England that throughout the South African War Germany was hostile to her. German opinion undoubtedly was hostile – bitterly hostile. But what of official Germany? Let my critics ask themselves what brought to a sudden stop, and, indeed, to absolute collapse, the European tour of the Boer delegates, who were striving to obtain European intervention? They were feted in Holland, France gave them a rapturous welcome. They wished to come to Berlin, where the German people would have crowned them with flowers. But when they asked me to receive them – I refused. The agitation immediately died away, and the delegation returned empty-handed. Was that, I ask, the action of a secret enemy?

"Again, when the struggle was at its height, the German government was invited by the governments of France and Russia to join with them in calling upon England to put an end to the war. The moment had come, they said, not only to save the Boer Republics, but also to humiliate England to the dust. What was my reply? I said that so far from Germany joining in any concerted European action to put pressure upon England and bring about her downfall, Germany would always keep aloof from politics that could bring her into complications with a sea power like England. Posterity will one day read the exact terms of the telegram – now in the archives of Windsor Castle – in which I informed the sovereign of England of the answer I had returned to the Powers which then sought to compass her fall. Englishmen who now insult me by doubting my word should know what were my actions in the hour of their adversity.

"Nor was that all. Just at the time of your Black Week, in the December of 1899, when disasters followed one another in rapid succession, I received a letter from Queen Victoria, my revered grandmother, written in sorrow and affliction, and bearing manifest traces of the anxieties which were preying upon her mind and health. I at once returned a sympathetic reply. Nay, I did more. I bade one of my officers procure for me as exact an account as he could obtain of the number of combatants in South Africa on both sides and of the actual position of the opposing forces. With the figures before me, I worked out what I considered the best plan of campaign under the circumstances, and submitted it to my General Staff for their criticism. Then, I dispatched it to England, and that document, likewise, is among the state papers at Windsor Castle, awaiting the severely impartial verdict of history. And, as a matter of curious coincidence, let me add that the plan which I formulated ran very much on the same lines as that which was actually adopted by Lord Roberts, and carried by him into successful operation. Was that, I repeat, an act of one who wished England ill? Let Englishmen be just and say!

"But, you will say, what of the German navy? Surely, that is a menace to England! Against whom but England are my squadrons being prepared? If England is not in the minds of those Germans who are bent on creating a powerful fleet, why is Germany asked to consent to such new and heavy burdens of taxation? My answer is clear. Germany is a young and growing empire. She has a worldwide commerce which is rapidly expanding, and to which the legitimate ambition of patriotic Germans refuses to assign any bounds. Germany must have a powerful fleet to protect that commerce and her manifold interests in even the most distant seas. She expects those interests to go on growing, and she must be able to champion them manfully in any quarter of the globe. Her horizons stretch far away."

APPENDIX II

THE BRITISH AND GERMAN FLEETS AUGUST 1914

The tables on the next thirteen pages give a comparison of the ships available to the two nations at the outbreak of war. For the sake of simplicity, I have included all ships that were on trials, or yet to fully commission, in the operational strength of each navy.

What is not mentioned in the tables is the relative protection carried by the capital ships of each navy. The distribution and thickness of armour plate on any two particular designs is impossible to compare without going into lengthy technical detail. A hypothetical vessel stated to have 15-inch armour on its waterline belt is not necessarily better protected to another that only has 12-inch protection over that particular area. Without going into the overall distribution and coverage of this armour, it is impossible to declare that one ship is better protected than the other. The ship with 15-inch armour might only have a short, thin belt of this, whereas the other vessel could have 12-inch plate covering much of its hull. What *is* pertinent is that, in the case of the *post*-dreadnought vessels, the German capital ships, most particularly their battlecruisers, had a greater proportion of their displacement devoted to armour than did their British contemporaries, and were thus better protected.

With regard to the quoted speed of the vessels, the figures give the *designed* capability of the class as completed. For the most modern ships, this is an accurate representation of their potential with a clean bottom, i.e. recently docked and anti-fouled. In the case of the older vessels, their boilers were often in a state of decrepitude and most were no longer capable of reaching, never mind sustaining, this level of performance, and many were a long way short of their designed speed. This proviso particularly applied to the large numbers of vessels commissioned from reserve, many of which had been destined for an early trip to the scrap yard had hostilities not intervened. At the other end of the scale, the modern battlecruisers of each navy often exceeded their designed speeds by 1-2 knots when circumstances required exceptional efforts.

Of the smaller vessels, many of the older cruisers and torpedo boat/destroyers served only as harbour defence units or in a stationary training capacity. Many were converted for auxiliary purposes.

The British and German Fleets August 1914

GREAT BRITAIN

Dreadnought Battleships

Class	Year	Tons	Guns	Speed (kts)	Units
Iron Duke	1911/14	25,000	10-13.5 inch; 12-6 inch	21	4
King George V	1910/13	23,000	10-13.5 inch; 16-4 inch	21.75	4
Orion	1909/12	22,500	10-13.5 inch; 16-4 inch	21	4
Neptune	1908/11	20,000	10-12 inch; 16-4 inch	21	3
St. Vincent	1907/10	19,250	10-12 inch; 20-4 inch	21	3
Bellerophon	1906/09	18,600	10-12 inch; 16-4 inch	20.75	3
Dreadnought	1905/06	17,900	10-12 inch; 27-3 inch	21	1
Erin*	1911/14	23,000	10-13.5 inch; 16-6 inch	21	1
Agincourt*	1911/14	27,500	14-12 inch; 20-6 inch	22	1
				Total	**24**

Building

Class	Year	Tons	Guns	Speed	Units
Queen Elizabeth	1912/15	27,500	8-15 inch; 14-6 inch	24	5
Royal Sovereign	1913/17	25,750	8-15 inch; 14-6 inch	21.5	5
Canada**	1911/15	28,000	10-14 inch; 16-6 inch	22.75	1
				Total	**11**

Semi-Dreadnoughts

Class	Year	Tons	Guns	Speed	Units
Lord Nelson	1904/07	16,500	4-12 inch; 10-9.2 inch	18	2
				Total	**2**

Pre-Dreadnoughts

Class	Year	Tons	Guns	Speed	Units
King Edward VII	1902/07	16,350	4-12"; 4-9.2"; 10-6"	18.5	8
Swiftsure	1902/04	11,800	4-10 inch; 14-7.5 inch	19	2
Duncan	1899/04	14,000	4-12 inch; 12-6 inch	19	5
Formidable	1898/04	15,000	4-12 inch; 12-6 inch	18	8
Canopus	1897/02	12,950	4-12 inch; 12-6 inch	18.25	6
Majestic	1893/97	14,890	4-12 inch; 12-6 inch	17	9
Royal Sovereign	1891/94	14,150	4-13.5 inch; 10-6 inch	16.5	1
				Total	**39**

* Taken over from Turkey, August 1914, before delivery to that country.
** Purchased on the stocks from Chile on the outbreak of war.

GERMANY

Dreadnought Battleships

Class	Year	Tons	Guns	Speed (kts)	Units
Konig	1911/14	25,796	10-12"; 14-5.9"; 16-3.4"	21	4
Kaiser	1909/13	24,724	10-12"; 14-5.9"; 12-3.4"	20	5
Helgoland	1908/12	22,800	12-12"; 14-5.9"; 14-3.4"	20.3	4
Nassau	1907/10	18,873	12-11"; 12-5.9"; 12-3.4"	19.5	4
				Total	17

Building

Class	Year	Tons	Guns	Speed (kts)	Units
Baden	1913/16	28,600	8-15"; 16-5.9"; 8-3.4"	22	4*
				Total	4

Semi-Dreadnoughts

Nil   Total   0

Pre-Dreadnoughts

Class	Year	Tons	Guns	Speed (kts)	Units
Deutschland	1903/08	13,191	4-11"; 14-6.7"; 20-3.4"	18	5
Braunschweig	1901/05	13,200	4-11"; 14-6.7"; 18-3.4"	18	5
Mecklenburg	1899/04	11,774	4-9.4"; 18-5.9"; 12-3.4"	18	5
Kaiser Friedrich III	1895/02	11,097	4-9.4"; 18-5.9"; 14-3.4"	17.5	5
Brandenburg	1890/93	10,013	6-11"; 6-4.1"; 8-3.4"	16	2
				Total	22**

*   Two never completed
**   In addition, Germany possessed 8 Coast Defence Ships of the Siegfried/Odin classes. Of 3,500 tons, they carried 3-9.4" guns at 15 knots.

The British and German Fleets August 1914

GREAT BRITAIN

Battlecruisers

Class	Year	Tons	Guns	Speed (kts)	Units
Lion	1909/13	26,350	8-13.5"; 16-4"	27/28	3
Indefatigable	1909/13	18,800	8-12"; 16-4"	26	3
Invincible	1906/08	17,250	8-12"; 16-4"	25	3
				Total	9

Building

Class	Year	Tons	Guns	Speed (kts)	Units
Tiger	1910/14	28,500	8-13.5"; 12-6"	29	1
				Total	1

Light Cruisers/Scouts

Class	Year	Tons	Guns	Speed (kts)	Units
Arethusa	1912/14	3,750	2-6"; 6-4"	28.5	2
Birmingham	1912/14	5,440	9-6"	25.5	3
Chatham	1911/13	5,400	8-6"	25.5	5
Weymouth	1910/12	5,250	8-6"	25	4
Bristol	1909/10	4,800	2-6"; 10-4"	25	5
Active (Scout)	1910/13	3,440	10-4"	25	3
Boadicea (Scout)	1907/10	3,300	10-4"	25	4
Early Scouts	1904/05	2,640-2,900	9-4"	25	8
				Total	34

Building

Class	Year	Tons	Guns	Speed (kts)	Units
Arethusa	1913/15	3,750	2-6"; 6-4"	28.5	6
Caroline	1913/15	4,219	2-6"; 8-4" (Later 4-6"; 2-3" guns)	28.5	6
Calliope	1914/15	4,228	2-6"; 8-4" (Later 4-6", 2-3" guns)	29	2
				Total	14

GERMANY

Battlecruisers

Class	Year	Tons	Guns	Speed (kts)	Units
Derfflinger	1912/14	26,600	8-12"; 12-5.9"; 12-3.4"	26.5	1
Seydlitz	1911/13	24,988	10-11"; 12-5.9"; 12-3.4"	26.5	1
Moltke	1908/12	22,979	10-11"; 12-5.9"; 12-3.4"	25.5	2
Von der Tann	1908/10	19,370	8-11"; 10-5.9"; 16-3.4"	25	1
Blucher	1906/09	15,550	12-8.2"; 8-5.9"; 16-3.4"	24.8	1
				Total	6

Building

Class	Year	Tons	Guns	Speed (kts)	Units
Derfflinger	1912/15	26,600	8-12"; 14-5.9"; 4-3.4"	26.5	1
Hindenburg	1913/17	26,947	8-12"; 14-5.9"; 4-3.4"	27	1
				Total	2

Light cruisers

Class	Year	Tons	Guns	Speed (kts)	Units
Karlsruhe	1911/14	4,900	12 – 4.1"	28	1
Magdeburg	1910/12	4,570	12 – 4.1"	27.5	4
Kolberg	1907/11	4,362	12 – 4.1"	26	4
Dresden	1907/09	3,664	10 – 4.1"	25	2
Nurnberg	1905/08	3,450	10 – 4.1"	24	3
Koenigsberg	1905/07	3,400	10 – 4.1"	23.5	1
Bremen	1902/07	3,250	10 – 4.1"	23	7
Nymphe	1897/03	2,660/2,715	10 – 4.1"	21.5	10
				Total	32

Building

Class	Year	Tons	Guns	Speed (kts)	Units
Rostock	1912/15	4,912	12 – 4.1" (Later: 7 – 5.9" guns)	28	3
Pillau	1912/15	4,390	8 – 5.9"	27.5	2
Wiesbaden	1913/15	5,180	8 – 5.9"	28	2
				Total	7

GREAT BRITAIN

Armoured Cruisers

Class	Year	Tons	Guns	Speed (kts)	Units
Minotaur	1905/08	14,600	4-9.2"; 10-7.5"; 16-3"	23	3
Warrior	1903/07	13,550	6 – 9.2"; 4 – 7.5"	23	4
Duke of Edinburgh	1903/06	13,550	6 – 9.2"; 10 – 6"	23	2
Devonshire	1902/05	10,850	4 – 7.5"; 6 – 6"	22.25	6
Monmouth	1899/04	9,800	14 – 6"; 10 – 3"	23	9
Drake	1899/03	14,100	2-9.2"; 16-6"; 14-3"	23	4
Cressy	1898/02	12,000	2-9.2"; 12-6"; 12-3"	21	6

Total 34

Protected Cruisers (1st, 2nd & 3rd Classes)

Class	Year	Tons	Guns	Speed (kts)	Units
Diadem	1895/02	11,000	16 – 6"; 14 – 3"	20.5	5
Terrible	1894/98	14,200	2-9.2"; 16-6"; 16-3"	22	1
Crescent	1890/94	7,700	1-9.2"; 12-6"; 12-6pdr	18	2
Edgar	1889/94	7,350	2-9.2"; 10-6"; 12-6pdr	18.5	6
Challenger	1900/05	5,915	11 – 6"; 9 – 3"	21	2
Highflyer	1897/00	5,600	11 – 6"; 9 – 3"	20	3
Vindictive	1896/00	5,750	10 – 6"; 8 – 3"	19	1
Eclipse	1893/98	5,600	11 – 6"; 9 – 3"	19.5	8
Astraea	1890/96	4,360	2 – 6"; 8 – 4.7"	18	3
Apollo	1889/92	3,400	2 – 6"; 6 – 4.7"	18.5	4
Topaze	1903/05	3,000	12 – 4"	22	4
Pelorus	1896/00	2,135	8 – 4"	18.5	6
Philomel	1889/91	2,575	8 – 4.7"	17.5	1

Total 46

Ocean going Destroyers

Class	Year	Tons	Guns	Speed (kts)	Units
'K,L,M' classes	1912/14	740/950	3 – 4" guns; 4 – 21" tubes	31/34	53
'G,H,I' classes	1908/12	760/900	2-4"; 2-3" guns; 2-21" tubes	27	59
Swift	1906/08	1,825	4 – 4" guns; 2 – 18" tubes	6	1
'F' class	1906/10	880/990	2/0-4"; 0/5-3" guns; 2-18" tubes	33	12
'E' class	1902/06	550	5 – 3" guns; 2 – 18" tubes	25.5	34

Total 169

Torpedo Boats/Old Destroyers

Class	Year	Tons	Guns	Speed (kts)	Units
TBD 1-36	1905/09	225/260	2 – 3" guns; 3 – 18" tubes	26	36
TBD 98-117	1901/04	180/205	3–3pdr guns; 3 – 14" tubes	25	13
'A,B,C,D' classes	1893/04	290/440	1-3"; 5-6pdr guns; 2-18" tubes	27/30	79

Total 128

Submarines

Offshore 39 Inshore 36 Total 75

GERMANY

Armoured Cruisers

Class	Year Units	Tons	Guns	Speed	(kts)
Scharnhorst	1905/07	11,600	8-8.2"; 6-5.9"; 18-3.4"	22.5	2
Roon	1902/06	9,500	4-8.2"; 10-5.9"; 14-3.4"	21	2
Prinz Adalbert	1900/04	9,050	4-8.2"; 10-5.9"; 12-3.4"	20.5	2
Prinz Heinrich	1898/02	8,900	2-9.4"; 10-5.9"; 10-3.4"	20	1
Furst Bismarck	1896/00	10,700	4-9.4"; 12-5.9"; 10-3.4"	18	1
				Total	**8**

Protected Cruisers

Class	Year Units	Tons	Guns	Speed	(kts)
Freya	1895/98	5,700	2-8.2"; 6-6"; 12-3.4"	19	5
Kaiserin Augusta	1891/03	6,060	12 –5.9"; 8 – 3.4"	20.5	1
Gazelle	1897/99	2,645	10 – 4.1"	21	2
Hela	1893/96	2,040	4 – 3.4"; 6 – 6pdrs.	20.5	1
Gefion	1892/94	3,770	10 – 4.1"	20	1
				Total	**10**

Ocean going Destroyers/Torpedo Boats

Class	Year Units	Tons	Guns	Speed	(kts)
Various classes	1911/14	820	2 –3.4" guns; 8 – 20" tubes	32.5	36
" "	1908/12	650	2 – 3.4" guns; 5 – 20" tubes	32.5	59
" "	1904/07	487/525	3/4-4pdrs; 3 – 18" tubes	28/29.5	36
" "	1899/03	400/420	3/4-4pdrs; 3 – 18" tubes	26.5/28	24
				Total	**155**

Old Torpedo Boats

Class	Year Units	Tons	Guns	Speed	(kts)
Various classes	1887/99	145/350	Various small calibres	22/25	59
				Total	**59**

Submarines

Offshore		22
Inshore		8
	Total	**30**

NOTES TO VOLUME ONE

CHAPTER ONE – THE ROYAL NAVY IN THE NINETEENTH CENTURY

(1) 'The final defeat…' Jack Sweetman: *The Great Admirals*; p.252

(2) 'There is no mortal…' Quoted in N.A.M. Rodger: *The Command of the Ocean*; p.574

(3) 'The British Empire…' Antony Preston & John Major: *Send a Gunboat*; p.7

(4) 'The Victorian age…' Robert K Massie: *Dreadnought, Britain, Germany and the coming of the Great War*; p.373

(5) 'Why do English…' A.T. Mahan: article; 1911

(6) 'To Admiralty officials…' Sweetman; p.252

(7) 'Freedom from foreign…' N.A.M. Rodger; p.582

(8) 'Britain invariably…' John Beeler: *The Birth of the Battleship*; p.16

(9) 'In reality…' John Charmley: *Splendid Isolation?*; p.400

(10) 'England is not…' Archibald Hurd: *Sea Power*; p.171

(11) 'The Navy which had…' Preston and Major; p.15/16

(12) 'The Fleet which was…' Admiral Sir Herbert Richmond: *Statesmen & Sea Power*; p.259

(13) 'Perhaps the most…' Beeler; p.21

(14) 'In a seaway…' R.A. Burt: *British Battleships – 1889-1904*; p.32

(15) 'The Crimean War…' Oliver Warner: *The British Navy*; p.127

(16) 'The fact was…' Admiral Lord Charles Beresford: *Memoirs*; p.344/5

(17) 'One problem was…' Robert K Massie: *Dreadnought*; p.391

(18)	'Nelson indeed…'	Oliver Warner; p.123
(19)	'Succeeding generations…'	Admiral Sir William James: *Admiral Sir William Fisher*; p.29/30
(20)	'Some of the gunnery…'	Ibid; p.48
(21)	'The Royal Navy at…'	Arthur J Marder: *Fear God and Dread Nought, Vol 1*; p.147
(22)	'I don't think we thought…'	
(23)	'In 1888, the Navy…'	James; p.6
(24)	'The pride of the English…'	R.A. Burt: *British Battleships*; p.7

CHAPTER TWO – THE BIRTH OF THE GERMAN NAVY

(1)	'When a nation…'	Bertrand Russell: *Let the People Think*; p.29
(2)	'The wars of liberation…'	Jonathon Steinberg: *Yesterday's Deterrent*; p.10
(3)	'When, in 1807…'	Sweetman: *The Great Admirals*; p.136
(4)	'By 1811,…'	T124 (Captain Russell Grenfell): *Sea Power*; p.105
(5)	'War is Prussia's…'	Quoted in Edward Legge: *The King, the Kaiser, and the War*; p.306
(6)	'Although the national...'	Steinberg; p.38
(7)	'A committee set...'	Ibid; p.37
(8)	'No ships,…'	Raymond K Massie: *Dreadnought*; p.161
(9)	'Under Bismarck…'	Lynn Abrams: *Bismarck & the German Empire*; p.42
(10)	'He needed a weapon…'	Werner Richter: *Bismarck*; p.281/2
(11)	'Another powerful...'	Ibid; p.282
(12)	'The colonial policy…'	Massie; p.89
(13)	'I am in despair…'	Cited in Legge; p.309/10

(14) 'William, secure in...'	Massie; p.36
(15) 'Bismarck was always…'	Gordon Craig: *Germany 1866-1945*; p.164/5
(16) 'Stosch started from…'	Alfred von Tirpitz: *My Memoirs. Vol. 1*; p.14
(17) 'Stosch took up again…'	Ibid; p.29
(18) 'This man…'	Ibid; p.28
(19) 'The Navy became...'	Steinberg; p.39
(20) 'By any measure…'	Massie; p.89
(21) 'It is a comment…'	Paul Kennedy: *The Rise and Fall British Naval Mastery*; p.181

CHAPTER THREE – A FLEET AGAINST ENGLAND

(1) 'It is perhaps right…'	Giles MacDonaugh: *The Last Kaiser*; p.460
(2) 'One of those strange…'	Steinburg; p.26
(3) 'He could make rings…'	Virginia Cowles: *The Kaiser*
(4) 'The Kaiser still shows…'	Bernhard von Bülow
(5) 'Initiative without tact...'	Quoted in Gordon Craig: *Germany 1866-1945*; p.224
(6) 'William's fluency…'	Michael Balfour: *The Kaiser and his Times*; p.145
(7) 'Wilhelm II, if…'	Herbert Asquith: *The Genesis of the War*; p.232/3
(8) 'Wilhelm II had none…'	Winston Churchill: *Great Contemporaries*; p.37
(9) 'When, as a little boy...'	Wilhelm II quoted in Massie: *Castles of Steel*; p.6
(10) 'He oscillated between…'	Massie; p.106
(11) 'It is hard…'	Simon Heffer: *Power and Place*; p.308
(12) 'The truth was…'	Virginia Cowles: *The Kaiser*; p.125-7

(13) 'The powers invested...'   Abrams; p.14

(14) 'The greatest point...'   Paul M Kennedy: *The Rise of the Anglo-German Antagonism*; p.403

(15) 'William II repudiated...'   A.J.P. Taylor: *The Course of German History*; p.157

(16) 'If Wilhelm II's course...'   Cowles; p.106

(17) 'What we gained by arms...'   Quoted in Churchill: *The World Crisis I*; p.5

(18) '(Bismarck) devoted...'   Ibid; p.5

(19) 'There can be no doubt...'   Werner Richter: *Bismarck;* p.369/70

(20) 'When the great star fell...'   Craig; p.178/9

(21) 'The weakness...'   Steinberg; p.52

(22) 'The Emperor wanted...'   Tirpitz: *Vol I*; p. 45

(23) 'One State Secretary...'   Eugen Richter: Leading article; *Freisinnige Zeitung*; Quoted in Steinburg; p.133

(24) 'Such a fleet...'   Holger H. Herwig: *Luxury Fleet*; p.42

(25) 'From the strategic...'   Craig; p.310

(26) 'Germany's growth...'   Steinburg; p.18

(27) 'The fleet increases...'   Quoted in Holstein

(28) 'Why did her leaders...'   Steinberg; p.27

(29) 'For all his great...'   Craig; p.310/1

(30) For details of the dispute, see   Terrell D. Gottshall: *By Order of the Kaiser*; p.177

(31) 'It had been easy...'   Winston Churchill: *The World Crisis: I*; *p.8*

CHAPTER FOUR – THE NAVAL RACE BEGINS

(1) '...British policy...'   R.K. Massie: *Dreadnought*; p.88

(2) 'In other words...'	Paul Kennedy: *The Rise and Fall of British Naval Mastery*; p.248
(3) 'The simplistic remedy...'	Ibid; p.248
(4) '...the shadow...'	Quoted in Ibid; p.246
(5) 'It was said...'	Ibid; p.138
(6) 'Bülow managed...'	Craig; p.273
(7) 'The seizure...'	Tirpitz: *My Memoirs Vol I*; p.122
(8) '...swept through...'	Massie; p.180
(9) 'When working out...'	Tirpitz; p.122
(10) 'To protect...'	Introduction to German 1898 Naval Bill
(11) 'Along with the risk...'	Massie; p.181
(12) 'The psychological...'	A.J. Marder: *British Naval Policy: 1880-1905*; p.288
(13) 'The balance...'	Ibid; p.293
(14) 'The question which...'	Adm. Sir Herbert Richmond: *Statesmen and Sea Power*; p.278
(15) 'More the passing...'	Marder; p.293
(16) 'On no one...'	Massie; p.298/9
(17) 'The Kaiser did not wish...'	Ibid; p.700
(18) 'Bülow's action was...'	Paul M Kennedy: *The Rise of the Anglo-German Antagonism*; p.249
(19) 'The years 1900-2...'	Marder; p.458/9

CHAPTER FIVE – FISHER

(1) 'One battleship was worth...'	Marder: *British Naval Policy 1880-1905;* p.30
(2) 'I wrote out the Lord's...'	Fisher: *Records*; p.7
(3) 'Penniless, friendless, and...'	Fisher: In many quotes and letters
(4) 'The more consequential...'	Jan Morris: *Fisher's Face*; p.94

(5) 'The materiel progress…'	Richard Hough: *First Sea Lord*; p.92/3
(6) 'It was fifteen years…'	Ibid; p.109
(7) 'I sent the wine around…'	Fisher: *Memories*; p.225
(8) 'These leagues of nations…'	Fisher: Various quotes from letters
(9) 'The supremacy…'	Fisher: Frequent expression; Quoted in various sources.
(10) 'From a 12 knot fleet...'	Quoted in Lord Charles Beresford: *Memoirs Vol. II*; p.467
(11) 'One does not wonder…'	Quoted in Hough; p.141

CHAPTER SIX – THE END OF SPLENDID ISOLATION

(1) 'Some historians…'	John Charmley: *Splendid Isolation?*; p.295
(2) 'The German's were…'	Virginia Cowles: *The Kaiser*; p.198
(3) 'London felt too weak…'	Paul Kennedy: *The Rise and Fall of British Naval Mastery*; p.252
(4) 'Equally alarmed…'	Ibid; p.253
(5) 'They walked…'	Robert K Massie: *Dreadnought*; p.251
(6) 'Behind this reply…'	Ibid; p.354
(7) 'Gradually, the larger…'	Ibid; p.359
(8) 'The political situation…'	E.L. Woodward: *Great Britain and the German Navy*; p.88/9
(9) 'Yet the situation…'	Ibid; p.89
(10) 'At first…'	Massie; p.367
(11) 'The personality of…'	Cowles; p.238
(12) 'As early as 1905…'	Charmley; p.399

CHAPTER SEVEN – THE DREADNOUGHT REVOLUTION

(1) 'The fighting efficiency...'	Cited in Arthur J. Marder: *Fear God and Dread Nought*; p.150

(2) 'The scheme…' Fisher: cited in Massis: *Dreadnought*; p.461

(3) 'Fisher's nucleus crew...' Marder: *From the Dreadnought to Scapa Flow Vol. I*; p.36

(4) 'The redistribution of the…' Ibid; p.40

(5) 'The homilies...' Reginald Bacon: *From 1900 Onwards*; p.155

(6) 'I don't care if...' Richard Humble: *Before the Dreadnought;* cited in Massie; p.466

(7) 'The Engine room...' Bacon: *The Life of Admiral Lord Fisher*; p.263

(8) 'The most powerful...' Richard Hough: *First Sea Lord*; p.241

(9) 'In deliberately sacrificing...' Marder: *From the Dreadnought to Scapa Flow Vol. I*; p.69

(10) 'However eminent...' Ibid; p.61

(11) 'Knowing as we did…' Bacon: *From 1900 Onwards*; p.103

(12) 'If we have the advantage...' Fisher: *Records*; p.91

(13) 'You can fight…' Fisher: Letter to a 'friend' and oft quoted in conversation.

(14) 'The "Invincibles"...' Fisher: *Records*; p.107/8

(15) 'Cawdor came...' R.C.K. Ensor: *England 1870-1914*; p.363

(16) 'It was his ruthless...' Lord Chatfield: *The Navy and Defence*; p.34

(17) 'His fitness for the task...' Hough: *First Sea Lord*; p.193

(18) 'The weaknesses...' Ibid; p.194

(19) 'Perhaps only one thing...' Wilmot: *Battleship*; p.42

(20) 'At every point...' Bacon: *Lord Fisher*; p.82

CHAPTER EIGHT – SCHISM IN THE ROYAL NAVY

(1) 'A man of action' Massie: *Dreadnought*; p.502

(2) 'But, to universal…' Penn: *Infighting Admirals*; p.70

(3) 'He was always…' Massie; p.501

(4) 'This impetuous man...' William Jameson: *The Fleet that Jack Built*; p.70

(5) 'Lord Charles Beresford...' Chatfield: *The Navy and Defence*; p.41

(6) '...Then there was a squall...' Ibid; p.41

(7) 'Everyone present...' Ibid; p.41/2

(8) 'Fisher, who spoke...' Massie; p.513

(9) 'In the two years...' Quoted in Jameson; p.86

(10) 'While Vice-Admiral...' Lord Charles Beresford: *Memoirs*; p.467/8

(11) 'If anything...' Fisher, in a letter to Earl Spencer 28/3/02 cited in Marder: *Fear God and Dread Nought*; p.238

(12) 'Private, No one to see…' Quoted in Marder: *Fear God and Dread Nought*; p.232

(13) 'There is a great deal...' Quoted in Jameson; p.86

(14) See *Infighting Admirals* by Geoffrey Penn for the background.

(15) 'Unfortunately for Beresford...' Massie; p.522

(16) 'It has come to my notice...' Beresford: Letter to the Admiralty

(17) 'They are all...' Quoted in Bacon: *Lord Fisher*; p.46

(18) '(the admiralty)…would...' Ibid; p.44

(19) 'Lord Charles saw…' Massie; p.525

(21) 'My Dear Admiral…' Letter from Lord Esher

(22) 'Needless to say…' Simon Heffer: *Power and Place*; p.257

(23) 'In conclusion…' Bacon: *Lord Fisher*; p.49

(24) 'Lord Charles, after...' Ibid; p.49

(25) 'He looked on...' Massie; p.535

(26) 'When he spoke...' Ibid; p.539

(27) '...were in practice...'	The committee's full report is available or précised in many accounts
(28) 'The committee have...'	Ditto
(29) 'In other words...'	Bacon; p.56
(30) 'Thus, after nearly...'	Ibid; p.57
(31) 'A tornado of energy...'	Geoffrey Penn: *Infighting Admirals*; p.230
(32) 'In the Navy we...'	Percy Scott: *Fifty Years in the Royal Navy*; p.202
(33) 'It was a satisfaction…'	Beresford: *Memoirs*; p.555

CHAPTER NINE – THE DIVISIONS INTENSIFY

(1) 'Germany might have had…'	Barbara Tuchman: *August 1914*; p.17
(2) 'One may say...'	E.L. Woodward: *Great Britain and the German Navy*; p.10
(3) 'An important school...'	Ibid; p.11
(4) 'In the case of...'	Jonathon Steinburg: *Yesterdays Deterrent*; p.23
(5) 'German society...'	Woodward; p.25
(6) 'It appeared to me...'	Lord Charles Beresford: Letter to the Admiralty
(7) 'English Imperialists...'	Tuchman; p.19
(8) 'Izvolsky had placed...'	Massie; p.604
(9) 'It is impossible...'	Grey of Falloden: *Twenty-Five Years*; p.192
(10) 'The Germans had...'	Ibid; p.202/3
(11) 'In the end…'	Winston Churchill: *The World Crisis Vol. I*; p.24
(12) 'Although the Chancellor...'	Ibid; p.24

(13) 'The great naval...' Lord Selborne: Memo: Quoted in Cabinet papers 7.12.03

CHAPTER TEN – THE *DAILY TELEGRAPH* INTERVIEW

(1) 'Bülow successfully...' Massie; p.689

(2) 'Uninfluenced by the...' Quoted in Bernhard von Bülow: *Memoirs*; p.423

(3) 'My father had returned...' Prince Wilhelm von Hohenzollern: *The Memoirs of the Crown Prince of Germany*; p.86/7

(4) 'In a perfectly loyal way…' Ibid; p.86

(5) '...thus the navy came...' Hew Strachan: *The First World War*; p.22

(6) 'Given the fact...' Ibid; p.21

CHAPTER ELEVEN – NEGOTIATIONS AND CRISIS

(1) 'As long as it was...' Grey of Falloden: *Twenty-Five Years: I*; p.219

(2) 'When Wilberg arrived...' Massie: *Dreadnought*; p.727

(3) 'A flag is easily...' Tirpitz: *My Memoirs:I*; p.210

(4) 'The despatch of...' Grey; p.220/1

(5) 'I thought what he...' Ibid; p.224

(6) 'I would make…' David Lloyd-George: Quoted widely.

(7) '...the first diplomatic…' Tirpitz I: p.211

(8) 'The end was almost...' Grey I: p.241

CHAPTER TWELVE – BRITANNIA TAKES TO THE SHORE

(1) 'He had in a very...' Grey; p.206/7

(2) 'The Utmost effort...' Adm. William James: *The Fleet that Jack Built*; p.53/4

Notes to Volume 1

(3) 'His short, sturdy...'   Ibid; p.53/4
(4) 'He was, without any...'   Winston Churchill: *The World Crisis I*; p.59
(5) 'In some men...'   James; p.47
(6) 'Wilson was...'   Ibid; p.50
(7) 'The King sent for...'   Richard Hough: *First Sea Lord*; p.277
(8) 'The King accepted...'   Simon Heffer: *Power and Place*; p.251

CHAPTER THIRTEEN – CHURCHILL AT THE ADMIRALTY

(1) 'He was far more...'   Marder; p.252/3
(2) 'How then...'   Churchill: *The World Crisis Vol. I*; p.195/6
(3) 'Winston certainly...'   Adm. Dudley de Chair: *The Sea is Strong*; p.150/1
(4) '...one of the young...'   Marder; p.260
(5) 'Churchill, who...'   Ibid; p.260
(6) 'When, a few...'   Ibid; p.260/1
(7) 'One of the private...'   de Chair; p.150
(8) 'Before doing so...'   Ibid; p.150
(9) 'Under vast pressure...'   Marder: *Vol. 1*; p.261
(10) 'The enclosed...'   Churchill; p.60
(11) 'Sir Arthur Wilson...'   Ibid; p.63
(12) '...looked rather young...' Quoted in various; apocryphal.
(13) 'Bridgeman did have...'   Marder; p.258
(14) 'In keeping with...'   Adm. Sir Peter Gretton: *Former Naval Person*; p.116
(15) '...the Royal Naval Air...' Ibid; p.128

(16)	'The life of...'	Churchill: Admiralty Memorandum; 17/10/1912
(17)	'No corresponding...'	Ibid
(18)	'During several months...'	Marder; p.271
(19)	'There is one thing...'	Kitchener: Quoted in Hough and Marder

CHAPTER FOURTEEN – OLIVE BRANCHES AND NETTLES

(1)	'We knew…'	Churchill: *The World Crisis Vol I*; p.71
(2)	'The extravagance...'	Tirpitz: *Vol I*; p.219
(3)	'A really business-like...'	Ibid; p.223
(4)	'Haldane did not…'	Tirpitz: *My Memoirs Vol I*; p.224
(5)	'There is however...'	Churchill; p.76
(6)	'…it was an honest...'	Herbert Asquith: *The Genesis of the Great War*; p.98
(7)	'The formula...'	Ibid; p.99
(8)	'England will...'	Quoted in various; Grey/Massie etc.
(9)	'Unlike McKenna's…'	Marder; p.283
(10)	'..one must remember…'	Tirpitz; *My Memoirs Vol I*; p.180
(11)	'The Germans…'	Quoted in A.H. Pollen: *The Navy in Battle*; p.119-20
(12)	'The only trump...'	Churchill; p.86/7
(13)	'The point I am...'	Ibid; p.87
(14)	'It would of course...'	Ibid; p.83
(15)	'Count Metternich...'	Asquith; p.103
(16)	'"no minister..."'	Tirpitz: p.232 and quoting O. Hammann
(17)	'His early death...'	Ibid p.219
(18)	'Take, as an instance...'	Churchill; p.84

(19) 'The Haldane mission...'	Marder; p.286	
(20) '...a confession...'	E.L. Woodward: *Great Britain and the German Navy*; p.430	
(21) 'The army was kept...'	Tirpitz II; p.290	
(22) 'Tirpitz's acknowledgement...'	Ibid; p.431	

CHAPTER FIFTEEN – TWILIGHT OF THE EMPIRES

(1) 'The great powers...'	Misha Glennie: *The Balkans*; p.127
(2) 'This rare unity...'	Alan Palmer: *History of the First World War*; p.55
(3) '...the thud of shells...'	Palmer; p.55
(4) 'To the Bulgars...'	Ibid; p.55
(5) 'Although the groupings...'	Churchill: *The World Crisis I*; p.7
(6) 'The First World War...'	Harold Macmillan: *Winds of Change*; p.59
(7) '...however much the British...'	Paul Kennedy: *The Rise & Fall of British Naval Mastery*; p.269
(8) 'Following meetings...'	Ibid; p.268
(9) 'His dynamism...'	Dan van der Vat: *The Ship that Changed the World*; p.28
(10) 'The influence of Germany...'	Ibid; p.25
(11) 'Not even the astutest...'	David Lloyd-George: *War Memoirs Vol. I*; p.36
(12) 'The Spring and...'	Churchill; p.143

CHAPTER SIXTEEN – A SINGLE SHOT

(1) 'I am sure...'	Quoted in Dedijer: *The History of the First World War Vol. I*; p.6
(2) 'Among the students...'	Misha Glennie: *The Balkans*; p.251
(3) 'The Serbian government...'	Vladimir Dedijer - in *History of the First World War I*; p.3

(4) 'Although the horrible...' Bernhard von Bülow: *Memoirs II*; p.136

(5) 'On July 13th...' Dedijer; p.8

(6) '...the six conspirators...' Glennie; p.304

(7) 'Although frequently wrong...' Ibid; p.251

(8) 'By killing...' Ibid; p.305

(9) 'It was a historic...' Robert K Massie: *Dreadnought*; p.861

(10) '...unexpectedly severe...' Grey: *Vol.1*; p.310

(11) 'The European powers...' Imanuel Geiss: in *History of the First World War I*; p.65

(12) 'The discussion had...' Churchill: *The World Crisis I*, p.155

(13) 'Germany now faced...' Massie; p.870

(14) 'Not until...' Churchill; p.165/6

(15) '...the majority...' Churchill: *Great Contemporaries*; p.88

(16) '...there was an invincible...' Churchill: *The World Crisis I*; p.173

(17) 'So unprepared...' John Buchan: *The King's Grace*; p.55

(18) 'Remembering…' Quoted in *The Times History of the War: Vol I*; p.25

(19) 'The lamps are going out...' Widely cited

(20) 'We are now in…' Quoted in *The Times History of the War: Vol I*; p.25

(21) 'It was 11 o'clock...' Churchill; p.186

(22) 'The German officers…' von Hase: *From Kiel to Jutland*; p.27

(23) 'We may now...' Churchill; p.172

SELECTED BIBLIOGRAPHY (3 VOLUMES)

Abrams, Lynn
Bismarck and the German Empire 1871-1918
Abingdon, Oxon: Routledge, 1995

Admiralty
Official Naval Despatches; No 3
London: The Graphic, 1914

Agar, Capt. Augustus, V.C.
Footprints in the Sea
London: Evans Brothers, 1959

Aspinall-Oglander, Cecil
Roger Keyes: Being the Biography of Admiral of the Fleet Lord Keyes of Zeebrugge and Dover
London: The Hogarth Press, 1951

Asquith, Herbert H.
The Genesis of the War
London: Cassell and Co., 1923

Bacon, Admiral Reginald
From 1900 Onwards
London: Hutchinson, 1940

The Life of Lord Fisher of Kilverstone (2 vols.)
London: Hodder & Stoughton, 1929

Bailey, Admiral Sir Lewis
Pull Together!
London: George G. Harrap, 1939

Balfour, Michael
The Kaiser and his Times
London: Harmandsworth, 1964

Barnett, Corelli
The Swordbearers
New York: William Morrow, 1964

Beatty, Charles
Our Admiral
London: W.H. Allen, 1980

Beeler, John
Birth of the Battleship
London: Chatham Publishing, 2001

Beesly, Patrick
Room 40
London: Hamish Hamilton, 1982

Very Special Intelligence
London: Hamish Hamilton, 1977

Bennett, Geoffrey
The Battle of Jutland
London: B.T. Batsford, 1964

Naval Battles of the First World War
London: B.T. Batsford, 1968

Beresford, Admiral Lord Charles
Memoirs (2 vols.)
London: Methuen, 1914

Berghahn, Volker
Germany and the approach of war in 1914
London: St. Martin's Press, 1993

Bingham, Cdr the Hon. Barry V.C.
Falklands, Jutland, and the Bight
London: John Murray; 1919

Bradford, Admiral E.
Sir Arthur Knyvet Wilson
London: John Murray, 1923

Breyer, Siegfried
Battleships & Battlecruisers 1905-1970
New York: Doubleday, 1973

Buchan, John
The Kings Grace
London: Hodder & Stoughton, 1935

Bülow, Prince Bernhard von
Memoirs (4 vols.)
Boston: Little, Brown, 1931-2

Burt, R.A.
British Battleships 1889-1905
London: Arms & Armour Press, 1988

Buxton, Ian
Big Gun Monitors
Annapolis: NUP, 1978

Selected Bibliography

Callwell, Maj.Gen C.E.
Field Marshall Sir Henry Wilson
London: Cassell, 1927

Campbell, John
The Fighting at Jutland
London: Conway Maritime Press, 1986

Campbell, N.J.M.
Battlecruisers (Warship Special 1)
London: Conway, 1978

Cecil, Hugh & **Liddle**, Peter (eds.)
Facing Armageddon
London: Leo Cooper, 1996

Chalmers, Rear-Admiral W.S.
The Life and Letters of David, Earl Beatty
London: Hodder & Stoughton, 1951

Charmley, John
Splendid Isolation?
London: Hodder & Stoughton, 1999

Chatterton, E. Keble
The Big Blockade
London: Hurst & Blackett, 1932

Gallant Gentlemen
London: Hurst & Blackett, 1932

Chatfield, Admiral of the Fleet, Lord
The Navy and Defence
London: Heinemann, 1942

Churchill, Sir Winston S
The World Crisis 1911-1918
New York: Scribners, 1923-29

Great Contemporaries
London: Collins, 1937

Clark, Christopher
Iron Kingdom
London: Allen Lane, 2006

Collier, Basil
The Lion and the Eagle
London: McDonald, 1972

Corbett, Sir Jeremy
Official War History Vols. 1-3
London: Longmans, Green, 1928

Cowles, Virginia
The Kaiser
New York: Harper & Row, 1963

Craig, Gordon A
Germany 1866-1945
London: Clarendon Press, 1978

Creswell, Cdr. John
Naval Warfare
London: Sampson, Low, Marston, 1936

Cunningham, Viscount A.B.C.
A Sailor's Odyssey
London: Hutchinson, 1981

Dawson, Capt. Lionel
Gone for a Sailor
London: Rich & Cowan, 1936

Flotillas
London: Rich & Cowan, 1933

De Chair, Adm. Sir Dudley
The Sea is Strong
London: Harrap, 1961

Dewar, Vice Admiral K.G.B.
The Navy from Within
London: Gollancz, 1939

Dixon, T.B.
The Enemy Fought Splendidly
Poole: Blandford Press, 1983

Domvile, Admiral Sir Barry
Look to your Moat
London: Hutchinson & Co, c.1938

By and Large
London: Hutchinson & Co, 1936

Dorling, Captain Taprell (Taffrail)
Men o'War
London: Phillip Allan, 1929

Endless Story
London: Hodder & Stoughton, 1931

Dreyer, Admiral Frederick C.
The Sea Heritage
London: Museum Press, 1955

Eade, Charles (ed.)
Churchill: By his Contemporaries
London: Hutchinson, 1953

Egremont, Max
Balfour
London: Wm Collins & Son, 1980

Ensor, R.C.K.
England: 1870-1914
Oxford: Clarenden Press, 1936

'Ephesian'
Winston S Churchill
London: Mills & Boon, 1927

Fawcett, H.W. & **Hooper**, G.W.W. (ed.)
The Fighting at Jutland
London: Hutchinson, c.1930

Fisher, Lord. Admiral of the Fleet
Memories and Records (2 vols.)
New York: George H Doran, 1920

Fear God and Dread Nought (3 vols.)
Correspondence of Admiral of the Fleet Lord Fisher
Ed. A.J. Marder
London: Jonathan Cape, 1952-59

Frewen, Oswald
Sailor's Soliloquy
London: Hutchinson, 1961

Glennie, Misha
The Balkans
London: Granta, 1999

Gordon, Andrew
The Rules of the Game
London: John Murray, 1996

Gottschall, Terrell D.
By Order of the Kaiser
Annapolis: N.I.P., 2003

Grenfell, Capt Russell ('T124')
Sea Power
London: The Right Book Club, 1941

Gretton, Admiral Sir Peter
Former Naval Person
London: Cassell, 1968

Grey of Falloden, Lord
Twenty-Five Years (2 vols.)
London: Hodder &Stoughton, 1925

Groener, Erich
German Warships 1815-1945
W. Germany: Bernard & Graefe, 1982

Hase, Commander Georg von
Kiel and Jutland
London: Skeffington & son, c.1921

Hawkins, Nigel
The Starvation Blockades
Barnsley: Leo Cooper, 2002

Hayward, Victor
HMS Tiger at Bay
London: William Kimber & Co., 1977

Heathcote, T.A.
The British Admirals of the Fleet
Barnsley: Pen and Sword Books, 2002

Herman, Arthur
To Rule the Waves
New York: Harper and Collins, 2004

Herwig, Holgar H.
'Luxury Fleet' The Imperial German Navy
London: Allen & Unwin, 1980

Hill, Richard
War at Sea in the Ironclad Age
London: Cassell, 2000

Hirst, Lloyd
Coronel and After
London: Peter Davies, 1934

Hickling, Vice-Admiral Harold
Sailor at Sea
London: William Kimber & Co., 1965

Selected Bibliography

Hoehling, A.A.
The Great War at Sea
New York: Galahad Books, 1965

Hohenzollern, Prince Franz Joseph von
Emden
London: Herbert Jenkins Ltd., 1928

Hohenzollern, Prince Wilhelm von
The Memoirs of the Crown Prince
London: Thornton Butterworth, 1922

Hore, Captain Peter
The Habit of Victory
London: Sidgwick & Jackson, 2005

Hough, Richard
The Pursuit of Admiral von Spee
London: George Allen and Unwin Ltd., 1969

Former Naval Person: Churchill and the Wars at Sea
London: Weidenfeld & Nicholson, 1985

First Sea Lord
London: George Allen and Unwin Ltd., 1969

The Great War at Sea
Oxford: OUP, 1983

Man O'War
London: J.M.Dent, 1979

Humble, Richard
Fraser of North Cape
London: Routledge & Kegan Paul, 1983

Hurd, Archibald
The Fleets at War
London: Hodder & Stoughton, 1915

The Command of the Sea
London: Chapman & Hall, 1912

The Merchant Navy
London: John Murray, 1921

Hythe, Viscount (ed.)
The Naval Annual 1913
Portsmouth: J.Griffin & Co, 1913

James, Admiral Sir William
A Great Seaman
London: H.F. & G. Witherby Ltd, 1956

Admiral Sir William Fisher
London; MacMillan & Co; 1943

The Sky Was Always Blue
London; Methuen; 1951

Jameson, Rear Admiral William
The Fleet that Jack Built
New York: Harcourt, Brace, 1962

Jane, Fred T. (var. eds.)
Jane's Fighting Ships
Var. 1898/1905/1914/1919

The British Battle Fleet
London: S.W. Partridge & Co., 1912

Jellicoe, Admiral of the Fleet Earl
The Grand Fleet
London: Cassell, 1919

The Crisis of the Naval War
London: Cassell, 1920

The Submarine Peril
London: Cassell, 1934

Jenkins, Roy
Churchill
London: MacMillan, 2001

Keegan, John
The Price of Admiralty
London: Penguin, 1988

Kemp, Lt. Cdr. Peter
Fleet Air Arm
London: Herbert Jenkins Ltd, 1954

Kennedy, Paul
The Rise and Fall of the Great Powers
New York: Random House/Vintage Books, 1987

The Rise and Fall of British Naval Mastery
Malabar, Florida: Krieger, 1982

The Rise of the Anglo-German Antagonism 1860-1914
Boston: Allen & Unwin, 1980

Selected Bibliography

Kenworthy, J.M.
Freedom of the Seas
London: Hutchison & Co., 1928

Kerr, Admiral Mark
Prince Louis of Battenburg: Admiral of the Fleet
London: Longmans, Green & Co., 1934

The Navy in my Time
London: Rich & Cowan, 1933

King-Hall, Stephen
My Naval Life
London: Faber & Faber, 1951

Knight, E.F.
The Harwich Force
London: Hodder and Stoughton, 1919

Knight, W. Stanley McBean
The History of the Great European War
London: Caxton, 1914-18

Knight-Patterson, W.M.
Germany; From Defeat to Conquest
London: George Allen & Unwin, 1945

Lambert, Andrew
Admirals
London: Faber & Faber, 2008

Langmaid, Capt. Kenneth
The Sea Raiders
London: Jarrolds, 1963

Layman, R.D.
Naval Aviation in the First World War
Chatham: Chatham Publishing, 1996

Layton, Geoff
From Bismarck to Hitler: Germany 1890-1933
London: Hodder & Stoughton, 2002

Legge, Edward
King Edward, The Kaiser and The War
London: Grant Richards Ltd., 1917

Lerman, Katherine A.
The Chancellor as Courtier: Bernhard von Bülow and the Governance of Germany 1900-1909
Cambridge: Cambridge University Press, 1990

Liddell Hart, Sir Basil
History of the First World War
London: Cassell, 1934

Lloyd-George, David
War Memoirs (2 vols.)
London: Odhams Press, 1938

Lochner, R.K.
The Last Gentleman of War
London: Century Hutchinson Ltd., 1988

Lowis, Cdr. Geoffrey. L.
Fabulous Admirals
London: Putnam, 1957

MacDonough, Giles
The Last Kaiser
London: Weidenfeld & Nicholson, 2000

Macmillan, Harold
Winds of Change
London: Macmillan, 1966

Mahan, Alfred Thayer
The Influence of Sea Power on History 1660-1783
Boston: Little & Brown, 1895

Marder, Professor Arthur J.
The Anatomy of British Sea Power
London: Putnam & Co., 1940

From the Dreadnought to Scapa Flow: The Royal Navy in the Fisher Era
London: O.U.P., 1961-65

Old Friends, New Enemies
Oxford: Clarendon Press, 1981

Fear God and Dread Nought
London: Jonathon Cape, 1952

Massie, Robert K.
Dreadnought: Britain, Germany and The Coming of the Great War
London: Jonathon Cape, 1992

Castles of Steel
London: Jonathon Cape, 2004

Milne, Admiral Sir A. Berkeley
The Flight of the Goeben and the Breslau
London: Eveleigh Nash Co. Ltd., 1921

Morris, Jan
Fisher's Face
London: Viking; 1995

Muir, Surgeon Rear Adm. J.R.
Years of Endurance
London: Philip Allan, 1936

Newbolt, Sir Henry
Official War History: Naval Operations Vols. 4 & 5
London: Longman Green & Co., 1922

Ollard, Richard
Fisher and Cunningham
London: Constable, 1991

Owen, Charles
No More Heroes
London: George Allen & Unwin, 1975

Padfield, Peter
Aim Straight: A Biography of Sir Percy Scott
London: Hodder & Stoughton, 1966

The Great Naval Race
London: Hart-Davis, MacGibbon, 1974

Palmer, Alan
Chap. In History of the 1st World War (Vol. 1)
London: Purnell for BBC Publishing, undated

Parkes, Oscar
British Battleships 1860-1950
London: Seely Service, 1957

Patterson, A. Temple
Tyrwhitt of the Harwich Force
London: Macdonald and Janes, 1973

Penn, Geoffrey
Infighting Admirals
Barnsley: Leo Cooper, 2000

Pitt, Barrie
Zeebrugge
London: Cassell, 1958

Pochammer, Hans
Before Jutland: Admiral von Spee's Last Voyage
London: Jarrolds, 1931

Pollen, Arthur.H.
The Navy in Battle
London: Chatto & Windus, 1919

Pound, Reginald
Evans of the Broke
Oxford: O.U.P., 1963

Preston, Antony & Major John
Send a Gunboat
London: Longmans Green & Co., 1967

Pugh, Philip
The Cost of Sea Power
London: Conway Maritime Press, 1986

Puleston, W.D.
Mahan
London: Jonathon Cape, 1939

Raeder, Grand Admiral Erich von
Struggle for the Sea
London: William Kimber, 1959

Raven, Alan & Roberts John
British Battleships of World War Two
Annapolis: USNI, 1976

British Cruisers of World War Two
London: Arms & Armour Press, 1980

Richmond, Admiral Sir Herbert
Statesmen and Sea Power
Oxford: O.U.P., 1946

Richter, Werner (Trans. Brian Battershaw)
Bismarck
London: Macdonald, 1964

Rodger, N.A.M.
The Command of the Ocean
London: Allen Lane, 2004

Roskill, Captain Stephen
Churchill and the Admirals
London: Collins, 1977

The Strategy of Sea Power
London: Collins, 1962

Hankey – Man of Secrets
London: Collins, 1970

Ross, Stewart
Admiral Sir Francis Bridgeman
Cambridge: Pearson Publishing; 1998

Ruge, F.
Scapa Flow 1919; The End of the German Fleet
London: Ian Allan, 1973

Scheer, Admiral Reinhardt
Germany's High Seas Fleet in the World War
New York: Peter Smith, 1934

Scott, Admiral Sir Percy
Fifty Years in the Royal Navy
New York: George H Doran, 1919

Silverstone, Paul
Directory of the Worlds Capital Ships
Shepperton: Ian Allan, 1984

Smith, Admiral H. H.
A Yellow Admiral Remembers
London: E. Arnold & Co., 1932

Steel, Nigel & Hart, Peter
Jutland 1916, Death in the Grey Wastes
London: Cassel, 2003

Steinberg, Jonathon
Yesterday's Deterrent: Tirpitz and the Birth of the German Battlefleet
New York: MacMillan, 1965

Stevenson, David
The Outbreak of the First World War
Basingstoke: Macmillan, 1997

Strachan, Hew
The First World War: Vol 1: To Arms
Oxford: O.U.P., 2001

Sweetman, Jack (ed.)
The Great Admirals
Annapolis: N.I.P., 1997

Tarrant, Victor
Jutland, The German perspective
London: Arms and Armour Press, 1995

Taylor, A.J.P.
The Course of German History
London: Methuen, 1971

The Times
History of the Great War (22 vols.)
London: The Times, 1922

Thompson, Julian (ed.)
The IWM History of the War at Sea – 1914-18
London: Sidgewick & Jackson, 2005

Tirpitz, Grand Admiral Alfred von
My Memoirs (2 vols.)
New York: Dodd, Mead, 1919

Tuchman, Barbara
August 1914
London: Constable, 1962

Van der Vat, Dan
The Ship that Changed the World
Edinburgh: Birlinn Ltd., 2000

Grand Scuttle
Annapolis: N.I.P., 1986

The Last Corsair
London: Hodder & Stoughton, 1983

Stealth at Sea
New York: Houghton & Mifflin, 1995

Warner, Oliver
The British Navy
London: Thames & Hudson, 1975

Wester Wemyss, Lady
The Life & Letters of Lord Wester Wemyss
London: Eyre & Spottiswoode, 1935

Weir, Gary E.
Building the Kaiser's Navy
Annapolis: US Navy Institute, 1992

Wilhelm II, Kaiser
My Memoirs (2 vols.)
London: Cassell, 1922

Willmott, H.P.
Battleship
London: Cassell, 2002

Wilson, H.W.
Battleships in Action (2 vols.)
London: Sampson Low, Marston, 1926

Wilson, H.W./ **Hammerton**, J.A. (eds.)
The Great War (12 vols.)
London: Amalgamated Press, 1914-19

Woodward, David
The Collapse of Power
London: Arthur Barker, 1973

Woodward, E.L.
Great Britain and the German Navy
New York: O.U.P., 1935

Yates, Keith
Flawed Victory: Jutland 1916
Annapolis, Maryland: N.I.P., 2000

Young, Filson
With the Battlecruisers
London: Cassell, 1921

INDEX

Adalbert von Hohenzollern: Prussian prince and founder of the navy
Creates Prussian Admiralty, 53-4; retires, 55, 63

Aehrenthal, Count Alois Lexa von: Austrian Foreign Minister 1906
231-2

Albert, King of the Belgians
430

Arabi Pasha: Egyptian army officer.
Attempted coup against Khedive; 147

Arnold-Forster, H.O.: Academic and politician. Ally and supporter of Fisher
126

Asquith, Herbert Henry: British Prime Minister 1908-16
On character of the Kaiser, 75; fails to support Fisher, 213-5, 217, 219; Agadir crisis, 272; 285; Admiralty changes, 292-3, 304-5, 308; desire to improve Anglo-German relations, 337; initiates Haldane Mission, 341; results of, 353-4, 356

Aube, Hyacinthe Laurent Theophile: French Admiral.
Advocate of torpedo boat warfare, 65

Augusta 'Dona': Empress of Germany and wife of Wilhelm II
116, 242

Bacon, Admiral Sir Reginald: Influential British naval officer and protégé of Fisher
Becomes head of submarine service, 135; commands *Dreadnought* 173, 175; on criticism of Fisher 192; on Beresford and McKenna, 213; criticises outcome of enquiry into Admiralty conduct, 218-9

Balfour, Arthur James: British politician. Conservative Prime Minister, 1902-06
Acquaintance with Fisher, 127; sets up commission to investigate army, 136; replaces Salisbury as Prime Minister, 138-9, 159; on Fisher's scrapping policy, 164; relations with Fisher and Beresford, 203, 214

Ballin, Albert: German Shipping Magnate
Suggests Anglo-German naval conversations, 261-2; resurrects this initiative, 338-41; Haldane Mission, 353; channels German response to Churchill's proposals, 362

Battenberg, HSH Admiral Prince Louis of:
2nd Sea Lord 1911-12; 1st Sea Lord 1913-14
Admiral Poore affair, 302; replaces Bridgeman as First Sea Lord, 313; supports naval aviation, 326; antipathy towards naval mission to Turkey, 402; suspends demobilisation of the fleet, 436

Beatty, David, Admiral of the Fleet Lord
Colonial service, 42; Naval Secretary to Churchill, 298, 311

Berchtold, Count Leopold: Austro-Hungarian Foreign Minister 1914
410

Beresford; Admiral Lord Charles: British Admiral and politician
On state of navy 37, 38, 42; Fisher asks for him as deputy at Alexandria 125; Second-in-Command, Mediterranean Fleet, 133-4, 191; feud with Fisher, 192-204, 207-11, 218-20, 213-21; shadows Russian Baltic Fleet, 227, 284-5, 281-2, 308

Berlin, SMS: German Light Cruiser
Role in Agadir crisis, 268

Bethmann-Hollweg, Theobald von: German Imperial Chancellor 1909-17
Succeeds Bülow as Chancellor, 185; support for Austria 232; wishes to improve Anglo-German relations, 240, 253; difficulties with naval policy, 254-5; policies of, 260-4; Agadir crisis, 266-7; supports Ballin/Cassell initiative, 338-40; Haldane Mission, and consequences, 343-5, 347, 354, 353-5; ignored by Tirpitz, 362; hopes for British neutrality, 390; on Belgian treaty, 394; policy during approach to war, 417-8, 430

Bismarck, Herbert von: Son of the 'Iron Chancellor'. State Secretary for Foreign Affairs
84-5

Bismarck, Otto Edouard Leopold von Bismarck-Schoenhausen: German statesman and Imperial Chancellor
Early career, 49-52; becomes Chancellor, 56-62; attitude to navy 64-66; colonies, 67; relations with Wilhelm II, 71, 77; Dismissed by Wilhelm, 83-6; anti-British policy, 90, 96, 118; relations with Russia, 103; replaced by Caprivi, 107; comparison with Tirpitz, 224, 230; structure of Germany, 252, 275, 369, 370, 384

***Blucher*, SMS:** German hybrid armoured/battlecruiser
184, 238

Bridgeman, Admiral Sir Francis: British naval officer. First Sea Lord 1912-13
Replaces Wilson 306; Churchill resolves to

force retirement of, 312-3, 326

Bülow, Prince Bernhard von: German Secretary for Foreign Affairs 1897-1900. Imperial Chancellor 1900-09

On the Kaiser, 75; character 107-8; responsibility for Germany's relative decline, 114; rebuffs Chamberlain initiatives, 112-13, 117-18; ferments Moroccan crisis, 151-7; Algeciras Conference, 118; suspicion of Britain, 222; reaction to Anglo-Russian détente, 230; threatens Russia over Bosnia-Herzegovina crisis, 233; attitude to naval matters, 239-40; *Daily Telegraph* affair, 241-3, 245-7, 250-1; forced resignation of, 253; legacy, 255, 260-3; and Weltpolitik, 391; on assassination of Franz-Ferdinand, 412

Cambon, Paul: French Ambassador to Britain during the entente negotiations
146, 228

Campbell-Bannerman, Sir Henry: Liberal Prime Minister 1906-8
292

Caprivi, General Count Leo von: Chief of German Admiralty 1883-88. Imperial Chancellor 1891-4
64-65, 107

***Captain*, HMS:** British turret ship battleship
Loss of, 34n

Cassell, Sir Ernest: British banker
Contacts with Ballin, 338-42: Anglo-German conduit, 353, 362

Cawdor, Earl of: First Lord of the Admiralty 1905
186

Chamberlain, Joseph: British politician. Colonial Secretary under Salisbury & Balfour
Character and policies, 105-8; reaction to Jameson raid, 112-3; overtures to Germany, 114, 117-8, 222; disillusion with and break with Germany, 117; friction with Foreign Office, 140

Chatfield, Admiral of the Fleet Lord: British naval officer
On Fisher, 189; on Fisher and Beresford, 195

Churchill, Winston Leonard Spencer: British politician and First Lord of the Admiralty 1911-15

On Wilhelm II, 76; on German diplomacy, 95; acquaintance with Fisher, 127, 185, 220; at Battle of Omdurman, 144n; on Fisher, 192; opposes naval estimates 236-7; on A.K. Wilson, 283, 285, 292-3; First Lord of the Admiralty, 294-336, 337, 340: 'Luxury Fleet' speech, 346; reaction to German 'Novelle', 348, 350; presents naval estimates to parliament, 356-60; proposes 'naval holiday', 362-3, 367, 370; on European balance of power, 393; Anglo-French naval distribution, 397-8; optimism on international relations in 1914, 403, 405; on Austrian ultimatum to Serbia, 419; on German ultimatum to France, 427, 429; on cabinet differences regarding war, 429; on declaration of war, 433; substitution of practice mobilisation in place of annual fleet exercises, 435; cancellation of demobilisation, 436

Coles, Captain Cowper: RN. British naval officer and designer
34

Craddock, Sir Christopher (Kit): British Admiral
42

Cromarty Firth: British Fleet anchorage
334

Cuniberti, Vittorio: Italian naval architect
Advocates *Dreadnought* type, 170

Custance, Admiral Sir Reginald: British naval officer. Beresford supporter
Opposes Fishers reforms, 190; supports Beresford against Fisher, 215-6, 219

Delcassé, Théophile: French politician and Foreign Minister. Architect of the Entente Cordiale
Fashoda incident, 145; initiates contacts with British Government, 146; First Moroccan crisis, 148, 151; forced to resign, 153, 155-6, 228-9, 276

***Devastation*, HMS:** British turret ship and forerunner of the modern battleship
35

De Chair, Admiral Sir Dudley: British naval officer. Secretary to First Sea Lord under Churchill
On difficulties with Churchill, 298; on the Admiral Poore affair, 301-3

Diederichs, Otto von: German Admiral
On acquisition of Tsingtao and differences with Tirpitz, 95

***Dreadnought*, HMS:** First all big-gun battleship
Origins of, 168-70; construction and qualities, 173-4; criticism and defence of, 174-6; consequences to German plans, 177-8, 181, 184, 190-1; effects on other warship types, 318

484

Edward VII: King of Great Britain and Emperor of India 1901-10

Family links to Wilhelm II, 77; difficult relationship with Wilhelm, 81-3; death of Queen Victoria and temporary reconciliation with Wilhelm, 115-6; political influence of, 121; friendship with Fisher, 125-7; contribution to entente with France, 146; support for Delcassé, 153; support for Fisher, 185, 207, 210-12, 215; contribution to détente with Russia, 228-30; 'encirclement' of Germany, 234, 281; death, 279-80; reported conversation with Sir Arthur Wilson, 284; friendship with Sir Ernest Cassell, 339

Enver Pasha: Turkish War Minister post 1913

401-2

Esher, Reginald Brett, 2nd Viscount: Influential establishment figure and supporter of Fisher

Friendship with Fisher, 127; chairs committee on army reform, 135, 217; support for Fisher, 207, 210-12; overlooked for panel of enquiry into Admiralty policy at Beresford's insistence, 215

Eulenberg, Count Philip von: Confidante of Kaiser Wilhelm II

Involved in scandal, 241

***Excellent*, HMS:** Royal Navy training establishment. Cradle of the Gunnery branch

123-7, 167

Fisher, John Arbuthnot, Admiral of the Fleet Lord Fisher of Kilverstone: Naval visionary and administrator

25; opinion of minor colonial and reserve warships, 40, 42; attitude to German naval expansion, 112; career and policies, 120-137, 138; reforms, 159-60, 163-4, 166-7; Builds *Dreadnought*, 168-70, 173-5, 177; and Tirpitz, 178; builds first battlecruisers, 181-4, 185; and his First Lords, 186; virtues and faults, 189-91; feud with Beresford, 192-207, 209-21; enquiry into Admiralty policy, 215-19, 282; death of Edward VII, 281-2; on A.K. Wilson, 284, 296; relations with Churchill, 306-08, 313-15; opposes establishment of naval staff, 314; chairs committee on oil, 317, 334; accurately predicts unrestricted submarine warfare, 321-2; supports creation of naval air service, 327; supports reform of personnel welfare and training, 327; supports ties with Turkey, 400

Franz-Ferdinand, Archduke: Austro-Hungarian Heir Apparent

379, favours Slav representation in government, 382; last words, 405; character, 409-10; scheduled visit to Sarajevo and assassination of, 413-5, 417-9, 439

Franz-Josef II: Emperor of Austria-Hungary

420, 424

Friedrich III: German Emperor 1888. Formerly Crown Prince

Liberal tendencies and opposition to Bismarck, 60-62, 77; advised by Stosch, 64; succeeds Wilhelm I and dies shortly afterwards, 73, 114

Gard, W.H: Naval constructor. Ally of Fisher. Chief Constructor, Malta dockyard when Fisher was C-in-C, Mediterranean

Discusses future battleship design with Fisher, 169; on *Dreadnought* committee, 170

Garvin J.L.: British journalist and editor. Ally of Fisher

211

George V: King of Great Britain and Emperor of India 1910-35

Family links, 77; relationship with Wilhelm II, 82, 281; sympathetic to Beresford camp, 219n, 281-2, 293; role in Lords reform, 395; reviews fleet, July 1914, 435

Gladstone, William Ewart: British Liberal politician and Prime Minister (4 times) between 1868-94

142, 257

Gordon, General Charles: British army officer, killed at Khartoum by the Dervishes

143

Gracie, Alexander: Engineer and businessman

On *Dreadnought* committee, 170

Grey, Sir Edward: British Foreign Secretary 1906-16

Character and political stance, 157; on committee of enquiry into Admiralty policy, 215; role in détente with Russia, 228-9; on Bosnia-Herzegovia crisis 1908, 232; on 'encirclement', 234, 254; relations with Metternich, 235; attitude to dialogue with Germany, 264-5; Agadir crisis, 267, 270, 272, 276; at Committee of Imperial Defence meeting 1911, 285; reactions to Haldane Mission and German 'Novelle', 350, 355; receives Austrian ultimatum to Serbia, 419; prophesy, 430

Haldane, Richard Burdon, Lord: Liberal politician, Head of the War Office 1905-14

On committee of enquiry into Admiralty policy, 215; at Committee of Imperial Defence meeting 1911, 285; considered as First Lord of the Admiralty, 292-3, 328; Mission to Berlin, 341-48, 350, 363, 366

Index

Hatzveldt, Count Paul von: German Ambassador to Great Britain
146n

Heinrich, Grand Admiral Prince: German naval officer. Younger brother of the Kaiser
434

Heligoland: Island in Heligoland Bight controlling approaches to German naval bases on the North Sea coast
Possession transferred from Britain to Germany 1890 in exchange for Zanzibar, 347; Queen Victoria disapproves of this, 347n

Hipper, Admiral Franz von: German Admiral. Commander of the High Seas Fleet battlecruisers 1914-18
66

Hohenlowe, Prince Chlodwig von: Imperial German Chancellor 1894-97
117-8

Hohenzollern, Prince Wilhelm von: German Crown Prince 1888-1918
On condition of Wilhelm II during *Daily Telegraph* affair, 247-8; criticism of Bülow's role, 248

Hollman, Admiral Friedrich: State Secretary of the Navy Office, 1890-97
86

Holstein, Freiherr Friedrich von: First counsellor to the Secretariat for Foreign Affairs
Comment on Wilhelm II, 75; comment on naval policy, 94, 239; policy towards Britain, 113, 222; role in first Moroccan crisis, 151-2; attitude towards Algeciras Conference, 155-6, 276

Hotzendorf, Franz, Conrad von: Austro-Hungarian Chief of Army Staff
Advocates pre-emptive war, 383, 409; unprepared for war, 421

Hulsen-Haeseler, General Count von: Chief of the Military Cabinet
246

Inflexible, **HMS:** Innovative British battleship commanded by Fisher
131-2, 194, 210

Ingenohl, Admiral Friedrich von: Commander-in-Chief High Seas Fleet, 1914
434

Invincible, **HMS:** First British battlecruiser
181, 183-4

Izvolsky, Alexander: Russian Foreign Minister 1906-12
Role in Anglo-Russian détente, 228-30; disastrous intrigue with Aehrenthal over the Balkans, 231-2; becomes Ambassador to France, 234, 276

Jameson, Dr. Leander Starr: Associate of Cecil Rhodes
Failed raid into Transvaal, 106n

Jellicoe, John Rushworth, Admiral of the Fleet, Lord
30n, 42; difficulties with Churchill, 302-3; earmarked as future fleet commander, 311; advocates use of airships, 325; threatens resignation over oil stocks, 334; measures to improve quality of shell not followed up, 335

Kelvin, Lord: Inventor and entrepreneur
On *Dreadnought* committee, 170

Kerr, Lord Walter: British Admiral and First Sea Lord prior to Fisher
134-6

Kiderlen-Waechter, Alfred von: German Secretary of State for Foreign Affairs 1909-12
Character, 261; role in Agadir crisis 266-69, 272-4

Kiel Canal
Work commenced during Caprivi administration, 65; requirement to enlarge in order to take *Dreadnought* size battleships, 177

Kitchener, Horatio Herbert, 1st Earl: British Field Marshall and Egyptian Sirdar
Defeats Dervish army at Omdurman, 144, 308; remark to Churchill on latter's fall from power, 336

Kruger, Paul: President of the Boer Republic of Transvaal.
'The Kruger Telegram', 106-7

Lansdowne, Marquis of: British Foreign Secretary under Balfour
Character and policy, 139; meets Delcassé, 146; notes decline of Germany's international position, 157, 228

Lichnovski, Prince Karl Max: German Ambassador to Great Britain 1912-14
146n; replaces Marschall, 361, 368

Lloyd-George, David: British politician. Chancellor of the Exchequer 1906-16
Opposes naval expenditure, 236-7, 332; role in Agadir crisis, 272-3; at Committee of Imperial Defence meeting, 1911, 285, 293; on war, 368; optimism on international relations 1914, 403, 429

Loubet, Emile: French politician. President during entente negotiations
Replaced, 153

Macmillan, Harold: British politician
396, 403

Mahan, Captain Alfred Thayer: American Naval Officer and historian
On prevalence of 'English' democratic values in the Americas, 23, 48; Wilhelm II's respect for his views, 76, 92; opposes *Dreadnought* type, 180

Marchand, Captain Jean Baptiste: French colonial army officer
148, 151

Marschall von Bieberstein, Baron Adolf: German Ambassador to the Ottoman Empire, and to Great Britain (1912)
263-4, 363; dies, 364

McKenna, Reginald: Liberal politician. First Lord of the Admiralty 1908-11
Replaces Tweedmouth as First Lord of the Admiralty, 193; dealings with Beresford, 218-9; represents Admiralty during enquiry into policy, 221; approves Fisher's plan to retire, 224; Churchill's appreciation of, 242; at Committee of Imperial Defence meeting, 1911, 288, 291; replaced as First Lord by Churchill, 295-6, 299, 307; Fisher's regard for, 310, 317, 359

Merrimack, **USS/** *Virginia*, **CSS:** Confederate States ironclad
30

Metternich, Count Paul Wolff: German Ambassador to Great Britain 1902-12
146; qualities of, 226; relations with Sir Edward Grey, 235, 272; post Haldane Mission negotiations, 350, 354-6; relieved of his post, 360-1; 367

Meux, Admiral Sir Hedworth: British Admiral. Supporter of Beresford
219

Milne, Admiral Sir Archibald Berkeley: British naval officer. C-in-C Mediterranean Fleet 1912-14
Fisher objects to his appointment, 308-9

Moltke, General Helmuth von: German Army Chief of Staff
Views on retention of Alsace-Lorraine, 84-5; military strategy of, 386

Monitor, USS: Union States ironclad
33

Morley, Lord (John): British Liberal politician and pacifist
On committee of enquiry into Admiralty policies, 215; against going to war with Germany, 429

Muller, Captain: German Naval Attaché in London. Tirpitz's 'mole'
367-8

Nassau, **SMS:** First German *Dreadnought*
177-8

Nicholas II: Tsar of Russia 1894-1917
Initiates first Hague Peace conference, 122; role in Anglo-Russian detente, 229-30; Bosnia-Herzegovina crisis, 1908, 232, 234; contradicts Wilhelm II re: *Daily Telegraph* interview, 244; 1905 crisis in Russia, 379; role in Russian mobilisation 1914, 421-2

Nicholson, Sir Arthur: British ambassador to Russia 1906
228-9

Nikita: King of Montenegro
Precipitates war with Ottoman Empire, 372, 375-6

Panther, **SMS:** German colonial cruiser
Role in Agadir crisis, 267-70

Pollock, Sir Frederick: British diplomat
On Germany's military and foreign policy, 358

Poore, Admiral Sir Richard: British naval officer.
Row with Churchill, 302-3

Princip, Gavrilo: Bosnian Serb anarchist
Character and motivation, 411; assassinates Archduke Franz-Ferdinand, 415-6, 435

Queen Elizabeth **class:** Fast battleships
318

Rhodes, Cecil: British entrepreneur, Colonial administrator and imperialist
105n, 159

Richmond, Admiral Sir Herbert: British naval officer and academic
27

Richter, Eugen: German radical politician
86

Roberts, Field Marshall Lord: British army officer and advocate of conscription
290

Rooseveldt, Theodore: American President 1901-09
Conversation with Kaiser, 78; Big Stick Theory, 133

Index

Rosyth: British naval dockyard
Incomplete, 334

Rouvier, Maurice: French politician.
Appeaser
Replaces Loubet, 153

Rozhestvensky, Z: Russian Admiral.
Commander of the Baltic Fleet 1905
Fires on British fishing vessels, 227

Salisbury, Lord, Robert Gascoyne Cecil:
British Prime Minister 1885-92, 1895-1902
Policies and 'isolationism', 103, 113, 116, 138-40; scotches binding Anglo-German alliance, 117-8; Fisher comes to the notice of, 128, 130; role in Fashoda incident, 144-5; 356n

Scapa Flow: British fleet anchorage,
334

Scheer, Reinhardt: German Admiral.
Commander of the High Seas Fleet 1916-18
66

Schlieffen, General Graf von: Chief of German Army Staff after Moltke
386; the Schlieffen plan, 389, 394, 423-4, 429

Scott, Admiral Sir Percy Moreton: British Admiral and Gunnery High Priest
Becomes protégé of Fisher 126, 166-7; the 'paintwork' incident, 207-9; views on Lord Charles Beresford, 221

Selbourne, Lord: British politician and First Lord of the Admiralty 1900-06
Supports Fisher's personnel reforms, 134-5; supports Fisher as future First Sea Lord, 135; adopts Fisher's full scheme of naval reforms 160, 186; on Germany's naval policy, 239

Senden-Bibran, Admiral Gustav von: Chief of the Navy Cabinet 1889-1906
95

Stead, W.T.: Influential journalist and editor.
Ally of Fisher
126-7, 211

Stolypin, Prince Peter: Russian Prime Minister 1906
232

Stosch, Albrecht von: General, later Admiral.
Chief of German Admiralty 1872-83
62-64

Stuart-Wortly, Colonel Edward
and *Daily Telegraph* affair, 241-3, 248

Tankosic, Major Vojin: Serbian army officer. Member of Black Hand organisation
411-4

Tattenbach, Count von: German diplomat
At Algeciras Conference, 154, 226

Tegethoff, Wilhelm von: Austrian Admiral, victor of Lissa
55

Thurston, J.R: British journalist and editor.
Ally of Fisher
211

Tirpitz, Grand Admiral Alfred von: State Secretary of the Naval Office 1897-1916
On Stosch, 63, 66; becomes State Secretary of the Navy Office, 89; produces first Navy Bill, 90-95; adverse effect on Anglo-German relations, 107, 109; on Bülow, 108; on Second Navy Bill, 110-1; 'a navy against England', 110-2; results of naval ambitions, 120-1, 122, 125, 137; Risk Theory undermined, 142, 148, 156-8, 166; reacts to construction of *Dreadnought*, 176; comparison with Fisher, 178; misled by plans for Invincible, 184, 185; and German public opinion, 224-5, 245; adverse effects on Anglo-German relations, 235-6, 239-40; 'a single issue politician', 251, 253, 262; Agadir crisis, 269, 275-6; concentration on battleships to detriment of all other forms of warship, 322; role during the Haldane Mission, 337-8, 341-5; introduces the 'Novelle', 346-7, 350, 353-6; on concentration of British fleet against Germany, 357; dismisses Churchill's 'naval holiday' proposals, 360, 361, 363; accepts limitations on naval ambitions, 367-9, 391; legacy of the 'Fleet against England', 399

Tweedmouth, Lord: First Lord of the Admiralty 1906-8
Inadequacies and illness of, 186; lacks will to confront Beresford, 202, 204, 207; replaced by McKenna, 212-3

***Vernon*, HMS:** Royal Navy Training establishment, cradle of torpedo development
124

Victoria: Queen of Great Britain and Empress of India 1840-1901
77-8, 81, 113-16, 119, 121, 138, 243, 280-1, 347n

Victoria, 'Vicky': Eldest daughter of Queen Victoria and wife of Kaiser Friedrich III
114

Vivian, Captain Gerald: British naval officer
Row with Churchill, 301-2

***Von Der Tann*, SMS:** First German battlecruiser
184

488

***Warrior*, HMS:** First British ironclad battleship
29, 31, 32n, 124

Watts, Sir Philip: Director of Naval Construction 1902-1912
On *Dreadnought* committee, 170

White, Arnold: British journalist and editor. Ally of Fisher
211

White, Sir William: Director of Naval Construction 1886-1904
36; 126, opposes *Dreadnought* type, 175

Wiesner, Friedrich von: Austrian diplomat
Dismisses Serbian Government involvement in assassination of Franz-Ferdinand, 413

Wilhelm I: King of Prussia and First German Emperor
56

Wilhelm II: German Emperor 1888-1918
56; cultivated by Bismarck, 61-62; self image, 68; character and influence, 73-76, 83-86, 89-92, 96, 157-8, 184-5; relationship with British Royal family, 77-78, 81-82; differences with, and dismissal of, Bismarck, 83-85; naval ambitions of, 89-92, 94, 117, 120-1, 137, 167, 225, 239-40, 291; the 'Kruger Telegram', 106; and Bülow, 107-9; promotes the Tirpitz Risk Theory, 110; 'a Fleet against England', 112-3; death of Queen Victoria, 115-6; role in first Moroccan crisis, 151-2, 200, 208; letter to Tweedmouth, 212; suspicion of England, 222; distrust of Metternich, 226, 361, 368; role in Bosnia-Herzegovina crisis, 1908, 232-3; 'encirclement', 234, 254, 280-1, 392; Eulenberg scandal, 241; *Daily Telegraph* affair 242-48, 251; dispenses with Bülow, 253; first dealings with Bethmann-Hollweg, 260-2; role during the Haldane Mission, 338-9, 344-5, 348-9, 353-4, 356; re Churchill and the 'Novelle', 359-62; adherence to Belgian neutrality Treaty, 390; not a warmonger, 391; 392; legacy of 'a Fleet against England', 399; role in granting Austria the 'blank cheque' to confront Serbia, 416-7; has second thoughts, 420-2, 434; 437

Wilson, Sir Arthur Knyvet, Bart, V.C.: Admiral of the Fleet
42; unattracted by post of First Sea Lord, 191, 200, 198; vetoed by Beresford as a member of the committee of enquiry into Admiralty policy, 215; evidence before committee, 216; Fisher earmarks as his successor, 219, 221; reaction to Agadir crisis, 271; becomes First Sea Lord, 282; character, 283-4; botches presentation to C.I.D., 285-9; forced retirement, 304-6, 312, 314, 325-6, 396,

Wilson, General Sir Henry: British army officer. Director of Military Operations 1912
286-8, 358

489

PRINTED AND BOUND BY:

Copytech (UK) Limited trading as Printondemand-worldwide,
9 Culley Court, Bakewell Road, Orton Southgate. Peterborough,
PE2 6XD, United Kingdom.